Publications of the Algonquian Text Society
Collection de la Société d'édition de textes algonquiens

H.C. Wolfart, *General Editor*

âtalôhkâna nêsta tipâcimôwina
Cree Legends and Narratives
from the West Coast of James Bay

wâskahikaniwiyiniw-âcimowina
ᐅᐧᐦᑲᐦᐃᐦᐊᓂ ᐊᐸᐃᐧᓂ ᐊᕐᒐᐃᐧᐊ
Stories of the House People
Told by Peter Vandall and Joe Douquette
Edited, translated and with a glossary by Freda Ahenakew, 1987

The Dog's Children: Anishinaabe Texts Told by Angeline Williams
Edited and translated by Leonard Bloomfield. Newly edited and with a
glossary by John D. Nichols, 1991

kinêhiyâwiwininaw nêhiyawêwin
ᑭᐦᐃᔭ ᐃᐧ ᐃ ᓂᓇ ᐦᐃ ᔭ ᐁ ᐃᐧ
The Cree Language is Our Identity:
The LaRonge Lectures of Sarah Whitecalf
Edited, translated and with a glossary by
H.C. Wolfart and Freda Ahenakew, 1993

âtalôhkâna nêsta tipâcimôwina

Cree Legends and Narratives

from the West Coast of James Bay

Told by Simeon Scott
Xavier Sutherland
Isaiah Sutherland
John Wynne
Joel Linklater
Silas Wesley
Hannah Wynne
Gabriel Kiokee
Andrew Faries
Gilbert Faries
Sophie Gunner
James Gunner
Willie Frenchman
Hannah Loon
Ellen McLeod
John Carpenter

Text and translation
Edited and with a glossary by C. Douglas Ellis

The University of Manitoba Press
1995

© The University of Manitoba Press 1995
Winnipeg, Manitoba   R3T 5V6

Printed in Canada on recycled, acid-free paper ∞
Design and typography by Norman Schmidt and A.C. Ogg

A set of six cassette tapes containing the complete Cree text of this book is available separately (ISBN 0-88755-163-7) **from the University of Manitoba Press.**

All royalties from the sale of this book revert to the Society's Publication Fund.

The editorial preparation of this book was made possible through the support of the Cree Language Project and the Linguistics Department at the University of Manitoba.

The publisher acknowledges with gratitude the assistance of Manitoba Culture, Heritage and Citizenship for support of its publishing program. This book has been published with the help of a grant from the Canadian Federation for the Humanities, using funds provided by the Social Sciences and Humanities Research Council of Canada.

Canadian Cataloguing in Publication Data

Scott, Simeon, d. 1979.

    âtalôhkâna nêsta tipâcimôwina = Cree legends and narratives
    from the west coast of James Bay

    (Publications of the Algonquian Text Society, ISSN 0829-755X)
    Text in Cree (roman orthography) and in English translation.
    ISBN 0-88755-159-9

1. Cree language – Texts. 2. Cree Indians – Folklore. 3. Cree Indians
– Social life and customs. 4. Cree Indians – Rites and ceremonies.
5. Cree language – Dictionaries – English. 6. English language –
Dictionaries – Cree. I. Ellis, C.D. (Clarence Douglas), 1923-
II. Algonquian Text Society. III. Title. IV. Series.

PM989.S36 1995   497'.3   C94-920203-7

ᐸᕁᑲᐧᐤ ᐅᒪ ᒪᕐᐊᕁᐃᑲᐊ
ᐁ ᐊᐊᕁᑯᑭᑊ
ᐊᓂᑭ ᐃᐣᓂᐧᐊᕁ
ᖃᔑᐧᐊᓄᕁ ᓄᕁᑕ ᒍᕐᓄᕌᓄᕁᑎᕁ
ᑲ ᑭ ·ᐃᕐᕁᐊᕁᕁ,
ᐁ ᐸᕐᕁᓬᐊᓄᕁᐧᐊᕁ ᐅᕁᐊ ᐊᒍᓬᕁᑲᐊ
ᑭᕐ ᐊᓄᕁᖅ ᐊᐸᑕᕁᑭ

This book is dedicated
in appreciation
to the people of the
Kashechewan and Moose Factory Bands
who have helped me
in the hope that these legends
will continue to be told

Contents

II Legends and Narratives: Kashechewan Cree

III Legends and Narratives: Moose Cree

Appendices

Introduction

The texts which follow were gathered over a ten year period, from 1955 to about 1965. Most were recorded during a three year residence at Albany Post (now Kashechewan) on the west coast of James Bay, or on visits to Moose Factory. A few, Texts 13 to 26, were recorded from a Cree speaker resident in Toronto. They represent a variety of narrative and conversational styles of Cree as spoken at Moose Factory and further north on the west coast of James Bay and were assembled initially to provide materials of linguistic interest. The different types of narrative, however, illustrate a life-style and, in the case of the traditional legends, a conceptual universe of considerable intrinsic interest and one which differs substantially from that of the typical non-Indian reader.

Dialect Variation

The texts have been grouped in three parts by dialect as shown on the map (Figure 1). The texts in Part I are in the n-dialect, so-called Swampy Cree, spoken north of Moosonee on the west coast of James Bay and inland into central Manitoba. Those in Part III were narrated by l-dialect or Moose Cree speakers from the area of Moose Factory. The intervening texts in Part II represent a mixed n-l usage, referred to as Kashechewan Cree for the purposes of this collection. Speakers who use this mixed dialect have grown up at Albany Post, some ninety miles north of Moose Factory and Moosonee and just across the Albany River from the Swampy Cree speakers at Albany Post. Their parents or grandparents in many cases were former members of the Moose Band and speakers of Moose Cree.

Recording and Translation

Recording was carried out under widely differing conditions, all the way from the informal setting of the village home to the controlled environment of a sound laboratory in Toronto, where the late Xavier Sutherland recorded the several accounts listed under his name. Procedure was uniformly for the narrator to record without interruption so as to lead to the most natural delivery possible. This has preserved a number of interesting stylistic effects:

FIG. 1. West Coast of James Bay: Cree Dialects

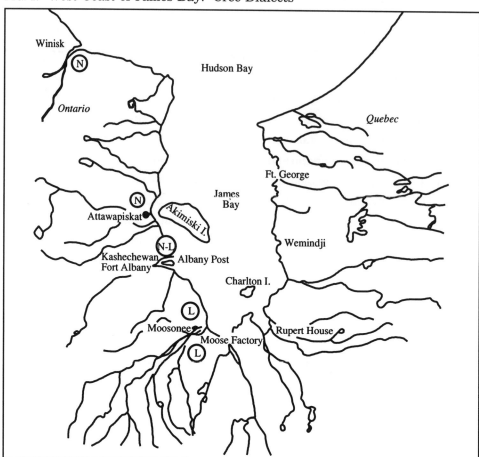

L   Moose Cree (l-dialect)
N   Swampy Cree (n-dialect)
N-L   Kashechewan Cree (mixed n-l usage)

stage whispers for eerie situations, onomatopoeia and outright imitations of animal sounds, child language, snatches of Ojibwa, etc. – and in certain cases the extreme contraction of a highly colloquial style. It has been attempted to represent all this in the transcription.

The narrators who furnished the legends, folktales, personal accounts, recipes and conversations were all native speakers of Cree but varied widely in their control of English: some spoke with ease, others with difficulty, and some were unilingual speakers of Cree only. Since the translations are 'informant inspired' and many Cree narrators were unable to reflect the subtleties of Cree style in English, a second and third informant often functioned in the rôle of translator. The transcribed text has been checked and rechecked with the recordings; and where Cree speaking listeners disagreed in their interpretation of the recording, variant readings have been given in the Notes. The resultant Cree text is, it is hoped, maximally reliable.[1]

The English version is the work of many persons, finally brought together by the editor. It is impossible to thank all who participated at one stage or another in the work, but among those who have been of major assistance in transcribing and translating are the late John Wynne of Albany Post and Anne Scott of Fort Albany, Joel Linklater of Albany Post and, later, Moosonee, the late Andrew Faries and the late James Gunner (Udgarden) of Moose Factory, the late Xavier Sutherland of Winisk, Angela Moore of Calstock, Bertha Metat of Fort Albany and Timmins, Mary Bird of Winisk and Timmins, Agnes Hunter of Timmins and Moosonee, Annie O'Brien of Timmins, and Elsie Chilton of Moose Factory (all in the Province of Ontario). The sincerest appreciation is also expressed to the many others who generously gave their assistance with specific problems as occasion required, in particular to Kenneth Ross of the Canadian Wildlife Service and Michael W.P. Runtz of Arnprior, Ontario, both of whom provided information on fauna of the North. No recognition would be complete without a note of sincere gratitude to Arden C. Ogg for her skilful reorganization and reformulation of

---

[1]   Early supplementary fieldwork was conducted on contract with the National Museum of Canada in the summer of 1964. Preliminary ordering and final preparation of the collection was made possible through Research Grants S76-1109 and 451-86-0391 respectively and Research Grant 410-86-0053 from the Social Sciences and Research Council of Canada and by sabbatical leaves from McGill University in 1977 and 1986. The sincerest appreciation is expressed to both.

The Cree speakers who recounted the narratives are listed below and with the Notes to each text. Those who furnished major help in transcription and translation are noted above. I can only express the warmest gratitude to them for their interest and patience. Particular acknowledgment is due to Mrs. Elsie Chilton of Moose Factory for her last minute help in elucidating the meaning of certain Cree forms and providing a more appropriate wording, both Cree and English, for the dedication; and to Gregory Spence of the Mushkegowak Council for his help in clarifying certain terms; and to the Reverend Redfern Louttit for kind assistance with translation problems. I am also indebted to my colleague, Professor Glynne Piggott, whose sense of Algonquian linguistic propriety has provided both encouragement and restraint in times of doubt.

Finally, to the colleagues who tolerated my monumental ineptitude while initiating me into the arcana of computer technology I tender the sincerest thanks. For errors, omissions and all manner of infelicity I accept full responsibility.

this material, a herculean task! Indeed, for the collective eagle eye and pointed queries of the editorial staff I am deeply obligated.

From time to time not merely a variant 'reading', but a correction of grammar is noted. Several speakers who assisted in the transcription and translation, in particular the late James Gunner, often remarked on an unfinished or incorrect word or aberrant grammatical form. For the most part, their comments have been passed on to the reader in the Notes.

The production of a satisfactory English version was beset by the difficulties common to all translation: how to produce a readable, running text which retained the essential flavour of the original without sacrificing either sense or exactness. One could enumerate a list of translation problems: the precise thrust of certain particles in Cree, the nuance of a verbal inflection, the handling of the neat contrast between nearer and more remote third person (proximate versus obviative) in Cree when no such grammatical apparatus exists in English, and so on. A lexical equivalent or near-equivalent is sometimes easy to find; but the semantic area or, more importantly, the cultural value of the closest Cree-English equivalent may be quite disparate.[2] One example may be cited, the transitive verb with animate object, *mîcilêw*. In Text 12:5 the meaning is 'he defecates on him', a translation which has clinical and stilted overtones albeit avoiding a socially less acceptable term. The Cree verb, however, is also used of a skunk spraying a person – an area of meaning totally absent from the nearest English equivalent. The English 'to mess on' was chosen as reflecting the folksy, unembarrassed Cree usage, the cultural value of which, however, is also contextually conditioned. One would be guarded of one's use of the Cree term in ordinary conversation.

The possibility of an interlinear translation with morpheme by morpheme analysis was considered and rejected, partly because of the extent of the material, partly since this would be useful to only a restricted readership and partly because such treatment is better suited to a more tightly focussed and specifically grammatical study.

---

[2] Where it was felt that additional words or phrases were essential to complete the sense of a passage, additions to the translation are given in square brackets.

Narrators

The several narrators are listed in alphabetical order.

John Carpenter, Text 68 (recorded 29 July 1965). At the time of the recording, he was an elderly person living in retirement at Moose Factory. He had spent time as a boy with the family of an Anglican mission priest and had a good control of English. A speaker of Moose Cree, he displayed a slight speech hesitation. John Carpenter died 24 April 1984.

Andrew Faries, Text 44 (recorded in 1958). One of the younger men living at Moose Factory in 1958, he was a fluent speaker of both English and Moose Cree, who had come as a child from Albany Post. Cree was his first language and he retained a familiarity with the Swampy dialect and was highly literate in both Cree and English. Andrew Faries died 8 May 1989.

Gilbert Faries, Texts 45-49 (recorded in the summer of 1958). A younger, middle-aged member of the Moose Band, at ease in both English and Moose Cree. In the employ of the government hospital in 1958, he was interested in local history and folktales.

Willie Frenchman, Texts 58-62 (recorded 30 July 1964). An elderly person at the time of the recording whose first language was Moose Cree, but who seemed to have had extensive exposure to English. His enunciation was often unclear and his control of English imperfect. His Cree also displayed grammatical erosion from time to time. Willie Frenchman died 24 June 1971 at the age of 89 years.

James Gunner (Udgarden), Text 57 (recorded 1964). A person in his mid-sixties at the time of the recording, and sometime employee of the Hudson's Bay Company. Of mixed Cree and Norwegian ancestry, James Gunner, as he was commonly known although the surname was actually Udgarden, was a fluent speaker of English and Cree, which latter he understood in several dialects (though he spoke primarily Moose Cree). His services were widely in demand as an interpreter, especially by medical services; and although his only textual contribution was as a participant in Text 57, his mark is on a large portion of this collection in transcription, translation and comment. James Gunner died 26 October 1976.

Sophie Gunner, Texts 50-57 (recorded July and August 1964). A lady of middle age in 1964 and wife of James Gunner. Originally from the area south and east of Moose, she was essentially a unilingual speaker of Moose Cree. Her speech was often characterized by rapid delivery. She was a repository of native technical lore of which Texts 50-54 offer a small sample. Sophie Gunner died 26 December 1976.

Gabriel Kiokee, Texts 41-43 (recorded 19 July 1965). A resident of Moosonee in his early thirties at the time of recording, who had been a deckhand on boats around James Bay. Originally from Attawapiskat, he was a unilingual speaker of Swampy Cree whose unmixed Swampy Cree speech was remarked on in Text 41:20. Gabriel Kiokee died in 1992.

Joel Linklater, Texts 34-38 (recorded 1956 or 1957); 41-42 (recorded 19 July 1965). A resident of Albany Post where he was in the employ of the Hudson's Bay Company in the mid 1950s, and later of Moosonee. Joel Linklater was a speaker of both English and Kashechewan Cree and was of material help in establishing contacts with other speakers. He also supplied major assistance in transcription, translation and comment.

Hannah Loon, Texts 63-67 (recorded 21 July 1965). An elderly, middle-aged widow in 1965, and a resident of Moose Factory. A highly alert and able person, she was a unilingual speaker of Moose Cree. As of November 1993 she was still very much alive and well at close to 100 years of age.

Ellen McLeod, Text 67 (recorded 21 July 1965). Sister to Hannah Loon and in the same age bracket, she had some English and was a speaker of Moose Cree. Ellen McLeod died 18 April 1985 at the age of 97 years.

Simeon Scott, Texts 1-12 (recorded between 1955 and 1957). A resident of Fort Albany and close to retirement at that time, Simeon Scott was in charge of a branch store of the Hudson's Bay Company at Fort Albany. A native speaker of Swampy Cree, he also spoke considerable English. Simeon Scott died 28 August 1979.

Isaiah Sutherland, Texts 27-29 (recorded around September 1957). An elderly hunter and member of the band at Albany Post in 1957. Isaiah Sutherland was a unilingual speaker of Moose Cree, although an occasional replacement of *l* by *n* was to be heard. His enunciation was often slurred. Isaiah Sutherland died 6 January 1970.

Xavier Sutherland, Texts 13-26 (recorded between 1960 and 1962). A native of Winisk (now Peawanuck), and in his late twenties at the time of recording, Xavier Sutherland had spent considerable time at school and was trained in silkscreen printing. He was a fluent speaker of English and Swampy Cree and of major help in recording, transcribing and translation. His tragic death in an airplane crash sometime after 1976 cut short a life of service to both the Cree and the larger community.

Silas Wesley, Text 39 (recorded in 1957 or 1958). One of the younger men in the Albany Band, in his early thirties at the time of recording. A trapper by profession, and resident of Albany Post, Silas Wesley was literate in English and a native speaker of Kashechewan Cree. He later served as Chief.

Hannah Wynne, Text 40 (date of recording unknown). A younger, middle-aged resident of Albany Post at the time of recording, wife of a hunter and mother of several children. Hannah Wynne had very little English and was a speaker of Kashechewan Cree. Hannah Wynne died 26 March 1982.

John Wynne, Texts 30-33 (recorded between 1956 and 1958). At the time of recording, John Wynne was an independent trader and manager of a branch store at Albany Post for his brother David Wynne of Moosonee. A man of some fifty-odd years, he was a native speaker of Kashechewan Cree, with a good command of English. He also provided considerable help in recording, transcription, translation and commentary. John Wynne died 13 June 1985.

Literary Genres[3]

The 'classical' literature of the Cree-speaking Algonquian people has been transmitted orally since time immemorial. The product of a largely unselfconscious literary tradition, it displays a variety of distinct literary types and sub-types; and this distinction is often internally and linguistically marked. A useful primary division may be made between so-called traditional and popular discourse. The former is represented by the often repeated and familiar narrative which may belong to a well-known body or canon of traditional accounts. The latter is, by its nature, more casual and often more impromptu. The main further distinction is between the *âtalôhkân* or (sacred) legend and the *tipâcimôwin* or account of some area of life experience. The *âtalôhkân* or *âtalôhkêwin* (the Moose Cree form of the word) is one of several well-marked literary genres represented in the corpus of Cree literature. It treats of a time when things were still in a state of flux in the world: animals and birds talked and strange, unspecified voices gave directions to isolated man. It has been described as the period before the

---

[3] A slightly fuller version of this survey appeared as the 1988 Belcourt Lecture under the title *"Now then, still another story –" Literature of the Western James Bay Cree: Content and Structure* (Winnipeg: Voices of Rupert's Land).

world jelled down to the way it is today. How old the tales are one can only speculate. The themes recur in the oral literature of related language communities where the leading figures may have different names; but the prototype must represent a level of antiquity comparable to anything in the Indo-European tradition.

The *atalôhkân* may recount the adventures of one or another culture hero, but it often displays many of the characteristics of myth, which has been defined as "a tale laid in a world supposed to have preceded the present order and which deals with sacred beings, semi-divine heroes and the origins of all things."[4] Myths, it has been pointed out, are often linked to religious practices and may include aetiological elements. The legend of Weesakechahk and the flood exemplifies this (cf. Text 7:8). Animals often play a rôle in myth, and human qualities may be ascribed to them. Some Cree tales, on the other hand, bear a stronger resemblance to the local legend or *tradition populaire*. In these are recounted extraordinary happenings believed actually to have occurred. These are told of various localities and involve strange creatures, some of which may be highly disagreeable. Stories of the windigoes (Text 12) are a case in point, or the tale of Ayas (Text 9), the return to life of Mistaganash (Texts 10, 63) or the story of Memishoosh the conjuror (Text 11). Narratives of this type often reflect the fear-ridden, even macabre mental world of life in the boreal forest peopled by threatening, non-human beings (Text 12) or depict the rivalries of interpersonal relationships (Text 11).

Among the *atalôhkâna* one sub-type is the *pâstâmowin*,[5] the tale of blasphemy and requital. It has a clear-cut moral purpose and to some extent fulfils the rôle of the fable. Another type of literary genre is the folktale or animal tale, a typical 'Just-So' story. It accounts for why things are the way they are: why the squirrel has red eyes (Text 46), why the muskrat has a long, tapered tail (Text 45), why the water in James Bay is salt (Text 68), and so on.

In contrast with the *atalôhkâna* stand the *tipâcimôwina*, or simply

---

[4] Thompson, Stith, *The Folktale*, New York, 1946; p. 9.

[5] *pâstâmowin* 'requital tale' or 'tale of blasphemy' (showing lack of proper respect for nature); cf. *pâstâmo-* VAI 'say something which brings one back luck', *pâstâho-* VAI 'do something which brings one back luck'; e.g., *'yâkwâ 'sa, ka-pâstâhon!* 'Look out, you're doing something which will bring you harm!'; cf. *pâstâm-, pâstâh- pâstân-* VTA: all seem to involve exceeding the limits by instrument, by word of mouth and by hand severally so as to incur an undesirable outcome (e.g., *pâstânam paspâpiwinâpiskoliw* 'he puts pressure on a piece of glass to the point where it cracks').

âcimôwina, which record real, or supposedly real, events. These are in a sense the 'action stories', but also much more. Some have taken on an almost canonical form from frequent repetition and hence belong rather to traditional discourse. Others of a more personal and less formal nature belong in the area of popular discourse. Set in a context involving real time or what could be real time, these accounts in turn break into a variety of sub-types: the action tale (Texts 31, 34-38), which often bears the marks of the apocryphal; the reminiscence (Texts 39, 40) – a favourite theme being that of the old days; and the aetiological account, such as 'How Ghost River got its name' (Text 30), where the action takes place in an unspecified past, although the location of the story may be well known. All of these belong to the living, oral tradition and constitute a rich and vital folk literature.

In addition to the foregoing, the present collection contains descriptions of local technology (Texts 50-54, 62) and several free (and unrehearsed) conversations (Texts 41-43, 67). One caveat must be kept in mind: neither the corpus from which the present selections are drawn nor their classification is exhaustive. Whole categories are unrepresented in the present account. There are, for example, no examples of hunting or certain other songs. The song of the muskrat is the only specimen of Cree verse included. Oratory, honed to a fine art by many speakers, is missing entirely from the collection. A record of such a vital area of language use would be instructive to possess. Translation literature has not been touched on. Far too much work by way of critical analysis remains to be done before any definitive results can be realized; but a tentative classification is represented in the chart below.

FIG. 2.

TRADITIONAL DISCOURSE		
âtalôhkâna	non-cyclical	unitary episode (e.g., arrival of man in the world)
		folktale (e.g., animal story)
	cyclical	'heroic' episode (e.g., Chahkabesh tale)
		'thematic' episode (e.g., *pâstâmowin*)
(tip)âcimôwina	historical narrative	
songs		
other		

POPULAR DISCOURSE	
(tip)âcimôwina[6]	accounts of personal experiences, events, reminiscences
descriptions	technology, recipes, etc.
oratory	(?)
correspondence	(?)

A brief discussion of several of the main literary genres may serve to elaborate their several distinctive characteristics.

Traditional Discourse

The **âtalôhkân**. The *âtalôhkân*, as shown in the discussion and diagram above, falls into at least four sub-categories, possibly more. The first of these consists of the unitary or non-cyclical narrative, each one of which stands more or less alone and involves a different protagonist: e.g., the story of Ayas (Text 9), Memishoosh the conjuror (Text 11), and so on. Here also belong members of the second sub-category, the folktales or animal stories, each one of which is complete in itself (i.e., non-cyclical). The third and perhaps best known category, that of the 'heroic' episode, belongs to a cycle of *âtalôhkâna* in which the activities or adventures of some well known culture figure are recounted in a series of tales with the same central character. The fourth category, that of the *pâstâmowin*, is what we have designated the 'thematic' episode. These 'moral' tales share a common thread of instructive purpose. They cannot be classed as *tipâcimôwina*, although they take place in what purports to be the real world, since the action described belongs to the realm of the fanciful: mosquitoes bite a man to death after being frozen all winter, the snow talks, and so forth.

Of the *(tip)âcimôwina* representing traditional discourse, the only example illustrated is the account of how Ghost River was so named (Text 30).

The Non-cyclical **âtalôhkân:** *The Unitary Episode.* The myth about the origin of man (Texts 1, 2) belongs to the category of non-cyclical *âtalôhkâna*. Its linguistic markings (in n-dialect form) indicate at the outset the genre to

---

[6] Certain historical narratives, although classed as *(tip)âcimôwina*, should probably be regarded as having become part of the traditional discourse, as the diagram shows.

which it belongs:

> *êko, kê-tipâcimoyân,* **âtanôhkân** *ê-'tâtanôhkâtisocik wînawâw tipinawê*
> *ininiwak kâ-itihcik.* (2:1)
> 'Now then I shall tell a story, a *legend* which those who are themselves
> called the [Indian] people tell about themselves.'

Much of the artistry is difficult to sustain in translation; and the
connotative meaning embedded in archaic terms such as *êhêpik* 'spider', or
the full effect of Ojibwa usage attributed to the lynx are inevitably reduced
for the non-Cree reader/hearer of the story. But artistry there is; and
evidence of careful structuring can be discerned in the piece. First, the
setting is established and the theme of the story laid out. The protagonists
appear initially engaged in normal activity – "walking along". Then the
significant intervention takes place: an unidentified voice puts a question to
the man and woman, and this motivates the chain of events.

The next figure on the scene is the Spider. The antiquity of the account is
authenticated by the use of the archaic term, *êhêpik*, immediately clarified by
the more current term, *otahnapihkêsiw* 'net-maker', further elaborated by the
epithet,

> *êwakwân' otahnapihkêsiw,* **êkâ wîskât kâ-câkinahk pîsâkanâpîniw**
> 'that is the one who is the net-maker, *who never exhausts the twine*' (1:4)

Another version describes him as the 'great net-maker', *miši-otahnapihkêsiw*.

As the central action begins to unfold, each new step is marked by a verbal
exchange:

Spider: "Do you want to go and see yonder land?" – and so on.
People: "Yes."
Spider: "Very well, I shall make a line to lower you."

The spider prepares "what looks like a bag" for the man and woman and,
as a last minute warning, advises that only one of them must look (out of the
bag) until contact with the earth is made. The journey then begins.

Once more the focus changes, signalled by the verbal exchange as one
passenger tells the other, "Now the land is in sight," and again, "Now the
rivers are in sight".

The narrator reminds the listeners of the dire penalty to follow
if both travellers peek – and then it happens: in their excitement they both
look. The gondola prepared by the spider slips sideways at tree level and

they find themselves lodged in the "great eagle nest" – the fruit of their disobedience! And there they are stuck.

Abruptly and dramatically comes the command: "Look down!" Once again the focus has changed. Various animals can be seen moving about and in turn the various creatures pass by. The first two speak; but the third, the bear, takes in the situation immediately and goes into action. He and the wolverine rescue the couple from the tree; but now comes what is one of the main points of the story. At the outset the couple had been told by the spider: "You will have someone there who will teach you how to survive." This turns out to be the bear who teaches them all they need to know to remain alive.

> *êko mâka, maskwa mâka kî-kistênimâkaniwan, – tâpiskôc ininiwa*
> *k'-îtênimêwak ininiwak maskwa. ê'kwâni mâka kâ-ohc'-îtên'tâkosit*
> *âhkih maskwah tâpiskôc ininiw kâ-kakêhtawên'tahk* ... (2:9)
> 'So then, the bear was respected, – the people thought of the bear the
> same as of a person. And that is the reason the bear is so considered,
> as it were, as a wise person ...'

In the area where the legend is told people do not eat bear meat.

Several features of a formal nature are to be noted:

The *type-index* of the narrative. The piece is linguistically marked as an *âtalôhkân*, or so designated by use of the corresponding verb.

The *timelessness* of the setting. The term *pêyakwâ* 'once (upon a time)' may appear; but these are essentially stories out of time and the occurrence of archaic terms, *êhêpik* 'spider' or *nimôlôm* 'my grandfather' (or perhaps 'my prey'), mark them stylistically as belonging to another era.

The *background features of setting*. The story opens in a mythical land somewhere "above". Here the development of the theme is forecast by an unidentified voice which puts the leading question, supplies instructions and sets the action in motion. Once, however, the initial setting has served its purpose, it is no longer heard of.

The *sequential ordering mechanism* of the discourse. Each stage of the narrative is introduced by its appropriate verbal exchange and proceeds in orderly fashion to the next. Advance to a new stage or even within the same scene is often signalled with a stock formula, *âšay manâ* 'now then', or *âšay manâ mâka* or *kêka manâ mâka* 'and finally then'.

The *major theme*. The major theme is readily apparent, in this case the coming of the first people to this world and the means of their integration into the environment. In the text under consideration the conclusion of the narrative links it to a folk practice, the local taboo against eating bear meat. A form of bear cult is common in arctic and subarctic areas of both the old and new world. While ritual activity surrounding the bear hunt was no longer practiced at Albany Post where the story was told, a residual trace of the old attitude remains in the legend.

The *characterization*. In the legend cited, characterization of the protagonists is weak. Initially willing to co-operate, they are later depicted as foolishly disobedient. The animals, in particular the lynx and the bear, receive greater attention in this respect. In other tales, such as that of Memishoosh the conjuror (Text 11), depiction of character is more focussed. Memishoosh's practice of communicating with the spirits, of casting evil spells, and his reprehensible penchant for killing off his sons-in-law leaves little doubt as to his anti-social tendencies. In both the Weesakechahk and Chahkabesh cycles, the main characters, while clearly type-cast, nonetheless display unmistakable personality traits.

The *ending*. The ending of the present *âtalôhkân* (Texts 1, 2) suggests no cycle of which it might form a part. It is self-contained, adding only that people multiplied from that point on, with a personal codicil by the narrator noting the arrival of the White-Men.

The Folktale. The second type of non-cyclic or 'unlinked' *âtalôhkân*, which belongs to the traditional literature, is the folktale. Four such are recorded in the present selection (Texts 45-48). Some of these are unfamiliar outside Cree speaking society, others are widely and well known. The story of how the muskrat got his long, tapered tail (Text 45) will serve as a good example of the genre. Of the four animal tales in this collection, it is the only one not to be marked as an *âtalôhkân*. The narrator repaired the oversight in each of the subsequent tales.

In terms of formal features the time is placed simply as 'once, long ago'. The framework shows the familiar two-stage arrangement and the major theme is the only one. While there is no unidentified voice, the muskrat is heard by an unidentified listener. Characterization is not important; and the conclusion sums up the whole point of a typical 'Just-So' story:

ê'kwâni mâka anohc wêhc'-îšinâkwanilik wacask osôw. (45:2)
'And that is why the muskrat's tail looks the way it does now.'

The Cyclical âtalôhkân: **The 'Heroic' Episode.** To turn from the
self-contained narrative to the episodic cycle, two series of *âtalôhkâna* told in
the Albany area are to be noted. They involve the two well known culture
figures already cited: Weesakechahk and Chahkabesh. Events and
experiences from the adventures of both are embodied in widely known
legends. As one narrator remarked: "There are a great many stories told
about Weesakechahk." Their cyclical membership is characteristically
marked by a linguistic label at the end of each episode:

ê'kwâni piko êskwâpihkêyâk. (16:5)
'That is the length of the story.'

Note the verb stem *iskwâ-* 'be so long, measure so long' does not occur in
simple form but incorporates the medial suffix ...*âpihk*... 'line-like, cord-like'.
The total stem, *iskwâpihkêyâ-*, is used of a line or cord and means 'be of such
a length (line or cord)'. As each episode is completed, the figure is that of a
line or cord (the series) having reached such a length, to be carried further by
the sequel. An alternative formula employs the form *êskwâpêkahk*, which
means essentially the same thing.

As is often the case with oral literature, the form of the discourse is not
verbally fixed in every detail. It is rather the theme and sequence which
remain constant. Certain stylistic devices internal to each sequence often
serve to characterize the main figure in the story: Chahkabesh's recurrent
declaration, "I'm going somewhere where I've never been before," – the motif
of dauntless Little Man, or the musings of Weesakechahk, the trickster, often
delivered in a tone suggestive of the devious plotter, "I wonder what I should
do about such and such." When a ruse is successful he exults; when *he* is
tricked he is furious. This simplistic over-drawing of character is, of course,
deliberate and expected. Different storytellers, nonetheless, often occasion
surprise by their verbatim adherence to certain formulae, while exercising a
liberty of improvisation in other respects. This underlying structural stability
of the literary piece may be illustrated by three narratives from the series.
The narrator in each case was the late Xavier Sutherland of Winisk, Ontario.

The stories are the familiar tales of Weesakechahk and the shut-eye dance
(Text 18), how Weesakechahk tricked the bear (Text 19) and Weesakechahk

flies south with the birds (Text 20). A reading will show that in all of these the narrative itself falls into two parts. In Part 1 Weesakechahk tricks the birds into closing their eyes so he can kill them, deceives the bear or convinces the waveys to let him fly south with them. Each separate focus as the stories unfold is introduced by either an appropriate soliloquy on the part of Weesakechahk suggesting what is to follow, or a brief exchange with the birds, the bear or the waveys severally. In each case Weesakechahk succeeds in his ruse. Then the scene changes. In Part 2 an overconfident Weesakechahk relaxes his cunning vigilance: he decides to sleep while the birds are being cooked, invites himself to be squeezed by the trees so he will have more room to put away food or disregards the wavey's warning about flight precautions. In each case he is in turn tricked or meets his come-uppance. Each story then normally concludes with an explanation of how Weesakechahk's behaviour accounts for some natural phenomenon or points up a lesson in proper behaviour drawn from his misdirected activity, or both. Clearly this transmission of the cultural repertoire fulfils the second of the ways in which the cultural heritage is passed on in non-literate societies.[7] It constitutes a paradosis or, at least, a statement of standardized ways of acting.

A brief review of three of the tales of Chahkabesh provides further interesting examples of a carefully crafted frame which allows nonetheless for individual improvisation in developing the theme. Chahkabesh himself was a little fellow, represented by one storyteller as about six inches tall. Like Tom Thumb he compensated by ingenuity for the disadvantages attendant on his minuscule size. His curiosity about the world around him knew no bounds. He lived in a wigwam with his older sister since they had been orphaned in childhood. He always addresses her as 'Big Shishter'. Palatalization is associated with diminutiveness; and the curious, palatalized speech effect with which he is depicted seems intended to characterize him as childlike and lovable, even if a mischievous and inquisitive little scamp. (When something has been mislaid, one may hear a Cree speaker laughingly remark, "It must be Chahkabesh [who has taken it].") His older sister was forever afraid that her little brother's uncontrollable curiosity would be the end of him; and sometimes it nearly was. Chahkabesh, however, always managed to extricate

---

[7] J. Goody & I. Watt, 'The Consequences of Literacy', in P.P. Giglioli, *Language and Social Context*, Penguin Books, 1972, p. 312.

himself from one hazardous situation after another – or *was* extricated – from all but the last one, that is. Disregarding his sister's warning not to do so, he stared up one night at the full moon and, as he had been warned, was drawn up. There he has remained ever since. You can see him in the shadowed part of the moon, Shadow Manikin,[8] which is what the name Chahkabesh seems to mean, standing with his pail with which he had been sent to fetch snow.

The tales of Chahkabesh exhibit a recurrent motif, a humorous picture of venturesome Little Man daring to explore unknown dangers and emerging triumphant, until the last adventure, that is, which nonetheless immortalizes him. His constant mentor is his 'Older Sister', mature Woman, voicing as always counsels of prudence and caution which have precisely the opposite effect of spurring him on to the very goals from which she attempts to dissuade him. The common pattern may be readily seen in almost any account of the exploits of Chahkabesh (cf. Texts 3-6, 13-17, 29, 56) and is sometimes delineated in greater detail as in Text 13:12.

First, the setting: Chahkabesh sees or hears something which excites his curiosity. He investigates and reports back to his sister, who promptly warns him not to take a chance by going there or doing what he proposes (whichever it may be) for fear of the dreadful consequences:

---

[8] *cahkâpês* has been translated as 'Shadow Manikin'; the name seems opaque as to meaning for all Cree speakers consulted to date. Forms such as *awikâstêhtin-*, *cahkâstêhtin-* 'make a shadow' allow for identification of *awik...* (which occurs in *awikâ-* 'get dark, become dusk') and *cahk...* as recurrent partials. A suggested etymology is to see *cahk...* as meaning something like 'put a dark mark' (on a clear surface). *cahkipêham* means 'he dots it, puts a dot on it', as over a syllabic to show vowel length. The medial ...*âstê*... presumably parallels the initial stem *wâstê*- VII 'be light'. A shadow is produced by something which obstructs or blocks the light (i.e., is 'obluccent'). Of a person walking past a window and momentarily blocking the light one would say, *cahkâstêpaliw* 'he makes a shadow (as he goes by)', or of someone standing in a doorway, *cahkâstêšin* 'he casts a shadow (blocking the light)'. A mother directing a child's attention to the moon might be heard to say, *kiwâpamâw nâ? ana kâ-cahkâstêšihk?* 'Do you see him? That one who casts a shadow?' Chahkabesh, then, is the Little Shadow Man who casts a shadow on the light surface of the moon.

" *'kâwina mîna wîskâc antê ohc'-îtohtê, kâ-k'-îši-pêhtaman anima*
kêkwân," itwêw.
"ê'kwâni, 'kwâni, nimišêh. kisêkimin. môna mîna n'ka-ohc'-îtohtân antê
kâ-k'-îši-pêhtamân anima kêkwân," manâ itwêw cahkâpêš. (14:2)
' "Don't ever go there again where you heard that thing," she said.
"All right, all right, Big Shishter. You're scaring me. I won't ever go
there again where I heard that thing," Chahkabesh then said.'

But, as the narrator commented:

'kwantaw mâk' ani ê-itwêt. 'kwâni piko mîna kê-wâpaninik 'ci-kîwêt
antê kâ-k'-îši-pêhtahk animêniw kêkwâniw, mâtih tâpwê ê-ytên'tahk.
(14:2)
'But he just said it off-handedly. Simply to go back there the next
morning to where he had heard that thing, that's what he really had in
mind.'

And now, following the setting, comes the characteristic two-stage
development:

Stage 1: Bright and early next morning off goes Chahkabesh, announcing
that he is going 'somewhere he has never gone before'. As he pursues his
goal he invariably gets into trouble.

Stage 2: He either escapes through great personal ingenuity or is
extricated by his sister who realizes that something has gone wrong and takes
steps to rescue him.

There may or may not be a lesson or explanation of some natural
phenomenon at the end. The episode concludes typically with some such
formula as:

'kwâni piko êskwâpihkêyâk. (14:7)
'That is the length of the story.'

As may be seen, the 'heroic' cyclic episode shares many features with the
unitary *âtalôhkân*. At the same time, certain marks of the cyclic episode
ought to be noted, in particular those of type-index signalling, theme or motif
indicators, and characterization.

Type-index signalling. Throughout the discourse considered, major action
sequences, changes of focus in the narrative, the winding up of the individual
episode and, frequently, its designation as belonging to one literary type or

another, are all characteristically if not without exception linguistically signed. In the cyclical, 'heroic' narrative the culture figure at the central focus is announced at the beginning of the episode. Where the action is staged in a legendary past, terms with a suitably archaic flavour may appear. Vocabulary shows the range typical of a hunting-gathering life-style.

Theme/Motif. The main theme is, as a rule, readily distinguishable and normally consistent with that of other episodes in the cycle. (This consistency extends to the principal actors: neither Weesakechahk nor Chahkabesh steps out of character.) It may be linked to a lesson in living or the explanation of a natural phenomenon or both. It may also be openly introduced: "I'm going where I've never gone before" – the theme of daring adventure – or be implicit in the characterization itself, as where Weesakechahk's low-level cunning backfires and the action culminates in the trickster being tricked. In each account the main theme appears to be followed closely though not verbatim by different storytellers, even though certain formulae recur with a surprising level of exact repetition.

Unlike the case with much heroic poetry in the Indo-European tradition, descriptive formulae are not a device to cope with the exigencies of metre. Hence, much of the motive for keeping an inventory of stock epithets is absent. The bear is characterized as *masko-cîpay êkâ wîskâc kâ-wayêšihiht* 'bear-spirit who can never be deceived'. This, however, serves merely to encapsulate the bear's great reputation for intelligence and so to underscore the cunning of Weesakechahk who crows: *n'kî-wayêšihâw!* 'I have deceived him!' The epithet of the bear or that of the spider 'who never exhausts his twine', unlike the resounding titles of Homeric figures, are not required to fill out the prosodic features of the piece. Apollo the Far-Darter, Swift-footed Achilles or Agamemnon, Lord of Men, are titles to call on in either half-line or full-line form as metre requires. They have no analogues in traditional Cree narrative. Nor is there call for the more generalized epithets dear to the Homeric bard, "the wine-dark sea", "the rosy-fingered dawn". Yet from time to time the language can be almost poetic, as in the description of moonlight on the night when Chahkabesh was taken up to the moon:

> *miconi mâka kî-mošišêyâpiskakocin tipiski-pîsim.* (6:12)
> 'The moon hung just like a clear stone.'

Artistry there is, but the canons and form are different. One must learn to appreciate what is there rather than look for what is not.

Characterization. Certain devices of characterization, linguistic and otherwise, can be singled out. Chahkabesh's littleness and childlikeness are emphasized by his trick of speech. He palatalizes: e.g., *nimis* 'Big Sister' becomes *nimiš*, rendered in translation as 'Big Shishter', or *itwêw* 'he says' is articulated as *icwêw*, roughly a stylistic equivalent of lisping in English. (In the case of *icwêw* the sequence *cw* violates the normally permitted cluster of sounds in the language, making it all the more noticeable.) When addressing his arrow Chahkabesh calls it *n'cakask* 'my awwow'. This baby-talk device is also used to represent the speech of certain devil-like creatures who are sub-human, cunning and childishly irresponsible in a malevolent way. An older windigo addresses a younger windigo as *n'kocic* 'my shon'. Weesakechahk, when being portrayed in a mischievous light, is often represented as feigning innocence, as in his exchange with the wild-fowl:

> "*hêy, wîsakêcâhk! kêkwân kâ-pimiwatêyin?*" …
> "*ôô …! 'kwantaw ô kêkwân kâ-pimiwatêyân. ninikamôwiniwat ô kâ-pimiwatêyân,*" *manâ itêw.* (18:2)
> ' "Yoo-hoo, Weesakechahk! What are you carrying?" …
> "Oh, just some stuff that I'm carrying about. It's my song bag that I'm carrying here," he said to them.'

Sometimes after a particularly gruesome action, e.g., the slaughter of the birds while they danced with eyes closed, he muses whimsically to himself with a high-pitched voice in a sort of horrid little boy style:

> "*šâ! tân'ka 'tê mâ' kê-tôtamwânê?*" (18:7)
> ' "Dear me, whatever shall I do with them?" '

Certain so-called paralinguistic features also serve to create the impression of spurious innocence: raised tone, diminished resonance of one kind or another, voice set, the hoarse whisper as, in the darkness of the dimly lit tent, one inquires cautiously who the mysterious stranger is who is sitting on the far side of the fire. This, of course, is hard to represent in transcription but, nonetheless, constitutes a vital part of the storyteller's art.

When Chahkabesh returns home to report something unusual which he has observed, Big Sister routinely warns: "Don't ever go there again," or "Don't ever do such and such again" – the oppressively, over-cautious adult – dare we say – female figure! And, in painting the sister's character, sooner or later we meet the inevitable 'I told you so'. As she cuts him out of the belly of the giant fish which had swallowed him, she smacks him and says:

> *"kikî-wîhtamâtin oš' êkâ 'ci-kapâšimoyin anima sâkahikanihk."* ...
> *"mâtika mâk' êkâ wîskâc kâ-tâpwêhtaman; mâtika mâka êy-ihtiyan."*
> (16:5)
> ' "I told you, didn't I, not to go bathing there in the lake." ... "See, you
> never believed it; and now look at the state you're in." '

Sometimes the account is even provided with sound effects: *zhuk, zhuk, zhuk,*
as the giants chisel through the ice looking for beaver (13:3); *tsin, tsin, tsin,
tsit,* as Chahkabesh directs his arrow to fall on the heads of the giants
(13:16), or *tingg, tingg, tingg*, as the giant women cut wood early in the
morning (14:4). The storyteller works within the context of well-defined
motifs and a commonly accepted framework, but clearly there is ample scope
for individual artistic expression in the smooth sequencing of events, the
lively representation of dialogue and situational context, and the rousing of
sympathetic response through the rehearsal of familiar themes with the
appeal which traditional stories have everywhere.

The 'Thematic' Episode (pâstâmowin). The fourth category of *âtalôhkân*,
the 'thematic' episode, is known in Cree as the *pâstâmowin*. Typical of the
pâstâmowina are Texts 21-23. The first one, The man who was devoured by
rabbits, opens with a straightforward statement of the type and goal:

> *pâstâmowin išinihkâtêw 'ma tipâcimôwin.* (21)
> 'This account is called a *pâstâmowin*.'

It continues:

> *'kwân' êši-kiskinohamâkaniwicik awâšišak ê-'pišîšišicik, êkâ
> 'ci-pâhpihâcik awênihkâna kotakiya wayêš ê-'htin'ci.* (21:1)
> 'This is the way little children are taught not to laugh at anyone
> else who is in trouble.'

Interestingly, each story of the *pâstâmowin* type is marked as one in a series,

> *'kwâni piko êskwâpihkêyâk.* (21:9)
> 'That is the length of the story.'

– but it is a cycle of themes rather than the recounting of a series of exploits
of a given hero.

One thing to be noted in passing: the first in the *pâstâmowin* series was
called a *tipâcimôwin*. The second, The man who was bitten by mosquitoes

(Text 22), is clearly marked as a traditional narrative, an *âtalôhkêwin*:

> *ê'kôma kotak âtanôhkêwin, pâstâmowin ohci.* (22:1)
> 'This is another telling of a legend about requital for blasphemy.'

As the stories are read certain characteristic features can be noted: a measure of type-indexing; a simple two-step pattern to the plot; little or no characterization of the actors; and a clear and unambiguous message. The stories then conclude with a 'one-of-a-series' marking.

The *pâstâmowin* is, in effect, a form of children's literature. It fulfils to some extent the rôle of the fable by teaching lessons in living. The language, as might be expected, is that of everyday life and relatively uncomplicated. The moral is not merely in the culmination of the account but is explicitly stated to make sure no one misses the point. There is magic, conjuring, but it all happens in an otherwise normal setting, the real world with people involved. Serious social values are inculcated; and many of these stories, possibly with editing, might well provide material for school texts.

**The tipâcimôwin*: Historical Narrative.* On a somewhat different level and yet part of the traditional literature must be included accounts of local history. These are *âcimôwina* or *tipâcimôwina*. One such (Text 30) tells how Ghost River got its name. Ghost River is a tributary one hundred miles upstream from the mouth of the Albany River. The story, as narrated in the late 1950s by the late John Wynne, tells of a successful ambush of invading Iroquois by the Crees who had been forewarned by a shaman. The resultant death of many Iroquois led to the name, Ghost River, being applied to the stream down which they paddled.

There must be many narratives of this general type which preserve factual (or what is regarded as factual) information. They might well serve to supplement or otherwise illuminate historic accounts or suppositions about prehistory.

The storyteller in this case tended to be sparing of words and the Cree style is terse and unembroidered: the bare minimum of setting, no characterization and a statement of events leading straight to the goal of the narrative. There is no dating, although it sounds like the period shortly before or just following that of European contact. No description of preceding or concomitant events is offered; and even the verb *kî-pêci-n'taw'palîstâtowâkopan* 'they had (it would appear) come to make war on each other' is in the dubitative mode. This latter suggests that the speaker assumes no personal responsibility for the historicity of the statement. And yet, it flashes a tantalizing glimpse of what must have been a significant moment in local history. One wonders whether there are other accounts among nearby bands or perhaps from among the invading Iroquois which might serve to fill out the record. Could several such accounts pieced together throw light on fragmentary annals of local history? Tales of exciting experiences or catastrophic events are often orally transmitted, the account of the Hannah Bay Massacre[9] being a case in point. In another instance a former Chief of the Kashechewan Band had been reading the biography of a personage well-known in the area a century earlier. The Chief was a highly literate and articulate person in Cree, although he read English with difficulty. He had been persevering with the book, however, and was much concerned with what he perceived to be factual inaccuracies. The subject of the biography was reported to have died at the Factor's House at Moose Factory, whereas the Indian hunters who brought him out of the bush by toboggan knew that he was dead before arrival. The hunters' account had been transmitted by word of mouth ever since, but never seems to have made the official record. It has remained within the oral tradition alone and, as such, was inaccessible to the author of the biography. As Toby Morantz has noted: "The fact that Algonquian historical accounts have survived more than three hundred years in recognizable form is further evidence of a sense of pride and interest in carefully transmitting the accounts."[10] Records of this kind must be regarded as part of traditional discourse.

Songs. Hunting songs, such a those used to propitiate the bear-spirit and promote good hunting, or those used in conjuring or for healing purposes are known to exist in other areas. Whether a memory of any such is retained in the Moose-Kashechewan area is not certain. Among the selections in the text, the only example of song is that of the muskrat (Text 45).

---

[9] Toby Morantz, 'Oral and Recorded History in James Bay', *Papers of the Fifteenth Algonquian Conference*, ed. W. Cowan, Ottawa, 1984, p. 181.

[10] *ibid.*, pp. 173-4.

Popular Discourse

The **tipâcimôwin**. At the level of popular discourse, the *(tip)âcimôwin* constitutes one of the most common literary genres. *tipâcimôwina* vary widely in type, from lively reports of personal experiences (e.g., Texts 34-39) or charming descriptions of childhood memories (Texts 24-26, 64-65), to reminiscences of long ago (Texts 40, 44, 49; 58-62). The account of a hunting experience (Text 35, Stuck frozen in a moose-hide), told by a narrator at Kashechewan, is a good example of the first type. The style is free-running, typical of informal narrative. The narrator tells it about someone he is supposed to have known, although one Cree listener remarked wryly that the story had a suspiciously high incidence of occurrence, and was told of more than one person! If it is indeed apocryphal, this attests even more strongly to its value as a theme in popular oral literature. Suspicious or not, it is a rollicking good yarn told with gusto and economy of expression. Once again, it is worth noting the presentation format: first, the setting, then the two-stage development, here set out in abbreviated form.

Setting: One winter a certain person, out moose-hunting, sighted a moose and killed him.

Stage 1: Since he was far from home and it was almost dark, he thought he would protect himself from the (winter) cold by sleeping wrapped up in the moose-hide.

Stage 2: The next morning he couldn't even stir as he was frozen stiff into the moose-hide. There he remained perhaps three days, until someone found him and built a fire which thawed out the moose-hide; and so he got out.

The Cree style is lively and the narrative is kept running, each new step being introduced by *âšay mâka* 'and now' or *êko mâka* 'and so (it was)'.

The *tipâcimôwin*, as a type, allows not merely for unrestricted choice of theme but for a wide scope of improvisation. A given theme or account may become identified with a given storyteller as a significant event in his or her life. This may then crystallize as his or her story to be told and retold on occasion and become, at least locally, celebrated. 'Old Alice can tell you about the time when ...' – a traumatic experience in her own life or that of the community, an exciting trip, where the setting and incidental features of the story may preserve information not documented elsewhere.

Description. Descriptions of technology (Texts 50-53, 62), recipes (Text 54) and the formulae for the preparation of medicines form a further category of popular discourse. While transmitted over a period of time, the format in which they occur is informal and they may be embedded in incidental conversational material. They nonetheless preserve an obvious thematic stability and discursive identity of their own.

Oratory, Correspondence. Of Cree oratory there is regrettably no example in the present corpus. The one piece of correspondence occurs in the context of a conversation (Text 43:3-7) where the spoken line on the recording is sometimes uneven since it was read from a handwritten, syllabic text.

Conversation. Three conversations (Texts 41-43) are included as examples, not of any literary form, but of a natural, desultory speaking style in the Swampy and Kashechewan Cree dialects. Both were unrehearsed and unsupervised. The editor was absent, except briefly at one point, and the recording was carried out by one of the speakers. Two further conversations (Texts 57, 67) furnish examples of natural speaking style in Moose Cree. The editor, while a non-participant, was present and recorded both.

I

Legends and Narratives:

Swampy Cree

Simeon Scott
Xavier Sutherland

tântê ka-ohcîwâkopanêništam-ininiwak

1   êko, kê-tipâcimoyân kotak âtanôhkân.[1] n'ka-tipâcimon ê-'tâtanôhkâsoyahk
kînanânaw ininiwak kâ-itikawiyahk. nêsta n'ka-âtanôhkân tântê
kâ-ohcîyahk wêhci-kî-pêci-… wêhci-kî-tašîhkâtotamahk ôm' âskiy kînanânaw
ê-'ninîwiyahk.[2]

2   êko isa, kê-kihcihtâyân nîštam.
     kotak askiy k'-îhtakwan išpimihk, itwâniwan. tâpiskôc ôm' âskiy
kâ-tašîhkâtotamahk[3] piko mâka pîtoš ê-itên'tâkwahk pimâtisîwin, nêšta pîtoš
ê-ispanik ê-tahkâyâk, ê-kîšowâyâk; mâka,[4] ôm' âskiy kâ-iš'-îhtâyâhk pišišik
w'-îspaniw ê-tahkâyâk.

3   êko anim' êšpimihk kâ-tipâcitocikâtêk askiy kâ-kî-ohcîcik nîšo
awênihkânak, pêyak iskwêw nêsta pêyak nâpêw, kî-kây… kî-tašihkêwak
nêmêniw askîniw išpimihk kâ-'htakwaninik. šâkoc[5] kî-kiskên'cikâtêw ôma
askiy kâ-tašîhkêyahk ê-ihtakwahk.
     êko pêyakwâ kâ-ayamihikocik awênihkâna, mêkwâc nêmêniw otaskîwâw
kâ-kîy-ohci-ohpikicik. k'-îtikowak, mâka, "kiwî-n'tawâpahtênâwâw nâ nêm'
âskiy, capašîš kâ-'htakwahk?"
     êwakômêniw kâ-kîy-âlimôtamâhcik[6] ôma kâ-tašîhkâtotamahk kî'nânaw.
"êhê," kî-itwêwak, "n'k'-êtohtânân."
     "anim' âskiy," k'-îtikowak, "pîtoš ispaniw, pîtoš itên'htâkwan ispîš ôma
kâ-tašîhkâtotamahk, kâ-tašîhkâtotamêk[7] anohc mêkwac ê-pimâtisiyêk. pîtoš
mâka ka-iši-miskênâwâw nêma n'tawâpahtamêkwê. tahkâyâw nêtê, nêst'
âskaw kišitêw."
     "pêpîtoš ispaniw nâspic. w'-îtohtêyêkwê mâka, ka-n'tawâpamâwâw êhêpik
ê-kišipâk ôm' âskiy kâ-iš'-îhtâyêk. êkot' ê-tasîhkêt."

4   êhêpik kâ-itiht, êwakwân' otahnapihkêsiw,[8] êkâ wîskât kâ-câkinahk
pîšâkanâpîniw, êko kâ-n'tawâpamâcik anihi, êhêpik kâ-itimihci. êko
kâ-otihtâcik.
     êko kâ-kakwêcimikocik, "tântê wâ-itohtêyêk. kiwî-n'tawâphtênâwâw nâ
nêm' âskiy, kotakîy capašîš kâ-'htakwahk?"
     "êhê," k'-îtwêwak.
     "kayâm," k'-îtwêw êhêpik. "n'ka-ošihtân pîšâkanapiy
kici-nîhtâpihkên'takok."[9]
     êko mâka, kâ-ošihtât pîšâkanâpîniw pîniš, ê-kînikwân-âpacihtât[10] pîniš,
pîniš išpimihk.

Where the first people came from

1   So then, I shall tell another legend. I'll tell a story, the legend about ourselves, the people, as we are called. Also I shall tell the legend about where we came from and why we came ..., why we who are living now came to inhabit this land.

2   Now then, first I shall begin.
     The other land was above, it is said. It was like this land which we dwell in, except that the life seems different; also it is different on account of its being cold and mild [here]. So then, this land where we are invariably tends to be cold.

3   So that is the land above which is talked about from which there came two people, one woman and one man, ... they dwelt in that land which was above. But it was certainly known that this world where we live was there.
     Now then at one time someone spoke to them, while they were in that land of theirs where they were brought up. He said to them, "Do you want to go see yonder land which is below?"
     The very one about which they were spoken to is this one where we dwell.
     "Yes," they said, "we will go there."
     "That land," they were told, "is different, appears different from this one which we dwell in, which you dwell in now during your lifetime. But you will find it different there, should you go to see that land. It is cold yonder. And sometimes it is hot."
     "It fluctuates considerably. If you wish to go there, however, you must go see the spider at the end of this land where you are. That is where he lives."

4   The spider, as he is called, that is the one who is the net-maker, who never exhausts his twine, – so they went to see him, who is called the spider. So they reached him.
     Then he asked them, "Where do you want to go? Do you want to go and see yonder land, the other one which is below?"
     "Yes," they said.
     "Very well," said the spider. "I shall make a line so that I may lower you."
     So then, he made a line up to, – working it around up to, up to the top.

"môn' êškwâ, môn' êškwâ wawâc âpihtaw," kî-itwêw.

êko k'-âyamihât ê-wîhtamawât, "n'tawâc 'ci-nîhtâpihkênât pwâmoših kîšihtât kê-yskwâpêkahkipan."

5 êko kâ-wîhtamawât, "anim' âskiy kâ-wî-n'tawâpahtamêk tahkâyâw nêšta âskaw kîšowâyâw. šâkoc mâka kata-ihtâw anta 'wênihkân kê-kiskinohamâtâk, kê-yši-miskamêk kici-pimâtisiyêk, ispî kîy-otihtamêkwê. misiwê kêkwâniw wîna, wîna ka-wîhtamâkowâw, kê-'t'-îsi-minopaniyêk."

êko kâ-ošihtât kê-'šiy-apin'ci,[11] ê-nîhtâpihkênât, nâpêw nêsta iskwêw. kî-pôsiwak anima tâpiskôc mîwat[12] ê-'sinâkwahk.

êko kâ-, kâ-wanašiwâtât mêkwâc ê-pim'panin'ci: "pêyak piko tâ-ytâpiw," k'-îtêw. "pêyak mâka môna ta-ytâpiw, pâtimâ kî-šamiškamêkwê askiy. tâpiskôc ka-itâpinâwâw."

6 êko ê-pim'pan'cik mêkwâc, pêyâk k'-îtâpiw. kêka kî-têpâpahtam askîniw. kî-wîhtamawêw mâka, "âšay têpinâkwan askiy."

mîna kî-wîhtamawêw, "âšay têpinâkwanwa sîpiya."

kî-wîhtamâkaniwanwak mâka, "kišâspin pêyak, ... kišâspin tâpiskôc itâpitwâwê pwâmoših otihcipanicik askîniw, miši-mikisiwi-wacistonihk 'ci-pîhcipan'cik êkâ mâka wîskâc 'ci-kî-wanawî-nîšâhtawîcik[13] anta ohci."

êkot' ânta kê-yhtâcik. ê'kwâni kâ-itihcik.

êko kâ-wîhtamawât, "âšay sâkahikana têpinâkwanwa. âsay maškwašîya."

êko tâpiskôc êtâpicik pwâmoših otihcipanicik mwêhci ê-kišipanaskisicik mistikwak ê-'htâcik. êko kâ-pimicipanicik nakiskaw; êko pâhcipan'cik miši-mikisiwi-wacistonihk. êkot' âni kâ-pîhcipanicik, ê-kî-pîkonahkik otonašawâtikowîniwâw.

7 êko mâka, "itâpik capašîš!"

kî-wâpamêwak misiwê awiyâšîša kâ-pimâtisin'ci ant' âskîhk: maskwa, atihkwa, amiskwa, nikikwa, ocêka, šakwêšiwa, kîhkwahâkêwa, pišiwa.

êko pêyakwâ kî-pimohtêw anta mwêhci tipiskôc atihk.

kî-itêwak mâka, "pêci-n'tawâ'minân. môna n'kî-nîšâhtawînân."

atihk itêw, "môna, môna wîskac n'kospâhtawîn."

kî-wâpahtinêw mâka oškašîya ê-'šinâkosin'ci.

êko mîna kâ-pimohtêt pišiw.

êko mîna kâ-itâcik, "pêci-n'tawâpaminân."

"môna wîskât, ... kâwîn îhkât n'kohpâtawîsi,"[14] k'-îtwêw pišiw.

môna tâpwêw. wayêšimêw. êkwâniy aspin mîna êy-omayâškahk.

"Not yet, not yet even half done," he said.

Then he spoke to them telling them, better for him to let them down even before he finished it the length it should be.

5 Then he told them, "That land which you want to go and see is cold and sometimes mild. But there will certainly be someone there who will teach you, where you will find a living once you have reached it. He, he will tell you every thing so you will get along well."

So he made a place for them to sit as he lowered them, the man and the woman.

They got in together, into that thing which looked like a bag.

Then he instructed them what to do during their trip. "Only one must look," he said to them. "But one must not look until you have made contact with the earth. You may both look then."

6 So, meanwhile as they went along, one looked. At last he caught sight of the land.

The one told the other, "Now the land is in sight."

Again the first told the other, "Now the rivers are in sight."

They had been told however, that "if one, … if they both look together, before they come to the land, they will go into the great eagle-nest and they will never be able to get out and climb down from there."

That's where they will be. That's what they were told.

Then the one told the other, "Now the lakes are in sight. Now the grass."

Then they both looked before they arrived, as they were right at the top of the trees. Then they went sideways for a short while; then they went into the great eagle-nest. That's were they went in, having violated their instructions.

7 Now then, "Look down!"

They saw all the creatures which live there on earth: the bear, the caribou, the beaver, the otter, the fisher, the mink, the wolverine, the lynx.

Then at one point the caribou walked there right across [from them].

They said to him, "Come and help us. We cannot get down."

The caribou said to them, "No. I never climb up."

He showed them what his hooves looked like.

Then the lynx came by.

So once more they said to him, "Come and help us."

"Never, … not effer am I climbing," said the lynx.

He was not telling the truth. He was deceiving them. Then away he went again past them.

8   êko maskwa kâ-pêci-takošihk.

êko kâ-itât…, kâ-itâcik,[15] "pêci-n'tawâ'minân."

môna kinwêš ohci-n'tohtam maskwa, êkwâni kâ-'t'-îši-šamatâskot
ê-n'tawâ'mât. nêsta kotak kîhkwahâkêw kâ-itiht. pêhpêyakwâ kî-'mohtêwak
ê-nîšâhtawîhtahâcik.

šâkoc mâka maskwa kî-nôsonêhokow anihi ininiwa.

êwakômêniw kâ-k'-îtikocik, "k'-âyâwâwâw anta 'wênihkân
kê-kiskinohamâtâk kê-'ši-pimâcihoyêk."

awa maskwa, kî-kiskinohamawêw misiwê kêkwâniw kê-'ši-pimâcihon'ci.[16]

9   êkota k'-âti-ohci-mihcêticik ininiwak ôko kistôtêw, awênihkânak
kâ-kîy-ohcîcik kotak askîniw. kî-pimâtisiwak ê-nihtâwikihâcik
ocawâšimišiwâwa pîniš ayâniskê. êwakwânima kînanânaw pîniš anohc
kâ-kîšikâk. ê'kwâni wêhc'-îhtâyahk ôm' âskiy.

10   nêsta pâtimâ kîy-ati-otihcipaniwak kâ-wâpisicik êy-ati-otihtâcik ininiwa
ôma askiy kâ-'š'-îhtâyahk.

ê'kwan' înikohk kêy-âtanôhkêyân.

8   Then the bear arrived.

So he said to them, … they said to him, "Come and help us."

The bear didn't listen for long; but then he started to get up on his hind legs to go and see them. Also another one, the wolverine as he is called. They made one trip each as they brought them down.

But the bear was followed by those people.

That was the very thing which had been said to them, "You will have someone there who will teach you to survive."

This bear, he taught them everything about how to keep alive there.

9   It was there that these people began to multiply from one couple, the persons who had come from another land. They lived giving birth to their children generation after generation. That is us right up until today. That is why we are in this country.

10   And by-and-by the White People began to arrive as they began to reach us people, who live in this country.

That is as much as I shall tell.

mâwaci-oskac ê-takošinowâkopanê ininiwak ôta askîhk

1   êko kê-tipâcimoyân, âtanôhkân ê-'tâtanôhkâtisocik wînawâw tipinawê
ininiwak kâ-itihcik.

pêyakwâ kî-tipâcimow pêyak kišêy-'iniw ê-'tâtanôhkâtêk ôm' âskiy kânata
kâ-iš'-îhtâyahk.

môna 'wênihkân ohc'-îhtâw ôta wêskac. kî-pišišikwâw ôm' âskiy. šâkoc
kî-ihtâwak ininiwak kotak askiy, išpimihk nêtê. êkotânta kâ-iši-pimâtisicik
ininiwak kâ-itihcik wêskac.

2   pêyakwâ mâka ê-kîšikâk k'-îhkin, pêyak ininiw, ê-pimohtêt ê-wîcêwât
mâka owîkimâkana ê-nîšicik piko kiyâpac. êko, kâ-pêhtahkik
pêhtâkosîwininiw, êkâ mâk' ê-wâpamâcik anihi k'-âyamin'ci 'wênihkâna.

kîy-ayamihikowak, êkâ mâka ê-wâpamâcik.

êko kâ-itikocik, "kiw'-îtohtânâwâw nâ kotak askiy?"

"êhê," mâka, k'-îtwêwak.

3   "êhê, ka-k'-îtohtânâwâw isa. atâmihk nêtê capašîš ihtakwan anim' âskiy.
nâspic mâka mistahi pîtoš ihkin, môna tâpiskôc ôta kâ-iš'-îhtâyêk. anim'
âskiy kâ-wî-n'tawâpahtamêk, nâspic tahkâyâw âskaw. âskaw mâka kišitêw.

êko mâka, ihtâw, – ihtâw 'wênihkân kê-wîhtamâtâk ê-kišipaskamikâk ôm'
âskiy kâ-iši-nîpawiyêk. êkot' âni mâka kê-'htohtêyêk, ka-wâpamâwâw antê.
êwakwâna mâka kê-wîhtamâtâk misiwê kêkwân, kê-tôtamêk nêsta kê-tôtâtâk
ispîy otihtêkwê."

êkwâni êti-kihtohtêcik. môna ohci-wâpamêwak anihi 'wênihkâna
kâ-ayamihikocik, piko pêhtâkosîwin' kîh-pêhtamwak. êko k'-êtohtêcik.

4   âšay mâka êti-kišipiskahkik[1] askîniw, êko kâ-wâpamâcik awênihkâna.
êhêpik išinihkâsoniwa. êhêpik mâka, êwakwâna otahnapihkêsiw,
mišiy-otahnapihkêsiw.

êko kâ-ayamihikocik anihi, twoyêhk kî-kiskênimikowak ê-pêci-… ispî
wêtihtâcik nêsta tântê wâ-tôtahkik.

êko kâ-kakwêcimikocik: "êkoši," k'-âti-kiskênimikocik, "kiwî-itohtânâwâw
nâ kotak askiy?"

"êhê," k'-îtwêwak.

êko kâ-itwêt êhêpik, "pitamâ isa n'ka-ošihtân pîšâkanâpiy. êkota
êwakwânima mâka kê-nîhtâpihkên'takok ašit kê-'šiy-apiyêk, n'ka-ošihtân.
ka-nîhtâpihkên'tinâwâw mâka ispîy ati-kinwâpêkahki. êko mâka anim' âskiy

The arrival of people here on earth at the very beginning

1   Now then I shall tell a story, a legend which those who are themselves called the [Indian] people tell about themselves.

Once a certain old person told a story, a legend told of this land, Canada, where we are.

There was nobody here long ago. This land was empty. To be sure there were people, another land, up yonder. There it was that there lived long ago those who are called 'the People'.

2   One day it happened that a certain person was walking along in the company of his wife, there still being only two of them. Then they heard the sound of a voice without seeing that person who was talking.

They were spoken to, and still they didn't see him.

Then he said to them, "Do you want to go to another land?"

And they said, "Yes."

3   "Yes, you can go then. Down there below is that land. But it is very greatly different, not like here where you are. That land which you want to go to see is sometimes very cold. But sometimes it is hot.

So then, there is, – there is someone who will tell you at the end of this land where you are standing. That's the way you will be going; you will see him there. And that is the person who will tell you everything which you are to do and which he will do for you once you reach him."

Then they set out. They did not see that person who spoke to them; they only heard the sound of the voice. So, off they went.

4   Now, however, as they came to the end of the land they saw someone. Spider was his name: Spider, that is the one who is the net-maker, the great net-maker.

So he spoke to them; immediately he knew they were coming to ..., when they arrived and what they wanted to do.

So they were asked by him, when he came to know them, "Well then, do you want to go to another land?"

"Yes," they said.

So the spider said, "First, then, I shall make a line; and I shall make that very line right here by which you will be lowered, along with a place where you will sit. And I'll lower you whenever the line begins to get

kâ-wî-n'tawâpahtamêk, mistahi pîtoš. kišitêw antê âskaw, nêsta nâspic
âskaw tahkâyâw. šâkoc mâka, kî-otihtamêkwê k'-ayâwâwâw anta 'wênihkân
kê-kiskinohamâtâk kê-'ši-pimâcihoyêk, ê-tôcikâtêk ê-'ši-pimâcihonâniwahk
anim' âskiy. nêsta ispî nîhtâpihkênitakokê môna, – môna tâpiskôc
ka-itâpinâwâw. pêyak piko ta-itâpiw. kišâspin itâpiyêkwê tâpiskôc,
miši-mikisiwi-wacistonihk ka-pîhcipaninâwâw. môna mâka wîskâc
ka-kî-wanawînâwâw anta ohci."

5   êko ispîy êti-kinwâpihkêyânik êy-ošihtât, "môn' êškw' wâwâc âpihtaw,"
itwêw. "šâkoc mâka âšay ka-nîhtâpihkênitinâwâw. n'ka-ispîhci-ošihtân
mâka mêkwâc ê-'ti-nîšâpihkên'takok. pêyak piko t'-êtâpiw. kišâspin
itâpiyêkwê tâpiskôt âšay kîh-wîhtamâtinâwâw kici-pîhcipaniyêk
miši-mikisiw'-wacistonihk. môna mâka ka-kî-nîšâhtawînâwâw. êkwâni
nîšwâ êtitakok."

     êko âšay pakitâpihkênêw. pêyak mâka k'-îtâpiw. kinwêš kî-pim'paniwak
ê-nîhtâpihkênihcik.[2]

6   kêka mâka kî-têpâpahtam kêkwâniw ana kâ-itâpit.

     êko kâ-wîhtamawât anihi êkâ kâ-itâpin'ci: "âšay niwâpahtên kêkwân,"
itêw. "âšay niwâpahtên askiy," itwêw. "âšay, âšay niwâpamâwak
mistikwak," itwêw. "âšay niwâpahtên sîpiya. âšay niwâpahtên nêsta
sâkahikana."

     'kwâni k'-ât'-îtwêt.

     "âšay, âšay niwâpahtên maškwašîya," itwêw.

     êko tâpiskôc êtâpicik.

     ispî mâka anima ê-'hkininik, kî-pimicipaniwak mwêhci mistikwa âšay
êy-otihtâcik.

     êko kâ-pîhcipanicik miši-mikisiwi-wacistonihk. êkotânta mâka kâ-ihtâcik,
– êkâ ê-kî-nîšâhtawîcik, ê-kî-pîkonahkik kâ-k'-îtihcik êkâ 'ci-tôtahkik.

7   êko mâka capašîš ê-'tâpicik kî-wâpamêwak awiyâšîša ê-pamâtakân'ci[3]
nêsta ê-papâmohtên'ci nêsta kotak' awiyâšîša.

     êko kî-wâpamêwak ê-pêci-nôkosin'ci atihkwa, mwêhci 'ci-pimohtên'ci anta
tipiskôc kâ-iš'-îhtâcik.

     êko mâka kâ-…, ispîy anta tipiskôc êhtân'ci, kî-ayamihêwak:
"pêci-nâtâhtawitotawinân. môna n'kî-nîšâhtawînân," k'-îtêwak atihkwa.

     "môna wîskâc … môna wîskât n'kospâhtawîn," k'-îtwêw atihk. "môna
n'kî-kospâhtawîwâkân ôko niškašîyak kâ-išinâkosicik," k'-îtwêw.

     kî-wâpahtinêw oškašîya. ê'kwânima k'-âspin-nêtê-mayâškawât.

     êko mîna, nâkê mâka kî-pêci-nôkosiw pišiw. êko, êko kâ-itâcik,

long. So then that land which you want to go to see is much different. It is hot there sometimes, and sometimes it is very cold. But to be sure, when you have reached it you will have someone there who will teach you how to survive there, what is to be done in making a living in that land. And when I am lowering you, you must not, – not look out together. Only one must look out. If you look out together you will go into the great eagle-nest. And you will never get out from there."

5 So when the line began to get long as he made it, he said, "It is not yet even half long enough. But now I will let you down. I'll make it up to length while I'm beginning to lower you. Only one must look out. If you both look about I have already told you that you will go into the great eagle-nest. And you will not be able to get down. So I am telling you twice."

So now he lowered them. One looked out. For a long time they went along as they were lowered by the line.

6 Finally the one who was looking out caught sight of something.

Then he said to the one who was not looking out: "Now I see something," he said. "Now I see land," he said. "Now, now I see trees," he said. "Now I see rivers. Now I see lakes too."

That's what he began to say.

"Now, now I see grass," he said.

Then they both looked.

But the moment that happened, they went sideways just as they were now reaching the trees.

So it was that they went into the great eagle-nest. And there it was that they stayed, being unable to climb down, because they had transgressed what they had been told not to do.

7 So then as they looked around below they saw creatures swimming and walking about, and other creatures.

Then they saw the caribou coming into view, so that he would walk right abreast of where they were.

So then when ..., once he was abreast of that point, they spoke to him: "Come up the tree to us. We cannot climb down," they said to the caribou.

"I never climb up," said the caribou. "I can't use these hooves of mine which look like this for climbing," he said.

He showed them his hooves. And with that he went right past them.

"pêci-nâtâhtawitotawinân. môna n'kî-nîšâhtawînân."

"kâwîn wîhkât n'gohpâtawîsi.[4] môna wîskât n'kospâhtawîn," itwêw pišiw, ê-kinâskit.

nâspic kaškihow ana pišiw ê-kospâhtawît. šâkoc mâka k'-îtwêw êkâ wîskâc ê-kospâhtawît. êko kâ-..., kâ-ati-mayâškawât aspin.

8   êko mîna nâkê pêci-nôkosiw maskwa.

êko kâ-..., kâ-pêci-takošihk anta êko kâ-itât,[5] "pêci-nîšâhtawîtahinân. môna n'kî-nîšâhtawînân." êkwâni maskwa twoyêhk kîy-otinêw mistikwa. otânâhk mâka k'-îhtâw pêyak kotak awiyâšîš, kîhkwahâkêw kâ-itiht. êkwâni, 'kwâni ê-nîšicik.

êko,*[6] pêhpêyak kî-nîšâhtawîtahêwak.

maskwa mâka, ispî kâ-nîšâhtawîtahât anihi pêyak nêsta kîhkwahâkêw pêyak, êko, kâ-ispaninik kici-nôsonêhwâcik maskwa.[7]

maskwa mâka, êwakwâna kâ-kiskinohtahât misiwê kêkwâniw, tân' êhkininik pimâtisiwininiw ôm' âskiy kâ-iš'-îhtâyahk. kî-kiskinohamawêw.

9   êko, êkotâni mâka k'-âti-ohci-mihcêticik ininiwak, ôm' âskiy kâ-iš'-îhtâyahk ê-'ti-n'tâwikihitocik. êko mâka, maskwa mâka kî-kistênimâkaniwan, – tâpiskôc ininiwa k'-îtênimêwak ininiwak maskwa. ê'kwâni mâka kâ-ohc'-îtên'tâkosit âhkih[8] maskwah tâpiskôc ininiw kâ-kakêhtâwên'tahk, wîna ê-kî-..., ê-kî-kiskinohamawât pimâtisiwininiw anihi ininiw' êšpimihk kâ-kî-pêci-ohcîn'ci.[9]

10   êko mâka kêka kîy-ati-mihcêtiwak ininiwak, ôma askiy kâ-iš'-îhtâyahk, pîniš wêmistikôšiwak ê-kî-pêci-otihtâcik.

êko mâka kî-minwên'tamwak ê-wâpamâcik 'êmistikôšiwak ininiwa awiyâšîši-wayâna êy-opîskâkanin'ci nêsta nâspic ê-mâminotâwên'ci amisko-wayâna, nikiko-wayâna ê-wînâmân'ci. kî-nânân'tôtamawêwak mâka opîskâkaniniwa itwâniwan, ê-minonamawâcik.

môna ohci-nisitohtâtowak.

ê'kwâni êskwâpêkahk tipâcimôwin.[10]

Then again, but later on, the lynx appeared. So, so they said to him,
"Come up the tree to us. We cannot climb down."

"Not effer do I climb. I never climb," said the lynx, as he lied.

That lynx is very able at climbing. But he *said* that he never climbed.
So ..., so he passed on right by them.

8   Then again later on, the bear appeared.

So when ..., when he arrived there then he said to them, "Come and take
us down. We're not able to climb down." With that the bear immediately
grasped the tree. Back of him there was one other animal, the one called
wolverine. Now, now there were two of them.

So they took them down one each.

However, when the bear brought down the one and the wolverine one,
then the time had come to follow the bear.

And the bear, that was the very one who guided them in everything, as
to how life went on in this land where we are. He taught them.

9   So, from that time the people multiplied, raising each other in
this land where we are. So then, the bear was respected, – the people
thought of the bear as a person. And that is the reason the bear
came to be considered, as it were, as a wise person, because it was
he ..., because he taught life to those people who had come here from
above.

10   So then, at last there began to be many people in this land where we are,
until the White-Men had come and reached them.

So then the White-Men were happy seeing the people having coats of
animal skins and very fine beaver skins, wearing otter skins. They looked for
a way to ask for their coats it is said, as they fancied them.

They did not understand each other.

That then is the length of the story.

cahkâpêš kâ-iši-nakwâtât pîsimwa

1 êko mîna kotak âtanôhkân, cahkâpêš[1] ohci.

pêyakwâ, pêyakwâ mîna ê-'šinawîkopanê[2] mihcêtoyêk wâsa ayitâcimikosiw cahkâpêš kâ-itiht. nanâhkaw âtanôhkâna mihcêt ohcîmakanwa. êwako…, êwakôma mâka pêyak kê-tipâcimoyân ê-'tâtanôhkâsot.

2 pêyakwâ ê-kišêpayâk kî-kihtohtêw cahkâpêš ê-papâmohtêt ê-nanâtaw'-pimâcihot.[3] kêka kîy-otihtam nâspic ê-išpânik wacîniw.

êko kâ-…, kâ-…, kâ-wâpahtahk tâpiskôc awênihkân ê-pimatahahk[4] ê-paskitâmaciwêt, ê-išinâkwaninik, ê-paskitâmaciwêtahahk.[5]

môna ohci-kiskên'tam awênihkâna kâ-tôtamin'ci; êko kâ-mâmitonên'tahk 'ci-tâpakwêt.

kî-tâpakwêw mâk' ânta cahkâpêš.

3 ispî mâka kâ-kîwêt, môna ohci-tipâcimow animêniw kâ-kî-tôtahk, wîkihk. môšak isa kî-wîci-tašîhkêmêw piko omisa, kâ-iškwâ-kîwasisiwâkopanê. môna mâka oht…, môna, môna mâka ohci-…, ohci-tipâcimostawêw animêniw kâ-kî-…, kâ-kî-ayitôtahk, ispî kâ-takošihk.

4 êko, is…, ispîy êti-tipiskâk kîy-ati-kawêšimowak ê-nipâcik tâpiskôc môšak kâ-tôtahkik.

êko, ispî kê-ati-wâpahkipan, môna ohci-wâpan. môna mâši. mitoni kêka kî-kîtaw'-pêhtâwak 'ci-wâpaninik.

5 êko, kî-mâmitonênimikow omisa, "tânika kâ-išinawîwanê mîna kâ-kî-kihtohtêyin?" k'-îtikow.

êko kâ-kiskisip…, kâ-kiskisipanit ê-kî-tâpakwêt, awênihkân' ê-'matahamin'ci anima kâ-ispâk waciy.

êko kâ-wîhtamawât omisa, anim' ê-kî-tôtahk.

êko kâ-itohtêt.

êko, ispîy êti-pêšinâkwahk kâ-k'-îši-tâpakwêt êkot' ânta piko mêtê-wâstênik mwêhci onakwâkanihk.

6 âšay kî-kiskisiw tân' êhkininik.

"manâ[6] oti pîsim n'kî-nakwâtaw," k'-îtên'tam.

êko tâpwê ê-'ti-pêšiwâpahtahk, kî-wâpamêw pîsimwa ê-nakwâson'ci. sakikwêpisoniwa manâ. hêh, hêh, hêh, hêh, hêh, êh, hêh, hêh.

7 êko, [suppressed laughter] êko kâ-…, kâ-k…, kâ-k'-îtên'tahk, môna kî-itohtêw. wêsâ kišitêw ant' êškotêhk.

êko, kâ-…, kâ-nâtawâpamât awiyâšîša 'ci-kîškatamin'ci anima

How Chahkabesh snared the sun

1   Now, once more, another story about Chahkabesh.

Once, once again stories are obviously told about Chahkabesh as he is called, the many different things he must have been up to. Many different legends have arisen. I am going to tell this one legend as it is told about him.

2   One morning Chahkabesh went off walking about in his search to sustain himself. At last he reached a very high mountain.

It was then that, that ... that he saw as though someone had trudged over the ridge, as it looked, making a trail over the ridge.

He didn't know who it was who was doing it; so he started thinking about setting a snare.

And there Chahkabesh snared.

3   When he returned home, however, he did not tell at home what he had done. He always lived only with his sister, of course, after they were supposed to have been orphaned. But he did not ..., not ..., but did not ...-n't tell her what had ..., what he had been doing, when he arrived.

4   So, wh..., when it began to get dark they started to go to bed, since they slept together which they always did.

Then, at the point when it would begin to dawn, dawn never came. Not even a little bit. At last they got tired waiting for it to dawn.

5   Then his sister started thinking about him. "What in the world must you have been up to again when you went away?" she said to him.

Then he suddenly remembered ..., remembered that he had set a snare on the trail made by someone going over that high hill.

So he told his older sister that he had done that.

Then he went there.

So, when he began to get close to where he had set his snare, at that very point light was showing at a distance right in his snare.

6   Now he remembered what had happened.

"I imagine I must have snared the sun," he thought.

Then in truth, as he was nearing it, he saw the sun caught in the snare. He was caught by the neck. Heh, heh, heh, heh, heh, eh, heh, heh.

7   Then, [suppressed laughter] then th..., thought ..., he thought, he couldn't go there. It was too hot there at the fire.

So, he wen..., he went looking for a creature to bite through that line

pîšâkanâpîniw [*more laughter*].

 êko kâ-..., môna kî-tôtamwak 'wiyâšîšak. iskwâsowak. wêsâ ê-kišitênik anta môna nêsta wîna kî-tôtam 'ci-kîy-âpahahk.

8 êko, âpikošîš mâka k'-âpišîš'šit, kîn'kisciy-âpikošîš,[7] êko kâ-itât, "kišâspin êkâ kîna kê-kî-tôtamowanê ...," êko kâ-..., kâ-iši-wêpinât anta.

 ana mâk' âpikošîš, kî-kîškiwêpahtam ana kîn'kisciy-âpikošîš

 êko kâ-..., kâ-..., kâ-wâstêpanik mâka kî-sâkâstawêpaniw.

kî-kêcikopaniw anima kâ-k'-îši-nakwâsot pîsim.

9 ana mâk' âpikošîš ka-wâpamâwâw ê-'šinâkosit tâpiskôc kâ-kî-pasot ê-išinâkosit. ê'kwâni mâka wêhc'-îšinâkosit itwâniwan anta ê-k'-îspanit iškotêhk. šâkoc mâka kî-kaškihtâw ê-kîškatahk animêniw pîšâkanâpîniw, kâ-k'-îši-nakwâson'ci pîsimwa.

10 êko mâka kâ-kîwêt; êko mâka têpâcimostawât omisa.

 "pîsim osa n'kî-nakwâcâw[8] nimis," manâ icêw. "ê'k' oš' âni êkâ mâši wêhci-wâpahk. anišâ mâka piko, kây-apišîš'šit mâwac âpikošîš n'k'-îši-wêpinâw antê kâ-kîškiwêpahtahk animêniw. môna kî-tôtamôpan wîna wâpoš. wâpoš kî-kocihêw. môna ohci-kaškihtâw wâpoš."

 'kwâni êtât.

11 êko mâka, kî-'yamihik' ômisa, êkâ wîskâc mîn' ânima 'ci-tôtahk, êkâ nêsta wîskâc kêkwâniw kici-mânên'tahk. mistahi kîy-ayamihik' ômisa cikêmânima ê-kî-sêkisin'ci êkâ mâš' ê-wâpaninik, wîna mâka ê-kî-tôtahk.

 ê'kwân' êskwâpêkahk anima wîna.

[more laughter].

Then were ..., the animals were not able to do it. They got scorched. Because it was too hot there he couldn't manage to undo it himself either.

8   So, the small mouse with the pointed nose, so he said to him: "If *you* can't somehow do it ..." Then h..., he threw him there.

But that mouse, he hurriedly gnawed it through, that mouse with the pointed nose.

It was then that ..., that ..., that it became light and the sun suddenly rose. That thing came off where the sun had been snared.

9   That mouse, however, you will see looking as though he was singed, looking like that. And the reason he looks that way, they say, is that he went in the fire. But he was certainly able to gnaw through that line where the sun got himself snared.

10   So then he went home; and then he told his sister.

"I shnared the sun, Big Sister," he shaid to her. "That's why it didn't even dawn. But there was nothing for it, I threw the very littlest mouse in there, and he gnawed through that line. The rabbit could not do it. The rabbit tried; but the rabbit wasn't able."

That's what he said to her.

11   So then his older sister spoke to him that he should never do that again, – and that he should never again misuse anything. His older sister spoke to him a great deal because she was frightened of course that it didn't even dawn, – and that it was his fault.

That then is the length of the story.

cahkâpêš kâ-kî-kohcipanihikot miši-kinošêwa

1   êko mâka kotak, kotak tipâcimôwin n'k'-âti-o... ošihtân.
      cahkâpêš pêyakwan.[1] âta mâk' ânim' ê-kîy-ayamihikot omisa, mîna
k'-îtohtêw sâkahikanihk, ê..., êy-otinât otakaskwa nêsta otahcâpiya.
      k'-îhtâwak mâk' anta mikisiwak ê-wacistonicik. sâkahikanihk, mistikwak
nânih sâkahikan.

2   êko mâk' anima sâkahikan kî-mâmišikitiwak kinošêwak, nâspic
ê-mišikiticik.
      êko mâka ispîy êtohtêt antê pwâmoš' îtohtêt kî-ayamihik' ômisa: " 'kâwina
'kâwina tôta nipîhk 'ci-pahkišihk kitakask. kišâspin, kišâspin pahkišihkê
nipîhk kitakask ka-wî-nâtahwâw mîna. kišâspin mâk' anima tôtamanê,
ka-kohcipanihikok anta kinošêwak aniki kâ-mâmišikiticik. êkwâni mâka
'ci-kîšihtâyin, môna wîskâc ka-kî-wanawîn anta ohci."

3   êko mâka, "hêh, nimiš,"[2] itêw. tâpiskôc, mihcêtw' ânima kî-..., kî-tôtam
cahkâpêš, "hêh, nimis," êy-itwêt. môna tâpwê ohc'-îtên'tam 'ci-tôtahk.
'kwantaw piko itwêw anima. têpinâhk 'ci-nahînawêhât omisa kêkwâniw
ê-ytikot.[3]

4   êko mâka kâ-itohtêt sâkahikanihk. kî-pimotêw[4] mâk' anihi kâ-..., mikisiw'
antê išpimihk ê-pâmihnân'ci.
      kêka mâka kî-kapastawêpaniniwa otakaskwa.
      êko mâka, ispî kâ-kapastawêpanin'ci, êko kâ-kapâšimototawât[5] otakaskwa.
      ispî mâka tâwic êt'-îhtât kî-kohcipanihikow miši-kinošêwa.

5   êko mâka ispî nêmatêt wîkihk, miconi kêka kî-kîtaw'-pêhoniwa
omisa.
      êko kâ-..., ê-..., kâ-..., kâ-itên'tamin'ci, "manâwina pahkopêkopan. êko
mâka kî-kohcipanihikow kinošêwa."
      êko kâ-itohtêt sâkahikanihk ana iskwêšiš.
      kî-miskamâ..., kî-miskawêniw' ant' ocahcâp'[6] êy-apin'ci pâhkwâhk.
      êko mâka, kî-nisitawinamêhikow ê-kî-tôtahk mwêhci animêniw
kêkwâniw kâ-kîy-ohcihikot. kî-kiskên'tam mâka ..., kî-kiskên'taminiwa[7]
mâka miši-kinošêwa watânîhk ê-ihtât.

6   êko kâ-otinahk kwâškwêpicikaniniw ana iskwêšiš.
      kî-kwâškwêpicikêw, ê-wî-kwâškwêpitât anihi kinošêwa kâ-mišikitin'ci,
"kišâspin mîskaw antê êhtâkwê nišîm," ê-itên'tahk.

Chahkabesh is swallowed by the giant fish

1   So then, another one..., I'll begin telling another tale.

It's the same, about Chahkabesh. Although his older sister had spoken to him that time, he went to the lake again, take ..., taking his arrow and his bow.

There were eagles there nesting. At the lake, there were trees at the lakeside.

2   Well then, at that lake the fish were enormous everywhere, very big.

So then when he went there his older sister spoke to him before he went: Don't, don't do anything so that your arrow falls in the water. If, if your arrow falls in the water, you will want to go after it. But if you do that, you will be swallowed there by those enormous fish. And then for a finish, you will never be able to get out from there."

3   So then, he said to her, "Right, Big Shishter." As Chahkabesh often di..., did, saying, "Right, Sister." He didn't really intend to do it. He didn't really mean it. Just as long as he satisfied his older sister because she had said something to him.

4   So then he made his way to the lake. He threw something at those wh..., eagles flying about up there.

Finally, however, his arrow fell into the water.

So then, once it had fallen into the water, he swam after his arrow.

But when he was out from the shore he was swallowed by a giant fish.

5   So then when he didn't show up at home, his older sister finally got tired waiting.

Then she thou..., thi..., thou..., thought, "Perhaps he must have waded out in the water. And so he has been swallowed by a fish."

So that girl went to the lake.

There she fou..., she found his arrow lying on the dry ground.

So then, she recognized from the signs that he had done exactly what he had been forbidden to do. And she knew ..., she knew that he was in the belly of the giant fish.

6   So, that girl took a fish-hook.

She angled, because she wanted to catch that big fish with a hook, "On the off-chance that my young brother may be there," she thought.

So, she actually did in fact hook the big fish.

êko, kêkât[8] tâpwê kî-kwâškwêpitêw kinošêwa ê-mišikitin'ci.

êko kâ-..., kâ-akwâsitâpêt.

miši-kinošêwa!

êko, êko mâka ispî kâ-akwâsitâpêt, êko kâ-..., kâ-pakocênât.

7   êko ispîy êti-mâcišwât, anta watânîhk anihi miši-kinošêwa, "pêhkât, pêhkât, nimiš. ka-mâcišon," wêhci-matê-'twêt cahkâpêš antê atâmihk, – atâmihk watânîhk kinošêwa.

êko mâka, pêhkâc kî-tôtam ana iškwêšiš ê-pakocênât anihi kinošêwa, pîniš ê-kaškihtât ê-wî-kocihât anta ohci ošîma.

8   êko mâka, êko mâka ispî kâ-..., kâ-wanawît anta ohci, cahkâpêš êko mîna kâ-ayamihikot omisa, – âšay ê-kî-ayamihikospan, mîna êkâ wîskâc kêkwâniw 'ci-tôtahk, êkâ kê-tôtahkipan.

ê'kwâni mâka, ê'kwâni êskwâpêkahk mâk' ôma tipâcimôwin.

Then she dra..., she dragged him ashore.

The giant fish!

So, so then when she had dragged him ashore, then did ..., she cleaned him out.

7   Then when she was beginning to cut him, there in that giant fish's belly, suddenly from deep inside, deep inside the belly of the fish came Chahkabesh's voice: "Carefully, carefully, Big Shishter. You'll cut me."

So then, that girl went slowly as she cleaned out that fish, until she was able to extricate her young brother from there.

8   Well then, well then when Chahkabesh had ..., had come out of there, then his older sister spoke to him again, – she had already talked to him, never again to do anything, – that he should not do it.

And that, and that is the length of this story.

cahkâpêš nêsta mâka maskwak

1   âšay manâ mîna pêyakwâ cahkâpêš, pêyakwâ ê-kišêpâyânik kihtohtêw.
pîniš manâ wâhnaw ê-ihtât ê-kospâmaciwêt wacîniw kâ-išpânik. êkâ
wîskât kâ-kî-ohc'-îtohtêt pwâmošiy anima, êkwênâk mâk' ant' ê-ytohtêt.
monâ ohci-wîhtamawêw omisa anima ant' ê-ytohtêt,
ê-ispîhci-wâhnaw-itohtêt ê-tahkotâmaciwêt mâškôc êkâ ê-'šinâkwahk anima
'ci-tôtahkipan. šâkoc mâka k'-îtohtêw.
2   âšay manâ ê-pimohtêt, kêka manâ wâpahtam ê-'miskanawên'ci awiyâšîša
ê-'mâtâhamin'ci.[1]
êko mâk' ê-'miskanawên'ci 'wiyâšîša ê-mamahkiškamin'ci.
monâ ohci-kiskên'tam kêko awiyâšîša.
âšay manâ mâka ê-'tiy-otâkošihk, âšay mâmitonên'tam ê-wî-kîwêt. âšay
manâ kîwêw.
3   êko manâ mâka ispî kâ-takošihk wîkihk, tipâcimostawêw manâ omisa:
"n'k'-îtohtân nêtê kâ-iš'-îšpâk waciy," manâ itêw. "êko mâka n'kî-mâtah...,[2]
n'kî-wâpahtên ê-pimatahahkik awiyâšîšak, nêsta mâk' ê-'miskanawêcik
ê-mâmahkiškahkik," manâ itwêw.
    "šâ-â mân' isa[3] kâ-itohtêyin antê," manâ itik' ômisa.[4] "monâ wîskâc ...,
monâ wîskâc ka-itohtâhtay antê. êwakwânik' oš' âni kâ-kî-kitimahitahkok,
kâ-kî-nipahâcik kinîkihikonawa."
    'kwân' êtât.
4   "hê, nimiš," manâ itêw. monâ tâpwê, –
    " 'kâwina mîna wîskât antê ytohtê," manâ itêw.
    "hê, nimiš," manâ itêw.
    monâ tâpwê ohc'-îtên'tam animêniw cahkâpêš kâ-itwêt. 'kwantaw piko
ê-wî-nahênawêhât omisa.
    " 'monâ mîna ta-ytohtêw,' n'ka-ytênimik iko," ê-ytên'tahk.
5   êko, wiyâpaninik, êko kâ-ošihât akaskwa nâspic ê-mamâhtâwên'tâkosin'ci
ê-itwâsot. êko kâ-..., êko kâ-..., kâ-..., iskani-kîšik kî-tašinawîw.[5]
    êko mâka, monâ ohci-kiskênimik' ômisa kêkwân wêhci-tôtahk anima.[6]
k'-îtênimikow piko, êy-ošihât otakaskwa.
    šâkoc mâka wîna, wîna kî-kiskên'tam kêkwân wêhci-tôtahk. ê'kwân'
ê-w'-îtohtêt mîn' anta kâ-k'-îši-... [pause], -mâtâhât awiyâšîša. êko kâ-..., êko
kâ-..., kâ-kâtawât omis' ânimêniw, êkâ ê-wîhtamawât.

22

Chahkabesh and the bears

1   Now then once again Chahkabesh, one morning off he went.

At last when he was far away he climbed up a high hill. He had never gone there before that, it being the first time he had gone there.

He did not tell his older sister that time that he was going there, since he was going so far to get to the top of the hill that it probably didn't look as though he would to it. Nonetheless off he went.

2   Now then, as he walked along, at last he saw it, an animal making tracks as it went over the ridge.

So then, the animal was making tracks with large footprints.

He didn't know which animal.

But now as evening drew on, he now reflected that he wanted to go home. Now then he went home.

3   So then when he had arrived at his home, he told his older sister about it: "I went yonder where there is a high hill," he said to her. "And then I spotted the tr... I saw animals going over the ridge, – and also making tracks with large footprints," he said.

"Oh, my! What did you go there for?" his older sister said to him. "You should never, never go there! They are the very ones, you realize, who caused us misery, who killed our parents."

That's what she told him.

4   "Right, Big Shishter," he said to her. Not seriously, –

"Don't ever go there again," she said to him.

"Right, Big Shishter," he said.

Chahkabesh didn't mean seriously what he said. He just said it casually because he wanted to please his older sister.

"She'll just think, 'He won't go there again,' " he thought.

5   Then, the next morning, then he made an arrow which would do marvellous things, as he thought. Then did ..., then did ..., did ... he busied himself all day.

However, his older sister did not know why he was doing that. She only thought that he was making his arrows.

But he, he certainly knew why he was doing it. It was because he wanted to go again to where [pause] ..., he had come upon the tracks of the animals. So he, so he, he hid that from his sister and did not tell her.

6   êko mâka ê-wî-kišêpâyânik, âšay kihtohtêw.

êko mâka, ispî wêhtihtahk nêtê mîna kâ-k'îši-'miskanawên'ci awiyâšîša, wacîhk kâ-kistatahamin'ci, êko, pwâmošiy anima, pitamâ kî-kakwêcihêw otakaskwa ânêspî..., tân' êspihtên'tâkosin'ci,[7] ê-piskosêkânik kî-pimotam.[8]

miconi mâka kî-pîši-wêpaham.

" 'kwâni mâka, n'cakask," itêw.

7   êko kâ-..., êko mâka, ispî kâ-otihtahk animêniw mêskanâniw kâ-'ši-mâtahât awiyâšîša, êko kâ-têpwêt.

êko kâ-matê-ohci-...,[9] -matê-ohci-wanawîyâhtawîcik maskwak.

pîniš mihcêt.

êko kâ-kâsot anta. kî-kâsostawêw ê-pêci-nôkosin'ci.

kîy-ayamihêw mâk' otakaskwa: " 'yâkwâmisî êko, n'cakask."[10]

êko, ispî pêcina..., pêci-pêšinâkosin'ci, êko kâ-pimotât.

'kwâni piko iyê..., 'kwâni piko k'-ât'-îšinâkosin'ci otakaskwa, ê-'ti-tâhtâhkišinin'ci piko, ê-yšinâkosin'ci misiwê pêhpêyak anihi maskwa, kî-..., kî-kâwahwêw[11] misiwê.

êko kâ-'škwâ-nipahât misiwê, êko kâ-n'tawâpamât.

misiwê kî-pakocênêw, ê-n'tôšwât onîkihikwa.

môna kêkwâniw anta ohci-miskam.

êko mâka kâ-kîwêt.

8   êko mîna kâ-wîhtamawât omisa ant' ê-kihtohtêt.

êko kâ-itikot: "tâpêkâ 'kâwina mîn' êtoht' ê-'t'tâpân,"[12] itêw.

êko mâka, "hê, nimiš."

" 'kâwina mîna wîskâc itohtê 'ntê," itêw. "êwakwânik' aniki kâ-kî-kitimahikot..., -kitimahitahkok wâsa k'-îtitihtay."

"âta oš' âna, n'kî-pakocênâwak misiwê; môna 'wênihkân mâka ihtâw anta, – môna 'wênihkânak anta k'-îhtâwak kinîkihikonawak."

êko, k'-âyamihikot omisa, êkâ mîna wîskâc anima 'ci-tôtahk.

9   êko pêyakwâ ê-'ti-otâkošihk mîna, ê-'yapicik, nâspic ê-min'-otâkošihk, pîniš ê-'ti-tipiskâk kî-kîšikâstêw mâka. mwêhci kî-wâwiyêsiw wayêš pîsim anima ê-kîš..., ê-tipiskânik.

êko mîna kâ-mâmitonên'tahk kêkwâniw ê-wî-tôtahk animêniw.

êko kâ-itât omisa, "n'ka-nâtahâkonân."

êko, wênawît.

6 So then, as it was about to be morning, he now went away.

So then, once he had reached the place again where the animals had made tracks, when they had packed down a trail on the mountain, then before carrying out his plan, he made trial of his arrow, to see how gr..., how strong it was. He shot at a mound of stones.

He shattered it in pieces.

"Right, then, my arrow," he said to it.

7 So wh..., and so, when he had reached that path where he picked up the tracks of the animals, then he shouted.

Then from away off came ..., from away off bears came crawling out.

At last there were many.

So he hid there. He hid from them as they came into sight.

He spoke to his arrow, though: "Be careful, my awwow."

Then, when they drew ne..., drew near, then he shot at them.

And then just ..., then his arrow just appeared as if it were just skipping along, the way it looked, one by one on each of those bears. He, he knocked them all down.

So after he had killed them all, then he went after them.

He gutted them all, searching for his parents.

He found nothing there.

So then he returned home.

8 Then again he told his sister that he was going away there.

So she said to him: "Seriously, as I was saying to you, don't go there again," she said to him.

So he said to her, "Right, Big Shishter."

"Don't ever again go there," she said to him. "Those are the ones who were caused sor..., caused us sorrow, as in fact I used to tell you."

"Nonetheless, I cleaned all of them out; but no one was there, – none of our parents was there."

Then his older sister spoke to him, that he should never do that again.

9 So one evening as they were sitting around, since it was a very fine evening, – at last as it began to get dark it was brilliant moonlight. The moon was just about perfectly round that da..., night.

So again he considered what it was that he wanted to do.

Then he said to his older sister, "I'll go to get some snow."

So, out he went.

"Don't look at the moon. He'll take you, he'll draw you," said his

SIMEON SCOTT

" 'kâwina kanawâpam tipiski-pîsim. ka-otinik, ka-ocipitik," itik' ômisa.
"ĥê, nimiš," itêw.

môna ohc'-îtên'tam tâpwê animêniw kâ-itwêt. piko têpinâhk 'ci-...,
ê-nahînawêhât omisa ê-'yamihikot. môna wîskât ohci-itên'tam, "tâpwê ôma
n'ka-tôtên kâ-išit nimis, 'c'-îtên'tahk." pîtoš k'-îspaniniw omitonên'cikan,
kâ-išiy-ayamihikot omisa.

šâkoc mâka k'-îtêw, "ĥê, nimiš."

10   êko êti-wanawît, ê-tahkonât otaskihkwa.

êko mâka, ispî mâka ê-kwâhkwâpahwât kôna, kî-kanawâpamêw
tipiski-pîsimwa, kinwêš.

kêka mâka kî-ocipitikow.

êwakwâna kâ-wâpamêk ê-matê-tahkonât otaskihkwa anohc. môna wîskâc
ohci-pêci-kîwêw anta ohci.

ê'kwâni pi...,[13] ê'kwân' ê-kî-..., ê'kwân' ê-kišipipaninik otipâcimikosîwin.
ê'kwâni.

âšay n'kîšihtân cahkâpêš tipâcimôwin mâhcic ê-'tâcimikosit.[14]

26

older sister.

"Right, Big Shishter," he said.

He didn't really mean seriously what he said. Just as long as to ..., as he was pleasing his older sister who spoke to him. He never thought, "I'll really do what my big sister said to me so she'll be satisfied." His mind changed about what his sister had told him.

But he said to her, "Right, Big Shishter."

10   So he started to go out, holding on to his pail.

And then, when he was scooping up snow, he looked at the moon, a long time.

And finally, it drew him up.

He is the actual one you can make out holding his pail now. He never came back from there.

That's the only ..., that was ..., that's the end of the tale about him. That's it.

Now I'm at the end of the last story told about Chahkabesh.

cahkâpêš kâ-kî-ocipitikot tipiski-pîsimwa

1   apišîš niwîy-âtanôhkân ê-ytâcimikosit cahkâpêš kâ-itiht. nayêwac piko
anta, n'ka-ohci-kihtâtanôhkân êkâ nâspic kici-kinwâk âtanôhkân
kâ-wî-tipâcimoyân.

2   cahkâpêš kâ-itiht, kî-pimâtisiw tâpiskôc kî'nânaw ê-ytâtanôhkâsot.[1]
mihcêt ininiwa mâka ê-'tât ..., ê-'tâcimiht.

nayêwac mâka piko anta n'kihcihtân êkâ ê-..., êkâ kinwêš kic'-îspanit
n'tâtanôhkân.

kî-pimâtisiniwa onîkihikwa tâpiskôc kî'nânaw nîštam k'-âti-nênîšiyahk.
kêka k'-îspaniw ôko kici-ayâwâcik iškwêšiša nîštam, mîna mâka nâpêšiša,
êwako cahkâpêš kâ-itiht.

3   pêyakwâ mâka ôko onîkihikomâwak kî-papâmohtêwak pakwataskamikohk
ê-nîšicik awa nâpêw owîkimâkana.

âšay ..., âšay ê-'ti-mâmišikiticik nawac ôko, ôho ocawâšimišiwâwa,
kî-nakatêwak, anta kâ-'ši-tašîhkêcik.

'kwantaw piko ê-papâmohtêcik pêyakwâ ê-kîšikâk inikohk, kî-ispaniw
kici-mêkwâškawâcik miši-maskwa. êkota kâ-'ši-wanihtâcik
opimâtisîwiniwâw,[2] maskwa ê-kî-nipahikocik ..., miši-maskwa ..., wacîhk
kâ-tašîhkêcik[3] maskwak kâ-mâmišikiticik.

êko ispî kâ-kîwasisicik, cahkâpêš omisa kî-wîci-pimâtisîmêw ê-nîšicik
tâpiskôc mêkwâc ê-wîci-tašîhkêmâcik onîkihikowâwa
kic'-îši-pimâcihitisocik.

4   ispîy ê-'ti-kîši-nihtâwikit cahkâpêš, mihcêtwâ kî-kihtohtêw wîpac
ê-kišêpâyânik ê-nanâtawâpahtahk kêy-ohci-pimâtisicik, omisa
ê-wîci-tašîhkêmât.

âskaw kinwêš k'-îtâpicîw iskani-kîšik.

êko pêyakwâ ..., pêyakwâ ê-kîšikâk kîy-itohtêw wacîhk anima
kâ-išpâpiskâk waciy.

ispîy êti-takošihk anta, kî-wâpahtam ê-pimatamwatânici awiyâšîša
kâ-mâmišikitin'ci. môna ohci-kiskên'tam kêko 'wiyâšîša.

k'-îhtâw anta pîniš iskani-kîšik ê-'pâmohtêt anta wacîhk.

kêka k'-îspaniw ..., k'-îspaniniw kici-kîwêt ê-'t'-otâkošihk.

5   ispî kâ-kîwêt, kî-tipâcimostawêw omisa. k'-îtêw mâka: "nimiš [chuckles],
n'k'-îtohtân nêtê wa..., kâ-išpâpiskâki waciya. n'kî-namêhâwak mâka
awiyâšîšak ê-mâmahkiškahkik[4] ê-pimitahahkik."

28

Chahkabesh is drawn up by the moon

1   I want to tell for a little a legend of what is told about Chahkabesh as he is called. I'm going to start the story off from just near the end, so the tale which I want to tell won't be very long.

2   Chahkabesh, as he is called, lived like us so the legend goes. He is tol... told about by many people.

But I'm beginning near the end there lest ..., so my tale won't go on for long.

His parents lived like us, when we were first starting as a couple. At last it happened that these first had a girl, and again a boy, the selfsame one who is called Chahkabesh.

3   Now at one point these parents of his were walking in the hinterland, the two of them, this man and his wife.

Now ..., now since these [children] were getting to be pretty big, these children of theirs, they left them there where they dwelt.

As they were just walking about casually for the space of one day, it happened that they ran into great bears. There it was that they lost their life, because they were killed by the bears ..., giant bears ... enormous bears who live in the hills.

So once they were orphaned, Chahkabesh lived with his older sister, the two of them, just as while living with their parents, so as to support themselves.

4   When Chahkabesh was almost fully grown, he often went out early in the morning in search of their livelihood, since he lived with his older sister.

Sometimes he was away a long time, all day long.

So once ..., one day he went to a hill, the high rocky hill.

Just as he arrived he saw the trail of the huge animals everywhere. He didn't know which animals.

He stayed there throughout the whole day, walking about on the hill.

Finally it was time ..., was time for him to return home as evening fell.

5   When he had returned, he told the story to his older sister. He said to her: "Big Shishter [*chuckles*], I went away fa..., to the high hills. I saw signs of animals making enormous footprints as they went over the ridge."

êko kâ-itikot omisa: "môna wîskâc antê ka-itohtâhtay. aniki 'wiyâšîsak
kâ-kî-mâtâhacik, êwakwâniki kâ-kî-kitimahitahkok, ê-kî-nišiwanâcihâcik
kinîkihikonawa. miši-maskwak aniki išinihkâtâkaniwanwak. 'kâwina mîna
wîskât ant' êtohtê."

6   "ʰêê, nimiš," k'-îtwêw cahkâpêš.

animêniw cahkâpêš kâ-itwêt, "ʰêê," kâ-itwêt, môna ohci-..., môna tâpwê
ohc'-îtên'tam kici-nanahihtawât, kici-tâpwêhtawât omisa. piko k'-îtwêw,
têpinâhk, kici-...nahênawê..., -nahên'tamin'ci.[5]

šâkoc kî-mâmitonên'tam mêkwâc anima ê-ytohtêt,[6] mêkwâc anima ê-ytwêt,
kic'-îtohtêt mîn' anta.

7   êko, mîna wêyâpahk, wîpac kêkišêp kî-waniškâw.

êko kâ-..., kâ-n'tawâpahtahk mistikoniw. êy-ošihât otakaskwa,
iskani-kîšik ê'kwâni kâ-tôtahk ê-mohkocikêwapit anta wanawîtimihk.

môna ohci-kiskên'taminiwa omisa kêkwâniw kâ-mâmitonên'tahk.
wîna piko kiskên'tam, animêniw kêkwâniw kâ-ohci-tôtahk.
kî-mâmitonên'tam kici-ošihât akaskwa kâ-mamâhtâkosin'ci,[7] ê-kiskisit
anihi awiyâšîša kâ-kî-wîhtamâkot omisa kâ-kî-kitimahikocik, êkâ êy-oh...,
wêhci-onîkihikocik.

êko, ê-'ti-tipiskânik, êko kâ-mâmitonên'tahk âšay kic'-îtohtêt anta,
wacîhk.

8   êko wîpac kêkišêp kî-kihtohtêw.

môna ohci-kiskên'taminiwa omisa tânt' êtohtêt.

kîy-itohtêw wacîhk.

pîniš êy-otihtahk kâ-iš'-îspisêkâniki.

êko kâ-mâmitonênimât anihi otakaskwa kâ-kî-ošihât kici-kocihtât tân'
êspihtên'htâkosin'ci.

êko kâ-pimotahk,[8] pêyak ê-piskosêkânik.

mitoni kî-pîsawêpaham.

"âhâ," itên'tam, "ê'kwâni ê-tipi-ayât, ê-tipi-ayât n'takask kaškihôwininiw,
aniki miši-maskwak ohci, kici-nišiwanâcihikocik ôhi n'takaskwa."

9   êko, ispî wêhtihtahk anima, kâ-'ši-pimitahamin'ci, êko kâ-têpwêt.

ispî payêhtahkik[9] ôko miši-maskwak, wâtiwâhk mêkwâc ê-tašîhkêcik
kî-wanawîwak anta ohci.

êko ispî wêyâpamât, ê-pêci-wanawîn'ci anihi miši-maskwa, kî-kâsostawêw,
anta kâ-iši-pimitahamin'ci.

pîniš mihcêt, ê-pêci-wanawîn'ci ê-kinwâpihkêmon'ci.

Then his older sister said to him: "You should never go there. Those animals whom you tracked, they are the actual ones who caused us misery because they destroyed our parents. They are called Giant Bears. Don't ever go there again."

6 "Ri-ight, Big Shishter," said Chahkabesh.

When Chahkabesh said that, when he said, "Ri-ight," he had no ..., really had no intention of obeying, of believing his sister. He just said it so long as, so as to ... satisf... that she would be satisfied.

Indeed he thought in his mind even as he was going, – even as he was saying it, that he would go there again.

7 So, the next day, he arose early in the morning.

Then he wen... he went and fetched a stick. As he made his arrow, that's what he did all day, sitting whittling there outside.

His older sister didn't know what he had in mind. Only *he* knew the reason he was doing that. He planned to make an arrow which would do wonders, as he remembered those creatures about which his older sister had told him which had caused them misery, and were the rea..., why they had no parents.

Then, as night came on, then he resolved that he would now go there to the hills.

8 So early in the morning he went away.

His older sister didn't know where he was going.

He went to the hills.

At last he arrived where there were mounds of stones.

Then he thought he would test how powerful his arrow was which he had made.

So he let fly at one of the hummocks.

He knocked it completely to pieces.

"Aha," he thought, "now it has enough, my arrow has enough power for those giant bears, so that they will be destroyed by my arrow."

9 So, when he arrived at that point where the animals had gone over the ridge, then he called out.

When these bears heard it, while they were dwelling in their dens, they emerged from there.

Then when he saw those bears coming out from there he hid himself from them at the spot where they went over the ridge.

At last there were many of them, as they came out moving in a long line.

êko k'-âyamihât otakaskwa: " 'yâkwâmisîwipan' îsa n'takask. ati-nânipanihi[10] piko."

ê'kwâni kâ-itât otakaskwa.

10   ispî pêci-pêšinâkosin'ci, kî-pimotêw miši-maskwa.

misiwê piko kîy-ati-tâhkišin, tahto k'-âti-pim'pa...,[11] kâ-'ši-pim'panit... -nciy otakaskwa.

misiwê kî-nîhtahwêw anihi miši-maskwa. misiwê kî-nipahêw.

êko kâ-pakocênât ê-n'tôšwât onîkihikowa. môna kêkwân ohci-miskam.

11   êko kâ-kîwêt wîkihk, nêsta kî-tipâcimostawêw omisa âšay mîna ê-k'-îtohtêt anta, " 'kâwin' itohtê," kâ-k'-îtikot.

êko kâ-itwêt ..., kâ-itikot omisa, "môna wîskâc anta ka-k'-îtohtâhtay. âšay kî-wîhtamâtihtay, êkâ mîna wîskâc 'c'-îtohtêyin anta."

"âc'[12] oš' âni n'kî-pakocênâwak, nimis, môna kêkwân n'c-ohci-miskên."

ê'kwâni kâ-itât omisa.

12   êko pêyakwâ, pêyakwâ mîna ê-'ti-tipiskânik, miconi kî-wâsêskwan. miconi mâka kî-mošišêyâpiskakocin tipiski-pîsim.

êko mâka, wî-'nâtahâkonêw. otaskihkwa mâka kî-tahkonêw kâ-mišikitin'ci.

êko kâ-itikot omisa ê-'ti-wanawît: " 'kâwina kanawâpam pîsim. ka-ocipitik."

"hê, nimis," k'-îtêw.

môna ohci-itên'tam 'ci-tôtahk animêniw. piko itwêw.

13   êko mêkwâc ê-pakitahwât kôna otaskihkohk, kî-kanawâpamêw inikohk tipiski-pîsimwa.

twoyêhk mâka kîy-ocipitikow. kîy-otinikow.

êwakwâna kâ-wâpamêk ê-matwê-tahkonât otaskihkwa an' âwênihkân kâ-matê-nîpawit anta tipiski-pîsimohk.

ê'kwâni ê-kišipipaninik otipâcimikosîwin.

Then he spoke to his arrow: "Look out where you're going, my arrow. Just travel along the side."

That's what he said to his arrow.

10   When they drew near, he let fly at the giant bears.

It just tipped every one when each one trotted along ..., when his arrow wen... – went along.

He knocked all those giant bears down. He killed them all.

Then he gutted them, searching for his parents with a knife. He found nothing.

11   So he went back home and told the story to his older sister, that he had already gone there again when she had said to him: "Don't go there."

Then she said ..., his big sister said to him, "You should never have gone there. I had already told you not to go there ever again."

"Even though I gutted them, Big Sister, I didn't find anything."

That's what he said to his older sister.

12   So once, once more as night came on, it was completely clear. The moon hung just like a clear stone.

So then, he wanted to go fetch some snow. And he took his pail with him, the big one.

As he was going out his older sister said to him: "Do not look at the moon. He'll pull you up."

"Right, Big Sister," he said.

He had no intention of doing what she told him. He just said it.

13   So while he was scooping up snow in his pail, he looked right up at the moon.

Straightway it drew him up. It took him.

He is the one you see, who can be made out holding his pail, that person who can be made out standing there on the moon.

That's the end of the story about him.

wîsakêcâhk ê-âtanôhkâsot kâ-kî-niskipotênik ômêniw askîniw

1   êko mîna kotak âtanôhkân, wîsakêcâhk êy-âtanôhkâsot.

pêyakwâ wâsa k'-îhkinôkopan, itwâniwan, ê-kî-niskipotêk ôm' âskiy. êko kâ-..., mitoni misiwê kî-niskipotêkopan.

êko kâ-mihtôtihkêkopanê wîsakêcâhk itwâniwan ê-wî-kakwê-pimâcihot.

êko mâka, kî-otinêw âtiht awiyâsîs' ant' ômihtôtihk, ê-kanawênimât.

mitoni kêka kî-kîškâyawâw nâspic itwâniwan ôma askiy.

2   êko kinwêš ant' ê-'htât, kêka kî-mâmitônên'tam kici-... [pause], -ošihtâspan askîniw. môna kiskên'tam êkâ wîskâc kici-pâhkwânik.[1]

êko mâka, "tânika kî-kâhcitinamân apišîs askiy," k'-îtên'tam. "n'ka-kîy-ošihtâhtay mâka, askiy anta, anta ohci. tâpiskôc ôma kâ-k'-îšinâkwahkipan kâ-kî-niskipotêk."

kî-kiskên'tam êkâ mîna wîskâc 'c'-îkastênik.

3   êko mâka, kâ-itên'tahk, "n'ka-pakit..., n'ka-pakitâpihkênâw pêyak 'ci-n'tawâpahtahk askîniw, 'ci-k..., 'ci-n'tawi-kâškipitahk askîniw. kišâspin mâka pêtâtê, apišîs êkot' ântê kêy-ohci-ošihtâyân askiy."

êko amisk kî-pakitâpihkênâkaniwan.

môna wawât nôminak[2] amisk inikohk nêstâpâwêt wêsâ '-kîškâyawânik.[3] nôhtaw kî-nistâpâwêw.

4   êko kâ-ocinât[4] wacaskwa, wîsakêcâhk. "kišâspin êkâ kîna n'cîc,"[5] icêw.

ê'kwâni mâk' kâ-mânênimât.[6]

êko, êko kâ-pakitâpihkênihc wacask. êko, êko kâ-..., kâ-kâškipitahk mânišîš askîniw. âšay mwêhci nistâpâwêw kâ-tôtahk, kâ-p..., kâ-..., kâ-ocipitât, âšay mwêhci ni..., niš..., n'nipiniwa, nistâpâwêniwa.

mânišîš mâk' akohkêniw' oškašîhk askîniw.

êko mâka kâ-pohpôcâcât anihi wacaskwa.

êko mâka kîy-ati-pimâtisiniwa mîna.

(ê'kwân' ê-wî-mînwâcihât anima kâ-tôtahk, anima kâ-pohpôtâtât.)

êko kâ-otinahk animêniw aškîsiniw k'-âkohkênik ocihcînihk. êko kâ-ošihtât askîniw anta ohci.

5   âšay mâka tipîspihcâtokê ê-'tên'tahk, êko kâ-itât, pêyak anihi awiyâsîša,

The legend of Weesakechahk and the flood

1   Now then, here again is another story, a legend about Weesakechahk.

Once upon a time, as you know, it must have happened, they say, that this land was flooded. So it had ..., must all have been completely flooded.

So Weesakechahk, they say, had supposedly made a raft in his desire to save himself.

Well then, he took some creatures there on his raft and looked after them.

At last this earth, it was said, was very deep in water.

2   So, being there a long time, at last he gave thought to ... [pause] making land. He didn't know that it would ever be dry.

So then he thought, "I wish I could get hold of a little earth. I could make land there from it, – like this, the way it had looked when it flooded."

He knew it would never again recede.

3   So then, he thought, "I'll low..., I'll lower one [creature] with a rope to go fetch earth, to ..., to go scratch the earth. If he brings some, then in that way I shall make a little land from it."

So the beaver was let down.

He wasn't in the water any more than a little while before he drowned because it was too deep. He drowned short of his destination.

4   Then Weesakechahk took the muskrat. "If it weren't for you, my little brother," he said to him.

And in saying that he was teasing him.

Then, then the muskrat was lowered with a line. Then, then he scra... scratched the earth a little. He was just drowning when he did it, when he bl..., when ..., when he pulled him out, he was just dy..., dr..., dying, drowning.

But there stuck into his claw a little earth.

So then, he blew the muskrat off.

And then he came back to life again.

(So then he blew on him, that's what he did to make him feel better.)

Then he took that little bit of earth which stuck to his paws. Then from there he made land.

5   Now, when he thought that this ground must be big enough, then he spoke

kîhkwahâkêwa, kîhkwahâkêw kâ-itimihci: "kînikwânipahtâ," itêw. "mâca 'sa ispahcâ, kwêskin."

êko kâ-kihcipahtât kîhkwahâkêw.

pîniš nisto-pipon k'-îtâpicîw ê-kînikwânipahtât. êko kâ-takošihk ispî nisto-pipon kâ-ispanik.

"âšay, wêsâ wês' âpišâšin kiyâpac," itwêw wîsakêcâhk.[7] "kiyâpac, kiyâpat, n'kiyâpat, n'ka-ošihtân; n'ka-nahkihtân kiyâpac," itwêw. êko kâ-ošihtât kiyâpac, kiyâpac; kiyâpac kîy-ošihtâw.

6   êko, mîna kî-kihcitišahwêw, kîhkwahâkêwa.

êko kâ-kihtohtêt kîhkwahâkêw, awênipan. pîniš pîniš, pîniš pîniš, môna wîskât ohci-takošin kêka.

kêka kî-kiskên'tam ê-mišânik nâspic askîniw wîsakêcâhk.

'kwân' êtwêt. "ê'kwâni mâk'," itwêw. "matêw[8] âšay. môna mâskôc kî-kînikwânipahtâw," itwêw.

êkot' âni, êkot' âni mâka kâ-ohcî..., kâ-ohcî..., -ohcîmakahk ôm' âskiy kâ-iš'-îhtâyâhk, itwâniwan.

môna wîskâc ohci-pâhkwâw anima[9] wîna kâ-kî-niskipotêk, 'kwâni näspic ê-kî-niskipotêkopanê.[10]

7   êko kî-..., wîsakêcâhk mâka kîh-ošihtâw kotakîniw, ê-'spîhci-kaškihot wîsakêcâhk misiwê kêkwâniw êy-icôtamokopanê.[11]

ê'kwân' êskwâpêkahk ôma tipâcimôwin wîna, âtawîna mihcêtininiwa ê-'ti-'yâniskê-tipâcimonâniwahk wîsakêcâhk pîniš kîwêtinohk mâhcic ê-kîy-at'-îtohtêt.

ê'kwânima kê-'ti-kîšihtâyân.[12]

8   êko mâka, kêka kî-nakatam wîsakêcâhk, itwâniwan, ôta kîwêtinohk ê-itohtêt.

kîy-ati-nanamêhâkaniwan mâk' itwâniwan, ê-'tapinawâpiskinikêt ê-kîwêtiniskât. nêsta êy-âtakâmišihk kîy-iši-wêpinêw mistasiniya têtâwakâm. êkotê 'ni k'-âtiy-âyîtohtêt.

êko, nêtê ê-kišikamiskânik kîy-otihtam. êkot' ânta mâka ê-'stênik otêhtapiwin, itwâniwan, ê-nikamot.

nêsta ê-nihtâwikin'ci oški-'škîš'a[13] ostikwânihk.

êko mâka ê-wanakošîn'ci wâpinêwa[14] oškîšikohk, oškîya ..., omîšâpôwinânihk wanakošîniwa itwâniwan. nikamow mâka tašinê.

9   êkot' âni pêyakwâ ininiwak nî..., ê-nîšicik ê-kî-pimohtêcik, anta kî-pêhtawêwak 'wênihkâna ê-nikamon'ci.

to one of the creatures, the wolverine, the one which is called wolverine. "Run around in circles," he said to him. "Go, run along, turn him over."

So the wolverine ran off.

Finally he stayed away three years, running around. Then he came back when three years were up.

"Now it's still too, too small," said Weesakechahk. "I'll make it more, more; I'll enlarge it more," he said. So he made it more, more; he made it more.

6   Then, he sent him away again, the wolverine.

So the wolverine went away, he was there no more. Until, until – until, until, at last he never came back.

Finally Weesakechahk knew that the land was very big.

Then he said, "That'll do," he said. "He's not here now. Perhaps he can't run in circles," he said.

That is where, but that is from ..., from ..., where this land on which we are living came from, they say.

It never dried out when it had been flooded, at that time when it must have been thoroughly flooded.

7   So –, but Weesakechahk made another one, he was so good at doing everything supposedly.

This is where this story ends, although there are a great many as one begins to tell one story after another until the last time that Weesakechahk had begun to go north.

Now I'll draw it to an end.

8   So then at last Wesakechahk left it here, they say, as he went north.

But signs were repeatedly left about, they say, as he made a windbreak with stones while there was a storm from the North; and being unable to cross because of the water, he tossed a large stone into mid-stream. And that is the way he wound his way about.

Then, he reached land's end. And right there, they say, is where his seat is located, as he sings.

Also, new little fir trees grow on his head.

So then, there are white partridges roosting on his eyes, – they roost on his eyebrows, it is said. And he is forever singing.

9   That way once t..., two Indians as they had walked along, heard someone there singing.

So, they went to see him. Then it was th..., they saw Weesakechahk

êko, kâ-n'tawâm'mâcik. êko kâ-..., kâ-wâpamâcik wîsakêcâhkw' ê-'pin'ci.
pêyak mâka ana kî-n'tawâpamêw nîštam. êko kâ-kakwêcimât wîsakêcâhk
kêkwâniw nêtawên'tamin'ci.

"nôminak isa 'ci-pimâtisiyân," manâ mâka itwêw. "kanakê
ê-'ci-kiši-n'tâwikicik n'tawâšimišak, 'ci-kî-pî-..., 'ci-kî-pimâcihocik mâka, ispî
namatêyânê," manâ itwêw.

"kayâm," manâ itwêw. "ka-mînikawin anima kâ-itwêyan," manâ itêw.

10   ê'kwâwa otânâhk kâ-ohcikâpawit kotak ininiw, "mayêw it' ê-'twêt,"[15]
k'-îtên'tam. "ta-kî-n'tôtamâpan 'ci-kâkikê-pimâtisit," k'-îtên'tam.

êko, kâ-..., kâ-n'tawâ'mât wînistam.[16]

"kêkwân mâka kîna nêtawên'taman?" k'-îtêw.

"kâkikê isa 'ci-pimâtisiyân," k'-îtêw.

"âstam," manâ itikow.[17]

11   êko kâ-otinât wîsakêcâhk. êko mâka kî-kînikwâni-wêpinêw manâ,
kî-titipani-wêpinêw. pikiw[18] mâna kâ-tôtâht, kâ-mâmâkomiht anima mâka,
kâ-wawiyêpanit, ê'kwâni kâ-tôtawât. nêtê mâka k'-îši-wêpinêw mostaskamik.

"kayâm isa kâkikê ka-pimâtisin," manâ itikow.

êwakwâni mâka kîy-asinîwipaniw, ininasiniy.[19]

êwakwâni mâka kâ-wâpamêk ana ininasiniy, kâ-..., kây-..., kâ-...,
kâ-šâšâkišihk[20] mistâskîhk.[21]

êwakwâna, ê'kwâna, êwakwâna ininiw kâ-kî-n'tôtamât kâkikê 'ci-pimâtisit.
ê'kwâni ..., ê'kwân' êskwâpêkahk tipâcimôwin.

sitting.

One of them went to see him first. So Weesakechahk asked him what he wanted.

"To live for a while, to be sure," he said, "at least until my children have finished growing, so they can m..., so they can support themselves when I am no more," he said.

"Right," said he. "You will be given what you say," he said.

10 Then this other Indian who stood behind thought, "That's the wrong way that he is saying it. He should have asked to live forever," he thought.

Then he wen..., went to see him in turn.

"And what do *you* want?" he said to him.

"That I may live forever to be sure," he replied.

"Come, then," he was told by him.

11 Then Weesakechahk took him. And then, throwing him around and around, he rolled him over and over. The same thing as is often done to pitch which is chewed, that is the very thing which he did to him when he went spinning around. And then he threw him away onto the bare ground.

"All right then, you will live forever," he was told by him.

At that point then, it formed into a stone, an ordinary stone.

And that is it, that ordinary stone which you see, which ..., which ..., which ..., which sticks out here and there on the mainland.

That is the one, that's the one, that is the [ordinary] person who asked him to live forever.

That is ..., that is the length of the story.

wîsakêcâhk kâ-itâcimikisot nêsta pinêsiwák kâ-papâmihnâcik

1 âšay manâ mîna pêyakwâ, wîsakêcâhk ê-'tâcimikosit, êko mâka ašic
awiyâšîša kâ-papâmihnâcik.[1] 'kwancaw tahkwâw ôm' âtanôhkân; šâkoc mâka
n'ka-tipâcimon.

2 pêyakwâ manâ kî-mawitônêw misiwê kâ-pimihnân'ci 'wê...,[2]
pinêsiwa cahkâpêš[3] ê-wîci-tašîhkêmât. kêka mâka k'-îtên'tam,
"cân'ka ... 'cê[4] kê-tôtamowâpânê misiwê 'ci-câkahakik?" manâ itên'tam.
âšay manâ kî-šîhkimêw 'ci-nîmin'ci. nîmihiwêw manâ, 'ci-nîmicik
aniki pinêsiwak, ê-wî-..., ê-wî-mîcisot oš' âni wêhci-tôtahk pêškiš.

3 êko, êko kâ-kihcišimocik, pinêsiwak misiwê ê-tahtowêkinâkosicik.
" 'kâwin' ayitâpik mêkwâc ê-nîmiyêk," manâ itêw.
"pasakwâpišimok mêkwâc ê-nîmiyêk," manâ itêw.
âšay manâ kihci-wêpinikâniwan ê-nîminâniwahk. nîmiwak manâ,
nîmiwak manâh pinêsiwak.

4 kêka manâ mâkah, kiskênimâkaniwan kêkwâniw wâ...,
'ti-kiskênimikow pêyak anihi awiyâšîša tâni wâ-tôtahk.
"manâwin' âwa mîna 'kwantaw niwî-tôtâkonân,
wêhc'-îtwêt ê-..., 'ci-pasakwâpiyâhk ê-nîmiyâhk," manâ itên'tam
mâkwa.[5]
mâkwa manâ mâkah kîmôc, kîmôt tôhkâpiw.
êko manâ mâka ê-wâp'mât, âšay manâ wî-nakwâtahonêw ...,
wî-nakwâtahonêw anihi kâ-nîmin'ci, "pasakwâpišimok," kâ-kî-itât.
"âšay kinipahikonaw wîsakêcâhk!" manâ it...,
wanawîpanihow manâ mâka anima kâ-'škwâ-itwêt,
nôso-wêpiškâtâkaniwan.

5 ê'kwâni mâka wêhc'-îšinâkwaninik ošôkan anima mâka itwâniwan,
anima kâ-ya-..., kâ-yšinâkosit, kâ-napošêkânik êšinâkosit, ê'kwâni
kâ-ytiškowâkopanê wîsakêcâhk ê-kišiwâhikot.[6]
êko manâ mâka k'-âti-..., k'-âti-pôni-pimâtisit ana mâkwa. kâ-yškw'
ânima, sâkahikanihk ê-ayakomot, âskaw ê-..., ê-'mâponot[7] piko šîpîšiša nawac
ê-..., êy-âpišâšininiki.

6 êko, êko pêyakwâ aniki kotakiyak awiyâšîšak ispî kâ-pa..., kâ-...,
kâ-nakatâcik wîsakêcâhkwa, êko kâ-..., k'-âti-otinât nîšo ..., nîšo 'skwêwa

Weesakechahk and the birds who flew south

1   Now then once more, a story about Weesakechahk, and along with him the creatures which fly about. This is just a short tale; but I will tell the story.

2   Once then Chahkabesh gathered together all the birds which fly as he lived with them. At last though, he thought, "What should I do to finish them all off?" he thought.

Now then, he persuaded them to dance. He threw a dance then, so those birds might dance, since he wanted ..., since he wanted to eat, of course, was the reason he did it.

3   So, so they started dancing, all the birds of every kind.

Then he said to them, "Don't look about while you're dancing."

"Swing with your eyes closed, while you're dancing," he said to them.

Now then there was a great shaking of feet as the dance went on. They danced then, then the birds danced.

4   But at last it was realized that he wanted something ..., one of the creatures realized what he wanted to do.

"Maybe this one wants to do something wantonly to us again, which is why he said ..., for us to shut our eyes as we danced," thought the loon.

And then stealthily, stealthily the loon opened his eyes.

So then as he [Weesakechahk] saw them, now he wanted to snare them ..., he wanted to snare those who were dancing, to whom he had said, "Dance with your eyes shut."

"Weesakechahk is killing us now!" he sai...,

Then he dashed out when he had said it and he was chased and kicked as he was leaving.

5   And that, they say, is why his lower back, which is flat in appearance, looks the way it does. That is the shape which Weesakechahk put on him when he made him angry.

Well then he grad..., that loon gradually died, after that, drifting about on the lake, sometimes as –, as he drifted with the current down quite li..., little creeks.

6   So, so one time when those other creatures had wa..., had ..., had left Weesakechahk, then Shingibish, as he was called, took ..., began to take

41

manâ, šinkipiš kâ-itiht. nîšo isk..., nîšo kî-kanawênimêw.

êko, šinkipiš išinihkâsow ana nikik ..., šîšîpa.

nîšo mâka kî-kanawênimêw ê-wîci-tašîhkêmât 'wênihkâna.

êko mâka kî-kiskênimêw anihi mâkwa nâspic ê-minwâšišin'ci. mâkwa mâka pišišik mîkis išîhokopan itwâniwan.

êko manâ mâka êyamihât anihi wîwa, "n'ka-maskamik kistinât mâkwa kišâspin wâpamikotê ..., wâpamikotê nîwa ê-'spîhci-minwâšîšit," manâ itên'tam.

êko manâ kâ-..., kâ-'yamihât wîwa: " 'kâwina ka-wayêšihikowâw[8] mâkwa. ta-'mâponô' 't'[9] âsay wîpac," manâ itêw. "pišišik mîkis ta-išinâkosiw," manâ itêw.

7   âšay manâ wêhci-'mâponot mâkwa. âsay manâ pêci-sêskaham. pêci-n'tawâ'mêw man' ânihi šinkipiša.

êkwâni manâ ê-kî-maskamât mâka wîwinîw ê-nîšin'ci.

nêsta manâ mâka pakwâtam šink..., šinkipiš anim' ê-kî-tôtâht. šâkoc mâka tašinê kî-nânakacihêw anihi mâkwa tânt' ê-'tiy-êhtin'ci.[10]

êko manâ pêyakwâ kî-nânakacihêw 'ci-nipân'ci. "nipâtê mâk' êkot' ânta kê-sêkahak," ê-ytên'tahk.

8   êko manâ nipâw mwâkwa. tâwatônêwêhkwâmiw manâ mâk' ê-nipât. miconi manâ šâpohkwâmiw.

êko manâ kâ-kišâpiskisahk êškaniniw šinkipiš; mêkwâc mâk' 'âstawêyâpiskitênik[11] manâ kî-pohcikonêwêyâsko-wêpahwêw mwâkwa ê-nipân'cih.

miconi manâ mâka kî-nâspitâskisow.

êkwâni mâka ê-kî-otinât mîna wîwa, anihi kâ-kî-..., kâ-kî-maskamiht.

anima mâka kâ-niscikikonêwênâkosit mâkwa, ê'kwâni kâ-k'-îtâskisot itwâniwan wêhc'-îšinâkosit.

êkwân' êskwâpêkahk anim' âtanôhkân cahkâpêš pîniš mâka mwâkw' ê-kišipipanik.

two ..., two wives then. Two wiv..., he kept two of them.

So, Shingibish was the name of that otter ..., duck.

He kept two persons with whom he lived.

Now then, he knew that the loon was very handsome. The loon, for his part, it was said, was dressed all in beads.

So then he spoke to that wife of his, "The loon will surely take her away from me if he sees her ..., if he sees my wife he's so good-looking," he thought.

So then he spo..., spoke to his wives: "Don't let the loon deceive you. He will drift along here soon now," he then said to them. "He will look like beading all over," he said to them.

7 Now then, suddenly the loon drifted by. Now he came to shore. He came to see that Shingibish.

And then he robbed him of both his wives.

And Shing..., Shingibish for his part didn't like being treated that way, and he kept an eye constantly on what that loon's movements were.

So then at one point he watched for him to sleep. "When he's asleep, that's the point at which I'll scare him," he thought.

8 Now then, the loon slept. But he slumbered with mouth wide open while he slept. He slept very soundly.

So then Shingibish heated up a chisel; and while it was white hot he shoved it down the throat of the sleeping loon.

He was instantly burned up.

And then he took back his wives again, the ones which ..., of which he had been robbed.

And that part where the loon appears dark-throated, it is because he had been burned, they say, that he looks that way.

That is the length of that legend, finishing up to Chahkabesh and the loon.

âtanôhkân wêskac, pêyak kišê-'iniw ê-itâtanôhkâsot okosisa âyâs kâ-išinihkâson'ci

1   êko, kê-tipâcimoyân âtanôhkân wêskac.

pêyak kišêy-'iniw ê-'tâtanôhkâsot okosisa âyâs kâ-išinihkâson'ci.
kî-wîci-pimâtisîmêw owîkimâkana nêsta okosisa anihi kîšikâwa. šâkoc awa
kišêy-'iniw ê-'ši-tipâcimonâniwahk ôm' âtanôhkân, môna ohci-minopaniw
owîkimâkana âskaw. (âhk' ôti piko, šâkoc itâtanôhkâniwan.)

2   šâkot âskaw mâskôc kî-mâšihkêpan'htwâw. okosisa mâka, mâ..., mâ...,
mihcêtwâ môna ohci-sâpên'taminiw ôm'[1] ê-tôtahk, âyâs kâ-išinihkâson'c'
ôkosisa.

pêyakwâ k'-îtên'tam, kici-kihtahonât anim' ê-tôtâkot ê-nanâskostâkot êkâ
kwayask, êk' êkâ kwayask ê-tôtawât owîkimâkana, ê-pakwâtamin'ci mâka
os..., okosisa.

ê-wâpamikot ôm' ê-tôtahk kî-ayamihikow mihcêtwâ.

kêka mâka kî-kisiwâsiw kišêy-'iniw.

êko kâ-itên'tahk tâwic wâhnaw ministikohk 'ci-n'tawi-pakitinât okosisa,
êkâ, êkâ nêsta ê-wîhtamawât ê-wî-nakatât anta; tâpiskôc êko kwayask
ê-wî-wîcêwât k'-îtôtam. ê-wayêšihât.

3   êko kây-..., êko kâ-nimitâwahahkik.

wâhnaw tâwic ministikohk.

êko ispî kâ-kapân'ci okosisa, êkot' ânta kâ-'ši-nakaci-wêpahwât.[2] môna
mâka mâši tâpwêht' ât' ê-têpwâtikot.[3]

'kwâni pêyakwan,[4] kî-..., kî-nakatêw anta. môna ohci-kitimâkênimêw.

êko mâka awah, aw' awâšiš, aw' ôškinîkiw, âyâs kâ-išinihkâsot,
kî-'pâmâšakâmêw[5] ant' ê-mâtot ministikohk, êkâ ê-'yât tântê
kê-kîy-ohci-âšaw'hahk.

4   êko, pêyakwâ ê-ytâpit, anta nipîhk, kî-wâpamêw 'wênihkâna ê-pêtâtakân'ci
awiyâšîša,[6] ê-otêškanin'ci.

êko mâka k'-îtikow ê-kakwêcimikot, "tân' ..., tân' êhtiyan?"

"môna, môna wayêš n'kîy-ohci-âšaw'hên, ê-kî-nakatahot[7] nôhtâwiy ôta
ministikohk," mâka itêw.

"kay-âšaw'hon'tin, nîna," itêw.

"êko mâka, têhtap' ôta nistikwânihk. mêkwâc mâka ê-pimiwinitân,
kišâspin pêhtawatwâwê ominiskiwak, wîhtamawin."

The legend of Ayas

1   Now then, I'll tell a tale of long ago.

The story is told of a certain old person whose son was called Ayas. He lived with his wife and son in those days. However, this elderly person and his wife, according to this legend, sometimes did not get along well. (It is just make-believe, but that is how the story goes.)

2   Indeed he may well have started fighting sometimes. His son fre..., fre..., frequently didn't relish his doing this, – Ayas his son was called.

At one point he thought he would take him away in a canoe because he did that to him, because he continually fought back, because he [the father] didn't treat his wife properly ..., not properly, and his son didn't like it.

Since he was observed doing this he was spoken to by his son many times.

Finally the old man got angry.

So he thought he would put his son far away offshore on an island and not, not tell him that he wanted to leave him there. So he made just as if he were going out properly with him as a partner. He wanted to deceive him.

3   So they ..., so they pulled away from shore.

Far away offshore on an island.

Then when his son had stepped ashore, that's where he dumped and left him. And he didn't even listen to him although he called to him.

It had no effect, – he lef..., left him there. He had no pity on him.

So then this, this child, this young man who was called Ayas, walked along the shore-line there weeping on the island, because he had no way to cross from it.

4   So, as he looked around at one point, there swimming up towards him from the water was a certain creature with horns.

Then the creature spoke to him and asked him, "What ..., what's the matter?"

"I've no ..., no way to get across because my father left me here on the island," he said to him.

"*I'll* take you across," he [the creature] said to him.

"Now then, sit here on my head; but while I'm carrying you, if you hear thunder, tell me."

ê'kwâni kâ-itât ..., ê'kwâni kâ-itikot.

5 êko, êko kâ-têhtapit awah awâšiš ostikwânilîhk ôh' awiyâšîša.

kêka kî-pêci-nôkwan ê-ominiskîskâk nêsta kî-pêci-nohtâkosiwak ominiskiwak.

môna oht..., môna mâši wîhtamawêw.

'kwâni pêyakwan, kêka kî-pêhtam aw' âwiyâšiš kêkwâniw ê-nohtâkwaninik.

"kêkwân kâ-itihtâkwahk?" itêw, ôh' awâšiša.

" 'kwantaw ani kink..., kitêškanak ani kâ-itihtâkosicik, ê-..., ê-kî-... cîwêyâšiwak,"[8] itêw.

6 êko ..., êko mîna k'-âti-kiht... k'-âti-kiht... k'-âti-... k'-âti-kihcipanihot awa awiyâšiš.

êko mâk' âšay '-pêšonâkwahk askiy.

êko, âšay pêhtawêw ominiskwa awa awiyâšiš.

âšay kî-..., âšay wî-pakici-wêpinêw anihi âyâsa. âyâs mâka k'-îtikot šâkot, "pistêw anima k'-âtîtakwahtihk, êkot' âni, êkot' âni at'-îši-pimohtê. môna mâka ka-šawinên nipiy." 'kwâni kâ-itikot.

êko mâk' êkwâni kâ-'ši-wêpipanihot mâka; kî-nimitâwêpanihow aw' awiyâšiš ê-pêhtawât ominiskwa. ê'kwâni mâka kâ-tôtahk âyâs, kîy-atih-... pimohtêw wakît pîstêhk, êkâ '-šawinahk[9] nipîniw; pîniš ê-..., pîniš ê-w..., êy-oš..., êy-otihtahk kâ-'ši-pâhkwânik.

êko, kêtahtawin kî-pâskiskwahikêw ominiskiw ê-pâskiskwahwât[10] anihi awiyâšîša.

7 êko, êko mâka kâ-..., êko mâka kâ..., kâ-pimohtêt nânih. nânêwêw ..., kî-nânêwêw kihcikamîniw aw' âyâš. kî-wâpamêw mâka ant' ê-'ti-nômakê-kihtohtêt watoya ê-pâhpahkišinin'ci, ê-waswêhwân'ci ..., ê-waswêhwân'ci anihi kâ-kî-pâskiskwahwât, anih' ê-waswêhwât ..., ê-waswêhkwakwahwât mâka anta kî-pâhpahkišininiwa watoya.

êko mâka âyâs ê-kanawâpamât anihi watoya, kî-ayamihikow ê-itikot: "mâtika mâka, ê-'spîhci-kopâsinâkosiyân êkâ kâ-wîhtamawiyan ê-pêtwêwitahkik ominiskiwak. 'kwâni mâk' ôma wêhc'-îšinâkosiyân." êko, kîy-ati-kihtohtêw âyâs ê-mihcinawêsit. šâkot pêškiš môna wayêš ohc'-îtên'tam, têpinâhk ê-kî-pimâtisit.

8 êko ê-pimohtêt, kîy-otihtam ..., kîy-otihtam mîkiwâmišiš ê-cimatêk. kîy-ati-pîhtokwêw mâka.

kî-wâpamêw anta ôhkôma ê-apin'ci.

That's what he said to him ..., that's what was said to him.

5   So, so this child sat on the head of this creature.

At last a storm appeared coming towards them and the thunder was rolling towards them.

He didn't ..., he didn't tell him at all.

No change. At last this beast heard the sound of something.

"What is it that made that sound?" he said to the child.

"It's only that ..., that's your horns which are making the sound, since they were ..., they are whistling," he said to him.

6   So ..., so again he kept on ... he kept on ... he kep... this beast kept on with his trip.

Now the land drew near.

And then this creature heard the thunder now.

Now, – now he wanted to drop Ayas off; and he said to Ayas firmly, "That froth, which is floating this way and that, right there, keep walking along, right there. You won't dislodge the water." That's what he said to him.

And then, he flung himself off. The creature swam quickly away because he heard the thunder. And so that's what Ayas did: he began ... to walk about on top of the froth, not budging the water, until he ... until he r..., until he ..., he reached where it was dry.

Then suddenly the thunderbolt struck, striking that creature.

7   So, so then he ..., so then he ... walked alongside. He skirted ..., this Ayas skirted the seaside. He saw, however, as he began to walk away for a while, blood-clots falling in all directions as the lightning bolt had knocked to pieces ..., as it had knocked to pieces that [animal] which it had struck, – it was the thunder which had ... had blown that one to pieces, knocking him to bits ... and because it shattered his face there the blood clots were falling all around.

So then, as Ayas was looking at that blood-clot, it spoke to him saying: "Look now, how miserable I appear because you didn't tell me the thunderstorm could be heard coming. That's why I look this way." Then Ayas began to walk away feeling sorry. Indeed, as long as he himself was alive, on that account he hadn't thought of it.

8   So as he walked along he reached ..., he reached a small wigwam which was set up. He began to go into it.

There he saw his grandmother sitting.

"A-a-ah my grandchild, Ayas," said the old woman. "My grandchild Ayas

"a-a-ah, nôsisim âyâs," itwêw kišêy-iskwêw. "takošin nôsisim âyâs."

âšay kiskisiw anihi ôsisima kâ-kî-nakatahomihci tâwic. êko mâka, kî-mihcinawêsiw mâka ôsisima ê-kiskênimât tântê wâ-itohtên'ci.

êko kâ-ayamihât: "nâspic âniman kâ-wî-..., kê-'ši-šâpoškaman, nôsisim," itêw. "môna kêhcin kê-kî-šâpoškên.[11] mihcêtiwak awênihkânak antê kê-'t'-îši-pimohtêyin, maciy-awênihkânak. môšak mâka ka-wî-maci-tôtâkwak tahto kê-'ti-wâpamacik. šâkot mâka, pitamâ n'ka-ošihtân kê-mîciyan."

9   awa kišê-'skwêw kî-'yâwêw askihkoša, ê-apišîšišit, – nâspic ê-apišîšišit askihk.[12]

êko mâka kîy-ošihtâw anta kêkwâniw tâpiskôc anôminâpoy mâškôc ê-'šinâkwahk, nêstapiko pahkwêšikanâpoy. nâspic ê-apišîšišic askihkoš. êko kâ-mînât ôsisima. êko kâ-itât: "kišâspin kaškihtâyanê ôma misiwê 'ci-mîciyan, ê'kwâni kici-šâpoškaman ..., 'ci-šâpoškawacik aniki maci-awênihkânak. êkâ mâka kitâyanê, môna ka-kî-šâpoškawâwak. ka-nipin pwâmoših otihtaman nêtê, kâ-iš'-îhtât kikâwiy nêsta kôhtâwiy."

10   êko ..., âšay mîcisow âyâs, nâspic ê-apišîšic askihk.

êko mâka, môna mâši kî-kitâw, môna mâši kî-kitâw. ât' êy-apišîšišit, tašinê, tašinê kîy-ati-kîšponêw ana askihkos êy-apišîšit.[13]

"êkw êcik' ân' tâpwê nipiyân,"[14] k'-îtên'tam.

kêka mâka, kêka kêka kîy-atiy-aciwipaniw anima ..., animêniw kâ-mîcit. kêka kî-kaškihtâw ê-kitât.

"ha-a-a, nôsisim. âšay mâka kî-..., âšay mâka kî-kaškihtân," itêw. "êko âšay ..., êko mâka ka-mînitin kêkwâna, nisto kêkwâna ka-mîn'tin," 'têw; "nisto kêkwâna ka-mîn'tin kêy-âpacihtâyin ôko maciy-awênihkânak kêy-ati-wâpamacik, kê-'ti-šâpoškawacik. êwakwâniki mâka kêy-âpacihtâyin kê-..., kê-naskowâkêyin." kî-mînêw mâka mîsâhk'-wayâna nêsta šâkwêši-wayâna pêyak, pêyak mâka cîstahikan.[15]

"ê'kwâni ê-'t'-îšinâkwahk anima, kêy-at'-îši-pimohtêt."

11   êko, êko kâ-..., êko wênawît âyâs.

"âšay n'kihtohtân nôhkom," itêw. "wâhnaw mâka ta-itohtêw âyâs."

êko ê-pimohtêt kî-wâpahtam mîkiwâm,[16] mîkiwâm ê-cimatêk.

âšay kî-pîhtokwêw mâka.

arrives."

Now she remembered that grandchild of hers who had been left in mid-stream. And then she was sorry because she remembered where her grandchild wanted to go.

Then she spoke to him: "It is very difficult where you wa..., where you will be passing through, my grandchild," she said to him. "For certain you won't be able to pass through it. There are many people there where you will be setting out to walk, wicked people. And they will always want to do you harm, each one whom you'll begin to see. But first I shall make something for you to eat."

9 This old woman had a kettle, a little one, – a very little kettle.

So then she made a thing there that looked probably something like porridge or flour-soup. The kettle was very small. So she gave it to her grandchild. Then she said to him: "If you are able to eat all this, that will take care that you get through, that you pass through those wicked persons. But if you do not eat it up, you will not be able to get through them. You will die before you reach yonder where your mother and your father are."

10 So ..., now Ayas ate, – since the kettle was very small.

But then, even so he couldn't finish it, – even so he couldn't finish it. Although it was little, steadily, steadily, that little kettle kept on filling him.

"It really seems that I'm going to die," he thought.

At last, however, at last, at last that stuff began to go down, that stuff which he was eating. At last he managed to eat it up.

"Ha-a-a, my grandchild. And now you've – ... and now you've managed it," she said to him. "So now ..., and now I'll give you some things, three things I'll give you," sh' said; "three things I'll give you which you must use when you begin to see those evil people, when you pass through them. And these are what you'll use to ..., to fight back with. And she gave him a sleeping-skin and one mink-skin and one pointed stick."

"That's how that'll begin to look, where he'll begin to walk."

11 So, so then, – so out went Ayas.

"Now I'm going away, Grandmother," he said to her. "Ayas will go far away."

Then, as he walked along, he saw a wigwam, a wigwam sticking up.
And now he went inside.
Two old women sat there. They were blind.

nîšo kišê-'skwêwak anta kîy-apiwak. môna wâpiwak.

êko mâka šâkoc kî-pîhtokwêw kîmôc. môna, môna, môna ayamihêw. nêtê k'-îtohtêw wêskwâhtêmihk. êkotê 'ni kâ-nahapit.

êko mâka môna kiskên'tamwak ôko kišê-iskwêwak awênihkâna ê-pîhtokwên'ci, êkâ ê-wâpicik.

êkot' ânta mâka k'-âpit.

12   kêkah, kêka pêyak kišêy-iskwêw k'-îtwêw, "êko minawê," itêw anihi wîci-kišêy-iskwêwa. "minawê êko."

êko kâ-otinât otaskihkw' âwa kišê-iskwêw. êko kâ-pakitinahk anta mîciminiw, pîhci otaskihkohk. iškotêhk mâk' anta kî-pakitinam 'ci-ohtênik.

mêkwâc mâk' ê-ohtênik, âyâs kîy-otinêw anihi askihkwa. pîtoš ant' âpišîš kî-pakitinêw, êkâ ê-kiskênimikot anihi kišê-iskwêwa.

êko, âšay ..., âšay âšay wî-miskawêw ..., âšay wî-natawênimêw otaskihkw' âna kišêy-iskwêw. kî-wanihêw otaskihkwa anta kâ-'ši-apinispan.

êko kâ-it..., kâ-itwêt, "âyâs mâškôc kâ-tôtahk. mâškôc kî-takošin âyâs," itwêw.

13   êko kâ-otinahk mistik.[17]

kî-nâtawi-miskawêw antê wêskwâtêmihk. kîy-..., kîy-ayi..., kî-ayitâskwanam animêniw mistikoniw.

êko mâka kî-miskawêw.

"mâtik' awah âyâs ê'kwâwa kâ-kîw-otinât n'taskihkwa," ê'kwâni êtwêt. "âyâs nâ kîna," itê...[18]

"êh'," îtêw, "nîna âyâs."

"êko, âšay ..., âšay nâ wîpac k'-wî-ati-wanawîn?"

"êhê, wîpat âšay n'k'-âti-wanawîn," 'têw.

"wîhtamawinân, wîhtamawinân isa mwêhci wî-wanawîyanê."

ôko mâka kišê-'skwêwak k'-îšinihkâsowak otôskwanêsiwak. otôskwaniwâhk kîy-ohci-nipahêwak awênihkâna. êko mâka, êko mâka k'-îtên'tamwak, "ispî wanawîtê ant' êškwâtêminihk, n'k'-êspanihonân êko mâka, kêy-otôskwanahwakiht anah. n'ka-nipahânân âyâs," k'-îtên'tamwak.

14   êko, êko kâ-otinât omîsâhkwayânah, hâyâs.

k'-îtâskwahwêw antê iš..., iškwâtêmihk.

êko kâ-itât: "âšay niwî-wanawîn." êko kâ-itâskwahwât antê. êko kâ-ispanihocik aniki otôskwanêsiwak ê-wâwâhcipiskwanêpanihocik anta, ê... iškwâtêmihk.

êko kâ-itâškwahwât anta omîsâhkwayâna âyâs.

êko mâka kîy-otôskwanahotowak aniki kišêy-iskwêwak, pîniš ê-nipahitocik

Now then he went in stealthily indeed. He didn't, didn't, didn't speak to them. He went over to the back part of the wigwam. There he seated himself.

Now then, these old women didn't know that anyone was coming in, since they were blind.

And that is where he sat.

12 At last, at last one old woman said, "Cook something." She said it to her fellow old woman. "Cook something."

So this old woman took her kettle. Then she put some food there, inside her kettle. And there on the fire she put it to boil.

While it was boiling, however, Ayas took the kettle. He put it in a slightly different place without that old woman knowing it.

Then, now …, now now she wanted to find it …, now that old woman was about to want her kettle. She lost her kettle from where it had been sitting.

Then she sa…, she said, "It's probably Ayas who did it. Perhaps Ayas has arrived," she said.

13 So she took a stick.

She went looking for him there at the back side of the wigwam. She …, she pro…, she prodded with that stick.

And then she found him.

"Here's this Ayas, the very one who has taken my kettle," she said then.

"Are you Ayas?" she sai…

"Yep," he said to her, "I'm Ayas."

"So, now …, now do you want to start going out soon?"

"Yes, I'll begin going out soon now," he said to her.

"Tell us, tell us exactly, when you want to go out."

Now these old women were called 'The Elbowed Ones'. With their elbows they killed people. And so, and so they thought, "When he goes out from the door there, we'll spring and then, we'll elbow that fellow. We'll kill Ayas," they thought.

14 So, so he took his sleeping-skin, did Ayas.

He held it on a stick at the d…, door.

Then he said to them, "Now I want to go out." Then he held it there. Then those elbowed ones jumped up, jostling with their backs there a…, at the door.

Then Ayas held up his sleeping-skin there.

So then those old women elbowed each other until they killed each other

tâpiskôt, "âyâs kâ-tôtawakiht," ê-'tên'tahkik.

15   êko mâka, – 'kwâni, 'kwâni mâka k'-âti-wanawît âyâs
kâ-'škwâ-nipahiton'ci. mîna kîy-ati-kihtohtêw.

    êko mîna mêkwâc ê-pimohtêt, êko mîna kâ-wâpahtahk mîk'wâm[19] mîn'
ê-cimatêk.

    êko mâka, otinîkêkanak ê-nîpitêhpisocik mihcêt, mihcêt ê-nîpitêhpitêki.[20]
awênihkân mâk' anta pimohtêtê, môna ta-šîpâsow.
ta-pâšici-kwâškwatiw piko. 'kwân êšinâkwahkipan ana kâ-iši-ihtât ana, ana
ininiw anta.

    pêyak mâk' acimošiša kîy-'yâwêw. kišâspin mâk' awênihkân
ê-kitawê-wêpiškawât anihi otinîkêkana, ênikohk mikisimow atim.

    êko mâka kâ-kwâškwatit ..., êko mâka piyâšici-kwâškwatit âyâs,
kî-kâhciciškawêw anihi oskana otinîkêkana.

    kî-nôhtâkwanwa mâk' anihi oskana.

16   êko mâka acimošiš hênikohk[21] kî-mikisimow.

    êko mâka kâ-kihcipahtât âyâs, kî-'mitišahokow[22] an' ana... anihi
atimošiša.[23]

    êko wê..., wênawîpanit ana kišê-'iniw; kî-'mitišahwêw anih' otêma.

    êko ..., êko ê-wîhpâpiskâk[24] kî-pîhcipanihow hâ... âyâs.

    êkot' âni mâk' ê-'tâpit an âtim ê-mikisimot ênikohk, êko mâka, kî-sâkit...
sâkit... ciwê..., -sâkit-ciwêpinêw[25] anihi šâkwêši-wayâna kâ-kî-mînikot
ôhkoma. ê'kwân' tâpiskôt šâkwêšiw mâka mân' êy-ocipanihot k'-îšinâkosiw
ana šâkwêši-wayân, antê 'ni... antê atâmihk animêniw êy-ohci-tôtahk anah
âyâs.

    êko, êko wiyâpamât ana, an' ininiw; šâkwêšiw piko k'-îtên'tam, êkwâni
kâ-'ši-kîwêkâpawit. "kâkê oš' âni tâpwê mîna kišišaw kêkwâniw
n'titênimâw," manâ itwêw ê-kîwêkâpawit anihi otêma ê-mikisimon'ci.

    môna kiskênimêw âyâsa ant' âtâmihk êy-ihtân'ci.

17   ispî mâka ê-'ti-nâwinâkosin'ci anihi ininiwa, âyâs mîna kî-kihtohtêw.

    êko mîna ê-pimohtêt, mîna kî-wâpahtam mîk'wâminiw kotakîniw
ê-cimatênik.

    êko mâka k'-îhtâw anta kišê-'iniw ê-mâ..., ê-..., ê-mâskisit..., ê-mâskânik
pêyak oskât, nâspic ê-mišânik. êko mâka kî-mihcêtwâ..., kî-nipahêwâkêw
animêniw opwâm, ê-pâhtakwahwât piko 'wênihkâna. êko mâka kî-nîšiniwa
ocawâšimiša, ê-wîci-tašîhkêmât.

    êko mâka k'-îspaniniw mâkah, âyâs, âyâs anta 'ci-nipât.[26]

    môna mâka mâši kawêšimow ana kišê-'iniw.

altogether, thinking, "It's Ayas to whom we're doing it."

15   So then, – then, and then Ayas began to go out after they had killed each other. Again he started to go away.

Then again while he was walking along, then again he saw a wigwam set up again.

So then, there were many shoulder blades hanging from a line, many strung from a line. And if anyone walks there, he's not supposed to go underneath [the shoulder blades]. He is only to jump over them. That's the way it looked where that, that person was staying there.

Now he had one pup; and if anyone were to touch those shoulder-blades and make them rattle, the dog barked really hard.

So then he jumped ..., so then Ayas, leaping over, caught those shoulder-blade bones with his foot.

Then those bones gave off a sound.

16   At that the pup barked for all it was worth.

And then, when Ayas ran away tha' that ... that puppy chased after him.

Then out ..., out came that old man; he ran after that dog.

So ..., so, as there was a cave in the rock, A..., Ayas jumped in.

The dog was looking around right there, barking like anything; so he threw threw ... out ... threw out that mink-skin which his grandmother had given him. Then that mink-skin looked like a mink sticking its head in and out [of the hole], there that ... as Ayas did that from down inside.

So, so that, that person saw him; he thought it was only a mink, so he turned back. "I thought it was really something important that he saw," he said as he turned back, because the dog was barking.

He didn't know that Ayas was down there inside.

17   When that person began to appear at a distance, Ayas once more went away.

As he was walking along again, then, once more he saw another wigwam set up.

Now then, there was an old person there cr... c... crippled ..., with one leg crippled, and very big. Now there were many ..., he killed with that thigh of his, just by crushing anybody [with the big leg]. So then, his two children were living with him.

Now then it was time for Ayas, – Ayas to sleep there.

kêka mâka kî-šâkotihkwašiw ana âyâs. kî-kawêšimohkâsow.
kî-kiskên'tam mâka šâkoc ê-ašahokot anihi ..., kî-nipâhkâsow nêst' ana, ana
kâ-..., ana kišê-'iniw kâ-mišânik opwâm.

ispî mâka nêskihkwâmin'ci, ê-itên'tahk âyâsa kî-n'tawâ'mêw.

êko pêyâ..., êkot' ê-'šiwatât[27] animêniw oskât kâ-... kâ-mišânik,
kâ-mâskânik, êko mâka kêtahtawin kî-pâhtakwahokow kêkwâniw âyâs
ê-nipât.

êko mâka kâ-n'tôpitahk ê-... ocîstahikaniniw kâ-kî-mînikot ôhkoma.
kî-cîstaham animêniw, animêniw opwâm... miskâtiniw nâspic
kâ-kosiko-mahcihtât ê-pâhtakoškâkot. pîniš ê-nipin'ci anihi kišê-'niniwa
'kwâni kâ-tôtawât.

18   êko mâka ispî, – ispî kâ-nipahât 'kwân' êši-wanawît 'kwâni mîn'
êši-kihtohtêt.

êko, mîn' ê-pimohtêt, kî-wâpahtam, mîk'wâmin'[28] ê-cimatêniki nîšo.

êko mâk' animêniw kâ-nîštamiškahk, kî-ohci-wanawîniw' êskwêwa.
kî-nisitawêniwêw[29] mâka okâwiya.

êko, awa kišê-'skwêw kî-wâpamêw okosisa ê-pêci-takošinin'ci mwêhci.

"âââ, n'kosis âyâs takošin. n'kosis, âyâs takošin n'kosis," 'kwâni
kâ-itwêt.

êko mâka, awa kišê-'skwêw kî-pêyakwêw anta mîk'wâmihk. wî-...

êko mâka, ana kišê-'iniw, kotakîniw mîk'wâmini' k'-îhtâw, kotakiy'
awênihkân' anta ê-wî-'ti-tašîhkêmât. (êko mâka owîkimâkan' antê
kî-pêyakoniwa 'kwantaw. êko, môna ohci-..., môna ohci-minototawêw.
kî-'wahkâtêw ... kî-'wahkâtêw owîkimâkana.) 'kwânima ..., 'kwâni
'kwantaw antê wêhci-wîkin'ci.

19   êko mâka anihi kâ-wîci-tašîhkêmât kotakiya iskwêwa pêyak awâšiša
kîy-... kî-... kî-'yâwêwak.

êko kâ-..., êkw âwa âyâs ispî kâ-pîhtokwêt wîkinîhk okâwiya misiwê
kî-mînikow tipâcimowininiw, ê-itôt..., ê-itôtâmihci.

êko, êko kâ-itwêt âyâs, "mâca n'tawi-pîhtokwê 'nima mîk'wâm. ê-...
pwâmoši pîhtokwêyin mâka, ati-pîhtokwêcina[30] mihta, miši-kotawê mâka.
ošihtâ iškotêw 'ci-mišâk." êko kâ-wanawît awa kišê-'skwêw kîy-ati-..., "êko
mâka ispî kišâkonêkê, macostê-wêpin an' âwâšiš." 'kwâni kâ-itât.

êko, êko kâ-w'nawît awa kišêy-iskwêw, êko k'-âti-pîhtokwêcinahk[31] mihta
kîy-ati-pônam piko, tâpiskôc kwayask kakwê...[32] kêkwâniw ê-wî-tôtahk
kîy-ati-tôtam.

20   êko, êko kâ-..., ispîy êti-mišâk iškotêw, êko mâka kîši...,

But that old person wouldn't even go to bed.

Finally, however, Ayas drowsed off. He made as if to go to bed, but he knew very well that he was being watched by that old one ... that one pretended to sleep as well ..., that one who ..., that old one with the big thigh.

When he thought Ayas was sound asleep he went after him.

Then there dr..., that's where he took his leg, that ..., that big one, that big one; but then suddenly something dropped on Ayas as he was asleep.

So then he felt for h..., his pointed stick which his grandmother had given him. He jabbed that, that thigh ... leg which he felt very heavy as it pressed down on him. That's what he did to him until that old person died.

18 So then when, – when he had killed him, then he came out, that's when he set off there again.

So, as he was walking along once more, he saw tents set up, two of them.

And then from that one which he came upon first, there came out a woman. He recognized his mother.

Then, this old woman saw her son coming towards her just as he arrived.

"Aaa, my son Ayas is arriving. My son, Ayas my son is arriving," that is what she said.

Now then, this old woman was alone in the tent. She want...

But then, that old man was in another tent because he wanted to begin living there with someone else. (And so his wife was alone there to no purpose. So, he didn't ..., didn't treat her kindly. He detested her ... he detested his wife.) That was ..., that was the reason why she dwelt there idly.

19 Now then that other woman with whom he lived, they d... d..., had one child.

So when, then this Ayas when he had entered his mother's tent, she gave him all the news, how they were ..., how they were treated.

So, so Ayas said: "Go ahead, go into that tent. As ..., but before you go in, push a log of wood in, and kindle a big fire. Make a fire so it's big." So when this old woman came out she began ... "and then when there's a hot flame, throw this child into it." That's what he said to her.

So, so this old woman came out, then when she began to push in wood she just started to build a fire; she began to do it as though she were about to do a proper thing.

20 So, so when ..., at the point where the fire was big, then she ..., she

55

kî-kišêwâtotawêhkâsow anihi awâšiša.

"pêšiw, n'ka-tahkonâw," itêw.

môna wî-mînêw ana. " 'kâwin' ohci-mîn."

kêka mâka kî-mînâkaniwan tâpwê, 'ci-tahkonât anihi 'wâšiša.
êko mâka kišêwâtot..., mêkwâc ê-kišêwâtotawât kî-macostê-wêpinêw
anihi 'wâšiša. miconi kî-kipotâmâpasow an' awâšiš.

êkwâni mâk' ê-'ši-wanawîpanit, 'šâstaw kisiwâsiw ana
kišê-'n'niw anim' ê-tôtâmihci ocawâšimiša. "mitoni ..., mitoni
ka-nipahitin," itêw anihi wî-..., wîci-kišê-'niw' aspin
ê-wanawîpanin'ci.

âšay mâka wanawîpaniw kišê-'niw: "âyâs n'kosis, âyâs n'kosis, âšay
ninipahik kôhtâwiy."

"kwâcistak ô, tâpwê oš' âni ka-wâp'mâw âyâs kikosis," manâ itêw
ana kišêy-'iniw. "mô... môna wîskâc ka-ohci-wâpamâw ana kâ-..."

âšay manâ wêhci-wanawîpanit âyâs anta okâwiya wîkinîhk.

âšay kâ-koškwâpišihk manâ okosisa êy-ohci-wanawîpanin'ci.

21 ê'kwâni mâka, aci-wâciyêmêhkâsow[33] manâ okosisa.

âšay manâ wani-kiskisiw animêniw kâ-ihkininik anta,
ka-kî-macostê-wêpinimici.

"âyâs êcika n'kosis kâ-cakošinokopanê,"[34] manâ icwêw.

êko manâ, cacašiwêkišimêw manâ 'misk'wayân'šiša kê-'ši-tâcâš...
-tâtâhkôskên'ci.

"miconi kî-pîkosicoš..., ki-pî..., kî-pîkositêšinôtokê âyâs n'kosis wâhnaw
ê-pimohtêt," manâ icwêw.

"ta-âpacihacik aniki[35] manâ," itâkaniwan;
îkatê-wêpênimâkaniwiniwa manâ anihi amiskošiši-wayâna.

22 âšay manâ ..., âšay manâ mâka,
kâ-iškwâ-misiwê-'kwân'-mîn'-ati-minopanik, êko manâ wêyâpaninik awa
oškinîkiw âyâs kâ-išinihkâsot, kî-môhkocikêw piko isk... iskani-kîšik êy-ošihât
akaskwa, nîšo.

êko mâka, ê-kanawâ'mât ..., ê-kanawâ'mât okosis' anim' ê-tôtamin'ci
nâspic kî-mikwaškâtên'tam. wayêš kî-itên'tam.

"tânika pâskat, tânika pâskac wâ-tôtamokwê?" k'-îtên'tam.

wî-nanihcîstawêw okosisa âšay wayêš ê-wî-..., ê-wî-tôtâkot.

êko kâ-kakwêcimât, "tâni wâ-..., tâni wâ-tôtaman anima kâ-..., kâ-tôtaman
kâ-ošihacik akaskwak?" manâ itêw.

"môna ..., môna ..., môn' âpatan 'ci-kiskên'taman. nîna piko, nîna piko

pretended to behave kindly to that child.

"Bring him here, I'll hold him," she said to them.

That woman didn't want to give him to her. "Don't you dare give it to her!"

At last, however, she was actually given it, so that she might hold the child. But then she behaved fondl..., while she was behaving fondly to him she threw that child into the flame. That child was thoroughly smothered with smoke.

But bursting out at that point, that old man was really angry that his child was so treated. "I'll kill you utterly ..., utterly," he said to his old partner as she ran out and away.

But now the old person came out: "Ayas my son, Ayas my son, now your father is killing me."

"Alas, surely indeed you will see Ayas your son," that old woman said to him. "You will no..., not ever see that one who ..."

Now then Ayas suddenly came out of his mother's tent there.

Now he was surprised that his son came bursting out of it.

21   At that, he then made as if to shake hands with his son.

Now then he forgot what had happened there, when his child had been cast into the flames.

"It must be Ayas, my son, who has arrived," he said to them.

So then, he spread little beaver-skins about where he would ste..., would step.

"He must have completely blis..., he bli..., Ayas, my son, must have blistered his feet walking a long way," he said.

"What's the use of those then?" someone said; then those little beaver pelts were thrown aside.

22   Now then ..., and now then, after everything was back to normal again, then in the morning this young man, Ayas, as he was called just whittled all ..., all day making arrows, two.

So then, seeing him ..., seeing his son doing that, he was very much worried. He had something on his mind.

"I wonder what, I wonder what on earth he wants to do," he thought.

He was nervous that his son now wanted ..., now wanted to do something or other to him.

So he asked him, "What do you wa..., what do you want to do in what ..., what you're doing that you've made arrows?" he said to him.

"There's no ..., no ..., no use for you to know. Only I, only *I* know this

n'kiskên'tên ôma kêkwân kâ-tôtamân," manâ itwêw, âyâs.

23   âšay manâ wêyâpahk.

êko mâka, êko mâka kâ-..., kâ-tôtahk animêniw kêkwâniw kâ-wî-tôtahk.
êko išpimihk kâ-iši-pimocikêt[36] anihi akaskwa.

êko mâka, kî-tâwahokow p..., ê-cipêkisinici akaskw' anah, ana kišêy-'iniw.
miconi mâka kî-nâspitahokow.

'kwâni mîna pêyakwan anihi kotakiya.

ê'kwâni mâkah, kâ-..., pêyakwan kâ-... kâ-tôtâkot ana kišê-iskwêw
kî-nipahi..., kî-nipahikowan anihi akaskwa, – anihi kâ-ošihât anah
âyâs.

êko mâka kâ-itwêt anima, êko k'-âti-pasitêk, k'-âti-pasitêk
mâk' âskiy, anima[37] kâ-iškwâ-tôtahk, ohcitaw ê-... ê-kî-tôtahk
'ciy-ati-pasitênik.

24   êko mâka ana kîy-ati-pasisow kišêy-'iniw. anima mâka
'ci-kiskisinâniwahk, kâ-kî-mânên'cikêt ..., kâ-kî-mânênimât wîci-kišê-'niniwa
kiskinowâcitikan ..., kiskinowâcitakwan ...,[38] kiskinowâcicikan ihtakwan.
kî-wâpahtênâwâw 'n' ânima mâna kâ-pîpotêpanik[39] kêkwân
kâ-tâtâhkoskâcikâtêki kâ-wîpâki kâ-o..., kâ-osâwâki.

êko mâka, êwakwâna kišê-'niniw kâ-kî-... kâ-k'-îspanit, ispî
kâ-'ti-câkâskitênik wîyaw ê'kwâni kâ-'ti-išinâkwahki anihi. anihi
cîpayi-pastêw' mâka kâ-'šinihkâcikâtêki 'kwânima kâ-pîkišêpanik ê'kwâni
kišêy-'iniw.

êko mâka, asiniy ana kâ-wâpamêk, ininasiniy kâ-mânâcašiškîšit.[40] kâ-...
kâ-... kâ-askîwâpiskisit kâ-išinâkosit, êwakwâna wîna, êwakwâna wîna
kišê-iskwêw.

êko mâka, aniki wînawâw, aniki w..., âyâs wîna êwakwânimah nânih
sâkahikan âskaw n... pîhtâpêwak nân..., pîhtâpêkohk kâ-cimasot âskaw
wâkinâkan, asâmâhtik ê-minwâšišit.

êwakwâni wîna, âyâs. ê'kwâni kâ-itwêkopanê âyâs, anima 'ci-išinâkosit
wîna. êkot' ânta nêsta wîna kâ-iši-kišipipanit.

25   "êko mâka, êwako t'-âti-âpacihêwak ininiwak kê-'ti-pimâtisicik
'ci-otasâmâhtikocik,"[41] k'-îtwêw anima kâ-k'-îsinâkohot.

êko wîna okâwiya kâ-minwâšihk sâkahikanihk askiy kâ-nôkwahk
'ci-minwên'tahkik ininiwak ê-pimohtêcik ê-kanawâpahtahkik ê-'šinâkwahk
askîhk ana kâ-nanêskamikâk[42] mâna, êw'kwâni wîna okâwiya kâ-...
kâ-išihon'ci.

ê'kwâni êskwâpêkahk tipâcimôwin, âtanôhkân âyâs ohci.

thing that I'm doing," Ayas said to him then.

23   Now it was the following day.

So then, so then he di..., he did that thing which he wanted to do. He shot those arrows up high.

And then, because the arrows were pointed, that, that old man was hit. He was killed outright.

Then again, it was the same with that other one.

And then, it was ..., it was the same ... the same thing happened to that old woman ... she was kil..., she was killed by those arrows, the ones which Ayas had made there.

So then when he had said that, then it began to burn, the earth began to burn, after he had done that, because ..., because he did it deliberately so it would begin to burn.

24   So then that old man began to burn. And that was to be remembered as a sign of his having abused, of his having scorned his old mate ..., a sign is ..., it is there as a sign. You have seen again and again that thing which makes smoke when trodden on, which are hollow, y..., and yellow.

Well then, that old man the way ..., the way things went with him, when his flesh began to be all burnt out, that's what those things looked like. And those "Ghost-smokes" as they're called, that one that steams, that's the old man.

So then, that stone which you see, Indian stone defaced with mud, which ..., which ..., which appears to have white moss on it, that one is her, that one is her, the old woman.

And furthermore, those ones are them, those ones are th... that one is Ayas alongside the lake sometimes al..., alongside the [lagoon] the tamarack which sometimes sticks up in the lagoon, a fine snow-shoe wood.

That one was Ayas. That's what Ayas must have said so that he looked like that. And that was the end of him too.

25   "And so the Indians of future generations will go on using them as snow-shoe frames," he said, that one which he made himself look like.

And his mother is the good land which appears on the lake so the Indians may take pleasure as they walk about looking at where the land runs out to little points, – that is the way his mother was dressed.

That is the length of the account, the legend about Ayas.

mistâkanâš kâ-kî-nipikopanê, êko mâka kâ-kî-waniškâkopanê

1   mistâkanâš wâsa, kî-tipâcimikosiw nêsta wîna, kâ-iši-pêci-ayišilawît,
ê-kî-tipâcimot oti, ê-kî-tipâtotahk opimâtisîwin. ê'kôma mâk' ânohc
kê-tipâcimoyân.

2   "n'kî-ni... n'kî-nipinâkopan wâsa," k'-îtwêw. "êko mâka n'kî-waniškân
mîna," itwêw.

"êko mâka, pêyakwâ manâ mâka kâ-koskosinâniwahk manâ mâka piko,
kî-t... n'k'-îtênimon, kêtahtawin ê-koskosiyân, âšay wêskac
ê-kî-nahîhkâkawâpânê matakwahpihk."[1]

'kwân' ê-'t... 'kwân' ê-'tâcimitisot.

3   " 'awasitê, awasitê šêmâcišinik,' n't-itwân," manâ itwêw.

"kišâ! kâ-... kâ-papêcihkwâskopanihoyân kêka; 'šâ, n'kî-nipinâkopân êcik'
ô, 'n'tên'tên.[2]

êko mâka, âšay ..., âšay niwaniškân; âšay tâpwê
n'kî-šâkocihtân, – niwaniškân anta kâ-k'-îši-pimišimikawiyân
êy-itâpiyân, kây-akotêk n'cîmân, m'pâskisikan ašic,
nimôhkomân.

êko mâka, k'-âti-otinamân n'cîmân, n'kîy-ati-kapastawêhên.

êko k'-âti-kihtâponoyân, kâ-'ši-ayihtâyâhkipan mâna, êškwâ
'-pimâtisiyâpân mâna, êkotê 'ni kâ-'t'-îtâponiyân.[3]

4   kêka mâka kîy-ati-tipiskâw.

kêka niwâpahtên kâ-cimatêk mîk'wâm.

êko kâ-kapâyân anta kîmôt. êko kâ-pîhtokwêyân, – êko kîmôt
k'-âti-pîhtokwêyân antê [whispered] 'kâmiškotêhk n'kî-nahišinin.

kêka matwê-... matwê-wâpan, -matwê-koškonâkaniwan mâka
n'kâwiy.

'kotawê,' matwê-'tâkaniwan.

nôhkomis, nôhkomis ana kâ-matwêy-itwêt.

êko, ê-matwê-waniškât n'kâwiy, n'kî-wâpamik ê-pimišinân [whispered]
akâmiškotêhk.

êko kâ-matwê-'tât nôhkomisa [whispered] 'awênihkân oš' ânta pimišin.
akâmiškotêhk.'

[deep voice] 'awênihkân ô kê-pimišinin'ci?' at'-êtwêw[4] nôhkomis.

Mistaganash who is supposed to have died and then to have risen

1   Mistaganash as you know then, there have been tales about him too, about his past activities since, – he told the story, that is, when he told about his life. Now this is the story that I'm going to tell.

2   "I must have ..., I must have died then," he said. "And then I arose again," he said.

"And then, once when people were just wakening, I th..., I thought to myself, suddenly as I awoke, that it was a long time ago that I had been put away at an old campsite."

That's the st..., that's the story he tells about himself.

3   " 'Move over more, move and straighten out,' I said," he said then.

"My, but ...! At last I made a rumbling noise moving about [in the coffin]; 'Tsk, tsk, I must have died, it would seem,' I thought.

So then, now ..., now I got up; I really mastered the situation, – I got up there where I had been laid down and looked around: my canoe hung there, my gun with it, and my knife.

So then, I started to take my canoe, I began to put it in the water.

Then I began to drift away with the current, to the different places where we frequently used to stay, when I used still to be alive, – that's where I went drifting by.

4   At last it began to get dark.

Finally I saw a tent sticking up.

So I went ashore there stealthily. Now I went in, – now I started to go in stealthily [*whispered*] to the other side of the fire, and I fitted in and lay down.

At last there were sounds of ... sounds of dawn, sounds of my mother being wakened.

'Start a fire,' someone could be heard saying to her.

My step-father, it was my step-father who was heard saying it.

Then, as my mother could be heard getting up, she saw me lying [*whispered*] to the other side of the fire.

So she was heard to say to my step-father [*whispered*]: 'Somebody is lying there. To the other side of the fire.'

[*deep voice*] 'Who is that who'll be lying down?' my step-father kept on repeating.

[*whispered*] êko, 'šâkoc oš' âni 'wênihkân pimišin anta,' matwê-'têw n'kâwiy.

[*slightly deep voice*] 'awênihkân awa kê-pimišihk kit-'tên'tên?' matwê-'twêw nôhkomis.

5 âšay niwaniškâpahtân âšay, 'nîna oš' ô n'kâwiy,'[5] n'tit... n'tittâ.[6]
kišâstaw minwên'tam nikâwiy hê-wâpamit. êko mâka kâ-'t'-...
k'-âtiy-ašamit ê-kišêpâyâk. kinwêš nawac anta n'kîy-apin; pâtimâ mâka n'kîy-ati-pôsin.

âšay ê-wî-n'taminahoyân ê-kiskisiyân n'kâwiy ê-sikinêsit ê-wâpamit, êko mâka, wî-nip... n'kî-nipahâw pêyak atihk.

'kwân' êši-kikišitêšihk[7] – ê'kwâni êši-kî-pôsihtâyân[8] êy-otêškaniwêhtihk ostikwân.

aa..., n'kanawâ'mik n'kâwiy ê-pêci-'mišakâyân. ê'kwâni mâk' êtwêt:
'šâ! tâšipwâm'[9] ê-mihcinawêsiyâpân n'kosis ê-nipit.'
'kwân' ê-icwêt[10] n'kâwiy.

êko mâka n'kîy-ati-wîcêwâwak; n'kî-wîci-tašîhkêmâwak n'kâwiy nêsta nôhkomis.

6 pêyakwâ mâka, kî-'t... kî-..., k'-îtwêw pêyak ininiw, 'ta-n'taminahôwak awênihkânak atihkwa ta-nâtawatihkwêwak.'

(môna mâši nîna m'pisiskên'tamohkâson.)

êko kâ-..., kâ-... kâ-itikawiyân, nêsta nîna 'ci-kihtohtêyân.

kî-ošihtâniwan mâk' anta kêkwân, ê-minwâšihk mîcim, awênihkân mâka ê-kîy-apwâniwahk.[11]

'awênihkân mâka mihcêt kê-nipahâkwê atihkwa mihcêtw' animêniw ta-tahtahkacikêpanihtwâw.'[12]

'kwâni kâ-itwêt ana kâ-tipên'tahk animêniw.

êko, kâ-kihtohtêyân nêsta nîna.

7 êko, âšay n'tôcihtên[13] kâ-'ši-wawân'takoskâk[14] ê-'šinâkwahk. ê'kot' ânta mâka kâ-išiy-... ê-ap... -apiyân.

âšay kêkwân m'pêhtên ispîy '-apiyân [*whispered*]: 'hêh, hêh, hêh,' kâ-icihtâkwahk.[15] âšay niwâpamâw atihk kâ-pêci-nôkosit, wâpišakicihp.[16]
(iyâpêwatihkwa ani kâ-itât.)

hâšay m'pâskiswâw ôcê ê-pim'pahcât: mîna kotakîy, mîna kotakîy, mîna kotakîy. pîniš pîniš mihcêt.

kêka n'câpasâpin. mâna n'kî-pêci-mêcawâhtay ê-šinâ... ê-'sinâkwahk, ê-'ši-namêhtâyân.

Then [*whispered*]: 'Someone is lying there for sure,' my mother could be heard saying to him.

[*slightly deep voice*] 'Who do you think this one is who'll be lying down?' my step-father could be heard saying.

5   I was already jumping up, already, 'It's me, Mother,' I sai... I said to her.

My, but my mother was happy to see me! So she began ... began to feed me as it was morning. I sat there a fairly long time; by and by, however, I went away in a canoe.

Now, as I was going to hunt, remembering that my mother was glad at seeing me, so then, going to kill ... I killed one caribou.

He still had his feet on, – then I loaded him with the antlers still on the head.

Aa ..., my mother looked at me as I paddled up. And this is what she said: 'Tsk, tsk! What a pity! I was sorry when my son was dead.'

That's what my mother said.

So then, I began to stay in their company; I began to live with my mother and step-father.

6   Once however, a certain person sai..., sa..., said, 'Some people will be hunting caribou, they will be going after caribou.'

(*I pretended not even to pay any attention.*)

Then was ..., was ... was I told, I too should go away.

Now something was made there, fine food, whoever had roasted it.

'Whoever kills the most caribou, he will stab it again and again.'

That's what the one who was in charge of that said.

So, I went away too.

7   Then, I now reached the place where the bush appeared tangled. And that's where I ..., sa..., sat.

Now I heard something when I sat down [*whispered*]: 'Heh, heh, heh,' it sounded like. Now I saw a caribou which was coming into sight, a caribou with a white forehead. (A real, old buck deer is what he meant.)

Now I shot him as he ran along towards me: again another and again another, and again another. Until, until at last there were many.

Finally I looked back. It look..., it looked as if I had been playing, the signs were so strange.

êko mâka ê-kîwêyân, âšay misiwê kîy-ohci-câhcakošinwak ininiwak kâ-cakošinân.

ââh, pêhpêyakwâ piko ispanihcwâwak, nênîšo âtiht.

âšay nînistam n'tôtinên anima.

kwâcistak! miconi kêka môna n'canawâniskêpanihon anim' ê-'spanihcwâyân.[17]

'šâ..., mâmân wês' âko[18] mihcêcwâ,' n'cikawin.

êko mâka nîna mâka n'kiy-ayân anima.

8   êko, âšay mîna pêyakwâ ê-kišêpâyâk, 'k'wawêšihok, ôk' oškinîkiwak,' icwâniwan.

êko mâka, nôhkomis ôma n'tik: 'tân' êhki kîna wêhci-êkâ-wêšihoyin ê-wêšihocik wêskinîkicik?'

âšay niwaniškân.

âšay n... âšay niwawêšihon nêsta pišišik nimihkonawên.[19]

êko mâka n'caci-mawâpin mâka, m'paspâpikâpawin mîkiwâm kâ-'škwâ-wêšihoyân. kêcahcawin piko m'pêhcên awênihkân ê-ytwêt: 'kinipin ininiw, kinipin ininiw, kinipin ininiw.'[20]

môna, môna m'pisiskên'camohkâhtay.[21] kêka mâka pêh... pêhkâc, pêhkât n'kîwêskwênin.

9   âšay niwâpahtên môhkomân ê-wî-tahkamikawiyân. âpihtawâpisk ninawacinên. âšay nimâšihi... nimâšihitonân ana ininiw.

šâ..., miconi maškaw... miconi nimaškawimahcihâw. 'mâmân ôw nimanitôw'-mâšihik,' n'tên'tên. êko mâka nêsta nîna niman'tôwi-mâšihâw.

âšay niwî-koci-tatinikonânak ininiwak.

'kwancaw piko kâ-papîwahâhkêyâhk.

âšay: 'wîhcama... wîhcamâmâhk ôhkomisa,' icwêwak; 'wîhcamâmâhk ôhkomisa,' icwêwak.

[deep voice] âšay kâ-pêci-nôkosit ê-ôhkomisiyân. ošâwasko-'pwoy išinihkâsôpan ê-ôhkomisiyân.

âšay piko m'pêci-sâminik: ' 'kâwin'. pêhkât, pêhkâc, pêhkâc; 'kâwin' kat'-êšinâkwan wâ-'šinâkwanokwê,' itwêw.

10   mân' ên'cohk n'kîy-ati-mâmâkošêkwahokowin[22] ê-'tamahcihoyân. âšay mâka pêhpêyak n'tat'-îspitikawinân, 'ka-kî-nipahicinâpan,' ê-ytitoyâhk; 'ka-kî-nipahicinâpan,' ê-ytitoyâhk. âšay, âšay mâkah, âšay nêtê wâhnaw ..., âšay wâhnaw nêtê ihtâw ana nêsta nîyak.[23]

So then, as I went home, already all the people arrived one by one when I arrived.

Aah, they had a go at it, only once each, some of them twice.

Now I took it in my turn.

Oh, my! At last I didn't allow any space between strokes as I went at it.

'Tsk, tsk, – it looks as though he's doing it a lot of times,' they said about me.

So then, *I* was the one who got that.

8   So, now once again it was morning, someone said, 'Get togged up, you young fellows here.'

So then, my step-father said to me: 'How is it you're not togging up, since these young fellows are dressing?'

Now I got up.

Now I … now I dressed and I had my face all red. And then …, and I began to visit, I peeped into a tent after I was togged up. Only suddenly I heard someone saying: 'You're dying Man, you're dying Man, you're dying Man.'

I wasn't … wasn't paying any attention. At last, however, slo…, slowly, slowly I turned my head.

9   Now I saw a knife about to stab me. I grabbed it half way up the blade. Now we wrestle … the other person and I wrestled with each other.

Tsk, tsk …, I felt his strength overc… overcoming me. 'It looks as though he's fighting me with his spirit,' I thought. So then, I too fought him with my spirit-strength.

Now the people wanted to separate us.

We just scattered them like feathers.

Now: 'Tell his … tell his step-father,' they said; 'Tell his step-father,' they said.

[*deep voice*] Now my step-father appeared. *"ošâwasko-'pwoy"* was my step-father's name.

Now he just came and touched me: 'Don't. Easy, easy, easy. Don't let happen what looks as though it must happen,' he said.

10   I began to feel just as though I were being pressed down on more and more tightly. And now one by one we were each being pulled apart. 'I could have killed you,' we were saying to each other; 'I could have killed you,' we were saying to each other. By now, but by now, now far off …, by now he was far away and so was I also.

âšay n'tayamihikawin êkâ wîskâc anima 'ci-côcamâpân. 'kwantaw, pêyak pêyak iškwêšiš anima kâ-ohcîhkâtawiyâhk 'kwantaw ..., atihk'-wayân'[24] âkwanîw."

ê'kwâni, ê'kwân' ..., ê'kwân' êskwâpêkahk tipâcimôwin.

Now I was told that I should never do a thing like that. It was pointless, on account of a certain, a certain girl that we were at each other ... she is just covered with an old scrap of deerskin."

That, that ..., that is the length of the story.

mêmišôš kâ-mitêhkêkopanê

1   mêmišôš išinihkâsow ôm' ânohc kêy-âtanôhkawak ...,
kêy-âtanôhkêyân.

mâmaskâc mihcêcwoyêhk[1] ayicâcimikosiw[2] mêmišôš kâ-itiht.
man'tôhkêkopan mâna. êko mâka mihcêtoyêk kî-ayitôtam
ê-manitôhkêt, nêsta wawâc ê-kî-nipahât âtiht êh..., anihi awâšiša
kâ-kîy-otinamâsot ê-'ti-n'tawikihât mâka ê-'ti-onahâhkišîmikopanê
mâka mâna.

2   êko pêyakwâ, ê-pimiškât man'šôš[3] mêmišôš, ê-mohci-otatâmahwât
piko otapihkana kîy-ohci-kihcipaniw[4] ocîmân.

êko, kâ-wâpamât awâšiša ê-'pâmâšakâmin'ci[5] ê-mâton'ci. êko, aw'
awâšiš kîwašišân, matêniwa onîkihikwa, kî-nipiniwa misiwê.

êko, kâ-otinât, "tân' êhtiyan?" 'tê[6] pitamâ.

"môna wayêš n'k'-îtohtân. môna n'kîy-âšaw'hên ôta," itêw. "matêw
nôhtâwiy nêsta matêw n'kâwiy."

"âstam," itêw. "ka-kanawênimitin. ka-n'tawikihitin," 'têw.

ispîy êti-mišikitin'ci, tâpwê kî-n'tâwikihêw. ispî mâk' êti-mišikitin'ci
kîy-ati-on'âhkišîmiw.[7]

êko, êspîy ..., ê-'ti-kišê-'yahâwin'ci 'ci-ocawâšimišin'ci, êko
kâ-itên'tahk kici-nipahât, ê-mitêhkawât ohci ê-pakonawâspin...
êê-w... ê-pakonawâspinatât[8] nêstapiko wâwâ... wâwâc ê-wîcêwât.
ê-wîcêwât ê-... âskaw kî-... kî-nipahêw anih' kâ-kî-'ton'âhki'mi...[9]
mihcêt anima kî-tôtawêw. 'kwân' ê-'t'-âtanôhkâsot.

3   êko pêyakwâh, anihi ... anihi pêyak on'âhkišîma kî-paskinâkow môšak.
môna kîy-ohci-kaškihtâw kici-wânihtak-ayitôtawât. awasitê kî-kaškihoniwa
ê-mitêhkên'ci ispîš wîna.

pêyakwâ mâka kî-nimitâwêhonêw. ê'kwani nîštam kâ-tôtawât. âšay
nîšiniwa ocawâšimiš' âna nâpêw. câwic wêsa nêcê 'kwat... it... akohcinôpan
êh... miniscik.[10]

"nâspic n'câ-wâwîpanak ê... kiyâskwak," manâ itêw on'âhkišîm.

"êko ninikon,[11] iši-šim... iš... iši-cimêtâh," ana itêw.

ê'kwâni mâmitonên'tahk, ê-wî-nakatahwât nêtê ispî
kî-kapân'tê.

Memishoosh the conjuror

1   Memishoosh is the name of the person about whom I shall now relate the legend ..., I shall tell a legend.

Very many different stories are told about the one called Memishoosh. He used to communicate with the spirits time and again. And in so many ways he did a lot of things as he conjured, and even having killed some ..., those children whom he had taken for himself to raise to make them his sons-in-law time and again.

2   So once upon a time as Man'shoosh, Memishoosh was paddling along, by just tapping repeatedly the thwart only, away went his canoe.

Then, he saw a child walking back and forth along the shore, crying. Now then, this child was an orphan; he had no parents; they were all dead.

Then, when he took him, he said to him first, "What's wrong with you?"

"I can't go anywhere. I can't cross here," he said to him. "My father is no more and my mother is no more."

"Come here," he said to him. "I'll take care of you. I'll bring you up," he said to him.

When he began to get big, he did indeed bring him up. And when he was nearly grown up he began to have him for a son-in-law.

Now then, when ... as he began to get older so they had children, then he thought to kill him through conjuring by a sickness spell ... by ... making him ill by casting an evil spell or eve... even accompanying them. By accompanying them in ... sometimes he ... he killed those sons-in-law of his. He did that to many of them. That's the story he tells about himself.

3   So once, that ... one of those sons-in-law of his always got the better of him. He wasn't able to do whatever he wanted to him. The latter was more powerful in conjuring than he was.

Once, however, he took him out in a canoe away from land. That was the first thing he did to him. By now that man had two children. Away out there in midstream there float ... wa... there floated er ... an island.

"The gulls ... are good at laying eggs," he said to his son-in-law.

"Well then, my son-in-law, let's paddle to ... to ... let's paddle to it," this one said to him.

That's what he had in mind, because he wanted to leave him there once he had stepped ashore.

šâkoc kî-minohtâkwaniniw otayamiwin, tâpiskôt tâpwê
ê-wî-nâtahahk wâwa, mê... mêkwâc ê-wâwin'ci kiyâskošiša.

4   êko kâ-pôsicik.

šâkoc kî-kiskên'tam awa ininiw tâni wâ-tôtâkot. kî-wîcêwêw šâkoc.
wâhnaw tâwic mâka k'-îš'... k'-îsi-cimêwak.

êko, kâ-otihtahkik[12] anima, manâwinân.[13] kî-mihcêtiwak anta
kiyâskošišak, kiyâskwak kinikaw ê-wâwicik.

êko, k'-âti-kapât anah, an' êniniw.

"nêcê oša mâna mâwac ninikon," icêw. nêcê išitišahwêw
wâhnaw. "êkotê 'ni mâna mâwac ê-'ši-mihcêtihkwâpan[14] wâw',"
icwêw.

êko, ispîy êci-nâwinâkosin'ci nawac, êko kâ-nimitâwê-wêpahahk.
kî-pôsipanihow ê-nakatahwât.

kî-têpwâtikow mâka.

môna mâši.

'kwâniy aspin.

5   êko mâka, ê-ispîhci-mihcêticik kiyâskwak anta kâ-wâwicik, acoskam
kî-pahkwêhtahwêwak anih' ê-wâ'mâcik anihi, anih' îniniwa ant' ê-yhtân'ci.

êko, kêka kî-..., kî-mâmitonên'tam kê-tôtahk aw' ininiw.

êko pêyak kîy-otinê... kî-ot... kîy-otihtinêw anihi kiyâskošiša.
kî-pahkonêw mâka.

ispîy mâka kâ-pahkonât, 'kwâni kâ-iši-pîhciškawât anihi kiyâsk'-wayâna.
'kwâni kâ-išiy-ohpahot.

6   môn' êškwâ otihtam mêmišôš anima kâ-kî-ohci-cimêt. picêlak mâskôc
wayêš têhtâwakâm ihtâw.

êko mâka, kîy-ati-mayâwahwêw. mêm... kîy-ati-mayâwahwêw osis'... osis'
ê-'miskân'ci.

môna kiskênimikow wîna. wayêš mâk' anta k'-îtôtam, âtawîna k'-îtôtawêw
ê-mânênimât.

êko, k'-âti-mayâwahwât, êko k'-âtiy-otihtahk wîkih.
kîy-atiy-akoci-wêpinêw anihi kiyâsko-wayâna kâ-kî-pohciškawât ê-pimihnât.
ê-mitêhkêt anima wêhci-kî-kaškihtât ê-tôtahk.

êko, kâ-mînât ocawâšimiša mîkwana, 'ciy-astahwên'ci otakaskonîhk.

7   êko mâkah, kinwêš nawac otânâhk kîy-otâpicîw[15] awa kišê-'niw.

êko mâka ispî mêtwê-mišakât kî-nâsipêpahtâniw' ôsisima.

êko kâ-itikot: "âšay wêskac wîna nôhtâwiy kî-takošin."

" 'awas," itwêw. "môna, môna wîskât ta-takošin kôhtâwîwâw," itwêw.

His word sure sounded good, as though he was really going to go after eggs, wh…, while the terns were laying.

4   So they embarked.

This person knew perfectly well what he [the stepfather] wanted to do to him. He went with him all right. They padd… they paddled there far out in midstream.

So, they reached that spot, 'The Collecting Place'. There were many terns there and gulls mixed with them laying eggs.

Then that, that person began to go ashore.

"That's the best place over there, my son-in-law," he said to him. He sent him far away yonder. "That way is where frequently there used to be the most eggs," he said to him.

Then, when he got a fair distance away, then he pushed his canoe out. He jumped in quickly leaving him behind.

His son-in-law called out to him.

No answer.

Away he went.

5   So then, since there were so many gulls there laying eggs, right away they tore chunks off that one, as they saw that one, that person who was there.

So, at last that person consid… considered what he would do.

So he took one … he too … he reached out to that tern. Then he skinned him.

But when he had skinned him, then he got inside of that gullskin. Then he flew up on the spot.

6   Memishoosh had not yet reached that place where he had canoed from. He was as yet only about at mid-stream.

Then, however, he began to pass him. Mem…, he began to pass his father-in-law … his father-in-law as he was paddling.

His father-in-law didn't know him. There he did something or other, although he did it to him to torment him.

So, he began to pass him; then, he began to reach his home. He began to throw the gull-skin up, which he had put on as he flew, so it would hang. The reason he was able to do that is because he did conjuring.

Then, he gave his child the quills, so he could put them on his arrows.

7   So then, that old man was away quite a while, back of the camp.

And then, when they heard him paddling, his grandchild ran down the bank.

Then he said to him: "My father has already arrived a long time ago."

"êhê," itwêw. "âšay kî-takošin nôhtâwînân. mâtik' ôki
mîkwanak kây-akohkêcik ê-..., n'takaskonâhk ê-kîy-astawêyâhk[16]
ê-kî-pêšiwât mîkwanah."

ê... kiyâpac môna ohci-tâpwêhtam.

êko k'-âti-kospit ê-'ci-pîhtokwêt mîk'wâmihk kî-wâ'mêw
êy-'pin'ci onahâhkišîma. môna ohci-'piskên'tam[17] ... môna
ohci-'piskênimikow, tâpiskôc kêko..., tâpiskôc ê-..., êkâ êhki'[18]
kêkwân.

'kwâni kâ-tôt..., kâ-tôtâkot.

8   êko mîna pêyakwâh, âšay mîna mâmitonên'tam, atoskam ê-wî-tôtahk,
anima kâ-itên'tahk, on'âhkišîma ohc' ê-wî-nipahât.

êko, "itohtêhtâ nêtê," itêw, pêyakwâ ê-kišêpâyâk. "ihtakwan nêtê
kwâškwatahonân," itwêw. "êkotê 'ni mâka kêy-itohtêyahk," itwêw.

êko, "kayâm," itwêw an' ininiw. kiskên'tam mîna kêkwân
wêhc'-îtikot.

êko, kây-itohtêcik ê-kišêpâyânik.

âšay man' âti-otihtamwak anta kâ-..., ê-mah... ê-ma... ê-mahki-wânâ'k[19]
êko mâk' ât'-n... tâpiskôc miši-šîpîšišihkân ê-yšinâkwahk. nâs'm[20] mâk'
âtâmihk nêtê ê-... ê-nôkwahk.[21] êko mâka, êkot' ânta mihcêt kâ-k'-îsi-nipahât
on'âhkišîma ê-nôhtêkâmêhân'ci. nêtê mâk' '-kî-pahkišinin'ci capašîš, môna
wîskâc ohci-kaškihtâniwa 'ci-wanawîn'ci.

ê'kwâni mâka mîna wâ-tôtawât ôho, onahâhkišîma, ôho kâ-...
kâ-kî-wîšâmât.

9   "êkow iši ..., êko mâka nâ... ninikwan, ...n," itêw.

'kwâni mâka piko ka..., kâ-iši-kwâškwatit anah, an' êniniw, nêtê mâk'
kî-pahkišin wâhnaw. môna ohci-..., môna ohci-nôhtêkâmêham.

êko mâka ..., êko mâk', "kîništam," itêw. "êko kî'štam kwâškwati," itêw ...,
itik' ônahâhkišîm'.[22]

âšay, nâspic kî-kostâciw. "êkwênâk šâkwênimoyân kwâškwacahonân,"
icwêw.

nâspit kî-šâkwênimow kici-kî-kaškihtât awa kišêy-'iniw wîna. âšay
kiskên'tam ê-paskinâht.

êko mâka kâ-'ši-kwâškwatit, 'kwâniy aspin capašîš kî-pahkišin. môna ...,
môna ohci-n... môna ohci-têpakâmêpaniw.

ê'kotê 'ni mâka, kâ-matwê-nôhtâkosit ê-matwê-môskôpinêt antêy
atâmihk.

"Be off with you," he said. "Your father will not, not ever arrive," he said.

"Yes," he said. "Our father had already arrived. Look at these quills fastened on ... which we have fastened on our arrows, quills which he brought."

As ... he still did not believe it.

Then when he began to climb up the bank to enter the tent he saw his son-in-law sitting. He didn't pay attention ... the latter paid him no attention, as though noth... as though nothing had happened.

That's what he did to him.

8   So once more, now again he planned, since he wanted to do with dispatch what he had in mind about his son-in-law in his desire to kill him.

So, one morning he said to him: "Let's go yonder. There's a jumping place there," he said to him. "That's the way we'll go," he said.

So this person said, "All right." He knew why it had been said to him again.

So, they went there in the morning.

Now then, they began to come to a place where ... it was hol... hol..., there was a deep hollow in the ground; so then ... it looked like a deep, narrow creek. It appeared away far down there. So then, that was the place where he had killed many of his sons-in-law as they fell short in jumping over it. For as they fell down into it, they were never able to get out.

This is what he wanted to do again to this one, his son-in-law, this one whom ..., whom he had invited along.

9   "So then ..., and so m... my son-in-law," he said to him.

But that was wh..., where that one jumped, that person; so he landed far away. He didn't ... he didn't fall short.

So then ..., so then he said to him, "It's your turn. So you jump in turn," he said to him ..., his son-in-law said to him.

By now he was very frightened. "It's the first time I feel nervous at a jump," he said.

This old man was very frightened about being able to manage it. Now he knew that he was beaten.

So then he jumped; then he fell away deep down. He didn't ... didn't reach far enough across in his jump.

And you can hear him, off there making a noise as he moans there away down below.

ê'kwâni mâka ê-ytâpit an' ini... ana ininiw, itwêkopan, mêhcêt[23] oskana
nêt' ê-wâpahtahk atâmihk, kâ-k'-îši-..., kâ-k'-îši-pahkišinin'ci onahâhkišîma
ê-nôhtêkâmêhân'ci ana mêmišôš.

êko mâka matwê-môskôpinêw.

êko kâ-kîwêt aw' êniniw. môna ohci-pisiskênimêw osisa.

10   êko mâka, ispîy têkošihk, êko kâ-wîhtamawât, kâ-wîhtamawât wîwa:
"tântê nôhtâwiy?" ê-ytikot.

"kêka mâ, ta-miškawâšihitisow kôhtâwiy êkâ '-nipwâhkât. atâmihk nêtê
kî-pahkišin kwâškwatahonânihk," it... itêw.

'kwâni mâk' ê-mâtot awa iskwêw, ê-mihcinawêsit ôhtâwiya. šâkoc mâka
mêmišôš kî-kaškihtâw 'ci-wanawît antah ..., pâtimâ wîskâta. kî-kaškiht'
âtoskam 'ci-wanawît anta ohci.

kî-takošin mâka.

'kwâni pêyakwan kâ-tôtahk aw ê..., aw' êniniw êkâ ê-pisiskênimât tâpiskôc
ê-..., kêkwân êkâ '-ohc'-îhkih.

11   êko mînah, mîna pêyakwâ, âšay mînah, mîna kî-mâmitonên'tam
kici-nipahât on'âhkišîma mêmišôš. môna wî-pôn'tâw, âta êkâ ê-kî-tôtahk
pîniš nîšwâ. âšay manâ, šâkoc mîna pêyakwâ.

êko mîn' ê-papâmohtêcik ê-..., ê-wanahikêcik ê-..., amiskw'
ê-wanahâmawâcik,[24] "êkota wanahikêtâ, ninikwan," manâ itêw.

êko mâka, kâ-kihtohtêcik. môna mâka k'-îspaniniw kici-kîwêcik;
nâspic mâka kî-kîšowâyâw anima ê-kîšikâk. mitoni mâka
kî-nipîwihtâwak otâsiwâwa.

êko mâkah, ê-'ti-tipiskânik, êko, êko kây-... kây-akotâcik ê... anta
kâ-'ši-nipâcik kâ-'ši-kotawâsocik ê-pâsahkik.

kî-kiskên'tam awa nâpêw kici-maci-tôtâkot osisa.

êko mâka, ê-mâmitonên'tamin'ci 'ci-kawacît kê-wâpaninik kišâspin
kâ-ihki mâna kâ-tahkâyânipanik.

(ê'kwân' êhkinikopanê. kiskên'tam mâk' anima kic'-îhkininik
ati-wâpaninikê, tâpiskôc kîn'nânaw âskaw kâ-wâpahtamahk anima
kici-at'-îhki..., wâpahkê nâspic 'ci-tahkâyâk, ât' ê-kîšowâyâk anim'
ê-kîšikâk.)

12   ê'kwânima mâka ê-... ê-'htiwâkopanê: kî-nipîwihtâw mâk' otayân' aw'
ê-..., ê-kîšowâyânik. kî-pâsinâsowak mâka; kî-akotâwak antê; man' âni mâka
kiyâpat ê-..., mahk'-îškotêwan.

cikêmânima ê-pâsahkik otayâniwâwa, ê-'ti-kawêšimocik kî-nôcihcâhkâsow
man' âni mâk' anihi mitâsa.

Then, as that per... that person looked about, he no doubt said, that he saw many bones there down below, where there had ... where the sons-in-law of that Memishoosh had fallen because they had jumped short.

Then he could be heard moaning.

So that person went home. He paid no attention to his father-in-law.

10 Well then, when he arrived, then he told it, he told it to his wife as she said to him, "Where is my father?"

"At long last your father will get himself into trouble from acting foolishly. He fell down yonder beneath the jumping place," he said to her.

Then this woman wept, in sorrow for her father.

Memishoosh, however, was able to come out there all right, later on after a while. Right away he was able to come out from there.

And he arrived.

It was the same thing which this p... this person did: he paid no attention to him as though ... nothing had happened.

11 Then again, once more, now again Memishoosh planned to kill his son-in-law. He didn't want to give up, although he had not been able to do it after trying twice. Now then, he would surely try once more.

Once more then as they were walking about as..., as they were setting traps as..., as they were setting traps for beaver, he said to him, "Let's set a trap right there, my son-in-law."

So then, away they went. It was not time for them to go home, but it was very mild that day and they got their leggings completely wet.

So then, as night came on, then, then th... they hung them up in ... there where they were sleeping where they made a fire for themselves, drying them out.

This man knew that his father-in-law was going to do him some mischief.

So then, the father-in-law was planning that the son-in-law would freeze the following morning if it happened that it went cold all of a sudden.

(That's how it must have been. But he knew that that would happen when morning began to dawn. Just as *we*, sometimes what we see is that it begins to happen ..., the following day it will get very cold, although it is mild on the day in question.)

12 So..., and that is ... is what must have happened to them: this one got his things wet wh... while it was mild. But they dried out their clothes; they hung them up there; and still there was a big fire.

Of course as they dried their things, as they were getting ready for bed, he pretended to work on those leggings.

êko, âšay, âšay kiskên'tam, âšay 'c'-îškwâtêniki piko kî-tôtam anihi mitâsa, anihi ... êkâ ..., on'âhkišîma otâsinîw.

êko, môna ohci-kiskên'tam wîn' otâsa ê-yskwâs... ê-yskwâsahk.

kîh-tôtâkow, ê-mîskôti-wêpinamin'ci anihy otâsa wîna 'c'-îskwâsahk.

êko mâka kî-apiskwêšimow wîn' otâsa ana ininiw.

êko mâka, ispî mâka mênâhkacênikih, "âš... kêkonên[25] kâ-wiyêkitêk?[26] manâ itêw. "wiyêkitêw kêkwân ninikwan," manâ itêw.

"manâwina kîna kitâsikitikwâna kâ-wiyêkitêki?" manâ êt'.[27]

"ôho 'ša nîna n'tâsikitikwâna kâ-..., k'-âspiskwêšimoyân," man' êtikow.

êko mâka, "nîn' êcika n'tâsikitikwâna kâ-wiyêkitêki," manâ itêw.

êko mâk' ê-ytâpit âšay kî-câkâskitêniwa.

13   êkoh, ê-kišêpâyâk, nâspic kî-tahkâyâw, kâ-matwêy-âskotihk mâna, kâ-ihkihk ê-'spîhci-tahkâyâk. ê'kwâni manâ 'hk[28] ê-kišêpâyâk.

êko, êko manâ ..., ê-kwîtawi-tôtahk mâka, kî-nihci-kâskisêwikinam oskâta, iskwâskitêskon'[29] êy-âpacihtât.

êko mâka, ê-'ti-kihtohtêcik otânâhk manâ kî-..., kîy-ati-pimohtêw on'âhkišîma ê-'mohtên'ci ê-sâsâkinikâtêt, tâpikâ '-tahkâyâk!

âšay manâ kêka kî-pêhtam awa kêkwâniw ê-matêy-âskotihk ê-'tihtâkwaninik awa ininiw.

k'-îtâpiw manâ.

kâ-cimason'ci manâ wâkinâkana ê'kwânihi osisa.

âš' ê-kî-wâkinâkaniwin'ci, ê-kî-..., ê-kî-kawacin'ci.

'kwâni mâka šâkot, ê-'twêt man' âna wâkinâkan: "t'-atî-... t'ât... t'-âti-ôtôtâpânâskwâhtikohkêwak, kê-'ti-pimâtisicik," manâ itêw anihi, ana wâkinâkan ê-..., ê-cimasot.

êwakwâna mêmišôš, kâ-k'-îšihot. êkot' ânta kâ-'ši-kišîpipanit.

ê'kwâni êskwâk tipâcimôwin mêmišôš ohci.

Then, now, now he knew, now he took steps so those leggings would burn, those ones… not…, his son-in-law's leggings.

He did not know that he was burning his own leggings.

His son-in-law got him to change those leggings of his around so he would burn them.

And then that person [the son-in-law] used his leggings for a pillow.

So then, when they gave off a burning smell, he said to him, "Re… what sort of thing is it which smells strongly? Something smells strongly, my son-in-law," he said to him.

"Maybe it's your leggings which smell strongly," he said to him.

"Well, these, you realize, are *my* leggings which I'm using for a pillow," the son-in-law replied.

So then he said to him, "It's my leggings then which are smelling strongly."

And then, as he looked around, they were already burnt up.

13 Well then, in the morning it was very cold, when the trees could be heard cracking, which is what happened it was so cold. That's what happened in the morning.

So, so then…, at a loss as to what to do, he burn-blackened his legs using the charred sticks.

And then, as they set out back, he began to walk bare-legged as his son-in-law walked along, even though it was cold!

Now then, at last this fellow heard something, which sounded to him as if the trees were cracking in the distance.

He looked around.

The tamaracks which stuck up, that was his father-in-law.

The tamarack had by now been bent, since he had … since he had frozen to death.

And that, to be sure, is what that tamarack said: "They'll begi…'ll beg… they'll begin to make sled runners, future generations," that tamarack then said to him as it stuck up.

That's how Memishoosh was dressed. Right there was the end of him.

That's the extent of the story about Memishoosh.

wîhtikôwak

1   âšay manâ šâkoc mîna pêyakwâ ê-ytâtanôhkâniwahk.

wêskac manâ wîhtikôwak, kâ-..., kâ-..., kâ-mâmâmawi-tašîhkêwâkopanê. êko mâka, âskaw ê-..., ê-n'taw'-minahot mâna, anim' ana pêyak. (êko manâ, wîhtikôwak is' išinihkâtâkaniwanwak nêst' ôk' ôciskwaciwak,¹ ê'kwâni pêyakwan.)

êko manâ šâkoc ..., âšay manâ šâkoc pêyakwâ kihcohcêw² pêyak ociskwaciw. (ociskwaciw isa n'ka-itwân. 'kwâni šâkoc ê-'tâtanôhkêcik ê... ininiwak.)

2   kihcohcêw manâ.

mihcêciwak man' âna mâka kâ-'ši-tašîhkêcik.

wîwikopan man' âna mâka kâ-kihcohcêt ê-n'caminahot.

'kwân' îniniw ê-'nâtawâ'mât. âšay manâ pêyakwâ mâtâhêw. mâtâhêw manâ ininiwa. âšay manâ nawahâcêw.

âšay manâ, kêka manâ kiskênimikow mâkah âšay ê-pêšinâkosit.

âšay [in a sing-song voice] manâ ošimow êni³ kînikwânipahtâw manâ '-piskwâskwayânik.

môna manâ mâši kî-kâhcitinêw.

âšay manâ pêyakwâ kînikiko-wêpaham ana mistikoniw ê-otiškawaskitât 'ci-pataskišihk ê-ytênimât.

3   ê'kwâwa ..., ê'kwâw' ociskwaciw, âšay manâ šâkoc, âšay âšay pêšinâkwaniniw anca kâ-k'-îši-kînikikohahk ... kâ-k'-îši-kînikiko-wêpahahk.

kiskên'tam manâ mâka nêst' âw' êniniw ê-mitêwit oti, m... ê-âcistawi-paskinâkot mâka ociskwatiw' nêsta wîna môna kiskên'tam tâni kê-'ti-ayitôtamin'ci.

paskostonêhotisow manâ mâka aw' ininiw. êko mâk' antê ê-'ti-nakahcišihk ê-'šinâkosit anta kâ-k'-îši-otiškawaskitâniwahk mistik.

"â..., 'ša, manâ!"

âšay ac'-îtâpiw anta kâ-k'-îši-otiškawaskitât mistikoniw.

âšay manâ kâ-matê-'mišinin'ci.

"ahâ! n'kî-mâmîskawicôcawâw," manâ kâ-icwêt.

'kwâni manâ mâk' êši-pohciwatêt sîwîyatihkân. 'ti-pohciwatêw manâ. âšay manâ mâk' ê-'miwatêt,⁴ otâmahokow manâ mâna otihtimana anta okaškamâhk.⁵

The windigoes

1   Now then, here once again is a legend.

Long ago the devils, so it seems, used to live in different groups; so then, sometimes one of them would, would frequently go hunting at that time. (So then, they were called "windigoes" and also "ochiskwajiws", – it is the same thing.)

Well then to be sure ..., now then, to be sure, at one point a certain ochiskwajiw went away. (I'll say "ochiskwajiw". That, in fact, is how the Indians t..., tell the story.)

2   Off he went then.

There were a great many of them there where they lived.

That one who went away hunting was supposedly married.

At that time he went looking for some people. Now then at one point he came upon their tracks. He picked up the trail of the people. Now then he tracked them.

Now then, at last then he was known to be getting close.

Now then, [*in a sing-song voice*] that one escaped, he ran around a clump of bushes.

He couldn't even lay hold on him.

Now once more he quickly put a point on a stick, facing it towards him [the devil], thinking he would run into it.

3   This..., this selfsame ochiskwajiw, now then as it happened, now now it drew near where he had sharpened it... where he had quickly put a point on it.

But now this person also knew how to conjure as well, n..., and that the devil was overcoming him and he also did not know what he was going to do about it.

But then this person made his own nose bleed. And then it looked as though he walked into it where the stick was set facing.

"Now, then!"

Now he began to look in the direction where he had faced the stick.

Now he [the devil] could be made out to be lying down.

"Aha," then he said, "I've discovered the right thing to do to him."

Then he put his caribou-stomach sack on his back. He put it on his back. And now then, tossing it over his back, he was struck on the shoulders, there at the nape of the neck.

"êhê," ana manâ kâ-itwêt. "n'ta..., m'pa...,"[6] '-cahkâskohtatât.

4   âšay manâ ..., âšay manâ '-pêti..., -pêšinâkwaninik mâka wîk... wîkiwâw.

êkota man' âni mâka, pêšoc atiy-akotâw man' ânimêniw wîwat, kâ-tôtahkik man' âskaw ininiwak k'-âtiy-akotâcik wîwatiwâw' ât' ..., ât' ê-pîhcihtininik apišîš kêkwâniw.[7] 'kwâni manâ ê-côtahk mâk' anima ê-..., ê-'tiy-akotât.

êko mâka k'-âci-pîhtokwêt wîkihk.

âšay manâh, kêka nâcipahtwâniwaniniw wîwat. âš' êtokê[8] kâ-ohci-kihtohtên'ci anihi kâ-kî-..., kâ-kî-pêtiwatêt.

âšay manâ šâkoc ê..., nawahâtêw.

âšay manââ, wâhnaw ê-'t'-îhtât ana ininiw kospâhtawîw manâ mâka nêtê. êkotê 'ni man' âna mâka mwêhc' ê-'spaninik 'c'-îši-nipât tipiskôc ana wîhtikôw, anta kâ-iši-kospâhtawîn'ci nêtê mâka išpimihk wîn' ê-nipân'ci.

5   êko manâ mâka, êti-wâpaninik.

mîcitikow manâ mâka.

"hâh..., š' âšay mâmîcânaskwan,"[9] manâ icwêw ociskwaciw, wîhtikôw.

âšay manâ šâkoc, kêka manâ mâka šikitikow mîna.

"âšay wêsâ šâk'[10] kimiwan," manâ itwêw.

âšay manâ itâpiw, kêka wâpamêw ant' ê-'kocin'ci, êy-akosîn'c' îš'imihk.[11]

âšay manâ, sikinêyâpamow âšay. "ê'kocê 'n' mâka kê-'ši-sêkihak," manâ icên'tam.

âšay manâ, ayâwêw manâ mâka nêsta wîna omiht... omihcikiwah awa ininiw.

"âšay manâ."

ê-pêci-pêšiwâpamikot manâ mâka, awa ininiw ôma itêw: "môhkaškama... môhki-kaškamêyâhtawî mâka êkâ 'ci-pinak..., -pinakêskiškamâtân,"[12] manâ it'.[13]

ê'kwâni manâ mâk' ê-tôtahk wîh... wîhtikôw ê-paskinâht miconi.

tahkamâkaniwan manâ mêkwâc anim' ê-tôtahk.

kâ-matê-pihtihkwašihk manâ. kâ-matê-nôhtâkosit ana ê-matê-môskôpinêt anta kâ-k'-îši-tahkamiht.

6   âšay manâ kîwêw.

k'-âti-p'm'wêhtahk[14] manâ, "n'tâšimik nimôlôm,"[15] manâ itw'. "n'tâšimik nimôlôm," âšay manâ pêhtamwak aniki kotakiyak wîhtikôwak, ociskwaciwak anca kâ-..., kâ-wîkicik.

"tân' êtwêt?" manâ itwêwak.

"Aha," he said then. "I dr..., I cra...," jabbing the stick in.

4 Now then..., now then there came...., there came into sight their hom... their home.

That was the right spot; he began to hang up that bag nearby. This is what the people sometimes do when they begin to hang up their bags even though..., even though there's only a little something inside. That's what he did that time as ..., as he began to hang it up.

And so then he started to go into his place.

Now then, finally they went and got his bag. Already, it would seem, that the one which he had brought back had..., had walked away.

Now then to be sure as..., he tracked them.

Now then, as that person got far away, he climbed up yonder. That was the very spot, it so happened, where that windigo was to sleep overhead, where the other one had climbed aloft to sleep.

5 But then it began to be morning.

He [the windigo] was messed on by him.

"Aha..., ts, now the clouds are dirtying," said the ochiskwajiw, the windigo.

Now then, to be sure, finally he was wetted on by him.

"Now then for su... it's raining," he said.

Now then he looked around; at last he saw him hanging, perched up aloft.

Now then, he felt happy at what he saw. Then he thought: "That's the way I'll scare the life out of him."

Now then, that person also had his sp..., his spear.

"Now then!"

When he [the ochiskwajiw] came close, however, this one said this to him: "Climb dow... climb down holding your neck out of the way so I won't... I won't drop the bark on you," he said to him.

That then is what the weeh... windigo did, being utterly beaten.

He was speared while he was doing that. He fell with a resounding crash. He could be heard making a noise as he moaned in the distance, there where he was speared.

6 Now he went home.

He could be heard moving off: "My gwandfawver is bwinging me bad luck," he said; "my gwandfawver is bwinging me bad luck." Now the other devils heard it, the ochiskwajiws who..., who lived there.

"What's he saying?" they said.

One said, "My gwan'fawver is bwinging me bad luck."

"n'tâšimik[16] nimônôm wâšâ," itwêw.

"môna, môna," manâ itwêw. "môna wîskâc âšay ... nimôlôm," manâ itwêw ana pêyak.

âšay manâ mîna, kâ-pêci-pêšohtâkosit: "n'câšamik nimôlôm," manâ itwêw. "ts, ts, ts, ts, ts, ts."

âšay mâmaskâtên'tam. "êkwênâk kâ-âšihkêmot môlôw," manâ itwêw.

âšay manâ pêci-takošin. kâ-sâkišinin'ci manâ okwayâhk mihcikiwa.

7   âšay manâ mâka mihcêtokamikisiwak oš' âni aniki ociskwaciwak ..., wîhtikôwak.

âšay manâ, môna manâ mâka kî-kêcikonimâkanawiniwa. môna kî-kêcikonahêwak aniki anta kâ-ihtâcik.

êko manâ mâka êtwêt ana pêyak: "nâcipahik, nâcipahik okakêhtâwên'tamow," manâ itwêw.

âšay manâ nâcipahâkaniwan okakêhtâwên'tamow.

âšay manâ kâ-pêci-paspâpit iškwâhtêmihk ohci.

âšay manâh, âšay wanašawêw. "apikanâsômâhk," manâ itwêw. "môna wayêš ta-ihtiw." nakacicê-wêpahamawêw mâka. "môna wayêš ta-ihtiw kêskaw... kêskiskawipanin'tê," ana itêw. kiskên'tam mâka mwêhci kê-ihtin'ci anima kâ-itwêt.

"êkwâni n..., ka-mîcisonânaw piko, kišâspin nâspitahohtê," ê-'tên'tahk.

'kwân' âšay wî-mîcisot anima kâ-itwêt anima. môna tâpwê itên'tam anima kic'-îhkininik.

8   êko, âšay manâ kisikanisomâkaniwiniwa.[17] êko man' âni mâka ê-kacicawêpahot[18] man' âspin kâ-cîtanâskopanit.

"šâ ..., êko êcik' âni kê-'hcit, nâ!" manâ kâ-icwêt ana, kâ-kakêhtâwên'tahk.

âšay manâ, âšay manâ, "tântê mâka kê-tôcikâtêk?" manâ it..., itâkaniwan.

"ta-minawâniwan isa," manâ itwêw. "ta-minawâniwan isa. ka-mîcisonânaw. wênâpêmit ta-minawêw," manâ itwêw. "êko mâka, k'-îškwâ-mîcisoyahkwê, pêhpêyak ka-iši-kihta..., -kihtatawêmonânaw," manâ itwêw. "ita mâka piko kê-'t'-îši-mâmîskoškâtoyahk êkot' ântê kê-'t'-îši-nânipahitoyahk," manâ itwêw.

9   âšay manâ šâkoc mâka, minawâniwan. wênâpêmit manâ mâka kî-minawêw.

êko manâ mâka, ispî kâ-iškwâ-mîcisocik, êko mâka kêhtohtêcik. êko mâka, kâ-kîy-at'-îši-mâmîskoškâtocik iko, êkot' âni manâ mâk'

"No, no," said another. "Not ever now ... my gwandfawver," said that particular one.

Now once more, he could be heard nearby as he approached: "My gwandfawver bwings bad luck to me," he said. "Ts, ts, ts, ts, ts, ts."

Now he was awe-struck. "It's the first time a gwandfawver gave an ill omen," he said.

Now he arrived. The spear could be seen sticking out of his neck.

7 And now, it seems, there were many families of those ochiskwajiws, windigoes.

Now then, it [the spear] could not be detached. Those who were there could not take it off.

Then one of them said: "Go get him, go get the wise one," he said.

Now then, the wise one was fetched.

Now he came peeking in from the door.

Now then, now he gave orders. "Crack open the bones," he said. "There'll be nothing wrong with him." He drove it through for him. "There'll be nothing wrong with him if it quickly…, if it goes through quickly," that one said to them. But he knew exactly what would happen to him when he said that.

"Then w…, we'll just eat, if he's killed stone dead," he thought.

So then he already wanted to eat at that point when he said that. He really didn't think that that was going to happen.

8 So, now his bones were warming up. Then he was speared through so he went rigid.

"Oh, my! It seems that is what's going to happen to him!" said that wise one.

Now then, now then, "What will be done now?" someone sai…, said to him.

"There'll be cooking for sure," he said. "There'll be cooking to be sure. We shall eat. The one who has a husband will cook," then said he. "So then, after we have finished eating, one by one away we'll go… away we'll go crying," he said. "Only, whenever we run into each other, that is where we'll kill each other," he said then.

9 Now then for sure, there was cooking. The married one cooked.

And now then, when they had finished eating, then they went away. So then, wherever they ran into each other, that's where they set upon each

êši-kwân'tâtocik. êko mâka, môna ohci-sêsikêhitowak ana ... aniki ... ana ...
aniki wîhtikôwak, aspin anima, ociskwaciwak kâ-itihcik. misiwê piko
pâhpêyak ihtâwak anim' âspin. ê'kwâni mâka wêhc'-îhkih itwâniwan ê-...,
anim' ê-kî-tôtamwâkopanê.

âtawîna k'-îhkin, ê-kîy-ati-wîwicik âtiht otawahkâniwâwa. pêyak mâk'
anima n'k-âtanôhkân anima kâ-kî-..., kâ-kî-tôtamokopanê. kinwâw
âtanôhkân anima.

10   ana pêyak wîhtikôw, kîy-ati-wîwikopan man' ânihi pêyak ot...,
otawahkâna. êko manâ mâka kêka kîy-ati-ocawâšimišiw. ê'kwânihi
mâka mâna wâcêwâkopanê okosisah ê-'nâtawâ'mâcik i... niniwa
ê-wî-mowâcik.

pêyakwâ mâka, kî-pas... kî-paskinâkowak ininiwah.

êko manâ, êk... êko manâ kêhtohtêcik ê-... kî-..., kî-ma...
kî-namêhêwak.

êko mâka kâ-'nâtawâ'mâcik.

êko mâka kâ-..., kinwêš môna ohci-miskawêwak anihi, anih' îniniwa.
šâkoc mâka kî-kiskênimikowak ê-..., pêšoc ê-yhtâcik. kišâstaw manâ piko
nânakânamâsokopan anêy ininiw ê-kiskên'tahk kici-takošinin'ci anihi
wîhtikôwa.

êko manâ, âšay mâka, âšay mâka kiskên'tam ê-pêšinâkosin'ci; êko manâ
kêhtohtêt.

11   ê-mahkikamâk manâ mâka sâkahikan kîy-ati-mitâwisiw.

êko manâ kâ-tôtahk 'ci-kihci-kîwêtininik, 'ci-kihci-nôtihk,
'ci-maci-kîšikânik.

êko manâ mâka, êko kâ-kâsot anta kapahtahanohk mihtânohk, nâspic
ê-yšpacistininik. êkota man' ânim' mâk' âtâmihk kâ-ihtât ant' ê-..., ê-kâsot,
êkâ ê-n'tawênimât 'ci-mowikot anihi ociskwaciwa, wîhtikôw' otih.

êko manâh, kî-kiskên'tam mâka awa, awa wîht..., ôko wîhtikôwak[19] okosis'
ê-wîcêwât.

âšay manâ itohtêw.

šâkot nêsta wîna, ê-kiskên'tahk apišîš tân' êtôtamin'ci, môna mâka šâkoc
ohci-pakitinikow mitoni ..., môn' ohci-pakitinikow 'ci-paskinawât.

12   êko mâka, wîwîkopan nêst' awa ininiw, akâ..., wîw' êsa nêsta wîcêwêw ant'
ê-kâsocik atâmihk mihtânohk.

êko manâ mâkah, kiskên'tam mâk' âwa wîhtikôw tân' êtôtamin'ci,
âcistawi-kiskênimêw. êkota man' ânim' mâka ê-'ši-matâwisicik sâkahikan[20]
êkota man' ânim' mâka ê-tatênimât šâkoc anta kapahtahanohk

other. So then that ... those ... that ... those devils haven't gone near each other since that time, the ones called ochiskwajiws. They all live one by one since that time. And that is how it happened, they say, because that's what they must have been doing.

It happened, however, when they began to marry some of their captives. I shall tell a tale of one at that time, however, about what he had been doing. That is a long legend.

10   A certain windigo, he had apparently begun to live with a certain captive of hi... his as wife. So then in time he began to have children. And it appears, he often used to accompany that sòn of his as they went after p... people in their desire to eat them.

At one time, however, they were overco... they were overcome by the people.

So then, so ... so then they went away because ... they had ... they had ... they saw signs of them.

So then they went looking for them.

Then, however, wh..., for a long time they didn't find those, those people. Even so, the people knew that they were near. Oh, my! That person must just have kept fending them off knowing that those devils were going to come.

So then, but now, but now he knew that they were close; so then he went away.

11   Then he came out onto a large lake.

So then he caused a great north wind to blow, to blow hard, so it was a bad day.

But then, he hid himself there on the leeward side in a snow-drift, in a high drift bank. And there he stayed at that time down under, hi... hiding there, because he didn't want to be eaten by that ochiskwajiw, – windigo, that is.

So then, this, this weeht... knew..., these windigoes that he was travelling with his son.

So now he went there.

Sure enough he too, knowing a little what the other was doing, he was in no way allowed by him..., he was not allowed by him to get the better of him.

12   So then, this person too must have been living with a wife, not..., indeed he was travelling with his wife, as they hid there down inside the snow-bank.

So now then, this windigo knew what they were doing, he was fairly sure that he knew. That is where they came out on the lake, that is the spot where he thought they would be in the wind in a high drift bank.

ê-yšpacistininik.

êko manâ, "êkoc' ôca câkoc n'kocic,"[21] manâ itêw.

âšay manâ cîhcîstahikêw,[22] mihtânohk ê-wî-miskahwât ant' ânt'
ê-'š'-îhtân'ci.

kišâstaw manâ nanihcîw aw' êskwêw, kišâspin cîsta...[23] mwêhci
mîskwaham antê kâ-iš'-îhtâcik, šâkot 'ci-nipahikocik.

" 'kâwin' êkoši, 'kâwin' êkoši, mâsihtâkosi, pâtimâ piko mwêhci ,
mîskwahokawiyahkwê," manâ itêw wîwa.

kâ-pawayâskopanik man' âskaw kônihk antê mistik kâ-cîhcîstahikâkêt ana
wî... ociskwaciw. êko manâ ê'kwânim' ê-tôtahk misiwê 'ntê.

"êkoc' ôca câkoc, n'kocic," manâ itêw.

'kwâni mâka kî-pônihtâw.

13 êko mâka ispîy ..., êko mâka ispî pwân'htân'ci, kî-kiskên'tam awah,
ê-kîwên'ci. kî-kiskên'tam nêsta mîna 'ci-pêci-takošinin'ci.

êko mâkah, kâ-wanawît anta ohci. êko mâk' kâ-ytohtêt, ê-..., kâ-ytohtêt
ê-..., ê-tatênimât ê-..., wîc'-ininiwa.

êko, êko mîna kâ-ytên'tahk ociskwaciw mîna 'ci-n'tawi-cîhcîstahikêt šâkoc
ant' ê-tatênimât.

hêko, kâ-oht..., kâ-ohci-kihciskanawin'ci manâ antah,
kâ-kî-cîhcîstahikêt.

"mâtika mâka, n'kocic," manâ itêw. "êkot' ôta šâkoc âta t...,[24]
ê-'tên'tamâpân kêkwân," manâ itêw.

êko, kâ-nawahahtâcik.[25]

14 kiskên'tam aw' 'iniw[26] 'ci-nawahahtikot. šâkot mâka kî-otihtêw
wîc'-îniniwa, kâ-iš'-îhtân'ci.

âšay manâ ošihtâniwan kê-yši-..., kê-'ši-takošihk ana ociskwaciw,
wîhtikôw oti ..., wîhtikôw okosisa ê-wîcêwât. kiskênimâkaniwan
nêsta okosisa 'ci-wîcêwât. êko manâ wêšihtâniwahk,
ê-sôsâskohtâniwahk anta iškwâhtêmihk pîhtokwêtê 'ci-pahkišihk
ê-išinâkwahk.

êko manâ, âšay âšay pêšiwê... pêšiwênimêwak aniki kâ-mitêwicik.
ê'kwâniki mâka kâ-kî-kiskên'tahkik kê-tôtahkik ê-kî-wîhtamâkocik
omitêwiniwâhk ohci, kê-tôtawâcik ôhi kê-k'-îši-paskinawâcik,
'ci-pîhtokwêyâponot manâ piko antê k'-îšinâkohtâniwaniniw mîkiwâmihk.

15 âšay manâh, kâ-pêtwêwinahkik pêyakwâ ani ê-'ti-tipiskânik.

âšay manâ šâkoc ê..., 'kwâni manâ mâk' ê-pîhtokwêyâhtahît anah, ana

So then he said to him, "Thish ish the plashe for sure, my Shon."

Now then, he prodded about, wanting to discover them there in the snow-drift.

Goodness gracious, but that woman was nervous, in case he before... he hit squarely right there where they were, so as to kill them for sure.

"So don't, so don't scream, unless he hits us right on," he said to his wife.

The stick which that weeh..., ochiskwajiw was prodding with made a shadow as it travelled repeatedly there on the snow. That's what he was doing all over there.

"Thish ish the plashe, right enough, my Shon," he said to him.

But at that point he stopped.

13 So then when ..., so then when he stopped, this one knew he was going home. He also knew that he would come back again.

So it was then that he came out from there. And he went, th... he went wh..., where he thought ... his fellow Indians were.

Then, then again the ochiskwajiw thought he would once more go prodding about, thinking he was there for sure.

So he sta..., he started to make tracks from that place where he [the ochiskwajiw] had been prodding.

"Look here, my Shon," he said to him then. "Right here, sure enough, is the place where I had been thinking there was something," he said to him.

Then, they tracked them down.

14 This Indian knew that he was going to be tracked down by him. But he succeeded in reaching his fellow Indians who were there.

Now then a pl... a place was made where that ochiskwajiw would come, the windigo, that is ... windigo travelling with his son. It was known that he would accompany his son also. So then it was made, – glare ice was made there at the door so that, as it appeared, he would fall when he entered.

So then, now now near ... the conjurors sensed that he was coming near. These were the ones, however, who knew what they would do, because they had been told from their conjuring what they must do to him to get the better of him: they made it to appear that way so that he would glide in right there in the tent.

15 Now then, they could hear approaching footsteps at one point as evening drew on. Now then right enough as ..., and then as that, that little ochiskwajiw, that first little windigo slid in, they broke his bones. Then that

ociškwacîšiš nîštam wîhcikôšiš, nâtwâkanê-wêpahwâkaniwan manâ mâka. êko mâka saskamôci-wêpiniht ana kihci-wîhtikôw animêniw wînininiw..., okosisa anta oskanihk ê-ohcîmakahk.

"câpwê wîkicimahtâniwâw kicêwâcicîwin,"[27] manâ itwêw.

'kwâni man' âst..., 'kwâni manâ..., 'kwâni manâ mâka nêsta wîn' ê-tôtâht anima, ê-kî-pîkohikâtênik ê-..., oskât.

êko mâka ê-nâtwâkanê-wêpahoht, 'kwâni mâka k'-ât'-îši-saskahwâhcik itwâniwan, aniki ê-kî-câkâskis..., kî-câkâskasomâkaniwiniwa mâka anihi kâ-pîhciskâkocik ê-..., ê-..., maskwamîya kâ-ohc'-ociskwacîwicik itwâniwan.

êko mâka, kî-tihkisomâkaniwiniw misiwê; ê'kwâni mâkah, môna 'wênihkân ana ihtâw ociskwaciw anim' êskonâhk. 'kwân' ê-kî-..., 'kwân' ê-k'-îš'-..., ê'kwân' ê-k'-îškwâ-câkihihcik aniki.

16 mihcêt ..., mihcêtwayêk itâtanôhkâsow antah, pwâmošiy ôma nîna kây-âtanôhkêyân. âšay mâka piko, 'kwân' ê-kišipipanik wîna, otâtanôhkâsowiniwâw ôko, ociskwaciw okosisa mâka.

big windigo had that marrow tossed into his mouth ..., which came from the bones of his son.

"Indeed," then he said. "It'sh a pity the way you're abushing my kindnesh."

And then they extingu... that then..., and he had the same thing done to him, his leg having been broken.

And then he had his bones broken; then straightway they had fire set to them, it is said, those ones having burnt..., those things were burnt up which were inside them as..., as..., the ice of which the ochiskwajiws consisted, it is said.

So then, it all melted; and that is why there is not any ochiskwajiw there since that time. Now they have..., now there they have..., now they have all been killed.

16   Many ..., in many ways he has been told about there, before I told this story. But right now, that's the end of the story of these ones, the ochiskwajiw and his son.

cahkâpêš kâ-natôkaminât mistamiskwa

1   pêyakwâ manâ mîna cahkâpêš.

"wîpac waniškâhkan nimišêh,"[1] manâ itwêw. "n'ka-kihtohtân. êkâ
wîskâc kâ-ohci-icohcêyân n'ka-icohcân,"[2] manâ itwêw.

"êhê," manâ mâka itik' ômisa. "wîpac isa n'ka-waniškân," manâ
itêw.

âšay manâ tâpwê kawišimow ê-'ti-tipiskânik.

2   wîpac manâ waniškâw kêkišêpâyânik.

kêkišêpânihkwêw manâ.

êko manâ mâka êti-awêspisot wîpac kâ-iškwâ-kêkišêpânihkwêt.

'kwâni manâ[3] 't'-îši-kihtohtêt. êkâ wîskât manâ kâ-ohc'-îtohtêt
at'-îtohtêw ...

pakwantaw nêtê atî-papâmohtêw. tahto-kîšikâw manâ 'kwân'
ê-tôtahk, ê-papâmohtêt, ê-nân'tawâpahtahk kêkwâniw,
kêy-ohci-mîcisocik.

3   mêkwâc[4] manâ mâka ê-pimohtêt, kêtahtawin man' âti-wâpahtam
sîpîniw. ati-matâpêw manâ. 'kwâni man' '-ât'-îši-mâhiškahk ispî
wiyâpahtahk.

wîpac manâ mâka ê-'ti-pimohtêt antê sîpîhk, pêhtam manâ
kêkwâniw.

kipihcipaniw manâ ê-pêhtahk. n'tohtam manâ.

"tâ'ka[5] kêkwân kâ-itihtâkwahk?" itên'tam. môna wîskâc
ohci-pêhtam kêkwâniw[6] ê-'tihtâkwaninik.

"zhk, zhk, zhk,"[7] manâ itihtâkwan'niw.

mîna man' âti-kihtohtêw. kiyâpac manâh pêhtam. âhcîhkên
ati-pêšohtâkwan'niw, mâmihk nêtê tasihtâkwaniniw sîpîhk.

kî-wîhtamâkopan manâ mâka omisa êkâ wîskâc 'ci-n'tawâpahtahk[8]
kêkwâniw ê-pêhtahk. pitamâ môšak 'ci-pêci-kîwêt, 'ci-pêci-wîhtamawât
kêkwâniw kâ-pêhtahk. êko mâka kê-kiskên'tamin'ci kêkwâniw animêniw
kâ-kî-pêhtahk.

'kwâni manâ tâpw' êtôtahk. 'kwâni manâ 'ši-kîwêt.[9] mwêhci
kâ-kî-pêci-ohtohtêt wîkiwâhk at'-îši-kîwêw, ê-n'tawi-tipâcimostawât
omisa.

4   hâšay manâ takošin ê-tipiskânik.

"nimišê,"[10] manâ itwêw, "ê-kî-pêhtamân kêkwân."

90

Chahkabesh reaches for the giant beaver

1   Once again then, this is a story about Chahkabesh.

"Get up early tomorrow, Big Shishter," he said. "I'm going away. I'm goin' away to a place where I've never gone before," he said.

"Right," his big sister said to him. "I'll get up early all right," she said to him.

Now then, he went straight off to bed as it began to get dark.

2   Early the next morning he got up.

He had his breakfast.

Then he began to get dressed right after he had finished eating breakfast.

That done, he set out on his way. He set off in a direction where he had never gone before.

He began to wander aimlessly about. Every day then, this is what he did, he would walk about searching for something for food.

3   While he was walking about, suddenly he spied a river. He came out into the open [from the forest]. Then, he began to work his way downstream, when he saw it.

Soon, as he was beginning to walk along there at the river, he heard something.

He stopped when he heard it. Then he listened.

"What can it be that's making that sound?" he wondered. Never before had he heard anything which sounded like that.

"Zhk, zhk, zhk," it sounded.

He started to go on his way again. Then once more he heard it. It was beginning to sound closer and closer. It came from just over there down the river.

His older sister must have warned him never to go investigating anything which he had heard. He should always come home first, so as to come and tell her anything which he heard. And so she would know what it was that he had heard.

That then in fact is what he actually did. He went right home. He began to go back to their tent exactly the way which he had come, to take the news to his older sister.

4   Now then, he arrived as it was dark.

"Big Shishter," he said, "I heard something."

91

"tân' êtihtâkwahk?" manâ itik' ômisa.

"zhak, zhak, zhak,[11] ê-icihcâkwahk," manâ itwêw.

"šââ! 'kwâni kwayask kâ-kî-pêci-kîwêyin," manâ itêw. "kišâspin k'-îtohtêyin antê kâ-k'-îši-pêhtaman 'nima kêkwân, mitoni ka-kî-nipahikohtâyak mistâpêwak," manâ itwêw, an' iskwêw. "kikiskên'tên n' âni kêkwân kâ-pêhtaman?" manâ itwêw.

"môna," manâ itwêw cahkâpêš.

"mistâpêwak oš' âni ê-nôcihâcik amiskwah, animêniw kâ-itihtâkwan'nik, êy-êškêcik mâka animêniw kâ-itihtâkwaninik kâ-pêhtaman," manâ itêw. "nôcihêwak oš' ân' âmiskwa mêkwâc ê-pipon'nik; êko mâka animêniw eh-... ê-kakê-pâskihwâcik,[12] êkot' âni mâka wêhci-n'tôkaminâcik. êkot' âni wêhci-nipahâcik ê-pêci-wanawîpanin'ci,[13] wî..., wîk'wâminîhk ohci. 'kwâni mâk' ê-tôtahkik animêniw kâ-pêhtawacik kâ-matêy-âpatisicik. 'kwâni kwayask ê-kî-tôtaman ê-kî-pêci-kîwêyin. 'kâwina mîna wîskâc ohc'-îtohtêy antê," manâ itik' ômisa.

"awas nimišêh, kišêkimin," manâ icwêw.[14] "môna mîna wîskât ka-ohc'-îcohcân ancê. pîtoš mîna n'ka-itohtân," manâ itwêw.

5 "wîpac mîna kêkišêpâyâkê koškonîhkan," manâ itwêw. "pîtoš mîna wayêš n'ka-itohtân êkâ wîskâc kâ-ohc'-îtohcêyân, êkocê 'ni kê-ytohtêyân," manâ itwêw.

âšay manâ tâpwê mîna ê-'ti-kêkišêpâyânik, wîpac manâ mîna waniškâw.

mîcisow manâ, kêkišêpânihkwêw. 'kwâni manâ mîna êti-'wêspisot wîpac. 'kwâni manâ mâka êti-kihtohtêt wîpac kâ-iškwâ-mîcisot.

patotê nêtê yši-kihtohtêhkâsow pitamâh. êkotê 'ni mâka mîna êt'-ohci-n'tawâpahtahk omêskanaw, êkâ kêy-ohci-wâpamikot omisah.

âšay manâ mîna at'-îtohtêw animêniw sîpîniw[15] kâ-kî-iši-pêhtahk kêkwâniw.

"êko mâka kê-kiskên'tamân tâpwê kêkwân kâ-kî-pêhtamân," itên'tam.

'kwâni môšak êtôtamokopanêh cahkâpêš. môšak wî-n'nâtawi-kiskên'tamôpan kêkwâniw kâ-kî-pêhtahk. 'kwâni mâka wâ-tôtahk mîn' ânohc: wî-kiskên'tam kêkwâniw kâ-kî-pêhtahk.

6 âšay man' âti-mâhiškam sîpîniw.

âšay manâ tâpwê 'ti-pêšohtâkwan'niw animêniw kêkwâniw kâ-kî-pêhtahk. kâ-mamatwêkahikêcik manâ nêsta, mistikoniw matê-otatâmâskwahamwak. kêy-inikohk matêy-âpatisiwak mistâpêwak.

"What did it sound like?" his older sister said to him.

"It sounded like 'zhuk, zhuk, zhuk,'" he said.

"Oh, my!" she said; "It's a good thing you came back home. If you had gone to the place where you heard that thing, the giants would most certainly have killed you," that woman said. "Do you know what that was that you heard?" she said.

"No," replied Chahkabesh.

"Why, it was the giants hunting beaver, that sound, – that sound which you heard [was made by them] as they chiselled through the ice," she said to him. "They hunt beaver during the winter, you realize; and then that's wh... they try to block off the lodges with sticks, and that's where they reach into the water for them. It's there they kill them as they come out of their lo..., lodges. That was what you heard them doing as they worked off in the distance. It was the right thing you did in having come home. Don't ever go there again," his older sister said to him.

"Go away, Big Shishter. You're shcaring me," he shaid. "I won't ever go back there again. I'll go somewhere else," he said.

5   "Please wake me again early in the morning," he said. "I'll go somewhere else to a place where I've never gone before, that's where I'll go," he said.

Now, when morning was really on its way again, he got up early once more.

Then he ate, he had breakfast. Then he began to dress himself early. And then he started out, soon after he had finished eating.

First of all, he pretended he was going away a little way off to one side. It was from there that he began to pick up his trail again, so his older sister would not see him.

Now then he set out along that river where he had heard something.

"Now I'll really know what it was that I heard," he thought.

That is what Chahkabesh apparently always used to do. He always used to want to go and find out what it was that he had heard. And that is what he wanted to do again this time: he wanted to know what he had heard.

6   Now then he began to walk down-river.

Now then that thing which he had heard began to sound really close. The ones who were making all kinds of noises could be heard in the distance knocking sticks together. The giants were working as hard as they could some way off.

âšay manâ tâpwê 'ti-sâkêwêškawêw êy-âpatisin'ci; môna manâ mâk' êškwâ
wâpamikow.

'kwâni manâ piko êt'-îši-n'tawâpamât. môna manâ kanakê
kostâciw.

kâ-matê-nânîpawicik manâ mistâpêwak. niyânânêwiwak
ê-matêy-âpatisicik, amiskwa ê-matê-nôcihâcik.

ati-pimohtêw manâ.

7   âšay manâ pêyak mistâpêw wâpamêw ê-pêci-nôkosin'ci.

pêci-apišîšišiw manâ mâka ê-pêci-p'mohtêt, cahkâpêš
ê-cahkokâpawišit.

"ĥêy!" manâ itwêw ana pêyak mistâpêw. "kanawâpam m' ân' 'ihkân[16]
kâ-pêci-nôkosit," manâ itwêwak. "cahkâpêš oš' ân' êtokwê mîna
kâ-pêc'-îšinâkosit," manâ itwêw ana kotak.

"ĥêy: mâtih pâhpihâta," man' itwêwak. "mâtih, 'n'tôkamin amisk,'
ta-itâkaniwan,"[17] manâ itwêwak. "êko mâka kata-pâhpihâkaniwan
kôkîhonikotê 'miskwa," manâ itwêw.

pâhpiwak manâ.

8   âšay tâpwê 'na pêyak kâ-okimâwit têpwâtêw: "ĥêy, cahkâpêš. âstam,
âstam," manâ itwêw.

"âšay mwêhci kêkât n'tôkaminamiskwâniwan," manâ itwêw.

âšay manâ k'-îškwâ-kakêpâskwahêwak anih' âmiskwa. hêko piko
kê-pêci-wanawî-cišahwâcik, nipîhk 'ci-pêci-ispanihon'ci.

âšay manâ mâka k'-îškwâ-kakêpâskwahamwak misiwê
wâtah.

âšay manâ tâpwê kâ-pêci-kâhcinâkosit cahkâpêš, kê-'nikohk
manâ kâ-pêci-pimohtêt. pêci-apišîšišiw. âšay manâ pêci-takošin.

"êko, êko cahkâpêš," manâ itâkaniwan. "êko, pêci-wanapi."

âšay k'-îškwâ-kakêpâskwahâ..., -kakêpâskwahikâniwan.

"êko piko kê-n'tôkaminihcik amiskwak," manâ itwêw ana mistâpêw,
"n'ka-pâhpihânân," ê-itên'tahk.

9   âšay manâ tâpwê 'ti-wawênapiw anta twâhikanihk cahkâpêš.
atiy-êyiskwanêw[18] manâ wanakwaya.

âšay manâ wanawî-cišahikêw ana mistâpêw, otatâmaham man' ânimêniw
wîstiniw.

âšay[19] manâ tâpwê wêhci-pêci-wanawîpanihocik amiskwak.
pêci-nânakacâskwašinwak anta kistâkanihk, ê-wî-kakw...,
ê-wî-kakwê-pêci-wanawîpanihocik.

And now he came right around the bend as they were working; but they hadn't seen him yet.

So then he simply continued on his way to see them. He wasn't at all afraid.

The giants were standing around away off. There were eight of them working over in the distance, busy hunting beaver away off.

He began to walk along then.

7   By now then, one of the giants saw him coming into view.

Somebody little was walking towards them, it was Chahkabesh, who stood short.

"Hey, there," said one giant. "Look at that person who's appearing," they said. "Why it must be Chahkabesh who's suddenly showing up," said another one.

"Hey! see here, let's make fun of him," they said. "See here, let's say to him, 'Reach into the water for a beaver,'" they said. "Then he'll be a laughing stock when the beaver makes him dive down [by pulling him in]," he said.

Then they laughed.

8   Now in fact the one who was their leader called right out to him: "Hey, Chahkabesh. Come on, come on," he said.

"It's just about time to reach into the water for beaver," he said.

They had already finished blocking the beaver off at the openings [out of the lodge on each side]. They were just ready to chase them out, so they would come right out [to the gates] in the water.

Now they had finished blocking off the outlets to all the dens.

And now, after hesitating at first, Chahkabesh came eagerly forward. Little as he was he came. And then he came right up to them.

"Now then, now then, Chahkabesh," he was told. "Come and get settled."

Already the outlets had been clo..., closed in.

"So the beaver will only have to be reached in for," said the giant, thinking, "We'll have a good laugh at him."

9   Now then Chahkabesh really began to settle himself there at the ice-hole. He started to roll up his sleeves.

Then the giant drove the beaver out, – he banged on that beaver lodge.

Now the beaver really came tumbling out of it. They bumped headlong into each other at the enclosure try..., trying to dash out.

Into the water Chahkabesh now plunged his hand.

âšay manâ cahkâpêš ospitôn kihtânam.

kwâcistak, kâ-taši-ninihkinâkosit manâ, wêhci-pêci-ašêstât tâpwê kêka.

"tâpêkâ ta-kî-ocipitikow piko," ê-k'-îtên'tahkik mistâpêwak.

môna manâ pâhpiwak âšay. kanwâpamêwak manâ piko. tâpwê kâ-pêci-ocipitât, ositinîhk manâ mwêhci tatinêw.

wêhci-sâkipanik manâ osôy, mistamisk osôy.

aspin manâ 't'-ôcipitât, kêka manâ misiwê pêci-sâkipitêw tâpwê.

10   ati-pasikow manâ.

pêyak p...[20] manâ ôt... ospitôn âpacihtâw nêtê wâhnaw ê-'ši-wêpinât kônihk.

"kwâcistak!" manâ itên'tamwak mistâpêwak.

'kwâni manâ 't'-îši-kikipanihot ana cahkâpêš, nêtê kâ-iši-pahkišin'ci[21] anih' âmiskwa. ati-otatâmahwêw manâ ocihciy ê-âpacihtât. mîna, mîna mân' otâmahwêw, ê-pihkwâhkocihcênit. 'kwâni manâ tâpwê kâ-'t'-îši-nipahât anima pik' ôcihciy ê-âpacihtât.

hah, k'-âti-papimâh... k'-âti-papim'-wêpinât manâh, ati-pipâhkwatiwêšimêw.

pîniš manâ nêtê wâhnaw ati-pimohtêw, ê-'ti-pipâhkwatiwêšimâhkâsot.

"hêy, tân' êtôtahk an' cahkâpêš?" manâ itwêw ana pêyak mistâpêw. "êkoš' âni mîna tâpwê kê-'ti-kimotit anih' âmiskwa, ana kâ-tôtahk," manâ itwêw.

"mâca n'tawâpamim," manâ itwêw ana kotak. "tâpwê mîna t'-ati-kimotiw."

11   âšay manâ anta pêyak mâwac ê-kostâtênimot: ispanihow.

"hêy, cahkâpêš," manâ itwêw. "pêšiw an' âmisk," manâ itwêw. ati-n'tawâpamêw man' ânt' ê-apin'ci.

kwâcistak manâ! mêkwâc man' ânt' ê-nîpawit cahkâpêš, wêhci-nawatinamwât manâ ospitôninîw ê-wîy-at'-otinân'ci anih' âmiskwa. nîšocihc manâ ocipahtwâw animêniw mispitôniniw, mistâpêwa ospitôninîw.

aspin manâ niyâtwânahk.

"êh-ê-ê-ê, ah-ah-ah," manâ itwêhkâsow ana mistâpêw. "ninipahik cahkâpêš," manâ itwêw.

kâ-nânîwêkotênik manâ ospitôn, ê-kî-nâtwânikâtênik.

" 'kwâni. 'kâ-tôtaw," manâ itwêw mâka ana kâ-okimâwit. "êškwâ, ka-nawinêhwânaw kî-kîwêtê," manâ itwêw.

'kwâni manâ tâpw' ê-'ti-kîwêt an' cahkâpêš, k'-âti-pimohtahât man' ânih' âmiskwa.

12   âšay manâ takošin wîkihk. pîhtokwê-wêpinêw manâ anih' âmiskwa.

Whew! He seemed to tremble there, backing it right out at last.

"He will be pulled in for sure," the giants had thought.

By now they were not laughing. They just looked at him. He had actually pulled a beaver out, and was gripping him right by the feet.

Next thing they saw, his tail was coming out, a giant beaver's tail.

As he tugged away at him, he finally pulled him right out altogether.

10   Then he started to stand up.

He used only one a... arm as he flung him away off on the snow.

"Whew!" thought the giants.

Then Chahkabesh went swiftly after it, to where that beaver had fallen in the distance. He began to pummel it using his hand. Again and again he beat it repeatedly, using his fist. Then he actually killed it, using only his hand.

Hah! When he continued thro..., when he continued throwing it around, he began to dry the water off its fur.

Gradually he got further and further away, pretending to be drying the water off his fur.

"Hey! What's that Chahkabesh doing?" one of the giants said. "Why he's starting to steal that beaver, that one who's doing it," he said.

"Go get it [the beaver]," said the other one, "or he'll certainly start again stealing it."

11   Now then, one of them who was the most daring jumped up.

"Hey, Chahkabesh," he said. "Bring that beaver here." He began to go after him as he sat there.

Good gracious! While Chahkabesh stood there he suddenly seized the giant's arm as he was going to reach for that beaver. With both hands he grabbed that arm, the giant's arm.

He broke it in two.

"Eh-e-e-e, ah-ah-ah," cried the giant. "Chahkabesh is killing me," he said.

His arm hung limp, broken in two.

"That's enough. Leave him alone," said the chief giant. "Wait a while. We'll get after him when he's gone home," he said.

Then Chahkabesh, setting out for home in real earnest, proceeded to carry off that beaver.

12   Now he arrived at his home. Then he tossed the beaver inside.

"šâ! tântê mîna kâ-ohci-kimotiyin aw' amisk kâ-pêšiwat," manâ itik' ômisa.

"môna n'tôhci-kimotin," manâ itwêw. "môna n'tôhci-kimotin. mwêhci n'kî-mêkwâškamâkân ê-kakêpahâtâniwahk. êko mâka, n'kî-itikawin, 'âstam, âstam, cahkâpêš,' " manâ itwêw. " 'pêci-n'tôkamin amisk,' n'k'-îtikawin."

"kikî-mînikawin nâ mâka awa kâ-iškwâ-nipahat aw' âmisk?" manâ itik' ômisa.

" 'hêy! âstam, âstam,' n'k'-îtikawin. 'pêci-n'tôkamin amisk,' n'kî-itikawin. êko man' âni ê-mînikawiyân anima kâ-itikawiyân," manâ itêw omisa.

"kîsis. nâspitêpi niwî-mowâw amisk," manâ itwêw. "êko ka-mowânaw amisk. kîsis."

"mâc' êsa mâka, n'tawâpam kôn," manâ 'tâkaniwan, " 'ci-tihkisamân nipiy.[22] wîpac mâka n'ka-ati-kîšinawân," manâ itwêw an' êškwêw.

âšay manâ tâpwê kîšinawêw. omistaskihkohk manâ iš'-ôswêwak anih' âmiskwa.

13 âšay manâ mawinêhikêwak mistâpêwak. n'tawâpamêwak manâ cahkâpêša.

'kwâni manâ êši-nîswâsicik ê-n'tawâpamâcik mista..., anihi cahkâpêša. pêyak manâ mâka[23] ana kâ-kî-mišwâkanikâtâkaniwit, kâ-kî-nâtwâkanikâtênik ospitôn.

mwêhci manâ mâka ê-'ti-kapatêskwêt ana iskwêw, âšay manâ pêtiwêšinwak mistâpêwak.

"mâcika mâka cahkâpêš kâ-kîw-îtitân, mitoni ka-pêci-nipahikawinânaw, kâ-k'-îtitân," manâ itwêw an' êškwêw. "âšay mâka cahkâpêš, kipêci-nipahikawinânaw. mistâpêwak âšay pêc'-îtohtêwak," manâ itwêw.

"môna. môna ka-nipahikawinânaw, nimišêh," manâ itwêw.

sîkwêpinam man' ânimêniw[24] 'kwâni man' êši-otihtapa-wêpinât anih' ôtaskihkwa. 'kwâni manâ êši-pîhtokwê-kwâškwatit.

14 âšay manâ pêci-pîhtokwêwak mistâpêwak.

"tântê cahkâpêš?" manâ itwêwak.

"anta otaskihkohk kî-pîhtokwêpanihow," manâ itwêw ana iskwêw.

kwâcistak man' âna pêyak mâwac ê-kostâtênimot wêpiškâtêw man' ânih' âskihkwa.

kwâhacistak, kâ-mohci-kîniniwak..., -kînikwâninâkosit manâ, mitoni nâtwâtihtâw osit.

98

"Oh my! Where did you steal this beaver from which you've brought?" his older sister said to him.

"I didn't steal it," he said, "I didn't steal it. I came right into the midst of things when it was all closed off [all the doors of the beaver lodge]. And then someone said to me, 'Come on, come on, Chahkabesh,' " he said. " 'Come and reach into the water for beaver,' I was told."

"But were you *given* this beaver after you had finished killing it?" his older sister said to him.

"They said to me, 'Hey, come on, come on. Come and reach into the water for beaver.' I was being given it when I was told that," he said to his older sister.

"Cook it. I want very much to eat beaver," he said. "So we'll eat the beaver. Cook it."

"Go on then. Fetch some snow," he was told, "for me to melt water, I'll soon begin to cook," that woman said.

Now then, she cooked in real earnest. In her big pot they boiled up that beaver.

13   Just then the giants came after him. They were coming to get Chahkabesh.

At that point there were seven of them as they came to get him, the gi..., Chahkabesh there. One had [gone home], the one who had been wounded, whose arm had been broken.

Just as that woman was transferring the beaver [from the cauldron to the pan], now then the giants' footsteps could be heard coming.

"Look, Chahkabesh! – just as I warned you. They'll come and kill us off altogether as I said to you," that woman said. "They're already coming, Chahkabesh, to kill us. The giants are already coming," she said.

"No. We won't be killed, Big Shishter," he said.

Then he poured out that [broth]. Then, he overturned that cauldron of his. Then he jumped into it.

14   By now the giants were coming in.

"Where is Chakabesh?" they said.

"He leapt into his cauldron there," said the woman.

"Huh," [said] the most fearless one of them; and he kicked the cauldron.

Good Heavens! He just sp..., seemed to spin around. He snapped his foot in two.

The cauldron which was lying upside down seemed like a rock which had

mâna piko âsiniy[25] kî-apîpan man' ê-'tên'tâkosit ana âskihk kâ-otatapišihk. âšay manâ mîna kotak ispanihow.

ocîhcîhkwanapipanihow[26] man' ânta pêšoc êy-apin'ci anih' âskihkwa. "n'ka-mohci-kîpaci-wêpinâw," manâ itên'tam. (mâna êkâ wîn' ê-išinâkosit man' ân' âskihk. kâ-otahtapišihk mâna piko mistasiniy kî-apîpan, man' ê-'tên'tâkosit.)

âšay m'[27] âna kâ-okimâhkatahk têpwâtêw: "cahkâpêš," manâ itwêw. "âšay kitin kitaskihk," manâ itwêw.

mân' êkâ wîna manâ ê-'šinâkosit an' âskihk.

"ka-otinimânaw omis' ê-tôtahk," manâ itwêw ana pêyak. "ka-kihtohtahimânaw' omisa, êkâ wîy-aši-kitinâtê otaskihkwa."

môna mâš'. mân' êkâ wîn' ê-'šinâkosit an' âskihk.

'kwâni manâ tâpw' êši-kihtohtahâcik anihi ..., anih' îskwêwa. 'kwâni êši-kihciwinâcik.

15 wîpac manâ mâka ê-'ti-iškwâ-niskiwênamin'ci, 'kwâni manâ 'ši-kî-..., êši-waniškâpanihot ana cahkâpêš.

âšay kihci-wêpinêw manâ otaskihkwa. wanawîpanihow manâ.

ati-moskipitêw[28] manâ nêtê otahcâpiyah, kâ-iši-nikwahwât. 'kwânimanâ êši-kihtahamêpahtât animêniw mêskanâniw kâ-kîy-at'-îši-kihtohtên'ci.

sâkahikan manâ mâk' antê 'tihtakwan.

ati-matâwisipahtâw animêniw sâkahikaniniw, kâ-ati-piskokâpawicik manâ mistâpêwak. mêkwayêš k'-âti-nîpawin'ci[29] ômisa.

16 âšay manâ wâkipitêw otahcâpiya.

ayamihêw man' ânih' otakaskwa: "n'cakašk,[30] n'cakašk, 'kâwina wîna nimišêh[31] oscikwânihk; 'kâwina wîna nimišêh oscikwânihk," manâ itêw. "mwêhci piko mistâpêwak oscikwâniwâhk at'-îši-pâhpahkišini: cin, cin, cin, cin, cin, cin, cit,"[32] manâ itwêw.

'kwâni manâ êši-pimocikêt kâ-iškwâ-itât.

kwâcistak, k'-âti-kwâškwâskwênâkosit man' âkask, mwêhci piko mistâpêwak ostikwâniwâhk. k'-âti-wani-tahtakwahwât manâ.

kâ-matê-pêyakwâskokâpawin'ci manâ omisa.

âšay manâ têpwâtêw: "nimišêh," manâ itwêw. "pêci-kîwê, n'tawi-mowât' âmisk," manâ itwêw.

kâ-pêci-nôkosin'ci manâ tâpwê wmisa.

17 êko man' âni mâka êt..., îši-kîwêw ê-wîcêwât.

"mâtika mâka kâ-ititân, nimišêh," manâ itwêw. " 'kâwina mikwaškâtên'ta, kâ-k'-îtitân. môna ka-nipahikawinânaw kâ-k'-îtitâpân," manâ itêw.

been sitting there.

Now another giant took over.

He quickly sat on his legs close by where the cauldron was sitting. "I'll just tip it over on its side," he thought. (Again and again the cauldron looked as if nothing had happened. It felt like a big rock as it lay there upside down.)

Just then the leader called out to him: "Chahkabesh," he said. "Turn your pot over now," he said.

But that cauldron still gave no sign of moving.

"We'll take his older sister, since he's doing this," said that one. "We'll take his older sister away, if he doesn't want to turn back his pot."

Still no result. The kettle didn't even appear to move.

Then didn't they actually take away that..., that woman! Then they carried her off.

15   As soon as their footsteps could no longer be heard, straightway up shot..., up shot Chahkabesh.

He heaved his cauldron right side up. He dashed outside.

He started to dig up his bow where he had buried it. Then he quickly ran off down the trail where they had started to go.

Now, there was a lake began there.

He came running out on that [frozen] lake, just as the giants were standing in a group. In the midst of them was standing his older sister.

16   Now then he bent his bow with a pull.

Then he spoke to that arrow of his: "My awwow, my awwow, not on my older shister'sh head; not on my older shister'sh head," he said to it. "Only keep falling right on the heads of the giants: tsin, tsin, tsin, tsin, tsin, tsin; tsit," he said.

Then when he had spoken to it, he let the arrows fly.

Whew! That arrow seemed to skip along, dead on the heads of the giants. He began to fell them one after the other.

His older sister could be made out standing like a lone tree.

Now then he called to her: "Big Shishter," he said. "Come home. Let's go eat the beaver," he said.

His sister then appeared coming towards him.

17   And so then he began..., he went home with her.

"See what I told you, Big Shishter," he said then. "Don't worry, as I said. We won't be killed as I had been telling you," he said to her.

âšay man' âti-pîhtokwêwak tâpwêh, kâ-piskwašihk manâ an' âmisk. môn'
êškw' ohci-mît…, mîcisôwak.[33]

"šâ! tântê mâka kê-tôtamân môskamiy?" man' êtwêw. "âst', tâpwê
niwî-minihkwân môskamiy. mâca isa mîna nâtahâkonê," manâ itik' ômisa.
"mîna mâka n'ka-kapastawêhên ôho mîcima," man' êtwêw.
" 'ci-môskamiwâkamipanik anima nipiy," man' êtwêw.

âšay manâ tâpwê nâcipahêw kôna.

tihkisam manâ nipîniw.

'kot' âni[34] mîna êši-kapastawê-wêpinahk anihi mîcima. 'kwâni mâka
ê-kîy-ak…, ê-kî-'yât môskamîniw. êko mâka mîcisocik tâpiskôc,
kâ-iškwâh-ošihtât môskamîniw.

'kwâni piko êskwâpihkêyâk.

By now they were actually entering the tent, where the beaver lay in a heap. They had not yet eat..., eaten.

"Tch! How shall I make broth?" she said. "Come on, I really want to drink some broth. Go get some more snow," his older sister said to him. "And I'll put these chunks of meat in again," she said, "so that that water will become broth," she said.

Now then he went out and fetched snow.

Then she melted water.

Then his sister tossed those chunks of meat in again. And then he had..., he had broth. So they both ate together, after she had finished making the broth.

And that's the length of the story.

cahkâpêš nêsta mâka mistâpêskwêwak

1 âšay manâ mîna pêyakwâ kihtohtêw cahkâpêš.

papâmohtêw manâh. mêkwâc manâ mâka ê-papâmohtêt pêhtam manâ kêkwâniw, "tangg, tangg, tangg,"[1] manâ kâ-itihtâkwaninik.

nîpawiw manâ ê-n'tohtahk.

"tânika kêkwân kâ-itihtâkwahk?" manâ itên'tam.

'kwâni manâ êši-kîwêt. "n'ka-n'tawi-wîhtamawâw nimišêh,"[2] manâ itên'tam.

2 hâšay manâ tâpwê takošin wîkihk, ê-tipiskânik.

"nimišêh, ê-kî-pêhtamân kêkwân," manâ itwêw.

"tân' êtihtâkwahk?" manâ itik' ômisa.

" 'tingg, tingg, tingg,[3]' ê-itihtâkwahk," manâ itwêw.

"šââ!" manâ itwêw ana iskwêw. " 'kwâni kwayask kâ-kî-pêci-kîwêyin," manâ itwêw. "mistâpêskwêwak oš' ân' ê-kêkišêpâ-manihtêcik, anima kâ-pêhtaman," manâ itwêw, "ê-matwê-kahikêcik oš' âni animêniw kâ-itihtâkwaninik," manâ itwêw. " 'kâwina mîna wîskâc antê ohc'-îtohtê, kâ-k'-îši-pêhtaman anima kêkwân," itwêw.

"ê'kwâni, 'kwâni, nimišêh. kisêkimin. môna mîna n'ka-ohc'-îtohtân antê kâ-k'-îši-pêhtamân anima kêkwân," manâ itwêw cahkâpêš.

'kwantaw mâk' ani ê-itwêt. 'kwâni piko mîna kê-wâpaninik 'ci-kîwêt antê kâ-k'-îši-pêhtahk animêniw kêkwâniw, mâtih tâpwê ê-ytên'tahk.

3 âšay manâ '-'ti-tipiskânik, "wîpac waniškâhkan," manâ itêw omisa. "wîpac n'ka-kihtohtân. êkâ wîskâc kâ-ohc'-îtohtêyân, êkotê 'ni kê-'tohtêyân," manâ itwêw.

âšay manâ tâpwê, "êh," manâ itikow omisa. "wîpac isa mâka kawišimo," manâ itikow.

'kwâni manâ tâpwê êtôtahk. wîpac manâ kawišimow. âšay manâ mîna wîpac waniškâw ê-'ti-wâpaninik, ê-kêkišêpâyânik.

kêkišêpânihkwêw manâ mâka. kâ-iškwâ-mîcisot manâ mâka, "šâ!" manâ itwêw. "tânika kî-nîmâwâpânê wîhkway,"[4] manâ itwêw. "ê-nipahak oša mâna pinêw ê-nawacîyân mâka; mitoni mâka m'pâsitênikon," manâ itwêw, "wêsâ êkâ ê-tômisit," manâ itwêw.

âšay manâ tâpwê mînik' ômisa pêyak wîhkwâniw namêsi-pimîniw. 'kwâni manâ mâka tâpw' êši-kihtohtêt, ê-'ti-payahtinâkwaninik.

4 pitamâ manâ mâka nêtê 'kwantaw iši-kihtohtêw...,

Chahkabesh and the giant women

1   Now once again, Chahkabesh went away.

He walked around for some time. While he was walking about he heard something which sounded like "tungg, tungg, tungg."

He stood listening to it.

"What can it be that's making that sound?" he wondered.

At that he started back home. "I'll go tell my big shishter," he thought.

2   And now he arrived right back at his home, as it was dark.

"Big Shishter, I heard something," he said.

"What did it sound like?" his older sister said to him.

"It sounded like 'tingg, tingg, tingg,' " he said.

"O-oh dear!" said that woman. "Then it was right that you came back home," she said. "It was the giant women, you realize, gathering wood early in the morning, that is what you heard," she said. "As they were noisily cutting it, indeed that is what made the sound," she said. "Don't ever go there again where you heard that thing," she said.

"All right, all right, Big Shishter. You're scaring me. I won't ever go there again where I heard that thing," Chahkabesh then said.

But he just said it off-handedly. Simply to go back there the next morning to where he had heard that thing, that's what he really had in mind.

3   Now since it was already getting dark, he said to his older sister, "Get up early. I'll be going away early. I'll be going somewhere where I've never gone before, that's where I'll be going," he said.

"Yes I will," his older sister said to him. "But be sure to get to bed early," she said to him.

That's just what he did. He went to bed early. Then he got up early again as daybreak was coming, in the morning.

He had his breakfast; but then, after he had eaten, he said, "Dear me! I wonder if I shouldn't have taken a food hamper, – of course I usually kill a partridge for a snack though; but I get very bad heartburn," he said, "when it's not fat enough."

Now then, his sister gave him one bladder of fish-fat. Then he set off in real earnest as soon as dawn broke.

4   At first, however, he just went ..., pretended he was going away

-hkâsow.[5] kâ-nihtâ-tôtahk mâna piko: "êkâ 'ci-kiskênimit nimis,"
ê-itên'tahk.

nêtê manâ mâka wâhnaw nawac êkotê 'n' ê-'ti-ohci-n'tawâpahtahk
omêskanaw, otâkošîhk kâ-kî-pêci-ohtohtêt.

'kwâni manâ mâk' ê-'t'-îši-nâtahamêt pîniš manâ mâka nêtê
pêšiwâpahtam kâ-k'-îši-pêhtahk ê-matwê-kahikâniwaninik.

âšay manâ tâpwê mîna pêhtam. pêyakwan manâ ê-'tihtâkwahk:
"tingg, tingg, tingg,"[6] ê-itihtâkwahk.

"âšay manâ mâka kê-wawêniyân," manâ itên'tam.

kêtawatêw manâ wîwat. wâpamêw manâ mâka wîskacâna,
ê-pêci-twêhon'ci mistikohk.

pimotêw manâ. kâ-pimiwêpahwât manâ piko.

'kwâni manâ êši-pahkwêpinât. pîhtôšakêpitêw manâ.

kâ-iškwâ-pahkonât manâ mâka, 'kwân' êši-pîhtômot animêniw
onamêsi-wîhkwâm.[7]

'kwâni manâ mâka êši-pohci-wêpiškawât anihi wîskacâniši-wayâna.

'kwâni manâ mâka êti-iši-kihcihnât.

5 nêtê manâ mâka kâ-tatawêkahikên'ci mistâpêskwêwa êkotê 'n' ê-'t'-îšihnât.

âšay manâ tâpwê wâpamêw mistâpêskwêwa, ê-manihtên'ci wanawîtihmihk
wîkinîhk. nânâtwâkahihtêwak manâ.

âšay manâ cahkâpêš pêšoc manâ ant' âtiy-akosîw.

kêka manâ mâk' âti-nîhci-twêhow. âhcîhkên manâ pêšoc ant'
âti-iši-kwâskwâškwatiw.

kêka manâ mitoni pêšoc.

âšay manâ kêka pisiskâpamêw ana pêyak mistâpêskwêw.

"šâ!" manâ itwêw. "tân êtôtahk awa wîskacâniš?" manâ itwêw.

"pimwâhtikonahihk pîwikahikaniniw," manâ itwêw ana kotak.
"ta-kînikwânâciwoswâkaniwan mistaskihkohk," manâ itwêw. "cahkâpêš oš'
ân' êtikwê mîna kâ-tôtahk," manâ itwêw.

'kwâni manâ tâpw' êtôtahk ana pêyak iskwêw. 'm'wâhtakonahêw[8] manâ
pîwikahikaniniw ê-âpacihtât.

kâ-mohci-ninihkikaškwê-wêpahwât manâh. 'kwâni manâ mâka êši-otinât.
pîhtokwê-wêpinêw manâ.

"êh," manâ itwêw anih' îskwêwa kâ-... kâ-kanawên'tamin'ci mîk'wâminiw
"kapastawê' 'wa mistaskihkohk," manâ itêw. "ta-kînikwânâciwosow," manâ
itwêw.

'kwâni manâ tâpw' êtôtahk ana kâ-apit iskwêw. kapastawêhwêw manâ

somewhere, as he was given to doing: "so my older sister won't know," he thought.

But then, away off, quite far in the distance, he began to look for his path in that direction which he had come from the day before.

Then he started to follow it until he began to come close to that place where he had heard the sound of noisy chopping in the distance.

Now then, he definitely heard it again. It sounded the same: "tingg, tingg, tingg," it sounded.

Then he thought, "Now I'll get ready."

He unslung his pack-sack. And then he saw a whiskey-jack coming to alight on a tree.

He shot at him. He simply knocked him down and killed him.

Then he began to skin him. He stripped the skin off the meat.

Then after he had skinned him, he tucked that fish-bladder inside his clothing.

Then he quickly put on the little whiskey-jack's skin.

Then he began to fly away.

5   He flew over to where the giant women were making the banging noise, that's the very way he flew.

Now he actually saw the giant women gathering wood outside their home. They were cutting wood into small lengths.

Now Chahkabesh perched close by there.

Finally he even alighted down on the ground. He kept hopping still closer and closer.

At last he was right close by.

Now at length one of the giant women noticed him.

"Oh, oh!" she said. "What is this whiskey-jack doing?" she said.

"Throw a chip at him," said the other. "He'll swirl around boiling in the big pot," she added. "It's likely Chahkabesh who's doing it again," she said.

Then that one woman did just that: she took a shot at him using a chip.

She just swept him away with talons trembling. Then she picked him up and tossed him indoors.

"Huh," she remarked to the woman who, who looked after the tent. "Put this fellow in the big pot," she said to her. "He will swirl around boiling all right," she said.

Then that woman who was sitting down did just that. She put him in the

mistaskihkohk. 'kwâni manâ mâka êši-akonât anta iškotêhk.

6   kêka manâ mâka osow an' askihk.

kâ-mohci-kînikwânâciwosot manâ cahkâpêš.

"mâmân êkwâni kêkât," manâ itên'tam cahkâpêš.

mêkwâc manâ mâk' êy-osot, pâskicênam manâ animêniw otôwîhkwâm kâ-kî-pêci-nîmât.

'kwâni manâ mâk' êši-kipihtâciwosopanit an' âskihk. mitoni manâ šôšawakohtin pimiy.

pêhtawêw manâ mâk' ana mistâpêskwêw ê-kipihtâciwosopaninici omistaskihkwa.

itâpipanihow manâ. kanawâpamêw manâ anihy âskihkwa.

"šâ!" manâ itwêw, ispî wiyâpahtahk pimîniw mitoni ê-šôšawakohtininik. "pêci-kanawâpamihk aw' âskihk," manâ iši-têpwêw wanawîtimihk.

'kwâni manâ tâpwê misiwê pêci-pî... pêci-iši-pîhtokwêpanihocik mistâpêskwêwak. pêci-wâskâkâpawîstawêwak man' ânihy âskihkwa. kanawâpamêwak manâ ê-mâmaskâtên'tahkik.

"šââ, šââ," 'kwâni manâ piko ê-'twêcik.

7   "mâmân êkwâni misiwê," manâ itên'tam cahkâpêš.

âšay manâ koškopanihow. 'kwantaw manâ piko wasaswê-wêpinam nipîniw, otahtahkwana êy-âpacihtât. 'kwâni manâ mâka misiwê êši-kakêpwâtâmwâskiswât misiwê, anihi mistâpêskwêwa. 'kwâni manâ êši-wanawî-kwâškwatit anta oh... mistaskihkohk ohci. 'kwâni manâ êš..., êt'-îši-sâsîkahahtâwât, animêniw môskamîniw â...,[9] anihi mistâpêskwêwa.

'kwâni misiw' '-kî-nipahât.

omišwâkana manâ mâka nêtê kâ-pimišinin'ci, anihi nâpêwa, kâ-kî-mišwâkanikâtâspan.[10] 'kwâni manâ ê-'ši-n'tawâpamât, sâsîkahahtawêw animêniw môškamîniw ê-âpacihtât.

kâ-mohci-catîtwâskopaninici manâ piko, êkwâni misiw' '-kî-câkihât mistâpêskwêwa nêsta misiwê omîšwâkana.

'kwâni piko êskwâpihkêyâk.

big cauldron. Then she hung it over the fire.

6   At last the pot boiled.

Chahkabesh just swirled around boiling.

"I would think it's about time now [for me to do something]," thought Chahkabesh.

While it was boiling he opened up his bladder which he had brought for food.

At that, however, that pot stopped boiling. The fat spread completely over the top.

But that giant woman heard her big pot stop boiling.

Suddenly she glanced over. She looked at the cauldron.

"Oh dear!" she said when she saw the fat completely spread over the top. "Come and look at this pot," she called outside.

At that they all came i... all the giant women came rushing in. They came and stood around that cauldron. They looked at it with amazement.

"Oh my, oh my!" was all they could say.

7   "I would think it is time now," thought Chahkabesh.

Now then, he made a sudden move. He splashed water just any way using his wings. Then he used the fire to make them all gasp for air, all those giant women. And then he leapt out from there... from the giant pot. And then he dr... began to pour that broth all over them...those giant women.

Then he killed them all.

But the wounded one was lying some way off, that man [giant] who had been wounded. Now then as he came looking for them, he [Chahkabesh] drenched him all over with that broth.

When he was stunned with shock, at that point Chahkabesh finished them all off, the giant women and the wounded giant altogether.

That's the length of the story.

cahkâpêš kâ-nakwâtâkopanê pîsimwa

1 âšay manâ mîna pêyakwâ kihtohtêw. wîpac manâ ê-kêkišêpâyânik
kihtohtêw. êkâ wîskâc kâ-ohc'-îtohtêt mîna itohtêw.

mêkwâc manâ mâka nêt' ê-papâmohtêt mêkwâc ê-kîšikânik, wâpahtam
manâ mêskanâhk ê-'šinâkwaninik kêkwâniw ant', askîhk. mwêhci manâ piko
ê-kî-tawâskitêk, išinâkwan askiy: išinâkwan mihcêtwâ kêkwân
ê-kî-pimohtêmakahk.

'kwâni manâ mîna êši-kîwêt, ê-n'tawi-tipâcimostawât omisa kêkwâniw
kâ-kî-wâpahtahk.

2 ê-takošihk manâ mâka wîkihk tipâcimow. "nimišê," manâ itwêw,
"ê-kî-wâpahtamân kêkwân mêskanâhk ê-'šinâkwahk. mwêhci mâk'
ê-kî-tawâskitêk ê-k'-îskwâtêk 'kwâni mwêhc' ê-'šinâkwahk. môna mâkaw
âtawîna wayêš n'tôhci-tôtên 'ci-tâpakwêyân," manâ itwêw.

"šâ!" manâ itwêw. " 'kâwina mîn' anima tôta kâ-itwêyan," manâ itik'
ômisa.[1] "k'kiskên'tên n' âni, ani kêkwân kâ-išinâkwahk mêskanâhk
kâ-išinâkwahk?" manâ itwêw. "êkot' oš' ân' ê-'ši-pimohtêt pîsim
ê-pêci-sâkâstawêk ê-wâpahk," manâ itwêw. " 'kâwina mîn' ohci-mikoškâciht'
ânima mêskanaw mîna wâpahtamanê," manâ itik' ômisa.

"okêy, nimišêh," manâ itwêw. "môna mîna wîskâc n'ka-ohci-n'tawâpahtên.
pîtoš mîna n'ka-itohtân wâpahkê," manâ itwêw. "wîpac mîna koškonîhkan
kêkišêpâyâkê," manâ itwêw.

3 âšay manâ mîna tâpwê kiyêkišêpâyânik waniškâw wîpac.

'kwâni manâ mîna êt'-îši-kihtohtêt ê-kêkišêpâyânik.

êkotê 'ni mîna tâpw' êt'-îtohtêt kâ-k'-îši-wâpahtahk animêniw mêskanâniw.
kihtohtahtâw manâ mâka nakwâkaniyâpîniw, "n'ka-tâpakwân," ê-itên'tahk.
"mâtih tâpwê pîsim anta pêmohtêkw'," ê-'tên'tahk, ê-wî-kiskên'tahk tâni
kê-yhkininik.

âšay manâ tâpwê tâpakwêw. mwêhci man' anta mêskanâhk iši-tâpakwêw.
'kwâni manâ mâka êsi-kîwêt anima kâ-'škwâ-tôtahk.

"wîpac waniškâhkan nimišêh," manâ itwêw. "wîpac mîna n'ka-kihtohtân,"
manâ itêw.

4 âšay manâ mîna tâpwê kêkišêpâyânik,[2] wîpac manâ waniškâw an' êskwêw.
âšay man' âpiwak.

"tânt' êkâ mâc' ês...[3] êškwâ 'êhci-wâpahk?" manâ itên'tam ana iskwêw.

Chahkabesh snares the sun

1   Now once more Chahkabesh set out. He left early in the morning. Again
he went somewhere he had never gone before.

While he was walking round and about some distance off during the day,
he saw something showing on the trail there, on the ground. The earth
looked just exactly as if a trail had been blazed: it looked as if something had
walked on it again and again.

So off he went home again, on his way to tell his older sister what he had
seen.

2   On arriving home, he brought the news. "Big Shishter," he said, "I saw
something which appeared on the path. Exactly as if a trail had been blazed
by burning, that's exactly what it looked like. But I didn't do anything,
however, about setting snares," he said.

"I should say not!" she exclaimed. "Don't you ever again do what you're
saying," his older sister said to him. "Do you know that... that thing which
appeared when it appeared on the trail?" she said. "Why that's where the
sun walks along when he comes rising at dawn. Don't you trouble that trail
any more if you see it again," his older sister said to him.

"Okay, Big Shishter," he said. "I won't ever go after it. I'll go again a
different way tomorrow," he said. "Waken me up early again in the morning,"
he said.

3   Now then when it was actually morning again, he got up early.

Then he started off again while it was still morning.

Off he set again right in that very direction where he had seen that trail.
But he took away with him some snare wire, thinking, "I'll set a snare. Let's
see whether the sun is really walking along there," he thought, since he
wanted to find out what would happen.

Now then he actually set a snare. Right there on the trail he set it.

And then he went home when he had finished doing that.

"Get up early, Big Shishter," he said. "I'll be going off again early," he
said to her.

4   Now then, when morning arrived again, that woman got up early.

Now then they sat.

"Why is it not even ye... not yet dawn?" the woman thought.

They sat for a long time; but still it didn't dawn.

kinwêš man' âpiwak; môna manâ mâka mâši wâpan.

âšay manâ kiskisipaniw animêniw mêskanâniw kâ-kî-wâpahtamin'ci.

"manâwina mîna wayêš kî-tôtam," manâ itên'tam an' êskwêw. "šâ! tân' êhkihk ô êkâ wêhci-wâpahk?" manâ itêw. "môna nâ wayêš kitôhci-tôtên kâ-kî-wâpahtaman mêskanaw pîsimo-mêskanaw?" manâ ytâkaniwan cahkâpêš.

"êhê," manâ 'twêw cahkâpêš, "tâpwê," manâ 'twêw, "n'kî-tâpakwân," manâ itwêw.

"šâ! 'kwâni mwêhci anohc ati-kihtohtê," manâ itikow anih' ômisa. "mâci. anta n'tawi-nâtawâpam⁴ ana pîsim. kî-nakwâtâtokwê 'na pîsim," manâ itwêw. "mâca piko. wîpac ati-kihtohtê," manâ it...têw ošîma.

"ê," manâ itwêw cahkâpêš. 'kwâni manâ tâpwê ê-'t'-îši-kihtohtêt.

5 tipiskâniw manâ mâka ê-pimohtêt.

môna mâši wâpan.

âšay manâ ê-'ti-pêšiwâpahtahk anta kâ-k'-îši-tâpakwêt kâ-matê-wâstêk manâ. wîy-ati-n'tawâpamêw manâ mâk' anihi pîsimwa; môna manâ mâka kî-tôtam, wêsâ '-kišâsikêt ana pîsim.

âšay manâ têpwâtêw pêyak, pêyak otôtêma. mâwac kâ-'pišîš'šit wâpikošîš, ê'kwânihi têpwâtât.⁵

"mâca n'tawâpahtip... n'tawâpam ana pîsim," manâ itêw. "êko mâka kîškaht' ânima nakwâkaniyâpiy," manâ itêw.

"kayâm," manâ itwêw anah wâpikošîš. "tâpwê n'ka-tôtên," manâ itwêw.

'kwâni manâ tâpw' êtohtêt ana wâpikošîš. n'tawi-kîškahtam man' ânimêniw nakwâkaniyâpîniw.

k'-âti-pimohtêt man' âna pîsim, kâ-'škwâ-kîškamât ana wâpikošîš. 'kwâni manâ mâk' êti-wâpahk wîpac kâ-iškwâ-kîškamâkaniwit ana pîsim.

hêko man' âni mâka wêhci-kînikistawêt, itwâniwan wâpikošîš mâwac kâ-apišîšišit, wêhci-paškostawêt itâkaniwan. anim' ê-kî-tôtawâkopanê cahkâpêš, hê-k'-îskwâson'ci mâka omînistowâkaninîhk.

'kwâni piko êskwâpihkêyâk.

Now then she suddenly recalled that trail which Chahkabesh had seen.

"I'll wager he's done something," the woman thought. "Goodness gracious! Whatever has happened that it's not dawn?" she then said to him. "You haven't done anything to the trail which you saw, have you, the sun trail?" Chahkabesh was asked.

"Yes," said Chahkabesh. "Actually," he said, "I set a snare," he said.

"Oh, dear! Then get on your way right now," that older sister of his said to him. "Off with you! Go and look there for the sun. You must have snared the sun," she said. "Just be off. Get on your way," she sai... said to her young brother.

"Right," said Chahkabesh. Then he set off right away.

5   It was dark as he walked.

It wasn't even dawn.

And now as he approached the spot where he had set the snare, there was a light shining in the distance. He wanted to keep on going after that sun; but he wasn't able to do so because the sun was shining too hot.

Now then he called one, one of his friends. It was the littlest mouse, that's the one he called.

"Go fet... go get that sun," he said to him. "And then gnaw through that snare line," he said to him.

"Very well," said that mouse. "I'll certainly do it," he said.

Then, true to his word, the mouse went on his way. He went to gnaw through that snare line.

The sun began to walk again, after that mouse had gnawed him through. At that it began to dawn as soon as the sun had been gnawed free.

And that, they say, is why he is sharp-snouted, the mouse who is very, very little, why he is said to have had his whiskers shaved off. At that time it was without a doubt because Chahkabesh had done it to him, when he got scorched on his whiskers.

And that's the length of the story.

cahkâpêš kâ-kî-kohcipanihikot mistamêsa

1   pêyakwâ manâ mîna cahkâpêš kihtohtêw manâ ê-nanâtawâpahtahk kêkwâniw.

âšay manâ mâka mêkwâc ê-papâmohtêt nêtê wâhnaw, ohci-wâpahtam manâ mâka sâkahikaniniw; mêkwâc mâka mêkwâc ê-pâhpâskâtikohtân'ci awiyâšîša, pimotêw manâ mâka pinêšîš' ê-akosîn'ci mistikohk. otakaskwa manâ mâka nêtê wâhnaw pahkišininiwa nipîhk.

anihi manâ mâka kâ-pâhpâskâtikohtân'ci awiyâšîša môna kî-tôtam 'ci-n'tawâpamât ê-kostâcit.

'kwâni manâ mâka n'tawâc êši-kîwêt ê-kîwê-tipâcimostawât omisa kêkwâniw kâ-kî-wâpahtahk.

2   ê-takošihk manâ mâka tipâcimostawêw.

"nimišê," manâ itwêw, "ê-kî-wâpahtamân kêkwâ…, sâkahikan," manâ itwêw. "ê-pâhpâskâtikohtâcik awiyâšîšak," manâ itwêw.

"n'takask mâka nêtê kî-pahkišin nipîhk," manâ itwêw. "môna mâka n'tawât n'tôhc'… n'tawâpamâw," manâ itwêw.

" 'kwâni kwayask êkâ wêhci-n'tawâpamât," manâ mâk' itikow.

"kikiskên'tên n' âni 'wênihkânak anik' kâ-pâhpâskâtikohtâcik nipîhk?" manâ itêw[1] anaw iskwêw. "kišâspin kî-pahkopêyin anta nipîhk, mitoni ka-kî-otamikohtayak namêsak," manâ itikow. "mistamêsak ka-kî-mâkomikohtayak[2] mâka ka-kî-kihcipanihikohtayak," manâ itêw ošîma.

"nimišêh, 'kâwin' anima icwê. kisêkimin anim' ê-'twêyin," manâ itwêw. "môna mîn' ântê n'ka-itohtân," manâ itwêw ana cahkâpêš.

"wîpac waniškâhkan mîna kêkišêpâyâkê," manâ itêw omisa.

3   âšay manâ tâpwê mîna ê-'ti-wâpaninik, wîpac manâ waniškâw ana iskwêw.

koškonêw manâ ošîma

êkwâni manâ mîna tâpw' êti-kihtohtêt ana cahkâpêš kiyêkišêpâyânik.

kâ-k'-îši-wâpahtahk piko sâkahikaniniw êkotê 'n' êt'-îtohtêt, ê-wî-n'tawâpamât awênihkâna kâ-pâhpâskâtikohtân'c'.

âšay man' âti-pêšiwâpahtahk, tâpwê âšay mîna kâ-pâhpâskâtikohtâcik namêsak.

'kwâni manâ '-'t'-îši-kapastawêpanihot.

Chahkabesh is swallowed by the giant fish

1   Once again then Chahkabesh set off in his search for
something.

But now, while walking around and around, away off yonder he
suddenly caught sight of a lake; and, in the meantime, while the
creatures were breaking the surface making bubbles he shot at a bird
perched on a tree. But his arrow fell far away in the water.

With those creatures making ripples as they broke the surface,
however, he was unable to go fetch it because he was afraid.

So then [he thought] he might just as well return home, go back
and tell his older sister what he had seen.

2   On arrival he told her the news.

"Big Shishter," he said, "I saw someth... a lake," he said. "With creatures
making ripples as they broke the surface."

"But my arrow fell away over there in the water," he said, "and," said he,
"it was better for me not... me not to go after it."

"It's a good thing that you didn't go after it," she said to him.

"Do you indeed know who those ones are who make the ripples breaking
surface in the water?" that woman said to him. "If you had gone in the water
there, the fish would most surely have grabbed hold of you," she said to him.
"The giant fish would have bitten you and they would have made off with
you," she said to her young brother.

"Big Shishter, don't shay that; you frighten me saying that," he said. "I
won't go there again," said Chahkabesh.

Then he said to his older sister, "Get up early again tomorrow morning."

3   Now sure enough when day was beginning to break, that woman got up
early.

She nudged her little brother awake.

Now then Chahkabesh set off again in earnest while it was morning.

Just where he had seen the lake, that's the way he set off as he was
anxious to go after whoever was making the ripples.

And now as he drew within sight of it, the fish were in fact already
breaking the surface in ripples again.

At that he jumped straightway into the water.

He began to swim.

ati-pimâtakâw manâ.

âšay manâ wîpac ê-pimâtakât, wêhci-k'-ôtamikot[3] manâ tâpwê namêsa.
'kwâni manâ tâpwê kâ-'ši-kohcipanihikot.

4   âšay manâ mâk' ana iskwêw kîtawi-pêhêw ošîma 'ci-pêci-kîwên'ci. kinwêš
manâ pêhêw ê-'ti-otâkošininik.

"šâ!" manâ itwêw. "mâškôc mînâ cahkâpêš kî-kapâšimow anta
sâkahikanihk," manâ itwêw. " 'kwâni 'kâ mâškôc wêhci-takošihk," manâ
itwêw ana iskwêw.

'kwâni manâ 'ši-kihtohtêt. okwâškwêpicikan manâ kihtohtahtâw.
omôhkomân mâka.

âšay manâ tâpwê wâpahtam animêniw sâkahikaniniw cahkâpêš'
kâ-k'-îši-pahkopên'c'.

'kwâni manâ 'ši-kapastawê'pinahk okwâškwêpicikan, âšay manâ piko
wêhci-manawêpahtahk ana namês kwâškwêpicikaniniw.

5   'kwâni manâ 'š'-ocipitât. akwâtâpâtêw manâ mâk' anta, askîhk.
kâ-mohci-mahkatayêsihk man' âna namês ê-mišikitit mistamês.
'kwâni manâ 'ši-mâci-wêpišwât ana iskwêw.

"nimišêh, nimišêh," kâ-matê-ytwêt manâ cahkâpêš. "ka-mâcišon,
ka-mâcišon. pêhkât, pêhkâc," manâ itwêw.

"n'âpatisiyan[4] ô kâ-itwêyin. kikî-wîhtamâtin 'š' êkâ 'ci-pahkopêyin
nipîhk," manâ itik' ômisa.

otâmahokow manâ.

'kwâni manâ mâk' kâ-pêc'-iši-kapatêyâhtawît anta namêsihk ohci. 'kwâni
manâ mâk' âši-kîwêcik ê-nîšicik.

"kikî-wîhtamâtin oš' êkâ 'ci-kapâšimoyin anima[5] sâkahikanihk," manâ
itwêw ana iskwêw. "mâtika mâk' êkâ wîskâc kâ-tâpwêhtaman; mâtika mâka
êy-ihtiyan," manâ itâkaniwan cahkâpêš.

êkwâni piko êskwâpihkêyâk.

116

He had hardly begun to swim when, sure enough, he was grabbed and pulled under by a fish. And then, without further ado, he was swallowed right down.

4   Now then, however, that woman got tired of waiting for her young brother to come home. She waited for him a long time as evening began to come on.

"Oh dear!" she said. "Chahkabesh has probably gone bathing again there in the lake," she said. "*That's* probably why he hasn't arrived," the woman said.

At that, she set off. She took her fish hook along with her, and her knife.

Now then she actually saw that lake where Chahkabesh had waded in.

Then, at that, she threw her fish hook in and immediately the fish took hold of the hook.

5   Then she pulled him. She pulled him ashore there, on the land.

That fish just lay with a huge stomach, an enormous, giant fish.

Then that woman slit him down.

"Big Shishter, Big Shishter," Chahkabesh could be heard saying. "You'll cut me, you'll cut me. Carefully, carefully," he said.

"Never mind that chattering," his older sister said to him. "I told you not to go into the water."

Then she smacked him.

At that then he stepped out from the fish; then they went home, the two of them.

"I told you, didn't I, not to go bathing there in the lake," that woman said. "See, you never believed it; and now look at the state you're in," Chahkabesh got told.

That is the length of the story.

cahkâpêš kâ-ocipitikot pîsimwa

1   pêyakwâ manâ mîna cahkâpêš 'kwâni mâhcic êy-ânimômâkaniwâspan[1] tâni kâ-ihtit.

ê-pêci-kîwêt manâ ê-k'-îškwâ-n'taminahot pêyakwâ ê-kîšikânik, "mâca, n'tawâpam kôn," manâ itêw ... m'...[2] itikow omisa.

wâsêskwanôpan man' âni mâka anim' ê-'t'-otâkošihk; nôkosîpan mâka tipiski-pîsim.

" 'kâwina mîna kanawâpam pîsim," manâ itikow. "kišâspin kanawâpamatê pîsim ka-ocipitik," manâ itikow.

"o-o-o, ê'kwâni, 'kwâni," manâ icwêw. "kisêkimin. 'kâwin' anim' êtwê," man' êtêw omisa.

2   âšay manâ 'ti-wanawît.[3]

wîpac manâ piko twoyêhk 'kwân' êti-kanawâpamât anihi pîsimwa. k'-ênikohk manâ kanawâpamêw.

'kwâni manâ mâk' kâ-'ši-ocipitikot anihi pîsimwa.

ê'kwâni mâk' ânohc wêhci-nôkosit nêtê cahkâpêš pîsimohk ê-matê-... ê-matê-nôkosit, ê-kîy-ocipitikot pîsimwa.

'kwâni piko êskwâpihkêyâk.

Chahkabesh is drawn up by the moon

1   Once again then, this is the last story which is told about Chahkabesh and what happened to him.

     As he returned home after he had finished hunting one day, his older sister said to him... m... he was told by his older sister: "Be off, fetch some snow."

     It was very clear that evening; and the moon could be seen.

     "Don't look back at the moon," she said to him. "If you look at the moon, he will draw you up," she said to him.

     "O-o-o, that's enough, that's enough," he shaid. "You're frightening me. Don't say that," he said to his older sister.

2   Now then he started to go out.

     Soon then, right away, he began to stare at the moon. He stared at it as hard as he could.

     And then he was drawn right up by that moon.

     And that is why Chahkabesh now appears yonder in the moon, away off... and appears away off, because he was drawn up by the moon.

     That is the length of the story.

wîsakêcâhk kâ-pimiwatêkopanê onikamôwiniwat

1   pêyakwâ manâ mîna wîsakêcâhk, pimâšakâmêw manâ sîpîhk.
n'tahâšakâmêw.

kêka manâ mâka ê-pimohtêt, wêhci-wâpamât manâ ê-'kwamon'ci
kâ-m...mihcêtin'ci pinêsiwa: wêhwêwa, niskawa, šîšîpa, mwâkwa, misiwê
piko tahtoyêk pinêsiwa.[1] kanawâpamêw manâ.

"šâ!" manâ itên'tam. "tâ'ka ytê[2] kê-kî-tôtamowâpanê 'ci-kî-nipahakik ôko
'wiyâšîšak," manâ itên'tam.

âšay manâ kiskisopaniw kê-tôtahk. kospipahtâw manâ mistikohk.
"n'ka-n'tawâpahtên askiy," manâ itên'tam, "êko mâka n'ka-pimiwatân.
wâpamitwâwê mâk' ê-pimiwatêwak, n'ka-pêci-têpwâtikwak," itên'tam.
"ta-wî-kiskên'tamwak awênihkâna kâ-p'mohtên'ci. ta-wî-kiskên'tamwak
kêkwâniw kâ-pimiwatêwak," manâ itên'tam.

âšay manâ manipitam[3] askîniw. mîwatihkâsow manâ. posciwatêw
mistahi askîniw. êko manâ mâka mîna n'têhâšakâmêt.[4]

2   âšay manâ awiyâšîšak wâpamêwak ê-pimohtên'ci. "šâ!" manâ itwêwak.
"awênihkân ana kâ-pimâšakâmêt," manâ itwêwak.

"hêy, wîsakêcâhk oš' âna," manâ itwêwak kotakiyak.

"mâhti, têpwâtâta," manâ it'tôwak.

âšay manâ tâpwê: "hêy, wîsakêcâhk! kêkwân kâ-pimiwatêyin," manâ
itwêwak.

mân', mân' êkâ wîn' êšinâkosit manâ wîsakêcâhk. kâ-pimohtêt manâ piko.
môna, môna môna kiskisiw ..., môna pisiskihtawêhkâsow.

âšay manâ mîn' awiyâšîšak têpwâtêwak: "hêy, wîsakêcâahk! kêkwân
kâ-pimiwatêyin?"

âšay manâ pêhtawêw mâka. kipihcipaniw.

"wa?"[5]

"kêkwân kâ-pimiwatêyin?"

"ôô...! 'kwantaw ô kêkwân kâ-pimiwatêyân. ninikamôwiniwat ô
kâ-pimiwatêyân," manâ itêw.

"ô mâht' îsa mâka nikamo; ka-pêhtâtinân," manâ itwêwak awiyâšîšak.

"mônah. môna n'ka-kî-tôtên ôtah. pâtimâ piko pîhtokwamihk
n'ka-kî-nikamon."

"kêkwân mâk' êkâ wêhci-ošihtâyin mîkiwâm?" manâ itwêwak awiyâšîšak.
"êkotâni mâk' iši-nikamo pîhci mîkiwâmihk."

Weesakechahk carries around his song bag

1   Once again then, Weesakechahk. He was walking along by the river. He was heading up-stream.

And then at last as he was walking along, all of a sudden he caught sight of ma..., many birds sitting on the water: waveys, geese, ducks, loons, – all kinds of birds. He looked at them.

"My goodness!" he thought, "I wonder what I should do to kill these creatures," he thought then.

Now, then, it occurred to him what he would do. He made his way up the bank to the trees. "I'll go fetch some moss," he thought, "and then I'll carry it along. But when the birds see me carrying it," he thought, "they'll come and call out to me. They'll want to know who it is that's walking along. They'll want to know what I'm carrying on my back," he thought.

Then he collected some moss. Pretending it was a bag, he slung a lot of moss over his shoulder. Then he continued to walk up-stream.

2   Now then, the animals saw him walking along. "Dear me," they said. "Who is that walking along the waterside?" they said.

"Why, that's Weesakechahk, you realize," the others said then.

"Come on. Let's call out to him," they said to one another.

Now they were ready to call: "Yoo-hoo, Weesakechahk! What is it that you are carrying on your back?" they said.

Weesakechahk gave no sign of hearing. He just kept on walking. He did not, not, not remember..., he pretended that he didn't hear.

Now the creatures called out to him again: "Yoo-hoo, Weesakechahk! What are you carrying?"

Now then he heard them. He came to a stop.

"Halloo!"

"What is it you are carrying?"

"Oh, just some stuff that I'm carrying about. It's my song bag that I'm carrying here," he said to them.

"Oh, but do sing; we shall hear you," then said the animals.

"No. I can't do it here. I'll only be able to sing later on indoors."

"Well, why don't you make a tent?" the animals then said. "And sing right there inside the tent."

"êškw' isa pitamâ. kiwî-pêhtênâwâw nâ '-nikamoyân? pitamâ 'sa n'ka-n'taw'-ošihtân mîkiwâm. êko mâka misiwê kê-pêci-pîhtokwêyêk; êko mâka kê-pêhtawiyêk ê-nikamoyân," manâ itwêw.

3   âšay manâ tâpwê kospipahtâw mistikohk, mamânipitam[6] askîniw, mistikwa mâka. wîpac manâ ošihtâw mîkiwâminiw. mišâhtâw. pêškiš mâka mêkwâc êy-ošihtât mîk'wâminiw, mamânipitêw watapîya. nakwâkaniyâpîhkêw mâka, watapîya êy-âpacihât. antê manâ mâka tašwâpihkêšimêw, "kêy-ohci-ocipahât wî-nipahâtê 'nih' awiyâšîša," ê-itwâsot.

âšay manâ kâ-'škwâ-kîšihtât wîkih, âšay manâ têpwâtêw anihi pinêsiwa: "êkoh,[7] âstamik. âšay n'k'-îškwâ-'šihtân mîk'wâm. êko mâka pêci-n'tohtawik ê-nikamoyân," manâ iši-têpwâtêw anihi pinêsiwa.

4   âšay manâ misiwê pinêsiwak pêci-kapatêsipahtâwak. pêci-mihcêtiwak manâ. êko mâka kê-pêhtawâcik ê-nikamon'ci manâ itên'tamwak.

misiwê manâ pêci-pîhtokêwak anta mîk'wâmihk. wâšakâmêpiwak manâh. têtâwic manâ mâka išiy-apiw ana wîsakêcâhk, ê-têhtapit wîwat, otaskîwat kâ-kîy-ošihtât.

âšay manâ mâka mâci-nikamow. 'kwantaw manâ piko ayîtahamâsow, ê-'ši-kiskên'tahk piko ayîtwêw.

kêka manâ mâka n'tawênimêw 'ci-nîmin'ci. "nîmik," manâ itwêw, "mêkwâc ê-nikamoyân."

tâpwê manâ mâka nîmiwak aniki wêhwêwak, niskak mâka, šîšîpak, misiwê man' ayîtahamâsow.

kêka manâ mâka wîhtamawêw, mwêhci w'kêt...,[8] mwêhci k'-âtiy-ayîtwêt ê-nikamot, 'kwâni mwêhci kê-'ci-tôtamin'ci.[9] iši-kinâskimêw.[10]

5   âšay manâ mêkwâc ê-nikamot, "pasakwâpišimôwin, pasakwâpišimôwin," manâ itahamâsow.

tâpwê manâ nîmiwak aniki pinêsiwak. pasakwâpiwak manâ ê-nîmicik. "ayasikwêšimôwin, ayasikwêšimôwin," manâ itwêw.[11]

'kwâni manâ tâpw' ê-tôtahkik: ayasikwêšimôwak ê-nîmicik mêkwâc.

âšay manâ mâka wawocipahêw anihi ôtôta... ôtôtapîma, nanakwâtaho-wêpinêw manâ. 'kwâni manâ mâk' êši-kipihkwêpitât anim' ê-pipêskwahpitât, anihi manâ mâka k'-âti-nipahât, 'kwân' êši-wawânawî-wêpinât.

pîniš manâ mâka mihcêt nipahêw; pitihkohtâwak mâka wanawîtimihk nêki k'-âti-wanawî-yêpinihcik.[12]

"Just wait a minute! Do you want to hear my singing? First I'll go make a tent. Then you'll all come inside; and then you'll hear me singing," he said.

3   Now then he went right up the bank to the trees and went around gathering moss and sticks. Soon he made a wigwam. He made it big. But even so, while he was making the wigwam he went around pulling up roots. Using the roots, he made snare lines. Then he spread them out there to one side, "from where he will suddenly pull them when he wants to kill those creatures," he said to himself.

Now then, when he had finished his dwelling, he called those birds: "Come along then. I've already finished the wigwam. So come on, then, and listen to me singing," he called out to those birds.

4   Then all the birds came running ashore. They came in great numbers. And now, they thought, they would hear him singing.

They all came pouring right into the tent. Around in a circle they sat; and right in the middle there sat that fellow Weesakechahk, sitting atop his bag, his moss bag which he had made.

And now he began to sing. He just sang any old way, saying anything which came to his mind.

Finally, however, he wanted them to dance. "Dance," he said then, "while I am singing."

Then those waveys danced in earnest, and the geese, – the ducks, every one sang along.

At last he told them, that exactly wh…, exactly what he was saying as he sang, – that is exactly what they should begin to do. In this he was lying to them.

5   Now then, while he sang, he intoned, "A shut-eye dance, a shut-eye dance."

Then those birds danced in real earnest. Now as they were dancing they shut their eyes.

"A dance with necks together, a dance with necks together," he intoned.

This is what in fact they proceeded to do: they held their necks together as in the meantime they danced.

But now he quickly snatched those roo…, those roots of his and looped them over their heads. Then he choked them, tying the roots together; and then as he began to kill them, he tossed them outside one after the other.

At last he killed many of them; but they made a beating noise outside, those ones who were being thrown out.

6   kêka manâ pêhtamwak aniki âtiht kotakiyak. "tântê ô nâspic wêhci-pitihkwatâcik?" manâ itên'tam.[13]

mwâkwa manâ mâka ohc'-îtâpiw kîmôc. pêhkâc ohciy-âpaham pêyak oškîšik, ê-wî-wâpamât tân' êtôtamin'ci.

mwêhci manâ mîna nakwâtaho-wêpinêniwa kotakiyah, ê-nîminicih. 'kwâni manâ 'ši-kipihkwêpitât. wanawî-wêpinêw manâ.

"âââšay kinipahikonaw wîsakêcââhk," manâ itwêw ana mwâkw' ê-kihcipahtât.

wanawîpahtâw manâ.

kwâcistak wîsakêcâhk manâ kisiwâsiw.

'kwâni manâ êši-tahkiškâtât ospiskwaninîhk. miconi manâ napaki-wêpiškawêw.

'kwâni manâ mâka kiyâpac êši-kihcipahtât ana mwâkwa. kapastawêpahtâw.

misiwê 'šic kotakiyak awiyâšîšak kihcipahtâwak. pinêsiwak 'kwâni êši-kapastawêpahtâcik, kâ-kîy-ohcipah..., kâ-kîy-ohcîcik.

'kwâni manâ mâka wêhci-napakisit itwâniwan mwâkwa, anim' ê-kî-tôtawâkopanê wîsakêcâhk, wêskac.

7   âšay manâ mâka kâ-iškwâ-nipahât mihcêt, "šâ! tân'ka 'tê mâ'[14] kê-tôtamwânê?" man' êtên'tam. minwên'tam manâ.

"êko mâk' kê-mîcisoyân," manâ itwêw. "êko mâka kê-mîcisoyân."

"šâ! tân'k' êtê mâka kê-itihkaswâwakwênak? n'ka-sakapwân kâkih, nêstapiko n'ka-nikwâwahahkatêpon. hêhê, 'kwân' tâpwê kê-tôtamân. n'ka-nikwâwahahkatêpon."

âšay manâ kotawêpanihow antê nêkâhk nânih sîpîhk. mistahi manâ kotawêw. kâ-'škwâ-kotawêt manâ mâka nêkâhk, êkota manâ, êkota man' âna mâk' êši-nakwahwât[15] anihi opinêsîma. sâsâkisitêšimêw manâ piko tânt' êši-nanikwahwât. mihcêt kî-nipahêw; misiwê mâka 'kwâni wâ-'ši-kîsiswât.

8   "šâ!" manâ itên'tam,[16] "tân'ka mîna pitamâ kî-nipâwâpânê! asay[17] tâpwê niwî-nipân. n'tayêskosin," manâ itwêw. " 'kwantaw piko kê-tôtamân. n'ka-nipân. pêyako-tipahikan nêstapiko nîšo-tipahikan. 'kwâni mâka mâškôc kê-kîsisocik koskosiyânê."

âšay manâ tâpwê kawêšimow. nipâw manâ.

mêkwâc mâka ê-nipât ...[18]

9   kêka manâ koškopaniw,[19] âšay kinwêš ê-kî-nipât.

"šâ! âšay mâwina kîsisotokwênak," 'twêw manâ.

6   Then, at last, several of those others heard it. "How is it they are making so much noise flapping?" they thought.

And then the loon suddenly peeked out stealthily. Carefully he opened one eye as he wanted to see what they were doing.

Just at this point he [Weesakechahk] again threw a noose over the others as they were dancing. Then as he choked them, he threw them outside.

"Naa-a-ow we're being killed by Weesakechahk!" said the loon as he ran away.

Then he tore outside.

My goodness, but Weesakechahk was furious!

Then he kicked him on the back. He flattened him right out.

But the loon kept running away all the more. He ran into the water.

All the other animals ran away along with him. The birds then ran into the water where they had run fr…, where they had first come from.

And that, they say, is the reason why the loon is flattened out: it is because Weesakechahk is supposed to have done that to him, long ago.

7   Now then, after he had killed a great many birds, he thought, "Dear me, whatever shall I do with them?" He was pleased.

"Well then, I'll eat," he said. "Well then, I'll eat."

"Dear me! I wonder though which way I should cook them? I'll roast them over the fire, I do believe; or I'll bury and cook them under the hot sand. Aha, that's what I'll do: I'll bury and cook them under the hot sand."

Then he quickly kindled a fire there in the sand beside the river. He made a great fire. And after he had made a fire on the sand, then right at that spot, right at that spot then he buried those birds of his. He put them with their legs sticking up where he buried them here and there. He killed a great many and he wanted to roast them all.

8   "Oh my," he thought, "wouldn't I like to have a sleep first! Now I really want to sleep! I'm tired," he said. "I'll just do that. I'll sleep. An hour or two. And then perhaps they'll be cooked when I wake up."

At that point he lay right down. Then he slept.

While he was sleeping …

9   At last Weesakechahk awakened with a start. He had already been asleep a long time.

mêkwâc manâ mâka ê-nipât, ininiwa kî-pêci-kakêmotamâkow,
mêkwâc ê-nipât. 'kwâni misiwê kâ-'š'-otinâcik anik' îniniwak anihi
pinêsiwa.   kî-kîškîškisamwak anihi osita, kâ-sâsâkihtininikih.
'kwâni manâ mâka mîna kâ-'ši-sâsâkihtitâcik anta nêkâhk, êkâ
'ci-kiskên'tahk ê-ytênimâcik.[20]

âšay manâ koskosiw mâka wîsakêcâhk.

ocipitam manâ anih' osita.

kâ-kišipawâcipitahk manâ piko.[21]

"šâ! âšay n'tôsâmawahahkatêpon," manâ itwêw. "wêsâ kinwêš
n'kî-nipân," itên'tam.

mîna mâka kotakiy' ât'-ocipitam kâ-sâkihtininikih. mîna manâ
piko kâ-kîškipaninikih.

"šâ! n'tôsâmawahahkatêpon tâpwê. âšay wêsâ mistahi kîh... -kîsisôwak.
kîy-osâmâskisôwak."

10   mîna manâ kotakiya ocipitam.

âšay manâ mâka kiskên'tam ê-kî-kimotamawâkaniwit.

misiwê manâ pik' ôsita piko mošê-sâsâkihtin'iwah.[22] misiwê
kî-kimotamâkow ininiwah.

êko manâ mâk' ê-šîwatêt, êko manâ mâka miton' ê-kisiwâsit
ê-kî-kimotamâkot intiyin.[23]

nâsipêpahtâw man' ântê nêkâhk.

tâpwê kâ-papâmiskanawêcik ininiwak. mêkwâc ê-..., kâ-nipât
ê-kî-pêci-kakêmotamâkot. 'kwâni misiwê kâ-'ši-kimotin'ci anih' owêhwêma.[24]

êko mâk' êy-apit, ê-šîwatêt

'kwâni piko êskwâpihkêyâk.

"Oh my! They must be cooked by now," he said.

While he had been sleeping, however, the people came and stole from him while he was asleep; then those people had taken all those birds. They had cut off those feet of theirs which were sticking up; and then they had stuck them back in the sand again, so Weesakechahk would not know [what had happened], as they thought.

Now Weesakechahk wakened up.

He pulled out the feet.

They came out rather easily.

"Oh dear! Now I've overcooked them," he said. "I've slept too long," he thought.

Again he began to pull at some others which were sticking up. Again they had been cut off.

"Oh dear, I certainly have overcooked them. Now they're coo..., cooked too much. They're overcooked."

10 Again he pulled some others out.

Now, however, he knew that he had been robbed.

Only all their feet were sticking up exposed. Everything had been stolen by the people.

Then he was hungry and thoroughly angry that his things had been stolen by the Indians.

He ran down to the water's edge on the sand.

There, sure enough, the people had made footprints. While he wa..., he had slept, they had come and stolen from him. Then they had come and made off with all his waveys.

And so he sat down, – hungry!

That is the length of the story.

wîsakêcâhk kâ-wayêšihâkopanê maskwa

1   pêyakwâ manâ mîna wîsakêcâhk.

pimâšakâmêw manâ sîpîniw, pêyakwâ '-k'-îškw'-âpihtâ-kîšikânik. mêkwâc manâ mâka ê-pimohtêt, ohci-wâpamêw manâ maskwa, ê-papâ-nihcikišininici, ê-môminênici ê-'ti-takwâkininik.

"šâ," manâ itên'tam: "tânika kî-n'tawâpamak," manâ itên'tam.

âšay manâ tâpwê n'tawâpamêw.

"ââh, nišîm," manâ itwêw. "tân' êtôtaman?"

"ââh, pakwantaw ô nimîcin mîniša," manâ itwêw.

"ââh, kêkwân wêhci-mîciyan?"

"êko wâs' âni môšak êtôtamân ê-'ti-takwâkihk," manâ itwêw ana maskwa. "nimôminân pwâmoši kawêšimoyân ê-wî-kakwê-tâhcipohitisoyân," manâ itwêw.

"ââh, môna ka-kî-wîcêwitihtay," manâ itwêw.

"cikêmânima," manâ itwêw. "wîcêwin isa wî-wîcêwiyânê," manâ itwêw ana maskwa.[1]

2   âšay manâ tâpwê wîcêwêw.

papâ-môminêwak manâ nêtê nôhcimihk. papâ-wîcêwitôwak.

"šâ," manâ itwêw. "âstam mâ nêtê nôhcimihk. n'kiskên'tên oš' ê-mihcêtihki mîniša," manâ itwêw.

âšay manâ tâpwê kospa-wîcêwêw. nêtê nôhcimihk wakîtâmatin ati-ayîtohtahêw.

kêka manâ kipihcîw wîsakêcâhk.

"šâ, nišîm," manâ itwêw.

"kêkwân?" manâ itwêw ana maskwa.

"hêêy, kiwâpahtên n' ânima kêkwân kâ-matê-nihcikihtihk?" manâ itwêw. "nêma wâhnaw," manâ itwêw.

"šâ," manâ itwêw ana maskwa. "môna n'ka-kî-wâpahtên," manâ itwêw. "môna oša niwâpin," manâ itwêw. "wêskac oš' êwakwâni wêhc'-îhtiyân," manâ itwêw ana maskwa. "môna niwâpahtên kêkwân kwayask," manâ itwêw.

"šâ..., nêma mâka wîna," manâ itwêw. "mâškôc wîna ôma ka-kî-wâpahtên kâ-matê-wâpâk. kâ-mišâk kêkwân kâ-matê-wâsitêk nêma awasitê wâhnaw."

"âh," manâ itwêw ana maskwa. "môna âpatan nîna n'tawâc 'ci-itâpiyân," manâ itwêw ana maskwa. "kikiskên'tên nâ êšinamân ê-itâpiyân?" manâ

Weesakechahk tricks the bear

1   Once again, then, a story about Weesakechahk.

He was skirting the river bank one afternoon. While he was walking along, he suddenly caught sight of a bear moving about like a dot against the background, as it ate berries in the early fall.

"Dear me," he thought: "I ought to go see him."

Now then, off he went to see him.

"A-a-h, Little Brother," he said. "What are you doing?"

"O-o-h, nothing important, I'm just eating berries," he replied.

"A-a-h, why are you eating them?"

"It's what I always do in the early fall," the bear said. "I eat berries before I go to bed as I want to try to make myself fat," he explained.

"Is that so? Couldn't I keep you company?" suggested Weesakechahk.

"Of course," he said. "Come with me by all means if you want to keep me company," the bear replied.

2   Now then, he went right along with him.

They walked around eating berries far into the forest. They kept each other company.

"My goodness," said Weesakechahk. "Come, look over there in the bush. I know a place where there are plenty of berries."

So the bear went up the slope with him. He took him around about, far into the forest on top of a hill.

Then at last Weesakechahk stopped.

"Dear me, Little Brother," he murmured.

"What is it?" inquired the bear.

"Sa-a-y, do you see that thing which is a dark blotch in the distance?" he asked. "That one, away far off," he said.

"Oh dear," the bear replied. "I can't see it. As a matter of fact, I don't see," he added. "Actually, because I've been this way for a long, long time," the bear explained. "I don't see anything properly," he said.

"Dear me, – that one away over yonder," said Weesakechahk. "Perhaps you'll be able to see this white thing in the distance. The big bright thing over there further off."

"Ah," then said the bear. "It's no use. I'm just as well not to look around," he said. "Do you know how it appears to me when I look about?" the bear

itwêw ana maskwa. "ê'kwâni piko ê-'ši-pîkišêyâk n'tišinên. âh, môna kanakê kwayask niwâpin," manâ itwêw. "môna âpatan 'ci-itâpiyân," manâ itwêw.

3   "šâ!" manâ itwêw. "tân'ka kipakwâtên êkâ ê-wâpiyan!"

"ââh, nâspitêpi m'pakwâtên," manâ itwêw. "môna wîskâc kêkwân n'kî-wâpahtên âta wâhnaw ê-itâpiyân," manâ itwêw ana maskwa.

"šâ," manâ itwêw wîsakêcâhk. "kikiskên'tên nâ, nišîm?" manâ itwêw.

" 'kwâni nêsta nîn' ê-'htiyâpân. nâspic môna niwâpihtay. pêšoc mâna piko niwâpahtêhtay kêkwân pâtimâ. nâspic mâka mâna nipakwâtêhtay anim' ê-'htiyâpân. n'kaškên'têhtay nâspic. kikiskên'tên nâ mâka tâni kâ-tôtamân wêhci-kî-ati-wâpiyân?" manâ itwêw.

"môna," manâ itwêw ana maskwa.

"kikiskên'tên nâ ôhô mîniša kâ-mîciyin anohc? ê'kwânihi kây-âpacihtâyâpân."

"tâpwê nâ?" manâ itwêw ana maskwa. "tâni kâ-tôtamapan?" manâ itwêw.

"oh, pikw ani' kâ-..., mâwac anihi kâ-mâmihkwâki mîniša, kâ-mâmahkicêyâki, ê'kwânihi kâ-iši-pâhpâškicênamâpân niškîšikohk."

"šâ," manâ itwêw ana maskwa. "tân'ka kikî-wîsakâpihtay!" manâ itwêw.

"oh, – môna mistahi n'tôhci-wîsakâpihtay. mânišîš piko," manâ itwêw. "êko mâka kâ-iškwâ-kicistâpawahtâyân niškîšikwa, nâspitêpi n'kî-nahâpihtay. 'kwâni mâka êhtiyân kiyâpic anohc, nâspitêpi ninahâpin. nâspic wâhnaw niwâpahtên misiwê kâ-iši-ayitâpiyân," manâ itwêw ana wîsakêcâhk.

4   "mâtika ka-tôtâtin," manâ itêw anihi maskwawa.

"oh, môna," manâ itwêw ana maskwa. "n'ka-wîsakâpin," manâ itwêw.

"môna, apišîš piko ka-wîsakâpin; êko mâka nâspic ka-minwên'tên k'-îškwâ-tôtâtânê," manâ itêw. "nâspitêpi ka-mino-itâpin; ka-wâpahtên misiwê kêkwân wâhnaw tântê piko kê-itâpiyan," manâ itwêw wîsakêcâhk.

"awas! môna niwî-tôtên," manâ itwêw maskwa. "wêsâ n'ka-wîsakâpin niškîšikohk," manâ itwêw.

"apišîš piko ka-wîsakâpin, mâškôc piko wayêš nisto-minikošiš ka-wîsakâpin," manâ itwêw. "k'-îškwâ mâka anima, ka-kicistâpawahtânânaw kiškîšikwa. êko mâka tohkâpiyanê, êêko mitoni kê-minwêtâpiyan. nâspic misiwê kêkwân ka-wâpahtên ê-papâ-nôkwahk nêtê wâhnaw."

"wâh, êkw is' êkoši," manâ itwêw ana maskwa.

5   âšay manâ tâpwê otinamwak mîniša. mâwac kâ-mišâniki kâ-mâmihkocêyâniki, ê'kwânihi wêtinahkik; 'kwâni manâ mâka tâpw' ê-'ši-nâsipêcik nêtê sîpîhk, nîštam kâ-k'-îši-wâpamâspan ê-mîcisonici,

inquired. "It simply looks to me as if it's all blurred. Oh, I don't see properly at all," he said. "It's no use for me to look around," said he.

3   "Oh dear," said Weesakechahk. "How you must hate it, not seeing!"

"A-a-h, you've no idea how I hate it," agreed the bear. "I can never see anything, even when I peer far away," he added.

"Oh my, oh my!" said Weesakechahk. "Do you know what, Little Brother? The same thing happened to me. I used to see very little. I often couldn't see a thing until it was very close to me. I used to dislike it very much when I ailed that way. I was very sad indeed. But do you know what I did so that I regained my sight?" he said.

"No," the bear replied.

"You know these berries which you're eating right now? Those are the very ones which I used."

"Really?" said the bear. "What did you do?" he said.

"Well, just those r..., you know, those real, red berries, the biggest of all the ones around? Those are the ones which I crushed into my eyes."

"Dear me," said the bear. "It must have made your eyes smart a great deal!" he said.

"Oh, my eyes didn't smart much. Only a little," he said. "But then, after I had washed off my eyes, I could see quite clearly enough. And that's the way I still am now," he continued. "I see quite well enough. I see everything away far off when I look around," concluded Weesakechahk.

4   "See here, I'll do it for you," he said to the bear.

"Don't bother," said the bear. "I'll have sore eyes."

"No, they'll only smart a little; then you'll like it after I've done it to you," he said to him. "You'll see quite well enough; you'll see everything away off wherever you look," said Weesakechahk.

"Get away: I don't want to do it," said the bear. "It'll make my eyes too sore," he said.

"It'll only hurt a little bit," he replied, "perhaps only for about three minutes; and then after that we'll wash off your eyes. And then when you open your eyes, the...en you'll see extremely well. You'll see every single thing as it appears moving about, far away in the distance."

"Oh, all right then," the bear agreed.

5   Then they gathered berries in earnest. The biggest ones which are red all over, those were the ones which they took; and then they went down the bank over there to the river where Weesakechahk had first seen the bear eating,

ê-môminênispan. âšay manâ n'tawâpamêw asiniy' anta pêyak, ê-apinici.

"haw," manâ itêw, "ê'kotôma iši-aspiskwêšimo awa ... aw' âsiniy," manâ
itwêw. "kê-ynikohk mâka tohkâpi," manâ itêw.

"êh," manâ itwêw ana maskwa. 'kwâni tâpw' êti-pimišihk.

6   âšay manâ tâpwê tohkâpiw ana maskwa. êko mâka, "wîsakâpiyanê,
kê-ynikohk pasakwâpîhkan," manâ itwêw. "êko mâka k'-îškwâ-wîsakâpiyanê
êko mâka kê-kicistâpawâtâyahk kiškîšikwa anta sîpîhk," manâ itêw anihi
maskwawa.

âšay manâ tâpwê k'-ênikohk tohkâpiw ana maskwa. 'kwâni manâ
ê-'š'-otinahk wîsakêcâhk ôho mîniša, k'-ênikohk manâ pâhpâškicê-wêpinam
anta oškîšikonîhk.

"a-h-a-h-a-h-a-h-a," manâ kâ-itwêhkâsot ana wîsakêc... ana maskwa.

âšay manâ mîna nêtê kotakiya mistasiniya ocipahêw ana wîsakêcâhk.

"pasakwâpi, pasakwâpi," manâ itwêw. " 'kâwin' ohci-tohkâpi."

âšay manâ pêcipahêw anihi asiniya. 'kwâni manâ
êši-napakicê-wêpahamwât ostikwâninîw, anihi âsiniya ê-âpacihât.

kâ-mohci-tihtipipanihot manâ piko an' âmisk ..., ana maskwa.

"aha," manâ itwêhkâsow wîsakêcâhk. "masko-cîpay," manâ itwêw, "êkâ
wîskâc kâ-kî-wayêšihiht. âšay mâka n'kî-wayêšihâw," manâ itwêw.

7   "šâ," manâ itwêw, kâ-iškwâ-nipahât. "tân'ka itê mâka kê-tôtamwânê?
n'ka-akwâwân kâkê," manâ itwêw. "ha, 'kwantaw piko kê-tôtamân," 'twêw ...,
ayamihitisow.

âšay manâ tâpwê manihtêpanihow. mihcêt mihta mâwacihtâw.
kâ-iškwâ-mistahi-kotawêt manâ mâka, 'kwâni k'-ât'-îši-akwâwân-apašohkêt,
kê-iši-akwâwêt anihi omîcimima. âšay manâ tâpwê 'ti-pahkwêpinêw anihi
maskwawa. êniwêhk manâ wîniniw ana maskwa! minokâmow.

âšay man' âti-papîhtošam omîcim. 'kwâni manâ mâka êt'-îši-ayakotât anta
misiwê manâ 'kwân' êt'-îši-ayakotât anta iškotêhk. ê-'ti-kâhkisahk,
kâ-mohci-tômihkâsonici manâ piko anih' omaskoma.

"šâ," manâ itwêw, "môna nâspic nišîwatân. tântê mâka
kê-kî-ohci-mîcisoyân mistahi?" manâ itwêw.

ayamihitisow manâ mîna. "šâ, pitamâ n'ka-... n'ka-nîwatiyâskocimon,"
manâ itwêw. "oh, 'kwantaw piko kê-tôtamân."

8   âšay kêciko-wêpinam opîsiskâkan. nêtê ispahtâw nôhcimihk, mistikwa
kâ-iši-cacêmasonici.

wâpamêw manâ mâka anta minahikwa ê-nîšwâskisonici.

êkot' âni êši-sîhtawipanihot, omistatâhk anta mwêhci êkot' ân' êši-...[2]

feeding on berries. Then he looked for a certain stone lying there.

"All right," he said to him; "use this stone for a pillow." Then he said to him, "Open your eyes as wide as you can."

"Fine," replied the bear. Then he proceeded to lie down.

6   Now the bear opened his eyes as wide as he could, and Weesakechahk said to him: "When your eyes smart, close them as tightly as you can. Then after you've had them stinging, we'll wash your eyes off there in the river," he said to the bear.

Now the bear opened his eyes as widely as he could. Then Weesakechahk, taking the berries, with a swift movement crushed them into his eyes as hard as he could.

"I-y-i-y-i-y-i," cried Weesakech..., the bear.

Then that fellow, Weesakechahk, quickly grabbed other great stones and said: "Close your eyes, close your eyes! Don't open them."

Then he came running with those stones. Then he threw [them and] flattened out the bear's head with the stones.

That beaver..., that bear suddenly just rolled over.

"A-ha!" cried Weesakechahk. "Bear spirit who can never be deceived. And now I have deceived him," he exclaimed.

7   "Oh my," he said then, after he had killed him. "Which way should I go about cooking him? I'll roast him on a frame over the fire, I imagine," he said. "Ha! I'll just do it any way," he said ..., he said to himself.

Now then, he quickly gathered firewood. He collected a great many logs. After he had kindled a big fire, then he began to set up the frame of roasting-poles where he could roast his food. Then he set to skinning that bear in earnest. Was the bear ever fat! He was nice and plump.

Now he began to slice his food up. Then he hung it up right there, he hung it all up there over the fire. As he started to sear it, that bear of his just dripped fat.

"Oh my!" he murmured. "I'm not very hungry. How will I be able to eat a lot?"

He was talking to himself again. "Dear me, first of all I'll..., I'll squeeze my belly with the trees," he said. "Hm-m-m, – I'll do it just this way."

8   Now he threw off his jacket. He ran off into the bush, up among the trees. There he saw two spruce standing together.

He squeezed himself in between them, squeezing himself right in there on his big stomach, where those two trees stood side by side.

êši-nîšwâskwamonici anihi mistikwa.

"êko mistikwak, pêci-nâcistâk," manâ itêw anihi mistikwa.

'kwâni manâ tâpwê pêci-iši-nâcistâcik aniki mistikwak. miconi
pêci-napakicêhikow anta omistatâhk. k'-ênikohk manâ pêci-nâcistâwak
pêhkâc aniki mistikwak.

" 'kwâni, 'kwâni, 'kwâni, 'kwâni, 'kwâni, 'kwâni," manâ itêw.

môna manâ kipihcîwak. [laughter] mwêhci manâ kêkât ... 'kwâni manâ
mâka ê-iši-tahkonikot anima, môna manâ tâpwêhtâkow " 'kwâni, 'kwâni,
'kwâni," ê-itât.

kâ-iškwâ-tôtahkik man' âniki mistikwak wêhci-tâpwêcik manâ, "êkwa
awiyâšîšak pêci-mîcisok. âšay kikî-kîšinawatikowâw wîsakêcâhk," manâ
itwêwak.

9   âšay manâ tâpwê mihcêt awiyâšîšak pêc'-îspahtâwak. 'kwâni manâ
pêci-iši-kimotamawâcik wîsakêcâhkwa: sihkosiwak, šâkwêšiwak, misiwê piko
tôwiy-awiyâšîšak pêci-mîcisôwak anihi ..., pêci-mowêwak anihi maskwawa
kâ-kî-kîsiswâkanawinici. nêtê manâ mâka k'-îši-wêpinamôpan otôtakišîm,
otôskwanim. wâhnaw nêtê kî-matê-pahkihtinôpan nôhcimihk.

âšay manâ kâ-kî-..., wîpac manâ piko kitânawêpanihôwak anik'
âwiyâšîšak. misiwê 'kwâni kâ-iši-mowâcik anih' âmiskwa ..., maskwawa.
môna kanakê kêkwâniw ohc'-îškwahtamwak.

kišâstaw manâ kisiwâsiw wîsakêcâhk!

'kwâni manâ êši-kwêskipanihot ana wîsakêcâhk. miconi maškawipanihow.
'kwâni manâ êši-nâtwâ-wêpinât anihi pêyak minahikwa, pêyakwayak itêhkê,
mîna kotakîya, kwêskitê itêhkê. 'kwâni manâ êš'-îspanihot anta
kâ-k'-îši-kotawêspan.

ah, môna manâ mitoni kêkwân iškwahcikâtêw.

kâ-mohci-mamihkowâskwaniniki manâ piko otakwâwânâhtikwa.

10   "šâ," manâ itwêw. êko mâka miton' ê-šîwatêt.[3]

"tân'ka itê mâka kê-tôtamwânê?" manâ itwêw.

"šâ!" kêskisipanit nêmêniw otôskwanim, otôtakišîm nêtê
kâ-k'-îši-wêpinahk.

âšay man' îspahtâw nêtê. n'tawi-nanâtawâpahtam.

pêtâw ant' otiškotêmihk.

ê'kwânimêniw piko kâ-mîcit animêniw ê-kîšikânik.

'kwâni mâka êši-kiskinohamâkêmakahk ôma, mêkwâc mistahi
ê-'htakwahk kêkwân kê-mîcinâniwahk êkâ wîskâc 'ci-wêpinikâtêk kêkwân
kâ-iškopanik.

Then to the trees he said, "Trees, come close together."

At that, those two trees indeed came close together. They utterly flattened out the hollow there in his stomach. As hard as they could those two trees slowly closed together.

"A'right, a'right, a'right, a'right, a'right, a'right," said Weesakechahk to them.

But they didn't stop. [laughter] Then almost exactly ..., then as he was being held at that point, they paid no attention to him as he said, "A'right, a'right, a'right."

Then, when the trees had finished doing it, they suddenly called out, "Come, Animals, and eat! Weesakechahk has already cooked for you," they said.

9 And now indeed, a great number of animals came running. Right away they came and stole everything from Weesakechahk: weasels, mink, every kind of animal came to eat that ..., came to eat that bear which had been cooked. But they threw away his innards, his liver far away, and they fell far off in the bush.

Now then when..., soon those animals finished everything up. Then they ate up the whole of that beaver ..., bear. They didn't leave anything at all.

My, but Weesakechahk was furious!

Then, Weesakechahk twisting around braced himself firmly. Then with his hand he snapped off that one spruce, in one direction, then the other one on the other side. Then he dashed over to where he had made the fire.

Ah, – not a single thing was left.

There were the spits with just blood stains remaining on them.

10 "Tch, tch," he exclaimed; and then he was very hungry.

"Whatever should I do," he murmured.

"Tch, tch!" Suddenly he recalled that liver of his and the innards which he had thrown away.

Now he ran over to that place. He began to search for them.

He brought them back to his fire.

That is all he had to eat that day.

And that teaches this lesson, that while there is plenty to eat, something which is left over should never be thrown away.

It has also been said that that is why you come on trees lying, one, one

êkoš' âni mâka wêhc'-îšinâkosicik mistikwak itwâniwan: nîšo mâna nêtê pêyak kâ-'ši-kawišihk mîna kotak ôtê kâ-iši-kawišihk, wîsakêcâhk animêniw kâ-tôtamokopanê itwâniwan.

'kwâni piko êskwâpihkêyâk.

way and the other, the other way. That must have been Weesakechahk's doing, so they say.

That is the length of the story.

wîsakêcâhk wêhwêwa kâ-wîci-pimihnâmâkopanê

1   pêyakwâ manâ mîna wîsakêcâhk.

pimâšakâmêw manâ nânih wînipêkohk, ê-'ti-takwâkininik. kêka manâ
mâka otihtêw wêhwêwa ê-mihcêtin'c', ê-mîcison'ci, pwâmoši pimâhamin'ci.

"šâ. tân'ka wîcêwakik!" manâ itên'tam.

"mâhti, n'ka-kakwêcimâwak," manâ itên'tam.

2   âšay manâ tâpwê n'tawâpamêw.

"hêy, nišîmak," manâ itwêw, "tâni tôtamêk, ô?"

"ah, nimîcisonân wâso,"[1] manâ itwêwak wêhwêwak.

"kêkwân mâka wêhci-mîcisoyêk?"

"nimîcisonân wâs' âšay wîpac 'ci-pimâhamâhk," manâ itwêwak. "nêtê
wâhnaw n'titohtânân, ê-takwâkihk mâna kâ-tôtamâhk," manâ itwêwak.

"šâ, tân'ka mâna kiminwên'tênâwâw nêtê kâ-itohtêyêk. wâhnaw n' âni
kititohtânâwâw?"

"êhê," manâ itwêwak wêhwêwak. "wâhnaw wâsa nêtê n'titohtânân," manâ
itwêwak, "êkâ wîskâc kâ-iši-pipohk."

"šâ, tân'ka kî-wîcêwitakok! mâhti ..., ka-wîcêwitinâwâw."

"êko isa n'tawâc. wîcêwinân," manâ itwêw wêhwêw.

âšay man' ânima kâ-iškwâ-itwêt ana wêhwêw, âšay manâ piko
wêhci-nîpawit kihci-wêhwêw. 'kwâni kâ-'ši-kwêskinâkosit mêkwâc anim'
ê-'tikot.

3   "ka-kî-wîcêwinân," ê-'tikot.

"êkw isa mâka," manâ itâkaniwan. "âšay wâsa nêsta kîna ka-mîcison,"
manâ itâkaniwan, " 'ci-wî-kakwê-tâhcipohitisoyan pwâmoši kihcihnâyahk,"
manâ itwêw ana wêhwêw.

'kwâni manâ tâpwê 't-îši-mîcisot[2] nêsta wîna wîsakêcâhk; maškošîya[3]
manâ k'-ênikohk mîciw.[4]

kêka manâ mitoni tâhcipôwak aniki wêhwêwak ê-mîcisocik.

"êko mâh!" manâ itwêw. "tânispî kê-kihcihnâyahk?"

"môna, môn' êškwâ," manâ itwêw ana wêhwêw. "pâtimâ kiyâpic kinwêš
nawac," manâ itwêw. "ka-mîcisonânaw mitoni 'ci-tâhcipoyahk," manâ itwêw.
"êko mâka kê-kihcihnâyahk."

âšay manâ tâpwê mîcisôwak kiyâpic.

4   âšay manâ mâka itwêw ana kâ-tipên'tahk kâ-nîkânît wêhwêw. "âšay,"
manâ itwêw. "âšay kê-tipiskâk ka-kihcihnânânaw," manâ itwêw.

Weesakechahk flies south with the waveys

1   Once again then, here is a story about Weesakechahk.

He was walking along beside the water-line in the early fall. At last he came upon a great many waveys feeding before they flew south.

"My, oh my! I'd like to go with them," he thought.

"Say! I'll have to ask them," he thought.

2   Then he went right off to see them.

"Hi there, Little Brothers," he said. "What's this you're doing?"

"Oh, we're feeding, as you see," they said.

"Why are you feeding?"

"We're feeding now, y'know, so we can soon fly away," they said. "We're going far away, same as we do every fall."

"Dear me," said Weesakechahk. "I imagine you like it where you're going! Is it far away that you're bound?"

"Yes," replied the waveys. "We're bound off yonder, where it's never winter."

"Mm, if only I could go with you!" said Weesakechahk. "Look here, I'll go along with you."

"You might just as well. Come along with us," said the leader wavey.

As soon as the wavey had said that, straightway Weesakechahk stood there, – a great wavey. He had turned into one in appearance while he was being spoken to.

3   "You can come with us," he was told. "But then," he was instructed, "you too must eat. You should make an effort to get yourself fat before we fly away," the wavey told him.

Then Weesakechahk too began to feed in earnest. He ate grasses for all he was worth.

At last those waveys were thoroughly fattened up with eating.

"Come on," said Weesakechahk. "When shall we fly away?"

"Not, not yet," said that wavey. "There's quite a long time yet to go," he said. "We have to eat so as to get really fat," he said, "and then we'll fly away."

And then they set to and ate some more.

4   Then, the chief wavey, the leader, spoke. "Ready?" he said. "Tonight," said he, "we shall fly away."

"kê-tipiskâk? kêkwân êkâ ..., kêkwân êkâ ê-kîsikâk?" manâ itwêw ana wîsakêcâhk.

"ê-tipiskâk is' êk' âwênihkân 'ci-wâpamitahkok," manâ itwêw. "mihcêt wâs' âwênihkânak ka-mikwaškâcihikonawak, mêkwâc ê-pimihnâyahk," manâ itwêw. "ininiwak ka-kitahokonawak. ka-pâskisokonawak; išpimihk mâka šâkoc ka-pimihnânânaw, êkâ k'-êš'-otihtahwât... -otihtahotahkok," manâ itwêw.

"ââ."

âšay manâ tâpwê mîcisôwak kiyâpac.

"pitamâ wâsa ka-sînitakišânânaw pwâmoš' ohpahoyahk êkâ 'ci-kosikwatiyahk,"[5] manâ itwêw ana wêhwêw. 'kwâni manâ mâka tâpw' êtôtahkik ê-sînitakišêcik.

5   âšay manâ mâka wayêš ê-'ti-âpihtâ-tipiskâk, âšay manâ w'wênikâpawiwak[6] kê-tôtahkik, ê-..., mêkwâc ê-pimihnâcik.

âšay manâ kakêskimâkaniwan wîsakêcâhk: "mihcêt ka-wâpamânawak ininiwak ê-p'm'paniyahk," manâ itwêw ana wêhwêw kâ-nîkânît. " 'kâwina mâka wîskâc ohc'-îtâpi," manâ itâkaniwan wîsakêcâhk. " 'kâwina wîskâc ohc'-îtâpi kâ-tatawêhtahkik. nêtê piko kâ-itâpiyan..., nêtê piko kâ-išihnâyin itâpi," manâ itâkaniwan.

"êhê," manâ itwêw.

âšay manâ tâpwê.

"pitamâ ka-kicistâpâwan'tisonânaw pwâmoši kihcipaniyahk," manâ itwêw ana wêhwêw kâ-nîkânît. 'kwâni manâ mâka tâpw' ê-tôtahkik: kicistâpâwanêwak omîkwâniwâwa. pahpawipanihêwak miconi 'ti-wâpiskisicik[7] mêkwâc ê-pim'pan'cik. âšay manâ ohpahôwak, '-tipiskânik. išpimihk manâ mâka pim'paniwak.

6   âšay manâ 'ti-wâpan'nik. âšay manâ pêhtawêwak ininiwa. kê-inikohk mâka kitahokowak.

" 'kâwina, 'kâwina itâpi," manâ itâkaniwan wîsakêcâhk. "nêtê piko itâpi kâ-itohtêyin," manâ itâkaniwan.

'kwâni manâ tâpw' êtôtahk. nâspic manâ w'-îtâpiw antê capašîs ..., wî-wâpamêw awênihkâna kâ-itwêhkâson'c'. âšay manâ kêtahtawin môna pisiskên'tam tâpw' ê-itâpit capašîs.

âšay manâ piko matê-pâskiswâkaniwan.

'kwâni manâ êši-pahkišihk. kaskatahtahkwanêhwâkaniwan. k'-ênikohk manâ mâk' otâmišin.

kâ-iškwâ-pahkišihk manâ wêhci-pasikot; k'-âti-pimohtêt manâ.

7   'kwâni mâka 'kâ[8] wîskâci-wêhci-nipahišihk êwako wêhwêwak[9] itwâniwan, wîsakêcâhk anim' ê-kî-tôtamokopanê. ê-pâskisocik mâka wêhwêwak môna

"Tonight? Why not ..., why not in the daytime?" asked Weesakechahk.

"So that at night we won't be seen by anyone. For many people will bother us while we're flying," he said. "People will call us. We will be shot at; but we'll sure fly away high up, where the shots won't reach th..., reach us," he said.

"O-oh," [replied Weesakechahk].

Now they really tucked away more food.

"First of all we shall purge ourselves right out before we take off, so we won't be heavy," said the wavey. And so that's what they did, they cleaned themselves right out.

5 Now then, as it was getting to be about midnight, they lined up in position, the way they would do in ..., while they were flying.

And now Weesakechahk was given instructions: "We shall see a great many people as we fly along," said the leader wavey. "Don't ever look about," Weesakechahk was warned. "Don't ever look about where they call. Just in the direction you're looking ..., just look in the direction you're flying," he was told.

"Yes," he replied.

Now they were all set.

"First we'll wash ourselves before we set off," said the leader wavey. And that's what they proceeded to do: they washed their feathers. They beat their wings so they would be good and white while they were flying. And then they took off at night. They went along high up.

6 Now the dawn began to break. They heard people. The people were calling them as hard as they could.

"Don't, don't look around," Weesakechahk was told. "Look only in the direction where you're going," he was warned.

That's what he did. But he wanted very much to look down below, – he wanted to see who was making the call. And then suddenly, he didn't notice that he was actually looking down.

At that point he was shot at from away in the distance.

Then at that he fell. His wing was broken. He fell and struck the earth as hard as he could.

After falling then, he stood up; then he began to walk.

7 And that, they say, is why that wavey goose never kills himself falling, because Weesakechahk is supposed to have done that.

wîskâc nipahišinwak. môšak pasikôwak kâ-'škwâ-pahkišihkwâwi.
'kwâni piko êskwâpihkêyâk.

When waveys are shot, they never fall dead. They always get up whenever they have fallen.

That is the length of the story.

nâpêw kâ-kî-kitamokokopanê wâpošwa

1   pâstâmowin išinihkâtêw 'ma tipâcimôwin.

'kwân' êši-kiskinohamâkaniwicik awâšišak ê-'pišîšišicik, êkâ 'ci-pâhpihâcik
awênihkâna kotakiya wayêš ê-'htin'ci. kiskinohamâkêmakan ôma
tipâcimôwin ê-tipâcimonâniwahk, ê-pêhtahkik awâšišak, 'c'-ohci-kiskên'tahkik
êkâ 'ci-mânênimâcik wîci-'wâšišiwâwa nêstapiko wîc'-îninîwâwa.

2   pêyakwâ manâ mîna wêskac nîšokamakisiwâkopan manâ 'wênihkânak,
ininiwak, tâpiskôc ê-tašîhkêcik ê-piponinik. namêsa manâ mâka nôcihêwak
mêkwâc ê-piponinik, wâpošwa mâka, ê-tâpakwêcik ê-ohci-pimâcihocik.
mêmîskoc manâ mâka kihtohtêwak ê-n'tawahocik pêyak pêyakwâ ê-kîšikânik,
mîna mâka kotak pêyakwâ ê-kîšikânik, mêmîskoc ê-n'taminahocik,
ê-n'tawâpahtahkik kêkwâniw kê-mîcicik.

wâpošwa manâ mâka nôcihêwak mêkwâc ê-piponinik. ê'kwânimêniw
mâwac wêhci-pimâcihowâkopanê mêkwâc ê-piponinik.

3   pêyakwâ manâ mâka kihtohtêw 'wa pêyak nâpêw kêkišêpâyânik,
ê-n'tawâpamât wâpošwa.

wîpac manâ mâka kâ-kihtohtêt wayêš nîšo-tipahikan[1] kâ-itâpicît. âšay
manâ piko wêhci-pêci-takošihk.[2]

kiskên'tamwak manâ mâka aniki k'-âpicik wayêš ê-k'-îhtin'ci, wîpac
wêhci-pêci-kîwên'ci.[3] ê-pêci-pîhtokwêt manâ mâka, 'toni[4] manâ
mihkowaniniw animêniw pêyak ocihciy.

ana manâ mâka kotak nâpêw wîpac manâ kakwêcimêw: "tâni kâ-ihtiyan
mâka êko?" manâ itêw. "tân' êhki' wêhci-mihkowahk kicihciy?" manâ itêw.

"oh, n'kî-mâkomik ôw' wâpoš," manâ itwêw ana kotak nâpêw kâ-takošihk.

pâhpipaniw manâ mâka ana kotak nâpêw kâ-tipâcimostawâkaniwit.
"tântê kê-kî-ohci-mâkomisk wâpoš?" manâ itwêw. "môna wîskâc mâkohcikêw
wâpoš, – môna mâka wîskâc mâkomêw 'wênihkâna," manâ itwêw ana nâpêw.
pâhpihêw manâ mâka wîci-nâpêwa.

4   "tântê wêhci-kî-tôtaman wêhci-kî-mâkomisk?" manâ itwêw ...,
iši-kakwêcimêw anihi nâpêwa.

"oh, pimâtisiw," manâ itwêw, "ê-wâpamak ê-apit nakwâkanihk," manâ
itwêw. "kî-sakikâtêpisok'an;[5] êko mâka pimâtisiw kiyâpac, kâ-otihtak," manâ
itwêw.

"niwî-at'-otinâw mâka," manâ itwêw; " 'kwâni mâk' ê-pêci-mâko-wêpamit,"
manâ itwêw.

The man who was devoured by rabbits

1   This account is called a tale of blasphemy and requital.

This is the way little children are taught not to laugh at anyone else who is in trouble. The story as it is told teaches a lesson, as the children hear it so they may know from it not to abuse their fellow-children or fellow-men.

2   Once again then, long ago, there were apparently two families of people staying together for the winter. They went after fish during the winter, and rabbits, setting snares from which they made their living. They went off hunting in turn one, one day, and again the other for one day, hunting turn and turn about as they went after something to eat.

They hunted rabbits during the winter. That was, it would appear, the most they had to live on during the winter-time.

3   Now then, this one man went away one time in the morning, going after rabbits.

He left early and was away for about two hours. He arrived back before he was expected.

Those who were sitting there knew that he had had some trouble, and that was why he had come home early. But when he came in, one of his hands was all covered with blood.

The other man quickly asked him, "What happened to you, then? What happened that your hand is bloody?" he said.

"Oh, I was bitten by this rabbit," said the other man who had arrived.

At that the man who had been told the story burst into laughter. "How can a rabbit bite you?" he said. "A rabbit never bites; isn't it so that a rabbit never bites anybody?" said that man. And he laughed at his companion.

4   "What did you do that he bit you?" he said ..., he asked the first man.

"Oh, he was alive," he replied, "as I saw him sitting in the snare," he said. "He was snared by the leg; and so he was still alive when I got to him," he said.

"I was just about to take him," he said. "Then he took a quick bite at me."

The other man laughed. He laughed at him as hard as he could.

pâhpiw man' âna kotak nâpêw. kê-'nikohk manâ pâhpihêw.

"cikêmânima, cikêmânima kî-mâkomik ê-pohcikonêwênat wâpoš," manâ
itwêw. "môna wês' âni wîskât mâkohcikêw wâpoš, kwayask wîna ê-tôcikâtêk,"
manâ itwêw. kê-'nikohk manâ pâhpihêw wîc-îniniwa anim' ê-k'-îhtin'c'.

5   kišîmâkaniwan manâ mâka ana kotak ana nâpêw kâ-kî-takošihk.

"êko is' âni," manâ itwêw. "êškwâ nêsta kîna ka-wâpahtên
pêyakwâ," manâ itwêw. "mâškôc nêsta kîna ka-mâkomik wâpoš," manâ
itwêw.

"hâ, cikêmânima!" manâ itwêw. "pohcikonêwênakê 'sa wîna wâpoš
n'ka-mâkomik," itwêw.

'kwâni manâ mâka tâpw' êši-kisiwâsit ana kâ-kî-takošihk. kišîmâkaniwan
man' âni mâka kî-pâhpihâkaniwan.

nihtâ-mitêwah... -man'tôhkêwâkopan[6] wêsa mâk' aniki 'wênihkânak
wêskac. nihtâ-man'toh ... -man'tôhkâtitowak. 'kwâni manâ mâka
kê-tôtawât anihi kâ-kî-pâhpihikot ê-kî-kišîmikot. ta-mitêhkâtêw.

6   âšay manâ mîna ê-'ti-wâpaninik, nêsta wîn' êko kê-kihtohtêt nâha kotak
nâpêw.

âšay manâ wîpac ê-kihtohtêt ê-kišêpâyânik pêyak manâ nakiškawêw
wâposwa, – kâ-pêci-pim'pahtân'ci manâ.

twoyêhk manâ mâka piko pâskiswêw wîpac, ê-pêci-pim'pahtân'ci.

wîpac manâ piko mîn' âšay nîšo pêci-nakiškâkow; mîna manâ piko 'kwân'
êši-pâskiswât nîšo.

âšay manâ piko mîna wîpac ê-'ti-pimohtêt, kâ-pêci-nistopahtâcik manâ
wâposwak. pêci-nakiškâkow.

kiyâpac manâ mâka kaškihtâw ê-pâskiswât '-nistin'ci.

kêka manâ mâka piko pêci-nêwiwak. kaškihtâw manâ mâka kiyâpac
ê-pâskiswât ê-nêwin'c'.

kêka manâ piko mihcêtiniwa '-pêci-nakiškâkot. kaškihtâw mâka
kiyâpac misiwê 'ci-pâskiswât, pwâmoših nakiškâkot, pwâmoš'
otihtikot.

kêka manâ mitoni pêci-mihcêtiwak ê-pêci-pim'pahitocik[7] wâposwak.

7   kiyâpac manâ pimohtêw.

n'tawâc manâ otinam mistikoniw ê-kinwâskwaninik. ê'kwânimêniw manâ
mâk' ê-âpacihtât ê-otatâmahwât, ê-wî-kakwê-nipahât misiwê pwâmoši
pêci-otihtikot.

kêka manâ mâka mitoni ayêskosiw. môna kî-tôtam misiwê 'ci-nipahât
wêsâ '-'ši-mihcêtin'c'.

"Of course, of course the rabbit bit you since you shoved your hand in his mouth," he said. "You know a rabbit never bites when the thing is properly done," he said. Then he laughed at his companion for all he was worth, that he had had that misfortune.

5 Then that other man who had arrived back was angered.

"That's enough," he said. "You too, you'll see one day yet," he said. "Perhaps a rabbit will bite you too," he observed.

"Ha, naturally," rejoined the other one. "If I put my hand in his mouth, to be sure the rabbit will bite me," he said.

At that point the one who had come back really got angry. He was offended and he was being laughed at.

They were apparently good at conjur..., at casting spells, those old-time people. They were good at casting sp..., casting spells on each other. So that's what he was going to do to the one who had laughed at him, because he had angered him. He would conjure him.

6 Now then as it was beginning to dawn again, that other man too was then going to go away himself.

Now, as he was going away early in the morning, he met up with a certain rabbit, – which came running towards him.

Right away he shot him as soon as he ran towards him there.

Soon two more came to meet him. Once again then, he just shot them both on the spot.

Now, soon afterwards, as he was walking along again, three rabbits came running towards him. They were coming to meet him.

Again he managed to shoot them, all three.

Then at last four came towards him. He was still able to shoot them even though there were four of them.

Then finally, there were a great many coming to meet him. He was still able to shoot them all before they met him, before they got to him.

Then at last the rabbits were utterly numberless as they came running towards him together.

7 Still he walked along.

Then he took a long stick. Using that he struck out at them in his anxiety to kill them all before they reached him.

But at last he became tired out. He couldn't kill them all because there were too many of them.

Finally they came and bit him again and again on his legs.

kêka manâ mâka pêci-mâmâkomikow anta oskâtihk.

wî-kakwê-mis... wî-kakwê-nipahêw manâ mâka misiwê môna manâ kî-tôtam.

'kwâni manâ mâk' êt'-îši-mâmâkomikot oskâtihk, êkâ '-kî-câkinipahât.

'kwâni manâ kêk' êti-pahkišihk anta mostaskamihk mostâkonak, k'-ênikohk ê-mâmâkomikot.

'kwâni manâ mâka k'-ât'-isi-kitamohikot anihi wâpošwa pâtimâ, oskana pišišik ê-pimihtin'niki. 'kwâni kâ-iši-nipahikot.

8   animêniw manâ mâka ê-'ti-tipiskânik, môna ohci-pêci-kîwêw wîkihk.

pêhikow manâ wîwa.

"šâ," manâ itwêw ana iskwêw. "tânika kâ-ihtikwê ninâpêm êkâ wâhci-pêci-kîwêt,"[8] manâ itwêw.

ana manâ mâka kâ-kî-pâhpahâkaniwit kiskên'tam tâni kâ-ihtin'ci anihi n..., nâpêwa, wîn' ê-kî-mitêhkâtât, ê-kî-kišîmikot.

"oh, mâškôc isa wâpaninikê ta-takošin," manâ itwêw. "mâškôc kî-mâkomikow wâpošwa êkâ 'hci-takošihk,"[9] manâ itêw anih' iskwêwa.

9   wiyâpaninik manâ mâka. âšay tâpwê namatêw ana nâpêw. môna ohci-pêci-kîwêw.

êkw îsa manâ itêw anih' îskwêwa ê-kî-nakatâkaniwin'ci "êkw îsa n'tawâc nawahâtâtâ," manâ itwêw. "mâhti, wâpahtât'..., wâpahtâtâ tâni kâ-ihtikwê," manâ itwêw.

'kwâni manâ tâpw' êši-kihtohtêcik wêyâpaninik. wîcêwêw anih' îskwêwa ê-wî-wâpahtinamohât tâni kâ-ihtin'ci anihi nâpêwa.

'kwâni manâ mâka tâpwê kâ-otihtâcik anta kâ-k'-îši-nipahikon'ci wâpošwa. mošê manâ pik' ôskana pimihtinwa kônihk. 'kwâni mâka êspîhci-kostâtikwahk pâstâmowin itwâniwan, ê-kî-pâstâmot ana nâpêw ê-kî-pâhpihât anihi kâ-kî-mâkomikon'ci[10] wâpošwa.

'kwâni piko êskwâpihkêyâk.

He wanted to try all ..., and then he wanted to try to kill them all; but he was unable to do it.

Then he was bitten all over the legs since he hadn't been able to finish killing them.

Then finally he began to fall down there on the bare ground, on top of the bare snow, utterly chewed up.

And then those rabbits ate him all up in no time, until nothing but the bones were lying there. That's the way they killed him.

8   Then as it was beginning to get dark, he hadn't returned home.

His wife waited for him.

"Oh my!" said the woman. "I wonder what must have happened to my husband that he hasn't come home."

The one who had been ridiculed, however, knew what had befallen that m..., man, since he had conjured him because he had been offended by him.

"Oh, he'll probably arrive tomorrow, I imagine," he said. "Maybe he got bitten by a rabbit and that's why he hasn't arrived," he suggested to the woman.

9   The next day dawned. Sure enough, that man didn't turn up. He did not come home.

Then he said to that woman who had been left, "I guess we'd better track him down. Come on, let's see ..., let's see what's happened to him," he said.

That's what they did, setting off in the morning. He went with the woman since he wanted to let her see what had happened to that man.

Then, sure enough, they reached him at the place where the rabbits had killed him. Only his bones lay bare on the snow. And that is how dreadful a blasphemy is, they say, because that man had said something which came back on him in that he had ridiculed the one who had been bitten by the rabbit.

That is the length of the story.

nâpêw kâ-kî-mâkomikot sakimêwa

1   ê'kôma kotak âtanôhkêwin, pâstâmowin ohci.

pêyakwâ manâ mîna nâpêw, mêkwâc ê-nîpininik, kâ-ihtâniwahk mêkwâc
ê-kišitêk, sakimêwak manâ mâka mihcêtiwak ...,[1] ê-'ti-otâkošin'nik mâka
osâm ati-mihcêtiwak.

mâkomikow manâ mâka mâna sakimêwa ê-'ti-tipiskânik. môna manâ
mâka wayêš kî-tôtam êkâ kêkwân' ê-ayât[2] kêy-ohci-nipahât.

kêka manâ mâka mitoni kî-kišiwâhikow anihi sakimêwa '-mâmâkomikot
tašinê.

âšay manâ itwêw, "êškwâ," manâ itêw anihi sakimêwa. "êškwâ
ka-nanêhkâcihitinâwâw," manâ itwêw. "môna ka-k..., môna tašinê
ka-kî-pimât'sinâwâw," manâ itêw.

2   âšay manâ mâwacihêw sakimêwa. pîhtahwêw manâ wayêš. mihcêt manâ
mâwacihêw.

êko manâ mâka wîpac ê-'ti-tahkâyânik, ê-'ti-mispon'nik, ê-'ti-pipon'nik, êko
mâka manâ itêw anihi sakimêwa: "êko mâka kê-tipahamâsoyân
kâ-kî-nanêhkâcihiyêk mêkwâc ê-nîpihk," manâ itêw.

'kwâni manâ kâ-'ši-wanawît ê-pipon'nik. wanawîtahêw manâ osakimêma.
'kwâni manâ êši-wâwanawî-wêpinât anta kâ-k'-îši-pîhtahwât.

wîpac manâ mâka piko ê-wanawî-wêpinât, 'kwâni manâ piko
kâ-'šiy-ayâhkwacipanicik aniki sakimêwak. môna manâ kî-pimihnâwak wêsâ
'-tahkâyânik.

"nah!" manâ itwêw. "êko m̂âk' êkâ wayêš kâ-tôtamêk ê-pipohk,"
manâ itwêw, "nâspic mâna kâ-wî-mâmâkomiyêkopan," manâ itêw.

3   âšay manâ ..., âšay manâ mîn' ê-'ti-sîkwaninik, ê-'ti-nîpininik
manâ, âšay manâ piko wîpac wêhci-pêci-mâkomikot pêyak sakimêwa.

nipahêw man' âtawîn'.

'kwâni manâ? môna manâ wayêš kî-tôtam 'ci-kî-nakânât anihi
sakimêwa. pêci-pâpîhtokwêwak tântê piko ê-'š'-îhtât. kêka manâ
mâka mitoni nanêhkâcihikow sakimêwa. nipîhk man' âta[3]
kapâšimow. kôkîw manâ. wîpac manâ mân' ê-sâkiskwênit, 'kwâni
mâna miton' êši-wîskwêpanihocik aniki sakimêwak.

êko manâ mâk' ê-'ti-mêkwâ-nîpin'nik miconi môna wayêš
kî-tôtam.

4   âšay manâ mâka kiskên'tam ê-kî-pâstâmot, ê-kî-nanêhkâcihât

The man who was bitten by mosquitoes

1   This is another telling of a legend about requital for blasphemy.

Once again then a man, during the summer, where people were staying while it was warm ..., there were many mosquitoes..., as it drew on towards evening they were especially numerous.

Now he was bitten repeatedly by mosquitoes towards nightfall. He could not do anything since he had nothing with which to kill them.

Then at last he was angered by the mosquitoes since they bit him all over continually.

Now then, "Just wait," he said, said he to those mosquitoes. "Just wait, I'll be cruel to you," he said. "You wo..., you won't be able to go on living," he said to them.

2   Now then he collected the mosquitoes. Then he put them into something. He gathered a great many.

So then as soon as it began to get cold, as it started to snow at the beginning of winter, then he said to those mosquitoes: "Now then I'll pay back your cruelty to me during the summer," he said to them.

Then he went out there in the winter. He took his mosquitoes out. Then he scattered them out around from where he had contained them.

As soon as he scattered them out around, at that point those mosquitoes froze right on the spot. They could not fly because it was too cold.

"Look," he said. "So then," he said, "there's nothing you can do in the winter, – you who wanted so very much to bite me over and over," he said to them.

3   So now ..., so now as spring was beginning, at the onset of summer, already by now a mosquito suddenly came along and bit him.

He killed that one though.

Was that all then? He couldn't do anything to stop those mosquitoes. They came in here and there wherever he was. At last the mosquitoes had him in utter misery. He even swam in the water. He dived. Time and again as soon as his head would come to the surface, then time and again the mosquitoes would go wrapping themselves all about him.

So then, since it was getting on to mid-summer, there was not a thing which he could do.

4   Now then he knew that he had brought evil on himself, because he had

sakimêwa ..., ê-kî-pâstâhât.[4]

êko man' âni mâk' ê-'ti-nîpininik, 'kwâni manâ mitoni
k'-ât'-îši-kitamawikot anihi sakimêwa, êkâ wayêš ê-kî-tôtawât. 'kwâni mâka
wêhci-kostâtikwahk 'ci-mânênimâkaniwîcik itwâniwan awiyâšîšak, êkâ
kêkwâniw ê-kî-tôtamâsocik ..., êkâ mâka nêsta 'ci-pâstâmonâniwahk.

been cruel to the mosquitoes ..., in that he had treated them blasphemously.

So then, as the summer went on those mosquitoes began to eat him up entirely, without his being able to do anything to them. And that, they say, is why it is dangerous for creatures to be abused, because there is nothing they can do for themselves ..., and also so that one does not bring requital on oneself.

nâpêw kâ-kî-wêpiškâtât kôna

1   pêyakwâ manâ mîna wêskac nîšiwâkopan manâ oškinîkiwak. pêyakwâ manâ mâk' ê-pipohk, ana pêyak ošîm'mâw[1] kî-sîhkaciw. 'kwâni manâ mâka kâ-ati-nipit anim' ê-kî-sîhkacit; 'kwâni tâpwê kâ-iši-kawacît pêyakwâ '-pipon'nik.

êko manâ mâka ana kâ-ostêsimâwit môna nâspic ohci-minwên'tam anim' ê-k'-îhkininik. kî-kisiwâsiw manâ. kî-pakwâtam anim' ê-k'-îhtin'ci ošîma.

2   êko manâ mâk' ê-'ti-sîkwan'nik, k'-âti-tihkisot kôn, ê-wâpamât manâ mâka anim' ê-'šinâkosin'ci, kî-n'tawâpamêw êy-apin'ci.

"nah, êko mâka ê-kakwâtakinâkosiyan," manâ itêw.

'kwâni manâ kâ-'ši-wêwêpiškâtât anih kôna, ê-kî-kišiwâhikot.

"kîna nâ kâ-kî-sîhkatimat nišîm?" manâ itêw. "êh ..., mâtih nîna, pêci-sîhkatimin," manâ itêw anihi kôna.

wêhci-naškwawašihikot manâ mâk' anihi kôna: "êškwâ isa ka-pêci-mawâpîstâtin mîna pipohkê," manâ itikow.

sêkimikow manâ mâk' anim' ê-ytikot.

3   âšay manâ mâka mêkwâc anim' ê-'ti-nîpininik, kwayask manâ mitoni kî-wawênîw, ê-kiskên'tahk tâpwê' ci-pêci-n'tawâpamikot mîna pipon'nikê ..., mîna 'ci-wâpamikot.

misiwê manâ mâwac kâ-... kâ-wahkêwâskitêniki mihta kî-mâwacihtâw, mihcêt kî-mâwacihtâw. misiwê mâka nêsta tahto-pimiy, awiyâšîši-pimiy. misiwê kîy-asawatâw askihkohk. pîhtikomihk mâka kîy-astâw.

4   âšay manâ mâka mîn' ê-'ti-pipon'nik, âšay man' âti-mikwaškâtên'tam. "âšay mîna wîpac n'ka-pêci-n'tawâpamik kôn," manâ itên'tam.

âšay manâ tâpwê, mâwac kâ-iši-tahkâyâk, wêhci-pêhtawênahk[2] man' âwênihkân pêyakwâ ê-apit ...[3] ê-'ti-tipiskânik. wêhci-pîhtokwêt manâ kôn kâ-'šinâkosit ininiw.

otiškotêm ana piko 'kwâni wâ-'šiy-âstawêpan'nik.

wîpac manâ sîkwêpahâhtam nip...[4] pimîniw. 'kwâni mâk' êši-pasitêpanik anima pimiy. mêkwâc manâ mâk' ant' ê-kîy-apit ana ..., ana ininiw, 'kwâni manâ wâ-'šiy-âstawêpan'[5] anim' êškotêw tašinê. tašinê manâ mâka, mâka macostêham omihtima mêkwâc ant' ê-apin'c'.

5   kêka manâ mâka, kêka kîy-at'..., kêkât kîy-ati-tihkisow ana kôn ê-apit, miton' ê-kisisâwêt.

'kwâni manâ n'tawâc kâ-iši-pasikot ana nâpêw kôna kâ-išinâkosit. "êko

The man who kicked away the snow

1   Once upon a time long ago there used to be, it would seem, two young
men. At one point in the winter, one of the younger brothers got a chill. At
that point, chilled through as he was, he was approaching death; then one
winter he actually froze to death.

So that older brother was not much pleased at what had happened. He
was angry. He did not like what had befallen his younger brother.

2   So then as spring drew on, when the snow had begun to melt, as he saw
the way it looked then, he went to see it as it lay there.

"See here, you look a miserable sight," he said to it.

Then he kicked that snow around, in his anger at it.

"Is it you who chilled my young brother?" he said to it. "Well..., here am I,
come and chill me," he said to the snow.

All of a sudden the snow answered him: "Just wait, I'll come and visit you
again next winter," it said to him.

He was frightened then at its speaking to him like that.

3   Now then, during the course of that summer, he made proper and
thorough preparations, knowing that it would certainly come to see him the
next winter ..., that it would see him again.

He gathered all the logs which ... which burn most easily, he gathered a
great many. Also every kind of grease, animal grease. He put it all in a pail.
And he set it inside the house.

4   And now as winter drew on again, now he began to worry. "Soon now the
snow will be coming to see me again," he thought.

Now then sure enough, when it was at its coldest, someone sitting at one
point suddenly heard footfalls ..., as night came on. Suddenly there came in
a person who looked like snow.

His fire was about to go out right away.

He quickly poured wat..., grease on it. Right away the grease flared up.
But while that ..., that person sat there, the fire kept wanting to go out all
the time. And all the time again and again he threw his logs into the fire
while the other one sat there.

5   But then at last, at last he began ..., that snow very nearly began to melt
as it sat there, as he put on full heat.

Then that man who looked like snow stood up. "So that's it," then he said.

155

wâs' âni," manâ itwêw. "êko wâs' ân' ê-kî-šâkocihiyan," manâ itwêw, "êkwâni
n'tawâc 'ci-kîwêyân," manâ itwêw. "môna mîna ka-mikwaškâcihitin," itikow.

'kwâni k'-ât'-îši-wanawît.

'kwâni mâka tâpw' ê-kî-paskinawât anihi kôna, môna mîna wîskâc
ohci-mikwaškâcihikow.

'kwâni piko êskwâpihkêyâk.

"So that's it, since you've overcome me, then I'd better go home," he said. "I won't trouble you again," he said to him.

At that he began to go outside.

And then indeed, having got the better of that snow, he was never again bothered by it.

That's the length of this story.

tipâcimôwin awahkânak ohci

1   ôma tipâcimôwin wîna awahkânak ohci.

pêyakwâ wêskac ê-'pišîš'iyâpân n'kiskisin ê-kî-'yâwakihtipan amisk êy-otawahkâniyâhk. mêkwâc ê-nipâyâhk, âpatisîpan k'-ênikohk. mêkwâc mâk' ê-kîšikânik, nipâpan k'-ênikohk.

êko mâka mêkwâc ê-tipiskânik ê-nipâyâhk, nîkinâhk, mîkiwâmihk, iškwâhtêmihk mâka, kâ-ohci-wanawînâniwahk, k'-ênikohk âpatisiw. kîškîškahtam nîpisiyâhtiko-mistikwa; êko mâka pêtâw iškwâhtêmihk.

2   ê-kêkišêpâyâk ê-waniškâyâhk, mitoni kî-kakêpaham n'tiškwâhtêminân. mêkwâc ê-tipiskânik 'kwân' êtôtahk: ênikohk âpatisiw ê-kipahahk iškwâhtêm,[1] tâpiskôc kâ-itôtahk sîpîniw.[2]

êko mâka ê-waniškâyâhk ê-kêkišêpâyânik âšay pimišin ê-nipât, mêkwâc ê-kî-âpatisit ê-tipiskânik.

About animals kept as pets

1   This story is about pet animals.

Once long ago when I was little, I remember that we used to have a beaver for a pet. While we were asleep, he used to work as hard as he could. During the day, however, he used to sleep for all he was worth.

So then, during the night as we were sleeping, in our home, in the tent, he would work as hard as he could at the door by which one went out. He cut willow sticks with his teeth, and then he brought them to the door.

2   When we got up in the morning, he had completely blocked up our door. During the night he did it: he worked as hard as he could closing up the door, just as he did to a river.

And then, when we got up in the morning he was already lying asleep, because he had been working in the meantime during the night.

nikik ê-itâcimikosit

1   awa wîna nikik.

pêyakwâ mîna n'kî-kiskisin ê-ayâwakihtipan nikik, ê-kîy-otâwahkâniyâhk. nikik mâka wîna nâspic kistâpatisîpan ê-'yâwakihtipan. nipâpan ê-tipiskânik; êko mâka ê-'ti-'êkišêpâyânik wîpac waniškâpan. wayêš mâka nîšo mîna âpihtaw ê-'spanik ê-k'-îškw'-âpihta-kîšikâk, âšay mîna pêci-kawêšimôpan.

2   êko mâka nêsta n'tâpacihâhtân mêkwâc ê-ayâwakihtipan.

ê-pakitahwâyâhk sîpîhk ê-pipohk, ispîš wîna mihcêtwâ 'ti-twâhtwâhikêyâhk,[1] mistik 'ci-âpacihtâyâhk, 'ci-pakitinakiht n'tahnapînân šîpâ maskwamîhk, môna wîskâc anima n'tôtêhtân. nîšo piko m'pêkotahwâhtân maskwamîy; êko mâka n'tahkopitamwâhtân nikik os...,[2] ocihcîhk pîšâkanâpîniw. pêyakot..., pêyakotwâhikanihk mâka êkot' âni kâ-ohci-kôkît; nêtê mâka mîna kotakîhk êkotê 'ni mîna kâ-ohci-pêtât[3] animêniw pîšâkanâpîniw.

3   'kwâni piko kâ-tôtamâhkipan[4] ê-'spîhci-wêhtisiyâhkipan ê-ayâwakihtipan nikik.

minwên'tâkosîpan mâka nêsta ê-kanawênimihtipan. môna wîskâc apîpan. papâm'pahtâpan tahtwâ ka..., ê-kîšikânik. êko mâka pêci-nipâpan ê-k'-îškw'-âpihta-kîšikânik.

A story about an otter

1   This one is an otter.

Once again I remember that we used to have an otter we had as a pet. That otter was very useful while we had him. He used to sleep at night; and then as it became morning, he would get up early. Around half-past two in the afternoon, however, he already used to come to bed again.

2   We also used to make use of him while we had him.

As we were setting nets in the river in winter, instead of our making lots of holes so we could use a stick to set our nets beneath the ice, we never used to do that. We used to cut only two holes through the ice; and then we would tie a line to the otter's ta..., to his paw. The single..., and at the single hole, that's where he dove from; and at the other one, further over again, that's where he brought that rope from again.

3   That's all we used to do; it was so easy for us since we had the otter.

He was good-natured too as we kept him. He never used to sit [quietly]. He used to run around every d..., in the day. And then he would come and sleep in the afternoon.

ôko wîna okâšakaskiwêsiwak

1   okâšakaskiwêsiwak nêsta minwên'tâkosiwak ê-otâwahkâninâniwahk.
mihcêtwâ n'kî-'yâwâwak ê-'ti-minoskamininik, – piponasiwak
kâ-'šinihkâsocik n'titên'tên. ê-apišîš'šicik mâka n'tôhci-kanawênimânânak
pwâmoši opîwâwicik.

2   namêsa mâka n'tašamânânak. mistahi mîcisôwak pêyakwâ '-kîšikânik;
êko mâk' ê-'ti-mišikiticik, êkot' ân' ê-'htâcik, môna wî-kihcihnâwak,
ê-sâkihiskik ê-kîy-otâwahkâniyan, ê-kiskên'tahkik nêst' êy-ohci-mîcisocik
kîkihk tahto-kîšikâw.

3   mîna mâka kotak kêkwân môna wîskâc kimikwaškâcihikwak wâpikošîšak,
kišâspin êhtât okâšakaskiwêsiw kîkihk. tâpiskôc pôsikâciš ê-'htât kîkihk êkâ
'skâc[1] ê-mikwaškâcihicik ..., êkâ wîskâc ê-mikwaškâcihiskik[2] wâpikošîšak.
'kwâni pêyakwan okâšakaskiwêsiw ê-'htât kîkihk môna wîskâc ka-wâpamâw
wâpikošîš pêšoc.

About hawks

1   Hawks too are nice to have as pets.

We had them many times just before break-up, – the ones which I think are called partridge hawks. We kept them from the time that they were small before they had feathers.

2   We would feed them fish. They ate a great deal once a day; and then, as they begin to get big, they stay there and don't want to fly away since they love you when you've had them as pets, because they know too that they eat at your home every day.

3   And one more thing mice never bother you if there's a hawk in your home. It's just as when there's a cat in your place mice never bother me ..., don't ever bother you. It's the same when there's a hawk in your home you'll never see a mouse nearby.

II

Legends and Narratives:

Kashechewan Cree

Isaiah Sutherland
John Wynne
Joel Linklater
Silas Wesley
Hannah Wynne
Gabriel Kiokee

wîsakêcâhk kâ-wayêšihâkopanê maskwa

1   ayahâw wîsakêcâhk ê-..., manâ wâpamêw maskwa, ê-'pâmohtên'ci.

manâ mâka itêw: "kiwâpahtên nâ nêma kêkwân, mîk'wâm kâ-išinâkwahk?"

"môla," manâ itwêw. "n'ka-wâpaht... mâtik' kiškîsikwa. n'ka-wâpahtên,"
'têw.

êko mâka wêyâpahtilât maskwa oškîšikwa.

" 'kiskên'tên[1] nâ nîla tân' êtôtamâpân anim' ê-yhtiyân, êy-âhkosiyân
niškîsikwa? mîniša m'pakitinêhtay n'škîsikwa. êko mâka ninipâhtay.
ka-milo-'mâtisin kî-nipâyanê. kišâspin mâka êk' ânima tôtamanê kâ-ititân,
môla ka-milo-macihtâyan kiškîsikwa."

2   êko mâka ispî kâ-nipân'ci, asiniya aspiskwêšimonahêw 'ci-nipân'ci.

êko mâka ispî kâ-nipân'ci, pimotêw asiniya ostikwânilîhk.

êkwâni mâk' ê-kî-nipahât.

ispî mâka kâ-nipahât, êko pêminawasot anihi maskwa ê-wî-mowât ...,
misiwê ê-'tikitin'ci kî-kîsisow.[2] mîniša mâka mihcêt ê-kî-mîcit ana
wîsakêcâhk môna kî-mowêw.

3   acilaw piko kî-kîsisow. ispî mâka kâ-kîsiswât, êh..., "pitamâ
n'ka-nîwâskocimon," itwêw.

mistikwa mâk' ê-lîhkitawisin'ci [chuckles] pakitinêw ôta âpihtaw ôt'
êši-pakitinêw mistikwa.

êko mâka, "pêci-nâcistâ," itêw, anihi mistikwa.

êko man' âni mâka miyâkohokot ant' âpihtaw ..., anta môla pakitinikow
anihi mistikwa.

pîniš, anihi manâ mâka mistikwa têpwê'w': "awiyâšîšak, mîcisok.
kitašamikowâw maskwa ê-kî-kîsiswât, wîsakêcâhk,"[3] itwêwak.

'ko mâka ispî kâ-kîsis..., kâ-mâcikonikot anihi mistikwa, pâhkân[4]
kâ-kitamawân'ci anihi awiyâšîša kî-pônihê..., kî-pônihikow.

'kwâni mâka, ê-kišiwâhikot anihi mistikwa, 'kwâni wêhci-pîmisicik[5]
mistikwak, ê-kî-pâpîminât anihi ê-mî... -mâcikonikot.

4   ispî mâka, kâ-'škw'-ânim'-êtôtahk,[6] âšay osam anihi otôskanima
kâ-k'-îškwahtamin'ci awiyâšîša; môla mâka[7] kêkwâniw pimîliw pik' ôhtinam.

êko mâka pâhtahahk wîhkwâhk, anihi mêna pimîliw.[8]

êko mâka manâ pimâtakâliw' anta wat...[9] amiskwa.

"nišîm," manâ itêw, "âstam. n'ka-'kwahpitên[10] ôma. tatahkikamihtitâ

Weesakechahk tricks the bear

1   Well, Weesakechahk as…, he saw a bear walking about.

Then he said to him "Do you see yonder thing that looks like a tent?"

"No," he said. "I'll see … look at your eyes. I'll see it," he said to him.

So then the bear showed him his eyes.

"Do you know what I used to do when I ailed that way, when I was sick with my eyes? I used to put berries on my eyes. And then I would sleep. You'll be better when you've slept. But if you don't do what I say to you, your eyes won't feel well."

2   So then when he slept, he made stones into a pillow for him to sleep.

So then once he was asleep, he threw a stone at him, at his head.

And then, he had killed him.

But when he had killed him, then he cooked that bear for himself because he wanted to eat him, – he cooked the whole bear. But because that [fellow] Weesakechahk had eaten many berries, he couldn't eat him.

3   He just cooked him up for the time being. When he had cooked him, however, uh…, "First of all I'll suspend myself from a tree," he said.

But since the tree was forked [chuckles] he put it here, – he put the tree half-way here.

And then he said to the tree, "Come nearer."

But then he was pinched there half-way …, there that tree didn't let him go.

At last those trees called out, "Animals, eat. Weesakechahk has cooked a bear and is feeding you," they said.

So then, when he had cook …, he was held by that tree until they had finished eating up that creature it stopped h… it stopped him.

And that is the reason, because that tree made him angry, that is the reason some trees are twisted, because he had twisted it while he was being h…, held.

4   Once, however, that he had finished doing that, he boiled those bones of his which the animals had left after eating; but he got nothing except grease from them.

So then he put it in a bladder, that grease.

So then there swam by a musk …, a beaver.

"Little Brother," he said to him, "Come here. I'll tie this thing. Cool off

nipîhk m'pimîm," manâ itêw.

ay'hâw isa mâkâ, an' âmisk wêpawêpâliwêpanihow[11] ê-kôkît. 'ko mâk' ispîy anima kâ-kôkît, pâškipaliliw alimêniw[12] pimîniw. 'kwâni misiw' ê-kî-wan'tât môn' ohci-mowêw anihi. môna wayêš ohc'-ilâpacihêw.[13]

5   êko mâka, ispîy anima kâ-'škwâ-itôtahk, âšay kišiwâhikow anihi amiskwa âšay mîna wî-kakwê-nipahêw anihi amiskwa, ê-kišiwâhikot. ispî mâka kâ-... kâ-... êyâšawakwâškwatiw[14] manâ šîpîšišiniw antê mâmihk, ispî mâk' anima, mêkwâc êy-âšawakwâškwatit, kêtahtawin papaskiwa ê-wâwin'ci, ayâ ... ohc'-ohpahoniwa, pitihkopalihoniwa.[15]

âpihtawikâm manâ mâk' êši-pahkišin anta nipîhk. âšay kêkât kî-nistâpâwêw ana wîsakêcâhk.

kišiwâhikow mâk' anihi pilêwa. ê'kwâni êši-tâtahkiškâtât mâk' anihi, anihi pilêšiša.

6   êkwâni, mâka môla kêkwâliw ohc'-ohtinam; êkwân' ..., ê-kî-..., ê-kî-šîwatêt[16] pîniš, eko mâka miconi kîy-ati-kawahkatêw ana wîsakêcâhk.[17] miconi kêka kîy-ati-kiši... -kišiwâhikow, anihi kâ-malakwahikot. k'-îskwâsow manâ mâka nêsta wâwât. miconi kî-n'šonâcihitisow.[18]

kêka manâ mâka, ê-'ti-kawahkatêt, 'kwantaw animêniw kâ-k'-îskwâsot mîciw.

7   êko mâka manâ êtwêt wîskacâniš ôt..., wîskacâniš' ayamihikow: "tân' êtôtaman ê-ayamiwanê wîsakêcâhk?"[19] manâ itikow. "kêkwânihkân ani kâ-mîciyan?" manâ itikow.

" 'kâ kitoh!"

"kimikiy oš' âna kâ-mîciyan," manâ itâkaniwan.

" 'kâ kito. nôhkom ošô kî-pâsamôpan ômêliw mihkoliw kâ-mîciyân."

"êhê," itwêw.

êko, 's' mâka ispî kâ-..., ê-matwê-ihtit, 'kwâni k'-âti-kawahkatêt anima pîniš miconi manâ oti. antê mâka mîna mâši, 'kwâni mâk' anim' êš..., êskosit anta wîna.

my grease in the water," he said to him.

Well then, that beaver waggled his tail as he dived. And then at the point when he dived, that grease exploded. So then, as he had lost the whole lot, he didn't eat that one. It was of no use to him for anything.

5 So then, when he had finished doing that, he was now angered by the beaver, again now he wanted to try to kill that beaver, in his anger at him. But when he had ... had ... he jumped back and forth across the creek there down-river. At that point, while he was jumping across, suddenly a hardwood-partridge, having eggs, uh... flew up with a roaring, flapping noise.

Half-way across the water, he fell into the water. Now that Weesakechahk nearly drowned.

He was angered by that partridge. Then he kicked away at that, that small partridge.

6 Then, – but he didn't get anything out of it. So then, having been hungry up to that point, then that Weesakechahk began utterly to starve. At last it began to make him thoroughly angr..., angry, that one which brought him bad luck. In addition to which he got burnt as well. He completely destroyed himself.

But now at last, as he was beginning to starve, he idly ate where he had burnt himself.

7 But then the blue jay said h..., the blue jay spoke to him: "What are you doing as you're talking, Weesakechahk?" he said to him. "Whatever is that which you are eating?" he was asked.

"Be quiet!"

"It's your scab for sure that you're eating," someone said.

"Keep quiet. My grandmother, you know, had dried this blood which I'm eating."

"Yes," he said.

Then, but when that, – as he was getting on with it, then he began to starve utterly, up to that time, that is. But even there again wh..., then that was the length of him there.

wîsakêcâhk ê-ošihât kê-kâkikê-pimâtisinici ililiwa

1   mîna mâka nêtê manâ matwê-pêht'wâkaniwan ê-nikamot,
ê-matwê-têpihtâkosit ê-nikamot.

ispî mâka ..., pêhtawêwak mâka nîšow 'ilîwak anih' ê-nikamon'ci.

"mâhti, n'tawâp'mâtâ," itikowak, itwêwak manâ.[1] êko manâ
nêtawâpamâcik.

k'-âpit man' ânta wîsakêcâhk, oskisk' ânta ostikwânihk manâ cimasoliwa
pêyak.

mâkâ ..., n'tawâp'mêwak anik' îl'liwak nîšow îl'liwa.

"kêkwân pêkosêlimoyin?" manâ itêw anih' îl'liwa.

" 'kwantaw ani kî-pêci-wîhtamâhtihtay nahi piko 'c'-îspîhcisîyân, êlikohk
ê-nipiyân," manâ itwêw an' êl'liw.

'ko mâk' ispîy animêniw pohpohtâtamwêw man' ostikwânilîhk.

2   'ko mâka ispî mînâ kotakiy' anihi êt'-otihtikot, "kêkwân mâka kîna?" manâ
itêw.

" 'ci-kâkikê-pimâtisiyân isa, kipakosênimitin," manâ 'têw, itikow 'nihi
kotakiya.

ocipitêw manâ. êko manâ mâk' êši-wâwiyê-wêpinât anima[2] tâpiskôc
tôhwân, kâ-išinâkosit.

asiniya manâ k'-âpin'ci ant' ê-k'-îši-wêpinât anih' îl'liw' ê-kî-kakêšiwinât.

ê'kwân' êlikohk kêskêl'tamân anima.

Weesakechahk creates an immortal

1   Once again he was heard from a distance, singing, – he could be well enough heard singing, from a distance.

When, however ..., but two people heard that fellow singing.

"Look here, let's go see him," it was said to them, they said then. So they went to see him.

When Weesakechahk sat there, a single jack-pine grew on his head.

B-u-t ..., those two people went to see him, two people.

"What do you wish?" he said to the one person.

"I just came to ask you that I may be of about average age when I die," said that person.

So then with that he blew at his head.

2   Now, when the other came to him, he said to him, "And what do you desire?"

"That I may live forever, I desire of you," he said to him, the other person said to him.

Then he pulled him. Then he spun him around like a ball looks.

That stone which lies there is where he threw that person when he crashed him down.

That's as much as I know about that one.

cahkâpêš kâ-kohcipalihikot mistamêsa

1   cahkâpêš manâ omisâ wîci-tašîhkêmêw ê-nîšicik.

'ko manâ mâka, "awênihkânak aniki anta kâ-sâsâkišikonêcik mâna namêsihk išinâkosiwak," manâ itêw omisa.

"namêsak aniki kâ-mišikiticik. 'kâwina pahkopê, ka-kohcipalihikwak," manâ itâkaniwan …, itik' ômisa.

môl' isa mâka tâpwêhtawêw omisa, ot… otakaskwa kapastawêpinêw.

êko mâka niyâtahwât aniy'[1] otakaskwa, kî-kohcipalihikow anihi namêsa.

2   nisto-tipiskâw mâka kî-watêmikow anihi namês' anta nipîhk. ôma manâ mâka itêlihtam ant' ê-watêmikot atâmihk ê-papâmâtakân'ci: "mân'si êkâ kâ-wî-kapastawê…[2] kêkwân nimis 'ci-kî-kohcipalihtwânispan' ".

êko manâ mâka, ispîy anima kâ-itên'tahk, omaskisin kî-kohci…, kî-kapastawêham an' êsa …, iskwêw. êko mâka kâ-kohcipalihtwât ana namês, ê'kot' âni kâ-ohci-nawatinahk ana …, animêniw maskisiniliw antê pîhci watânîhk anihi ôw…, namêsa.

ispî mâk' ânima …, êko manâ mâka kâ-côhcôhkipit…, kâ-côhcôskipitahk[3] anta ohci pâhkwâšihk ê-kiskêl'tamin'ci omisa, 'ko mâkâ, kâ-kwâsipitâl'ci anihi namêsa.

3   'ko mâkâ, ispî nêtawêl'tahk anihi omisa 'ciy-otinikot, kî-mâciswêw anihi namêsa an' êskwêw, watâlîhk ê-n'taw'šwât ošîma.

" 'kat, 'kat, nimis; 'kâwina mâcišon," an' êtêw.

êko manâ mâka, misiwê mâk' anima namês kâ-išinâkwaniliki ê-kohcipalihtwât, kâhkâpisit kâ-išinâkosil'ci namês ê'kwân' ê-'šinâkosit misiwê 'l' it'[4] cahkâpêš.

êko mâkâ, " 'kâwina mâcišon, nimis. pêhkâc piko," itêw.

ispî mâka manâ, kâ-'škw'-ânim'-âyitôtahk, êko kâ-kâškahokot anihiy omisa. ot… osto… otônihk manâ mâka anta k'-îškwâtahok'w apišîš, êkâ oti…, ê'kwâni mâka wêhci-opîwâwitonâniwahk anta mitônihk, anim' ê-kî-iškwâtahokot.

4   'ko mâkâ, ispîy anima, "awênihkân 'ša n'ka-…[5] n'kî-mâtâhâw nimis," manâ itêw omisa.

ispî mâk' kâ-mâtâhât anihi 'wê'hkâna,[6] "pîsim ana," man' itikow.

" 'kâwina 'pâmêliht' ânima. môna ta-wâpan," manâ ytikow.

Chahkabesh is swallowed by the giant fish

1   Chahkabesh lived together with his older sister, the two of them.

So then he said to his sister, "Who are those ones there who keep breaking surface with the dorsal fin, they look like fish?"

"They are big fish. Don't go into the water, – they'll swallow you," he was told ..., his big sister said to him.

But of course he didn't believe his older sister; he threw his ... his arrow into the water.

Then he went after that arrow of his in the water and was swallowed by the fish.

2   For three nights that fish had him in his belly there in the water. And at this point he thought as he was held in the belly there of the fish swimming down below, "I wonder why my sister didn't throw something so he could have swallowed it."

So then, when he thought that, that woman swa..., threw her moccasin in the water. And then when that fish swallowed it, on the spot he grabbed that ..., that shoe there inside the belly of that ..., the fish.

At that point ..., so then he widened it ..., when his older sister knew that he [the fish] nibbled at it in the shallows, then she p..., dragged that fish ashore.

3   So then, when he wanted that older sister of his to take him, that woman cut the fish, searching with the knife in his belly for her little brother.

"Careful, careful, Big Sister; don't cut me," he said to her.

Now then, since a fish swallows all kinds of things, he looked as if he were discoloured, that's what Chahkabesh looked like all over, he said.

So then, "Don't cut me, Big Sister. Just go slowly," he said to her.

When then she had finished doing that, his sister scraped him off. But she left a little unscraped on his ..., his h ..., his mouth, not that is ..., and that is why there are whiskers around the mouth, because she left it unscraped.

4   So then, at that point, he said to his older sister, "I'll ..., I saw tracks of somebody there, you know, Big Sister."

But when he had seen the tracks of that person, she said to him, "It's the sun. Don't bother with that. It won't dawn," she said to him.

'ko mâk' êspîy animêliw môna tâpwêhtawêw 'misa; kî-tâpakwêw anihi, tâpiskôc '-tâpikwât awiyâšîš' kî-tôtam.

pîsim wêcik' ânih'.

'ko manâ mâka ispî kâ-'tôwi-pêhtât[7] an' êskwêw 'ci-wâpan'nik, "tân' ihki wêhci-'kâ-wâpahk?" 'tik'[8] ômisa.

"šâ! n'kî-tâpakwâhtay 'sa awênihkân kâ-kî-mâtâhak ê-pasatahahk."[9]

"manâ k'-îtitihtay 'kâ 'ci-tâpak'wat[10] pîsim oš' âna k'-îtitin mâk' oš' âna 'kwâni wêhci-'kâ-wâpahk."

misiwê manâ mâk' âwiyâšîša antê k'-îšiwilêw antê 'ci-paskamân'ci; môna mâka kî-tôtam. ispî mâka, kây..., k'-âyât..., kâ-kînikisit an' âpikošîš, êwakwâna kâ-paskamât anihi pîsimwa kâ-ohci-wâstêpalik.

'kwâni mâka ê-cahkâsikêt pîsim mîna.

But at that point he didn't believe his older sister; he snared him, he did it as when he snared an animal.

It was obviously the sun.

So then, when that woman got tired of waiting for it to dawn, [she] his older sister said to him, "What's the reason it's not dawning?"

"Oh my! I had snared someone whose worn-down trail I saw."

"Didn't I tell you not to set a snare for the sun and I *said* it to you. *That's* why it's not dawning."

Then he sent every animal there to gnaw; but he couldn't do it. But then th..., the ..., that sharply pointed mouse, that's the one who gnawed that sun free, so that all of a sudden the light came.

And then the sun began to shine again.

tântê kâ-ohci-wîhcikâtêkopanê cîpayi-sîpiy

1   kî-pêci-n'taw'palîstâtowâkopan[1] nâtawiyêwak[2] nêsta mâka ililiwak.
kî-kosâpahtam'wâkopan mâka manâ pitamâh, ê-nân'tawi-kiskênimitocik tânt'
ê-pêc'-îhtâcik.[3]   êko mâka kâ-kiskêlimitotawiht tânt' êš'-îhtâcik[4]
ê-kosâpahtahkik ohci omitêwiniwâhk.

2   êko ililiwak kâ-wawêlîcik 'ci-âšawa…, 'ci-ašahwâcik nâta'yêwah,
'c'-îši-'mâpolon'cih.[5]

       mihcêt mâk' 'anâ[6] kî-nipahêwak ôma ê-tôtahkik nîkân ê-kî-wâpamâcik
tânta k'-îši-ašahwâcik.   mihcêt nêsta kîy-otinêwak ê-'wahkâtâcik.[7]

       ê'kwâni mâka cîpayi-sîpiy wêhc'-îcikâtêk anohc kâ-kîšikâk anima
cîpayi-sîpiy.

How Ghost River got its name

1   The Iroquois and the People must have come to make war on each other. They had been looking into the future because they wanted to know how far from each other they were in their approach. So then it was made known to him [the conjuror] where they were from their forecasting by their conjurings.

2   So the People prepared to cro... to lie in wait for the Iroquois for them to drift downstream.

And they killed many then by doing this, having foreseen where they would lie in wait for them. They also took many as slaves.

And that is the reason why Ghost River is today called by that name, Ghost River.

nîšo ililiwak ê-nakiškawâcik wâpaskwa

1   pêyakwâ ê-kišêpâyâk ê-n'taminahocik ê-nîšicik 'wênihkânak,
môna ohci-kihciwitâwak môs'-asinî-pâskisikaniniw, ê-mispohk ohci,
êkâ 'y-kî-nakatahkik ocîmâniwâhk ê-'šaw'hikêcik. ispî mâka
wâ-pêci-kîwêcik, kî-wâpamêwak kêtahtawin wâpaskwa
ê-'ši-kîškâyawânik.

2   ana mâka wâpask kî-namipalihototâkowak,[1] kî-kapatêsipalihowak mâk'
ê-kap…, ê-kapatêtâpêpahtwâcik ocîmâniwâw.

     pêyak mâk' âna kîy-ošimow. êko mâka kâ-têpwâtât ana, "êlikohk, êlikohk,
kihcipahtâ! âšay ki'micišahok," ana k'-îtêw.

     ispî mâk' êtâpipalihot, kî-wâpamêw wâpaskwa kwêskakâm itêhkê
ê-kihcipahtân'ci [laughs].

Two men meet a polar bear

1   One morning as two persons were hunting, they did not carry a moose-shot rifle since, because of the snow, they were not able to leave it in their canoe as they came across [one of the small, northern rivers on the west coast of James Bay]. But when they were about to come home, they suddenly saw a polar bear where it was deep.

2   That bear passed them close by, but they quickly got out of the canoe asho..., dragging their canoe ashore on the run.

One of them got away. Then that one shouted to the other, "As hard as you can, as hard as you can, run away! He's already running after you," he said to him.

When he quickly turned to look, however, he saw the polar bear running away across the water [laughs].

ê-pâšikwâtahk kîwêtinohk

1   pêyakwâ '-wanahikêcik ê-nêw'cik 'wênihkânak, kî-mêkwâškamwak nâspic ê-mâci-kîšikânik. môna 'wâc ohci-kaškihtâwak 'ci-..., 'ci-cimatâcik oci..., omâhkîmiwâw ê-'spîhci-lôtininik.

2   kê'šêpâyânik mâka, mitoni kî-liskicistin'niw omâhkîmiwâw, otêmiwâwa nêsta.

    ot..., pâhkân mâka ê-'kišêpâyânik kî-môlâkonêhiwêwak otêmiwâwa, môna ohci-wal..., môna ohci-kaškihtâwak 'ci-walawîcik animêniw ê-kîšikânik.

A northern blizzard

1   Once as four people were out trapping they ran into an extremely bad day. They were not even able to ..., to set up their ..., their tent, it was so windy.

2   In the morning, however, their tent was completely buried with drifting snow, their dogs as well.

Their..., presently, however, in the morning, they dug into the snow for their dogs. They did not go ou..., they were not able to go out that day.

atimwak ê-kotaskâtitocik

pêyakwâ mâka mîna kî-kakwê-'taskatitôpanîk[1] atimwak, âtawâpiskâtowastimwak, êko mâka kêšîciwanowastimwak.

k'-îtên'tamwak âtawâpiskâtowastimw' awasitê ê-kisisawisîn'ci ispîš kêšîciwanowastimwa. šâkoc mâka kêšîciwanowastimwak kî-..., kî-kišîpaliwak.

ê'kwâniki kâ-paskilâkêcik [chuckles].

A dog-team race

Once again some dogs were trying to beat each other in a race, Attawapiskat dogs and Albany dogs.

They thought that the Attawapiskat dogs were smarter than the Albany dogs. But the Albany dogs ra..., they sure ran fast.

They were the ones who won [*chuckles*].

ê-'nâtawimôswâniwahk kwêtipawahikani-sîpîhk

1   pêyakwâ '-kîšikâk ê-'nâtawimôswêyâhk,[1] pêyak ililiw ê-..., ê-wîcêwak,
kêšîciwanohk ohci sîpîhk kwêtipawahikan kâ-icikâtêk
ê-iši-'natawimôswêyâhk, êko mâka, ê-'ti-p'miškâyâhk kêkât n'î-pêhtawâw[2]
môs nôhcimihk, "mhaa, mahaham,"[3] ê-'twêhkâsot.

êko mâka, môna pêhtawêw ana kâ-cîmak.

n'kosko-wêpiškên mâka cîman apišîš 'ci-kiskên'tahk âšay môsw'
ê-pêci-nôkosin'ci.

2   êko mâka kâ-kipihcîyâhk anta.

ispî mâka, ê-pêci-matâpêt ana môs, kî-pêci-pahkopêw. kî-kipihcîw mâk'
anta.

êko mâka kâ-mâci-pâskiswakiht, môsasiniy' pâskisikan'[4]
êy-âpacihtâyâhk.

kêka mâka kî-kisiwâsiw êkâ ê-nipahakiht, ê-mišwakiht, êkâ mâkah mâš'
ê-pahkišihk. êko kâ-kîšihtât ê-kihcipahtât têtâwakâm sîpîhk, ê-misaskênâk
anâwis êy-âpihtawipênik kêkât wîyaw.

3   êko mâka kâ-nawahwakiht. nâspic k'-êlikohk ê-'miškâyâhk, kêk' âwasitê
kîy-ati-nâwinâkosiw, ispîš ê-'spîhcipaliyâhk nînanân.

êko mâka kêkah, mîna kâ-... kâ-wî-sêskipahtât nôhcimihk iši.

êko mîna kâ-kihcihtâ'hk[5] ê-pâhkiswakiht. môna mâka
n'kîy-ohci-nipahânân 'nta mêkwâc ê-nôkosit. ispî mâka, ê-'ti-liskipalit
lîpisîhk, kêkât n'k'-îši-pâskisikân ê-'ti-koškopaliki lîpisîya.

êkwâni mâka kâ-ohci-..., kâ-ohci-pahkišihk nipîhk iši.

Moose-hunting on the Kwetabohigan River

1   One day as we were moose-hunting, as ..., as I was accompanying a certain person from Albany Post on the river which is called Kwetabohigan, as we were hunting moose there, well then, as we were beginning to paddle, I just barely heard a moose in the forest, making the sound, "mhaa, mahaham."

Then, however, the person with whom I was canoeing didn't hear him.

I rocked the canoe a little, so he would know that a moose was coming into sight.

2   So then we stopped there.

But when that moose came out of the bush, he waded into the water. But he stopped there.

And then we began to shoot him, using moose-shot in the guns.

At last, however, he got angry since we were not killing him, but were wounding him, though he was not falling. So he finished by running away in mid-stream in the river where there was hardly any bottom with almost half his body in the water.

3   And so we went after him. As we paddled for all we were worth, finally he began to draw further away faster than we were travelling.

And then at last, once more he was ..., was going to run ashore again towards the bush.

So we again started shooting at him. But we did not kill him there while he was in sight. When, however, he began to disappear into the willows, I shot him almost as the willows began to sway.

And it was then that he suddenly ..., he suddenly fell into the water.

ê-âhkwatâhkwacit môs'-wayânihk

1   pêyakwâ ê-pipohk, kî-..., ê-k'-îtohtêt pêyak ililiw ê-'nâtawâmôswêt,[1]
ê-'nâtawâpamât môswa kêy-ohci-pimâtisit ..., êko kâ-wâpamât môswa
animên' 'nâtawâmôswêt,[2] kî-nipahêw mâka.

âšay mâka wâlaw k'-îhtâw kâ-'š'-îhtât otašîhkêwinihk.

âšay mâka wîy-â..., mitoni tipiskâniw.   môna mâka k'-îspaliw
kici-kîwêt.

êko mâka kâ-itêlihtahk ispî kâ-pahkonât anihi omôsoma kici-tôtahk
ê-iši-..., êkâ 'šîhkacit[3] ê-tipiskânik ê-nipât, ê-..., ê-pipohk,
ê-tahkâyânik ohci.   êko kâ-... kâ-itêlihtahk kici-wîskwêkonît anihi
môs'-wayâna.

2   êko kâ-kawêšimot ê-wîskwêkonît anihi wâpoš'-wayâna ..., anihi
môs'-wayâna.

êko mâka ispîy ê-'kišêpâyânik, ispîw[4] ê-wî-waniškât, môna 'wât[5]
kîy-ohci-kaškihtâw kici-koškot, êy-âhkwaci'n'ci[6] anihi môs'-wayâna.   êko
kâ-ihtât ant' êkâ '-'kî-walawît anihi môs'-wayânihk.

mâškôc mâka wayêš nisto-kîšikâw k'-îhtâw anta pâtimâ kâ-takošihk
kotakiy' 'wênihkâna ê-'nâtawimâkaniwit ê-wanihiht, êkâ ê-kî-kîwêt.   êko
kâ-pêciy-â... kotawâniwahk êy-âpawiswâkaniwit ana môs'-wayân,
kici-walawît an' ê'liw[7] ant' ohci, môs'-wayânihk.[8]

Stuck frozen in a moose-hide

1   One winter a certain person had, having gone to search for moose, as he was looking for moose for food, then he saw a moose at that point as he was moose-hunting. And he killed him.

But now he was far away from where he was at home.

And now it was about to d..., it was completely dark. It was not possible, however, for him to go home.

So now he thought when he had skinned that moose of his that he would take steps so as ... not to get chilled through at night as he slept in ... in winter from the cold. So he thou..., thought that he would wrap up in that moose-hide.

2   So he went to bed wrapping up in that rabbit-skin ..., that moose-hide.

So then when it was morning, when he wanted to get up, he wasn't even able to stir, as that moose-hide was frozen. So there he was, not able to get out of that moose-hide.

And he was there perhaps about three days until someone else arrived in the search for him because he was lost, since he wasn't able to go home. So they came and a ..., made a fire as that moose-hide was being thawed out so that that person might get out from there, from the moose-hide.

ayâkwâmisîtotaw môs!

1   pêyakwâ ê-takwâkihk k'-âti-mâci-pâm'pahtâcik môswak
ê-wî-âmaci-môsocik ilikohk, ê-kîy-ati-kihtohtêyân mâka ôta ohci
kêšîciwanohk, cîpayi-sîpîhk ê-'t'-îtohtêyân, pêyak ililiw 'îcêwak.[1]

pêyakwâ mâka nêt' ê-'ti-kapâyâhk, ê-kotawêyâhk, nawac
ê-'ti-pêšonâkwahk cîpayi-sîpiy, ispî mâk' ê-wîy-ati-pôsiyâhk, niwâ'mânân[2] môs
nawac ê-nâwinâkosit, ê-matwê-nîpawit lâlih sîpîhk.

2   êko ê-'pâmohtêyâhk anta, kêka pêci-kihtohtêw.

êko kâ-'pâmohtêyâhk anta, tâpiskôc ê-nêwihki niskâtinânîy[3]
ê-'mohtêwâkêyâhk nisitinâna nêsta nicihcînânîy, kimiwaniyân mâka
êy-akwaniyâhk.

êko kâ-pêc'-îši-kihtohtêt ana môs, "nîci-môsw'," ê-ytên'tahk. pîliš nâspic
kî-pêšonâkosiw.

ispî mâka kêka nâspic ê-pêšonâkosit, êko kâ-otatâmâpiskîšimakiht,[4] êh...,
olâkan êy-âpacihtâyâhk.

êko nâspic kâ-koškopalit, nâspic k'-êlikohk kî-kihcipahtâw.

Beware of the moose!

1   One fall when the moose were beginning to run about, at the mating season, I had begun to set out from Albany Post here, on my way to Ghost River in the company of a certain person.

At one point as were landing there, we built a fire, as Ghost River was getting quite near; but when we wanted to push off again we saw a moose appear a fair distance off, standing within sight at the waterside.

2   Then as we walked around there, finally he left and walked towards us.

So we walked there, as though we had four legs, using our feet and our hands to walk on, covered over with a raincoat.

So the moose came walking away towards us, thinking, "It's a fellow moose of mine." Until he got within very close view.

But when at last he got within close sight, then we banged on the rocks, uh..., using a dish.

Then he was very startled, and ran off as hard as he possibly could.

ê-wanišininâniwahk nôhcimihk

1   pêyakwâ ê-kîšikâk ê-papâ-itohtêyâhk anta ê-iši-..., kâ-'ši-n'tawên'cikêyâhk
ê-papâ-kanawâpahtamâhk n'tônikanânîy,[1] êko mâk' ê-'ti-kihtohtêyâhk âšay
ê-..., mâk' ê-'t'-otâkošihk, n'tati-kihtohtânân ê-n'tawi-kanawâpahtamâhk
n'tônikanânîy. nê... ništ..., nisto mâk' ililiwak niwîcêwâwak, ninêwinân
mâmaw.

2   êko mâk' ê-'ti-kihtohtêyâhk, aniki nîšow ililiwak ništam sîpiy
ati-kihtohtêwak ê-n'tawâ'htahkik[2] otônikanâwâw'.[3]

     êko mâka nî'nân[4] ana kotak n'kîy-ati-kihtohtânân kotakîy sîpiy
ê-n'tawâpahtamâhk.

     êko mâka, ispî kâ-otihtamâhk anima sîpiy, n'kî-paskêwilitonân. êkwân'
nîna n'timihk itêhkê kâ-'ši-kihtohtêyân; kotak mâk' âna mâmihk itêhkê.

3   êko mâka n'timihk nêt' ê-'t'-îhtâyân, mitoni kî-ati-tipiskâw pîliš ê-'ti-...,
pâtimâ kâ-'t'-otihtamân ê-'škwâ-kišipastêki nitôw'nahikana.

     âšay mâka tipiskâw, nêsta mâka êkwêlâk wâpahtamân askiy. môna
ninakacihtân.

     ispî mâk' ê-kîwêyân mitoni âšay kaski-tipiskâw. ispî mâka nistam sîpiy
ê-'tiy-âšawakâšiyân ê-kîwêyân, kiyâpac ninisitawinên âtawîna ant'
ê-kî-wâpahtamân pêyakwâ, mwêhci âtawîna kwayask ê-'tohtêyân.[5]

     mîna mâk' ânima kotakîy ê-'tiy-âšawakâsiyân, âšay mišâw anta maskêk
ê-..., ê-paškwâk.[6] mêkwayêš mâka 'kwantaw maskêkoh' cimatêw
nimâhkîminân kê-'ši-kîwêyân. êko mâka piko n'ka-wî-kakwê-mišotên mwêhci
'ci-kî-miskamân, pâtimâ kê-k'-îhtâyân anta nîkihk anim' ê-tipiskâk.

4   êko mâka ispîy ê-'ti-'mohtêyân, kêka êlikohk ê-'ti-'mohtêyân, ilikohk
kê-'spalihkipan 'ci-kîy-otihtamân nîki, môna n'nisitawinên tântê ... tântê
kê-'ši-takwahkipan[7] nîki.

     êko mâka kâ-itên'tamân, "môna n'tawâc awasitê n'ka-kihtohtân."

     êko mâka kâ-kapêšiwinihkâsoyân antah, êkâ mâhkiy ê-'yân, êkâ
nêsta nipâkan ê-'yân; êko mâka n'kî-nipân anta maskêkohk,
ê-mošêhkwâmiyân.

5   êko mâk' ê-'ti-kîtawi-pêhicik aniki kâ-wîcêwakik, mâškôc wayêš mitâht
ê-'spalik nêstapiko mitâht mîna âpihta' ê-'spalik ê-tipiskâk, kî-kihtohtêwak
ê-sêkisicik, "mâškôc cîkahotasôtokwê[8] nêstapiko wayêš tôtâsôtokwê,"
ê-ytên'tahkik. êko mâka kâ-pimohtêcik nêtê kâ-itohtêyân, môna mâka

Lost in the bush

1   One day as we were walking about there where ... where we were hunting as we looked over our traps, well then, as we were beginning to go away, already as ... however, as evening drew on, we began to move away as we looked over our traps. Fo... thre... I was in the company of three people, we were four altogether.

2   So then as we began to move off, two of the people began to follow the first river as they went off to see their traps.

So then, the other person and myself, we began to walk away following the other river.

So then when we had reached that river, we parted from each other. Then I moved away up-river; the other one down-river.

3   Well then, as I began to get up-river, it began to get all dark till it started to ... until I reached the end of my traps.

And now it was night. It was also the first time I had seen the country. I wasn't familiar with it.

At the time I was on my way home it was by now utterly black dark. As I began to ford the first river on my way home, I still recognized it, even though I had just seen it once. I was going in the right direction nonetheless.

Again as I began to ford the other river, the swamp was now big and ... clean. Somewhere in the middle of the muskeg stood our tent where I had to go home. So then [I thought], I'm just going to try to hit it straight on so I can find it exactly, with the resolve of being at home later on that evening.

4   So then once I began walking along, finally as I began walking right along, just about the time it would take to reach my place, I didn't recognize where ... where my home would be.

So then I thought, "I'd just as well not go any further."

So then I made a sort of camping place for myself there, since I had no tent and since I didn't have a bed-roll either; so I slept there in the muskeg, sleeping without any cover.

5   So then as those whom I was with began to get tired waiting for me, probably about ten or half-past ten at night, they went their way frightened, thinking, "Perhaps he's cut himself with an axe or done something or other to himself." And so they walked to where I had gone, but they couldn't ... uh – they weren't able to go there directly, and they didn't know exactly where

kî-ohci-...,[9] êh-... kwayask kaškihtâwak kic'-îtohtêcik, môna nêsta wînawâw kiskên'tamwak mwêhci tântê kâ-itohtêyân.

êko mâka ispîy ê-wî-pêci-kîwêcik, kêkât kî-wanišinwak nêsta wînawâw. âtawîn' âpišîš pîtoš kî-pêciy-oht'htêwak, kâ-kîy-at'-îši-kihtohtêcik êya..., ispî kâ-kîwêcik; âtawîna kî-miskamwak mîna wîkiwâw.

6   pâtimâ mâka, mîn' ê-wâpahk, ispîy ê-'ti-payahtênâkwahk kâ-kihtohtêyân. apišîš n'kî-kîwân[10] nimêskanaw: "mâhti tânt' êhtâwânê," n'ên'tên.[11] ispî mâka kâ-sâkaskêhamân,[12] môna nâwinâkwan nîki nâsic pêšonâkwan kâ-k'-îši-nipâyân, – mâškôc piko nîšo-tipahikan, askîwi-tipahikan ê-'spîsinâkwahk.

I had gone.

So then at the time when they were wanting to go home, they too almost got lost. In any case, they came from a slightly different direction from that in which they had gone out, in ..., when they were coming home; nonetheless they found their home again.

6   But by-and-by, in the morning again, once it was beginning to get bright, I set out. I went back a little on my trail. I thought, "Let's see where I may be." At that point, however, when I came out of the bush into the swamp, my tent wasn't far off, it was near where I had slept, – perhaps up to two miles, land-measure.

ê-kî-kîwê-miskahk kâ-kî-wanitâspan opâskisikan

1   pêyakwâ ê-miloskamihk ê-wanihikêyâhk pêyak oškinîkiw ê-cîmak,
ê-'miskowanihikêyâhk.

êko nêtê, pâkašîhk n'timihk sîpîhk ê-htâyâhk, pâkašiy kâ-'cikâtêk sîpiy,
apišîš mâmišîhk[1] cîpayi-sîpîhk kâ-ohci-paskêyâk,[2] – êko mâka nêtê ê-'tiy-a...,
-natawên'cikêyâhk ê-wanahikêyâhk[3] pêyakwâ mâka ê-w... mêkwâc
ê-walastâ'n nitônahikan,[4] ôta mâk' ê-mâskostêk wakît cîmânihk[5] m'pâskisikan
k'-âpacihtây'n ê-pâskiswakik amiskwak, aspin kapastawêpaliw.

2   êko kâ-manikahamân mistikwa tâpiskôc kwâškwêpicikan ê-'šinâkohtâyân
ê-kakw'-otin'ân[6] m'pâskisikan. môna mâka n'kîy-ohci-kaškihtân 'c'-otinamân.

"tân'ka 'tê kê-tôtamwânê kici-kîy-otinamân m'pâskisikan?" m'â n'ên'tên.[7]
ê-..., ê-..., môna mâka mâši n'kî-kaškihtân 'ci-otinamân.

êko kâ-kêtâspisopalihoyân.[8]

êko kâ-..., ê-..., ê-'ti-kapastawê..., ê-'ti-kapastawêšimoyân, môna, môna
mâškôc nâs'ic mâka milwên'tam; kostâciw mâškôc mâk' âpišîš kâ-cîmak. êko
kâ-išit: "côwil, côwil," ê-kostâcit ê-'ti-kapastawêšimoyân.

3   êko kâ-otinamân m'pâskisikan.

mâškôc apišîš aliwâk n'kotwâs misit ispiht... ispihtâtimâw nipiy anta
kâ-kî-ohc'-otinamân m'pâskisikan.

Retrieval of a lost rifle

1   One spring as we were hunting I was canoeing with a certain young chap, as we were trapping beaver.

So, away there we were up-river at Pagashi, the river called Pagashi, a little below where it branches off from Ghost River. So then since we were beginning away yonder …, to look for game as we set traps, at one point as … while I was setting my trap, with the gun which I used in shooting beaver lying here on top of the canoe, it fell off into the water.

2   So I chopped off a stick, making it look like a hook, in an attempt to get my gun. But I couldn't manage to take it.

"I wonder what I should do so as to be able to get my gun," I thought then. I couldn't even manage to reach it.

So I undressed quickly.

Then when…, as…, I began to go into the wa…, I began to go into the water, but the person with whom I was canoeing didn't … didn't much like it; he was probably a bit scared. So he said to me: "Joel, Joel," in his fright as I started to go into the water.

3   Then I got my gun.

The water was perhaps a little in excess of six feet … deep where I took my gun from.

šâwanohk ê-iši-âpatisinâniwahk

1   kî... kîwêtinohk n'k'-îtohtâhtân nôhtâwiy ê-wîcî-tašîhkêmak
ê-papâ-wanahikêyâhk; môna mâka kêkwân n'tôhci-'yânân mâhkiy, mitoni môna
kêkwân, n'kî-papâ-mošêhkwâminân pišišik, ê-papâmohtêyâhk
ê-papâ-wanahikêyâhk, wâlaw ê-'t'-itohtêyâhk âskaw pîliš pêyako-tawâstêw. âskaw
môna n'kî-nipânân ê-tahkâyâk ohci ê-tipiskâk, mêmîskoc mân' ê-kotawêyâhk.
      nâspic âliman mâka n'k'-îtên'tên êy-awâšišîwiyân ohci ništam kâ-wanahikêyân.
2   n'kî-mâmitonên'tên mihcêtwâ, "n'tawâc âpatisîwin
'ci-kakwê-kâhcitinamân." êkoši mâk' êskali-'pon[1] n'kî-'pâ-wanahikân[2]
ê-'pâ-wîcêwak nôhtâwiy, ê-papâmohtêyâhk ê-'pâ-wanahikêyâhk.
      êko mâka n'kî-..., ê-'ti-nîpihk, n'k'-îtên'tên kici-n't'ê-'nâtaw-âpatisiyân.[3]
wâlaw mâka n'kî-kihtohtân, wayêš nîswâso-mitâhtomitana-tipahikan ôta ohci.
ê-n't'êy-âpatisiyân,[4] nêtê wâlaw kâ-iši-kîšin'cik[5] awiyânak, n'k'-îtohtân. êko
mâka, n'kîy-âpatisin antê n'kotwâs pîsim.
3   êko mâk', mîna pîtoš n'k'-îhtin anta kâ-kî-n't'êy-âpatisiyân. ê-kišitêk ohci
môna nâspic n'tôhci-min'wên'tên. êko mâka, kâ-itên'tamân mîna
kici-pêci-kîwêyân. n'kî-pêci-kîwân mâka ispîy êy-itên'tamân mîna
'ci-pêci-kîwêyân.
      âtawîn' tâpwê n'kî-milopanin antê mê... ilikohk kâ-k'-îhtâ'n,[6]
kâ-kîy-âpatisiyân. mistahi n'kî-'yâwâw šôliyân; misiwê kêkwân
n'kî-mîšakipalin.
      êko mâka, n'kî-pêci-kîwân. mîna n'kî-pêci-n'tawâ'mâw nôhtâwiy.
      nisto-'pon mâka n'kîy-âpatisin antê. ispî mâka nisto-'pon kâ-'škw-âpatisiyân
êko mîna kâ-mâcih... kâ-wanahikêyâhk ôtê, n'tihtâwinihk kêšîciwanohk.
4   êko mâka, âšay misiwê kêkwân mîn' anima ..., mîna n'tayân
kâ-'pâmohtêyâhk.[7] n'kî-'pâmohtânân âskaw, mihcêtwâ mâka šâkoc mîna
n'kîy-âlim'pim'palin ê-'pâ-wanahikêyâhk ohci. âskaw ninôhtêpalin mîcim pîliš
nisto-kîšikâw, ilikohk.[8] šâkoc mâka môna wayêš n'tôhc-îtên'tên pîliš anohc
kâ-kîšikâk.
      êko mâka ..., kotak kêkwân n'kîy-âlimên'tên: kâ-'škwâ-...,
kâ-'škwâ-ohci-pêci-kîwêyân nêtê, n'kî-nôhtêpalin kâ-k'-îši-..., kâ-i...,
kâ-iši-milopaliyâpân. pîtoš ôtê n'k'-îši-miskên kâ-'ši-tôtamân. šâkoc mâka,
môna n'tôhci-manêsin mîcim wîna, kotakîy mâka 'kwânihkân[9]
n'kî-wan'htân..., kâ-k'-îši-milopaliyân nêtê mêkwâc êy-âpatisiyân.
      'kwâni mâka êskwâk n'tipâcimôwin.

A job outside

1   My father and I had gone n..., north as I lived with him while we went about trapping. We had no tent to speak of, not a single thing, we just constantly slept in the open as we travelled about setting traps. We would go far away sometimes up to a period of one week. Sometimes we couldn't sleep because of the cold at night, as we took turns repeatedly kindling a fire.

It was very hard, I thought, when I first began to trap from childhood.

2   I thought many times, "Just as well I should try to get work." So then all winter I wandered about trapping in the company of my father, as we walked around setting our traps.

So then I..., as summer began, I thought I should go off to look for work. I went far off, about seven hundred miles from here. In looking for work I went far away where skins are tanned. And so I worked there six months.

3   Then, something else happened to me when I had gone looking for work. Because of the heat I didn't like it very much. And so, I thought I would go back home. And once I thought of coming home again, I came home.

Nonetheless I certainly got on well there wh... as long as I stayed there, where I worked. I had a lot of money; I had plenty of everything.

But then, I came home. I came back to see my father.

Three years I worked there. But when I had finished working three years, then I began again ... I trapped here, in my village, Albany Post.

4   So then, now everything again ..., I have it again when we walk around. We used to walk around sometimes, but I sure often found it hard again to make ends meet from our setting traps about. Sometimes I went short of food for up to three days. But in fact I didn't particularly think of it until today.

So then ..., something else I thought difficult: after ..., after coming back home from there, I lacked what ... wh... what I used to enjoy there. I found what I'm doing here quite different. But, I wasn't hard up for actual food; I missed other kinds of things however ..., which I enjoyed there while I was working.

And so that's the extent of my story.

pêyakwâ wêskac

1   pêyakwâ wêskac ê-papâmohtêyâhk nêtê wâlaw nôhcimihk, nâspic
ê-mihcêtiyâhk wêskac-ililiwak:[1] nôhtâwiy, pâtrik stîpin, cân kôsîs,
sayman kôsîs, âlik lâsaras, hêntriy lâsaras[2] ..., 'kwân' ê-'tašiyâhk. nâspic
ê-mišâk mîk'wâm, wêskat mêkwât kwayask ê-papâmâtisiyâhk[3]
ê-papâm'piciyâhk.

nâspit kî-kihciy-âliman wêskat kâ-kî-pêci-'mâtisicik ililiwak, pwâmoših
takwahk misiwê kêkwân ôma k'-âpacihtâcik 'êmistikôšiwak.

2   ôma tipâcimôwin nâspit mišâw, kici-kî-tipâcimowâspan ililiwak
kâ-kî-pêc'-îši-miskahkik mêkwâc askîhk kâ-papâmâtisicik.

nâspit kîy-âliman. kî-kihciy-âliman. môna wîskât kêkwân kîy-ohci-...
kêkât âpatan 'êmistikošiwi-mîcim. piko, pakwataskamik'-mîcim kây-âpatahk,
kâ-papâmohtêmakahk wâlaw.

êkot' âni kâ-ohci-'mâtisiyâhk, ôma k'-ât'-ispîhtisîyâhk nînanân. âskaw
nisto-kîšikâw môna pêtâniwan mîcim kê-mîciyâhk anta nîkinâhk.
ê-'spîhci-âlimahk pakwataskamik'-mîcim kici-kî-nipahtât ililiw mîciminiw,
nâspic ayêskosiw ililiw ê-wî-kakwê-nipahtât mîciminiw.

3   êko mâk' anima kâ-tipâcimoyân kâ-mihcêtiyâhk nâspic mihcêt atihkwak
kî-nipahâkanânak.[4] n'kî-pimipicinân ê-pimohtêyâhk ê-'tohtêyâhk
kâ-k'-îši-nipahihcik aniky atihkwak.

nâspit mâka n'kî-milwê..., n'kî-milwên'tênân ant' ê-mihcêtiyâhk.[5]

êko mâka, n'kî-nâcipahânân' aniky atihkwak, nêtê wâlaw kiyâpac
ê-pimišihkik kâ-k'-îši-... kâ-k'-îši-kapêšiyâhk. n'kîy-otâpânân, otâpânâsk
n'tâpaciyânân.[6] pêhpêyak n'tôtâpânân atihkwak ê-misiwêsicik, 'kwân'
ê-'ši-misiwêsicik. n'kaškihtân nêsta nîna ê-kihciwilak pêyak atihk,
ê-pimohtêyân nîna piko nîna n'îyocipitak[7] atihk ê-pimohtêyân.

môšak n'kîy-âlimisin nêsta nîna ê-pimiwitâyân kêkwân
ê-pimiwitam'wakik[8] nîc'-ililiwak kêkwâniw, kâ-kî-pêci-papâmohtêyâhk.

4   môšak wâlaw n'kî-papâmohtânân. nâspit n'kîy-âlimisinân mêkwât nîn'nân
kâ-pêciy-ohpikiyâhk. misiwê[9] kêkwân kî-namatakwan wêmistikôšiwi-mîcim.
êko mâka, anohc ôma k'-âti-pimâtisiyâhk ôma k'-ât'-îspîhtisîyâhk,
nimilopaninân n'tên'tênân askonâk[10] k'-âpacihtâyâhk kwayask
wêmistikôšiwi-mîcim.

nâspit n'kîy-âlimisinân wêskat êkâ 'hcy-âpacihtâyâhk[11] kêkwân, mistahi.
nâspic apišîš piko, n'kîy-âpacihtânân.

The old days

1   Once long ago we were walking about far off there in the bush. There were a good many of us old-timers: my father, Patrick Stephen, John Koosees, Simon Koosees, Alec Lazarus, Henry Lazarus, that's how many we were. The tent was big, away back while we lived wandering about as we travelled around camping.

It was really hard long ago for the people who used to live at that time, before there was everything which the White-Men use now.

2   This story is very long, which people could tell, about what they used to find then while they were living wandering around the country.

It was very hard. It was enormously hard. White-Man's food was never … almost never used. It was only country food which was used, which roved far and wide.

That's the way we lived, those of us of our age. Sometimes for a three-day stretch there was no food brought for us to eat in our camp. Because it was so difficult for a person to kill country food, a man got very tired wanting to try to kill food.

3   So then, at the time I'm telling of, when there were a good many of us, a great many caribou were slain. We went about with our gear, walking on foot as we went to where those caribou were killed.

But we very much li… we liked it with a lot of us there.

So then, we went after those caribou, since they still lay far away from where … where we camped. We hauled, we used a sled. One each we hauled whole caribou, whole as they were. I can take one caribou away too, walking just by myself alone I can, pulling the caribou as I walk.

I always had a hard time too in carrying anything, in carrying anything for my neighbours, when we were coming along.

4   We always travelled around far away. *We* had a very hard time while we were growing up. All kinds of White-Man's food did not exist. So then, living as we do now, getting to our age, we think we're doing well since we've been using White-Man's food properly.

We had a very hard time long ago never having used anything, much. We used only a very little bit.

5   ay'hâw mâka, kâ-itwêyân, mêkwâc anima, môna kêkwân nêsta
kîy-ohci-tipahikâtêw ayôwin. âpihtawahtay ..., âpihtawahtay piko k'-îtakisow,
šâkwêsiw êy-atâwêyâhk mêkwâc anima, kâ-itwêyân. wayêš mâškôt mâka
niyâlan nikik n'tên'tên, ê'kwâni wayêš. môna n'kiskên'tên wîn' âmisk.

nâspit kîy-âliman wêskat, ê-pimâtisit[12] ililiwak. môšak wâlaw
n'kî-papâmohtânân ê-pipohk ê-tahkâyâk, ê-nipâyâhk mîkiwâm piko
êy-âpacihtâyâhk, iškotêw piko alit'-iškotêw[13] ê-kotawêyâhk mîkiwâmihk
ê-nipâyâhk.

6   môna tâpiskôc anohc. apišîš mâka wêhtan anohc itên'tâkwan, anohc
kâ-p'mâtisiyâhk. kâ-p'mâtisicik k'-ât'-oški-p'mâtisicik awâš'šak,
ê-'ti-papâmohtêcik misiwê kêkwâniw âtawîn' âpacihtâwak anohc wîna.[14]

šâkoc mâka, môna k'-îhkin tašin' 'wênihkân 'ci-kî-milopanit. âskaw
pêyako-tawâst' ê-'pâmohtêt 'wênihkân môna miskam kêkwâniw
kêy-ohci-pimâtisit, wanahikan' âta ê-nôcihtât. mihcêt anim' êhtiwak
'wênihkânak. mihcêt iši-miskamwak ôma kâ-itwêyân.

7   nêsta nîlanân mwêhcy ôm' anohc kâ-kîšikâk, otihcipaliw êkâ sôhk'
ê-milopaniyâhk, ôma mwêhc' anohc kâ-kîšikâk kâ-tipâcimoyân.

êkâ nêsta sôhka ê-milopanit n'..., awa ni..., ni..., nîciyâkan,[15] anohc
kâ-piponinik. piko mâka êši-kaškihtâyân nêsta nîna, ê-wî-kakwê-tôtamân
kêkwân ê-wî-kakwê-pimâcihoyân, ê-itên'tamân.

nêst' êkâ sôhk' ê-milopanit awa nâpêšiš k'-âyâwakiht pêyak, ê-wîy-âhkosit
êy-atôskêt, awa nâpêšiš k'-âyâwakiht.

'kwâni piko anima tipâcimôwin mitoni kwayask kê-tipâcimoyân[16] pikoh.
animah ..., kwayask n'tipâcimon piko animah.

5   Well then, at that time when I was speaking of, fur wasn't paid anything
for either. Half a dollar ..., only half a dollar was the price when we traded
mink during that period, that I am speaking of. But it was perhaps five
dollars for an otter, I think, – somewhere about that. I don't know what
beaver brought.

It was very difficult long ago as people lived. We always wandered off in
the cold winter, using only a wigwam to sleep, lighting just an open fire in
the tent as we slept.

6   Not like now. It seems a little easy now, as we live at present. New-born
children who are living, as they begin to walk about, now have the use of
everything.

Certainly though, it's impossible for someone to make out well all the time.
Sometimes a person walking about for one week doesn't find anything to live
on, even though he tends his traps. That happens to lots of people. Many
find it as I say.

7   We too, right now today, it turns out that we're not doing awfully well,
right now today that I'm telling the story.

And things aren't going very well either with m..., my... this husband of
mine this winter. Just that I'm managing for my part, since I want to try to
do something with the idea of trying to make a living.

Also, this one boy whom we have is not getting on terribly well, since he
tends to be sick when he works, this boy whom we have.

So then that is the story which I shall tell utterly straightforwardly

That one... I'm just telling that properly.

Ayamihitowin [I]

1 JL: kêko kišê'liw mâka kâ-tipâcimat ôta?

GK: âšay 'sa, ... ay'hâw ana, cân coc.

JL: cân coc.

W1: [in background] 'matêtokwê n'têlimâw ana.

GK: 'matêw mâškôc an' n'têlimâw 'nohc.

JL: o?

GK: kî-tipâcimôpan nêtê otâkošîhk asinîhk, asiniy ana kâ-cimasot,[1] k'-îši-...[2] n'kîy-apihtân antê, ê-ayamihtâyâhk ...

JL: kêkw asiniy ana?

GK: ôma ..., ana ..., ôma kâ-'matâwis'amohtâniwahk[3] mêskanaw.

JL: o? kâ!

GK: kâ-kî-nipahikocik otâpâniniw ...[4]

JL: o?

GK: ... kêkwân piko ê-tôcikâtêk misiwê piko kêkwân kâ-kî-nanipahikocik kâ-pêci-âpatahki ê-ošihtâniwahk ôma otâpân'-mêskanaw.

2 JL: o?

GK: anim' ôtê kâ-nôkwahk antê 'sinîhk.

JL: êhê! êkotê 'ni mâka k'-ayamihêw'kanawâpit ...[5]

GK: êkotê 'ni mâka kâ-nânîpawiyâhk. n'kî-pêci-n'tawâpamikonân ant' ê-nânîpawiyâhk.

JL: hmm.[6]

GK: kîy-ati-tipâcim' ôs' âna mâka. kîy-ânimôtam apišîš animêniw.

JL: o?

GK: wêskac ê-kî-tipâcimostawât[7] kišê-'niniwa, wêskac nawac ê-... wêskac kišê-'yahâw nawac ana kišêy-'iniw. ôma itwêw, wêmistikôšiw oti. 'mayêw wîna 'kwantaw 'iniw.[8]

3 JL: o?

GK: êko mâka k'-ânimôtahk animêniw otâpânêskanâniw itwêw wêskac ..., nêma! 'mayêw wîna ôma kwâkran[9] kâ-p'mitamohk.

JL: o?

GK: ... awasit' antê kâ-p'mitamohk, kâ-'ši-pim'paniki ayahâwa, kihci-otâpâna[10] šâposkamik kâ-ispaniki.

JL: kâ-šâposkamikipaliki anihi?

GK: êhê. êko mâka, k'-ânimôtahk anihi, wêskac ê-tipâcimostawât

A conversation [I]

1 JL: Which old man is it that you're talking about here?

GK: Now then ..., well uh, that was John George.

JL: John George.

W1: [in background] must be dead.

GK: I think he's probably dead now.

JL: Oh?!

GK: He was telling the story over yonder yesterday at the stone, – that stone which stands up, where ... We were sitting over there, reading it.

JL: Which stone is that?

GK: This one ..., that one ..., this road that comes out of the bush.

JL: Oh?! Oh, that's the one!

GK: ... those who were killed by the train.

JL: Oh?

GK: ... whatever was being done, every single thing which killed them off from the time it was used in building this railroad.

2 JL: Oh?

GK: That [writing] which appears this way on the stone there.

JL: Yes. That's where the Bishop ...

GK: That's where we stood around. He came to see us as we stood around there.

JL: Mhm.

GK: He began to tell a story, you know. He talked a little about it.

JL: Oh?

GK: He had told it to an old man quite a long time ago, as... a long time ago, as ... a long time ago, – this old man was a pretty old person. This he said, – a White-Man, I mean. He wasn't just anybody.

3 JL: Oh?

GK: So then that railway that he was talking about he said a long time ago ..., that one yonder! It's not that one that crosses in Cochrane.

JL: Oh?

GK: ... the one which crosses further along, the what-do-you-call-'ems which go along there, the real ... the trains which go right through the country.

JL: Those ones which go right through the country?

GK: Yes. So he talked about them, long ago as he was telling the story to the

kišê-'yahâwa, êkâ'wâc pêyak ê-yhtakwanokopan' âpacihtâwin.

JL: m-hm.

GK: kêkwân mašîn wîna môna kêkwân takwanokopan.

JL: o?

GK: 'kwâni piko mošê piko anihi[11] ê-papâm'picicik,[12] mistatimwak ê-'m'watêcik anihi kêkwâna, mistatimwak êy-âpatisicik.

JL: otâpacihtâwiniwâw.

GK: êhê.

4 JL: m-hm.

GK: êko mâka nêsta, mistikwa piko êy-âpahtahk 'kwantaw kêkwân êy-oskâtihkâkâniwahk âšokanak êy-ošihihcik.

JL: o?

GK: mistikwak pišišik 'kwantaw.[13]

JL: o?

GK: môna wîna kêkwân pîwâpisk ihtakwanokopan êškw' anim...

JL: o?

GK: ... mošê piko ê-pim'piciwâkopan' tawikahikanihk.[14]

JL: o? hm.

GK: tawikahikâtêkopan pikw êkota mâk' ê-'ši-pimohtêcik aniki ohwâsak[15] kâ-'m'watêcik kwayê'.[16]

5 W1:   [to child] mâc' ântê wanawîtimihk, mâca.

GK: ... kâ-'m'watêcik ayahâwa.

W1:   [to child] wîhtamawik êkâ 'ci-pêci-pîhtokwêcik. tântê wêhc'-itêlimâcik ...[17]

GK: kâ-'m'watêcik ani.

JL: o?

Child: awênihkânak?

GK: [to child] 'kâwila mah ayami. kipêhtâkosin oš'[18] anta.

JL: [laughs] ê-pêhtâkosiyin wâsa ka-ytwân [laughs].

6 GK: êko mâka, anima mâka tawâskokahikan'[19] anihi môna kêkwân ihtakwanôpan ihtâwin. ê'kwâni piko pakwataskamik.[20]

JL: o?

GK: tâpiskôc piko pakwataskamik ê-'mohtâniwahk.

JL: a-ha [laughs].

GK: ê-pimohtâniwahk, ê-pim'picit ôt' 'wênihkân êkâ kâ-wâpahtahk kêkwâniw êkâ nêsta kanak' êškwâ kêkwân ihtâwin ê-'htakwahk. mêkwêskamik piko.

JL: â.[21]

old people, when there mustn't have been even one piece of equipment.

JL: M-hm.

GK: Any machinery, there mustn't even have been any of that.

JL: Oh?

GK: At that time, as they travelled about without equipment, with horses carrying those things, horses doing the work.

JL: Their belongings.

GK: Yes.

4 JL: M-hm.

GK: And then too, only logs were used and any old thing for making supports out of, when trestles were built.

JL: Oh?

GK: Any kind of trees throughout.

JL: Oh?

GK: There can't ever have been any metal used up to that time ...,

JL: Oh?

GK: ... as they must have travelled about just as they were at the railway cut.

JL: Oh? Hm.

GK: I guess a trail used to be cut only at the point where the pack horses walked,

5 W1: [to child] Go on outside, go on!

GK: ... which carried the thing-a-mees.

W1: [to child] Tell them not to come in. How do they think he...?

GK: *They're* the ones who did the carrying.

JL: Oh?

Child: Who are they?

GK: [to child] Don't talk! You can hear your voice there, you know.

JL: [laughs] You'll speak and naturally you'll be heard.

6 GK: So then, at the time of those railway cuts, there was no village of any kind there. It was just hinterland.

JL: Oh?

GK: Just like walking in the open country.

JL: A-ha. [laughs]

GK: Like someone walking, travelling here who never saw anything because there was as yet no kind of village at all. Only muskeg country.

JL: Ah.

GK: môna kêkwân takwanokopan. 'ma takwan ihtâwin; nêsta mâka 'ma
takwan âhkosîwikamik, 'ma takwan ..., 'matêw[22] n'tohkonon.

JL: â-hâ.

GK: êko mâka, mihcêt mâk' ânimôcikâsowak ê-kî-nipicik, êy-âhkosicik
'kwantaw pakwataskamikohk, êkâ ê-...

JL: êhê!

GK: ... êkâ ê-'htât n'tohkonon.

JL: o!

7 GK: ê'kwâni mâk' êtwêt ana kâ-tipâcimot, mâškôc 'sa êy-apwêsicik nêsta,
êkâ mâk' ê-minwâšininik ê-mino-tašîhkêcik ê-piponinik
ê-tahkâyânik.

JL: ê-tahkipanicik![23]

GK: 'kwantaw mâka piko šâk mâškôc iši-tašîhkêwâkopan nêsta.

JL: o!

GK: êkâ mâka nêsta pêyakwanohk ê-k'-îhtâcik,[24] ê-pim'picicik piko tašinê,
tašinê ..., ê-'t'-îsk'-ôšihtâcik[25] mêskanâniw.

JL: o!

GK: ê'kwânimêniw k'-ânimôtahk otâkošîhk.

JL: o?

8 GK: "ispîhci-mistahi '-kî-mino-tôtâtahkok[26] kî'nânaw," itwêw. ôm' ânohc
mâka kîn'nânaw kâ-yšinâkwahk ôta kâ-yš'-îhtâyahk[27] êkâ
'-ohci-mošihtâyâhk ânimisîwin kanakê ôma mêkwâc
kâ-pêci-ošihtâniwahk, mošê[28] piko ê-kîy-ošihtâniwahk.

JL: êhê!

GK: ê-'šinâkwahk oti kîn'nânaw anohc wîna ôca[29] kâ-'mâtisiyahk.

JL: ... ê-mohci-pîhtinikêkâpawiyêk!
    [voice in background]

GK: êko mâka, ê-mohci-pîhtinikêkâpawiyahk piko. kotakiyak mâka wîna
kâ-kî-pêci-ošihtâcik kâ-... kâ-pêciy-âpatisicik, âta misawâc
ê-kî-pêciy-âpatisicik ê-tipahamâhcik kîy-ânimisiwak nâspic.

JL: â?

9 GK: êko mâka wîna ..., anohc mâka wîna kâ-yši-tipahikâniwahk nêsta,
ê-min'-ôhtisîyahk; wînawâw mâka wîn' awasitê ..., awasitê êkâ kêkwân
ê-ohci-... -tipaham'wâwatipanênak.[30]

JL: kêkât mâškôc mošêy âpacihâkaniwiwâkopan.[31]

GK: [interrupting] êhê. kêkât moš' ê-kîy-âpatisicik. anohc mâka kî'nânaw
mitoni moš' ê-pimâtisiyahk mâka tâpwê nôkwan manâ.

GK: There can't have been a thing: there was no settlement; there was no hospital either, there wasn't ..., there was no doctor.

JL: A-ha.

GK: And then, many people are reported to have died, since they had some sickness or other in the hinterland, without any ...

JL: Yes.

GK: ... without there being any doctor.

JL: Oh!

7 GK: And that's what the one telling the story said, perhaps when they perspired too, y'know, with no good place for them to stay in the winter when it's cold.

JL: ... catching a chill!

GK: And any old shack is where they must have lived too.

JL: Oh!

GK: And they couldn't live in just one place, travelling about all the time, all the time, as they completed each lap of the road.

JL: Oh!

GK: That's what he was talking about yesterday.

JL: Oh?

8 GK: "They treated us so well!" he said. It's such a big difference now, here where we're living. We didn't feel the hardship at all while the building was coming along as it was being done for next to nothing.

JL: Right!

GK: I mean the way it looks now, here where we're living.

JL: ... just standing with your hands in your pockets!

[voice in background]

GK: So then, just standing with our hands in our pockets. But the others there, who had come to build who ..., who came to work, although they had come to work anyway and were being paid, they had plenty of hardships.

JL: Ah?

9 GK: And then..., but *now* with the wages we're getting too, we're being well paid. But those ones, it was less..., less they must have been earn..., you must have been paying them.

JL: They must have been working for practically nothing

GK: [interrupting] Right. They worked for almost nothing. But now it really looks as if we live completely for nothing.

JL: ê-hê!

GK: … moš' ê-pimâtisiyahk.

JL: ê'ko wâs' âni.[32]

GK: ê'ko wêhci-pimâtisîyahk mâk' anta kêkwâna kâ-kîy-ošihtâcik.

JL: êkâ mâka 'wâc apišîš wayêš ê-'lâpatisiyahk êy-ohtisiyahk mâka kî'nânaw.

GK: m-hm! ê-hê.

10 JL: êkâ mâk' êy-ohci-ohtisicik aniki kâ-kîy-ânimisicik.

GK: êhê. nêsta mâka, ê-kî-min'-ôšihtâcik animêniw kêkwâniw[33]
kêy-ohci-p'mâtisîwâkêyahk.

JL: â hâ.

GK: tâpiskôc mâk' ê-kî-nihtâwikihcikêcik, êko mâka ê-at'-ohcipan…[34]
-ohtinahk šôniyân ê-'tiy-âpatisiyahk, êh?

JL: ê… hê.

GK: 'kwâni mâka pikw êšinâkwahk tâpwê misiwê[35] âpatisîwin.

JL: ê… hê.

GK: awênihkân …, kîšâc,[36] kîšâc ê-pasikowitât kêkwâniw
kêy-ohci-pimâtisit mêkwâc ê-mino-pimâtisit nêstapiko mêkwâc
êy-oški… ê-pimâtisit, … ki'y-at'-ohci-pimâtisin'ci[37] nîkân ocawâšimiša
'ntê itêhkê.

11 JL: [coughs]

GK: môna wîn' âpatan awênihkân ê-ytên'tahk pâtimâ kiciy-ayâwâcik …
kišê-'ahâwiyânê êkâ kêkwân kî-tôtamâsoyânê.[38] môna. môna
kîy-âpatisîmakan anima.

JL: ha … ha![39]

GK: mâmaskâtên'tâkwan oti ôma ê-'spîhci-mâmaskâsinâkosit mâna
'wênihkân[40] tahtwâw ê-'yamihê'-kîšikâki ê-papanit otâpânihk!

JL: ê… hê!

GK: misiwê mâka mîna ma…

JL: [in background] šôniyânihkâkêw mâk' animêniw.

GK: … ati-šôniyânihkâkêw, misiwê 'nimêniw 'wênihkân.

JL: êhê.

12 GK: nêsta mîn' ôta k'-âtiy-âšawakâmipanihâcik[41] wêmistikôšiwa. mîna
ê-pêci-âšawakâmipanihâcik, âsay, âšay nâspic mistah' îspaniw antê
šôniyân.

JL: êhê.

GK: wêškac mâka wîna môna kîy-ohci-takwan anima tôwi-kêkwân kanakê;
âpatisîwin piko 'ci-whci-pimâtisit[42] 'wênihkân. 'kwâni piko ê-n'tawihot.

JL: It does!

GK: … living for free.

JL: That's it, sure enough.

GK: So we subsist from the things which they built.

JL: Even though we work at it only a little, *we're* getting paid.

GK: We are! Right.

10 JL: Because *they* didn't get paid, the ones who had the hardship.

GK: Yes. And also, it's a good job they made of that thing from which we'll
        be making our living.

JL: A-ha.

GK: As if they had planted, then there began to result…, we got money from
        it as we began to work, eh?

JL: Ye-es

GK: That's what every job really looks like anyway.

JL: Right.

GK: Anybody [is wise] … ahead of time, in opening up something ahead of
        time from which he can make a living while he's doing well or while
        he's still young … in life … so his children will have something to live
        on in the future on ahead.

11 JL: [*coughs*]

GK: There's no use in a person's thinking that later on they will have it …
        when I'm an old man and can't do anything for myself. No. That can't
        work.

JL: Right!

GK: It's amazing, that is, the unusual sight of so many people coming on the
        train every Sunday.

JL: Right, indeed!

GK: But everybody again is mak…

JL: [*in background*] He [the Railway] is making money out of that, though.

GK: … everybody's beginning to make money on that.

JL: Yes.

12 GK: And again when they take the White-Men across here. When they
        bring them across again, by now, by now there's very big money
        involved there.

JL: Yeah.

GK: In the olden days, that kind of thing didn't exist at all; there was only
        work that a person could make his living from. Only hunting.

JL: ê'kwân' nêsta mwêhci êtâcimospan wêmistikôšiw nîpinohk antê kâ-k'-îšy-âpatisiyân.

GK: mhm.

JL: antê, a... oskôtim[43] kâ-yhtakwahk.[44]

GK: mhm.

JL: alîkiš[45] kâ-itihcik aniki wêmistikôšiwak.

13 GK: mhm.

JL: êwakwâniki!

GK: kââ!

JL: ay'hâw mitoni cîtawišôkaninâkosiw wâkisiw ê-'mohtêt ana kišê-'niw ana.

GK: mhm.

JL: ê-kî-tiskôsot.[46]

GK: mhm.

JL: ê-kî-pahkišin'ci ê-kî-tasôsot asiniya?

GK: mhm.

JL: ê-pahkisikâniwahk?

GK: mhm.

JL: cîpayikamikwa oš' âni mâka nêst' ihtakwanw' anta.

GK: êhê.

14 JL: êkâ mâka 'wâc ê-kî-kihcipalikopanê 'wênihkân ê-nip..., ê-nipâ..., ê-nipahišihk, ê-nipahikot kê'wâ'hkân'niw. pakwantaw pikw ê-yši-nahîhkawâkaniwit.

GK: ê'kwâni mwêhci kâ-itâcimot anima. nôkosiwak kiyâpac aniki tôwi-cîpayâhtikwak ant' ê-'mišihkik[47] aniki.

JL: êhê.

GK: tahto-nîpin oti k'-âhcî'hcik ôko kâ-wâpipêhikâsocik oti, wâpipêhwâkaniwanwak wâsa,[48] aniki kâ-kihci-'wênihkâniwicik kâ-k'-îši-nânipicik.

JL: êhê.

GK: ant' ê-pimišihkik nîstam kâ-pêci-takwahk mêskanaw ôm' âskîhk.

JL: êkot' oš' âni mâka nêsta wakic oskôtim[49] cêmasot an' âsiniy?

15 GK: êhê.

JL: ana tôwihkân mâk' ôca kâ-cimasot kâ-tipâcimât.

GK: êhê.

JL: kâ-masinâsocik oti kâ-kî-nipicik.

GK: mhm. ê'kwâna.

JL: That's exactly what the White-Man used to tell too, there where I worked last summer.

GK: M-hm.

JL: There, th... where the dam is.

GK: M-hm.

JL: Those White-Men who are called 'Frog'.

13 GK: M-hm.

JL: Those are the ones!

GK: Oh, so that's it!

JL: Well, that old man looks completely stiff in the hips, he's bent over walking.

GK: M-hm.

JL: It's because he had a back injury.

GK: M-hm.

JL: Because he was trapped when a rock fell on him.

GK: M-hm.

JL: When they were dynamiting?

GK: M-hm.

JL: And of course the graveyards are there too.

GK: Yes.

14 JL: And then nobody could apparently even be shipped out when he d..., when he die..., when he died from a fall ..., when he was killed by something or other. They just buried him any old place.

GK: That's the same thing exactly as he was saying. Crosses of that kind are still to be seen where those people are lying.

JL: Ya-as.

GK: Every summer the ones that are painted white are changed, that is, they're painted white y'know, those persons of some importance who had died here and there.

JL: Yes.

GK: There they were lying when the railroad first came in this country.

JL: And it's right there of course too, on top of the dam that stone stands up?

15 GK: Right.

JL: And that's the kind, that stands up there, that he told them about.

GK: Yes.

JL: With those listed, that is, who had died.

GK: Uh-huh. That's the one.

JL: mihcêt oš' âni nêst' anta kî-nipiwak.

GK: cikêm' ânima! tahto man' âni pikw anima ê-... pêyak ohci
kâ-k'-îši-kîšihtâniwahk; mîna mâka kotak
ê-'tiy-âniskôhcêhtâniwahk[50] otâpânêskanaw, ê'kwâna pêyak
asiniy k'-ânimôcikâtêk[51] anima.

JL: â. êhê.

GK: ihtâtokwê mâk' ana nêst' an' êy-ânimôcikâtêk mâmaw,[52] ...

JL: mhm.

GK: ... misiwêskamikâk. ê-mišikitit ana tôwa, tâpiskôc cîpayi-mistikwat,
was' ânih tâpiskôc itên'tâkosiw.

16 JL: êhê. ê'kwâni.

GK: ê'kwân' êtastêk an'm.

JL: môna mâka nêsta kêkwân 'htakwanokopan kêkât kêkwân'hkân
êy-âpatisîmakahk.

GK: môna.

JL: mêkwâc kâ-ošihtâniwahk anima.

GK: ê'kwânimêniw nêsta kâ-tipâtôtahk ana kâ-tipâcimot kâ-'twêyân.

JL: mhm.

GK: môna nêsta kêkwân ihtakwanokopan kêšišaw kêkwân wînâhcikan
êškw' anima.

JL: âhâ.

GK: aw... astisak ihtâwâkopan ...,[53] kâ-maškawisicik piko.

17 JL: êhê.

GK: êko mâka wîna môna kêkwân êškwâh nâspic takwanokopan kêkwân'
kâ-kakîšiwâki,[54] anim' ispiš wêškac oš' âni animêniw k'-ânimôtahk
wêškac ...

JL: o?

GK: ... wêškac animêniw. môna wîn' ânohc. kišê-'yahâw it..., wâsa itwêw
anihi kâ-kîy-âniskêy-âcimostâkot kiyâpac mâka
kîy-ati-âniskêy-âcimostawâkaniwan nêst' ana kâ-kî-tipâcimostâkot.

JL: âšay mâškôc kêkât n'kotwâsomitana niyâlošâp piponwa n'titêlimâw
ana, ana wêmistikôšiw nîla kâ-tipâcimak.

GK: mhm.

JL: "n'tôškinîkihtay mâk'," itwêw ...

18 GK: [*interrupting*] mhm.

JL: nîswâsošâp, nîswâsošâp ošâ n'titihtawâw.

GK: mhm.

JL: Quite a great many died there.

GK: That's for sure! ... Every time just that one ... where one section had been completed; and again when another railway line is connected, that is the particular stone [erected] when that matter is talked about.

JL: Oh! Uh-huh.

GK: But that stone must be there with the account all together, ...

JL: M-hm.

GK: ... [from] all over the country. That big kind, like a coffin, it seems like that [i.e., a headstone such as one for a coffin].

16 JL: Yes. That's it.

GK: That's the way it is.

JL: There must have been almost nothing, no kind of machinery,

GK: No.

JL: ... while that was being constructed.

GK: That's what that fellow who was telling the story told all about, whom I mentioned.

JL: M-hm.

GK: Also, up to that time there must hardly have been anything by way of clothing,

JL: Ye-es.

GK: Thi..., there can't have been any gloves..., only the hard ones.

17 JL: Right.

GK: And then too, there can't yet have been much of anything warm, right up 'til then a long time back, the time he's talking about long ago ...

JL: Oh?

GK: ... that story of long ago. Not right now. The old fellow sai... said of course that when he in turn had been told this story by that person, it still kept being passed on by that person also who had told it to him.

JL: I think perhaps he's nearly sixty-five years old, that White-Man *I'm* talking about.

GK: M-hm.

JL: "I was a young man," he said ...

18 GK: [interrupting] M-hm.

JL: Seventeen, he was seventeen evidently, I understood him to say.

GK: M-hm.

JL: tahto-piponêsikopan.

GK: mhm.

JL: kâ-ošihtâwâkopanê 'nimêniw.

GK: cikêm' anima wêškac šâkoc anima.

JL: iskwâ wês' âni mâk' anima?

GK: mhm.

JL: nîšwâ mitâhtomitana niyânânêw'mitana ... nê'šâp oša n'tên'tên.

GK: kââ!

JL: ispîhc'-îšpâw antê otih nîhci,

GK: mhm.

19 JL: ê-nîšâhtawîpaliyâhk ê-kî-n'tawi-kanawâpahtamâhk.

GK: mhm.

JL: pêyak mâk' an' âsiniy, pêyak mâk' an' âsiniy kâ-wanastêk[55] ê-'ši-šihkâpêšihk?[56]

GK: mhm.

JL: '-ohci-nakâhikâtêk[57] anim' oskôtim.

GK: â... hâ.

JL: êkwâni pêyak ana kâ-nimitâwêšihk, êkot' ân' êši-'mišihk pêyak anta pîhci asinîskâhk ...

GK: mhm.

JL: ... ê-k'-îši-kipopalit pikw anta

20 GK: kââ! m... hm.

JL: ha ha!

GK: wêškac wês' an' tâpwê.[58]

JL: âšay wâsa ta-kî-pîhtwânânaw.

GK: mhm.

JL: pitamâ. (ay'hâw oš' âni wêhci-n'tawêlimisk 'ci-ayamiwat anta, êkâ ê-kilika-wêpinaman ê-ayamiyan.)[59]

GK: môna wâsa wîna ê-kinaka-wêpinahk 'wênihkân. pêyakwan piko ê-'ši-kîšawêt[60] âtawîna tâpw' 'wênihkân, manâ?

JL: a... ha!

GK: pêyak ...,

21 JL: âpihta' wâsa mâka ..., âpihta' wâsa mâka kilika-wêpinamwak ôta wîla[61] ê-'yamicik.

GK: pêpîtoš išinihkâtamwak kêkwâna mihcêt ...,[62] mistahi. môna mâk' anima kinakiš... itwêmakan wîna kîna kitayamiwin ...

JL: môna.

JL: That's how old he must have been.

GK: M-hm.

JL: When they were building that, I gather.

GK: Of course that was a really long time ago.

JL: It was after that, though?

GK: M-hm.

JL: It was actually two hundred and eighty ... four feet, I think.

GK: Is that so?!

JL: That's how high it is there, that is, below,

GK: M-hm.

19 JL: ... as we went down by elevator when we had gone to look at it.

GK: M-hm.

JL: [you know] one of those stones..., one of those stones tapering down over that way?

GK: M-hm.

JL: ... by which that dam is reinforced.

GK: Yes I do.

JL: So one of those buttresses, one fell right there in amidst the cement...

GK: M-hm.

JL: ... and just closed it in there.

20 GK: Is that so! Well!

JL: Ha-ha!

GK: That was really a long time ago.

JL: It's time for a smoke now.

GK: M-hm.

JL: That's all for now. (He wants you to talk there because you don't mix up your language.)

GK: Yes, that's not someone mixing it up! I'm a person who really talks the same language regardless, eh?

JL: Right!

GK: One ...,

21 JL: Here they mix it up half and half though ... half and half as they talk.

GK: They call many things by different names..., a good deal. But you don't mee... your way of talking doesn't sound that way...

JL: No.

GK: ... since you speak properly. Everything has a name in Cree; but

215

GK: ... ê-'ninîmoyin wîna kwayask. misiwê piko kêkwân' êninîmôwinihk iši-wîhcikâtêw'; âtiht mâka wîna 'ci-kinika-wêpinahkik wêmistikôšîmowin; mayêw anima wîna ininîmowin.

JL: mayêw [coughs]. tân'k' itê[63] mâka mîna k'-êtâcimoyin?

GK: môna n'kiskên'tên.

JL: êškwâ pitamâ. êškwâ pitamâ. ê'kwâni pitamâ.

GK: m... hm.

JL: ê'kwâni. [to CDE, who has just come in] kipaha pitamâ. môn' êškwâ.

when some people mix it up with English, that's not Indian talk.

JL: It isn't [*coughs*]. I wonder what story you'll tell now.

GK: I don't know.

JL: Wait a bit! Wait a bit! That's enough for now.

GK: M-hm.

JL: That's enough. [*to CDE, who has just come in*] Shut it off first. Not yet.

Ayamihitowin [II]

1   JL: âšay pitamâ …

      GK: âšay, âšay wêškac n'kî-pônihtâhtay kâ-papâm'paniyâpân mân' ôtê wînipêkohk.[1]

      JL: o?

      GK: nakiska n'kî-pôn'htân, …

      JL: o?

      GK: … ê-wî-kakwê-kâhcitinamân âpatisiwin.

      JL: a… ha.

      GK: mihcêtwâ mâka n'kî-pêc'-îtohtân ôta mošê êkâ '-kî-'yâyân âpatisiwin. nakiskaw…, wêsâ mâka nakiskaw n'titohtêhtay ê-nîpihk piko.

      JL: m…hm.

2   GK: êko mâka, mîna mîna m'pêc'-îtohtân tahto-nîpin. n'titohtâhtay mâk' âtawîna nôhcimihk ê-n'ṫawihoyân, …

      JL: a… ha.

      GK: … mêkwâ-pipon.

      JL: o?

      GK: êko mâka, ê-minoskamihk mîna m'pêc'-îtohtâhtay ôta.

      JL: o?

      GK: kêka, kêka n'kîy-ati-kâhcitinên apišîš âpatisiwin. môna m'pônihtân.

      JL: o?

      GK: 'toskam[2] n'kocihtân, 'toskam.

      JL: o?

      GK: kêka 'sa mâka n'kîy-at'-îhtân ôt' ê-pipohk.

3   JL: o?

      GK: âšay mâka wayêš nîswâso-pipon ôta kâ-'htâyân awasitê mâškôc.

      JL: o?

      GK: nêstapiko niyânânêw'-pipon âšay ispanîtokwê.[3]

      JL: o?

      GK: êko mâka, kêka 'sa mâka n'kîy-ati-kâhcitinên apišîš âpatisiwin ôt' ê-'htâyân.

      JL: o?

      GK: kihciwê kihciwê kêkât piko tâpwê kwayask n'kîy-ati-âpatisin.[4]

      JL: a… ha.

      GK: pîniš mâk' ôm' ânohc kâ-'t'-êti-kâhcitinamân[5] tâpwê 'ci-ati-âpatisiyân

A conversation [II]

1 JL: First of all now ...

   GK: Now, it's a long time now since I had stopped travelling here regularly on the Bay.

   JL: Oh?

   GK: I quit it for a while,

   JL: Oh?

   GK: ... because I wanted to try to get work.

   JL: O-ho!

   GK: I often came here for nothing, 'cause I couldn't have any work. For a time..., for too little time I used to come in the summer only.

   JL: M-hm.

2 GK: So then, I used to come again and again every summer. I used to come even though I went hunting in the bush,

   JL: O-ho.

   GK: ... in mid-winter.

   JL: Oh?!

   GK: And then, when it was open water I would come here again.

   JL: Oh?

   GK: At long last I began to get a little work. I didn't let up.

   JL: Oh?

   GK: I kept on trying and trying.

   JL: Oh?

   GK: And finally then, I began to stay here in the winter.

3 JL: Oh?

   GK: And by now I've been here probably around seven years or more.

   JL: Oh?

   GK: Or it must already be eight years.

   JL: Oh?

   GK: And then, at last I began to get a little work since I was here.

   JL: Oh?

   GK: Finally there was nothing else for it, I began to work properly in earnest.

   JL: Yes, I see.

   GK: Up to this time, however, I kept on getting job after job, so that now

ôma 'iš.[6]

JL: a... ha.

4 GK: âšay mâka môna n'tawâc ôma nâšic n'tên'tên, n'ka-pônihtân ôm' ê-'patisiyân nêstapiko n'ka-n'tawihon 'c'-îtên'tamân, ...

JL: m... hm.

GK: ... 'ci-wanihikêyân otih.

JL: êhê. n'kiskên'tên nêsta âšay êkâ ê-'kitêk ayôwin.[7]

GK: mhm. n'kiskisihtay âšay êkâ ê-'kitêk ayôwin. âšay môna kî-whci-pimâtisinâniwan anima. apišîš wîna pikw[8] ê-tôcikâtê k'wân,[9] ...

JL: êhê.

GK: ... pâtimâ piko ê-mišâk[10] ayôwin kâ-iši-wanihikâniwahk, nêsta mâk' ênikohk 'tôtaman.

JL: m... hm.

5 GK: môna mâka wîn' anim' ihkin âpatisiwin.

JL: a... ha.

GK: kitanwêpin tahtwâ kâ-kîšikâk. kin'taw'-pîhtokwân kîhkihk.

JL: a... ha.

GK: mîna mîna kitati-kihtohtân, piko ê-yhtakwahk tašinê kê-k'-îš'-îhtâyin.

JL: aha.

GK: êko mâka wîn' ê-n'tawihoyin nâspic âniman.

JL: a... ha.

GK: nâspic âniman. tahtwâ kâ-kîšikâk kitôšihtân pîtoš kîki. mîna kikotawân.

JL: ê-kapêšiyan.

GK: ... ê-kapêšiyan. mîna kitâpatisin anta.

6 JL: môna mâka kikêhcinâhon 'ci-kaškihtâyin kêkwân ... anim' ê-kîšikâk kâ-walawîyin.

GK: môna. môna wîskâc. môna wîskâc ...

           [simultaneously]

JL: êko mâka wîn' êy-âpatisiyan mâka wîna, kikêhcinâhon tân' i'kohk[11] kê-kaškihtâyin.

GK: êhê. êk' ôtih mâka wîna pîsimohkânihk mâk' ê-'ši-tipahamâkawiyin nêsta.

JL: êhê.

GK: ê-kî-tipahamâkawiyin nêst' anima. nêsta mâka awâšišak wînawâw tipinawê 'ta-kîy-ati-pimâcihitisôwak nîkân itêhkê kišâspin êkâ

I have a steady job, right up to now.

JL: Ah, yes.

4 GK: Now I'm not very much inclined to think that I'll quit this work or to think that I'll go hunting ...,

JL: M-hm.

GK: ... trapping, that is.

JL: Yes. I know that fur doesn't pay much now either.

GK: M-hm. I was thinking back that by now fur didn't pay much. One can't live on that now. Only a little bit can be done ...,

JL: Yes.

GK: ... unless the fur is big on the trapping grounds, and you work hard.

JL: M-hm.

5 GK: But employment is not like that.

JL: Right.

GK: You take it easy every day. You go into your home.

JL: Right.

GK: You keep on going off to your job, because there'll always be a place where you can live.

JL: Right.

GK: But then when you go hunting, it's very hard.

JL: Right.

GK: It's very hard. Every day you make your home in a different place. You light up a fire again ...,

JL: As you're camping.

GK: ... as you're camping. Again you work there.

6 JL: You can't be sure of earning anything ... on that day that you go out.

GK: No. Not ever. Never ...

[simultaneously]

JL: So then, when it comes to your working, you're sure how much you'll make.

GK: Yes. And for that matter it's by the clock that you're paid as well.

JL: Yes.

GK: You were paid for that as well. And the children themselves too, they'll be able to begin supporting themselves in the future if they don't stop

pônihtâtwâwê 'nima kâ-yskôniwicik. êniwêhk 'ta-'ti-kaškihôwak nêsta.

JL: m... hm.

7 GK: âšay nôkwan misiwê 'nima nâspic ê-'ti-kaškihocik
ininiwî-'wâšišak.

JL: a.

GK: ... êkâ otih kâ-pônihtâcik...,

JL: mhm.

GK: ... ê-kiskinohamâhcik, ...

JL: mhm.

GK: ... kêy-ihtit 'sa mâka piko šâkoc 'wênihkân ê-'ši-kisisawisît. ê'kwâni
piko šâkoc kê-yšinâkwahk ât' ê-kaškihot.

JL: ê... hê.

8 GK: 'ta-ihkin nêsta 'wênihkân êkâ nâspic 'ci-kî-..., piko ...-pimâcihitisot
kišišaw wêsâ ..., kâ-wî-kihtimit.

JL: a... ha.

GK: nêstapiko wêsa kâ-wî-šaškatên'tahk êy-âpatisit.

JL: êhê. êhê. côsip tôwa [laughs].

GK: wêsâ kêkât... wêsâ mâmâš âpatisiw. wêsâ mistahi nôcihtâw
'kwantaw'-kêkwâniw, ...

JL: mm.

GK: ... êkâ wayêš kâ-itâpatahk, êkâ kanakê kâ-wîcihikot
'ci-kî-pimâcihitisot.

JL: êko wâs' âni pêškiš mâka nêsta kâ-wanâhikot 'wênihkân.

GK: ê'kwâni kâ-wanâhikot 'wênihkân wêsâ, wêsâ ê-kakêpâtisit.[12]

JL: êhê.

9 GK: âskaw awa 'ta-ayapîpan 'ci-mâmitonên'tahk wîkihk.

JL: êhê.

GK: ... kêkwâniw kê-tôtahk 'ci-ohci-pimâcihot. kêka mâka
ta-kiskên'tamôpan.

JL: êhê.

GK: ta-wâpahtamôpan tâpiskôc kâ-akimat kišôniyânim[13] tân' inikohk
kê-mêstinaman kêkwân ê-wîy-ošihtâyin.

JL: m... hm.

GK: ê'kwâni pêyakwan mwêhci êspanik, ê-mâmitonên'taman êy-apiyan.[14]

JL: m... hm.

GK: môna wîna pišišik piko 'ci-mêtawêyin, nêstapiko 'c'-îtohtêyin misiwê
kêkwân, šôw[15] kâ-ytocikâtêk, nêstapiko kotakîy ê-'ši-mêtawâniwahk

going to school. They'll be really competent too.

JL: M-hm.

7 GK: Already all that is evident as the Indian children develop marked ability.

JL: Yeah.

GK: ... the ones, that is, who don't give up ...

JL: M-hm.

GK: ... being taught,

JL: M-hm.

GK: ... it will depend for sure on a person's particular cleverness. That's just what it will look like for sure, even though he's got ability.

JL: That's right.

8 GK: It'll happen too that a person won't be very well able to ... only... support himself capably ..., who wants to be too lazy.

JL: Right.

GK: Or anyone who gets too fed up with working.

JL: Yes. Yes. A fellow like Joseph [pseudonym]. [laughs]

GK: Almost too ... he works too haphazardly. He's too much occupied with something of no importance.

JL: M-hm.

GK: ... which is no use for anything, and doesn't help him at all to make a living.

JL: But even so, that's what spoils a person too.

GK: That's what spoils a person when he's too, too stupid.

JL: Yes.

9 GK: Sometimes this fellow would sit around at home to think things over ...

JL: Yes.

GK: ... what he would do to support himself. But finally it would come to him.

JL: Yes.

GK: He should see it as when you count your money [so you know] how much you'll spend when you want to make something.

JL: M-hm.

GK: That goes exactly the same way, when you sit and think it over.

JL: M-hm.

GK: Not just for you to be constantly playing, nor to go to every show which is put on, or other kind of entertainment so that you go every day in

'c'-îtohtêyin tahtwâ ê-kîsikâk êkâ 'ci-patahaman.

10 JL: a... ha.

GK: êniwêhk mistah' ispaniw anima, êy-akihcikâtêk wîna.

JL: a... ha.

GK: êy-akihcikâtêk. šâkoc mâka wîna êkâ wîskâc kêkwâniw êy-akihtahk ininiw, môna kanakê kiskên'tam tâni kâ-kî-tôtahk otânâhk misiwê kêkwân:

JL: môna.

GK: tân' inikohk kâ-mêstinât šôniyân' anta;

JL: a... ha.

GK: tân' înikohk kâ-ošihât šôniyâna; tân' înikohk kâ-âpacihât mîciminiw nêstapiko wînâhcikan ...

JL: a... ha.

[simultaneously]

GK: ... pêyakwâ ê-pipohk. misiwê mâka kâ-tôcikâtêki anihi, êniwêhk osâw[16] ispaniw antê, šôw nêstapiko pinkoh nêstapiko kotakîy ê-'ši-mêtawâniwahk.

JL: ... ê-'tohtâniwahk.

11 GK: êhê. ê'kwân' êši-macipan'cik âtiht anima, wêsâ misiwê kêkwân kâ-wîy-âpacihtâniwahk.[17] môna 's' âtawîna nimacênimâwak ôma kâ-'twêyân; šâkoc mâka n'titwân piko 'ci-akihtahkipan misiw' 'wênihkân kêkwân, tân' inikohk kê-âpacihtât kici-kiskên'tahk tân' inikohk kê-yspanit kêkwâniw ê-wî-wšihtât.

JL: êhê.

GK: tân' inikohk mêstinât nêsta šôniyâna ant' ê-'tohtêt šôw, êkâ mâka wayêš ê-'tâpatahk.

JL: êhê.

GK: ... tâpiskôc moš' ê-kî-wêpinât.

JL: nôkosiwak anim' ê-'šinâkosicik âtiht nâspic mistahi.

GK: m... hm. mihcêt.

12 JL: mâcik' âniki kâ-mâmihcêticik!

[simultaneously]

GK: m... hm.

JL: pêyakwâ ê-'htohtêcik anima kâ-cahkâstêpanihcikâniwahk, kistinâc anta nîšohtay mêstinêwak šôliyâna, ...

GK: mhm.

JL: ... anim' ê-tôtahkik.

order not to miss it.

10 JL: Uh-huh.

GK: That sure costs a lot when it's reckoned up.

JL: Uh-huh.

GK: When it's reckoned up. But for sure, when a person doesn't ever reckon up anything, he has no idea at all what he's done in the past with everything:

JL: No.

GK: ... how much money he spent there.

JL: Uh-huh.

GK: how much money he made; how much he used on groceries or clothing ...

JL: Uh-huh.

[simultaneously]

GK: ... in one year. But all those things which are carried on, most money goes there, the show or bingo or some other games that people play.

JL: ... going to them.

11 GK: Yes. That's why some people have a bad time of it who want luxuries. I'm not running them down, nonetheless, in what I'm saying. I'm only saying that everyone should keep an account of things, how much he uses so that he knows how much it will come to when he wants to do something.

JL: Yes.

GK: How much money he spends also going to the show, when it doesn't do him any good.

JL: Yes.

GK: ... as though you had thrown it away for nothing

JL: Some of them appear very much that way.

GK: M-hm. Many.

12 JL: Look at the large families!

[simultaneously]

GK: M-hm.

JL: When they go to the show once, they most likely spend two dollars there,

GK: M-hm.

JL: ... in doing that.

GK: tâpwê.

JL: môna mâka pêyakwâ piko ê-..., ê-... cahkâstêpalihcikâniwan[18] ê-...

GK: m... hm.

JL: ... pêyakwâ '-tawâstêk.

GK: kanakê nêwâ cahkâstêpanihcikâniwan pêyakwâ ê-tawâstêk.

JL: âskaw oša[19] mêšikwan'-tipiskâw w'n'[20] antê ministikohk.[21]

13 GK: êhê. ê'kwâni kâ-yspanik ôta nêst' aspin kâ-ihtakwahk ôma lîcin.[22]

JL: êhê. aniki mâka kâ-minwên'tahkik ê-kanwâpahtahkik anim'
         ê-cahkâstêpanihcikâniwahk ...

GK: m... hm.

JL: miton' ê-..., môna patahamwak.

GK: m... hm.

JL: mitoni piko mêsakwanâpan.

GK: m... hm.

JL: mistahi mâk' ispanîtokwê pêyako-tawâstêw.

GK: m... hm.

JL: mistahi ta-whcîmakanôpan mîcim ...

14 GK: šâkoc. tâpwê mistahi ta-yspanîpan ...

JL: ... ispîš wîna ê-nanôhtêpanicik ... 'ci-ohci-pimâtisicik.

         [*simultaneously*]

GK: ... šôniyân ana ... êhê. mâcika, nîšo tawâstêw' êkâ ê-'tohtêyin šôw, nîšo
         tawâstêwa mâka, kanawênimat[23] ana kišôniyânim.

JL: a... ha.

GK: êniwêhk mistahi ta-'spanîpan mîcim 'ci-kîy-otinikêyin...
         'ci-kîy-ohci-pimâtisiyin.

JL: m... hm.

GK: ... âta mitâhtwahtay êy-ispanik.

JL: ê... hê.

GK: mistah' anima mitâht'ahtay.

JL: a... ha. [*clears throat*]

15 GK: êniwêhk âtiht môna tâpwê kêkwâniw nahastamâsowak n'tênimâwak
         ininiwak ôta. môna kêkwâniw wanastâwak, nîkân
         kêy-ohci-'ti-pimâtisin'ci ocawâšimišiwâwa kanakê.

JL: môna wês' âni mitoni mân' otih mâmitonên'tamwak tâni kê-tôtahkik, ...

GK: êhê. m... hm.

JL: ... apišîš otih kêy-iši-kinopanik êy-âpatisi..., êy-âpatahk kêkwân.

GK: That's true.

JL: They don't have only one er..., er..., show, when...,

GK: M-hm.

JL: ... in one week.

GK: There's a show at least four times in one week.

JL: Sometimes, as you know, it's every night over on the Island.

13 GK: Yes. That's what's been happening here too since there's been this Legion.

JL: Yes. But those who like it looking at the moving-picture show...

GK: M-hm.

JL: They utterly uh..., they won't miss it.

GK: M-hm.

JL: Just pretty well every day.

GK: M-hm.

JL: It must cost quite a lot in a week, though.

GK: M-hm.

JL: A good deal of food would come from it ...

14 GK: Right enough. It would come to quite an amount...

JL: ... instead of their running short ... of their source of livelihood,

[simultaneously]

GK: ... that money. Yes. Look now, for two weeks by not going to the show, for two weeks, you save your money there.

JL: Uh-huh.

GK: It would sure come to a lot of food you could buy to live on...

JL: M-hm.

GK: ... even though it amounts to [only] ten dollars.

JL: Yes indeed.

GK: Ten dollars is quite a lot.

JL: Uh-huh. [clears throat]

15 GK: I sure think that some people here certainly don't put anything by for themselves. They don't set up anything from which their children will live in the future at all.

JL: They don't give any thought, that is, to what they'll do,

GK: Yes. M-hm.

JL: ... how a little something, that is, will stretch out in work..., in being used.

GK: môna nêsta mâka ê'kwâni piko têpinâhk ê-'ši-n'tawi... ê-mîcisocik, ...

JL: a...ha.

GK: ... êy-ašamikocik kihc'-okimâwa.[24]

JL: âtiht oti.

16 GK: ê-... môna mâka kanakê wîcihitisôwak.

JL: m... hm.

GK: môna wî-wîcihitisôwak nîkân-itêhkê. ocawâšimišiwâwa mâka êškw' ânimêniw ta-mošihtâniwa.

JL: êhê.

GK: kâ-k'-îhticik wâsa piko aniki kâ-kîy-ohpikihitahkok, ...

JL: ... kâ-k'-îši-kiskinohamâtahkok ...

GK: ... kâ-k'-îši-kiskinohamâtahkok mâka, nêsta kî'nânaw kicawâsimišinawak ê'kwânimêniw kê-'ti-mošihtâcik.

JL: m... hm.

GK: mâtik' anim' mâka, šâkoc âpatan ê-kî-kiskinohamâkawiyahk kisisawisîwinihk itêhkê.

JL: êhê.

17 GK: mihcêtwâ nîna n'kî-'yân anima nâspic.

JL: ê'kwâni.

GK: ... ê-k'-îši-wîhtamâkawiyân kêkwân mêkwâc nêsta 'ci-'ti-waniškâyân ê-'ti-wâpahk. atoskam atoskam ê-'ti-waniškâcišâhokawiyân, n'kî-tôtên.

JL: ê'kwâni mân' ê-'tak ana ..., ana n'kosis.

GK: m... hm.

JL: ay'hâw, ê-... anim' ot' ê-šikicišahwak kê'wâ'hkâniw[25] 'ci-tôtahk.

GK: ê-hê.

JL: âšay mîna mitoni nâpê' n'tiš'-âpacihikawihtay, n'tilâpacihikawihtay[26] anim' ê-'spîhtisîyân kâ-'spîhtisîyan nêta.

GK: m... hm.

18 JL: "môna n'kîy-ohci-'yân nîna nâspic mistahi 'ci-mêtawêyân awasitê 'spîš êy-âpatisiyân ..., nîkihk," n'titâw.

GK: ê'kwân ê-'hkihkipan[27] tâpwê.

JL: "n'kî-šîhkacišahokawin 'ci-âpatisiyân," n'titâw.

GK: misiwê 'wênihkân 'kwâni kâ-ytit wêskac. anohc mâka, âšay mitoni môna kanakê kiskinohamâsowak âpatisiwininiw awâšišak.

JL: kišâstaw oš' âni mân' âskaw niwîyatisîhkâhtay.

GK: m... hm.

GK: And not only that, as long as they go off..., to eat,

JL: Uh-huh.

GK: ... receiving government rations.

JL: Some, that is.

16 GK: In..., but they are of no help to themselves at all.

JL: No.

GK: They don't want to help themselves for the future. But their children will still feel it.

JL: Yes.

GK: The way they lived who brought us up...,

JL: ... the way they taught us...

GK: ... the way they taught us though, your children and mine will have the same feeling too.

JL: M-hm.

GK: Look at that though, – it sure is useful to have been taught along smart lines.

JL: Yes.

17 GK: *I* had that [kind of teaching] many times, a great deal.

JL: Quite!

GK: ... I was told something during that time too, that I should get up early in the morning. Since I was told to get up, whether I would or no, I did it.

JL: That's what I keep telling that..., that son of mine.

GK: M-hm.

JL: Well, as... it's to urge him to do something here.

GK: Yes.

JL: I already used to do a man's work, I used to do that job when I was about as big as you there [*looking at a picture of GK*].

GK: M-hm.

18 JL: "I didn't have very much opportunity to play, rather than work ..., in my home," I say to him.

GK: That's the way things used to be.

JL: "They got after me to work," I say to him.

GK: That's what every person said to me long ago. But now, now the children absolutely don't learn work at all.

JL: Gosh, but sometimes, y'know, it used to be funny when I did it.

GK: Yeah.

JL:	n'tawâš'šîwihtay oš' âni.

GK:	m...hm.

JL:	nêw mâk' atimwak n'kîy-âpacihâhtay êy-âwacitâpêyân mihta.

GK:	m... hm!

JL:	pâtimâ mitoni mân' âskaw nêtê 'kâmihk n'tiši-wâpamâhtay n'têmak ê-nakacipahicik êkâ ê-kî-... êkâ kwayask ê-kî-šâkohakik [laughs].

19	GK:	êko mâka ...

JL:	ê'kwâni mâka mâna ê-'tâcimostawakik, ê-ytak an' ê-wîhtamawak. anohc mâk' awâšišak êkâ wâci pêyak kâ-kiskinohamâhcik,[28] 'wâc apišîš ê-kiskinohamawâkaniwicik, šâkoc 'ci-âpatisicik[29] mâna n'titâwak.

GK:	m... hm. tâpwê! tâpwê kîy-âniman wîna wêskac ispîš anohc. ê-wêhtahk mâka nâspic kici-kî-pimâcihot awênihkân anohc.

JL:	m... hm.

GK:	ât' ê-kîy-ânimahkipan wêskac ê-pimâcihonâniwahkipan šâkoc mâk' êkâ kêkwân ê-takwahkipan piko.

JL:	m... hm.

GK:	mitoni mâka kwayask ê-pimâcihitisospan 'wênihkân ...

JL:	... šâkoc ê-wî-mîcisonâniwahk.

20	GK:	m... hm. anohc mâka wîna, misiwê kêkwân takwan mašîn kwayask 'ci-kî-pimâcihitisot 'wênihkân.

JL:	m... hm.

GK:	papâm'paniw tântê wâ-itohtêt. kâ-..., nêstapiko 'kwantaw piko pakwataskamihkohk kâ-yhtâcik papâmihnâwak.

JL:	kâ-pim'paniki pîwâpiskwa êy-âpatahki.

GK:	êhê. êncinim misiwê êy-âpatahki nêsta.

JL:	ililîwêpina mâka.[30]

GK:	môna kêkwân ani..., môna kêkwân ati-... môna kêkwân ati-...

JL:	kâ-pim'paliki pîwâpiskwa.

GK:	môna 'wênihkân apwîy[31] ihtâw [laughs].

JL:	môna, môn' âpatisiw apwoy.

GK:	âšay, âšay môna ka-kî-kihtohtân, wîna apwîy piko.[32]

21	JL:	a... ha. 'wênihkân mâka ...

GK:	'kwâni kêy-itwêyin anima ...

JL:	... êkâ ê-'htakwahk pimiy ...

GK:	m... hm.

JL:	'matakwan.

GK:	m... hm.

JL: I was a youngster, after all.

GK: Yeah.

JL: I used to use four dogs when I was hauling wood.

GK: M-hm.

JL: Sometimes I would see my dogs outrun me across the river since I hadn't... hadn't mastered them properly [*laughs*].

19 GK: And then...

JL: Then that's what I tell them about, when I talk to him and tell him. But now not even one of the children who are taught, not even taught a little, I keep telling them that they should work.

GK: Yeah. That's true! It was really hard long ago, right up till now. But it's very easy for a person to be able to make a living now.

JL: M-hm.

GK: Even though it used to be hard in the olden days to make a living this was because there was nothing [to make a living from].

JL: M-hm.

GK: One could support oneself quite easily ...

JL: ... but for sure people were [still] wanting to eat.

20 GK: M-hm. But nowadays there is every mechanical thing so that a person can make a living properly.

JL: M-hm.

GK: He drives wherever he wants to go. Wh..., or those who are scattered about the hinterland fly around.

JL: Using motorized equipment.

GK: Yes. With every [kind of] engine being used also.

JL: Use a Cree word for it.

GK: There's nothing there ..., nothing starting to ... nothing starting to ...

JL: Motorized equipment.

GK: There's nary a paddle [*laughs*].

JL: A paddle's of no use, no use.

GK: Now, now you can't go anywhere by paddle alone.

21 JL: Uh-huh. But someone...

GK: That's what you'll say, at that point...

JL: ... when there's no fuel...

GK: M-hm.

JL: There isn't any.

GK: M-hm.

JL: môna n'kî-tôtên.

GK: 'matakwan kâs.

JL: 'matakwan pimiy.

GK: m... hm.

JL: [laughs]³³

GK: a... ha. ê'kwâni ê-'twâniwahk anohc; wêskac mâka wîna môna kêkwân.

JL: a... ha.

22 GK: nêwac piko kimanipahâw kitapwoy, nêt' ê-w'-îtohtêyin, nêstapiko
           mistik.

JL: a... ha.

GK: pakwânêkin mâka kin'tôpit...,³⁴ kin'tawâpahtên kiwâpwayân nêstapiko
           apahkwâsonêkin, 'kwâni. ê'kwân' ê-wî-pim'paniyan.

JL: ê'kwâni mâk' âšay ê-pim'paliyan anima.

GK: kitohpwêkahikân mâk' ê-nâmowinâk.

JL: a... a.

GK: môna kitâstakâtên tânt' ê-'tohtêyin,

JL: [laughs]

GK: ... tâpiskôc iko ê-'yâyân êncin kititên'tên mwêhci
           ê-nâmowinâšiyin.

23 JL: tâpiskôc ê-'yâyin pîwâpisk kâ-pim'palik.

GK: tâpiskôc ê-'yâyân pîwâpisk oti. môna nâspic âniman wîn' ânohc ...
           'ci-kî-pimâcihot 'wênihkân. môna tâpiskôc kayâs. wêskac tâpwê
           kîy-âniman. êniwêhk mihcêtwâ n'kî-mošihtân nêsta nîna.

JL: a.

GK: n'kî-kiskên'tên mihcêtwâ ê-kî-mošihtâyân.

JL: a... ha.

GK: mâcika nêtê mihcêtwâ n'kîy-âpacihâw *Hudson Bay Company* nêtê,
           êy-atâwêspan âtawâpiskâtohk n'timihk.³⁵

JL: o?

GK: ê-mohc'-otâpâniwahkipan.³⁶

JL: a... ha.

24 GK: 'kwâni manâ mâka ê-'t'-âpatisiyâpân anim' êy-âpacihak kampaniy
           anima êy-otâpêyân, ê-n'tahi-'tâpêyân êy-ohtisîyân niyânošâpwahtay.³⁷

JL: a... ha.

GK: *hundred-fifty found* mâk' êy-otâpêyân.³⁸

JL: ililîmo.³⁹

GK: êhê.

JL: I can't do it.

GK: There's no gas.

JL: There's no oil.

GK: M-hm.

JL: [laughs].

GK: Uh-huh. That's what they say now; but long ago there wasn't anything.

JL: Yeah.

22 GK: You just picked up your paddle right off when you wanted to go there, or a stick.

JL: Right.

GK: You felt for a shirt ..., you fetched your blanket or a piece of canvas, that's all. That was it when you wanted to have a ride.

JL: And that's what [you'd use for a sail] then riding about.

GK: You'd hoist your sail in a fair wind.

JL: Yeah.

GK: You don't consider it a bother where you want to go,

JL: [laughs]

GK: ... you think it's exactly like having an engine, when you're sailing with a fair wind.

23 JL: As when you have an engine that goes along.

GK: As when you have an engine, that is. It's not very difficult nowadays ... for someone to make a living. Not as in olden times. Long ago it was really difficult. A great many times I've felt this way myself.

JL: Yeah.

GK: I knew I'd felt it many times.

JL: Oh, yes.

GK: Look, time and again I've worked for the Hudson's Bay Company over there, when it was trading up-river at Attawapiskat.

JL: Oh?

GK: When they just used to haul.

JL: Oh, yes.

24 GK: Then when I was beginning to work, as I was working for the Company at that time hauling, hauling upstream, I earned fifteen dollars.

JL: Uh-huh.

GK: And hauling a hundred and fifty pounds.

JL: Speak Cree.

GK: Yes.

JL: ililîmo.

GK: mitâhtomitana niyânomitana ...

JL: ... tipâpêskocikan.

GK: ... tipâpêskocikan.

JL: o?

25 GK: 'kwân' inikohk...

JL: [coughs]

GK: ... êy-otâpêyâpân.

JL: o?

GK: n'tôtâpâhtay piko.

JL: â?

GK: âskaw wês' âta wîna pêyak atim, nîšo atimwak. kêka mâk'
       âtawîna kîy-at'-îspaniw tâpwê mihcêt atimwak
       ê-'tiy-âpacihakihcik,

JL: a... a.

GK: ... ê-'ti-mihcêticik[40] ot' atimwak ê-'ti-mihcêticik n'têminânak.

JL: o? tân' tahto-tipahikanêyâk mâk' aniy antê?

GK: mihtahtomitana nîšitana niyânan.

JL: o?

26 GK: ay'hâ', sîpîhk ...

JL: tân' tahto, ... tân' tahto-nipâyêkopan ant' ê-ytohtêyêk?

GK: wâ, – mihcêtwâ. mihcêtwâ n'nipânân šânkwâ.[41]

JL: o?

GK: šânkwâ '-otâpâniwahk wîna.

JL: hm. mîna mâka, šânkwâ nâ mâka mîn' ê-kîwêyin?

GK: môna. nêwâ.

JL: nêwâ.

GK: nistwâ âskaw.

JL: o? o? kikišîpalinâwâw wîn' ê-kîwêyêk?

GK: n'kišîpaninân ê-pišišikohtêyâhk[42] wîna.

27 JL: êkâ wîna ê-misponiskâyêk.

GK: mitâhtomitana nîšitana niyânan tipahikanêyâw.

JL: a... ha.

GK: kišîpaniw isa wîn' êkâ kêkwân ê-mohci-pimohtêyin piko.

JL: a... a.

GK: môna tâpiskôc êy-otâpêyin.

JL: Speak Cree.

GK: A hundred and fifty...

JL: ... 'pound weight'.

GK: ... pound weight.

JL: Oh?

25 GK: That's how much ...

JL: [coughs]

GK: ... I used to haul.

JL: Oh?

GK: I only used to haul.

JL: Uh?

GK: Although sometimes I had one dog, two dogs. At last, however, the time gradually came, that we used a good many dogs.

JL: Oh!

GK: ... since dogs, that is, began to be plentiful, – since our dogs began to be plentiful.

JL: Oh? How many miles is it to there?

GK: A hundred and twenty-five.

JL: Oh?

26 GK: Well, er – by river ...

JL: How many,... how many times used you to sleep going there?

GK: Oh, – a number of times. We slept a number of times, nine times.

JL: Oh?

GK: Nine times in the actual hauling.

JL: Hm. And again, nine times again as you went home?

GK: No. Four times.

JL: Four times.

GK: Three times occasionally.

JL: Oh? Oh? You made speed on your way home?

GK: We travelled fast, going back empty.

27 JL: As long as you didn't run into a snow-storm.

GK: It's a hundred and twenty-five miles.

JL: A-hah.

GK: It goes fast, of course, when you're just walking without [hauling] anything.

JL: U-hah.

GK: Not [the same] as when you're hauling.

JL: a... ha.

GK: môna is' âni mâka wîna kwayask anima!

JL: o?

GK: môn' isa kwayask.

JL: o?

28 GK: ôma wês' êšinâkwan[43] wîna sîpiy [gesture].

JL: ê-wâwâkatamohk.[44]

GK: ê-wâwâkatamohk sîpiy mâka šâkoc âpatan.[45]

JL: a!

GK: tašinê piko sîpiy.

JL: a... a.

GK: iši kwayask isa mâka wîn' êspaniw êkâ..., kâ-'mihnâmakahk anohc wîna.

JL: a... ha.

GK: kîy-ati-tipahikêw oš' âni mâk' âtawîn' âpišîš[46] kampaniy anim' ê-'spî...,
        atimwak ê-'t'-îhtâcik.

JL: a?

GK: kîy-ati-tipahikêw.

JL: [coughs]

29 GK: kêkât niyânomitana kîy-ohtisiw awênihkân ê-n'tahipahtwâcik
        atimw' êy-âpacihâcik.

JL: â.

GK: wêhtanôpan mâka wîn' anima. nistwâ, nêwâ kinipâhtay.

JL: a?

GK: âpihta mâka' ê-nipâcik ê-kišîpanicik atimwak
        ê-mâhipahtâyin.

JL: a... ha.

GK: ê-minotêwêyâk[47] ê-sîkwahk mêkwâc.

JL: mâcika kâ-ytâcimospan mîn' ây'hâw,
        kampani-kihci-okimâw.

GK: m... hm.

JL: nêtê cîpayi-sîpîhk mêkwâc kâ-ihtâyân.[48]

GK: mm.

30 JL: nêtê mâka nêmiskâw[49] k'-êcikâtêk k'-îtohtêw.

GK: m... hm.

JL: tipâcimow wês' âni mâk' ê-pâhpit.

GK: mm.

JL: "m'pêci-n'tawâp'mikonân pêyak kišê-'l'liw miton' ê-kišê-'l'lîwit," 'twêw.

JL: Yeah.

GK: But *that's* not a straight cut.

JL: Oh?

GK: It's not straight, you realize.

JL: Oh?

28 GK: For the river looks like this [*gesture*].

JL: ... a crooked road.

GK: But the river, [though] a crooked road, is used, nonetheless.

JL: Oh, really!

GK: Only the river, all the time.

JL: Uh-huh.

GK: But nowadays, of course, the plane goes in a straight line, not...

JL: A-ha.

GK: The Company began to pay a little, y'know, though, once there were dogs.

JL: Oh?

GK: It began to pay.

JL: [*coughs*]

29 GK: Someone could earn almost fifty dollars when they were running the freight up-river using dogs.

JL: Yeah.

GK: But at that time it was easy. You used to sleep three, four times.

JL: Yeah?

GK: With the dogs sleeping half-way when they travelled fast as you ran down-river.

JL: Uh-huh.

GK: With a hard snow-crust in springtime.

JL: Look at the report again, er... which the Hudson's Bay District Manager gave.

GK: M-hm.

JL: While I was over at Ghost River.

GK: M-hm.

30 JL: He went over there to Namiskau as it's called.

GK: M-hm.

JL: And he told about it laughing of course.

GK: M-hm.

JL: "A certain old fellow saw us, a very old fellow," he said.

GK: m... hm.

JL: "... antê nêmiskâhk."

GK: m... m.

JL: "kê'wâ'hkân[50] 'ima nâspic wêhciy-âlimahk kê'wân'hkân anohc, ê-...
itwêw?" itwêw.

GK: m...hm.

JL: "êkâ mâka wîskâc anim' ê-kîy-ohc'-îtakihtêk kêkwânihkân, mêkwâc
êy-âlimahk ê-pimiwitâsonâniwahk ê-mohci-pimohtâhtâniwahk
kê'wânihkâna itwêw," itwêw.

GK: m... hm.

31 JL: "anohc mâka kâ-'mihlâmakahki êy-âpatahki, nâspic âliman kêkwân,
itwêw," itwêw.

GK: m... hm.

JL: "âta mâka êkâ wayêš ê-'lâpatisit ana kâ-pimiwatât ê-mohci-apit iko,
ê-tahkonât tahkon-apwoya ..."

GK: m... hm.

JL: "... išpimihk ê-pimiy-akocihk, itwêw," itwêw.

GK: m... hm. [*both laugh*] šâkoc wîna kiskên'tam tâni kê-itwêt. [*more laughter*]
šâkoc mâka kišîpaniw 'ci-nipispan ana is... âta kâ-wêhtisit[51]
ê-pimiwitât.

JL: a... ha.

32 GK: ê...[52] môna 'wâc *one minute* t'-êspanîpan. môna wâwâc pêyak
ominikošiš.

           [*simultaneously*]

JL: môna wâwâc pêyak ominikošiš.

JL: môna kiskên'tam tânispî.

GK: êhê. môna kiskên'tam tânispî.

JL: ha... a.

GK: êhê. môna ta-kiskên'tam. ê-pimohtahtâspan wâsa mâka wîna
'wênihkân kiskên'tamôpan ê-išpânik nêstapiko êkâ k'-ênikohk
'ci-nâsipê-wêpinât otôtâpânâskwa.[53]

JL: êkâ 'ci-pîkošimât otôtâpânâskwa.

GK: êkâ 'ci-pîkošimât otôcâ... câpânâskwa nêsta mâk' êkâ 'ci-takwahokot,
ê-...

JL: [*laughs*]

33 GK: ta-wâpahtamôpan mâka wîna.

GK: M-hm.

JL: "... there at Namiskau."

GK: M... hm.

JL: "Why is that stuff getting very expensive, as... he [the old man] observed," he [the District Manager] went on.

GK: M-hm.

JL: "Nothing ever used to be so expensive," he said, "even while it was so hard transporting it by canoe and just portaging things," he [the Manager] continued.

GK: M...hm.

31 JL: "But now that aircraft are used, an article is extremely expensive, he said," he [the Manager] went on.

GK: M-hm.

JL: "... even though that carrier does nothing by way of working at it as he only just sits there, holding the rudder handle ..."

GK: M-hm.

JL: "... coasting along up there, he said," he [the Manager] concluded.

GK: M-hm. [both laugh] He sure knew what to say. [more laughter] He'd sure be dead in a flash, though, that fl... even though he had an easy time carrying a load.

JL: Uh-huh.

32 GK: Y... it wouldn't even take one minute.

JL: Not even one minute.

[simultaneously]

JL: Not even one minute.

JL: He doesn't know when.

GK: Right. He doesn't know when.

JL: Uh-huh.

GK: Yes. He won't know. When someone was carrying a load, though, he used to know when it was high and not to throw his sled down the hill.

JL: So as not to smash his sled.

GK: So as not to smash his sl..., sled and also so it didn't jam him against anything, as ...

JL: [laughs]

33 GK: But the point is, he would *see* it.

JL: But he will sure run the risk of cutting himself setting up camp [alone].

JL: šâkoc mâka ta-nîsânisîw 'ci-cîkahotisot ê-kapêšit.

GK: êkot' ân' ê-tipiskânik.

JL: êhê. ê-tipiskânik ê-kapêšit.

GK: ê-tipiskânik mâwac.

JL: [laughs] êko wâs' ân' ê-kîtaw-itâcimoyahk nôhtaw kêhcin.

GK: êko wâs' âni.

JL: [laughs]

GK: mihcêtinw' oš' âni tipâcimôwina. 'wênihkân, môna wîna piko
        ê-w'-îskwa-mâmitonên…, ê-mohci-mâmitonên'taman mâka wîna môna
        k'-îhkin.

JL: môna wâsa.

34 GK: kî-masinahamawâw[54] mâka wîna, kanakê pêyako-tawâstêw
        ta-kî-mišâpan kitipâcimôwin.

JL: êhê.

GK: môna mâka wîna k'-îhkin anima ê-mohci-mâmitonên'hcikâtêk piko.
        [sighs] wês' âti-nôhtêpaniw itên'tâkwan.

JL: êhê.

GK: … ê-'ti-mâmawi-kiskisinâniwahki anih' kêkwâna k'-ânimôcikâtêki.

JL: ê-mâmawipaliki ašic.

GK: m… hm. kišâstaw 'ša kî-mânâtan ôma kâ-'šinâkwahk kâ-wâpahtaman
        môsonîhk wêskac.

JL: ê-pasakopêyâk.

GK: êhê.

JL: ê-kî-kihtâpêyâk mitoni.

35 GK: êhê. nêtê oš' ân' n'kî-wîkihtay,[55] ôma nâsipêtimihk, mâcik'
        anima kâ-cimatêk nîki kotak. ê'kwânima. ê'k' oš' ânima nîki.[56]

JL: o?

GK: ay'hâw ani cêkap n'kî-mînâw animêniw, cêkap smâl.

JL: o?

GK: êwakw' âna kâ-wî-išicišahohtipan[57] mân' ant' êy-išîhtâspan ana …,
        wî-…,[58] owâhkomâkana.

JL: êhê.

GK: kêtahtawin mâna, "wanawîtimihk kâ-piskwastêki n'tayâna,"
        itwêpan.

JL: tâpwê nâ?

36 GK: m… hm. wêsâ mâka n'kitimâkênimâhtay 'sa mâka.

JL: ê-walawî-wêpinikâtêniki?

GK: That's the case in the dark.

JL: Yes. Camping in the dark.

GK: Mostly so at night.

JL: [laughs] Well that's it, we'll most likely be running short of things to talk about for sure.

GK: Well, that's it.

JL: [laughs]

GK: There are a good many stories y'know. For a person only to finish thinking..., as you just think about them it can't amount to anything [you have to tell them].

JL: I wouldn't think so.

34 GK: But you can *write* to him, one week at least and your story would have been a big one.

JL: Yes.

GK: It can't amount to anything, though, when it's only just being thought out. [sighs] It's running too short [the stock of conversation], it seems,

JL: Yes.

GK: ... remembering all together those things which are talked about.

JL: When they come running together.

GK: M-hm. Gosh, y'know, this looked pretty bad what you saw at Moosonee long ago.

JL: When it was marshy.

GK: Yes.

JL: When it used to be completely swampy.

35 GK: Yes. I used to live over there, y'know, this place down the bank, see there my other house that sticks up. That's the one. That used to be my place, y'know.

JL: Oh?

GK: Well, I gave that one to Jacob, Jacob Small [pseudonym].

JL: Oh?

GK: That's the one they were repeatedly going to send to where that one..., his wi..., his relatives were.

JL: Right.

GK: All of a sudden he was saying, "My things are piled up outside."

JL: Really?

36 GK: M-hm. I was feeling terribly sorry for him though.

JL: Because they were being thrown out?

GK: êhê. n'kî-kitimâkênimâhtay mâka. "kišâspin wêsa mâka
tipahamawiyanê nîšwâ mitâhtomitana niyânomitana, twoyêhk
ka-kî-mînitin anima nîkih," n'titâht'.[59]

JL: o?

GK: ê'kwâni mâka wêhci-kîy-ošihtâyâpân anim' êy-apišâšihk anohc.

JL: aha.

GK: wêsâ oš' âni mâka n'kî-tacipanihikohtay payihtaw, ...

JL: aha.

GK: ... ê-'ti-tahkâyâk 'kwân' 'êhci-taš'-îšinâkwahk ôma.

JL: a... a.

37 GK: môna mâk' anima ..., môna mâka n'tawâc niwî-wawêšihtâhtay ôma.

JL: êhê.

GK: niwî-ošihtâhtay kotak kwayask ..., kwayask ..., kwayask

[simultaneously]

JL: kotak kiwîy-ošihtân. o?

GK: 'ci-minwâšihk.

JL: a... a.

GK: ê'kwâni mâka wêhci-taši-nanêhkâsinâkwahk anima.

JL: mîna mâk' atâwâkêyanê ôma ...

GK: m... hm. mîna mâka n'ka-ošihtân ôma pitamâ, êko mâka
kêy-atâwâkêyân nîki.

JL: o?

38 GK: nîn' oš' âni mâka misiwê kâ-'ši-namêhtâyân ... kiwâpahtên nâ
wâskâhikan kâ-cimatêk ôma kâ-paškwâk?

JL: ôtê pîniš? o?

GK: nînanân kâ-iši-namêhtâyâhk anima.

JL: o?

GK: n'kî-paškokahikânân misiwê 'ntê.

JL: o?

GK: ôma nêsta kâ-wâpahtaman kâ-paškwâk misiwê n'kî-paškwakahikâhtay.

JL: o?

GK: ôtê nêsta itêhkê nâmowin kâ-išinâkwahk misiwê n'kî-paškokahên.

JL: a?

GK: [coughs; sighs] payihtaw isa mâhtâwi-tôcikâtêw ôta nâspic.

JL: o?

39 GK: êniwêhk ta-kihci-minwâšinôpan ôma yhtâwin kišâspin kâ-tôcikâtêk antê
kîwêtinohk tôcikâtêk.

GK: Yes. I was feeling sorry for him though. "If you pay me two hundred and fifty dollars, I'll be able to give you my house right away," I said to him.

JL: Oh?

GK: That's why I had that little one made now.

JL: Uh-huh.

GK: But I was held back too much on account of ...,

JL: O-ho.

GK: ... the cold weather setting in, that's why it looks this way.

JL: Oh, yes.

37 GK: But that one I wasn't ..., but I wasn't going to fix up this one.

JL: Right.

GK: I was going to make another one properly ..., properly ..., properly,
    [simultaneously]

JL: You were going to make another one. Oh?

GK: ... so it'd be nice.

JL: A-ha.

GK: That's why it looks so wretched that way.

JL: But if you sell this one again...

GK: M-hm. I'll make this one again first, and then I'll sell my house.

JL: Oh?

38 GK: It's *my* work, all where I've left traces ... Do you see the house standing here in the clearing?

JL: Right up to here? Oh?

GK: It's us who left evidences in that.

JL: Oh?

GK: We cleared everything there.

JL: Oh?

GK: And this clearing which you see, I did all the clearing.

JL: Oh?

GK: And all that appears to this side leeward I cleared.

JL: Ah?

GK: [coughs; sighs] The trouble is, things are very strangely done here.

JL: Oh?

39 GK: This town would be really fine indeed if what was done there in the North were done.

243

JL: o?

GK: môna oš' âni mâka kîy-âpatisiw 'wênihkân ôta êkâ kanakê 'pišîš 'ci-kîy-ohtisit.

JL: a... a.

GK: êko mâka, wîn' ântê âtawâpiskât n'kîy-ošihtâhtay nîki. anta *Indian Agent* n'kî-tipahamâkohtay.[60]

JL: a?

GK: awa šôniyânikimâw.

JL: a... a.

GK: môna wîna n'tôhci-tipahamâk ...

JL: â.

40 GK: ... piko n'kî-..., n'kî-nôtâhtikwâhtay; 'kwantaw piko ê-nôtâhtikwêyân, ê-wî-kocihtâyân 'ci-wâskâhikanihkâsoyân âtawîna môna kêkwân n'tayâhtay.

JL: o?

GK: ispî mâk' ê-wâpahtahk ôma šôniyânikimâw ê-tôtamin'c' îniniwa, n'kîy-ati-wîcihitonân mâka. n'kîy-ati-mihcêtinân, kikiskên'tên.[61]

JL: â?

GK: n'kîy-ati-wâwîcihitonân isa mâka. môn' 'nt' ohci pâpêyak pikw ihtâw ininiw.

JL: o?

GK: mêmîskoc. êko mâka, kîy-ati-mihcêtiwak mâka mistikwak.

JL: â... â.

41 GK: nâspic kîy-ati-mihcêtiwak anta mistikwak kâ-yši-tâškopocikâniwahk.

JL: â... â.

GK: êkw isa mâk' ê-wâpahtahk ôm' ana šôniyânikimâw k'-îtêw ôho nâpêwa tâpw' ê-wâpahtamwât ê-wî-kakwê-wîcihitison'ci.

JL: â... hâ.

GK: k'-îtwêw mâka 'ci-wîcihât 'ci-wâskâhikanihkâson'ci pîniš.

JL: o?

GK: tâškipocikaniniw mâka kî-tipaham anta pimîniw.[62]

JL: a.

GK: môn' ohci-tipaha... otinâkaniwanwak[63] aniki nimistikominânik ant' ohci.

JL: a.

JL: Oh?

GK: Nobody can work here though, y'know, without being able earn at least a little.

JL: A-ha.

GK: But then, up there at Attawapiskat I had built my house. I was getting paid by the Indian Agent there.

JL: Oh?

GK: This paymaster.

JL: A-ha.

GK: He didn't pay me in cash, as such...

JL: Ah.

40 GK: ... only I..., I had got logs; I was getting logs just for something to do, since I wanted to try to make a house for myself even though I didn't have anything.

JL: Oh?

GK: But once the Indian Agent at this point saw the people doing it [assembling materials], we began to help each other. There began to be quite a few of us, y'know.

JL: Ah?

GK: We began to help each other all 'round. There was no Indian there only on his own.

JL: Oh?

GK: [We took it] in turn. And then there began to be a good number of trees.

JL: A-ha.

41 GK: There began to be a very good number of trees there where they did the sawing.

JL: A-ha.

GK: So when that Indian Agent saw it he said to these men that he really saw that they wanted to help themselves.

JL: A-ha.

GK: And he said that he would help them up to the point that they made houses for themselves.

JL: Oh?

GK: And he paid the oil for the saw there.

JL: Ah!

GK: Those trees of ours from there were not char..., charged.

JL: Ah.

42 GK: ê'kwâni misiwê kâ-yš'-êyâwakihcik.

JL: môn' ohciy-âpihtawinâkaniwanwak.⁶⁴

GK: môna.

JL: a.

GK: misiwê n'kî-'yâwânânak.

JL: o?

GK: êko mâka k'-ât'-ošihtâyâhk wâskâhikan. nînanân mâka n'kîy-ati-nîšinân, cîmis kâ-tahkwâpêt.⁶⁵

JL: o?

GK: mâwac nîstam ê-kîy-at'-ošihtâyâhk ani' wâskâhikana.

JL: o?

GK: môna kêkât n'tôhci-tâpwêhtawâhtay. mât... macên'tâkosiwak wâsa mâka wîn' ant' ininiwak nâspic anima kâ-išikîšwêcik.⁶⁶

JL: a... ha.

43 GK: "wêmistikôšîhk ka-ytakimikawin," pišišik kâ-itwêcik. 'kwantaw mâka an'-îtwêwak anima kâ-ytwêcik.

JL: ha... a.

GK: misiwê 'wênihkân kâ-wâpamat, ôko kâ-pimâtisicik anohc ininiwak misiwê wêmistikôšîhk ohci-pimâtisiwak.

JL: a... ha.

GK: môna 'wâci pêyak 'kwantaw pakwataskamik ihtâw ininiw,

JL: m... hm.

GK: ... êkâ 'êmistikôšîhk k'-ohci-p'mâtisit.

JL: môna wâsa.

GK: mâcika mâk' ânohc. mino-tašîhkêwak mâk' anta nîkihk. nôhtâwiy ant' ihtâw.

JL: â.

44 GK: nišîm nêst' ant' ihtâw, âskaw nêsta kotakiyak 'wênihkânak pîhtokwêwak anta.

JL: o?

GK: cîmis stîpin nêsta kî-pîhtokwêw anta.

JL: â.

GK: wîna mâka pêyak nâšic kâ-kîy-ayamispan ê-pakwâtahkipan anihi wâskâhikana ê-wšihtâniwaniniki.

JL: â? ê-wîy-ohcihiwêt.

GK: ê-wîy-ohcihiwêt, êkâ ê-sâpên'tahk wêmistikôšîhk 'c'-îtakimimihci 'wênihkâna.

42 GK: And so we had them all.

JL: They were not divided in half.

GK: No.

JL: Ah.

GK: We had them all.

JL: Oh?

GK: So then we began to build a house. We began to team up, James Short-trace and I.

JL: Oh?

GK: Because we had begun to make those houses right at first.

JL: Oh?

GK: I almost hadn't believed him. But the people who speak that language are very un..., unfriendly, y'know.

JL: A-ha.

43 GK: "You'll be classed as a White," they persisted in saying. They're just talking nonsense in saying that.

JL: Ho-oh.

GK: Every person whom you see, these Indians who are living now all are living off the White-Man.

JL: A-ha.

GK: There's not even one Indian left in the hinterland,

JL: M-hm.

GK: ... who doesn't live off the White-Man.

JL: There's none.

GK: But look here now. They live well there in my house. My father's staying there.

JL: Oh.

44 GK: My younger brother is there too, and sometimes other persons come in there.

JL: Oh?

GK: James Stephen [pseudonym] came in there too.

JL: Ah.

GK: He was one of those who had been saying that he hated those houses being built.

JL: Oh? Because he wanted to prevent it.

GK: He wanted to prevent it because he didn't like the idea of anyone being classed as a White-Man.

JL: â.

GK: âšay mâka wêwêlat, âšay mâk' âpacihtâw. ihtâw anta nîkihk nêsta wîna âšay ê-kwîtaw'-îš'-îhtât, kiwâpahtên.[67]

45 JL: a... a.

GK: mihcêt isa mâka kîy-ati-tôcikâtêwa.

JL: a... a.

GK: 'kwâni mâka êšinâkwahk ôma ihtâwin.

JL: a... a.

GK: ôma k'-îšinâkwan.

JL: a... a.

GK: ... ôta wapistikwayâwak ê-'htâcik.

JL: a... a.

GK: ôho... kâ-'t'-îtaskitêki ôma [gesture] ... wâskâhikana ...

JL: â... â.

GK: ... misiwê, ôma kîy-at'-îtaskitêwa.

JL: a... a.

46 GK: mîna hê-nîpihk, mîna kotakîya.

JL: a... a.

GK: tastawic mâka mêskanaw k'-îhtakwan anihi ôtê mâka [gesture].
     [simultaneously]

JL: a... a.

GK: ê'kwâni mâk' êtaskitêki anohc ôma.

JL: a?

GK: mihcêtinwa mâka.

JL: a... a.

GK: payihtaw mâka kî-nôhtê-kipihcihtâwak mâka kêk' âniki. tâpwê k'-îskwâpaniw kêk' ânima.

JL: a... a.

GK: kêka môna 'wênihkân tâpwê mâka wîcihâkaniwan.[68]

47 JL: ê'kwân' ê-... 'šinâkwahk, n'tišinêhtay.

GK: m... hm.

JL: ka-matwê-papêmâwatamwanwa mêskanawa, n'tišinêhtay.

GK: êhê. minwâšin. tašinê ...

JL: ay'hâw, n'kî-pôsipalihtay pêyakw' ânc' kâ-'mihlâmakahk ê-'spanik.

GK: m... hm.

JL: kâkê mâka, môn' isa mâka n'kiskên'têhtay naspâtakâm ê-'ši-têhômakahk.

JL: Ah.

GK: But now he openly, but now he uses it. He is there in my house, him too, since now he's at a loss for a place to stay, ya see.

45 JL: A-ha.

GK: Well, many of them began to be built.

JL: A-ha.

GK: And that's how this village looks.

JL: A-ha.

GK: It looked this way,

JL: A-ha.

GK: ... when the Frenchmen were staying here.

JL: A-ha.

GK: These ones which began to stand in a row [like this] [gesture] ... the houses...

JL: A-ha.

GK: ... all of them, they were beginning to stand like this.

JL: A-ha.

46 GK: Again in the summer, again the other ones.

JL: A-ha.

GK: And in the middle there was a road to this side of them [gesture].
      [simultaneously]

JL: A-ha.

GK: So this is how they stand now.

JL: A-ha.

GK: And there are many of them.

JL: A-ha.

GK: The trouble is, though, they finally put a stop to this. At last that [the logging and building] actually came to an end.

JL: A-ha.

GK: Finally nobody was actually getting helped.

47 JL: That's the was it looks, I used to think.

GK: M-hm.

JL: The paths will criss-cross [into blocks], I used to think.

GK: Yes. It's nice. All the time...

JL: Well er..., I had jumped on the plane once, there as it was going.

GK: M-hm.

JL: I thought, though, I didn't know that it was landing on the wrong side.

GK: m... hm.

JL: ispî 'sa mâk' ê-takopanik antê, '-'ti-kînikwânipanik kâ-'mihlâmakahk.

GK: m... hm.

JL: aspin[69] mâka naspâtakâm itêhkê 'ši-têhômakan.

48 GK: ê'kwân' ê-tôcikâtêk. ê'kotê'ni šâkoc êkw êš'-îhtakwahk kihci-sîpiy.[70]

JL: a... a.

GK: âšay kîškâyawâw otih.

JL: a... a.

GK: âtawînâta kaškihtâwak ê-apišâšihk anta kâ-'mihnâmakahk
         êy-âpacihtâcik šîpânakohk[71] ê-têhocik mêkwâc mâka pikw ê-mišâk nipiy.

JL: o?

GK: môna wîna ê-'pišâšihk nipiy.

JL: nêstapiko ê-mêkwâpêkahk.

GK: ê'kot' âni mêkwâc oc'[72] ê-mêkwâpêkahk kâ-'šinâkwahk n'titwân.

49 JL: a... ha

GK: êko wâs' ân' pâtim'[73] ê-'šâk,[74] ê-mêkwâpêkahk.

JL: a... ha.

GK: ê'ko... tê mâk', ê-'ši-têhonâniwahk wîn' ê-mêkwâ'hk[75] nêtê ...

JL: kwêskakâm itêhkê.

GK: ... kwêskakâm itêhkê. anohc oš' âni kâ-wâpahtamân k'-ât'-îšinâkwahk
         kâ-pâhkwâpiskâk misiwê.

JL: aha.

GK: kâ-pâhkwâk môn' anim' êšinâkwanôpan wêskac.

JL: o?

GK: ... anohc anima kâ-yšinâkwahk.

JL: o?

50 GK: minwâšinôpan ani wîna wêskac. anohc mâka atô..., atô...
         at'-osâminâkwan.

JL: hm!

GK: pêyakoyêk mâka nâspic wêhtan ê-minwâšihk anta ê-..., nipiy
         êy-ihtakwahk.[76]

JL: o?

GK: ... âtawâpiskâtohk. sâkahikan' anta nâspic minwâkaminwa, ...

JL: o?

GK: ... pêšoc anta.

JL: o?

GK: M-hm.

JL: But once it arrived there, as the plane began to circle around ...,

GK: M-hm.

JL: There it was, – it landed on the wrong side [of the river].

48 GK: That's what's generally done. It's because that's where the main river is.

JL: A-ha.

GK: It's already deep there, that's to say.

JL: Oh.

GK: In spite of everything, when they use a small plane they're able to land behind the island while the water is high, though.

JL: Oh?

GK: Not at the point where there's little water.

JL: Or at high tide.

GK: That's what I mean, while it appears to be high tide, that is.

49 JL: Uh-huh.

GK: 'Cause that's the only time there's a lot, when it's high tide.

JL: A-ha!

GK: And that's where, they actually land at low tide over there ...

JL: On the other side of the river.

GK: ... on the other side of the river. It's only lately that I see all the dry rock that's beginning to show.

JL: Uh-huh.

GK: What's dry used not to show long ago.

JL: Oh?

GK: ... what shows now.

JL: Oh?

50 GK: A long time ago it used to be nice. Now, though, it's be... it's be...,
it's beginning to look quite a sight.

JL: Hm!

GK: At one place, though, it's easy to get good [drinking] ... er,
water.

JL: Oh?

GK: ... at Attawapiskat. Some lakes there have very good water,

JL: Oh?

GK: ... near there.

JL: Oh?

GK: pêc'-ocihcipaniw anima pêyak antê ..., mistosokamikohk antê itêhkê anima, opistikwayâwak omistosokamikowâhk.

JL: aha.

GK: kîy-ošihtâniwan sâkahikan ê-kîškâyawâk anta.[77]

51 JL: a?

GK: pêšoc antê 'htâwinihk.

JL: n'kî-wâpahtêhtay oš' âni, n'kî-wâpahtêhtay oš' âni pêyak, ay'hâw, ...

GK: m... hm.

JL: ... ant' ê-'tohtêyâpân ê-pipohk.

GK: êhê.

JL: ê-papâmahamêyâhkipan mistosikamik manâ ant' êtêhkê 'htakwanôpan.

GK: êhê. anim' âwas itêhkê kampaniy-astâsonikamik kâ-ihtahkwahk ... ê'kwânima mâwac mênwâšihk.

JL: ê'kwâni mâka [...] [drowned out by next utterance]

GK: wâkinâkaniskâhk[78] kâ-'htakwahk.

52 JL: anta kâ-ohci-cêhkatamohk mêskanaw kampaniy kâ-'ši-wîkit.

GK: êhê. ê'kwânima.

JL: ê'kwânima kâ-kî-wâpahtamâpân.

GK: êniwêhk mihcêtinwa wâs' âni mâka nâspic.

JL: o?

GK: mihcêtinwa nêtê; 'wasitê mišâw' ôta ê-yhtakwahki.

JL: o?

GK: ... 'ntê 'têhkê.

JL: o?

GK: mîna mâk' nêtê 'têhkê nôhcimihk mâškôc pêyak mîn' âpihtaw tipahikan nôhcimihk.

JL: o?

GK: nêstapiko nîšo-tipahikan wayêš ...

JL: o?

53 GK: ... ihtakwanwa mîna ant' ê-mišâki ..., awasit' ê-mišâki ispîš anima.

JL: aha.

GK: pišišik sâkahikan piko, pišišik išinâkwan ôma kâ-wâpahtaman, mâmihk itêhkê nêsta kihciy-akâmihk itêhkê.

JL: o?

GK: misiwê, misiwê ka-wâpahtên sâkahikan pišišik.

JL: aha.

GK: It comes right near at one place there …, on that side of the cattle-barn, the Frenchmen's cattle-barn.

JL: Uh-huh.

GK: They made that lake deep there.

51 JL: Oh?

GK: Near to the settlement there.

JL: I had seen it y'know, I had seen it y'know one, well, er…,

GK: M-hm.

JL: … [time] when I used to go there in the winter.

GK: Yes.

JL: When we had been walking around following the road, the barn used to be there on the other side.

GK: Yes. That one, back of where the Company warehouse is…, that's the best one.

JL: That's the one, though … [*drowned out by next utterance*]

GK: The one that's among the junipers.

52 JL: Where the trail meets the bush, where the Company has its home.

GK: Yes. That's the one.

JL: That's the one I used to see.

GK: Are there ever a lot of them, though!

JL: Oh?

GK: They're plentiful further on; they're bigger ones here.

JL: Oh?

GK: … on the further side.

JL: Oh?

GK: And again, on the far side of the bush, perhaps a mile and a half in the bush.

JL: Oh?

GK: Or about two miles.

JL: Oh?

53 GK: … there are big ones again there …, bigger ones than that.

JL: Uh-huh.

GK: It's only lake throughout, what you see here looks like lake after lake, down-river and also on the other side of the river.

JL: Oh?

GK: All, all that you see is simply lake…

JL: Uh-huh.

GK: êkwân' êši-minwâšik nipiy anta. môna tâpiskôc kâ-yšinâkwahk
       kêšîciwanohk. êniwêhk âniman 'ci-kî-'yâniwahk ê-minwâšihk nipiy anta.

JL: aha.

54 GK: ê-namatakwahk sâkahikan.

JL: môna mâka nêsta nâ-... môna mâka nêsta tâpwê minwâkamin
      nipiy,

GK: mm.

JL: ... anta kâ-... pîhtâpêkohk[79] kâ-wîkicik opistikwâyâwak.[80]

GK: êhê. môna.

JL: mahkatêwâkam'paniw wâs' ê-wâpâkaminikâtêk.

GK: ê'kwâni. 'kwân' ê-'šinâkwahk. ay'hâw, môna wâsa sâkahikanihk
       tâpwê 'nima kâ-ihtakwahk.

JL: aha.

GK: wîhpi-minahikoskâwitinwa[81] oš' âni sâkahikana.

JL: anta pîhtâpêk.

GK: anta pîhtâpêk.

JL: m... hm.

55 GK: pîtošinâkwanwa mâka wîn' anihi, maskêkohk kâ-'htakwahki, wakic
       askîhk nawac kâ-'htakwahki.

JL: aha.

GK: nêsta mâka minwâšinwa[82] maškwašiy' ê-nihtâwikihk' ant' atâmihk.

JL: o... ho.

GK: nâspic isa mâka minwâkamin anima nipiy, kikiskên'tên, tâpiskôc
       mwêhci ôm' kâ-ošihtâcik ôta kâ-... mâmihk[83] wêmistikôšiwak ôko
       kâ-wâpâkamik nipiy.

JL: êhê.

GK: miconi mwêhci kâ-yspîhci-wâšêyâkamihk[84] askîwi-pimiy.

     [simultaneously]

JL: ... wâšêyâkamin.

JL: aha.

56 GK: miconi kiwâpahtên misiwê kêkwân' antê 'tâmihk.

JL: êhê.

GK: atâmâtim ant' ê-'spîhci-payahtênâkwahk.

JL: ê'kwâni mwêhci mîna, 'kwân' êšinâkwahk anima ..., akâmihk anta
      ministikohk kâ-ošihtâcik.

GK: m... mhm.

JL: âhkosîwikamikohk anima, maškawisîwikamik.

GK: So then, the water's good there. Not like the way it looks at Albany. Is it ever hard for good water to be had there!

JL: Uh-huh.

54 GK: Because there's no lake.

JL: And also no... and the water's not really good either,

GK: M-hm.

JL: ... there at the... Lagoon where the Frenchmen have their home.

GK: Yes. No.

JL: The tea stays black, you know, even when milk is put into it.

GK: That's it. That's what it looks like. Well, of course, what's there doesn't really [look like] a lake.

JL: Uh-huh.

GK: The lakes [which have good water] are enclosed, y'know, by a continuous high ridge of spruce.

JL: The lagoon there.

GK: The lagoon there.

JL: M-hm.

55 GK: These ones look different, though, – the ones in the swamp which are pretty much on top of the soil.

JL: Uh-huh.

GK: And the grasses are nice too, growing there on the bottom.

JL: O-ho.

GK: And of course that water's very good, you know, exactly like this white water which they make, here wh... these White-Men down-river.

JL: Yes.

GK: Every bit as clear as coal-oil.

[simultaneously]

JL: ... it's clear water.

JL: Uh-huh.

56 GK: You can see everything there on the bottom.

JL: Yes.

GK: It looks so clear beneath the bank.

JL: That's exactly it again, that's exactly how that looks..., what they made there across the river on the island.

GK: M-hm.

JL: That one at the hospital, the power house.

GK: êhê. m… hm.
      [simultaneously]

JL: [laughs]

GK: m… hm. minwâšininiw. minwâkamininiw.

JL: m… hm.

GK: 'kwân' tâpw' êši-minwâšihk antê.

JL: mihcêt kêkwâna nanâhkaw[85] êšinâkwahki pakitinikâtêwa.

57 GK: m… hm. âta mâka êkâ '-ošihtâniwahk anima wîna kâ-itwêyân, êko
         wâs' âni mâka šâkoc êšinâkwahki šâkoc anihi tôwa
         maskêkohk kâ-'htakwahki sâkahikana …

JL: sâkahikan' otih.

GK: êhê. mwêhci askîwi-pimiy.

JL: aha.

GK: 'kwâni mâka mwêhc' êšinâkwahk anima,
      kâ-ošihtâniwahki nipiya kwayask.

JL: âšay mwêhci kêkât kišipâpihkêpaliw mitênaniy.

GK: âšay mwêhci câkipaniw mitênaniy.

JL: êhê. âšay nawac tahkwâpihkêyâcokê[86]
      kâ-'šinâkwahk.

GK: mhm. cikêmânima.

JL: [coughs]

58 GK: wêskac wâsa kâ-kihcipanikipan.

JL: aha. êko wâs' ân' ê-nôhtêpaliyahk kê-'tâcimoyahk. [looks out window]
      hm! kâ-pîkwêhkopâk ê-'šinâkwahk tâpêk' âni pikw ê-nîpîšišiwahk,
      wêhc'-îšinâkwahk …

GK: ê-nîpisîwahk, ê-nî…, ê-nî' pikw[87] anima
      kâ-'šinâkwahk.

JL: paškonâkwanotok' wîn' ê-pipohk.

GK: ta-minwâšinôpan mâka nêsta tašinê paškotâniwahk apišîš êkâ
      kici-sakimêskâkipan.

JL: êhê.

GK: ay'hâw, wês' âni mâka piko kâ-'šinâkwahki piko nîpisiya.

JL: êhê.

GK: âšay oš' âna kî-paškohtâniwan.

JL: aha.

59 GK: wâkinâkaniskâpan oš' ôma misiwê 'nohc ôma.

JL: o?

GK: aniki mâka wâkinâkanak ê'kwâniki kâ-manihtâtihcik aniki.

GK: Yes. M-hm.
   [*simultaneously*]
JL: [*laughs*]
GK: M-hm. It's nice. It's good water.
JL: M-hm.
GK: It's really good there.
JL: A lot of things of different colours are put into it.
57 GK: M-hm. Even when what I'm speaking of [purifying the water] isn't done, nonetheless those kinds, the lakes which are in the swamp, sure look that way...
JL: The lakes, that is.
GK: Yes. Exactly like coal-oil.
JL: Uh-huh.
GK: That's exactly what it [the water from muskeg ponds] looks like, the waters which they purify.
JL: Now the tongue [the leader tape on the recording reel] is running almost right to an end.
GK: The tongue is just about used up.
JL: Yes. It looks as though the tape must be pretty short.
GK: M-hm. Naturally.
JL: [*coughs*]
58 GK: It's a long time, mind you, since it started.
JL: Uh-huh. So we're running short of what we'll talk about. [*looks out window*] Hm! It looks as if the willows are thick, I'm sure, only because the leaves are growing, that's why it looks that way ...
GK: Because there are lots of willows, in the su..., it only looks like that in the summer.
JL: It must look *bare* in the winter.
GK: It would be nice though too if it were cleared to the ground a little all the time so there would not be a lot of mosquitoes.
JL: Yeah.
GK: Well, what you see there, mind you, is just willows.
JL: Yes.
GK: It's already been cleared, y'know.
JL: Uh-huh.
59 GK: This used to be all a juniper stand, you realize, just recently.
JL: Oh?
GK: And those juniper, they're the ones which are chopped up for wood.

JL: o?

GK: ê'kwâniki kâ-'ši-manihtâtihcik, ê-... mâwac kêkwân kâ-nipîwahk.

JL: o?

GK: asâmâhtikwak.

JL: o?

GK: 'kwâni mâka pikw anim' ê-n'tawâpamacik ê-'ti-kîškîškiponacik ê-pêci-pîhtokwahacik mâka, ...

JL: hn!

60 GK: ... mânišîš ê-kisisocik, 'kwân' ê-'t'-îši-macostêhwacik nâspitêpi wcêhkamahkolêw.

JL: a... ha. cikêmanim' ê-pikîwicik.

GK: m... hm. ê-pikîwahk os' âtawîna pêškiš nêsta.

JL: êhê.

GK: aškiškâhtikwa mâka nêsta 'kwân' ê-'hkihki.

JL: misiw' wâsa wîna pikîw wâkinâkan atâmihk nêsta.

GK: êhê.

JL: môna piko walakêskohk.

GK: êhê. êko wâs' âni mâka pikw ê-'hki' misiwê pikw aškiškâhtik.

JL: aha.

GK: kišâspin mâka wîna kîwêtinohk nêtê ihtâyin, môna ta-kî-pasitêw kitiškotêm aškiskâhtik.

JL: aha.

61 GK: âta 'wâc ê-pâhwâk.

JL: a... a. [laughs]

      [pause in conversation]

GK: âšay kišipâpihkêpaliw.

Voice: [in background] kêkât kîsihtâniwan.

GK: kêkât kîsihtâniwan. m... hm.

JL: êko wâs' ân' âšay ê-kišipâpihkêpanik. âšay.

      [end of first side of tape]

GK: ê? [GK directs JL's attention to a rocket ship in a comic paper at which he has been looking.]

JL: mâcik' ô' mâk'[88] ê-'šinâkwahk, na!

GK: êhê. mâcika mâk' ê-'šinâkwahk!

JL: ê... ê.

JL: Oh?

GK: Those are the ones where they're chopped up [for wood], as the greenest thing …

JL: Oh?

GK: Snow shoe frames.

JL: Oh?

GK: And that's it, you just go and fetch them and you begin to saw them one after another, bringing them in …,

JL: Hm!

60 GK: … heat them up a little, then as you begin to put them in the fire it burns up with a flash.

JL: A-ha. Naturally, because they're pitchy.

GK: M-hm. Because it's pitchy, of course, that's partly why.

JL: Yes.

GK: Green wood acts the same way though.

JL: There's pitch at the core of every tamarack too, mind you.

GK: Yes.

JL: Not just in the bark.

GK: Right. But that, of course, is the trouble with all green wood.

JL: Uh-huh.

GK: And if you're up there in the North, your fire won't be able to burn with green wood.

JL: Uh-huh.

61 GK: Even though it's dry.

JL: Uh-uh. [laughs]

        [pause in conversation]

GK: Now the tape is coming to an end.

Voice: [in background] It's almost finished.

GK: It's almost finished. M-hm.

JL: That's it, now the tape's at an end. Now.

        [end of first side of tape]

GK: Eh? [GK directs JL's attention to a rocket ship in a comic paper at which he has been looking.]

JL: See what this looks like, here!

GK: Yes. See how it looks, though!

JL: Yeah.

62 GK: ê-'šinâkwanokopanê mâka kêkwân ê-p'miwitâsowâkêt
êmistikôšiw.

JL: êhê.

GK: ê'kwâni mâk' ê-'ši-wînihcik ôko.

JL: ha! âšay mîna šâkoc kihtâpihkêpaliw.[89]

GK: [to a child coming in] tântê kâ-'tohtêyin? âstam êko, pêc'-api ôta,[90] kî'stam
êko.[91]

JL: [to the same child] kêkwân? kitayân nâ tipâcimôwin? [amused laughter; the
child, a toddler, is carrying an iron poker.]

GK: ta-pahkicipitêw anihi pîwâpiskohikana ...

JL: ta-takositêhokow.

GK: ta-takositêhokow.

JL: êko, kihtâcimo mîna.

63 GK: ta-wî-... t'-âyâhciw-akocin[92] mîna mîna êy-âpatisit.

JL: ta-minîyokaškwêw.

GK: ta-minîyokaškwêw mîna kê-wâpaninik.

Voice: [in background] tân' êšinihkâsot apiscawâšiš ana?

GK: torotiy.

Voice: [in background] aha.

GK: torotiy išinihkâsow.[93] [to child] pikinwat.[94] "tâpask ana tâpw' ê'kwân'
êšinihkâsot," manâ itên'tam.

JL: nôhtêpaliw tipâcimôwin.

GK: nôhtêpaniw wâsa.

JL: tânispî mâhcic kâ-'tohtêyin âtawâpiskâtohk?

GK: nîpinohk oša n'-k'-îtohtân.

JL: nîpinohk nâ k'-îtohtân?

64 GK: nîpinohk wâsa n'k'-îtohtâhtay kâ-'mihnâmakahk ..., mêkwâc holiday
kây-ayâpân.

JL: o? môna nâ ...-hc'-itohtâhtay?[95]

GK: ê?

JL: môna nâ mîna kitôhc'-itohtâhtay?

GK: môna.

JL: o?

Child: papa!

JL: 'kwâni pêyakwâ pikw aspin.

GK: ê'kwâni.

JL: o.

62 GK: The thing which the White-Man used to use for carrying must have looked like that.

JL: Right.

GK: That's what they're named.

JL: Ha! The tape is starting up again now for sure.

GK: [to a child coming in] Where did you go? Come here then, come and sit here; it's your turn then.

JL: [to the same child] What is it? Have you something to tell? [amused laughter; the child, a toddler, is carrying an iron poker.]

GK: She'll pull out that flatiron so it falls ...

JL: It will fall and crush her foot.

GK: It will fall and crush her foot.

JL: So, start your story again.

63 GK: She's going ..., she'll limp up when she goes to work again.

JL: Her toe nails will be full of pus.

GK: Her toe nails will be full of pus the next day.

Voice: [in background] What's that small child's name?

GK: Dorothy.

Voice: [in background] Uh-huh.

GK: Her name is Dorothy. [to child] *pikinwat.* I suppose he's thinking, "I wonder if that's really her name."

JL: The story's running out.

GK: It's running out all right.

JL: When did you last go to Attawapiskat?

GK: I went last summer.

JL: Last summer you went?

64 GK: Last summer I went by airplane ... while I was having a holiday.

JL: Oh? You hadn't gone?

GK: Eh?

JL: You hadn't gone again?

GK: No.

JL: Oh?

Child: Papa!

JL: That's only once since.

GK: That's right.

JL: Oh.

GK: I'll take them [fresh produce from Moosonee to Attawapiskat]

GK: êškw' êsa mîna n'k'-êšiwitân picênak.

JL: aha.

65 GK: mîna n'k'-êtohtân.[96] ati-tatêpipaniyânê ispî ...

JL: aha. êko wâs' ân' ê-kitaw-itâcimoyahk. tân'ka it' êhtâkwê, –
êmîl nâkoc'[97] îs' ihtâkopanê nêsta.

GK: m... hm. ta-kî-kaškohôpan wâs' ân'. môna wâsa ta-kî-wânên'tamôpan
k'-êtâcimot, ...

JL: êhê.

GK: ... êkâ wîskâc ê-wânên'tahk tâni k'-êtwêt.

JL: môna wâsa wîskâc wânên'tam k'-êtwêt ê-'yamit.

GK: m... hm. [long pause]

JL: ha! mân'šîš wâsa kê..., mân'šîš wâsa kinakiškâkonâniwanokopanê
êkot' âni ta-kî-minwên'cikâtêpan ê-'yaminâniwahk.

GK: êko wâs' ântê pâtimâ kê-kî-'yamiyahkopan.

JL: êhê. [laughs]

66 GK: mayê' 'tê wâsa kâ-kî-tôtamahk.

JL: êhê.

GK: ka-kîy-ayamihtâhtânaw mâka piko kî-masinahamawahkopanê
kâ-itwêt.

JL: kî-masinahikâtêkopanê otih.

GK: ê'kot' âni.

JL: nêstapiko mâmâš kîy-ati-masinahikâtêkopanê kê-kîy-ati-kiskisomikot[98]
'wênihkân ...

GK: m... hm.

JL: ... kê-'tiy-êtwêt.

GK: ê... aha.

JL: kêt-ohc'-ati-kihci-wêpinahk.

GK: êy-ohci-...-ohci-kihci-wêpinahk.

JL: ha. tâpêkâ nâspic ê-minwên'tahkik awâšišak ê-kanawâpahtahkik.[99]

67 GK: nâspic!! môna wîskâc ...

JL: m... hm.

GK: ... ka-kîy-ohcihâwak awâšišak ê-kanawâpahtahkik ôho.

JL: êhê.

GK: êkâ mâka wîna wîskâc ê-nôcihtâcik ayamihêw'-masinahikan.

JL: ê'kwâni. ê'kwâni mwêhci ê-'hcicik kâ-itwêyan.

GK: m... hm.

JL: êkoš' âni mâna nîna ê-tôtawak an' awâšiš, ...

later some time.

JL: Uh-huh.

65 GK: I'll go again. When I start to have more [money] ...

JL: Uh-huh. Well, that's that, we're tired of telling about things. I wonder where he is, – I wish Emile Nagochee were here.

GK: M-hm. He would have been able to manage all right. He wouldn't have been stuck for what to tell about,

JL: Right.

GK: ... because he's never stuck for what to say.

JL: He's sure never stuck for what to say when he's talking.

GK: M-hm. *[long pause]*

JL: Ha! If we were feeling a little, mind you..., a little high, mind you, that way one would be in a mood to talk.

GK: Then by-and-by we would have been able to speak there all right.

JL: Yes. *[laughs]*

66 GK: That's not the right way that we did it.

JL: Right.

GK: But we could have read it if we had in fact only written down what he said.

JL: It could have been written down, that is.

GK: That's the way.

JL: Or if it had in fact been written down roughly it could begin to remind a person ...

GK: M-hm.

JL: ... what he was to say.

GK: Yeah ... uh-huh.

JL: Where he's to start from.

GK: From where ... from where he's to start.

JL: Huh. I'm sure the youngsters like looking at them.

67 GK: Very much so! You can never...

JL: M-hm.

GK: ... prevent children from looking at these things.

JL: Right.

GK: But they never busy themselves with a prayer book.

JL: That's it. That's exactly the situation you were saying.

GK: M-hm.

JL: That's what I do repeatedly to that child.

GK: m... hm.

JL: ... ê-...âšikitâskošihk ê-kanawâpahtahk anihi.

GK: mhm.

JL: kêtahtawin mâna âskaw n'tôhci-wêpinamawâw animêniw ...

GK: m... hm.

JL: ... masinahikaniniw kotakîniw.

GK: m... hm.

JL: [laughs]

GK: m... hm.

GK: M-hm.

JL: ... when he lies flat on his back looking at those things.

GK: Mhm.

JL: All of a sudden I sometimes toss him that ...

GK: M-hm.

JL: ... another book.

GK: M-hm.

JL: [laughs]

GK: M-hm.

Ayamihitowin [III]

1 W1: a? kê-mâtocik.

GK: êko mâka, ayami.

W1: êko mâka, ayami. tâni kê-ytwêyân? n'ka-masinahên isa piko kê-ytak. [*child's voice heard indistinctly in background*] môna os' âna mâka nêsta nisitohtam.

GK: tân' êtwêspan otih, ayamihêw'-iskwêw kâ-ytwêt?

W1: kâ-it...

GK: "n'côcêmik," kâ-ytwêt.

2 W1: [*laughs*] nêsta kâ-wî-... mîna nâspici-... mîna kâ-pakosênimot 'ci-pêc'-îtohtêwat.

W2: môna wayêš ohc'-îtwêw.

GK: môna wayêš ohc'-îtwêw mîna "pêc'-îtohtê" 'c'-îtisk?

W1: môna wayêš.

Child: êhê, n'tâmahok.

GK: [*to child*] 'kawin' ôtê 'ci-pêc'-îtohtê. 'kwantaw nêsta kîn' antê nânîpawi.

W1: [*laughs*] nipwâhkâ kîna torotiy. êškwâ pitamâ niwî-'yamihtân. nimasinahamâkawin oš' ô. [*laughs and opens a letter*]

3 GK: mâhti pêtâ. n'ka-'yamihtân. tân' êtwêt ômêniw? 'wênihkân ô?

W1: [*reading letter*] "apišîš kimasinahamâtin. êko mâka, kikakwêcimitin êkoši pêciy-ašamik kâ-šîwâki, kâ-itamân ..., kî-tôtamanê kâ-ytwêyân. êkoši mâka môna wîskâc n'koci..., n'koci..., n'kocistên, 'kwân' 'hc'-îtwêyân."[1]

GK: [*in background*] tântê kâ-kî-pêci-masinahamâkawiyân?

W1: "êkwâni mâka wâciy'. êkoši mâk' apišîš ka-ititin. ê'kwâni ci..., cimiy mâka mîna pêci-kîwêtê, mîniyanê kâ-ytitân. mâhcic mîn' êkoši mâka kâ-šîwâki, kâ-ytitân."

GK: ôma ..., ôm' ayamihtâ.

W1: ôma ayamihtâ.

4 GK: awênihkân kâ-kî-pêci-masinahahk ômêniw?

W1: nîcihkawêsiw. "kimasinahamâtin. kêyâpac pêmâtisiwanê nêsta kîna, kêyâpac mâmâš ê-pimâtisiyân nêsta nîna. môna mâka šâkoc mistahi n'tayân tipâcimôwin. piko pahpakwac kimasinahamâtin, o..., kimasinahamâtin. âskaw, ê-kiskisitôtâtân, kâ-pêci-n'tawâpamiyapan môsonîhk kâ-p'mâskošinâpân. môna mihcêt awêna m'pêhtên nâspic

266

A conversation [III]

1 W1: Eh? They're going to cry.

GK: So then, speak.

W1: So then, speak. What shall I say? I'll just write down what I'll say to him. [*child's voice heard indistinctly in background*] But she doesn't understand it either, mind you.

GK: What was she saying, that is, when the nun spoke?

W1: She sai...

GK: "She's kissing me," she said.

2 W1: [*laughs*] And she wanted her ... again for good... she hoped that she [the child] would come again.

W2: She didn't say anything.

GK: She didn't say anything [just] to say to you again, "Come back."

W1: Not anything.

Child: Yes, she banged me.

GK: [*to child*] Don't come here. You too, stand around any place over there.

W1: [*laughs*] You be quiet, Dorothy. Wait a minute, I'm going to read. I've got a letter here. [*laughs and opens a letter*]

3 GK: Let's see, bring it here. I'll read it. What does he say in this? Who is this?

W1: [*reading letter*] "I'm writing you a short note. So I'm asking you: bring them food, fresh fruits, I mean ..., if you can do what I say. I never ta..., ta..., taste them; that's why I say it."

GK: [*in background*] Where's that letter I had written to me?

W1: "Well good-bye then. I'll tell you a little, though. That Ji... Jimmy [*pseudonym*] when he comes back again, if you give me what I tell you. For the last time again, it is fresh fruits which I say to you [to bring]."

GK: This..., read this.

W1: Read this.

4 GK: Who was it who wrote this?

W1: My brother. "I am writing to you. If in fact you too are still alive, I'm more or less alive too. I sure don't have any big news, though. Only to keep busy I'm writing to you, o..., I'm writing to you. Sometimes I remember you, when you came to see me at Moosonee when I was lying on my back. I don't hear that anyone is very sick... except for

wîna 'ciy-âhkosit … sapêt² piko, ê'kwâna mâškôc iko 'wasitê
ê-'tiy-âhkosit …, âniy otih, wîci-kišê-'niniwa."³

W2:   [to child banging something] ê'kwâni!

W1:   "môna wîskâc wayêš išîwîniwa." [to child] êh! [continues with letter] "piko
âskaw ê-nâtawâkahên'cêšit⁴ 'kwâni piko ê-tôtahk tašinê êy-itapit.
awâšišihk êy-itapit."

5   "môna wîskât kêkât ninipân," itwêw, "ê-'ti-otâkošihk⁵ ê-otami-nôtinit
sayman, otih. tâni mâka piko êhtikwê ânohc? twâmas mâka wîna,
êwakwâna mîna kây-âhkosit.⁶ môna kê-… kêkwân awêhtâkwan tân'
êtwêkwê ê-'yamîšihtât.⁷ môna nisitosiw ocihciya. kêtahtawin pikw
ânima ê-kîy-ohc'-îhtit sîkwanohk. mêkwâc mâk' êy-ašawahikêkopanê
'nima kâ-ihtit. tânika sôhka mihcêtoyêk wêhci-ihkinokopanê ôt' askîhk
ê-pimâtisinâniwahk. kôhkomisinaw mâka wîna cân kî-pîmihkwêpaniw,
itâkaniwan. âhkosiwikamikohk ihtâw." [to older girl minding child] mâhcâ,
wanawîhtay êko.

GK: t'âpacihat ani piko pêyak.

6 W1: [continues reading] "anohc ê'kwâni mâk' âtawîna pêyakwan ê-'htiyân nêsta
nîna kêyâpac, mâmâš ê-'mâtisiyân nêsta kišêy-'iniw. ê'kwâni kêyâpac
êšinâkosit …, mâna tašinê kâ-kôskôskêpanispan … "

GK: "… kâ-kôskôskêpanispan."

[simultaneously]

W1:   … kâ-wâpamatipan.⁸

    " 'kwâ⁹ nîcihkawêsiw, môna n'kiskên'tên 'ci-kî-pêc'-îtohtêyân anohc
kâ-nîpihk môsonîhk, nêstapiko šâkoc mitoni sikatapiyânê nakiskaw
kê-pêc'-îtohtêwânê. kêkât misiwê 'wênihkân ašamâkaniwan ôta
kâ-ihtâcik ininiwak. mô' 'cê¹⁰ pî… htikohtâcik ê-mâmî…,
ê-mâmîmicimêcik.¹¹ êkwâni mâka …, êkwâni mâka, n'kotwâsomitana
nîna kêkât ê-mînikawiyân, ê-ispîhci-macênimikawiyân, âta mâka hêkâ¹²
hê-minomâtisiyân. môna mâka šâkoc pišišikwâw m'pwâkitim."

7   "âta hêkâ êy-ašamicik, êkâ manâ wtâni¹³ hêy-ohci-ašawahikêwak¹⁴
ê'kwânima êkâ wêhci-wî-mînicik. âskaw wês' âtawîna n'taminahon.
môna mâka wîskâc awêna niwî-cîmik, ê-n'taminahowak. tânika hê…
otâni hêtênimiwâkwê êkâ wêhci-wî-wîcêwicik. ninôcihikwak isa mâka
wîna kêskênimitwâwi mîciminiw ê-pêtâwak.¹⁵ ê'kwâni nîcihkawêsiw.
âšay wî-a…, wî-…, wî-atih-… wî-ati-ošâšihtâkwan nimasinahikan."

Sabet, she's probably just getting a little worse…, Annie's [pseudonym] old man, that is."

W2: [to child banging something] That's enough!

W1: "He never does anything." [to child] Eh! [continues with letter] "Only sometimes he chops a little bit of wood. That's all he does, just sits around all the time. He sits around like a child."

5 "I almost never sleep," he says, "in the evening, since Simon [pseudonym] is busy fighting with me. I don't know how he must be now. As for Thomas [pseudonym], he got sick again. Not a thi…, thing that he says makes sense when he prattles on and on. He doesn't have feeling in his hands. It just suddenly happened to him last spring. It happened to him while he was sitting in a blind. I wonder why so many different things happen to one while living in this world. As for our uncle John [pseudonym], they say his face is twisted on one side. He is in the hospital." [to older girl minding child] Go along, take her outside then.

GK: What's the use of only one [being sent out]?

6 W1: [continues reading] "But right up to now, though, I'm still about the same, I'm still more or less alive and the old man also. He still looks the same …, he limps all the time the way he used to …"

GK: … the way he used to limp.

[simultaneously]

W1: … as when you used to see him.

"Well then, my brother, I don't know that I'll be able to come to Moosonee this summer or, if I get tired sitting around, whether I may come for a while. Almost every one of the people who are here is on rations. They don't even br… ing it in when they go for food. But then…, but then, because *I* was given almost sixty dollars, they think so badly of me, even though I'm not in good health. My pocket certainly isn't empty though."

7 "Even though they aren't giving me rations, just because I don't sit in a blind as far as they're concerned, – that's why they don't want to give it to me. Sometimes I do go hunting. But no one ever wants to go in the canoe with me, when I'm hunting. I wonder what they must think of me that they don't want to come with me. They keep bothering me, though, mind you, whenever they know that I'm bringing in food. That's that, my brother. Now my letter is going to…, going, is going to begin… is going to begin to sound snippy."

"wâciyi mâka, wâciyi,"

"nîna âlik âšîš."

8 GK: awênihkân mâk' ômêniw omasinahikan?

W1: šâpatîs.

GK: šâpatîs. kâ!

W1: šâpatîs man' ânihi ocôšimiša.

GK: [begins to read letter] "apišîš kimasinahamâtin êko mâka kiwî-kakwêcimitin êkoši pêciy-ašamin, apišîš a...

W1: ... kâ-šîwâki ...

GK: ... kâ-šîwâki ...

W1: ... kâ-itak ...

GK: ... kâ-itaman ...

W1: ... kî-tôtamanê kâ-itwêyân ...

GK: êkoši mâka môna wîskâc n'kocistênân ...," tân' êtwêt?

W1: "ê-..., môna wîskâc n'kocistênân ...

GK: ... êkoši mâka. môna wîskâc n'kocistênân wêhc'-îtwêyân." ê'kwâni, mâna ...

[simultaneously]

W1: "ê'kwân' 'êhci-i..., êkwâni mâka wâciyi. êkoši mâka mîn' âpišîš ka-ititin. côsif[16] mâka mîna pêci-kîwêtê, mîniyanê kâ-ititân. mâhcic mîna êkoši ... ha! ..."

9 GK: môna n'kocistênân isa; mâtik' ôtê mâka 'kwantaw pakwataskamikohk kâ-apiyan.[17]

W1: mâtika mâka, êkâ êy-ohci-n'ta... êkâ êy-ohci-n'tohtawiyin k'-âyamihitân 'sa piko, ka-ytâw.

GK: kimacipalihikon mâka kâ-šîwâki ... êko mâka mîciyan kâ-šîwâki, 'kwantaw ê-k'-îši-kihtohtêyin cêyakoc, ani êy-âpatisiyan.

W1: tântê mâka mîna kê-itwêyahk?

GK: kêkwân mâka wîna ani? tâni wâ-itwêyin? mwêhci [child speaks] tâni kê-itwêyin? nêsta kîn' âstam. 'kwêšic[18] pêci-'yami.

10 W1: ayami ...

GK: ayami ôta 'ci-nohtâkosiwat[19] ana kâ-a...[20]

W1: n'kî-pêhtâk. tâni kê-itwêyân?

GK: ... kâ-otayânit.

W1: ninihtâ-kanawâpahtên ...[21]

GK: ninihtâ-kanawâpahtên ...[22] ayami â..., ayami ta-nîpawiw ana.[23] ta-nohtâkosiw nêsta wîna. [child talks into microphone]

"Good-bye then, good-bye,"

"I am Alec Asheesh [*pseudonym*]."

8 GK: And whose letter is this?

W1: Jean-Baptiste's [*pseudonym*].

GK: Jean-Baptiste. Ah, yes!

W1: Jean-Baptiste's step-child there.

GK: [*begins to read letter*] "I'm writing you a short note, and so I want to ask you, please bring me food, br... a little...

W1: ... fresh fruit ...

GK: ... fresh fruit ...

W1: ... as I told him.

GK: ... I mean ...

W1: ... if you can do what I say ...

GK: And so we never taste them." What does he say?

W1: "Because, – we never taste them...

GK: ... so then. We never taste them is why I say it." That's it, frequently ...

[*simultaneously*]

W1: "That's why ... but good-bye then. Well, then, I'll tell you a little more again, – but when Joseph comes home again, if you give me what I say to you. Well then, for the last time again ... ha!"

9 GK: We don't taste them, that's all; you see what happens when you're sitting in the hinterland.

W1: Look here, now, you'll tell him that you didn't lis... that you didn't listen to me when I was talking to you.

GK: You have a bad time with perishables ... so then you eat the fresh things, having taken off in that direction instead, working there as you do.

W1: · What are we going to say next?

GK: What indeed [will we]? What do you want to say? Just [*child speaks*] what will you say? You too, come here. Girlie, come and talk.

10 W1: Talk...

GK: Speak here so you can be heard by that, one who...

W1: He can hear me. What shall I say?

GK: ... who owns it.

W1: I'm used to looking at it ...

GK: I'm used to looking at it ... Speak, uh... speak. She'll come to a standstill. She'll make a sound too. [*child talks into microphone*]

W1:   nohtâkosiw oš' âni nêsta wîna.

GK: ôta. ôta iši-ayami.

11 W1:   tân' êhki'? a?

GK: a! 'kâwina nâspic wâlaw itâpihkêpita.

W1:   "mâmá," itwê. ha! "mâmá."

Child: mây...

W1:   "pây pây," itwê.

Child: pây.

W1:   pây pây.

GK: "pây pây," itwê.

Child: pây-o. [laughs]

GK: "halo-o," itwê. [mother laughs] mîna!

W2:   "halo," itwê.

Child: pây pây.

W1:   kakwêcim kêkwâniw. mâhti kê-itwêkwê.

12 GK: "halo-o," itwê. mîna.

W1:   "halo-o," itwê. halo!

Child: pây!

W1:   halo.

Child: halo-o. pây.

W1:   pây.

GK: mîna: "pây," itwê.

W1:   "pây," itwê.

Child: [makes a noise]

GK: "halo," itwê.

Child: halo. [several exchanges follow between parents and child with infant noises.]

GK: âšay wîna kî-iškwâ-tipâcimow, wîna torotiy. apišîš kîy-ayamiw, wîna siyâkên.[24] [indistinct, brief background conversation]

13 W1:   tântê cicima?[25]

GK: tântê?

W1:   tântê cicima?

Child: pâ.[26]

W1:   nipâw.

GK: nipâw nâ? tântê?

W1:   tântê?

Child: pâw.

W1:   titima.

W1: Of course she'll make a sound too.

GK: Here. Talk here.

11 W1: What's happening? Eh?

GK: Eh? Don't pull the line [microphone wire] too far.

W1: Say, "Mama". Huh! "Mama".

Child: Mây...

W1: Say, "Bye-bye".

Child: Bye.

W1: Bye-bye.

GK: Say, "Bye-bye".

Child: Bye-o. [laughs]

GK: Say, "Hallo-o". [mother laughs] Again!

W2: Say, "Hallo".

Child: Bye-bye.

W1: Ask her something. Let's see what she'll say.

12 GK: Say, "Hallo-o". Again.

W1: Say, "Hallo-o". Hallo.

Child: Bye.

W1: Hallo.

Child: Hallo-o. Bye.

W1: Bye.

GK: Again: say, "Bye".

W1: Say, "Bye".

Child: [makes a noise]

GK: Say, "Hallo".

Child: Hallo. [several exchanges follow between parents and child with infant noises]

GK: Now she's finished telling a story, Dorothy has. She spoke a little bit at any rate. [indistinct, brief background conversation]

13 W1: Where's Titima?

GK: Where is she?

W1: Where's Titima?

Child: T'eep.

W1: She's asleep.

GK: Is she asleep? Where?

W1: Where?

Child: T'eep

W1: Titima.

[*simultaneously*]

GK: titima.

Child: pâw.

W1:   nêtê …

GK: "êhê," itwêw.

14 W1:   êhê.

GK: ê'êciw.[27]

W1:   êhê. âšay 'cika mîna pêyak k'-âhtakwakatât oški-'yâniw awa.[28] kâk' oš' âni nîšow êyâw[29] n't'têlimâhtay …, kâk' oš' âni piko pêyak êyâw n'titêlimâhtay.

W1:   tântê wêhci-kî-pîhcipanik anta?

GK: anta oš' âni ati-ispaniw.[30] pêyakwan ôma mwêhci kâ-išinâkwahk. tânêk' ântê 't'-îtâpihkêmohtâniwahk šâpo [*gesture*]. tâpask môna ta-k'-îhkinôpan.

W1:   [*laughs*]

GK: êhê! âšay kêkât kišipipaniw mâka pikw îtiht.[31]

W1:   k'wî-nipân?

GK: mîn' âyami.

W1:   [*speaks to child*]

GK: "niwî-nipân," itwê. "mêmê,"[32] itwê.

W1:   "mêmê," itwê.

Child: 'pân.

GK: 'pân.

W1:   [*laughs*]

GK: m'pân. [*laughs*] mâcika mâka kâ-itwêt: "niwî-nipân. 'pân". tânika itê mâka kâ-itohtêkwê? êkwâni mâka … antê ê-nânîpawit.

W1:   tântê aspin êtohtêt?[33]

GK: tânt' êtikwê piko? 'kwantaw manâ ôtê, antê mêskanâhk nânîpawiw. *fresh air* man' âni tôtam.

15 GK: [*looking out window*] tântê ô? êko êcik' âni mâka piko mîna aspin tôtahkik ôko, kâ-pêci-pakitinâcik mistikwa?

W1:   ê'kwâni.

GK: môna wêcika mîna wâ-'ti-wâskâhikanihkêcik.

W1:   âšay aspin misiwê.

GK: misiwê nâ kihtohtêwak?

W1:   m-hm. n'tawi-mohci-nâcipahêwak manâ mîna ošôniyânimiwâwa kê-kî-ohci-mani-cîstâskwâniwâspan.

GK: tâpwê isa minwâšininiw ômêniw otayân awa.[34] ê-kostahk mâka

[simultaneously]

GK: Titima.

Child: T'eep.

W1: Over there.

GK: She says, "Yes".

14 W1: Yes.

GK: Tee tick.

W1: Yes. I see he's already put a new reel on. I thought, he seems to have two ..., I was thinking ..., he seems to have only one, I was thinking.

W1: How can it [the sound] go into there?

GK: It's there of course it begins to go. There's just this one from the way it looks. I wonder if it would work if the line were put through there [gesture]. It probably wouldn't work.

W1: [laughs]

GK: Yes. It's almost at the end, he'll be told.

W1: Do you want to sleep?

GK: Talk again.

W1: [speaks to child]

GK: Say, "I want to sleep". Say, "Rock-a-bye".

W1: Say, "Rock-a-bye".

Child: S'eep.

GK: S'eep.

W1: [laughs]

GK: "I s'eep." [laughs] See what she said! "I want to sleep. 'eep." I wonder whereabouts he's gone. So then ..., standing around there.

W1: Where's he gone off to?

GK: Who knows where? Probably just over this way, he's standing around over there on the road. He's probably just taking fresh air.

15 GK: [looking out window] What's going on? So these people are doing the same thing again who came and placed the lumber.

W1: That's right.

GK: They're not going to start building a house right away.

W1: Now they're all away.

GK: Are they all leaving?

W1: M-hm. They probably just went to get their money in order for them to get some more nails.

GK: This fellow's equipment [CDE's tape recorder] sure is really nice! One of

ininiw 'ci-têpi-tôtamâsot ôma êšinâkwanilik[35] ê-âpacihtât wêmistikôšiw.[36]

the Indians is afraid though of doing it adequately for himself when a White-Man uses something that looks like this.

III

Legends and Narratives:

Moose Cree

Andrew Faries
Gilbert Faries
Sophie Gunner
James Gunner
Willie Frenchman
Hannah Loon
Ellen McLeod
John Carpenter

ANDREW FARIES

nîštam kâ-pâpalik kâ-pimihlâmakahk môsonîwî-ministikohk

1 m'pakosêlimikawin kici-tipâcimoyân pêyak tipâcimôwin.
êko mâka, nîštam kâ-pâpalik kâ-'milâmakahk[1] nika-âlimôtên,
kâ-kî-išiy-itâcimostâkawiyân 'nîkihikwak[2] ohci.

2 wêskac pêyakwâ pwâmoši ihtakwahki anihi kâ-ohci-ayaminâniwahk,
mâškôc âšay aliwâk nistomit... nistomitana piponwa otânâhk, kî-pâpaliw
mêkwâc, mêkwâc ... a...., mêkwâkîšik ê-nîpihk kêkwâ... kêkwânihkân.
ililiwak kî-wâpahtamwak nêt' ê-pêci-nôkwanilik, kîšikohk. môla mâka
kîy-ohci-kiskêlihtamwak tâni kê-itêlihtahkik. nâspitêpi kî-pakwâtamwak;
wâwâc nêšta 'kwâni kâ-iši-mâwatôpahâcik otawâšimišiwâwa,
ê-pîhtokwêpahâcik wâskâhikanihk.

3 kišêy-ayahâwak mâka kâ-pimâtisiwâspan mêkwâc anima,
kîy-itêlihtamwak âšay 'ci-iskwâpalilik askîliw. pêyak mâka ililiw êy-ôt...,
ê-'tôtêsit n'timihk sîpîhk ihtâpan, côsif nâkocîy ê-ytiht, mâskitôhtan[3]
išinihkâtêpanîk ililiwak ôta kâ-ihtâcik. ispî mâka wayâpahtahkik
kâ-'milâmakanilik išpimihk kîšikohk omôsasinîwi-pâskisikaniwâwa
kîy-otinamwak, kî-mâci-pâpâskisamwak mâka êy-itêlihtahkik, "wîhtikow âšay
kî-pêci-nipahikonaw."

4 êko mâk', kâ-takopalik kâ-'milâmakahk môsonîhk itêhkê
kîy-iši-têhômakan. kêkât mâka misiwê ê-ytaskânêsicik ililiwak ôta
môsonîwi-ministikohk kîy-âšawahamwak ê-n'tawê-wâpahtahkik omêliw
kê'wâ'hkân[4] nâspic kâ-kišiwêmakahk, kîšikohk kâ-papâm'palik. mihcêt mâka
kîy-ihtâwak antê ê-wâwâskâpawicik ê-kanawâpahtahkik animêliw
kᵃ-'milâmakanilik. mêkwâc mâka anim' ê-nîpihk kîy-ihtâw kišêy-ililiw, sômis
ê-ytiht, cimiy âšîš ê-itâkaniwit, kwayêsk ê-wîlâkaniwit. nâspic
kî-kišê-ylilîwiw; kîy-itêw mâka otôtêma ê-kî-wâpahtahk pawâmowinihk
kêkwânihkâniliw kîšikohk ê-pêci-nôkwanilik. "êko mâka," kî-itwêw,
"nika-wâpahtên pwâmoši nipiyân." êko isa mâka kâ-ihkih'.[5]

5 anima mêkwânîpin[6] kâ-pâpalik kâ-'milâmakahk kîšikohk, kâ-kîy-itwêt awa
kišê-yl'liw. pwâmošiy ati-âhkwatinilik mâka mîna ê-piponilik,
kî-pôni-'mâtisiw.

280

The first airplane comes to Moose Factory

1   I have been asked to tell a certain story.

So then, I shall talk about the first airplane which came, which I was told about by my parents.

2   Once long ago, before there were radios, perhaps by now over thirt... thirty years ago, there came during, during ... uh ..., at midday in summer a thing ... a kind of thing. The Indian people saw it coming into sight away yonder, in the sky. But they did not know what to think. They didn't like it at all; and at that point they even gathered their children on the run, making them scurry into the houses.

3   The old people who were living at that time, though, thought that the world was now coming to an end. One person, however, with his fa... with his family, was staying up-river, Joseph Nagochee by name, – "Lame-heel" the people hereabouts used to call him. When they saw the airplane high in the sky, they took their moose-shot guns and they began to shoot repeatedly at it, thinking, "A windigo has now come to kill us."

4   So then, when the plane arrived, it landed on the Moosonee side. And people of nearly all nationalities crossed here to Moose Island [i.e., Moose Factory] because they wanted to see this sort of thing which made a very loud noise, which moved around in the sky. And there were many standing around there, looking at that airplane. During that summer there was an old person, Soomis as he was called, spoken of as Jimmy Asheesh when he was given his proper name. He was a very old person; but he said to his friend that he had seen in a dream a kind of thing coming into sight in the sky. "And so," he said, "I shall see it before I die." And that is what happened.

5   That was it: it was midsummer when the plane arrived in the sky, as the old man had said. But before it began to freeze the next winter, he passed away.

wacask wêhci-išinâkwanilik osôw

1   pêyakwâ wêskac ê-tipâcimâkaniwit wacask, kî-napakâliw osôw, ê-mišâlik
mâka tâpiskôc amisk. êko mâka, nâspic ê-pakwâtahk awa wacask,
ê-papâmâtakât. ê-papâmâtêmot mâka, ê-ytâkaniwit šîpîšišihk
ê-miloskam'ilik[1] ê-papâmâtakât. êko mâk' ôma, ê-ytahamâsot:
       "nipapâ-pwâwihôtân nisôyê,[2]
              nisôyê, nisôyê;
       m'pâ'-pwâwihôtân nisôyê,
              nisôyê."

2   êko mâka, ispîy ê-'ti-pêhtawâkaniwit, kî-mâcišikâtêliw osôw îtaw itêhkê.
ê'kwâni mâka anohc wêhc'-îšinâkwanilik wacask osôw.

How the muskrat got his long, tapered tail

1   Once long ago, as the story is told of the muskrat, his tail was flat and big like a beaver's. Well then, this muskrat disliked it very much as he swam around. He went around crying, so it is said of him, swimming in the creek during open water [in late spring, after the ice has broken up]. And so he took up this refrain:

"I'm dragging it around, My Tail,
      My Tail, My Tail;
N'draggin' it around, My Tail,
      My Tail."

2   So then, when he began to be heard, his tail was cut off on each side. And that is why the muskrat's tail looks the way it does now.

acicamoš wêhci-mihkwacâpit

1   êko, ê-'tâtalôhkawâkaniwit acicamoš wêhci-mihkwacâpit.
pêyakwâ wêskac ê-natawâpamâkaniwit kici-nîkânisît 'wiyâšîš
mistikoskâhk, acicamoš k'-îtêl'tam wîla kici-nîkânîspan. êko mâka ispîy
ê-wâp…, ê-wâpamikot kotakîya 'wiyâšîša, kî-mâci-mâlêlimêwak.
kî-pâhpihêwak mâka ê-ytâcik: "âwas kîla! wêsâ kitapišîš'šin. môla wîskâc
ka-kî-okimâwin ôta mistikoskâhk ê-'pišîš'iyan."

2   êko mâka, nâ'c[1] ê-pakwâtahk acicamoš, nâ'c êlikohk kî-mâtow. nâš'c êlikw'
[2] mâka nêst' ê-sinikocâpin'tisot, pîliš, pîliš miconi ê-kîy-ati-mamihkwâtakâpit,
ê-'spîhc'-êlikohk-mâtot.[3]

Why the squirrel has red eyes

1   So then, the legend is told of why the squirrel has red eyes.

Once long ago when an animal was being sought to be leader in the woods, the squirrel thought that *he* should be foremost. Now then, when the other animals saw ..., saw him, they began to make fun of him. And they ridiculed him, saying to him: "Be off with you! You're too little. You'll never be able to be master here in the woods because you're little."

2   And so, since the squirrel hated it very much, he cried very hard. And he also rubbed at his eyes very hard, until, until he began to have entirely red eyes from crying so hard.

mwâkwa wêhc'-îšinâkwaniliki osita

1   êko mâka, ôma mîna ê-'t'-âtalôhkawâkaniwit mwâkwa wêhc'-îšinâkwanilik
omisita ...[1] osita.

pêyakwâ wêskac, 'wêyâšîšak nêsta pilêsiwak, kî-mâwacihitowak
ê-wî-makošêcik. êko mâka, sâkahikanihk ant' ê-'htâcik, mêkwâc ê-makošêcik,
kî-mâci-nôcihêw kotak..., kotakîya pilêsiwa, awa mwâkwa. êko mâka
kotakîyak aniki pilêsiwak môla nahêl'tamwak anima ê-wî-maskahtwêt
šinkipiš wîwa, awa mwâkwa.

2   êko mâka kâ-..., ê-kisiwâsit aw šinkipiš, kî-pimicišahwêw ô' mwâkwa.[2]
êko mâk' ê-'ti-kihcipahtâl'ci nâ'c êliko' kî-nôsô-tahkiškâtêw. miconi mâk' antê
o..., otânâhk k'-îši-wêpiškam osita ê-kî-mâskiskawât mâka. iskonâk mâka,
ê'kwâni mâka wêhci-anim'-êtakotêliki osita, cîkic anta onahkitîhk awa
mwâkwa.

Why the loon's feet are near the tail

1   Now then, this again is the beginning of the legend about the loon, why this one's feet ... his feet look the way they do.

Once upon a time long ago, the beasts and the birds got together because they wanted to have a feast. And so, as they were there on the lake, in the course of the feasting, this loon began flirt around with oth..., other birds. So then the rest of those birds weren't pleased with the fact that this loon wanted to take away Shingibish's wife.

2   And so when ..., being angry, Shingibish chased after this loon. And then, as the latter ran away, he kicked him very hard as he ran off. And he utterly knocked his ..., his feet back there having crippled him. And ever since, that's why the loon's feet hang that way, right near his tail-end.

maskwa wêhci-tahkwâliwêt

1   anohc, ôma ê-'t'-âtalôhkâtâkaniwit maskwa, wêhci-tahkwâlik osôw.
pêyakwâ wêskac kî-n..., kî-wâpamêw mahkêšiwa namêsa ê-'yâwâl'ci. êko
mâk' ôm' êtwêw maskwa: "tântê wêhci-kaškihtâyin kîla ê-kâhcitinat
namês?"

êko mâk' ôm' êtwêw mahkêšiw: "nâhtâ[1] wêhtan ê-wî-kâhcitin...âkaniwit
namês. ê-pakwaniyâk antê sîpîhk, maskwamîhk, êkota piko ê-'ši-kiht...,
-kihtâpêkinamân nisôw. êko mâk' ê-môšahak namês, ê-nôcihtât nisôw,
n'kwâškocipalihon. mêkwâc ê-mâkohtahk nisôw,[2] nimôskipitâw mâka.
ka-kaškihtân, nêsta kîla, kišâspin wî-mâkonat...,[3] wî-kâhcitinatê namês,"
itêw ma..., maskwawa.

2   êko mâka, "tâpwê," kâ-itêl'tahk maskwa, "n'ka-kocihtân, nêsta nîla."
êko mâka kâ-kihtâpêkinahk osôw, ê-kinwâlik oti osôw. êko mâka
ê-môšihât namêsa, namês' ê-nôcihtâl'ci osôw, môl' êškwâ kwâškocipalihow.

"êkoši pitamâ mihcêt, kata-wanakohkêwak," itêl'htam awa maskwa,
ê-wîy-okâš'kimit oti. mihcêt namês' n'tawêlimêw.

3   êko mâka pîliš, ê-'ti-akwaškwatinilik osôw, "âšay mihcêtiwak," itêl'htam,
"namêsa,"[4] ê-'ti-kosikwa-mahcihtât osôw.

êko mâk' ispî kâ-kwâškocipalihot, êkotê 'ni kâ-kîškipitahk[5] osôw, âšay
ê-kîy-akwâhkwahtinilik.[6]

Why the bear has a short tail

1   Now, this is the beginning of the legend about the bear, why his tail is short.

Once upon a time long ago he f..., he saw a fox that had a fish. And so at this the bear said: "How is it that *you* are able to catch fish?"

And so at this the fox replied: "It's very easy when one wants to catch a fish. At that hole there in the river, in the ice, it's just at that very spot that I di..., dip my tail in. And then, as I feel a fish playing around with my tail, I suddenly give a jump. While he's biting my tail, I pull him to the surface though. You can do it too, if you want to catch hold of him ..., if you want to catch a fish," he said to the b... bear.

2   So then the bear thought, "Certainly, *I'll* be able, too."

So then he dipped his tail in, his long tail, that is. And then as he felt a fish, a fish playing with his tail, he didn't yet give a jump.

"So wait a little and many, – will be hanging on here and there," thought the bear in his greedy desire, that is. He wanted a lot of fish.

3   And so at last, as his tail began to freeze to the ice, he thought, "Now there are a lot of fish," as he began to feel his tail heavy.

And then at that point when he gave a sudden jump, that's the way he tore off his tail, since it had already been stuck to the ice.

wêskac môsonîwi-ministikohk

1   mân'šîš niwî-tipâcimon ê-'ši-kiskisiyân,[1] wêskac âšay ôta nawac
ê-kîy-ohc'-îhtâyân.[2]

      nîštam ôta kâ-pêc'-îtohtêyân, cîmânihk n'kîy-ohci-..., n'kî-pêci-pôsin
kêšîciwanohk ê-kîy-ohci-pêšîwikawiyân[3] kiskino..., kiskinohamâtôwikamikohk
mâk' ôtê ê-kî-pakitinikawiyân. n'kiskisihtay mâna nîštam ôta kâ-pêc'-îhtâyân
ililiwak mâna ê-pôsiwâspan nâspic mâna wîpac mâna ê-..., ê-takwâkihk
pôsîpanak, misiwê ocawâšimišiwâwa ê-wîcêwâcik.

2   iskan'-pipon mâka ê-'tâpicîwâspan aniki, iskwêwak, awâšišak mâka.
nâpêwak wîla mâna âskaw takošinôpanak ê-k'-îškwâ-walawîmakahk[4]
otayôwiniwâwa ê-pêtâcik. iskani-pipon mâk' itâpicîpanak mâna, ê-n...
ê-natahocik oti. pâtimâ mâka mîna ê-miloskaminilik mišakâpanak. ispî
mâka mân' ê-mišakâcik ililiwak, mêkwâ-nîpin, nâhtâ' 'âna[5]
miši-makošâniwanôpan. âtiht mâna nâpêwak išicišahwâkaniwinôpanak
kici-nâtawamôswêcik[6] nêstapiko wâpošwa, môso-wîyâsiliw ê-pêtâcik
kici-makošêwâkaniwahk. êko mâka mâna mistiko-nâpêwikamikohk[7]
iši-makošâniwanôpan. nâ'c mân' ê-kinwâki mâna mîcisonâhtikwa
pakitinikâtêwa. nêtê mâka mâwac nîkân itêhkê kotak mîcisonâhtik
pakitinikâtêpan. êkota okimâwak, ayamihêwikimâwak, kâ-kiskinohamâkêcik
mâka ..., êkotê ê-iši-apihâkaniwit[8] nîštam, wîlistamiwâw[9] ê-mîcisocik,
pwâmoš' îliliwak makošêcik.

3   nâhtâ' kistêl'hcikâtêpan anim' ê-kîšikâk. êko mâka,
ê-k'-îškwâ-mîcisonâniwahk, êkotê ê-mâci-kwêci... -kwêcihitonâniwahk,
ê-pim'pahtâcik otih, awâšišak pîliš kišê-'l'liwak. n'kiskisin pêyakwâ
kišê-'l'liw, cân martin ê-'tâkaniwit. êko mâka, nêsta wîla pim'pahtâpan.
mêkwâc mâka ê-pim'pahtât, kâ-p'mi-kalakâpiskipalihât pîhcipihkwâna[10]
opwâkitimihk ê-pîhcišinil'ci. miconi mâk' ê-kosikwaniliki o..., ê-kosikwanilik
opîskâkan ê-'šinâkosit, šâkoc mâka kêkât kî-nîkânipaliw, âta misawâc
ê-kišê-'l'lîwit.

4   êko mâka nêsta, oškinîkiwak nêsta pim'pahtâwak. nâhtâpwê
milwêl'htâkwanôpan. êko mâk' ê-..., pêyakwâ antê mêkwâc
ê-kanawâpahtamâhk ê-mêtawâniwahk (êlikôš išinihkâsôpan, ôta oškinîkiw,
awâšiš oti, tâpiskôc mâškôc n'tispîhcisînân) êko mâka n'kišiwâhitonân anta
mêkwâc ê-mêtawêyâhk. êko mâka, mêkwâc ê-milo-mêtawâniwahk, nâ'c
êlikw'[11] nimâšihkânân nîlanân. miconi kihciwê n'kisiwâsinân. nâ'c mâka

The old days at Moose Factory

1   I want to give a brief account of my memories, since I've been around here now for quite some time.

When I first came here, it was by boat I ca..., I sailed, having been brought from Albany Post to schoo..., and was put here in the school. I remembered again and again from the time I was first here the Indians used often to go away by canoe, very frequently they used to go away early in ..., in the fall, all their children going with them.

2   Those people would stay away the whole winter, women and children. The men, for their part, frequently used to come in sometimes after the New Year, bringing their furs. But they frequently used to be away the whole winter hun..., hunting, I mean. Later on, however, when it was open water again, they used to paddle. Furthermore, at the time when people were habitually paddling, in midsummer, there used to be a very big feast indeed. Several men used to be dispatched to go look for moose or rabbits, bringing back moose-meat to be used for the feast. And then the practice was, there would be a feast in the carpenter shop. Very long tables would be regularly set up. But over there at the extreme head of the table another table used to be put. That's where the bosses, the clergy and teachers ..., there's where first seated, they ate at the first sitting, before the people feasted.

3   That day was highly thought of. And then, after the feast was over, at that point they began to com..., to compete with each other, in racing that is, children up to old people. I remember one time an old fellow, John Martin as he was called. So then, he too used to run. But while he was running, he made the cartridges which lay in his pocket rattle. And although he appeared as if his ... were very heavy, his jacket was very heavy, nonetheless he was nearly in the lead, even though he was old.

4   And then also, the young men raced too. It was really enjoyable. And then uh ..., one time there while we were watching the sports (a young fellow here, a child I mean, Little Ant used to be his nickname, we were both perhaps the same age) well then, we got each other mad while we were playing there. So then, while the fun and sports were going on, *we* were wrestling as hard as we could. We got really very angry. And the old

n'šîhkihikonânak nêsta kišê-'liwak kici-mâšihkêyâhk. môla isa šâkoc
kîy-ohci-kiskêl'htâkwan awênihkân kâ-šâkotwât. tâpiskôc mâškôc
n'kî-iši-wêpahotonân [laughs].

5   êko mâk' ê-k'-îškwâ-makošâniwahk ê-kîšikâk, ê-k'-îškwâ-mêtawâniwahk
mâka, êkwâni mâk' âti-...,[12] ê-'ti-miši-nîminâniwahkipan. âskaw mâna
ê-makošâniwahk, mîna mâka makošân'ôpan,[13] šîšîpak ispîy êy-ohpahocik.
êkwâni mîna pêyakwan êtôcikâtêkipan: nâpêwak mâna
kihcicišahwâkan...iwîpanak,[14] kici-nataw'šipêcik. êkwâni mîna pêyakwan
êtastâniwahki mâna, mîcisonâhtikwa ê-walastâniwahki. ay'hâw mâka
nêsta kihcy-okimâw ê-pâpihlâsp... ê-pâpilispan,[15] kihci-..., kihcy-okimâw oti
..., kihcy-okimâw. miconi mâna nîpitêkâpawiwak, nîpitêkâpawiwak ililiwak,
nâpêwak pâskisikan' ê-'yâcik, nêtê akwâpicikanihk,[16] lâlipêk ant'
ê-nîpawicik.

6   êko mâk' ê-pêci-pimaholâkaniwit ana kihcy-okimâw, êkot' ânta
mâci-pâpâskisikêwâspan ê-'spîhci-wâpahtamolâcik ê-kistêlimâcik anihi
kâ-pêci-mišakâl'ci, ê-kistisîl'ci oti. êko mîna cîkic anta,
kampani-wâskâhikanihk, êkot' ânta mîna kotak[17] '-nîpawicik nâpêwak,
ê-pêci-kospit mâk' awa kihcy-okimâw, êkota mîna nâ'c êl'k[18] '-pâpâskisikêcik,
nâspic kî-wâpahtamolêwak anihi kihcy-okimâwa, ê-'spîhci-kistêlimâcik
ê-kistakisol'ci.

7   mihcêt kê'wâ'hkân[19] n'ka-kîy-âlimôtêhtay ôta, ê-mâcistahk nêsta. môla
wîskât išinâkwan âšay ê-mâcistahk anohc kâ-'šinâkwahkipan mâna wêskac.
pêyakwan n'kî-wâ'htên[20] ê-..., kêkât ê-kî-pâsicipotêk ôma ministik. êko mâka,
pâtimâ k'-âyamihcikêt ayamihêw'kimâw kî-..., kî-kîwêpaliw anima nipiy
mêkwâc ê-'yamihcikâniwahk.

ê'kwân' ispîš wîl' anohc kê-ytwêyân. môla misawâc mâškôc n'ka-tâpwêtâk
niwâhkomâkan n'tohtawitê, ântriw fârîs ôta kâ-itâkaniwit.

fellows too were urging us on a lot to wrestle. It really couldn't be known who had won. We probably knocked each other around just about even [*laughs*].

5   So then after the feast while it was day, and after the sports, then began ..., a big dance used to begin. Sometimes frequently, in the course of feasting, the feasting would take place all over again, when the ducks started flying. Then the same thing would be done all over again: the men would be sent out repeatedly to look for ducks. The same arrangements would often be made again, in setting up tables. And er ..., the chief Manager too used to fly in ... used to come in by boat, the Chief ..., District Manager, that is ..., the District Manager. They would stand completely in line, the Indians would stand in a line, the men with their guns, there on the Flats, standing there alongside the water.

6   So then as the District Manager was being brought in, at that point they would begin firing their guns, showing him the extent of their respect for that one who was paddling in, as an eminent person, that is. Then again nearby, at the Company house, with other men standing right there again, while the Chief Manager was walking up to the bank, – right here again by shooting off their guns for all they were worth they showed that District Manager that they had held him in such esteem as a person of prestige.

7   I could tell about many kinds of things here, about break-up too. It never looks at break-up now the way it frequently used to look long ago. I've seen the same fl... this island almost flooded. And then, after the clergyman had prayed the water w..., receded while they were having the service.

    That's all I have to say now. In any case I probably won't be believed by my relative if he listens to me, Andrew Faries as he's called here.

ê-ošihâkaniwit môso-wayân

1   môso-wayân ..., âšay? môso-wayân, ê-ošihakiht nîštam ohci misiwê
nipaškotawêšwânân. misiwê n'tôtinênân opîwaya. êko k'-îškwâ-kîšihakiht
anima, nikapastawêhwânân tapihk, pêyako-tipiskâw m'pakitinânân
kici-akohcihk nipîhk. hêko[1] mistik nâcipahtwâniwan nôhcimihk ohci; êko
m'pakitinânân anta wakic mistikohk. êk' ôskan n'tâpacihtânân, môs'-oskan.
ê-paškwahokiht ana môswa, môso-wayân ê-ošihakiht, êko
k'-îškw'-ânima-tôtawakiht,[2] mîna n'kapastawêhwânân, nipîhk ê-kîšihakiht,
misiwê omihkow kici-wîkatêpalilik, êkâ wâci mân'šîš kit'-ihtakwahk.[3] mâškôc
nisto-kîšikâw n'takohcimânân âskaw, micon' êkâ nôkwahk nipîhk pâtimâ
mihkow.

2   nipîm'pâtâskwahwânân mâka, n'takolânân mistikohk.[4] êko iškwâ anim'
ê-tôtawakiht, êko, môswa wîl'tihp[5] n'tâpacihtânân, ostikwânihk ohci môswa.
n'itêhênân[6] anima olâkanihk, pêsin tâpiskôc ê-kicistâpâwalonâniwahk.
n'itêhênân anima wîl'tihp êlikohk; kôn[7] mâka nipakitinânân ê-pipohk wîla.
môla m'pônihtânân ê-itêhaw..., ê-itêhamâhk anima, stwâpihk[8]
n'tôkît-astânân.[9] pîliš, pîliš ê-'ti-kîšitêk, êkow ê-k'-îškwâ-kîšitêk, êko
pîm'pâtahok[10] mîn' ana môso-wayân. nâh'c êlik'[11] m'pîm'pâtahwâw miconi
kici-pâhkopalit. êko pêkitinak, pêkitinamân anima, tapihk m'pakitinên;
n'sîkinên anima wîl'tihpâpôw. êko, misiwê nimisitêpitên anima wîl'tihp;
misiwê n'tâhtêkipitâw. nišašiw'nên misiwê kici-têpipalik anima.

3   êko k'-îškw'-ânima-tôtawakiht nisto kîšikâwa nipakitinânân anta kiciy-apit
tapihk. êko k'-îškw'-ânima nisto-kîšikâw, âšay n'tôt..., n'tôtinânân 'nta ohci,
mistikohk n'takolânân, ê-wâšêyâskotamâhk[12] mistik. êkot' êy-akolakiht anta
kici-pâsot, n'tôcicipitânân[13] ê-'ti-pâsot ana. môla m'pônihânân êy-oci...
-ocipitakêt pîliš ê-'ti-pâsot. êko kâ-iškwâ-pâsoci anima, ê-wîy-osâwâ-pâsokiht
wîla, nipasâhtakwâtânân, 'stâhkwanak[14] n'tâpacihânânak ê-wî-..., 'ci-lôskisit
ê-..., ê-itêl'htamâhk ana môso-wayân.

4   êko k'-îškw'-ânima-tôtawakiht, êko mîna kapastawêhokiht. sôp
n'kipiškišwânân; n'tôswânân ana sôp. êko kêpastawêhokiht anta sôpâpôhk.
akohcin mîna; mîna nisto-tipiskâw n'takohcimânân ana môso-wayân. êko
n'tôcocipitânân ant' êy-akohcihk sôpâpôhk. môla nipônihânân, mîna mîn'
ê'kwân' ê-tôtawakiht nipiy m'pâtinânân.

êkow êškw'-ânima-tôtawakiht, êko mîna êkolakiht mistikohk, êko
sîn'pâtahokiht, mistik n'tâpacihtânân, m'pîm'pâtahwânân nâ'c êlikohk. êko

Tanning moose-hide

1   Moose-hide ..., now? Moose-hide, when we make it from the beginning
we cut *all* the hair off. We take off all its whiskers. Then after we
have finished doing that, we submerge it in a tub, for one night we put it
to steep in water. Then a pole is fetched from the bush; then, we place it
on top of the pole. Then we use a bone, a moose bone. We scrape off the
upper layer of skin from the moose, as we make the moose-hide; then after
we've done that to it, again we submerge it, as we finish it in the water, so
that all his blood disappears, and not even a little bit is there. Sometimes
we let it soak for perhaps three days, until there is no blood showing in the
water at all.

2   We wring it by twisting with a stick, and we hang it on a pole. Then after
we've done that to it, then, we use the moose's brain, from the moose's head.
We stir that in a dish, like a wash basin. We stir that brain vigorously; but
we put in snow [instead of water] in the winter. We don't stop stir..., stirring
that, but we set it on top of the stove. At long last it begins to cook; now after
it's cooked, then I wring that moose-hide again. I wring it as hard as I can so
it will go entirely dry. Then I put it, I put that thing, I put it in a tub; I pour
that brain-liquid of his into the tub. Then I spread all that entire brain of his
all over; I move it all around. I work the whole hide around so that that will
be enough.

3   Then after we have done that to it, we put it there to sit in the tub for
three days. Then after that three-day period we ta... take it from there, we
hang it on a pole, whittling the pole clean. Hanging it there to dry, we pull
away at it as it begins to dry. We don't stop pulling and pulling away at it
until it begins to dry. Then whenever it's finished drying, since we want to
smoke it yellow, we use wood chips, we use brushwood since we want ..., so it
will be soft with ..., with that idea in mind for that moose hide.

4   So after we've done that to it, then we put it back in the water. We cut up
soap in small pieces; we boil that soap. Then we put it there in the soap
liquid. It soaks again; we soak that moose hide again for three nights. Then
we keep stretching it as it floats in the soapy water. We don't stop; doing the
same thing to it over and over again, we wring the water out.

So as we've finished doing that to it, we then hang it on the pole again;
then we wring it out, we use a stick; we wring it by twisting it as hard as we

kîšinakiht picêlak.[15] pîliš, pîliš miconi ê-pâsot môla m'pônihânân; mistik
nêsta n'tâpacihtânân n'tôtatâmahwânân[16] ê-..., ê-..., mistik ê-piskwâk antê
nîkân,[17] ê-mišâk. ê'kwân' wêtatâmahikâkêyâhk an' '-otatâmahwâkiht
kici-lôskisit, ê-pêyakohkawakiht[18] wîla.

5   ê-nîšohkawakiht mâka wîla môla n'tawêl'htâkwan mistik.
'-nîšohkawâkaniwit êy-oci... -ocipitâkaniwit lôskisiw. pîliš pîliš ê-'ti-pâsot,
êko kâ-iškwâ-pâsoci, êkâ wîla ... ê-wî-wâpihakiht mâka wîla, môla n'...,
môla n'takwâpaswânân. môla pîkotôhtak n'tâpacihtânân. ê'kwâni pikw
ê-'ši-nakatakiht anim' ê-'šinâkosit, ê'kwâni mâka ê-'ši-maskisinihkâkêyâhk.
êko mâka wîla ê-wî-osâwâ-pasokiht, pîkotôhtak n'tâpacihtânân. mâwac
ê-pîkotôwahk mistik n'nân'tawâ'htênân[19] nôhcimihk. âskaw
wâkinâkan'-pîkotôhtak mâwac milwâšin, nêst', ayahâw, minahiko-pîkotôhtak
âskaw.

    êko n'tôsâwâ-paswânân. êko kâ-iškwâ-osâwâ-pasokihci, êkw êkolakiht
walawîtimih' 'ci-wêwêpâšit, êkâ nâšic kici-milâkosit[20] anima êy-osâwâ-pasot,
êkâ kici-milâkwahk anima pîkotôhtak. 'kwân' êh-tôtawakiht môso-wayân
êy-oš'akiht.

6   pîtoš mâka mîna tôtamwak wîla nâpêwak, wîla nâpêwak wîla '-ošihâcik
môso-wayâna, kâ-k'-îši-wâpahtamân nêtê '-pêci-pimâtisiyân ê-'wâšišîwiyân.
pîtoš tôtamwak nâpêwak wîla. ana môso-wayân môla otinamwak opîwaya,
êkwân' ê-'ši-akolâcik mistikohk ê-kînikâk mistik. 'kwân' ê-'ši-okîcišimâcik[21]
ant' akolêwak. êko, mihkikwan išin'kâtêw anim' ôskan. êwakwânimêliw
tâpisikonamwak ocihciwâhk, otatâmahwêwak anihi ... mêliw[22] ê-manahahkik
otamaskâliw. môla tâpiskôc nîlâ'n[23] kâ-tôtamâhk iskwêwak, pî... im...,
ay'hâw, oskan kâ-âpacihtâyâhk. otatâmahwêwak pîliš ê-kîšihâcik pîliš
misiwê ê-mananahkik anim'[24] otamaskay kâ-icikâtêk.

7   êko[25] picêlak mênišahkik animêliw 'pîwâliw.[26] êko picêlak wîlawâw
oskaniliw wêtinahkik kwêskitê 'nim'[27] ê-mananahkik kâ-mahkatêwâk watôw
kâ-išinihkâcikâtêk. nâpêwak wîl' ê'kwân' ê-htôtahkik.

    pâpîtoš 'sa 'htôtamwak misiwê 'wênihkânak ê-ošihâcik nêsta môso-wayâna.
âskaw nêst' ê-n'tawêlimiht nâspic kici-wâpisit môso-wayân, akolâkaniwan
mistikohk ê-pipohk walawîtimihk. kinwêš, mâškôc pêyako-pîsim âskaw
akocin antê. miconi mâka wâpisiw ê-pâwanacit.

    ê'kwân' êhtôhtâht âskaw môso-wayân êy-ošihiht.

can. Then we finish it just then. Right up until it's entirely dry we don't let
up; we use a stick as well, we beat it repeatedly w... w... a stick with a knob
on it there at the front end, a big one. That's what we use to hit away with in
beating that moose hide to be fluffy soft, when we work it alone.

5   When two of us work at it though a stick is not needed. When it's
worked at by two people, being pulled this way and that, it is soft. Until,
until it begins to dry, then whenever it has finished drying, not that ...,
when we want to whiten it in particular, we don't ..., we don't smoke it. We
don't use rotten wood. We leave it the way it looks and make moccasins out
of it as it is. But then when in fact we want to make it yellow, we use rotten
wood. We look for the most rotten wood in the bush. Sometimes juniper
rotten wood is the finest, – also er ..., spruce rotten wood sometimes.

    Then we smoke it yellow. Then every time after we have smoked
it yellow, then we hang it outside to blow in the wind, so it won't
have a strong smell, being as it's smoked yellow, so that that rotten
wood won't smell. That's what we do to it when we make moose
hide.

6   But as for the men, they do it differently again when men are making
moose hide, which I've seen since I was living away over there as a child.
Men for their part do it differently. They do not take the hairs of the moose
hide; then they hang it on a stick, a pointed stick. Then laying it on
something, they hang it up there. So, that bone is called the shin-bone. They
slip that thing on their hand; they beat away at it ... that, removing the bits
of meat by hand. Not like what we women do, wr... w... well, uh, who use a
bone. They beat it until they finish, until they remove by hand all that meat
residue as it's called.

7   It's only then that they cut the hair off. It's only then that *they* take the
bone, scraping off on the other side that black, clotted blood as they call it.
The men do it that way.

    All people, frankly, do it in different ways when they make moose hide.
Sometimes also when the moose hide is required to be very white, it is hung
up on a pole in winter outside. For a long time, sometimes perhaps for a
month it hangs there. It gets completely white as it dries with the frost.

    That's what is done to it sometimes when moose hide is made.

askiy kâ-âpacihtâniwahk ê-tahkopitâwasonâniwahk

1   askiy êy-âpatahk ê-..., awâšiš ê-âpacihtamohâkaniwit nâcipahtwâniwan nôcimih', ê-pahkwêpicikâtêk.[1] môla wîla misiwê kâ-wâpahcikâtêk[2] askiy, môla misiwê âpatan. ihtakwan an'm' askiy kâ-âpacihtâcik, awâšišak êy-âpacihtamohihcik[3] ê-..., ê-tahkwapisocik wâspisoyânihk, êkâ pakwayânêkin êy-âpatahk. nâcipahtwâniwan mâka nôhcimihk anim' ê-pahkwêpicikâtêk askiy; akotâniwan mâka, mistikohk ayakotâniwanwa. pâsikâtêwa miconi kwayêsk; êko pawapicikâtêwa k'-îškwâ pâs..., pâstêki. pako... pako..., pawapitâkaniwanwak nêsta êkâ ê... 'c'-îhtâcik anta man'côšak.[4] misiwê wîkatêpitâkaniwanwa. pîhtahikâtêwa mâka mîwatihk, kanawêl'cikâtêk,[5] hê-âpacihtamohihcik awâšišak ê-pipohk wîla ê'kwân ê-tôcikâtêk. nahastâniwanwa nahastamawâkaniwanwak awâšišak.

2   êko mâka nêst' êkâ ê-'yâ'spanak[6] wîla mîwatiliw wêskac awê'hkânak, nôhcimihk akotâwak šîpâ mistikohk, šîpâ mistikohk iši-kâhtinikâtêwa ê-sakâ... ê-sakâskosicik[7] ê-... s'tâhkwanak.[8] êkotê 'ši-šêšêkonikâtêk. êkw ê-nôhtêpalicik anik' awâšišak anihi 'y-âpacihtâcik askîliw, nâcipahtwâniwanwa piko, ohci-nâcipahtwâniwaniliwa, hêy-âpacihtamohihcik. nâspic mâka kî-payêhkisiwak awâšišak anihiy ê-pêci-âpacihtâcik askîliw. môla tâpiskôc anohc pišišik pakwayânêkinwa '-âpacihtâcik. môla milwašin anima '-'ši-nihtâwikihâcik ocawâšimišiwâwa anohc kâ-p'mâtisîcik. nîla mâka wîla kâ-pêciy-ohpikihâwisoyân pišišik askiy n'kîy-âpacihtân. n'kî-wîcihik nêsta ninâpêm ê-nâcipahtwâyân, ê-wîhkwayêkiwatiyâhk apahkwânihk, an'm askiy ê-matâpêtiwatêyâhk.

3   wayahtâkanihk mâka m'pîhtahêhtân nîl'ân[9] ihtâwinihk ôt' ê-yhtâyâhk êkâ nôhcimihk[10] ê-yhtâyâhk. wayahtâkana mihcêt nimâwacihtâhtân; êkota mâka pîhtahamâhk, nisto wayahtâkan' âskaw. n'kanawêl'htênân. ê'kwâni mâk' âskani-pipon micon' îspaliwa n'cawâšimišinân anima askiy, pîliš mîna ê-'ti-pâskâhkotêk, ê-'ti-nîpihk. ê'kwâni kâ-pêci-tôtamâhk ê-p'mâtisiyâhk, êy-âpacihtâyâhk askiy.

The preparation of moss for babies' diapers

1   The moss which is useful u..., used for a child is sought after in the bush, being pulled off in chunks. Not every kind of moss that is seen, not every one is useful. There is that moss which they use, when the children have it used for them a..., as they are being tied up in the moss bag, without any cloth. That one is gone after in the forest, pulled off in chunks; and it is hung up, they are hung up here and there on the trees. They are dried thoroughly; then they are shaken and pulled after they are dr... dried. They are pl... pl..., they are also shaken out so th..., there are no worms there. They are all pulled away. They are then put in a bag which is kept. In that way the children have it used for them in winter. They are put away, the children have them put away for them.

2   So then, when people of long ago did not in fact have a bag, they hung it in the woods under a tree, they were pushed under a tree where the brushwood was thi..., thick wh... That's where it was squeezed in. Then when the children ran short of them as they were using the moss, they were just fetched, they went and fetched them from that place as they were used for them. And the children were very clean when they came to use that moss. It's not like now when they use cloth exclusively. It's not nice the way people now living raise their children [i.e., with diapers only]. When I, in fact, brought up my children, I used moss consistently. My husband helped me fetch it too, as we bundled it in a canvas tarpaulin, carrying that moss out from the bush.

3   We used to put it in barrels when we were here in the settlement and were not in the bush. We used to gather a lot of barrels; that's where we used to put it in, three barrels sometimes. We kept them in store. And that moss lasted our child the whole winter, until the snow began to clear away again with the onset of summer. That's what we did living then, when we used moss.

ê-ošihâkaniwit wâpoš'-wayân

1   ê-ošihâkaniwit mâka wâpoš'-wayân, wâšwâkaniwinwak[1] wâpoš'-wayânak,
ê-..., ê-'skosit wâpoš'-'iyân wâ..., wâšwâkaniwan. êko mâka,
ê-'škwâ-wâšwâkaniwit, pakitinikâ... otinikâtêw mistik ê-môhkocikâtêk nêw
micihcin ê-yskwâskwahk. tâpisikohtatâniwan mâk' antê oškîšikohk, antê,
ê-pakwanêcâpit awa wâpoš'-'iyân. pîmihwâkaniwan[2] mâka êlikohk,
pîmâstêhwâkaniwan.[3] êko šêhkâtâpêt antê kotak antê awâšiš[4] ê-'htât
'ci-šêhkâtâpêt ant' ê-'skwâpihkêsit ana wâpoš'-'iyân. tihtipanipaliw mâka ana
wâpoš'-'iyân. êko êškw'-ânima-tôtawâkaniwicik êko 'kolâkaniwicik[5]
walawîtimih'; nîmâskwahwâkaniwanwak mâk' išpimihk kici-wêwêpâšicik
kinwêš. êko mîn' nîhtanâkaniwicik aniki wâpoš'-'iyânak. êko, wêšihâkaniwit
picêlak wâpoš'-'iyân 'nt' ohci.[6]

2   wâ-ispihtêkahat mâk' ana piko wâpoš'-'iyân, tahto-misit kitiskwâskohtân
kimistikoma[7] ê-kîhkêyâskwapitaman otih. êkw antê wâšakâm ê-'tahpitaman
antê 'šâkanâpiy antê, ê-wâspitaman tâpiskôc otâpânâsk ê-wâspitaman
ê-tôtawat. êko kêhcihat ana wâpoš'-'iyân antê. kikwêskwêskohtân antê
ê-tâhtâpišahot. âskaw mâka, awas'tê mitâhtomitana mîna niyâlomitana
kîy-âpatisiwak ana,[8] pêyak ê-mišêkisit ani..., an' ê-mišikiticik 'wê'hkânak nîšo
..., nisto ê-têpašêkocik ê-..., ê-itikitit, ê-'spihtêkahâkaniwit.

3   kinwêš 'sa t'šîhkawâkaniwan wîl' ê-mišêkisit wîla. mîna, mîna mâk'
âhtahpitâkaniwan ani piko ê-'t'-îskwêkisit ana, pêyakwan anima nêw
misit piko ê-'skwâki mistikwa, pikw ê-'spihcâk mîk'wâm, ê-'skwâskitêk.[9]
âyâp... âyâpahwâkaniwan mâka; mîna, mîna iskwâskopitâkaniwan
mâna, ê-'skwêk' ... ê-'skosit nâpêw ê-mišikitit, n'kotwâs misit âskaw
ê-'skwêkihâkaniwit nîswâs misit. 'kwân' ê-tôtawâkaniwit wîla wâpoš'-'iyân
ê-wšihâkaniwit.

4   n'kî-wâpahkân nêst' ê-wšihtâniwahki mâka, ê-'šihomakahki[10] 'wên'hkân
awâšiš ê-pohciškahk, nêsta kišê'yahâw, pîskâkan ê-wšihtâniwahk ant' ohci
wâpoš'-'iyânihk. mihcêtwâ n'kâwiy n'kî-wâpamâw '-'šihtât[11] animêliw
pîskâkaniliw. môla mâka nîla wîskât n'kîy-ohci-kocihtân 'ciy-ošihtâyân.
n'kî-wâpamâw mâka 'lâta,[12] tânt' êhtôtahk êy-ošihtât. n'ka-kašk'tâhtay mâkâ
'lâta kici-ošihtâyân nêhîla[13] n'itêl'htên. šâkoc mâka môla ihtâw wîl' ânohc
wâpoš kici-kî-tôcikâtêk anima. mihcêtwâ n'kî-wâpamâw nišîm,
ê-wšihtamawâkaniwit anima, wâpoš'-'iyâni-pîskâkan nêsta palacîsa,
ê-ytâspitâkaniwit pikow ê-kîšôhâkaniwit awâsiš. 'kwân' mâka nêsta wâ...

Making rabbit-skin blankets

1   In the making of a rabbit-blanket, the rabbit-skins are cut in strips, the rabbit-skin is cu..., cu..., cut into strips to ..., to its full length. And then, when it's been cut in strips, a stick is pu..., is taken, planed four inches in length. It is inserted there in the eye, in the rabbit's eye-hole. Then it is spun around quite a bit; it is twisted into strands. Then another one keeps drawing it away as fast as it's twisted, a child who is there, to draw it away the full length of the rabbit-skin in a strand. That rabbit-skin winds up, though. So after that's been done to them, then they're hung up outside; and they're hung high up on a pole to blow back and forth for a long time. Then those rabbit-skins are taken down. Now, only then is the rabbit blanket made from that point.

2   Whatever size you want to make that rabbit-skin you make your stick so many feet in length, tying it in a square, that is. Now you tie the rope 'round about that way, lacing it the way you lace it when you're doing it for a sled. Then you start making that rabbit-skin there. You go back and forth, threading it through there. And sometimes they worked more than one hundred and fifty of them, for a big one ... for two ..., three large people to squeeze under when ... when it was so big, when it was made such a size.

3   A big one takes quite a long time. Again, again it is tied to another place according to the length it develops; and similarly the wooden frame is only four feet in length – a wigwam is only of such a size – and so high. But they keep on unty..., untying it; again, again it's raised up repeatedly, being the length ... as long as a man is big, sometimes being made six feet, sometimes seven in length. That's what is done to it when a rabbit blanket is being made.

4   I have also seen a suit of clothes made for a child to put on, and also for an old person, a coat made out of rabbit-skin. Many times I've seen my mother make that kind of coat. I have never tried to make it myself, though. I have seen, however, what she did in making it. But I could also manage to make one myself I think. But right now there is no rabbit so that can be done. Many times I have seen my young brother with that made for him, a rabbit-skin coat and breeches, and being dressed only that way the child was made warm. The same as when a mo..., moss-bag is made for a small child, – looking like a moss-bag to keep the child warm.

wâspis'-'iyân[14] nêsta awâšiš ê-... ê-'pišîšišit êy-ošihtamawâkaniwit, wâspis'-'iyân tâpiskôc ê-'šinâkohtâniwahk 'ci-kîšôhâkaniwit awâšiš.

'kwân' nîla kâ-pêci-wâpahtamân ê-'wâš'šîwiyân.

That's what *I've* seen when I was a child.

ê-ošihtâniwahk aškimaniyâpiy

1   aškimaniyâpiy mâka wîla êy-ošihtâniwahk ê-... kâhkapin[1] išinihkâsow 'na
môso-wayân. môl' ôti kêkwân pakitinikâtêw, piko paškwahwâkaniwan,
opîway' otinikâtêwa[2] watôw mâka. êko wâšwâkaniwit, mihcêtwâ
n'kî-pêci-tahkonên anim' '-ošihtâniwahk 'šâkanâpiy, n'kâwiy ê-wîcihak
kiciy-ošihtât. êkoh, ê-itâp'palihoyân mâk' antê pakwantaw mišêtwâ[3]
kî-pahpaškišam mâna, kêka mâka n'tayamihik, ê-... ê-kišiwâhak anim'
ê-tôtamân 'ti. "nîla wês' ôma k'-âpacihitân ôma. kanawâpam awa
kâ-tahkonat awa môs'-'iyân," n'tik. "tahkona mâk' ôma kwayêsk, nêsta
kanawâpahta," n'tik, ê-'tâp'palihoyân mâk' ê'kwân' ê-š-paškišikâtêk[4] anima
'šâkanâpiy.

2   niwâšwânân, anima. "nâspic kinwêš n'tašîwîn," n'titêl'htên ê-wâšwak ana
môs'-'iyân oti, pêyak ê-wâšwak môs'-'iyân'šiš ê-wîcihak ê-tahkonamân anim'
ê-wâšwak..., apišimaniyâpiy[5] kâ-icikâtêk nêst' aškimaniyâpiy, misiwê
ê-'t'-îši-nâkohtât anima.

hêkoh, ê-kanawâpamak anim' ê-tôtahk, misiwê 'nima n'kî-kocihtân
'c'-ati-kiskin'wâpiyân anima, âpatisîwin kâ-wâpamak ê-tôtahk, ê-'škimêt oti[6]
asâma pîliš ê-'tiy-'škimâtât anihiy asâma. môla niw'-îkatêsin
ê-kanawâpamak ant' êy-apiyân ê-kanawâpamak ê-'škimêt, –
ê-'ti-kîšihât micon' anihi ê-'škimâtât asâma. êko pêyakwâ n'titâw,
"n'ka-kocihtân anima 'ci-tôtamân," n'titâw.

3   êwk'[7] kâ-išit, "nî... mê... kêkwân nîštam kê-tôtaman an'ma? otin an'
asâm, ana kâ-kî-mowât an' atim, – atipisihk," n'tik.

"âpaha mâk' anihi 'šâkanâpiya misiwê," n'tik. "îkatên' anta ohcih. êkot
ân' mâ' kêy-ohci-kiskêl'htaman anim' âpatisîwin kâ-wî-kiskêl'htaman," n'tik.

tâpw' ê-tôtamân anima, wêtinak an' âsâm êy-âpahok, misiwê
n'tâpihkopitâw anah.

4   âšay n'kî-kocihtân anima kici-tôtamân animah. n'kî-kaškihtân mâka
atipisihk wîla ê-'škimêyân. ositiyêhk mâk' ant' âsâm, môla
n'kîy-ohci-kaškihtân kici-ošihtâyân. mîna, mîna ..., êko n'kî-kocihtân. kêka
mâka n'kî-kakwêcimâw wîla kici-kiskinohamawit. kâ-kiskinohamawit mâka;
âšay n'kîy-ati-onâpêmin kâ-'škw' anima. n'kî-kaškihtân mâka
ê-kîšaškimêyân[8] aniky asâmak wîlât'. awâšišasâmak n'kîy-aškimâtâwak.
nisikilêsin mâk' ê-kî-kiskinohamawit misiwê kêkwâliw kê-...
kâ-kî-pêc'-îtâpatisit wîla, mêkwâc k'-âwâš'šîwiyân ê-kanawâpamak.

Making babiche for snow-shoes

1   When [snow-shoe] netting line is being made as ..., that moose-hide is called *kâhkapin*. Nothing is put on it [as a cure], it is only shaved; the hairs are taken off, and any clot. Then when it's cut into strips, I've many times come to hold that line as it's being made, as I helped my mother to make it. Then, when I would suddenly look around inattentively, she would often cut it; but finally she spoke to me because I annoyed her that I was doing that. "It's me you're working for at this. Keep your eyes on this moose hide which you're holding," she told me. "Now, hold this properly, and watch it," she said to me, as I quickly looked around at that point when the line was being cut off.

2   We cut it in strips. "I'm taking a long time," I thought, cutting that moose hide in strips, that is, as I helped her in cutting one small moose hide, as I held that material cutting it in strips ..., the 'small netting line' as it's called and also the 'netting line', as she made it all to look like that.

     Now as I watched her doing that, I tried to begin taking note of that, the work which I saw her doing, netting snow-shoes that is, – until she began to net those snow-shoes. I didn't want to be out of the way as I sat there and watched her, looking at her as she netted, – as she began completely to finish netting those snow-shoes. So at one point I said to her, "I'll try to do that," I said.

3   So she said to me, "Fir..., wh... what is the first thing you must do? Take that snow-shoe which that dog ate, – at the end," she said to me.

     "Open up all those lines," she said to me. "Remove them from there. That's the way you'll learn that work which you want to know," she said to me.

     Indeed by doing that, taking that snow-shoe and undoing it, I unravelled it all.

4   Now I tried to do that. I managed to net the small end of the snow-shoe. But where your feet are on the snow-shoe, I couldn't manage to do it. Again, again ... so I tried. At last, however, I asked her to teach me. Then she taught me; now, I've got married after that. I was able though to finish netting those snow-shoes ..., nonetheless. I netted a child's snow-shoes. I'm glad, though, that she taught me everything which she would ..., the kind of work she used to do while I was a child watching her.

atihkamêk owâhkona ê-kîsisomihci

1   namês mâka wîla o..., atihkamek kâ-itâkaniwit, ê-oš'htâniwahki o...,
otakašiya, oskwan'piy¹ 'šin'kâcikâtêw. mihcêt ê-nipahakihcik ah... namêsak
atihkamêkwak, n'toš'htânân otakašiy' ê-kîsisamâhk. "oskwan'piy" mâka
n'tišin'kâtênân. misiwê n'sînênân² anihiy otakašiya. êko pânaskihkohk
m'pakitinênân ê-kîs'samâhk. kinwêš, kinwêš n'kîs'sênân anta, pîliš micon'
ê-pâhkwahkâtêki, 'ti-sâsihkâtêki 'ti-prâwniwahki³ miconi. êko mâ'šîš
pahkwêšikan m'pakitinânân, n'tispahwânân ayahâhk..., olâkan'šihk ...
n'tispahwânân mâka. êko pêkitinamâhk anta, ê-kîs'samâhk anihi. nâš'c
mâka wîhkašinwa.

2   êko mâka nêsta kotakiy an'⁴ atihk..., an' namês, mihkwacakâš
kâ-išin'kâsot, wâhkonak mâka kâ-itihcik anta, ê-'yawâcik aniki
m'pakocênânânak. n'tasicikaswânânak an'ki wâhkonak. awasitê mâka
wîhkašin anim' oskwanipiy ê-wšihtâyân, ispîy ê-pakitinakihcik aniki
pahkwêšikanak mâk' asic ê-'ti-pakitinakihcik apišîš ant' ê-'ti-tispahwâkihcik.
ê'kwân' ê-tôtamâhk mâka wîla ê-... ošihtâyâhk anima oskwanipiy. apišîš
pahkwêšikan m'pakitinânân n'tispahwânânak olâkanišihk. awasitê mâka
wîhkašin anima ê-'šinâkohtâniwahk pahkwêšikanak apišîš
ê-pakitinâkaniwicik. êko mâka nêsta mihkwacakâšo-wâhkanak âskaw
pakitinâkaniwinwak anta, asicikaswâkaniwanwak anta. 'as'tê⁵ wîhkacin⁶
mâka anim' ê-'šinâkohtâniwahk.

A favourite dish from whitefish roe

1   Now for that fish's ... which is called the whitefish, in processing its ..., its
innards, it is called 'liver-water'. When we catch a good number uh ..., of fish,
whitefish, we clean the innards and cook them. And we call it 'liver-water'.
We squeeze out the whole of those innards. Then we put them in a frying pan
and cook them. We cook them there a long, long time until they're boiled
completely dry, so they may come to a fry, so they become all brown. Then we
put in a little flour; we mix it in a thing, a small dish, and we mix it. Then
we put them there [in the liver-water], as we cook them. And they are very
delicious.

2   And then also that other caribou ..., that fish, the so-called red sucker,
what's called the roe there, we cut them open as they have it. We cook those
roe along with them. That liver-water is tastier, though, as I make it, when,
as we put the flour with it, we gradually put a little flour in as we continually
stir it. That's what we do when we make that liver-water. We put in a little
flour, that is, and we stir it in a small dish. It's more delicious when it's
dressed that way, with a little flour put in. And so red-sucker roe also is
sometimes put in it, and cooked along with it. And it's more delicious when
it's dressed that way.

wîsahkwêcâhk nêsta mâka pilêsiwak, nêsta wêhci-omikîwicik mistikwak

1   pêyakwâ 'sa wêskac ê..., wîsahkwêcâhk[1] išinihkâsokopanêh nâpêw
     ê-papâmohtêt, pimiwatêw mâk' askîyah ..., wâp'mikow mâk' ôhi pilêsiwa,
     wêhwêwa, misiwê tôwihkân pilêsiwa. wâpamikow ê-p'mohtêlit ...
     ê-p'miwatêt.
        "kêkwâ'hkân anima kâ-p'miwatêyin?" 'tikow manâ mâka.
        êko manâ wt', ê-itât mâka: "ninakamohiniwat,[2] ôma kâ-p'miwatêyân,"
     'têw manâ wtih.
        "kêkwân mâk' ani wêhci-wî-nakamoyin?" 'têw manâ ..., itikow manâ wtih.
        "niwî-n'tomâwak awîyâšîšak, pilêsiwak nêsta kici-pêc'-îtohtêcik antah,
     kîšihtâyânê ôma,"[3] itêw mâka. "êko mâka wî-pêc'-ît'êyêkwê,[4]
     ka-kî-pêc'-îtohtânâwâw," itêw.
        "kayâm," itwêwak mâka ôko wêhwêwak, misiwê tôwihkân wêhwêw...
     pilêsiwak.
2   êko mâ' kâ-itohtêcik kîy-ošihtâw askîk'wâmiliw[5] nâhic[6] ê-mišâlik, awa
     wîsahkwêcâhk kâ-itiht, nâpêw. kâ-itohtêcik antê, ê-pîhtokwêcik mâka
     kîy-olapihêw[7] misiwê kî-têtipa-apihêw antê. êko kâ-kitohcikêw'hamâsot.
        nîmî..., nîmîliwa mâka nîmîhkâsowak antê pîhci mîk'wâmihk,
     askîk'wâmihk.
        " 'ssiwê[8] tahkonamok mâka kitakahkwaniwâwa antê," itêw.
        wâšakâmênah'ik tâ'skô' ê-'ti-nîminâniw'h' ê-tôtah'ik.[9]
        êko m'â wt' ê-wî-..., mwâkwa nêst' anta k'-îhtâw. misiwê tôw'hkân pilêsiw.
     êko manâ wti mâk' awa mwâkwa, wî-kostâciw wîla. tašinê manâ wti apišîš
     âpaham oškîšikw' âskaw, napatê âskaw itâpiw ê-kanawâpamât
     ê-kitohcikêw'hamâsolici.
        kêka manâ wtih, 'šâkanâpîliw mâka kî-kâhcitâpahtam
     êy-olâpihkênamil'ci.
        êko, "ayasikwêšimok," itêw manâ 'tih.
        'kwân' mâka tâpw' ê-htôtah'ik misiwê itinamwak ostikwâniwâw anta
     pêšoc ê-kîn'kwân'šimocik.
        'kwâni mâk' ê-'šy-ohcipahtwât kêk' ošâkanâpîm, antê misiwê
     tâpisiko-wêpahwêw.
3   mwâk' osa mâka wîla '-kî-..., -k'-îtâpit apišîš, 'kwân' ê-'ši-walawîpahtât
     manâ wtih walawîpaliw. nôsôtahkiškâtêw mâk' anihi mwâkw'

Weesahkwechahk and the birds, and why the trees have scabs

1   Once upon a time long ago as ..., a man supposedly by the name of Weesahkwechahk, as he walked about, was carrying a load of moss ..., and he was seen by these birds, waveys, and every kind of bird. They saw him as he walke..., walked about carrying it.

"What kind of thing is that which you're carrying?" they said to him then.

So this is what he told them: "This is my song-bag that I'm carrying," he said to them then.

"What do you want to sing for?" he said to them then ..., they said to him, that is.

"I want to invite the animals, the birds too to come when I finish this," he said to them. "So then, if you want to come, you may come," he told them.

"Right," these waveys said, every kind of wavey ... of birds.

2   So then when they went, this man, Weesahkwechahk as he was called, made a very large lodge. When they went there, he seated them all as they entered, he seated them all around there. And then he played himself a tune.

And they were dan..., dancing and pretending to dance inside the tent, the lodge.

"All of you hold your wings there," he said to them.

They held them around as though starting to dance, as they did it.

Now then, since he want ... the loon was there too. Every kind of bird. So then this loon, he was getting to be scared. He kept on opening his eyes a little from time to time, looking sidelong at times with one eye as he watched him [Weesahkwechahk] playing himself a tune.

Then at last he caught sight of a line as he [Weesahkwechahk] was setting it up.

So then, "Dance with your necks together," he said to them.

And then, in very truth, they all did that: they held their heads there that way, as they danced around there close.

And then, suddenly grabbing his line, he [Weesahkwecahk] lassoed them all there.

3   But as for the loon, having peeked around a bit, then dashing right out at that point, he went outside in a hurry. As he began to run out he

SOPHIE GUNNER

ê-'ti-walawîpahtâl'ci. ê'kwâni mâk' ani wêhci-...-napakâlik ošôkan,
ayitâtalôhkâsow ana mwâkwa, ê-kî-tahkiškâtât ana wîsahkwêcâhk.

kâ-piškošimât manâ ot' anihi, ê-kî-nipahât mâka pilêsiwa,
wêhwêwa, misiwê tôwihkân pilêsiwa, niska nêsta.

êko manâ wtih, 'wânêl'tahk, "tân'ka 'tê kê-išitêpoyân ôkih?" itêl'htam
manâ wt'. êko manâ wtih kêka itêl'htam, "n'ka-likwahwâwak antê
n'tâmih'. n'ka-likwahahkatêpon," itwêw, man' oti. "tâpiskôc
ê-sakapwâniwahk kic'-îtihkasocik anikih. 'kwâni kê-tôtamân," itwêw
man' ot'h.

4   êko manâ'tih, êko tâpwê kâ-paškopicikêt manâ wti, âšay paškopitêw manâ
wti misiwê 'nihiy opilêsîma. êko wêš'htât 'škotêliw manâ wtih, têtâwic anta,
mîk'wâmih' ..., otaskîk'wâmih'. êko manâ wtih, šêšêkošimât[10] antê,
têtipa-šêšêkwahwât anihi, lêkâhk anta n'tâmihk; sakapwêw anihi.
owêhwêma sakap..., sakapwêw antê tâpiskôc kit'-îtihkasol'ci.[11]

êko manâ wtih, nâhic wî-nipâwiyiw 'êkâ[12] man' ot'h. êko manâ wt'
êtêl'htahk, "tân'ka 'tê kê-tôtamân êkâ kici-wanahakik aniki?" itêl'tam manâ
wti. "kistinât n'ka-pêci-kimotamâk 'wiyâšîš kê-tipiskâlik," itêl'htam manâ
wti. môla nêsta wî-nipâw. êko manâ wti kêka, âšay itêl'htam:
"n'ka-ayamihâw n'cisk," itêl'htam. êko manâ wtih tâpw' êtôtahk.

âšay ê-'ti-nahišihk, "n'cisk," itwêw manâ wtih, " 'wê'hkân wâpamatê
'ntê, ê-pêci-pîhtokwêt," itêw manâ wtih, "wîhtamawin," itêw. "nôhtâkosi!"
itêw.

5   âšay manâ wti kawišimow.

âšay mwêhc' ê-'ti-liskihkwâmit nâhic ê-'ti-milohkwâmit âšay manâ wti
nôhtâkosiliwa ociska.

êkwâ ê-'ši-waniškâpahtât itâpiw ant' iškwâtêmih'. môla 'wên'hkâna
wâpamêw. êko manâ wti mîna nêhišihk.

nânâkêh mîna âšay manâ wtih, âšay mwêhci ê-'ti-nipât mîna, âšay mîn'
nôhtâkosiliwa'n' ot'h. môl' 'ê'hkâna[13] wâpamêw.

itâpipalihow manâ wt'h.

âšay kišiwâhikow, anihi ociska. " 'kâwila wîla wîyâšimin," itêw. "pâtimâ
piko tâpwê wâpamat' 'ê'hkân[14] antê," itêw, "nôhtâkosi," itêw. "êko mâka
kê-waniškâyân 'ci-n'tawahak," itêw.

6   âšay manâ wti tâpwê mîna, ê'kwâni, ê'kwân' ê-kî-kišîmât anihi ociska,
môla mîna kî-whci-nôhtâkosiliwa. ê'kwâni kâ-'ši-nipât. môla kî-'hci-koskosiw
pâtimâ ê-kišêpâyâlik.

310

[Weesahkwechahk] pursued that loon and gave him a kick. And *that* is why ... his backside is flat, so the story goes about the loon, because that Weesahkwechahk kicked him.

Then he threw those [birds] in a heap, when he had killed them: birds, waveys, every kind of bird, and geese also.

But then, he was puzzled: "I wonder how I'll cook these," he thought. So then at last he had an idea: "I'll bury them there underneath. I'll bake them under the sand to eat," he said then. "So they'll be cooked as if they're roasting. That's what I'll do," he said then.

4 Now then, now he plucked in earnest, – now then he plucked all those birds of his. So he made a fire then, in the centre of the tent ..., of his lodge. So then, he shoved them in under there, shoving them in separately there beneath the sand; he roasted them. His waveys he roas... he roasted there so they could be all evenly cooked.

So then, he badly wanted to yawn, at last, that is. And then he thought, "What shall I do so I don't lose those [birds]?" he thought. "For sure an animal will come and steal it from me tonight," he thought. He didn't want to sleep either. So then, finally, now he thought: "I'll talk to my rear end," he thought. So then, that in fact is what he did.

Now, as he began to lie down comfortably, he said: "Rear end, if you see anyone coming in there," he said to him, "tell me," he said to him. "Make a noise," he said to him.

5 Now then, he went to bed.

Now right as he was drifting off to sleep, beginning to sleep well, at this point his rear end made a noise.

Then leaping out of bed and running he peeked around at the door. He didn't see anyone. So then he lay down comfortably again.

Again now, a short while after, right at the point where he was beginning to go to sleep again, now again it made a noise. He didn't see anybody.

He quickly glanced around.

Now he got annoyed at that rear end of his. "Quit fooling with me," he said to him. "Only after you've really seen somebody there," he said to him, "make a noise," he told him. "And then I'll get up to look for him," he said to it.

6 Now in fact, then, then when he had spoken again rudely to that rear end of his it did not make any more noise. Then he went off to sleep. He didn't waken up until the following morning.

It was already completely broad daylight as he awakened, and it was

âšay miconi pahkahkâpaniliw kwêskosit, manâ wt'h âšay wâsêyâliw.[15]
"âhay[16] pîsim nôkosiw," itwêw manâ 't'. 'kwân' êši-waniškât.
"kwâcistak!" itwêw manâ 'ti. "nâhitêpi[17] n'ka-milohcikân," itwêw manâ
wti.

âšay manâ wtih, ocipitam ositah, nîšê... ê-niyê...[18] -sâsâkihtatât misiwê
têtipa '-kî-sâkihtatât, ê-lik'hwâkatêpot. 'cipitam manâ wti 'n'mêliw
ositiliw; môl' 'ê'wâhkân[19] man' oti, kâ-kîšipâk anim' osit. kî-kîškahcikâtêw
anima.

7   mîna kotakîy[20] ocipitam. mîna kotakîy..., micon' têtipâ pîliš. 'mwât[21]
pêyak kêkwân[22] miskam. nâhtâ k'šiwâhikow mâk' ocisk' anim' ê-kî-tôtamilici
ê-kî-cîšimikot otih, êkâ '-kîy-ohci-tôtamil'ci kâ-k'-îtašiwâtât.
"ka-kiskêlimin 'lâta[23] ê-'hkâniwiyân anohc," itêw. "nâhitê[24] kikišawâhin,"
itêw.
'kwâni m'nâ wt' ê-'ši-nâsipêt, kâ-mišikitit mâka mân' asiniy
kâ-wâwiyêsit, 'kwâni manâ wt' ê-'ši-kospihtahât 'n'hiy asiniya. têtâw
iškotêw manâ wti pakitinêw. 'coni[25] wâstêyâpiskihkasow anihi asiniya.
awât...[26] ê-'š'-akwayâskwahwât anihi, 'kwâ' êši-okîtapit anta. nâ'c
êl'ohk nôhtâkosiliwa manâ wti ociska. môla kipihtawêliwa
ê-nôhtâkosil'ci.

8   "â, hâ, â, hâ," itêw manâ wtih. "k'wâ'htên nâ mâka êkâ
kâ-kîy-aci-tôtaman[27] kitâpatisîwin?" itêw man' ati.[28] "êko mâk' kêskêlimiyan,"
itêw man' ot'h.
êko man' ot', êko manâ wti mâka,[29] kâ-iškw'-ânim'-ihtit,[30] êko kêhtohtêt,
papâm'htêw m'n ot'.
âšay nâšic wîy-ati-mîc'sow mâka, '-papâmohtêt ê-nân'tawâ'htahk kê-mîcit.
âšay miconi kispakatamwaniliw omikiy anta ociskîhk ê-k'-îskwâsot'sot.

9   êko manâ wtih, ê-m... -n'tonikêt mâka, manâ wtih mâna, ê-kalakisit[31]
nêsta. 'kwâni mâ' 't' âni[32], ê-'ši-manipitah' animêliw, omikiy animêliw, 'kwâni
êši-panaškat'nah' mistikohk ê-pimohtêt. ê'kwâni mâka mâna kâ-wâ'htamah'
kâ-itwâtalôhkâtêki ê-'tâtalôhkâsicic aniki mistikwak, anima wîsahkwêcâhk
omikiy kâ-itwâniwahk, anima pikîwak aniki k'-âhkohkêcik; nêsta anihi[33]
nîpisîhk kâ-êy'kwahkêki[34] ê'kwâna[35] kâ-mahkatêwatamwaki mikîhk
kâ-išinâkwahki kâ-omikîwicik aniki, 'sâcîš'šak[36] nêsta nîpisiya. êwakwân'
ana wîsahkwêcâhk an'mêliw âhki omikiy an'm ê-'twâsonâniwah',
ê-kî-papanaškatinahk animêliw omikiy.

already clear.

"Now the sun's out," he said. Then he got up.

"Oh my!" he said. "I'll have a real, good feed for sure," he said. Then he got up.

Now then, he pulled its feet, with both feet … bo…sticking up, having stuck all of them out separately, burying them to cook [under the sand]. Then he pulled that foot out; there was nothing on it, just the end of the foot. It was bitten right off.

7   Again he pulled out another one. Again another …, right the whole way around. He found not even a single thing. He got really furious at his rear end for having done that, for cheating him, that is, for not having done what he ordered it to.

"You'll know who I am now," he said to it. "You're making me really mad," he told it.

Right away he went down the bank. There is a kind of big stone which is frequently rounded; then straightway he took that stone up. He put it in the centre of the fire. That rock was altogether white hot. Then, levering it off, at that point he sat upon it there. Then his rear end made a noise as hard as it could. It didn't quit making a noise.

8   "A-ha, a-ha," he said to it then. "Do you see now that you didn't keep on with your work?" he told it then. "So now you know who I am," he said to it.

Now then, so now then, after that happened to him, then he went away, he went for a walk.

Now he wanted very much to eat, though, as he walked about searching here and there for food. Now his scab was getting altogether thick on his rear end there where he had burnt himself.

9   So then, as he f… felt all around there, he kept on getting itchy too. Then, pulling off that, that scab, he then plastered it on the trees as he walked along. And that's what you see again and again, that are told about in legend, when stories are told about trees: that is Weesahkwechahk's scab, they say, the blobs of pitch which adhere are that; also, those things which adhere to willows, which are black things stuck on the surface, which look like a scab, and with which small poplars and willows are scabby. It's that very same Weesahkwechahk whose pretend scab it was, as they imagine, which he had stuck around here and there.

cahkâpêš nêsta mâka mistâpêskwêwak

1   pêyakwâ 'sa wêskac ê-..., cahkâpêš išinihkâtâkaniwinokopan ililiw. ê-papâmohtêt mâka, kî-nîšo-tašîhkêwak mâka pik' ômis' awa cahkâpêš.

papâmohtêw mâk' ana: papâpilâškâw '-papân'tawihot nêsta. kêka manâ wti pêhtawêw 'wê'hkâna ê-matêy-âtahikêl'ci ê-'tihtah'... itohtêw mâk' antê kâ-'ši-matêy-âtahikâniwanilik manâ wtih. wâpamêw kêkât mic..., mištâpêškwêšiša nîšo ê-matê-mâtahwâlici amisk'-wayân' ê-kišêpâyâlik wîpac.

2   êko manâ wti nêt' ê-wâpamât, kîmôc antê n'tawâp'mêw. kêka wâpamikow mâka, ê-..., ê-pêci-n'tawâpamât kîmôc ê-pêci-n'tawâpamât.

âyâkowiyâskošimow mâka.

kêka pêšoc nawac ant' ê-'htât, nîpawiw anta mistikohk, ê-mîskwâskošimot. kanawâpamikow mâk' anihi apistâpê...[1] anihi mištâpêskwêwa ... mištâpêskwêšiša. êko manâ wtih, ê-'htôtawât ana, sâkasâkinam[2] manâ wti 'nimêliw 'cayâniš[3] antê 'na mistâpêw mi..., an' cahkâpêš.

3   êko manâ wtih pâhpiwak nâh'c êl'oh' ôki mistâpêskwêšišak.

"kêkwâ'hkân ani kâ-pâhpihtâyin?"[4] itikowak mâk' êkw ôkišê'skwêmiwâwa. antê pîhc' îhtâliwa 'kâwiwâwa mîk'wâmihk.

"wîskacâniš ana kâ-pâhpihakiht," itwêwak man' at'. " 'kihtakihtaholêw anihi watoya. mamaskamitowak mâka, ani wêhci-pâhpihakiht. niwîyasinawânânak," itêw.

âšay manâ wti mîna nânâkêh ..., âšay mîn' ê'kwân' ê-'htôtahk awa. pêci-sâkipalihtwâw antê otayân, pêci-sâkinam man' ot', ê-sâsâkikâpawit.

âšay manâ wtih mîna pâhpiwak nâ'c êl'oh' ôki mistâpêskwêšišak.

4   âšay manâ wtih awa kišê-iskwêw, kîmôc itâpiw antê pîhtikom ohcih mîk'wâmihk. kanawâpamêw manâ wtih kîmôc.

wâpamêw anihi cahkâpêš' ê-pêc'-sâsâkâskonamil'ci antê mistikohk ê-nîpawil'ci.

ê'kwâni m'na wt' êši-walawîpalit awa kišê-mistâpêskwêw. mâkwanêw okaškamâlîhk anihi cahkâpêša. pîhtokwê-wêpinêw manâ wti o..., wîkihk.

5   mêkwâc mâka kî-kîšinawasokopan, ê ..., amisk' ê-kîšinawasot

Chahkabesh and the giant women

1   Once upon a time long ago as ..., there was a person supposed to have been named Chahkabesh. As he was travelling about, this Chahkabesh and his older sister lived just the two of them together.

That one [Chahkabesh] walked about; he wandered about hunting here and there too. Finally then he heard someone making a noise scraping moose-hide as he imagined. He went over to where there was a noise of hide being scraped. He saw then almost ent..., two giant girls making a noise scraping beaver skins very early in the morning.

2   So then, when he saw them away over, he stealthily sneaked up on them there. At last, however, he was seen by them as ..., as he came sneaking up, as he came stealthily sneaking up on them.

But he kept ducking behind the trees.

At last when he was getting pretty close, he stood there at a tree, standing behind the tree. But he was watched by the small gian..., that giant woman ..., giant girl. So then, as he was doing that to them, that giant ..., that Chahkabesh kept sticking out [from behind the tree] that little thing of his [his penis].

3   So then these giant girls laughed very hard.

"What's that that you're laughing at?" their old woman said to them. Their mother was there inside the tent.

"It's that little whiskey-jack that we're laughing at," they said. "He keeps on carrying off that clot. But they keep stealing it from each other, which is why we're laughing at him. They look funny to us," she said to her.

Now then a little bit later – then he started doing that again. He came and quickly poked his thing out there, he came and stuck it out then, standing with his body showing every now and then.

Now then these giant girls laughed again for all they were worth.

4   Now then this old woman peeked about stealthily there from inside in the tent. She watched him then stealthily.

She saw that Chahkabesh come sticking it out in the open every now and then as he stood there by the tree.

Right away then that old giant woman ran out in a hurry. She seized that Chahkabesh by the scruff of the neck. She threw him into her ..., her tent.

5   Meanwhile, however, she must have been cooking for herself, uh...,

mistaskihkohk. ê'kwâ' man' ot' êši-pîhci-wêpinât anta otaskihkoh' anihi,
cahkâpêša.

kwâcistak! manâ wti, kâ-kînikwânâciwasot manâ 't' wîla cahkâpêš.

"kanawâpamihk, mâ, cahkâpêš," itêw manâ wtih
kâ-k'-antê-misiwê-'tahil'ci[5] anih otânisa, ocawâšimiša nêsta.

kâ-kîn'kwânâciwasot m'na wt', nâš'c êlik' kwâškwâškwêyâciwosow!
"misiwê kanawâpamihk. pêšoc itiskwêlik," itêw m'nâ wt'.

6   âšay manâ wtih misiwê 'ti-'yâkosikâpawiwak ant' askihkohk. kêtahtawêl,
manâ wtih cahkâpêš ohciy-ošawêyâkam'palihow manâ wtih. misiwê manâ
wt', êyahâw, kipotâmaswêw anihi ê-kanawâpamikot anta. 'kwân'
ê-'š'-otihtapipalihât anihi askihkw' anta, mostaskamik anta, pîhci
mîk'wâmihk. 'kwân' manâ 't' êtapit anta.

"   'kwân' êši-mâtahcikêyân," itwêw manâ 't'. "nimowâw an' amisk," itwêw
manâ 'tih.

7   "kêka wêhci-pêci-... pêhtê... pîhtokwêt 'ê'hkân,"[6] itwêw manâ 't'. "pîht...
pêtwêwêšinwak," itwêw manâ wti, "ôk' ôti mistâpêwak."

"   'kwâni manâ wt' êši-mâci-otatâmahwâcik anihi askihkwa," 'twêw manâ
'ti, "kâ-'ši-pîhcišiniyân," 'twêw manâ 't'h.

"môla nêsta kî-kwêtipahwêwak anihi n'taskihkwa," itwêwak manâ 't'.
"n'mîtison kiyâpac manâ 'ti. kêka micon' ati-nânapakahwêwak anihi
n'taskihkwa," itwêw manâ 't'. "n'tôhci-walawî-kwâškwatin ant' askihkohk.
niwalawîpahtân," itwêw man' ot'.

8   " 'âpiscililîš[7] êcik' âwa kâ-tôtahk,' n'tikwak," itwêw manâ 'tih.

"ê'kwân' êši-kihcipahtâyân, ninâsipêpahtân mêskanâhk," itwêw 'na 't'h.
"n'kîwêpahtân," itwêw m'na 't'h.

"n'tayamihik nimis ê-'ti-pîhtokwêyân," itwêw m'na 't'h. "âšay oš' âwa wîl'
âwa mîna wayêš k'-îšilawîtokwê, awa kâ-tôtah' n'tik," itwêw ma' 't'.

"môla n'k'-îton," itwêw mana 'tih. "n'tatimapin," itwêw mana 'tih. "kîmôc
nipâhpihâw nimis," itwêw mana 'tih. "n'kiskêlimik mâka wayêš ê-'šilawîyân,"
'twêw mana 't'.

ê'kwân' êskwâk.

cooking a beaver in a big pot. Then she quickly tossed that one, Chahkabesh, into her pot there.

My Goodness, though! Chahkabesh, for his part, spun around boiling.

"See, look at Chahkabesh," she said to all those daughters of hers who were there, and her children as well.

He spun around while boiling, bouncing up and down like anything while he boiled. "All of you look at him. Put your faces close," she said to them then.

6 Now then they all began to crane their necks there at the pot. All at once, Chahkabesh quickly churned the water brown. Then all of them, uh, he smothered those ones with steam as they looked at him there. Then he quickly overturned that pot there, on the bare ground inside the wigwam. So then there it sat.

"So then I start eating," he said. "I'm eating that beaver," said he.

7 "At last somebody is come ..., heard ..., probably came in," he said. "The footsteps of these giants can be heard," he said.

"So then they're beginning to bang away at that pot," he said, "where I'm lying inside."

"They can't pry that pot of mine over either," they said. "I'll eat some more then. At last they're beginning to flatten out completely that pot of mine," he said. "I'll jump out from the pot there. I'll dash out," he added.

8 " 'It's a little person who's doing this,' they said of me," he said.

"So then I'll quickly run away, I'll come down the bank on the path," he said. "I'll run home," he said then.

"My older sister talked to me as I began to go in," he said. "I'm sure he must have been up to some mischief, this one who did it, she told me," he added.

"I didn't say anything," he said. "I had my back towards her," he went on. "I secretly laughed at my older sister," he added. "She knew though that I'd been up to something," he said.

This is the length [of the story].

ayamihitowinišiš: n'tahikâtêkwê nêstapiko êkâ?

A: ki'wêl'tên nâ... ki'wêlêl'htênânaw nâ mâka kê-... kici-ispaliyahk
ililiwaskîhk[1] anohc? môla nîla n'titêl'htên. wêsâ lipâtan; n'titêl'htên
'ci-... êkâ kwayêsk ê-'šinâkwahk kîšik.

B: kîla 'sa ê-'ši-nahêl'htaman. kîla mâtânah[2] môšak kiwî-okimâwin.

A: êkoš' isa mâka. ê'kwâni wîl' ânohc n'titêl'htên. môla, môla nâhic
n'nahêl'htên wîla ê-lipâtahk 'ci-pim'paliyân anim' ot'..., piko âta ispîš
ê-w'-îspaliyahk.

   'kwâni mâka n'tawâc êkoši m'pônêl'htên nîla.

B: nahêl'htamanê môl' 'êš[3], nêst' nîla n'titêl'htên.

Snatch of a conversation: to go up-river or not?

A: Are you decide... are we making up our mind ... to go to the Indian
        Reservation right now? *I* don't think [we should]. The weather's too
        dirty; I think that ... the sky doesn't look right.

B: Just as you please. You always seem to want to be the boss.

A: Let it go at that. That's what I think right now. I don't very much
        relish the thought of travelling in dirty weather. It's just that ...,
        although we only want to go this short distance ...

        Never mind then; I may as well stop thinking about it.

B: If you're satisfied at that, I don't mind it either.

ê-išilawînâniwahk ê-oškinîkinâniwahkipan

1   êkwâna mâka, mâk' kâ-kî-tôtamân nîstam, *eighteen foot canoe*[1]
kâ-otinamân, pêyak *French* n'kî-wîcêwâw, êko nêsta pêyak kišê-'l'liw,
kišê-sîpî'-'liliw.[2] êko mâka k'-âšaw'kâmiyâšiyâhk ôma ohci[3] môsonîhk, ôta
ohcih môsonîwi-ministikohk. kwayêsk akâmaskiy n'kîy-itâšinân, *Cha...,*
Charlton Island[4] kâ-išinihkâtêk. êko n'kî-..., n'kî-..., n'kîy-apinân anta
pêyako-kîšikâw; nâ'c êlikohk kî-lôtin; môla n'kî-pimiškânân. êko mîna
kâ-pôsiyâhk, misiwê kotak *island*[5] n'k'-îši-âšawahênân, nêw'šâp tipahikan
ispîhci[6] âšaw'kâmayâw.

2   mîna n'tôhci-... k'-âšaw'kâmêyâšiyâhk pêyakwan ê-kîšikâk anima, *Cape*
Hope Island[7] n'k'-îši-mišakâmêyâšinân, *forty* ... nêmitana niyâlošâp tipahikana[8]
ispîhtakâmêyâw. ê'kot' ânta mâka nâš' kâ-'ši-m... -lôtihk. kêkât n'kî-kostâcin
ê-pimâšiyân antê tâwic. mwêhci kišê-cîmân kâ-'ši-pimipalik n'k'-îši-pimâšinân[9]
piko a..., piko cîmân'šiš êy-âpacihtâyâhk. niyâlo-kîšikâw mâka n'kî-tašîwînân,
kišê-sîpîhk êy-otihtamâhk[10] ôta ohci môsoni'-ministikohk.

3   êko mîna kâ-pêci-kîwêyâhk. nîšo kîšikâwa n'k'-îhtânân kišê-sîpîhk. êko,
n'kî-... nâš' kî-lôtin. âšay nîšitana-n'kotwâs'šâpo-konakisiw *October*. âšay
nâš't takwâkin. nâš'c êlikohk mispon kâ-pimâšiyâhk. môla 'wâ'htênân[11]
tântê kêy-itohtêyâhk;[12] pakwantaw ê-wâšahâk n'k'-îši-...
n'k'-îši-wîhkwêyâšinân.[13] ê'kot' ânta kây-ihtâyâhk nisto-kîšikâw,
nâtaw'-maskwamîwan.[14] kêka n'titâw, *French* ana, niwîciwâkan: "mâhti,
ôtê nôhcimihk n'ka-itohtân," n'titâ', "kici-... mâht' êšinâkwahk antê
kwêskitê, ôma kâ-macitêwêyâk," n'titâw.

4   ê-'ti-matâpêyân sîpiy kâ-p'mihtihk, môla môla 'wâc[15] *half a mile* n'tô...
m'pimohtân. niwâpamâwak ahlapiyak nêtê, ê-šâk'šihkik[16] akâmihk itêhkê
ôma sîpiy. ôma mâka sîpiy *Paint Hill*[17] 'šinihkâtêw. ê'kot' âna mâk'
kâ-p'pon'šiyâhk, pîliš mitâhto-kîšikâw pwâmoši *Christmas*.[18] êko mîna
kâ-iši-kîwêyâhk nêtê kišê-sîpîhk, *ten days* pwâmošê *Christmas*, êkotê
kâ-ihtâyâhk mâka mîna, pâtimâ *fifteenth of January*[19] n'kî-pêciy-ot...
-kihtohtânân kišê-sîpîhk ohci ôtê ê-itohtêyâhk môsonîhk. n'kî-niyâlinân mâka
nîšow il'liwak n'kî-kanawêlimikonânak.

5   êko mâk' anta kâ-ihtâyâhk, *Paint Hill*, môla kêkwân âlahkonâw
n'kî-whci-mowânân, môla nêsta tiy, môla šôkâw. môla m'pîhtwânân ..., piko
namês, pilêw, wâpoš, êko âhk'skiw, nêsta âhkik, misiwê wma kêkwân
n'kî-mîcinân, âhkiko-pimiy ê-wsi-kîs'swâkaniwit,[20] ê-sâsot namês. êko nâspit

Stories of youthful exploits

1   Well then this is what I first did, when I took an eighteen foot canoe, I accompanied a certain Frenchman, and a certain old man also of Fort George. So then we sailed across from this place to Moosonee, from here, Moose Island. Straight across the water we sailed, to Cha..., what is called Charlton Island. Then we ..., we stayed there one day; it blew very hard; we couldn't paddle. So then we embarked again, we all crossed to another island, it was fourteen miles distant across the water.

2   Again we de... we sailed across that same day, we sailed towards Cape Hope Island, at a distance of forty ... forty-five miles. There however, it was very, m... windy. I was almost scared as I sailed away out there. We sailed right where the ship went, only th..., we were using a small boat. It took us five days to reach Fort George from here, Moose Island.

3   So then we came home again. We were two days at Fort George. Then, we..., it was very windy. Already it was the twenty-sixth of October. It was already late in the fall. It snowed very hard when we sailed. We couldn't see where we would go; we sai... we sailed into the very end of a bay, any old bay. Right there we stayed for three days; it got very icy. Finally I said to that Frenchman, my companion: "Let's see; I'll go this way in the bush," I said to him, "to..., let's see how it looks there on the far side of this point," I said to him.

4   As I came out of the bush on the river which lay there, I didn't even wa... walk half a mile. I saw nets over there, protruding above the surface on the far side of this river. And this river, it was called Paint Hill. And that is where we wintered until ten days before Christmas. Then we went back to Fort George away over there, ten days before Christmas. And right here we stayed again, until after the fifteenth of January we came ..., we went away from Fort George to here, on our way to Moosonee.

    We were five, and two Indians were keeping check on us.

5   So then, when we were there at Paint Hills, we ate nothing by way of bread, nor any tea, no sugar. We weren't smoking ..., only fish, partridge, rabbit, then pheasant, and seal, all this kind of thing we ate, with fried

n'kî-kâkwâtakimahcihonân kêka, êkâ '-sâpimahcihoyâhk anim'
ê-'ši-mîcisoyâhk. êko mâka nêtê kâ-iši-kîwêhtahikawiyâhk, kišê-sîpiy, ê'k'ôta
kâ-ihtâyâhk. êko mâka '-pêci-kîwêyâhk šâkitâto-kîšikâw,
n'kî-p'm'pahikonânak atimwak, ôta kâ-otihtamâhk mâka, *about* mâškôc
nîšitanawêkonakisiw *January*. nîšošâp mâk' askîwêtimwak[21]
n'kîy-âpacihânânak; êko, tahtwâw ê-..., ê-kapêšiyâhk, pêyakwâw '-mîcisocik
atimwak n'nakatênân.

6   êko mâka nîla ôta kâ-nâspic'-îhtâyân; kî-kîwêwak niwîcêwâkanak. nîšo
okimâwak n'kî-pêci-wîcêwânânak, wâpišîšin-okimâwak[22] kâ-išinihkâsocik.
kikiskêlimâwak aniki misiwê, êh?

       âšay n'kîšihtân anima wîla.

fish heated with seal oil. So we felt very miserable in the end, since we didn't feel well in ourselves from eating that way. And then we were taken back there to Fort George, and that's where we stayed. So then on our return trip over nine days, we were pulled by dogs, and when we arrived here it was perhaps about the twentieth of January. We used twelve Husky dogs. So, every time we ..., we camped, we left enough food [at the campsite] for one feed for the dogs.

6   Now *I* stayed for good; my partners went home. We were accompanied by two managers, "opposition" [Reveillon Frères] managers as they were called. You know all those ones, eh?

Now I've finished that one.

wêskac ê-iši-pimâtisinâniwahk

1   *now*, – nîštam ililiwak wêskat êši-pimâtisicik ê-wî-kakwê-p'mâcihocik
nôhcimihk ê-n'tahokocik, pišišik mîcim kî-mîciwak môla kêkwân
wêmistikôšîwi-mîcim, piš'šik mîcim, môla nêsta tîy. misiwê kêkwân piko
kâ-nipahtâcik mîcisôwak. mistahi mâka mîcîpanak mîcim ispîš wîla anohc
kâ-tôcikâtêk ê-mîcisonâniwahk. êko, nêsta nîla n'kî-ihtân antê nawac
ê-awâš'šîwiyân, nôhcimihk. âskaw kêkât n'kî-kawahkatânân, micon'
ê-kitimâkisiyâhk ê-mîciyâhk, piko wâpoš, môla kêkwân pimiy, misiwê ôma
kâ-k'-îhtiyâhk. âtiht ililiwak kî-kawahkatêwak. kî-kawahkatêwak ililiwak
nôhcimihk nêtê. môla miskawâkaniwinwak.

2   êko, êko kî-..., kî-..., kî-nipahêpanak mâka âskaw atihkwak,[1] mihcêt
nipahêpanak atihkwa âskaw, ê'kwâni wêhci-pimâtisiyâhkipan. êko mâka,
kêka n'kî-miskawânânak ê-kawahkatêcik ililiwak. n'kiskêlimâwak tân'
êšinihkâsocik ôk' îliliwak kâ-kawahkatêcik. êko n'kî-kocihtânân
'ci-pimâcihakihcik. môl' âta wê...[2] 'mwâci pêyak kîy-ohci-...
-nâspici-kawahkatêwak.[3] n'kî-'šamânânak. êko, wêskac mâk' awas'tê,
awasitê kî-kawahkatêpanak ililiwak. âskaw misiwê nipîpanak
ê-kawahkatêcik. pêyak piko iskôpan.[4] môla kî-kawahkatêw pêyak. êko
pakwantaw n'taw'-papâmohtêw, tâpiskôc, ah, wîhtikôw ê-ytakimâkaniwit.
êkwâni, mm ..., êkwâni môla wîskâc kî-nipiw, pakwantaw ê-papâmohtêt
nôhcimihk.

3   âskaw mâka otihtêpan ililiwa, ê-..., ê-wî-kakwê-n'šiwanâcihât. môla mâka
k'-îtôtawêpan. êko 'sa mâka ililiw ê-yhtât, ê-kišê-'l'lîwit, ê-mitêwit mâka ...,
ê-mitêwit il... aw' ililiw. êkwân' êši-mâhkwapitahk ostikwân, tâpiskâkan
kâ-mihkosit. êkwâni ê-'šiy-ohpipalit nêtê yšpimihk, êko wî-..., wîhtikôwa
nôspinêhokow. wâlaw nêtê n'taw'-pakitinêw ôhi wîhtikôwa, aw' ililiw
kâ-mitêwit. êko mîna pêci-kîwêpaliw aw' ililiw. pêci-pahkišin ant'
êškwâhtêmihk. êko misiwê tipâcimow tântê kâ-išiwilât ôhi wîhtikôwa. êko
mâka kî-... kotakiy' ililiw' ê-wtihtât ôhi..., awa wîhtikôw, ê'kot' ân'a
kâ-nipahikot ôh' îliliwa.

4   êko mâka, pâskisikan 's' âyâpanak piko pêyakwâhtik ê-matwêtêk
pâskisikan êyâwak ililiwak anima išpîš.[5] môl' êškwâ kâ-milwâšihki
pâskisikan' êyâpanak. êko mâka, pêyakwâhtik pâsk'swêw. môla, môla, môla
šawahwêw. êko mâka mîna ocipitam[6] opâs'sikan, êkâ kî-..., êkâ kêkwân
ê-pîhcitihk, êkâ '-pîhcipihkwâtahk. pâskisikêw kiyâpat êkâ '-pîhcitihk anta

Life in the old days

1   Now, – the way people used to live at first long ago as they tried
to make a living hunting in the bush, they ate nothing but country
food, no White-Man's food, – just country food, no tea either. They ate
only whatever they killed. They use to eat a lot of food as much as
what is now usual to eat. Well then, I was there too in the bush when
I was fairly young. Sometimes we almost starved, poor as we were in
foodstuffs, only rabbit, nothing fat, – all this happened to us. Some
people starved. People starved away off in the bush. They were not
found.

2   Then, but then sometimes they used ..., used ..., used to kill
caribou, sometimes they killed many caribou, that's what we used
to live on. So then, finally we found people starving. I knew the
names of these people who were starving. So we tried to rescue
them. Nonetheless there was hardly any ..., not even one was
really starving. We fed them. So, longer ago though, – the people
used to starve more. Sometimes they would all die of starvation.
Only one would be left. One couldn't starve; so he went walking
aimlessly about, considered as, ah – a windigo. Then, one,
mm ..., then he could never die, walking about aimlessly in
the bush.

3   But sometimes he would come up to a person, be..., because he
wanted to try to destroy him; but he was unable to do it to him. But
then there was a man, an old person, and a conjuror ... a conjuring per...
this person. So he wrapped his head up in a red kerchief. Then he rose
away up high so the win... windigo followed him. He took this windigo far off,
this person who conjured. Then this person came back again. He came and
fell in the door. Then, he told all where he had carried off this windigo. So
then he ..., as this windigo came to some other Indians, these ..., that's where
he got killed by these Indians.

4   So then, they used to have as a gun only the single-shot gun ... the
people had up to that point. They didn't yet have the good guns. So then,
he fired one shot at him. He didn't ... didn't ... didn't harm him. So
then again he pulled the gun, even though ..., even though there was
nothing in it, even though he hadn't loaded it. He shot again although

kêkwân. êko picêlak nipahêw.[7] miconi tâtwahwêw ê-'spihcikitit wîyawilîhk,
ôhi wîhtikôw.[8] ê'kot' âni mâk' êši-..., kišipipalit ana wîhtikôw.

ê'kotê 'ni êhtiwâspan wêskac-ililiwak tânta wêhcîspan,[9] ôki ililiwak
kâ-kawahkatêt,[10] pêyak iskopalîpan. môla kî-kawahkatêw. a, ah.

ê'kwâni mâk' êskwâk anima.

not a thing was in it there. Then at that point he killed him. He ripped him completely, the full length of his body, this windigo. And that was the ... end of that windigo.

That's how the old-time people used to be, originally; when these people starved there was always one left. He couldn't starve. A, ah!

And that is the length of that story.

ê-nipahihcik ililiwak, ê-mowihcik mâka

1   a, a..., ôki nîšow ililiwak kâ-kî-tôtahkik ôhtâwiya ê-wîcêwât, kî-...,
kî-nipahêwak ililiwa nîšitana piponwa anim' êšpihc[1] kî-tôtawêwak
pwâmoši kotakiya kâhcitinikocik ililiwa. êko, êko kî-papânîšiwak
iskani-pipon. môla kiskêlimikoliwa ililiwak ê-nipahâcik ililiwa,
ê-mowâcik mâka. piko mâka wanihâkanawîpanak ililiwak mêšikwan'
pipon.

       pâtimâ ê-pêci-mâhahkik, ê-sîkwahk[2] ê-'škwâ-n'tawihocik, êko
picêlak mwêhc' îliliw mâk' itêl'htâkosiwak êsp..., ôk' îl'liwak ôma
kâ-tôtahkik. kâ-nipahâcik wîc'-îl'liwâw', môla kiskêlimâkaniwanwak
ôma ê-tôtahkik ê-pipohk. êko mâka ê-nîpihk mwêhci kwayask il'liwak
itêl'htâkosiwak.

2   êko mâka, kî-..., kêka kî-miskawêwak ililiwa ê-kawahkatêl'ci; êko,
kî-âtawêlimêwak mâka. wêsâ kawahkatêwak; môla kî-mowêwak. êko,
kî-nân'tawihow a..., oškinîkiw. môla kišê-'l'liw nân'tawihow, piko oškinîkiw.
êko, pêyakotênaw kî-miskawêw ililiwa. êkwân' ê-pêši-nipahât misiwê. êkw
iškwêšisa nîšo kî-pêtiwatêw ant' êliliwa kâ-'ši-kawahkatêl'ci, ê-pêci-mîlât
ôma,[3] ililiwa iskwêšiša nîšo. pêci-pitihkwahtin anta kêkwân iškwâhtêmihk
walawîtim. êko itêw, "anihi iškwêšisa anta ihtâliwa kotakiya," awa, awa
kišê-'liliw.

3   mayêw isa wîhtikôw kišê-'l'liw, ililiw piko. êko, "ocipita, ocipit' ânima
mîwat," itêw ôh' iškwêšiša.[4] "n'nahâhkaniskwêmê,"[5] itêw, " 'cipita. pasiko,
'šipaliho." ana iškwêšiš ocipitam. kawahkatêw mâka âpihta.
wêhci-pêci-sâkistikwânêpalit 'škwêšiš. kwâcistak! êkwân' êši-sêk'sicik nâsic.
m'coni môla kiskêl'htamwak kê-itêl'h...[6] tâcikwê[wak]. mâtôwak misiwê
ê-wâpamâcik ililiw' ê-pêci-pîhtokwêpit... -ocipitâcik.

       "wa," itwêw. " 'kâwila sêk'sik," itwêw ana kišê-'l'liw. "môla wês' âni
môšak anima n'tiši-mîcisonân. piko âskaw," itwêw. "êko mâka mîna
kata-n'tawôhôw[7] n'kosis wâpahkê," itêw. "êko mâka, ka-nipahtamâkowâw
mîcim," itêw. "nîlanân mâka, n'ka-'îkatêsinân ôta ohc'," îtêw.

4   êko, êko tâpwê n'tawihow mîna aw' ê-kišêpâyâk ôškinîkiw,[8] okosisa
kišê-'l'liw. êko, ê-..., pêyak môswa nipahêw. âšay pêtiwatêw ôhi môswa.
wîwašiw piko, ê-'spîhci-maškawît. pêyak môs, ê-mišikitit. pêci-pitihkwahtin
mîn' anta mîwat.

       "hâw, n'nahâhkaniskwêm. ocipita mîwat," itêw.

People killed and eaten

1   Uh, uh …, what these two people did as he went with his father, they kill…, killed people for a period of twenty years, they did it to them before they were caught by other Indians. So, they were together wherever they went all winter long. The people did not know about them that they were killing Indians and eating them. It was just [they noticed] that the people were being lost every winter.

Bye and bye as they were coming down by canoe in the spring when they were finished hunting, then at that point these people appeared exactly like an Indian …, these people who did this. The ones who killed their fellow Indians were not known to be acting this way in the winter. And so in the summer they were considered as quite proper people.

2   So then, th…, at last they found people who were starving; so, but they rejected them. They were starving too much; they could not eat them. So, they hunted around, uh…, the young man. The old man didn't hunt around, just the young man. So, he found one family of people. Then he killed them all. Then he carried home on his back two girls of the people who were starving there, giving them this thing, two people, girls. There was a noise of something falling there at the door outside. So this, this old man said to them: "There's one other girl there."

3   The old man was, of course, not a windigo, only a person. So, he said to this girl: "Pull it, pull that bag, Daughter-in-law," he said to her. "Pull it. Stand up. Jump up quickly!" That girl tugged it. She was half-starved. All of a sudden a girl popped her head out. My goodness! At that point they became very frightened. They had no idea what to thi…, they screamed. They all wept at seeing the people as they dragged … pulled them in.

"O-o-oh!" she said. "Don't be frightened," said the old man. "We don't necessarily always eat like that. Only sometimes," he said. "So then, my son will hunt again tomorrow," he added. "And then he'll kill some meat for you," he told her. "But as for us, we'll get away from here," he said to her.

4   So, so indeed this youth, the old man's son, hunted again in the morning. Then, uh …, he killed one moose. Now he brought back this moose on his back. He just carried him, he was so strong. One moose, a big one. Again the bag resounded loudly there.

"Now then, Daughter-in-law, pull the bag," he said to her.

môla kaškipitam, môswa wêhci-pêci-... [laughs] ê-misiwêsit môswa,
ê-wîwašit mâka. êko's' âni mâ' kâ-'ši-nakatâcik anta. pahkân nêtê
wîlawâw k'-îtohtêwak wâlaw.[9] "pitamâ 'ci-... ta-âhcikwêwak,"[10]
itwâsowak.

5   êko kišê-'l'liw, kâ-kî-nipahtamâht môswa, âšay kîšinawêw. misiwê
kîsiswêw môswa ê-'tikitit.[11] êk' omistatay[12] mâka môswa ..., kikiskêl'htên
omistatay môswa ... ê'kot' ânta ê-k'-îši-..., -kîšponahtât môškamiy, misiwê
môškamiy; misiwê kîsiswêw môswa ê-'tikitit. êko ispîy ôma
kâ-iškwâ-'tôtahk, kâ-'škwâ-mîcisocik misiwê, âšay ê-milomahcihocik,
êko nikamow êlikohk awa kišê-'l'liw. hêlikohk nikamow. n'totamâw
êlikohk k'ci-kimiwahk. mêkwât mâka mêkwâ-pipon, nâš'c natotamâw
'ci-kimiwahk. tâpwê êlikohk kimiwan. êko, kâ-iškwâ-kimiwahk êlikohk,
êko n'totamâw mîna micon' 'ci-wâsêskwahk, 'ci-âhkwatihk. êko,
kihtohtêwak, môla kiskêl'...[13] môla nôkwan omêskanâwâw tânt'
êši-kihtohtêcik. kwayêsk lâlih kihcikamîhk itohtêwak.

6   êko nâspic, mâwac kâ-iš'-îšpacistihk[14] mihtâliw (kikiskêlimâw mihtâliw,
drift-snow ê-mišikitit), êkotê 'ni kâ-ši-wâtihkêcik nêtê. wîkiwâw kî-'šihtâwak
atâmihk kônihk. êkot' âni kâ-ihtâcik misiwê, 'n'ma mîcim ant' êtê. êko môla
kiskêlimêwak ôki, ispîy ê-nân'tawâpamâcik ôki, awa kâ-nipahiwêt. môla
kiskêl'htamwak tânt' ê-'htâl'ci.

7   êko ê-'ti-sîkwahk, âšay papâmohtêwak ê-nân'tawâpamâcik. êko mištik
âpacihtâwak tânt' ê-tatêlimâcik, ôtê 'tôtamwak. kêkât mâna pakwanêyâw.
kêkât mâna pakwanêhamwak kâ-pêci-šîpwâstêpalik mâna mištik antê, antê
kêkât ê-pakonêyah'ik. kî-kiskêlimêwak tânt' ê-'š'-îhtâlici. môla piko mwêhci
kî-miskawêw.

    mî-î-îna mâna p'miwêyâkonêhikêwak ê-cahkahwâcik kôna. môla
kî-paskocêhamwak kâ-'š'-îhtâl'ci. êko miconi ê-'ti-nîpihk, ê-..., micon'
ê-'ti-nîpihk, kâ-walawîcik anta ohci micon' êkâ ê-'htât kôn, ê-...,
kî-pôsiwak.

8   êko n..., kî-itohtêcik kâ-'ši-n..., -tašîhkêcik. môla 'sa ihtâwin takwan,
'matakwan êškwâ ihtâwin. môla wâskâhikan. pikw îliliwak ihtâwak. êko
mâka kâ-..., kâ-kiskêlimihcik anima, êwakwânihi kâ-mamišimikocik mâk' ôhi,
ôhi kâ-kî-kiht..., -kîtonawâcik antê 'tâmihk kônihk, êwakwânihi
kâ-kî-mišimikocik.

She couldn't budge it because the moose ... [laughs] because it was a whole moose; but yet he had carried it. So then they just left it there. They went separately far away. First so that ... they made as though they would move away.

5 Then the old man now cooked the moose which had been killed for him. All of it, big as it was, he cooked. Then the moose's stomach, however ..., you know the moose's stomach ... there is where he ... filled it full of gravy, all the gravy; he cooked the whole moose, big as it was. So when he had finished doing this, after they had all eaten, now since they were feeling good, this old man then sang out lustily. He sang right out. He begged for it to rain hard. Meanwhile, being in the middle of winter, he begged earnestly for it to rain. It really rained hard. Then, after it had rained hard, then he asked for it to be completely clear again, to freeze. So, they went away, they didn't kn... their trail wasn't visible where they went. They went straight alongside the sea.

6 So, where the drift bank was very, was highest (you know a drift bank? – big "drift-snow"), it was right there that they dug a tunnel. They made their home beneath the snow. And that's where they stayed, all the food being alongside. So these people didn't know, when they were searching about, this one who did the murdering. They did not know where they were.

7 So as early spring began, they were already walking about searching for them. So they used a stick where they thought they were; they did it this way. Again and again there was almost a hole through. Repeatedly they almost made a hole where the stick could be discerned coming through there, there as they almost made a hole. They knew where they were. Only he couldn't exactly find them.

Agai-i-n and again they made a noise coming and going on the snow as they poked at the snow. They could not break open where they were. So then as summer was pretty well beginning, uh..., as summer was pretty well beginning, they went out from there since there was hardly any snow, as ..., they travelled away by canoe.

8 So th... they went to where they w... were living. There was, of course, no settlement, no settlement existed as yet. No house. Only people were there. So then when ..., when they were found out at that time, they were the ones who were informed on by these ones, these ones whom they were un..., whom they were unable to find there beneath the snow, they were the ones who had informed on them.

êko, kî-ništiliwa awa mâka nâpêw okosisa. kî-mîlêw otânisa
kici-wîkimâlici ôhi, ôhi oškinîkiwa. êko kâ-n'taw'hocik. âšay
wî-nipahêwak, ê-'ti-takwâkihk. âšay tâpwê, âšay n'taw-êškêwak.
âšay maškwamiy ihtâw. âšay kišê-'l'liw tipâcimow misiwê
kâ-kî-tôtahk, ê-'pit wîkihk. âšay nipahêtokw' ôhi misiw' oškinîkiwa,
wîsta' êtêl'htam ..., itêl'htam. misiwê tipâcimow kâ-kî-pêci-tôtahk
išpit nîšitana piponwa.

9   êko kî-..., nêtê mêkwâc ôm' ê-tôtahk ê-n'tôkaminât amiskw' âwa
oškinîkiw pêyak, wî-tahkamêw êškaniliw. otâmâskwaham kotak
êškaniliw. patahwêw wîstâwa. 'kwân' êši-kwâškwatotât'cik.[15]
pêsinâkwan mâka ê-mišâk sâkahikan, nâspic ê-mišâk. êkwâni
kâ-mâci-mâšihitocik,[16] môla wîla kêkwân âpac'htâwak, môla môhkomân,[17]
pik' ôcihciwâwa. pîliš maskwamiy têtâwakâm mâšihitowak. pêyak
âšay miconiy ayêskosiw awa kâ-ostêsimâwit; miconi šâkohikowak ôhi
kâ-nipahiwêl'ci wîstâwa. êko mîna kotakiya, kotakiya kwâškwatotawêw
âpihta kâ-ohcît.[18] mîna, mîna šâkwêhêw. êkow ispîhci-pakwanêhamwak
ôm' ê-'spîhci-mahki-pakwanêyâk kici-têpišihk 'wênihkân ê-pohci-wêpiniht.
êkot' âni mâk' âna ô kâ-oškinîkit mâwac' šîm'mâw ..., ê'kwâna
kâ-kî-šâkwahât, êkota kâ-pohci-wêpinât.

10   êko mâka ana m..., n'tâmihk ê-papâmâtakât ôtê, maskwamîhk, miconi
tâškipaliw maskwamiy. mîna 's' piko ..., mîna wî-pêci-walawîw ant' ohci;
tatâhkamêwak mâka, êškan.[19] kêka môla nôhtâkwan kêkwâ'hkân. êko mâka
kâ-nakatahkik. êko k'-âti-kîwêcik.
    "êko mâka kâ-n'šiwanâcihakiht, nîstâwinân," itwêw 'wa kišê-'l'liw.
    "sôhkatân'[20] mâka kiwî-tôtênâwâw, wêhci-kî-n'taw'-êškêyêk,"[21] itêw awa,
awa kišê-'l'liw, ôht..., ôhtâwiya kâ-kî-nipahiht.[22]
    êko mâka, êko mâka otâmikâtêhwâkaniwin ôta. paskocê-wêpahikâtêliw
oskan. opimiy mâk' antê kâ-pîš'tihk[23] wînihk, nisitwâw...
saskamoci-wêpilâkaniwin.
    "nisitokanêw nâ?"[24] itâkaniwan.
    "êhê, cikêmân'm, nisitokanêw."
    "tântahtôtênaw kâ-mowât ililiw êkâ 'ci-nisitokanêt?" itwêw.
"mihcêtôtênaw kî-mowêw," itwêw. "tântê mâk' êkâ kêy-ohci-nisitokanêt?"
itwêw.
    "otâmahwâkaniwin cîkah'aniliw ostikwânihk. 'kwân'
ê'ši-nipahiht. ê'kwân êši-oh...[25] -iskwâsot anta walawîtim.

So then, this man had three sons. He gave his daughter to be wife to this, this young man. So they went hunting. Now they wanted to kill game as fall was beginning. Already in fact, already they were chiselling [for beaver]. Already there was ice there. Now the old man told about all that he had done, as he sat in his tent. He must already have killed all these young men, his brothers-in-law he thought ..., he thought. He told everything that he had done for the previous twenty years.

9 So he, while this one young man was doing this away off, groping under-water for beaver, he wanted to stab him with the chisel. The other one struck the chisel on the handle. He missed his brother-in-law. Then they jumped on each other. There was a large lake nearby, very large. Then they began to wrestle each other; they didn't use anything, no knife, just their hands. They wrestled each other out to the ice in the middle of the lake. Now one, this older brother, was utterly tired out; the brother-in-law who did the killing was completely overcoming them. Then again he jumped on the other one, the other one, the middle brother. Again, again he got the better of him. Now they made a hole big enough so someone thrown into it would fit. And right there, the one who was the youngest brother ..., that's the one who beat him, and there he threw him in.

10 Now then, that one who ..., as he was swimming about under the ice this way, the ice was severely cracked. Again, of course, only ... he wanted to come out from there again; but they kept poking away at him with a chisel. At last there was no noise of any kind. Then they left it. Then they began to return home.

"Now then we destroyed him, our brother-in-law," said this old man.

"So that's what you wanted to do, the reason you went to chisel beaver," this one said to him, this old man whose fa..., whose father had been killed.

So then, so then he got clubbed on the leg here. The bone was burst open. The fat, however, which lay inside the marrow, it taste ... he had it thrust into his mouth.

"Has the bone a flavour?" someone said.

"Yes, of course, it has a rich flavour."

"How many families has the man eaten that it shouldn't be rich in flavour?" he said. "He has eaten many families," he went on. "How wouldn't it have a rich flavour?" he said.

"He was hit on the head with an axe. He was killed right there. It was right there he was lif... he was burned there outside. He was entirely

câkâhkaswâkaniwin."

11   êkot' 'n' âni[26] kâ-'ši-câkipalit awa kišê-'l'liw, aw' nêsta okosisa. êkotê
kâ-'ši-nipit. nîšitana piponwa mâka ôma kî-tôtam, êkâ '-kiskêlimikot
wîc'-îl'liwa. kwayêsk pikw ililiw k'-îtêlimikow. a ah.

êkotê 'n' êskwâk mâk' anima.

consumed."

11   That is where this old man was consumed, this one and his son. That's where he died. Twenty years he carried on this way, unknown to his fellow men. He had always been considered a proper person. Uh-huh.

And there's the length of that [story].

kotakîya kêkwâna kâ-kî-tôcikâtêkwâpan

1   nîla kâ-kî-tôtamâpân ana ..., *now, I'm gonna start it from what I been
doing myself, you see?*

pêyakwâ antê n'k'-îtohtân wâšâ'k[1] ê-pêyakwêyân ê-takwâkihk
ê-n'taw'-nipahak wêhwêw. êko, âpihta n'kî-nipân ê-'spiht'-nâkwahk
kê-'ši-nipahak wêhwêw.[2] êko, n'kî-'šiwihikân mîna kotak ê-kîšikâk. nî...
mwêhci âšay kihcihlâwak wêhwêwak, šâwanohk êy-ispihlâcik.[3] êko,
nîswâsomitana niyâlal[4] n'kî-nipahâwak wêhwêwak anim' ê-kîšikâk; êko
mitâht niskak, êko nistomitana šîšîpak. ê'ko išpit[5] kâ-n'nip...[6] -minahwêyân.

2   êko, nisto mâk' anta iskwêš'šak ihtâpanak, pêyak mâka kišê-'l'liw, otânisa
awa kišê-'l'liw. êko mâka, n'k'-îtâwak kici-pakocênâcik misiwê niwêhwêma;
êkot', kâ-oš'htâyân *stage*,[7] têšipitâkan kâ-išinihkâtêk. êkota kâ-...,
maškošîya[8] n'kî-pakitinên; êkota kâ-'ši-pakitinakik misiwê. êko
n'n'kîšinawatikwak ôk' iskwêšišak nîšo wêhwêwa, ê-pêci-kîwêyân.

âšay micon' takwâkin. micon' âpihtaw niskâtihk n'tiskwâkonân kôn. êko,
m'pêci-p'mohtân. âpihta mîna n'kî-pêci-nipân. mîna kotakiy otâkošihk, âšay
otâkošin nawac m'pêci-otihtên ôta sîpîhk. mâskôc pêyak tipahikan
ispîhtakâmêyâw. âpihtaw mâka ôma n'kî-iskopân miconi, êy-âšaw'hâtak'ân.[9]

3   âšay mâka, *about a quar'*... pêyak šikâk[10] micihcin ispîhci-kispakiciw[11]
maskwamiy. êko m'pêci-p'mohtân êy-âšaw'hâtak'ân. âšay 'ti-pahkišimow.
êko, miconi kêka n... ôta [*gestures towards the waist*] n'tiskopân. n'tôtâmahwâw
mâka maskwamiy; m'pâskisikan n'tâpacihtân ê-..., êy-otâmahok maskwamiy
ê-'t'-îtohtêyân. êko mâwac ôm' âstamitê kâ-itêhkêhtihk,[12] môla
n'kî-âšaw'hên[13] ê-'spîhci-kišîciwahk. nâspic kîškâyawâw. êko n'tawât
n'kîwân. nîpisîhk n'titohtân[14] ê-kinwâskwahki nîpisiya. kêka niwâpahtên
kêkwâ'hkân ê-makwahtihk ôm' ê-ispîhci-makwahtihk ê-mišâk maskwamîhk
n'tâmihk. n'tôtâmahên. 'kwân' êši-pahkišihk maskwamiy. êkota n'tiskwapân
âpihta niskâtihk, kiyâpic. âskipôta mâka m'pohciškên kâ-kinwâki. micon'
môskinêpêwa. misiwê ninipîwin. ôta n'kî-mâhkwapitâwak nistikwânihk
nimâcîsimak. êkot' ôta pikw ê-'ši-pâhkosiyân, micon' îskan'-tipiskâw kêkât
ê-p'mâtak'ân, ôma pêyak tipahikan. êko, cîmân anta kî-kapatêyâhotêkopan
nâš'c ê-mišâk, kâ-nîswâskwahki cîmâna,[15] *Hudson Bay* ocîmâna. môla
n'k'-îtohtân nêst' ant' ê-'spîhci-kîškâya...[16] wâšakâm. ê-wâlâk is' âni[17]... êko,
n'tawât n'kihtohtân mîna.

More early activities

1   What I had been doing that ... now, I'm going to start from what I had been doing myself. Do you see?

Once I went to Hannah Bay alone in the fall on my way to hunt the wavey. So then, I slept half way to where I was going to kill waveys. Then, I watched the third day. I ... right at that point the waveys were flying away, in their flight south. So, I killed seventy-five waveys that day; then ten geese, then thirty ducks. That's as much as I kill... I hunted.

2   So then, there were three girls there, and one old man. These were the old man's daughters. Then, I told them to gut all my waveys; then I made a stage, a so-called *têšipitâkan* ... It was there that ..., I put grass on it; that's where I put them all. Then these girls cooked two waveys for me as I came back home.

Now it was well into fall. The snow was a good half way up my legs. So, I was walking back. I slept half way again. The next evening, it was already on towards evening, I arrived here at the river. The river was about one mile wide. I was half way up in the water, as I waded across.

3   But now, about a quar... the ice was about a quarter of an inch thick. So I began to walk across, wading. Already the sun was beginning to set. So, at last I completely ... I was in water up to here [*gestures towards the waist*]. I struck the ice; I used my gun in ... hitting the ice as I began to go. Well then, the one that was nearest me I couldn't cross, it was flowing so swiftly. It was very deep. So at last I turned back. I went into the willows where the willows are long. Finally I saw a kind of thing covered over, covered up to this level, big beneath the ice. I hit it. Then the ice fell away. At that point I was half way up my leg in water, more. I had on long 'husky-boots'. They were entirely full of water. I was all wet. I tied my matches to my head here; this was the ony place that I was dry, as I took pretty near the whole night wading this one mile. Now, a canoe there must have been driven ashore by the waves, a very big one: there were seven canoes, Hudson Bay canoes. I couldn't go there either because it was so deep all around it, – because it was concave, that was the reason; so I ... so, I'd no choice, I went off again.

4   'kwâni, môla n'kî-'hci-âšaw'hên. êkot' ânta kâ-nipâyân. nâtâ[18]
niwî-nipân. nêsta niwî-minihkwân. niwî-mîcison. êkot' ânta okîc[19]
êši-kotawêyân anta mistikohk, mistik wêcik' âwa kâ-makošihk anta,
paskwahciy. êkot' ânt' êši-nipâyân. ôtê [gesture] itaskitêwa[20]
paskwahciya nîšo. êko n'takwanahotison. 'udson Bay blanket mâka
piko m'pimohtahtân ê-lâhkašihk. ê-nipâyân anta, mit... niwî-...,
awê'hkân pêci-n't..., ôtê n'tihtôtâk 'wê'hkân. n'titâpin. ôma
kâ-pêci-tôtahk, ay'hâw, *one of them* ... waniki,[21] kâ-kâšikašk'wêcik
pilêšîšak, ôtê m'pêci-tôtâk. ê'kwâni, môla n'kî-wîhkocin[22] niwâpwayân[23]
ê-'spîhciy-âhkwatihk. [interruption] ôta nistikwânihk ôma n'tihtôtâk ana.
ana pilêšîš mišikitiw; ôma kâ-tôtahk ê-kanawâpamit.

5   êko, êko n'tati-wan..., niwî-wîhkocin.[24] môla n'kî-tôtên. micon' âhkwatin
niwâpwayân. kêka n'kî-wîhkocison.[25] 'kwân' êši-kwâškwatiyân anta
kâ-k'-îši-p'mâtak'ân. môla 'wat'[26] nimatwênâw[27] maskwamîy ê-'spîhciy, âh...,
âhkwatihk. micon' mâka ê-šâpwâpâwêyân ê-kî-nipâyân ant' iskan'-tipiskâw.
êko pêci-kihtohtêyân. miconi niwatênên maskwamîhk: anima nêsta
kâ-kišîciwahk[28] miconi m'pimohtân. êko nêtê kâ-otihtamân ê-'ši-piskwahtihki
mihta, êkota kâ-kotawasoyân. n'sîn'pâtinên n'tayâna. m'pâšên. êko
nisâsâkilisitân. miconi 'mošêškatân ant' ê-papâ-nânîpawiyân ê-pêyakoyân
ê-pâsamân n'tayâna.

6   êko mâka âšay êti-kîšowâyâw ê-kišêpâyâk. âšay n..., âšay
m'pêci-kihtohtân ôt' akâmihk. m'pîpotênikân. môl' êškwâ maskwamîwan[29]
ôta wîla sîpîhk. n'kâwîpan âšay m'pêci-nâtahok ..., *my mother*. êkotê 'ni
kâ-ihtiyân: nâhta' n'kî-âlimisihtay. kêkât n'kî-kawatâpwâwân. môla mâka
n'kîy-ohci-âhkosin nê... *next day*; môla n'kîy-ihci-w'êš-ihtin,[30] âta ê-kî-nipîw'ân
iskan'-tipiskâw.

    [laughs] ê'kwâna mâk' êskwâk anima.

4   That was it, I didn't cross it. That's where I slept. I certainly wanted to sleep. I also wanted to drink. I wanted to eat. So at that point I made a fire on top of a log, a stick which happened to be covered over there, a stump. That's where I slept. Two stumps stood at this angle [gesture]. So, I covered myself up. I just took a Hudson Bay blanket with me because it's light. As I slept there, ent... I want ... somebody came to me ... somebody did this to me. I looked about. The thing which he came and did, well, uh ... "one a dem" ... those ones, the birds which have sharp talons, he came and did this to me. Well then, I couldn't wriggle out, my blanket was so frozen. [interruption] Here on my head that one did this to me. That bird was big; this is what he did looking at me.

5   So, so then I began to un... I wanted to wriggle out. I couldn't do it. My blanket was completely frozen. At last I freed myself; then I jumped back into where I had been wading. I didn't even crack the ice, it was so fro... frozen. But I was completely soaked through from having slept there all night. So I came away. I was supported completely on the ice; even there where the current was fast, I walked right along. Then when I arrived away over there where the driftwood was piled up, at that spot I made a fire for myself. I wrang out my clothes. I dried them. Then I was in bare feet. I was completely naked there as I stood around walking here and there, all alone, as I dried my clothes.

6   Now then, it was already beginning to get mild as morning came. Already I ... already I was coming away here across the water. I made a smudge fire. It was not yet icy here on the river. My late mother now came to get me ... my mother. That's what happened to me: I had had a real hard time. I almost lost my life through being in the water. But I was not sick ... next day. I had no bad effects, even though I had been wet all night.

    [laughs] And that is the length of that one.

ê-waškwayi-cîmânihkâniwahk

1   nîštam ê-kihcihtâniwahk tânt' êtôcikâtêk â... oškwayi-cîmân[1]
êy-oš'htâniwahk, pitamâ nâtahikâtêw' ôškwaya[2] mihcêt. êko, kišê-'l'liwak ôta
ihtâwak ê-... êy-oš'htâcik mihcêt a... oškwayi-cîmâna wêskac, *Company*,
'udson Bay Company[3] '-oš'tamawâcik cîmâna. êko mâka, môl' âlimisîpanik
ê-wš'htâcik; nâš'c wêhtan êy-ošihtâniwahk oškwayi-cîmân. piko 'kwân'
ê-'tiy-olâskwahaman kiwâkinâwak mâsakîskak; ê'kwân' êši-'ci-šîpâhacik,[4] a...
awa... aspihtitâkanak kâ-išini..., kâ-napakisicik, kâ-môhkotacik[5] mistikwak.
mâsakîsk mâka piš'šik kitâpacihâw.

2   êko mâka watapîy, watapîy n'tâmihk mištikohk kâ-pimâpihkêšihk askîhk,
êwakwâna '-kaškikwâcikâkêyan êy-ošihtâyin ôma apaci... ay'hâw,
oškwayi-cîmân. êkotê' n' ê-tôcikâtêkipan êy-ošihtâniwahk ôhi cîmâna. môšak
mâna n'ka-kanawâpamâhtayak kišê-'l'liwak ê-wš'htâcik. n'kaškihtâhtay
mâka nêsta nîla ê-wî-..., 'ci-wîcihêw'ân êy-oš'htâniwahk. kiyâpac mâkââ,
n'ka-kîy-oš'htâhtay oškwayi-cîmân, wî-koc'htâyân 'ci-wš'htâyân, anohc êê...
kiyâpac. tânt' êtôcikâtêk piko, oškway n'ka-nâtahêhtay, mâsakîskak mâka,
ê'kwâni piko. êko mâka, mâka ... *Hudson Bay* mâka ôh' êy-ošihtamâht
cîmân', ê'kwân' ê-'tiy-âniskê-'tâmâspan ililiwa. êko môla mâk' an', ... môl'
âlimakihtamôpan kêkwân anim' êspihc. môla tâpiskôc anohc kâkikê.

3   ê'kwâni piko 'tê kâ-tôcikâtêkipan anih' êy-ošihtâniwahkwâpan
oškwayi-cîmâna. milwâšinôpana mâka. maškiwâwa nêsta môla ... môla
pîkwahtinôpan' ê-p'miškâyan, ê-..., asiniy âskaw ê-miškwahot. pâwistikohk
nêsta ê-pîwitaman nâhtâ' milwâšinôpan. mihcêtwâ mâk' antê n'kî-n'tahên
sîpiya ôh' êy-âpacihtâyân nêsta ê-mâhamân, ê-n'tawihoyân wêskat. ê'kwân'tê
mâka,[6] piko êtôcikâtêk ê-wš'htâniwahk.[7]

     ê'kwâni mâk' ôma êskwâk wîla.

Making birch bark canoes

1   First at the outset the way it's done in making a birch bark canoe, first of all many pieces of birch bark are gathered. Well then, there are old people here wh... who used to make many uh ... birch bark canoes long ago, the Company –, making canoes for the Hudson Bay Company. And so, they used to have no difficulty making them; it was very easy making a birch bark canoe. Only at that point when you start making the frame you bend the cedars; then you push them in, uh ... the flooring stays as they are cal... the flat ones, the boards which you plane. You use cedar throughout.

2   So then [you take] a root, a root which lies in a line beneath a tree in the ground, this is what you lace it with as you make it, use this ... well, uh ... a birch bark canoe. That's how it used to be done when making these canoes. I would always watch the old people again and again as they made them. And I myself used to try also because I want ... in order to help as they made them. And still, I could make a birch bark canoe, should I wish to try to make one, right now, uh ... still. The only thing that would have to be done, I'd fetch birch bark and cedar, that's all. And, and then ... when these boats were made for the Hudson Bay, then they in turn sold them to the people. So then they weren'... nothing used to be expensive at that time. Not like it always is today.

3   That's all that used to be done in making those birch bark canoes. They used to be good, though. They were strong too and didn't ... didn't break up as you were paddling, as ... as you sometimes hit a rock. And as you were running on the rapids it was really very good. And many times I've gone upstream using these and downstream too, as I hunted long ago. And that's all they used to do in making them.

    That then is the length of this one.

mišcâkalâš kâ-kî-nipikopanê, êko mâka kâ-kî-waniškâkopanê

1 opaskowi-pîsim nîšitana-pêyak ê-kîšikâk.[1]

mišcâkalâš kî-..., ê-kîy-išinihkâsot, nâspic mâka kî-n'tâ-n'tawihot mišcâkalâš. kî-nôtinitôwak mâka ililiwak wîla mâka nêsta kî-mâš'hkêw. kî-têpwêw mâka kotak ililiw: "âšay nipahitowak ôko ililiwak." kî-pâhpahtâw mâka ošâwasko... ošâwaskwapîway. kî-mâš'hêw mâka mišcâkalâša. ošâwaskwapîway mâka nâspic kî-k..., kî-kisiwâsiw, mišcâkalâš[2] ê-..., ê-iši-..., ê-mâš'ikot. ôko..., ôko 'sa nâspit mâka ôhk... ôhk... ôhkomisa, ôhkomisa k'-îšinihkâsoliwa, ošâwaškwapîway kî-išinihkâsoliwa ôhkomisa. "piko nimâkonikawin ê-..., mâna piko n'kî-mâciwêpišokawin, ê-'tamahcihoyân," piko itwêw, ê-mâkonikot ôhkomisa ê-ohcihikot ê-mâšihkêt.

2 pêyakwâ mâk' ê-kîšikâlik, kî-pôsiw ispî kâ-iškwâ-mâšihkêcik. kî-... [clears throat], êko mâka, kâ-itwêt awa mišcâkalâš, êwakwâwa mišcâkalâš: "n'kî-nipinâkopan 'êcik' âni." êko mâka, awasitê, kî-..., awasitê mâka kî-šîh..., kî-sîhciškawâkaniwan.

"kêkwân 'nima... kêka k'... wêcik' âni âšay nikoskosin. nikî-nipinâkopan 'êcik' âni. âšay niwaniškân. mitoni osâwaškâw wêniškâyân. ispî kâ-kwêtipîyân n'tôtinâw n'cîpêy-ospwâkan[3] ê-pîhtwâyân. êko kâ-kîwêyân nâspic n'kiskêlimik nikâwiy, ê-kî-..., ê-kî-takošiniyân ê-'kišêpâyâk. âšay niwâpamik nikâwiy. mâtow nikâwiy: 'tâpêkâ nâspic ê-sâk'hak n'kosis, nâspic ê-n'tâ-n'tawihot.' "

'êcik' âni, êkwâni k'-âti-pôsiyân, ê-n'tawatihkwêyân.

3 kâ-matê-nâsipêt nikâwiy, wiyâpamit ê-pêtâstamiškâyân. âšay pêci-nôkosiw, ê-pâmiškât.[4]

"paskwahcîliw kâ-pêtahotât."

nitôt..., n'tôtihk,[5] n'tô..., cîmânihk, nîkân n'cîmânihk ê-kî-pakitinamân.[6] "iyâpêwatihkwa wêcik' âni kâ-nipahât."

âšay mâka kiskêl'htam nikâwiy mîcim ê-pêtâyân.

mâtow nikâwiy: "tâsipwâ nikosis ê-kî-mihtâtak kâ-nipit, ê-ispîhci-n'tâ-n'tawihot."

Mishchagalash who is supposed to have died and then to have risen

1   The twenty-first day of July.

Mishchagalash was ... as he was called, Mishchagalash was very good at hunting. The people fought with each other and he too wrestled. The other person hollered: "Now these people are killing each other." But *ošâwasko... ošâwaskwapîway* laughed at it. He wrestled with Mishchagalash. But *ošâwaskwapîway* go... got very angry, being ... being wrestled with ... there ... by Mishchagalash. These ones ... these ones, of course, very much his unc... his unc... his uncle, his uncle's name, *ošâwaskwapîway* was his uncle's name. "I was only grabbed as... again and again I felt just as if I were slashed," he just said, as his uncle seized him and stopped him from fighting.

2   Now one day he went away by boat when they had finished wrestling. H... [clears throat], so then, this Mishchagalash, this very Mishchagalash said: "It would seem I had died." So then, more, he was ... then he was more conf... he was confined.

"What is that ... at last uh ... it seems now I am awakening. It would seem I had died. Now I am getting up. The grass was yellow when I got up. When I had turned over I took my ghost-pipe and smoked. Then when I went home my mother knew me very well, since I had ... since I had arrived in the morning. Now my mother saw me. My mother wept: 'To be sure I love my son very much; he was much given to hunting.' "

It seems, then that I started to go away by canoe, looking for deer.

3   My mother went down the bank in the distance, as she saw me as I came paddling facing her. Now she came into sight, paddling towards me.

"It's a stump which he's bringing back."

My cra... in my craft, my cr... in my canoe, I had put it in the bow of my canoe.

"It's a buck deer, it seems, which he has killed."

And now my mother knew that I was bringing food.

My mother wept: "No wonder, it's my son for whom I was sorry when he died, because he was such a good hunter."

HANNAH LOON

pakwacililiw

1   wêskac êy-awâšišîwiyân n'kî-kanawêlimik ê-..., nôhtâwiy ispîy êkâ
kâ-pimâtisît[1] nikâwiy ôta ê-..., ê-yhtâspan *Moose Factory*[2] êy-âpacihât
kampanîwa.

êko mâka môla ohci-pimâtisîw n'kâwiy. n'kî-pêti-nâtahokonân mâka
nôhtâwiy ê-kanawêlimiyamiht,[3] ê-n'tawihot nêtê, wâškêyokâw kâ-išin'kâtêk,
kâ-k'-îši-otaskîspan môšak, ê-pêci-pimâtisît. êko mâka, n'kî-n..., -n'tahênân
mâk' anima sîpiy, wâškêyokâw'-sîpiy ê-išin'kâtêk, ê-pôsihiyamiht ê-pâmiškât
ê-nâtahâhk otêyâna,[4] ê-'stahcikot antê.

2   êko mâka, m'pêhtawânân 'wê'hkân ê-'miškâyâhk. matê-otatâm'ham
kê'wâhkâniliw. môl' ani wîskât mâka pêhtâkwan 'wênihkân wîskât
kici-kalakihtât. êko mâka matê-..., ê-twêhikêt[5] [beats a frying pan]. kinwêš
mâka nawac otatâmahwêw pîliš mâka n'tati-lâwinâkosinân. kiyâpac
matê-otatâmaham, anima, askihkwa,[6] kêkwân ê-'tihtâkwahk [beats frying
pan again].[7]

êko mâka nôhtâwînân n'titânân. iškwêšišak mâk' anta kî-nîšiwak
ê-pôsihât, nîla mâka nêšta. êko kî-kôstâciwak ôko kâ-mišikiticik
iškwêšišak. êko itwêwak: "pakwaciliwiw 'š' âwa kâ-matê-kalakihtât."

"mayêw ana pakwacil'liw. pakwantaw ani kititihtênâwâw. mistikwak
wês' âni mân' ayamiwak nêsta.[8] kaškihtâwak wês' ân' ê-'yam'cik mistikwak."
ê'kwân' êtwêt nôhtâwiy.

3   (hêntriy sêlors mâka k'-îšinihkâsow awa nôhtâwiy.) ê'kwâni mâk' êtât ôho
iškwêš'ša, otânisa. pêyak mâka kotak iškwêšiš ê-..., ê-wîcêwâkanihât
ocawâšimiša, ê-kaškêl'htamil'ci ohci. kostâciwak mâka ôkô 'škwêšišak.

êko mâka kâ-pêci-mâhamâhk anima sîpiy. môla mîna
ohci-matê-kalakihtâw. môla n'kî-whci-pêhtawânân mîna. ê'kwânim' êšpiš[9]
kâ-pêhtawakiht piko ê-matê-otatâmâpiskáhikêt.

344

The Bushman

1   Long ago in my childhood I was taken care of as … by my father when my
mother died, as … as he used to stay here at Moose Factory working for the
Company.

So then, my mother died. My father came to get us by canoe to take care of
us, since he was hunting away off, at Grassy Bay Creek as it was called,
where he always used to have his trapping grounds, while he was alive. So
then, we went u… up that river called Grassy Bay River, with him taking us
by canoe as he paddled fetching his trapping outfit, caching it there.

2   Well then, we heard someone as we were paddling. He was hitting away at
something in the distance. It was never heard of that anyone should ever
disturb the quiet. So this is the banging sound which he made [beats a frying
pan]. He beat upon it for a long time, but at last we began to get further and
further away. He could still be heard in the distance beating it, that thing, –
it sounded somewhat as if he were beating on a kettle [beats frying pan again].

So then we told our father. Now there were two girls there that he was
taking with him in the canoe, and myself as well. Well then, these two big
girls were afraid. So they said: "This is a Bushman for sure who's making
that noise in the distance."

"That's not a Bushman. You imagine you're hearing things. The trees
frequently talk too, you know. You know the trees are able to talk." That's
what my father said.

3   (Henry Sailors was my father's name.) And that's all he said to these
girls, his daughters. There was one other girl though uh … who came along
as a companion to his children, since she was lonesome. But these girls were
frightened.

So then we came down that river. He didn't make any further noise. We
didn't hear him again. It was only at that time that we heard him, drumming
away in the distance on metal.

mêkwâc e-awâšišîwiyâpân

1   mêkwâc ê-'wâšišîwiyân nimis n'kî-kanawêlimik. tayna cam k'-îšinihkâsow.
ispîy ê-kaškihtâyân ê-wêspitit'soyân êkâ '-okâwîyân, êko mâka, nâspic tâpwê
mâna n'kî-âlimisinân, n'k'-îtêl'htên, mêkwâc ê-'wâšišîwiyân.
   tâpwê kîy-âliman, n'titêl'htên mâna ô..., anohc ê-mâmitonêl'htamân.
âskaw môla n'tôhci-ayân kê-pohciskamân maskisina. n'kî-sâsâkilisitân. âta
nêsta ê-maskwamîwâkamihk[1] ê-wâpahtamân, kiyâpat môla n'tôhci-ayân
maskisina. n'kî-pahkopân mošê[2] n'sitihk. âskaw maškošîya
n'kî-n'taw'-manipitên, ê-'šikêyân[3] êkâ ê-'yâyân kê-pohciskamân âskipôta, mošê
piko ê-'pâmâtakâyân kônâpôhk. êko mâka, kî-kitimâkan mâka šâkoc mêkwâc
anima, nêsta kî-manêwan mîcim.
2   šâkoc mâka nâspic kîy-âhkosiw môšak aw' ililiw kâ-kî-kanawêlimicik.[4]
kîy-âhkosiw awa ililiw[5] onâpêma, – ânkas cam k'-îšinihkâsow.
   êko mâka, ê-pôsiyâhk mân' ê-nîpihk ê-nân'taw'-mîcisoyâhk nêtê tâwic,[6]
nîšo mâka awâšiša kî-'yâwêw. kî-nîšo-p'ponêsiw pêyak: êko mâka kotak
mâskôc kî-pêyako-'ponêsiw. ôko mâk' awâšišak mâna n'kî-kanawêlimâwak
ê-'pâ-n'tawihonâniwahk, '-'nâkacihakik.
   êko mâka, nîla n'kî-wîcêwâw nêsta nimis ê-n'tawahot, '-kî-âhkosit awa
'liliw ê-wî-kak'-'mâcihakiht,[7] 'ci-mîcisocik ôko 'wâšišak nêst' aw' ililiw. êkow
âliman âskaw ê-pêci-kîwêholakiht aw' ililiw nâspic ê-âhkosit. nîšwâ
n'kî-kiskêl'htên ê-kî-pêci-kîwêholakiht ôt' ê-pêšiwakiht, ministikohk. nêtê
m'pap..., ê-'pâ-nân'taw'-mîcisoyâhk anima kâ-ihtit mâkah.
3   mîna mâka n'kî-pôsihtân pêyakwâ. êko nêtê kâ-iši-cimêyâhk,[8]
North, North Bluff,[9] macitêwêyâw, kâ-išin'kâcikâtêk, âstam'tê
'nima kâ-piskwâhkâw.[10] êkot' anta kâ-kapâyâhk. pêyako-kîšikâw
itêl'htâkwan ê-'miškâniwahk wîla tâpinâ p'm'palîpan cîmân antê ...,
apwoy piko n'âpacihânân ê-'miškâyâhk. êkw isa mâk' anta
n'kî-kapânân. nâspic âhkosiw a' kišê-'l'liw. nâspic wîsakêl'htam.
môla 'wên'hkân kâ-pimâtisît ispîhci-wîsakêl'htam itihtâkosiw êy-âhkosit.
piko n'tayakopâtinânân kišâkam'têliw. môla nêsta ihtakwan nipiy.
nâspic wâlaw ihtakwan nôhcimihk. akâwât piko têpinâkosiw ililiw
ê-kwâpikêt nêtê nôhcimihk. wâlaw milwâpôw ê-n'tawâpahcikâtêk.
4   êko mâka, êkot' ê-'piyân ê-kanawêlimakik awâš'šak, pîliš nisto-kîšikâw
anta n'tihtânân ê-kakwê-... êkâ ê-kî-pimohtêt aw' ililiw, nîlanân

Childhood memories

1   While I was a child my older sister took care of me. Her name was Dinah
Chum. When I was able to dress myself, since I had no mother, well then, –
we really had a very difficult time again and again, I thought, while I was a
child.

It was really hard, I frequently thought, h... as I reflect on it now.
Sometimes I didn't have shoes to put on. I went barefoot. Even though I saw
it was icy water, I still didn't have shoes. I had to wade barefooted.
Sometimes I went pulling grass for my socks, since I had no husky boots to
put on as I just walked around with nothing in the slush. Well then, one sure
was poorly off at that time, and food was scarce too.

2   But this person who was taking care of me was often very ill. This person
was ill; her husband, – Angus Chum was his name.

So then, as we repeatedly went off by canoe in the summer in search of
food away along the coast, she had two children. One was two years old; and
the other was probably one year. These children I frequently took care of,
looking after them as they wandered around hunting.

Well then, *I* used to accompany my older sister too as she was hunting
because this person was ill and we wanted to try to keep him alive, so as for
these children and this person to eat. So it was sometimes difficult as we
were bringing this person back by canoe since he was very ill. Twice I knew
that we brought him back here by canoe, bringing him to the island [Moose
Factory]. We were wand... as we were wandering about over there looking for
food, the time that happened to him.

3   Again we set off by canoe once. So we canoed over there to North ... North
Bluff, "The Point" it's called, this side of that sandy shoal. That's where we
went ashore. It seemed to take about one day to paddle since the canoe wasn't
driven by power there ... we used to paddle only as we went by water. But
then we went ashore. This old person was very ill. He was in great pain. He
wouldn't be expected to live [from the sound of it], he suffered so much in his
illness. We just bathed him with hot water. There was no water either. It was
very far off in the bush. A person was hardly within range of sight getting
water there in the bush. It was a long way for good water to be fetched.

4   So then, I stayed in camp right here taking care of the children, we stayed
there for three days trying ... because this person could not walk, just

piko ê-kanawêlimakiht, nimis, nîla mâka. n'kî-'pišîš'šin mâka; mâskôc môla
'wâc n'kî-'hci-mitâhto-p'ponêsin, ômah kâ-itwêyân.

êkw isa mâka, kêka mâka ispî kâ-nisto-kîšikâk, n'kî-pêci-kaškihtânân
ê-pôsihakiht ê-nâsipêtâpêyâhk apahkwânihk ê-p'mitâpêyâhk piko,
'ci-pôsi-tahkoskêt cîmânihk ê-'yši-'tâpêyâhk. êl'êhk mâka, n'tâlimisin,
n'titêl'htên, êkâ nêsta tâpwê ê-'htakwahk kê-mîcinâniwahk, êkâ
ê-kî-têpi-tôcikâtêk nêsta kêkwân, êkâ nêsta 'wê'hkân ê-n'tawihot anta,
êy-otami-kanawêlimakiht awa êy-âhkosit ililiw, ê-pêci-p'mišakâyâhk mâka
piko.

5   êko mâk' âta mân' ê-koci-p'mâšakâmêpicikêyân nîla, ispî sîpiy
ê-pêci-otihtamâhk,[11] nâspic mâkah êkâ tâpwêh..., mâskôc 'sa, mân'šîš
niwîcihiwânâtokwê. 'šâkanâpiy n'kî-otinên ê-'mâšakâmêpicikêyâhk.

êliwêhk mâka miscêtiwak nêsta sakimêwak! kêkât mâna
n'kipotâmoškâkowak.[12] nimis mâka piko ê-tahkohahk anta, 'wâšišak mâka
nîšo ant' ê-pôsik...[13] ê-kanawêlimakihcik, êy-âhkosit mâk' aw' ililiw
ê-pêšiwakiht, ê-pêci-kîwêholakiht. êliwêhk mâka kinwêš kîy-âhkosiw aw'
êliliw. anim' ê-nîpihk, tašinê kîy-âhkosiw ..., ispîš âta kâ-pêšiwakiht ôta,[14]
êkâ ê-'htât n'tohkolon. môla mat' âna kîy-ohc'-îhtâw n'tohkolon wêskac. môla
kêkwân n'kî-wîcihikonân.

6   mîna mâka pêyakwâ ê-pôsiyâhkipan, êkwâni mîna pêyakwan
kâ-tôtamâhk. nîlanân piko n'kî-pôsinân ê-iskwêwiyâhk ..., êko mâka, wâlaw
nêtê kâ-iši-cimêyâhk. wâlaw nawac n'k'-îši-cimânân. mîniša mâka
n'kî-'pâ-'nâtawâp'tênân anima, jam mâna êy-ošihtâyâhk, namêsak nêsta
ê-mowakihcik, ê-pakit'hwâyâhk.

n'kî-'wâšišîwin mâka nîl', anima kâ-itwêyân. wîlawâw mâka, kotakiyak
nêsta kî-... kotak cîmân iskwêwak kî-pôsiwak, nîlanân nêsta, môla nâpêw'[15]...
môla nâpêw kî-whci-wîci...êwêwak,[16] ê-pôsicik ê-n'tawahocik.

7   êko mâka nêtê kâ-..., wâlaw kâ-iši-cimêyâhk, '-pâmiškâyâhk. êko
mêkwâc ê-kanawêlimakik ôko' wâšišak kî-nîšiwak, nêsta nîla môla
nâcit[17] n'kî-ohci-mišikitin. mâskôc âšay nawac nimišikitihtay
misawâc.

êko, n'kanawêlimâwak ôko' wâšišak nîšo. mîniša mâka nêtê
n'tawâpahtamwak, wâlaw ê-ytohtêcik. kêka m'pêhtawâw 'wênihkân
êlikohk nâs'c ê-matê-mâtot.

"tân'k'êtokwê kâ-itwêhkâsot awa nîc'-iškwêšiš?"

tâpiskôc n'k'-îspihcikitinân.

ourselves taking care of him, my older sister and myself. I was little, though; perhaps I wasn't even ten years old, at the time I'm speaking of

So then, however, at last when three days were up, we arrived at the point where we were able to take him in the canoe by hauling him down the bank on a canvas and just dragging him around so that he stepped into the canoe as we dragged him. But did I ever find it hard! – I thought – with there not really being anything to eat, and with nothing able to be adequately done, and with no one hunting there, as we were busy taking care of this sick person, and as we came in by paddle only.

5   Well then, although I repeatedly tried to track the canoe, once we reached the river, really wasn't any ... I may perhaps have been a little help. I took the line as I tracked.

My, but the mosquitoes were bad too! Frequently they nearly choked me. My big sister, was just steering there, as we took the two children in the canoe, minding them as we were, bringing that sick person, as we brought him back by canoe. Was this person ever sick for a long time, though! That summer he was ill continually, – even up to the time we brought him here, since there was no doctor there. It would appear there was no doctor there long ago. We had no help in anything.

6   And once again, we went away by canoe, then we did the same thing again. We went off by canoe, just the women alone ... and then, we canoed away far off. We went quite far by water. We walked around getting berries at that time, making jam again and again. We ate fish too, setting out our nets.

I was just a child though, at the time I'm talking about. But they, the other ones as well ... the women went off in another canoe, and we too, no man ... they didn't go ... with any man, as they went off hunting.

7   So then we went away yonder ... we went far away by water, paddling. So during the time I was taking care of them there were two of these children, and I myself was not very big. Perhaps by now I was fairly big any way.

So I took care of these two children. And they fetched berries away yonder, going far away on foot. Finally I heard someone weeping very hard in the distance.

"I wonder what the matter is that my girlfriend is taking on so?"
We were both the same size.
"What must be the matter with her that she is making that sound?"
I thought.

"tâytik'[18] kâ-itwêhkâsot?" n'titêl'htên.

kêka wêhci-pâpahtât. pâpahêw ošîma; tihkinâkanihk akwahpisoliwa.

"tân' êhtiyan?" n'titâw.

"n'kâwiy w'-îskwâsot'sow," itwêw. "wî-pahk'sot'sow. nišîmiša mâka tahkonêw anta pêyak. n'ka-n'taw'-maskamâw mâka ôho. ana n'šîmiša n'ka-maskamâw."

8   êkota kâ-nakacipahât anihi ošîma; n'kanawâpamâw mâka. kî-matê-maskamêw[19] mâka okâwiya anihi ošîma. êkwân' ê-kî-kihcipahât nêtê, patotê k'-îspahêw.[20]

êko mâk' awa kâ-pahkisot pihkoliw iskwêw. k'-îskwâsotisow. êko mâka, k'-îskwâsow kâ-pâpahtât, n'mâhkîminâhk ant' ê-pêc'-îspahtât. nâhtêp' iškotêw ê-pêc'-îšinâkosit.

êkwân' êšiy-ocipahak aw' awâšiš kâ-kanawêlimak mêmêpisonihk k'-âkocihk; n'kihcipahâw. pêyak n'sakiniskêpahâw. nîšo n'kihcipahâwak ôko 'wâšišak. nêtê piko n'taw[21] nin'taw'-...-âkôšimôlon, ê-wî-pimâcihakik.

êko kîwêpa'how[22] mîn' an' êskwêw. pêšoc kî-pêc'-îspahtâw. miconi kî-pêci-pasitêw pêšoc anta kâ-iši-wîkiyâhk, maškošîya,[23] ê-pêc'-îskwâsot ant' ê-pêci-pâpahtwâc ê-iskwâsot. êko, mêkwâc nêtê ê-kîwêpahtât mîna, mîna kotakîliw kî-matê-pahkisam pihkoliw, nâspic ê-kišiwê'têlik,[24] mwêhci miši-pâskisikan ê-itwêwêtêlik. êwakwânim' onâpêm' opihkomilîw misiwê '-kî-câkâhkasahk.

9   êko mâk' ôko nimis nêtê wâlaw ê-n'tawi-mawisocik, misiwê nêst' otânis' aw' êskwêw. mâmišikitiwak aniki iskwêwak. êko, ê-pêci-kîwêpahikocik nâspic kî-sêkisiw a' nimis. "mâskôc n'cawâšimišak iskwâsowak," k'-îtêl'htam. "nišiwanâcihowak n'cawâšimišak."

êkw awa iskwêw ..., êko iskwêw nêtê[25] kâ-itohtêt, lâlipêk nêtê kî-n'taw'-nîpawiw šîwâpôhk; šîwâkamin mâtâna nipiy nêtê. môla 'w'ihkân kî-minihkwêw. môla ... miconi mâka kî-kîsisow.[26] êkotê mâka twoyêhk kâ-'spahitocik antê, ê-pâpahitocik.[27] nimis mâka êkota kâ-ohci-kâhcitinikot kêkwân, êkâ '-wî-milow-ihtit. mâskôc kî-kîškwêyêl'htam "n'cawâšimišak iskwâsowak," ê-itêl'htahk.

10   awa mâka iskwêw, môla kinwêš kî-whci-pimâtisîw[28] mâskôc ispîš k'-âti-kîwêholâkaniwit. kîwêtinohk mâka ohcîwâkopan ôko ililiwak ê-pêci-kîyôtêcik '-pâmiškâcik ôtê *Moose Fac...* môsonîhk ê-pêci-pâmiškâcik

At last, all of a sudden, she came running. She came running
bringing her little sister; the latter was covered up and fastened in a
cradle board.

"What's wrong with you?" I said to her.

"My mother is going to burn herself," she said. "She is going to blow
herself up. She's holding my little sister there alone. I'll go take away this one
from her. I'll take my baby sister away from that woman."

8   There she left her young sister and ran; and I kept an eye on her. In the
distance she grabbed that young sister of hers away from her mother. Then
having run away off with her, she ran with her to one side.

And then this woman exploded some gunpowder. She burned herself. So
then, she got burned as she came running towards me, as she came running
to our tent. She looked very much like a fire as she approached.

At that I grabbed hold of this child whom I was minding, who was hanging
in a hammock; I ran away with her. All by myself I ran with her by the arm.
I ran away with these two children. I ran around looking for cover, as I
wanted to save their lives.

So, that woman turned back again in a hurry. She had come running
towards us close by. The burning grass was approaching close to where we
were tenting as she came there burning, running it towards us in flames.
Then, while she was running off back again yonder, she was heard exploding
more gunpowder, as it made a very loud report, sounding just like a cannon,
having at that point burned up all her husband's powder.

9   Now then, these women, including my older sister, went gathering berries,
and all this woman's daughters. Those women were big, each one of them. So,
as they were being run back here, my older sister was very much afraid.
"Perhaps my children are burning themselves," she thought. "My children are
destroying themselves."

Then this woman ... so the woman who had gone away yonder, she went
and stood away over along the edge of the salt water; the water is salty away
off there. Nobody can drink it. Not ... She was thoroughly cooked. And right
away they ran each other to that spot, running towards each other. But my
older sister was caught by something there, since she wasn't in very good
state of mind. Perhaps she was distraught, since she was thinking, "My
children are burning themselves."

10   But this woman, she didn't live long, – I'd say up to the time they left to
take her home by canoe. These people had come visiting from the North,

piko;[29] ê-'ti-kîwêhocik mâk' ôma kâ-ihki. n'kî-'ti-wâpamânânak[30] piko antê; wêhci-kî-... kî-wâpamakihcik ôma ê-ihticik.

paddling around here to Moose Fac... just paddling around to Moosonee. It was as they started home that this happened. We first saw them there; this is why we sa..., how we saw this happen to them.

ê-mâšihitocik wîskacâniš nêsta mâka wâpikošiš

1   pêyakwâ mîna ôtê pakwantaw ê-tašîhkêyâhkipan, a... sâhkamistikohk[1]
n'tihtânân. êko mâk' ani, nôhc...[2] tâwic antê mâna n'kîy-omâhkîminân
nîpisîskâhk[3] wayêš, ê-n'pahakihcik mahkêšiwak. êko mâka, pêyakwâ nî...,
ê-'piyân pîhtikwamihk, nâspit tâpw' êlikohk matê-nohtâkosiw wîskacâniš.
"tân' êhtikw' awa kâ-itwêhkâsot wîskacâniš?" n'titêl'htên. n'tâpin[4] kêka.
kinwêš âta pitamâ môla n'kî-whc'-îtâpin. kêka '-pakwaniyâk mâka
n'tôhc'-itâpin m... mâhkîhk. êkot' 'êhci-kanawâpamak. k'-âkosît
wîskacâniš nîpisîhk. n'kanawâpamâw. "tân' êhtikw' awa
kâ-itwêhkâsot?" wêhcis...[5] môskît âpikošîš kêka, kônihk.
môskâkonakîw.

2   êkwân' êši-kwâškototawât wîskacâniš anihi âpikošîša.[6] mâkomêw
anta okwayâlîhk. k'-âti-'mahôlât[7] mâna.
        šâkohikow.[8]
        kihciwilêw, mâna.
        môla manâ ... âhcipaliholiwa mân' ê-p'maholât. ê'kwâni mân'
êši-kiciskipalihikot êy-âhcipaliholici. aspin mâna pahkišin âpikošîš
mohcihk ..., kônihk. 'kwâni mîn' êši-šêkopalihot[9] kônihk. êkwâni mîna
ê-'š'-ašawâpamât mîna wîskacâniš anta. wîskacâniš ašawâpamêw.
wîskacâniš mâk' ana mîna pêci-walawîw ... âpikošîš.
n'kanawâpamâw.
        âšay mîna kwâškwatotawêw wîskacaniš anihi âpikošîša. mâkomêw
mîn' anta okwayâlîhk. kiciskinêw mâka mâna ê-p'maholât '-âhcipaliholici,
o-mâkomât[10] piko.
        âšay mîna šêkopalihow âpikošîš. kêka pêci-walawîw mîna. âšay têhow.
âšay mâšihitôwak anta walawîtimihk. êko nôtin'tôwak.
        môla kî-šâkohêw ôho âpikošîša ô[11] wîskacâniš. šâkohikow. nâspitêp'
êlikohk nôhtâkosiw 'w' wîskacâniš.
        "mâht' îhtikw' awa kâ-itwêhkâsot," n'titêlimâw ..., [imitative screech] ...
'twêhkâsot. kâ-itwêhkâsot ê-sêkihâkaniwit a... a..., wîskacâniš.

3   êko nâ'c êlikohk m'pâhpin kêka. mâmâkowêpimêw wîskacâniša âpikošîš.
oskâta piko nîpawîw.[12] êko mâka, kwêskwêskikwâškwâškwatiwak,[13]
kwêskwêskikwâškwâškwatiwak, nêsta wîskacâniš
kwêskwêskikwâškwâškwatiw, ê-šâkohikot anihi. otakahkwana mâka wîla
mân'šîš wîcihikow awa wîskacâniš wîla; âpakošîš mâk' awas'tê maškawîw,

A fight between a whiskey-jack and a mouse

1   Once again when we had been living somewhere in this area, uh … we were at West River. Now, at that time, in the bu… we regularly used to have our tent out towards the sea in the willows more or less, as we killed foxes. Well then, once I …, as I was sitting inside, a whiskey-jack was making an awful racket. "My! Whatever's wrong with this whiskey-jack that he's making this noise?" I thought. I looked around finally. For a long time, at first though, I didn't look. But at last I looked through a hole in the t…, tent. From there I looked at him. The whiskey-jack was perched on a willow. I looked at him. "What's wrong with this one who's making this noise?" Suddenly there pop… a mouse slowly emerged at last, in the snow. It emerged from the snow.

2   At that point the whiskey-jack jumped at the mouse. He bit him in the neck. He flew away with him repeatedly.

The mouse got the better of him.

He carried him off, again and again.

Then not … he [the mouse] struggled as he carried him off again and again, – to such an extent that he was quickly dropped as he struggled. Again and again the mouse fell away on the ground …, on the snow. Then he quickly dug in the snow again. Then once more the whiskey-jack would watch the spot again. The whiskey-jack kept a lookout for him. But out came that whiskey-jack again …, that mouse. I looked at him.

Now the whiskey-jack jumped at that mouse once again. He bit him in his neck. He dropped him again and again as he carried him off struggling, just biting him.

Now once more the mouse quickly took cover. Finally he came out again. Now he landed. Now they had a tussle with each other out in the open. Then they battled each other.

This whiskey-jack was not able to get the better of this mouse. He was worsted by him. This whiskey-jack was making a dreadful lot of noise.

"Look now, whatever's wrong with this fellow that he's making such a racket?" I thought as he made a noise like this [imitative screech]. That's what the whiskey-jack said because he was scared: "â... â...".

3   So at last I laughed really hard. The mouse bit away at the whiskey-jack. He was just standing on his [hind] legs. And then, they were jumping at each other back and forth, jumping back and forth at each other, and the

mâka, n'titêlimâw nîla, ê-kanawâpamak. môla mâka n'kî-tôtên êkâ ylikohk 'ci-pâhpiyân ê-kanawâpamakik, ê'kwân' ê-kî-wanâhakik ê-mâšihitocik mêkwâc.

whiskey-jack was jumping back and forth as he was getting the worst of it from that mouse. This whiskey-jack was helped a little by his wings; but to my mind the mouse was stronger as I looked at him. I couldn't help but laugh hard as I watched them, to the point that I disturbed them while they were fighting with each other.

ayamihitowin

1 HL: tântê …, tân' êhtiyêkopan ani nêtê kîlawâw wâšâhk[1] kâ-ihtâyêkopan,
mêkwâc kâ-wîci-tašîhkêmatipan ê-n'taw'hot kôhtâwiy, êlin? tânt' anih
kâ-išilawiyêkopan …, kâ-pêci-takošiniyêkopan pêyakwâ ôta,
ê-'wâšišîwiyân …, n'tawâš'šîwihtay nîla nimis kâ-kanawêlimispan.

EM: m… hm.

HL: tântê mâka kâ-išilawîyêkopan wêhci-kî-takošiniyêkopan anta kîlawâw
piko kâ-takošiniyêk?

2 EM: môla wî-pêc'-îtohtêw *Christmas*. "itohtêtâ kîl'ânaw mâka," n'tik ana
nimis. "nôsônêhwâtânak ôko kâ-kihtohtêcik k'stêsinawak," itwêw. êkw
'sa mâka, "kayâm," n'titâw. "kihtohtêtâ. kîšinawatâtâw 'sa, pitamâ
mâmâš kôhtâwinaw pwâmoših kihtohtêyahk mâka," n'titâw.
n'kîšinawatânân mâka. misiwê 'kwân' kwayêsk n'tôtam'wânân.
n'kî-pêci-kihtohtânân âšay. 'mahtakwan cîkahikan. kâ-mišâk[2] piko
cîkahikan ihtakwan. êkwânimêliw wêtinahk nimis,
m'pêci-kihtohtânân. ê-'htâyâhk anta, kâ-mišikitit asiniy,[3] âšay
n'tatiminêhwânânak[4] ôko nistês'.[5] "tâ' êhtiyêk?" itwêw. môla
n'kî-whci-'yamihânânak. n'kâsohtawânânak [*laughs*].[6]

3 HL: [*interrupts*] … ta-kî-pêci-kihtohtêpanak, ot' âni, 'nik' îliliwak.[7] êhê …,

EM: n'nipânân anta. ninipânân anta ê-nîšiyâhk. pâtimâ anta, nêtitišîhk
anta pâtimâ n'kî-wâpamânânak.

HL: kî-pêci-nîkâni-kihtohtêwak man' âni wîlawâw.

EM: êko mâka, n'tik nistês: "tântê kôhtâwîwâw?"
    "n'kî-nakatânân. môla wî-pêci-kihtohtêw. môla w'-îtohtêw
ihtâwinihk *Christmas*. nîlanân mâka m'pêci-kihtohtânân.
n'têhtapihikon …[8] têhtapihâkaniwan mâka wîla. môla nîla
n'tôtinikawin. m'pim'pahtân nîla."

HL: kimis mêriy otinâkaniwan.

4 EM: nimis piko mêriy otinâkaniwan. m'pim'pahtân nîla. êko mâk' êtwêt:
"otinam animêliw ocîkahikaniwâw," itâkaniwan wîliy nistês. "tânt' ôt'
ôk' êtohtêcik?" "n'taw'-nôtâhtikwêwak manâ ô pîhtawânakâhk,"[9] itwêw
wîla âhcipêl [*laughs*].[10]

HL: … ê-mâlêlimitâk.

EM: ê… hê.

HL: êkâ '-ocîkahikaniyêk mâk' ani šâkoc.

A conversation

1 HL: How ..., What happened to you folks while you were staying at Hannah Bay, while you were living with your father as he was hunting, Ellen? What had you been up to ... that you had arrived here once when I was a child ..., I was a child when my older sister used to take care of me?

EM: M-hm.

HL: What had happened to you that led you to come when only you folks arrived?

2 EM: He wasn't going to come at Christmas. But my older sister said to me, "Let's go, you and me. Let's follow our older brothers who are going away," she said. So then I said to her, "All right. Let's go; but let's hurry and cook up some things first for our father before we leave," I said to her. And we cooked for him. We did everything properly for him. Now then, we left to come. There was no axe there. There was only the big axe. With my older sister taking that one, we came away. By the time we were at Big Stone we had already caught up with them, including my older brother. "What's wrong with you two?" he said. We didn't speak to them. We hid from them [laughs].

3 HL: [interrupts] ... Those people ought to have left to come anyway. Yes ...

EM: We slept there. We slept there, the two of us. Bye and bye there, bye and bye we saw them there at Netitishi.

HL: *They* had come away in advance.

EM: And then, my older brother said to me, "Where is your father?" "We left him. He didn't want to come away. He didn't want to go to the settlement for Christmas. But *we've* left to come. I got a ride ... she got a ride, though. But I wasn't taken. I ran along."

HL: Your older sister, Mary, was taken.

4 EM: Only my older sister, Mary, was taken. I ran along. And he said, "Take that axe of theirs," – my older brother, Willie, was told. "Where are these two going?" "They're off logging to Peehtawanagaw," said Archibald [laughs].

HL: ... just teasing you.

EM: Uh-huh.

HL: Because you two sure didn't own an axe.

EM: m'pêci-pim'pahtân tašinê nîla. pim'pahâkaniwan wîl' otâpânâskohk.
   kêka n'kî-wâpamâw oškinîkiw, cîmis n'têhtapihik otôtâpânâskohk.
   n'takošininân ôta. kâ-nîši-kîšikâk wêhci-takošihk awa nôhtâwiy.
   pâhpiw. m'pâhpihikonân. m'pâhpinân nêsta nîlanân.

5 HL: tân' êtisk mâk' ana cîmis mêkwâc ê-pêci-ayêskosiwat êy-otâpâtisk?

   EM: tâni piko?

   HL: manâ kit…, manâ kitayâwâhtay? môla mâtâna[11] wayêš ihkin …!

   EM: nîla ê'kwân' ispîš kâ-wî-tipâcimoyân.

   HL: a? a! [interruption][12]

   EM: ôma ispîš kê-wîhtamâtân.

   HL: êhê …

   EM: môla wîla …

   HL: ê'kwân' êskwâk ê-'tâcimoyin anima …

   EM: êhê.

EM: *I* ran along all the time. *She* was carried on the sled.

Finally I saw a young fellow, James [*pseudonym*]. He gave me a seat on his sled. We arrived here. On the second day my father suddenly arrived. He laughed. He laughed at us. We laughed too.

5 HL: But what did James there say to you while you were tired as he was hauling you?

EM: Who knows?

HL: Didn't you ..., didn't you have him as a boyfriend? There's nothing wrong with that ...!

EM: That's as much as *I'm* going to tell.

HL: Oh? Oh! [*interruption*]

EM: This is as much as I'll tell you.

HL: Yes.

EM: Not about that.

HL: Then that's the extent of your story.

EM: Yes.

wêhci-kî-šîwâkamihk wînipêk

1 wêhci-kî-šîwâkamihk wînipêk,[1] n'k'-âtalo...,[2] n'kay-âh..., -âlimôtên.
wêsk..., wêskac wêsa kî-makošêhêpan awiyâšîša ê-išinihkâsoc[3]
wîsahkwêcâhk. misiwê mâka kî-n'tomêw 'wiyâšîša. kêkwân'tokwê piko
kâ-mîciwâkwê môla n'kiskêl'htên. šâkoc mâka misiwê 'wê'hkân, misiwê
'wiyâšîš k'-îhtâw anta. êko mâka, êko mâka kî-ati-... pêyak piko 'wênihkân'[4]
môla kîy-ohci-n'tomêwak,[5] kîhkwahâkêwa. ê'kwâna êkâ
kâ-kîy-ohci-n'tomâcik. anima ..., anima mâka is..., ispihc[6] kîhkwahâkêw
misiwê 'wênihkâna kî-kostikow. kî-kostikow 'wiyâšîša pîliš anohc. ê'kwâni
mâka êkâ wêhci-n'tomâwâkopanê.

2 kêka 'sa mâka mêkwâc ê-..., ê-'ti-..., âpihta ê-'ti-k'-îškwâ-mîcisocik, êko
man' oti pêyak k'-îšic'ahwâ'n[7] 'ci-ašawâpit.
  "mâht' ê-pêci-nôkosilikwê!"[8]
  "nîla nêsta mâka," itwêw mahkêšiw, "nîla mâwac n'kišîpalin."
  "môla," itwêw. "môl..., môla kîla ka-kaškihtân," itwêw šihkošiw.
  "nîla n'ka-itohtân," itwêw šihkošiw. "n'ka-kî-šî... šîpâ... -šêkwâkonêwin[9]
ê-papâm'pahtâ'n ê-'šawâpamak."

3 êkwân' isa mâk' kâ-itâcik, kici-n'tawi... kic'-îtohtêl'ci. êkw isa mâka âšay
tâpwê pêcih-wâpamêw ê-pêci-nôkosil'ci. kîwêpahtâw man' otih mâk' awa
šihkošiw. n'taw'-wîhtamawêw wîci-'wiyâšîša.
  "âšay tâpwê pêci-nôkosiw," itêw. êko mîna wêwêlâpamâcik[10] 'wênihkâna
kêko[11] nakiškawâl'ci.
  êko, "nîla n'k'-êtohtân," itwêw maskwa.
  "môla," itâkaniwan. "wêsâ kîla kih..., kipêhkâcîn," itâkaniwan.
  êko 'sa mâka, êko 'sa mâka wîlah, mahîhkan: "mêh..., nîla n'k'-êtohtân,"
itwêw. "nîla, nâhtâ n'kaškihon,[12] wayêš ê-tôtawak 'wênihkân," itwêw.

4 "môla," itwêw, kêka šikâk wêhci-ayamit. "nîla, n'k'-êtohtân," itwêw. "môla
wîla nîla 'wênihkân n'kostâw," itwêw.
  ê'kwân' tâpwê kâ-itâkaniwit. šikâk isa mâka kî-pakitinâkaniwan
kic'-îtohtêt.
  âšay šâkoc itohtêw šikâk. wîpac nâšic kî-nakiškawêw. âšay man' otih
kakwêcimâkaniwin kîhkwahâkêw: "tânt' êtohtêyin?"
  "nêsta nîla niwî-pêci-makošân kâ-makošihiwêt ana wîsahkwêcâhk," itwêw.
  "môla kîla ka-itohtân. môla kin'tawêlimikwak 'wiyâšîšak. kikostikwak.
wêsâ misiwê kê'wâ'hkân[13] kiwî-têh... -tipêl'htên. kiwî-'ti-n'šiwanâcihtân

Why the water in James Bay is salt

1   Why James Bay is salt water, I'll tell the leg..., I'll t... tell about it.

Long ..., long ago, as it happened, Weesahkwechahk, as he was called, made a feast for the animals. And he invited all the animals. Whatever they must have eaten I don't know; but everyone, every beast was there. So then, so then they began ... one person only they did not invite, the wolverine. That was the one whom they did not invite. Then ..., and ever since then the wolverine has been feared by everybody. The animals have been afraid of him right up to now. That must be why they had not invited him.

2   At last, however, while, as they began ..., when they were half way through eating dinner, one of them was sent to keep a look-out.

"See whether he's coming!"

"I'll go too," said the fox. "I go the fastest."

"No," said [another]. "*You* ca..., can't do it," said the weasel. "*I* shall go," the weasel said. "I'll be able to un... under ... tunnel under the snow as I run about keeping a look-out for him."

3   So then they told him, to go to ... to go. And now, sure enough, he came and saw him as he came into view. Then this weasel ran back. He went to tell his fellow creatures.

"Now he's really coming into sight" he said to them. So again they went around the circle making a choice of someone who would meet him.

So then, "I will go," said the bear.

"No," he was told. "*You* are too s... slow," he was told.

And so then, and so then the wolf said: "I will go. *I'm* very good at dealing with a person one way or another."

4   At last the skunk spoke up. "No," he said. "*I* shall go. *I* am not afraid of anybody."

That's what he was told. And so the skunk was allowed to go.

Now the skunk set right out. Very soon he met him. Now then, the wolverine was asked: "Where are you going?"

"I too want to come to the feast which that Weesahkwechahk has given," he said.

"*You* must not go. The animals don't want you. They are afraid of you. You're too anx... anxious to be in ch... charge of everything. You want to spoil

mâka misiwê kêkwân," k'-îtêw. [coughs]

5   êko 'sa [coughs] … 'sa wîci-wî… môla 'sa mâ'[14] milwêl'htam kîhkwahâkêw
ôm' ê-'tâkaniwit. "atoskam nîla n'k'-êtohtân," itwêw. âšay man' ôti mâka
w'-îtohtêw. kwêskitiyêpalihow 'sa mâk' awa šikâk. ê'kwân' isa mâk' anima
kâ-… kâ-ohcipalik kêkwân êkâ ohci…, ê'kwân' isa mâk' êši-mâkomât.
mâkomêw kîhkwahâkêw ê-wî-kakwê-kiponât šikâkwa.

mitoni 'sa mâka kî-kîškwêhokow ôma šikâk, – ôma kîhkwahâkêw. môla
kiskêl'htam tânt' êhtât. mitoni kî-kîškwêhokow. êko mâka kâ-kîwêt mâk'
awa šikâk. "môla kata-takošin," itwêw.

6   wâlaw 'sa mâk' anta mêkwayêš,[15] ôma k'-îši-makošêwak wâlaw, wâlaw
kihcikamîhk ohci. âšay man' ôtih mâka wîh-… nâsipêw 'wah, êkâ
ê-kî-wâpit, ê-wî-kîškwêt nêst' awa kîhkwahâkêw. âšay man' ôti
nâsipêw ê-tatêl'htahk kihcikamîliw. kê-… kê-… nânakacâškošin[16] isa mâk'
êkâ ê-wâpit.

"awên'kân kîla?" itêw mistikwa.

"minahik," itwêw.

âšay mîn' ati-p'mohtêw. mîna nakacâškošin: " 'wê'hkân[17] kîla?"

"waškwayâhtik," itwêw.

mîn' an' ât'-…, ati-kihtohtêw. mîna nakacâškošin: " 'wê'hkân
kîla?"

ay'hâw, "waškwayâhtik," itwêw.

kêka kîhkwahâkêw itwêw, "ê'kwâni pêyakwan ôt' ê-ihtâyân
mêkwêyâmatin. môla n'kiskêl'htên tânt' êhtakwahk. êkoši mîna
n'ka-kocihtân," itwêw.

7   kêka mîna kî-'ti-kihtohtêw. mîna nakacâškošin. " 'wê'hkân[18] kîla?" itwêw.

"i'lâstik," itwêw.

"âšay, âšay," itwêw. "âšay n'-'ti-pêš'wâpahtên[19] nipiy," itê…[20] itwêw
'sa mâk' awa kîškwahâkêw. kiyâpac ati-kakihtohtêw.

kêka mîna ê-nakac…, -nakacâškošihk âšay, mîna kî-…, " 'wê'hkân kîla?"
itwêw.

"mâsakîsk, nîl'," itwêw.

"ê'kwâni pêyakwan ôta ê-'htâyân," itwêw awa kîhkwahâkêw.

êko 'sa, êko 'sa mâka mîna k'-âti-kihtohtêt. êko mâmâš nawac
kî-p'mohtêw. âšay mîn' ati-n'… nawac ati-… mîna nakacâškošin
kê'wâ'hkâniliw.

" 'wênihkân kîla?"[21] itwêw.

ay'hâw, "wîkopîy," itwêw.

everything," he said to him [coughs].

5   So then [coughs]... then his fellow ... f... but the wolverine didn't like being spoken to this way. "I'm going all the more," he said. Now then, he was about to go. But the skunk suddenly swung his backside around. And so, naturally, that ... that thing came out not from ..., then he bit him. The wolverine bit him as he wanted to block the skunk.

    At this point the skunk, – at this point the wolverine was knocked utterly senseless. He didn't know where he was. He was knocked crazy. So then the skunk went back. "He will not be arriving," he said.

6   It was far away in the country where they had their feast, far, far away from the ocean. But now the wolverine wanted ... to go down the bank, because he couldn't see and he wanted to run amuck. Now then, he went down the bank, making a guess that the sea was there. To ... to ... he kept bumping into trees since he couldn't see.

    "Who are you?" he said to a tree.

    "A spruce," it said.

    Now he started to walk along again. Again he bumped into a tree. "Who are you?"

    "A birchwood," it said.

    Once more he beg..., began to go away. Again he bumped into a tree. "Who are you?"

    Well, "A birchwood," it said.

    At last the wolverine said, "I might as well stay here among the knolls. I don't know where it is. So I'll try again," he said.

7   At last he began to move off again. Again he bumped into a tree. "Who are you?" he said.

    "A balsam," it replied.

    "Now, now," he said. "Now I'm beginning to draw close to the water," th..., said this wolverine. He began to move about aimlessly some more.

    At last as he bump... bumped into a tree again, again he ... "Who are you?" he said.

    "I'm a cedar," it answered.

    "It amounts to the same thing if I stay here," said the wolverine.

    Now then, but now then he started walking away again. So he walked about pretty much at random. Now again he ... pretty well began ... he bumped into something again. "Who are you?" he said.

    Well, uh, "Willow bark," it said.

8   ânt' âši²² sikilêsiw. "âšay pêšoc n'tat'-îhtân kihciwê-nipîhk,"²³ itêl'htam
awa kîhkwahâkêw. êko 'sa mîn' âti-kihtohtêt, âšay 'sa šâkoc mîna
nakacâšk'šin. " 'wê'hkân kîla?"

"atôspîy," itwêw.

âšay nâht' ati-sikilêsiw ê-'ti-p'mohtêt. kêka, kêka môla kê'wân'kân
miskoškam. kêka pêhtam kê'wân'kâniliw, mwêhci ê-lôtihk ê-'tihtâkwanilik.
âšay 'nta kiskêl'htam ..., môla mâka kiskêl'htam tântê tatwê...
ê-tatwêkamahâšikêt.²⁴ kêka [coughs] kêka mâka kî-'ti-p'mohtêw. kê...
kêhcawil,²⁵ kêhcawil nakacišin mîna kê'wâ'hkân. "kê'wâ'hkân²⁶ kîla?" itwêw.

"asiniy, nîla," itwêw.

kêka nâhtâ sikilêsiw. kêk' âšay pêhtam. kêk' âšaw...²⁷ kêka iš... kê...,
kêka kiskêl'htam ê-'ti-pahkopêt. êkw âšay 'ti-... kî-'ti-pahkopêw pîliš
ê-'ti-liskipêt. kê'²⁸ k'-âti-kistâpâwalot. ê'kwânima mâka wêhci-kî-šîwâk,
šîwâkamihk²⁹ kihcikamiy.

8   Now he was very glad. "Now," thought this wolverine, "I'm beginning to be near the proper water." So now he began to walk away again, and now he bumped right into a tree. "Who are you?"

"The black alder," it said.

Now he became very happy as he walked along. At long last he didn't discover anything with his feet. Finally he heard something sounding just like the wind. Now he knew that there ..., but he didn't know where the rol... the rollers were coming in over there. At last [cough], but at last he began to walk on. Su..., suddenly he bumped into something again. "What are you?" he said.

"I'm a stone," it said.

At last he was very happy. Now at last he heard it. At last he jum... finally then fi... finally he knew he was beginning to wade out. So now he began... he began to wade up until it started to be covered with water. At last he began to wash himself. And that is why the ocean is salt.

Appendices

Editorial Conventions

Transcription

The transcription used in this volume might be described as taxonomic phonemic and follows the standard convention of Algonquianists working in Cree. In this case separate letters mark the twelve consonants of Moose Cree (plus *r* which occurs in borrowed words) and the seven vowels (four long, so marked with a circumflex, and three short). Swampy Cree (the n-dialect) also uses the same inventory of consonants and vowels, except for *l* which occurs only in borrowed words. The mixed n-l usage referred to as Kashechewan Cree for the purposes of this book makes use of the larger inventory of Moose Cree.

The table that follows lists the letters used to represent the distinctive sounds of the Cree dialects represented in this volume.[1]

Consonants
Stops
    p voiceless or lightly voiced[2] bilabial as in *pit* or *bit*
    t voiceless or lightly voiced apico-alveolar as in *tin* or *din*
    c voiceless or lightly voiced lamino-alveopalatal as in *ch*eer or *j*eer
    k voiceless or lightly voiced dorso-velar as in *k*it or *g*et

Nasals
    m voiced bilabial as in *man*
    n voiced apico-alveolar as in *net*

Liquids
    l voiced lateral continuant as in *let*
    r voiced retroflex, alveopalatal as in *run* (in borrowed words only)

Fricatives
    s voiceless or lightly voiced slit alveolar as in *sip* or *zip*

---

[1] The purpose of this section is not to provide a full account of the phonology of Cree, but rather to illustrate the main spelling conventions used in these texts. Readers interested in phonological or other issues may have direct access to the initial database through the cassette copies of the original recordings, available from the publisher.

[2] See the discussion of voicing, below.

š   voiceless or lightly voiced grooved alveopalatal as in *ship* or *measure*

Vowel-like consonants or glides

w   voiced bilabial as in *willow*

(but with typically less lip rounding than in English)

y   voiced palatal glide as in *yellow*

h   voiceless 'glottal fricative' as in *hollow*

Vowels

Long vowels

î   high front unrounded as in *seen*

ê   mid front unrounded as in *they* (but without y-glide)

ô   high back rounded; ranges from the vowel in *bone* to that in *boon*

â   low, front to back, unrounded; ranges from the vowel in *had* to that in *wall*

Short vowels

i   lower high front unrounded; ranges from the vowel in *pin* to that in *get*

o   mid to high back unrounded; ranges from the vowel in *more* to that in *foot*

a   low to mid, centre to front; ranges from the unrounded vowel in *hat* to that in *hut*

In the texts, the hyphen is used exclusively to mark the link between members of a compound stem: [3]

cîmân 'canoe'

miši-cîmân 'ship'

kâ-kî-tôtahkik 'what they did'.

Phonetic Variation

The texts exhibit a great deal of speech variation, including not only major, typical variants (allophones) of the distinctive sounds, but also various kinds of alternations and stylistic devices. The editorial conventions observed in each of these instances are outlined below.

---

[3] In the Notes and the Glossary, the hyphen is used to mark the point at which inflectional material may be added to a stem; see also the beginning of the Glossary.

Contraction. Contraction accounts for a large part of change in the phonemic shape of morphemes and is signalled by the use of the apostrophe. In simple syncope, the elision of one or more distinctive sounds is marked by an apostrophe, e.g.,

> *kâ-n'tawâpahtahk* for *kâ-natawâpahtahk* 'which he goes to see'
> *mâk' anima* for *mâka anima* 'but that one'
> *n'tên'tên* for *nititênihtên* (Swampy Cree) 'I think'
> *kê'wâ'hkân* for *kêkwânihkân* 'what sort of thing'.

An exception to this practice is in the spelling of forms which never occur in uncontracted shape, e.g.,

> *tântê* 'where' (cf. **tânitê*)
> *anta* 'there' (cf. **anita*).

Vowel merger, especially the merging of the final vowel of one word with the initial vowel of the next, is common. Where the vowels are the same, dropping of the first is often followed by lengthening of the second. In this case apocope is marked with an apostrophe and the increase of length on the succeeding vowel by use of the circumflex, e.g.,

> *anim' âskiy* 'that land' for *anima askiy;*

contraction may also take place between two members of a compound stem, e.g.,

> *wêhc'-îtwêt* for *wêhci-itwêt* 'why he says'.

The vowels may be similar in position, differing in length only:

> *w'-îspaniw* 'he wants to go' for *wî-ispaniw.*

Where the vowels differ in position, with the first clearly retained and the second elided, this is clearly indicated in the transcription, e.g.,

> *ê-'pin'ci* 'as he sits' for *ê-apinici*
> *kâ-'htakwahk* 'where it is' for *kâ-ihtakwahk.*

Another common instance of apocope is the frequent elision of the conjunct prefix *ê-*, despite its grammatical function. Here again an apostrophe is used to show that something has been dropped, e.g.,

> *wêsâ '-kîškâyawânik* 'because it was too deep' for *wêsâ ê-kîškâyawânik*
> *êkâ '-šawinahk* 'not moving the water' for *êkâ ê-šawinahk.*

Glides. Within a simple stem, two long vowels which would otherwise be adjacent are separated by the insertion of a *y*, *w* or *h* glide:

> *tâpwêyêlimêw* 'he believes in him' represents *tâpwê...êlimêw*.

This is frequently carried over to a sequence of long vowels between members of a compound stem, e.g.,

> *kây-âhtokwêt* '(when) he moved elsewhere' for *kâ-âhtokwêt*
> *kîw-îkatênam* 'she put it away' for *kî-îkatênam*

or simply between final and initial vowels of separate words in sequence:

> *anah âyâs* 'that one Ayas' for *ana âyâs*.

Words with initial or final vowel often show an h-onset or off-glide:

> *hêko* 'so, then' for *êko*
> *ililiwah* 'people' for *ililiwa*.

This is recorded in the transcription only where it seems related to some emphatic utterance or other stylistic effect. The optional *h* off-glide which occurs after vowels may occur as an intervocalic glide, but occurs elsewhere as an aspirate.

Sometimes in rapid speech a final vowel remains and the succeeding initial vowel is reduced to the corresponding glide, i.e., *o* to *w* and *i* to *y*; e.g.,

> *manâ wt'* 'then, I suppose' for *manâ oti*
> *ê-ytât* 'as he speaks to him' for *ê-itât*.

The glottal stop, [ʔ], commonly occurs as a realization of *h* in two words: *êhê* [ɛhɛʔ] 'yes', where it appears to be invariant in final position, and *êhêpik* [e·ʔe·pɪk], the archaic term for 'spider', where it is the more usual but not exceptionless realization of *h*. Consistency would require the regular transcription of *êhê* as *êhêh*, but since the optional *h* off-glide is elsewhere an aspirate, the final *h* is simply and regularly omitted in transcribing *êhê*, which appears to be unique in this respect; and *êhêpik* is phonemically spelled.

In the preverb *matwê* 'perceptible at a distance' the *w* glide is typically produced with the lips in relatively straight position. For some speakers, the *w* becomes inaudible:

> *ê-matwê-tahkonât* 'holding it in the distance'
> *matwê-'tâkaniwan* 'she was told some way off'

kâ-matê-'mišinin'ci 'he could be made out to be lying down'

matê-otatâmâskwahamwak 'they could be heard knocking sticks together in the distance'.

Voicing. Voicing is not distinctive in Cree although some sounds are characteristically voiced, e.g., *l, m, n*, while others may or may not be, depending on the sound environment. *p, c* and *k*, but not *t*, may be voiced (i.e., sound more like *b, j* and *g* as in *get*) between a long, stressed vowel and a short one: V́_V. The same holds for *s* and *š*. In careful speech one hears *wâpamêw* 'he sees him' as [wɔ·pame·w], whereas in faster or more casual usage one may hear [wɔ·bm̥e·w] or even [wɔ·m̥·e·w]. Similarly, normal, casual speech forms with other stops and sibilants are:

nôcihtâw 'he works at it' as [nó·jihta·w]

mâka 'but, however' as [má·gʌ]

pâskisikan 'gun' as [pa·skízɪgʌn]

and

âšay '(by) now, already' as [á·žʌy] or [á·žɛy]

but

âta 'although' as [á·tʌ].

All stops, however, including *t*, may be voiced following a nasal. This happens with regularity as a result of vowel syncope, e.g.,

pimipaliw 'he/it goes along' as *pim'paliw* [pɪmbʌlʊw]

*anita 'there' as *anta* [ʌndʌ]

nicîmân 'my canoe' as *n'cîmân* [nǰí·ma·n]

nikî-pôsin 'I embarked' as *n'kî-pôsin* [ŋgi·pú·sɪn].

Where the preceding segment is a nasal, vowel syncope is commonly followed by regressive assimilation. This may also be represented in the orthography, e.g.,

nipâskisikan 'my gun' as *m'pâskisikan* (the *p* may also be lightly voiced)

but

nikiskêlihtên 'I know (it)' as [ŋkɪskɛlte·n], [ŋgʌskɛlte·n] or [ŋkʌskɛlte·n]

Certain other environments also lead to voicing (cf. *pâskisikan* above) or sustain voicelessness, e.g., *âpaham* [á:pəhəm]. Non-distinctive voicing alternations are not recorded in the transcription.

The pattern of voicing in certain intervocalic positions is sometimes carried over to *h*, which is then realized as *y*:

ayamihêw 'he speaks to him' may be heard as *ayamiyêw*.

(Note that the *h* : *y* contrast is otherwise distinctive:

ahâwêw 'long-tailed duck'

but

ayâwêw 'he has him'.)

Phonemic Variation

Although the difference between *a* and *i* is normally of contrastive importance, there are many forms in which these two phonemes appear to be interchangeable, e.g.,

pamâtakâw 'he wades (human), swims (fish or quadruped)' for *pimâtakâw*

ayawiši-namês 'fresh fish' for *ayawaši-namês*

wana-kiskisiw 'he forgets' for *wani-kiskisiw*

askonâk 'since' for *iskonâk*

mahkwacakâš 'red sucker' for *mihkwacakâš*

This alternation is recorded in the transcription, with a footnote indicating the more common form.

s shows a variant phonetically close to *š* and sometimes hard to distinguish from the latter. I have elsewhere, especially in pedagogical material, written it as *ṡ*:

nêṡta [ne·ṡtʌ] 'and, also'.

It is difficult to specify the conditioning factor since both [s] and [ṡ] allophones seem to occur in identical environments:

nêsta [ne·ṡtʌ] 'and, also'

and

mêstinêw [me·stəne·w] 'he uses him up'.

In spite of their periodic phonetic proximity, the difference between *s* and *š* is of contrastive importance:

nakiskaw 'a short while'

and

nakiškaw 'meet him';

môla nitôsihtân 'I'm hard of hearing'

and

môla nitôšihtân 'I'm not making it'.

In the present volume, only the contrastive distinction of *s* versus *š* is maintained.

Stylistic Variation

Palatalization and baby-talk are common characteristics of the speech of Chahkabesh and other 'little devils'. This is reflected in the transcription by the use of *c* for *t* or *š* for *s*. Where this occurs in Cree, the English translation attempts to mimic it, most often by replacing *s* with *sh*.

Various imitative sounds that fall outside the usual set of distinctive sounds appear in the text. These include the sound of wood cutting, of chiselling through ice, and even the sound of a moose call. They could be represented using standard phonetic notation, but are instead written as:

tangg, tangg, tangg for [tʌŋŋ, tʌŋŋ, tʌŋŋ] (14:1)

zhak, zhak, zhak for [žk, žk, žk] (13:4)

mhaa, mahaham for [mhə̄ə̄ mə̄hə̄hə̄m] (34:1)

In the few other locations where speakers depart markedly from the regular sound system, a phonetic rendering is likewise given in the Notes.

A number of further orthographic issues crop up: the vexatious problem of representing speech where enunciation is blurred, even though the listener may know what is intended; the attempt by the Cree speaker to represent Ojibwa speech or the intrusion of English words into an otherwise Cree narrative. The representation of blurred, mumbled or overly rapid speech has been phonemically represented as far as possible, with full forms for the more severe contractions or other changes provided in the Notes. Ojibwaisms, where they occur, seem to have been made by the speaker to conform to Cree phonology and have been spelled in terms of the latter. English terms which have become part of the local Cree lexicon (e.g., *askipôt* 'husky-boot', *wâpišîšin* 'opposition') or that of the individual Cree speaker have been phonemicized in the Cree text.

Grammatical Correction

Items added by the speaker after the fact appear in the Notes, except in the very few cases where they represent accidental erasures from the recording, or where they are essential to the sense of the following text; in such cases they appear in parentheses, followed by a footnote.

Borrowed Words

English to Cree. Sustained contact with English speakers over several centuries has left its mark on West Coast James Bay Cree in the form of loans of various types. A number of these occur in the texts. Some, proper names in particular, have been borrowed outright. Others represent varying degrees of loan blend, where a stem borrowed from English is combined with one or more elements from Cree; e.g., *prâwn* (English *brown*, used as a cooking but not a normal colour term) is combined with the suffix *...iwan-* to produce the verb stem *prâwniwan-* VII 'be browned'. This, put into the conjunct indicative with the prefix *kici* 'in order to' yields the form *kici-prâwniwahki* 'so they may be browned'.

In some cases a loan retains much of its English pronunciation. In others, where it has been more fully incorporated into the language, conformity to Cree pronunciation and grammatical patterns, as in the example cited above, confer on the borrowed term virtual native language status. Several general levels in the integration of loans may be distinguished throughout the texts, although the lines are not always clear cut. These are discussed with illustrative examples under five headings:

(1) Unintegrated loans are characterized by the intrusion of English terms into Cree where a Cree equivalent already exists.

A particularly generous measure of unintegrated loans occurs throughout Texts 58 to 62. The speaker in this case, Willie Frenchman, was from the Moosonee-Moose Factory area and had a long history of contact with English speakers. Roughly half of the English interpolations into his narrative are proper names:

Charlton Island (58:1)
Cape Hope Island (58:2)
French (58:1, 3)

October (58:3)

Christmas (58:4)

Paint Hill (58:4, 5)

January (58:5)

Hudson Bay (61:3; 62:2)

Other English terms include:

island (58:1)

forty (58:2)

half a mile (58:4)

about (58:5)

now (59:1)

drift snow (60:6)

stage (61:2)

about a quar' (61:3)

my mother (61:6)

next day (61:6),

and the full sentence:

Now, I'm gonna start it from what I been doing myself, you see? (61:1).

Other terms appear in the discourse of other speakers:, e.g.,

holiday (42:64)

fresh air (43:14)

jam (65:6)

and the place names *Moose Factory* (64:1, 65:10) and *Cochrane* (42:3).

(2) Some unintegrated loans are recognizably English but influenced to a varying extent by Cree pronunciation. The forms in this category appear in the texts in standard English spelling, but with a footnote which suggests the Cree-influenced pronunciation. For example,

eighteen poot canoe for *eighteen foot canoe* (58:1)

pifteent' of January for *fifteenth of January* (58:4)

one a dem for *one of them* (61:4)

Moose Pactory for *Moose Factory* (64:)

'udson Bay blanket for *Hudson Bay Blanket* (61:4)

Company, 'udson Bay Company for *Hudson Bay Company* (42:23, 62:1)

Nort, Nort Plap for *North, North Bluff* (65:3),

and an interesting example of hyper-correction:

hundred-fifty found for *hundred-fifty pound* (42:24).

(3) Partially integrated loans often conform readily to the Cree sound system and occur easily in the speech of unilingual speakers as members of one or another Cree stem class but are still recognized as imported terms. In the case of

lîcin- NI Legion hall at Moosonee (42:13),

the speaker, Gabriel Kiokee, was a Swampy Cree (n-dialect) speaker who used the shape in which the word was easily borrowed into the Moose Cree dialect of Moosonee, with retention of initial English /l/. Further nativization would be expected to lead to a Swampy Cree form with the shape *nîcin-*. The relatively recent arrival of the item on the cultural scene is sensed in the phrase, *ôma lîcin* 'this "legion" '. With fuller integration and understanding of the term *Legion* one would expect a reference to the Legion Hall to show a form such as *lîcinikamikw-*.

A further example is that of *intiyan êcint* 'Indian Agent' (42:39). The common Cree term is *šôliyânikimâw-* NA 'paymaster'. With the disappearance of the office of Indian Agent and the establishment of banking services in the North, there is some evidence of a semantic shift of *šôliyânikimâw-* from 'Indian Agent' to 'Bank Manager' (cf. *šôliyânikamikw-* NI bank).

(4) Fully integrated loans have a particular interest in that they show the assimilation of terms, not merely into the sound system of Cree but into the full set of grammatical patterns as well. The first of such loans to appear in the text, *kânata* NI 'Canada' (1:1), while stemming originally from an Iroquoian source, has found its way into Cree through English and requires no further comment. Two old loans, however, *palacîs-* and *šôliyân-*, will serve as illustrations of the full integration process.

palacîs- NA 'britches, trousers' (52:4) refers to the whole garment and, unlike the English, is singular. English /b/ is devoiced and /r/ replaced by Cree /l/, resulting in /pl/ which, as an initial cluster foreign to Cree, is broken up by the insertion of /a/, producing the first syllable /pal/. The remainder of the English word is then adjusted to conform to Cree phonology and the total form is treated as a Cree word, i.e., *opalacîsa* 'his trousers', displaying third person possessor prefix and obviative suffix for a noun of the animate gender.

šôliyân- NA 'money' (39:3, 41:9) is borrowed in all probability from English *shilling*. The stem participates freely in any and all of the grammatical constructions proper to a Cree stem, e.g.,

ošôliyânima 'his money'
šôliyânihkâkê- VAI 'use it to make money' (41:11)
šôliyânikimâw- NA 'Indian Agent, paymaster' (42:39).

Other instances of loanwords occurring in the text demonstrate inflection for personal possession, number, locative case, or are first members in a derived stem as the following examples show:

ohwâsak NA [pl.] 'horses' (41:1)
mašîn- NI 'machinery' (41:3)
iskôniwi- VAI attend school (SC); (42:6); *iskôliwî-* (MC)
šâk- NI shack; 41:6
pinko- NI bingo; 42:10
šôw- NI (picture) show; 42:9; n. 42:16
êncin- NI engine; 42:20
kâs- NI 'gas', gasoline; 42:21
kampaniy- NA Hudson's Bay Company; 64:1
opwâkitimihk NI [loc.] in his pocket; 49:3
tapihk NI [loc.] in a tub; 50:1
šôkâw- NI sugar [sometimes NA]; 58:5
wâpišîšin- NI the 'Opposition' (to the Hudson's Bay Company; i.e., Reveillon Frères); 58:6
stwâpihk- NI [loc.] stove 50:2
pêsin- NA/NI basin [gender varies with speaker]; 50:2
sôp- NA soap; 50:4
sôpâpôhk NI [loc.] in soapy water; 50:4
kici-prâwniwahki VII [conj.indic.] so they may be browned; 54:1
pânaskihkw- NA frying pan, skillet; 54:1
tîy- NI tea; 58:5
nimâcîsimak NA [pl.] my matches; 61:3
askipôta NI [pl.] husky-boots; 61:3

Normally a loan in the form of a single stem is imported from English. When thoroughly integrated this may then be blended with grammatical elements of Cree. Forms such as *kici-prâwniwahki* and *šôliyânihkâkê-* illustrate something of the scope of this process.

(5) Loan translations occur from time to time. One such suspected example is *kâ-wâpisicik* 'the White People' (1:10), which appears instead of the more common terms *wêmistikôšiwak*.

Another such suspected case is the phrase referring to the parents of Chahkabesh and his sister:

êkota kâ-'si-wanihtâcik opimâtisîwiniwâw (6:3)
'There it was where they lost their life'

The phrase is immediately further clarified as,

maskwa ê-kî-nipahikocik ..., miši-maskwa
'because they were killed by the bears ..., giant bears'.

In the preceding text Chahkabesh's sister warns him away from the bear tracks which he wants to follow with the words:

êwakwânik' oš' âni kâ-kî-kitimahitahkok, kâ-kî-nipahâcik kinîkihikonawa. (5:3)

They are the very ones, you realize, who caused us misery, who killed our parents.'

In both cases the verb *nipah-* VTA 'kill s.o.' conveys the sense fully and clearly without the cumbersome *kâ-'ši-wanihtâcik opimâtisîwiniwâw*. It may be that the narrative style was felt to be enhanced by the phrase from the well-known biblical passage,

ana kê-wanihtâkwê opimâtisîwin nîna ohci, kata-miskam. (Matt. 10:39)
'Whoever loses his life for my sake will find it.'

Whatever the case, the phrase in Text 6 smacks of translation and possible prestige through association with a literary source (cf. also Lk. 17:33; Jn. 12:25). At the same time it must be noted that, when a native speaker other than the narrator was queried, the response was that this sounded like proper Cree and not at all like a translated English expression.

A further term, also suspected of being a loan translation, is *mistâskîhk* 'on the mainland' (cf. n. 7:21). Although seldom heard and apparently awkward sounding, its occurrence in the context of a traditional narrative might also suggest archaic usage. This, however, is only speculation.

Other possible loan translations are less certain still and should perhaps be seen as a growing preference for a different construction type. It has been suggested that long standing and intensive contact between Cree and English speakers has favoured replacement of synthetic constructions with those of a more analytic type. The title of Text 62 is of interest in this connection. The form which commended itself to Agnes Hunter, a Swampy Cree speaker from Peawanuck, an area of less intensive contact with English, was *ê-waškwayi-cîmânihkâniwahk*, literally 'birch-bark-canoe-making' – one compound word in Cree, with the suffix *...ihkê-* 'make'. The narrator of the text, however, refers more than once to *oškwayi-cîmân êy-ošihtâniwahk*, using the separate VAI-T stem *osihtâ-* 'make s.t.'. In Texts 50, 52 and 53, the titles, based on the text, exhibit the more analytical construction with verb and unincorporated object. If there is indeed an observable tendency to move from synthetic to more analytic construction types (and pending further study this remains little more than an impression), then the door may well be open to loan translation on a more ample scale.

One further loan translation may be noted: *alîkisak* 'frogs' (41:12). It occurs only once in the narrative and the context makes clear that it is not generally used in Cree in this connection.

Ojibwa to Cree. There is contact from time to time between members of Cree and Ojibwa bands (cf. n. 10:6). A number of Ojibwa loanwords appear in Cree and several are used in the texts.

n'tittâ 'I said to her' (10:5): felt by James Gunner to be an Ojibwaism, it may be used as a traditional element in the story. The context in which it occurs, however, has a ghostlike atmosphere of unreality, and the non-Cree term may well serve to lend an air of heightened strangeness to the scene as Mistaganash, returned from the dead, addresses his mother in Ojibwa, or what is supposed to be Ojibwa.

ninikon or *ninikwan* 'my son-in-law' (11:3): the term is used by the scheming father-in-law in a threatening context. Elsewhere (e.g., 11:9), *ninahâhkišîm*, the normal Cree term, appears. (The portrayal of the lynx (1:7, 2:7) as hostile and Ojibwa speaking may be recalled.)

Two further forms and a proper name call for mention:

kêkonên 'sort of thing' (11:12), a suspected Ojibwaism. The expected Moose Cree form would be *kêkwânihkân*.

šânk, šânkwâ 'nine, nine times' (42:26). The Moose Cree form is *šâkitât*. This is probably a reshaped loan, originally from Ojibwa *šânkwâsswi* (Piggott & Grafstein), *zhaangawi* (J.D. Nichols) 'nine'.

šinikipiš- 'Shingibish' (8:5, 47:1): a type of diver duck, probably the small or hooded merganser. The form *šihkipiš* is attested at Attawapiskat, north of Kashechewan.

Cree to English. Certain Cree loans have become so fully integrated into English as to be considered fully English words. *Moose, muskeg* and *moccasin* (with *skunk* from Eastern Algonquian) belong in the lexicon of the unilingual English speaker and all occur at one point or another in the present set of texts. One term, however, calls for comment: *kâhkapin-* NA 'fast drying (moose) hide' (53:1). The word belongs to a specialized technology and there appears to be no convenient and generally accepted equivalent in English; hence the retention of the Cree term, with an explanatory note, in translation.

The term *têšipitâkan-* is carried over to the English translation of 61:2, not as a loan from Cree, but rather as elucidation provided by the narrator. The use of 'stage' in the Cree text should similarly not be regarded as a loan from English, but rather as an explanation of the term which follows in Cree. The same thing may be said of the phrase 'my mother' and, possibly, 'next day' later in the narrative (61:6). Perhaps much of Willie Frenchman's intrusion of English into his narratives (Texts 58 through 62) should be understood this way.

Place Names[4]

Cree place names, when transliterated, are sometimes represented by more than one English spelling: *Netitishi* or *Nettichi, Kwetabohigan* or *Kwetipawahikan*. Different names for the same place in Cree and English, e.g., *wâškêyokâw* or *Grassy Bay Creek*, or a different point of reference for the same name, e.g., *kêšîciwan*, which may designate the present day village of Kashechewan or the former village at Albany Post, may further compound uncertainty. All three problems have been encountered in listing and transcribing place names around the coast of James Bay and inland. Two sets of names in particular call for comment: the first, *Moosonee* and *Moose Factory*; the second, *Albany Post, Fort Albany* and *Kashechewan*.

The term *Moose* is used by itself locally to refer to the general area of Moosonee and Moose Factory several miles upstream from the estuary of the Moose River. *Albany* was formerly used in parallel fashion to denote the

---

[4] cf. also the dialect map which appears in the Introduction, p. xiv.

general area about the Albany River which included Albany Post and Fort
Albany. Albany Post was always called *kêšîciwan* in Cree, but when the
community moved to a new site on the north channel of the Albany River,
kêšîciwan, officially spelled *Kashechewan*, was adopted as the name of the
new village.[5] Unfamiliarity with the area in question and with local usage in
particular can lead to perplexity. Accordingly, an effort has been made
throughout the texts and supplemental material not only to use uniform
spelling for each point named but to designate each as specifically as possible,
even at the risk of repetitiveness. Whenever possible, spellings from the
Ontario Gazetteer have been adopted for transliterating Cree names. Where
a separate English name exists, this is used in the English version.

Cree place names transliterated in the text:

âtawâpiskât	Attawapiskat (33:1, 42:23, 42:39, 42:50, 42:63)
kêšîciwan	Kashechewan
kwêtipawahikani-sîpiy	Kwetabohigan River (34)
môsoniy	Moosonee (42:34, 43:4, 44:4, 58:1, 58:4, 65:10)
nêmiskâw	Namiskau (42:30)
nêtitišiy	Netitishi (67:3)
pâkašiy	Pagashi (38)
pîhtawânakâw	Peehtawanagaw (67:4)
pîwânak	Peawanuck
wînask[6]	Winisk

Cree place names for which an English name is used in the text:

akwâpicikan	The Flats (49:5, n. 49:16)
cîpayi-sîpiy	Ghost River (30)
kâ-mihcâpiskâw	Big Stone (67:2)
kâ-mišikitit asiniy	Big Stone (n. 67:3)

[5] The name is pronounced by most English speakers as *Kesáchewun* (stress on the
second syllable). Improved water supply, better fishing and more ready access to
firewood were among the reasons alleged for the move which took place in 1959.

[6] On May 16, 1986, the village of Winisk was devastated within minutes by a flood at
the spring break-up of ice in the river. Due in large measure to the energetic efforts of
Chief George Hunter the community was relocated, as of June 1986, at a new and
safer site, Peawanuck, about thirty-two kilometres further up-river (cf. Janice E.
Graham, 'After the Flood: Relocation to the Promised Land', W. Cowan, ed., *Papers of
the Eighteenth Algonquian Conference*, Ottawa: Carleton University, 1987; pp. 137-
145).

kêšíciwan	Albany Post (name of old village prior to 1959; 33, 36:1, 39:3, 49:1)
kišê-sîpiy	Fort George (58:3)
macitêwêyâw	North Bluff (65:3)
môsonîwi-ministik	Moose Factory Island (local English usage normally omits Island)
pîhtâpêk[7]	Fort Albany (proper name in 42:54; not in 9:24)
wâškêyokâw	Grassy Bay Creek (64:1)
wâškêyokâw'-sîpiy	Grassy Bay River (64:1)
wînipêk	James Bay (68)

Local points for which no Cree name occurs in the text:

Cape Hope Island (58:2): *wîpicînakw-* (lit., 'walrus island')
Charlton Island (58:1)
Cochrane (41:3) as *kwâkwan*
Paint Hill (58:4) now called *Wemindji*; cf. MC *wîliman'ci*, n. 58:17.

The following list provides the names of points of land and creeks from Moose Factory to the Albany River, along with their distance (in miles) from Moose Factory.

miles	English name	Cree name (and literal translation)
7	Sandy Island	*wêhwêwi-sîpiy ministik* (wavey-river island)
9	Ship-sands Island	*kišê-cîmân ministik* (ship island)
9	Hay Creek	*kaškêwêhonân* (portage)
11	White Top Creek	*paskwahcîwi-sîpiy* (stump creek)
	(so-called from long plants with white tops)	
12-13	Little White Top Creek	*paskwahcîwi-šîpîšiš*
14	Otter Head Creek	*nikikostikwân(iš)*
16-18	North Bluff Shoal	*kâ-piskwâhkašihk*
18-20	North Bluff	*macitêwêyâw*
19-21	North Bluff Creek	*macitêwêyâwi-sîpiy*
22	White Owl Creek	*wâpikalowi-sîpiy*
23	Jarvis Bluff	*šêkwâhkâw*

---

[7] Fort Albany was more specifically referred to in Cree as *pîhtâpêk* 'the lagoon' or 'the pond', because of the pond produced there by the damming of a creek at the Roman Catholic mission.

26	[English name unknown]	*kišipâskwayâw* (end of trees)
29	Little Piskwamisk	*piskwâmiskošiš* (little hump)
31	Piskwamisk	*piskwâmisk* (hump)
40	[English name unknown]	*paskwahciy* (stump)
47	Long Ridge	*kâ-kinwâwahkâw* (long sand ridge)
50	Halfway Point	*wâpask'âw* (white bears abound)
65	Cockispenny Point	*kâhkâkîšiminak* (crow duck berries)
69	No-Man's Land	*minâwinân*; cf. *manâwinân* (collecting place (for eggs))
71	[English name unknown]	*lâwâpiskâw* (deep rock)
75	Netitishi	*nêtitišiy*
78	Canoes River	*kinošêwi-sîpiy* (pike river)
80	[Cree name used]	*wâpisîwi-sîpiy* (swan river)
90	Albany Post	*kêsîciwan*

Personal Names

Personal names from English or French are commonly used in Cree with greater or lesser adaptation to Cree pronunciation. Standard Cree orthographic conventions are used for these in the text, standard English spelling in the translation. The names, including pseudonyms, are as follows:

âhcipêl	Archibald (67:4)
âlik âšîš	Alec Asheesh (pseudonym, 43:7)
âlik lâsaras	Alec Lazarus (pseudonym, 40:1)
âniy	Annie (pseudonym, 40:1)
ânkas cam	Angus Chum (65:1)
cân	John (pseudonym, 43:5)
cân coc	John George (41:1)
cân kôsîs	John Koosees (40:1)
cân mârtin	John Martin (49:3)
cicima	Titima (doll's name, 43:13)
cêkap	Jacob (pseudonym, 42:35)
cimiy	Jimmy (pseudonym, 43:3)
cimiy âšîš	Jimmy Asheesh (44:4)
cîmis	James (pseudonym, 67:4, 67:5)
cîmis kâ-tahkwâpêt	James Short Trace (42:42)
cîmis stîpin	James Stephen (pseudonym, 42:44)

387

côsif	Joseph (43:8)
côsif nâkociy	Joseph Nagochee (44:3)
côsip	Joseph (pseudonym, 42:8)
côwil	Joel (38:2)
êlin	Ellen (67:1)
êmil nâkoc'	Emile Nagochee (42:65)
hêntriy lâsaras	Henry Lazarus (40:1)
hêntriy sêlors	Henry Sailors (64:3)
mêriy	Mary (67:4)
pâtrik stîpin	Patrick Stephen (40:1)
sayman	Simon (pseudonym, 43:5)
sayman kôsîs	Simon Koosees (40:1)
sapêt	Sabet (42:4)
šâpatîs	Jean-Baptiste (43:8)
tayna cam	Dinah Chum (65:1)
torotiy	Dorothy (42:63, 43:12)
twâmas	Thomas (pseudonym, 43:5)
wîliy	Willie (67:4).

When a full name is given, it is inflected as a unit, and only one obviative ending appears, e.g.,

wâpamêw âlik lasarasa 'I saw Alec Lazarus'.

Cree family names have sometimes been translated into English for trade or official purposes: *kâ-apišîšišit* 'who is small', a family name at Moose Factory, was commonly rendered *Small*; *âšimok* 'small loon', as *Loon*. Others, such as *Hunter*, may be English surnames or may, in fact, be translations of a Cree original. The practice followed in the texts is to carry over traditional Cree language personal names and occasional nicknames into the English version in their Cree form. Further comment or translation is provided in the Notes, e.g.,

cîmis kâ-tahkwâpêt (42:42)
êlikôš (49:4)
mâskitôhtan (44:3)
ošawâsko-'pwoy (10:9)
ošâwaskwapîway (63:1)
sômis (44:4).

The names of certain Cree mythical personages are well enough known beyond Cree circles to be recognizable by many English readers, even where minor variations in spelling occur. The slight voicing heard on Cree /p/, /t/, /c/, /k/ in certain positions is shown in English spelling by /b/, /d/, /j/, /g/, e.g., *cahkâpêš* 'Chahkabesh'.

The two culture heroes who figure most frequently in the present texts are *cahkâpêš* 'Chahkabesh', now the Man in the Moon, and *wîsakêcâhk* 'Weesakechahk', or, in Moose Cree form, *wîsahkwêcâhk* 'Weesahkwechahk', a trickster figure. A brief glance at the table of contents will show the texts in which each appears. Other legendary characters whose names occur:

šinkipiš	Shingibish (8:5, 47:1)
âyâs	Ayas (9:2)
mêmišôš	Memishoosh (11:1)
mišcâkalâš (MC)	Mishchagalash (63:1)
mistâkanâš (SC)	Mistaganash (10:1)
ociskwaciw	ochiskwajiw (12:15)
wîhtikôw	windigo or cannibal devil (12)
pakwacililiw	Bushman (64).

Notes

Notes to Text 1

Non-cyclical *âtalôhkân*. Recorded c. 1955 at CDE's home at Albany Post. Titles by Agnes Hunter (C) and CDE (E). Cf. also Text 2.

1 Note the interplay of *tipâcimo-* VAI 'recount a story or an event which happened to someone' and *âtalôhkê-* VAI 'narrate a legend, a myth'.

2 *ililîwi-* VAI 'be alive'. If someone found a moose on the river bank or a person lying on the shore, he might be asked, *ililîwiw nâ nêstapiko nipiw?* 'Is he dead or alive?' When inquiring about an old friend, however, the term used would be *pimâtisi-* VAI 'be living': *kiyâpac nâ pimâtisiw?* 'Is he still alive?'

3 *tašîhkâtot-* VTI 'use it as a dwelling'; cf. *ê'kot' ântê têšîhkâtotahk* 'that is the spot he uses for a dwelling', referring, for example, to an island; if referring to a house, *têšîhkêt* VAI would be used.

4 On listening to the recording, James Gunner noted that the narrator should have said *êko mâka* here instead of just *mâka*.

5 The style is curious and sounds adversatively emphatic, as though someone had tried to conceal this world from the inhabitants above but they *had indeed* found out about it; i.e., it was *indeed* known; cf. *šâkoc kî-itohtêw* 'He *did* go!'

6 Note use of *l* by a Swampy Cree speaker. Many residents of Albany Post were formerly members of the Moose Band which earlier reached as far north as Albany Post. Moose Cree has retained the historic *l*-sound which fell together with *n* in Swampy Cree.

7 The narrator forgot that he was addressing a listener and momentarily assumed the rôle of the voice addressing the couple in the story.

8 The common term for spider is *ahnapihkêsiw-* or *otahnapihkêsiw-*; *êhêpik kâ-itiht* 'the one who is called (the) spider' is an archaism.

9 *nîhtâpihkên-* VTA/I 'lower s.o./s.t. on a rope (by hand)'; cf. the synonym *lâšâpihkên-* VTA/I.

10 Perhaps the narrator had in mind *kînikwânâpihkêhtatâ-* VAI-T 'loop it around and around something' (VTA *kînikwânâpihkêšim-*); cf. *pîmastên-* VTI 'twist it'; *pîmastêyâpihkên-* VTI 'twist the rope'.

11 A Cree-speaking listener with seafaring experience commented, "Must have been like a bosun's chair, I suppose."

12 The more usual Albany Post term for a bag or sack is *wîhkwêyâw-* NI.

13 James Gunner interpreted the recording as though he heard a hiatus here, with the narrator checking himself after *wanawî-*. He may have begun to say *-wanawîcik* 'get out', and altered it to *-wanawî-nîšâhtawîcik* 'get out and climb down'. The recording, however, seems to show an uninterrupted sequence as transcribed.

14 Affected Ojibwa speech.

15 *kâ-itikot* might have been expected here. Note the switch of proximate-obviative focus. The narrator seems to have confused speaker with addressee.

16 i.e., *kê-iši-pimâcihonici* 'that they (3') might so survive'.

Notes to Text 2

Non-cyclical *âtalôhkân*. Recorded during the winter of 1955 or spring of 1956 at CDE's home at Albany Post. Titles by Agnes Hunter (C) and CDE (E). Cf. also Text 1.

1 The narrator may have intended *êti-kišipaskamikâk* (cf. *kišipaskamikâ-* VII 'be the end of land'), but used *kišipisk-* VTI 'come to the end of it (land, trail, etc.)'.

2 On listening to the recording, a Moose Cree speaker thought *ê-nîhtâpihkênâkaniwicik* to be better stylistically. This essentially stylistic difference nonetheless calls attention to the spread of the derived VAI of undergoing in Moose Cree and neighbouring dialects at the expense of the VTA form with indefinite actor and 3rd person goal; cf. Ellis, 'Cree Verb Paradigms', *IJAL* 37, 1971, §10, p. 84.

3 cf. *pimâtakâ-* VAI 'wade (a man), swim (a fish or quadruped)' (Watkins–Faries); *pamâtakâ-* may be due to the interchange of /i/ and /a/ in many forms, e.g., *ayawiši-namês* versus *ayawaši-namês* 'fresh fish', or it may be a contraction of *papâmâtakâ-*.

4 Impressionistic Cree version of Ojibwa; cf. 1:7. Note the ethnocentrism reflected in the comment on the Ojibwa speech of the lynx.

5 *kâ-itât* 'he said to him/them'. Note the switch of proximate-obviative focus; the narrator seems to have confused speaker with addressee. *kâ-itikot* 'they said to him' would have been expected.

6 Accidentally erased from the recording.

7 James Gunner, a Moose Cree speaker, noted that *maskwâwa* would be expected here.

8 *âhki* IPC 'let's pretend, let's make believe', used in children's games, e.g., *âhki môswa kâhcišotâw* 'let's play (make-believe) moose'. In some contexts the meaning seems roughly synonymous with *...hkâso...*, e.g., *nôcîskwêwêhkâso-* VAI 'pretend to flirt'. Final /h/ glide of speech is here preserved in transcription for (possible) value.

9 This service rendered by the bear is alleged as one reason for the taboo on eating bear-meat in this area.

10 Note how, with the transition to historical events, the *âtalôhkân* is concluded as though the storyteller were recounting an actual event, a *tipâcimôwin*, rather than narrating a legend.

Notes to Text 3

Cyclical *âtalôhkân*. Recorded during the winter of 1955 or spring of 1956 at CDE's home at Albany Post. Titles by Agnes Hunter (C) and CDE (E). Cf. also Text 15.

1 *cahkâpêš*. A mother directing a child's attention to the moon would say something like *kiwâpamâw nâ? ana kâ-cahkâštêšihk*. 'Do you see him? That one who casts a shadow.' Cf. Introduction, footnote 8.

2 cf. *išilawî-* VAI 'fare so'; e.g., *tân' êšilawît?* 'What's he doing?, What's he up to?', *tân' êšilawîcik?* 'How are they making out (as of sick persons)?' The expression in the latter case is actually non-committal, instead of a direct query such as *âhcikow nâ ati-ihtiw, nêstapiko ati-milo-ihtiw?* 'Does he fare worse or is he better?'

3 The Moose Cree form is *ê-nân'taw'-pimâcihot*.

4 The use of *pimatah-* VTI 'trudge' is an archaism according to Agnes Hunter.

5 The recording is unclear here; cf. *paskê-* VAI 'branch off (from the main trail)'; *paskitâmaciwê-* VAI 'go over the ridge'. If there is a break in construction after *ê-*, then *paskitâmaciwêtâk* alone could mean 'let's walk over the ridge'.

6 The recording sounds more like *manâ wina* 'perhaps', interpreted by another Cree

listener as *manâ oti* 'then namely'.

7 lit., 'pointed mouse'. The small, fat field mouse is known as *amisko-wâpikošîš* 'beaver mouse'.

8 i.e., *n'kî-nakwâtâw*. Chahkabesh characteristically palatalizes, often, for example, addressing his older sister as *nimiš*. Note that the palatalization here is inconsistent, i.e., *nimis* occurs unchanged, but *itêw*, which follows, becomes *icêw*, with the narrator carrying Chahkabesh's 'cute' mispronunciation (palatalization) over into his own narrative.

Notes to Text 4

Cyclical *âtalôhkân*. Recorded c. 1956 at CDE's home at Albany Post. Titles by Agnes Hunter (C) and CDE (E). Cf. also Texts 16, 29.

1 Alternative reading: *pêyakwâw* 'once upon a time'. If this is, in fact, what is recorded, then the narrator begins again at *âta*.

2 Chahkabesh palatalizes, a sort of 'cute little' speech characteristic in which *s* becomes *š*, and *t* becomes *c*; cf. 5:6, *n'cakask*.

3 lit., 'In her having something said-to-her-by-him'.

4 Perhaps the verb should have been *kî-pimotaškwâtêw* VTA 'he shot at them', a term more appropriate to a sling-shot or bow and arrow, which the following lines suggest.

5 *kapâšimototaw-* means 'swim after'; 'wade after' would be *nâtakâtotaw-*.

6 i.e., *ocahcâpiya êy-apin'ci*.

7 'she knew' first time in proximate, second in obviative as narrator recalls subject, *omisa*.

8 *kêkât* 'almost'; *kêka* 'finally' would make better sense here: 'At last she actually …'.

Notes to Text 5

Cyclical *âtalôhkân*. Recorded 1956 or 1957 at CDE's home at Albany Post. Titles by CDE, with the Cree title checked by Agnes Hunter.

1 There may be some confusion here with *pimatah-* VTI 'go over a/the ridge'; cf. 6:7, where it takes the form *pimitaham*. The recording here has *ê-'mâtâhamin'ci*. One informant wondered whether the intent of the speaker was *ê-pimahâtâpên'ci* (cf. *pimahâtâpê-* VAI 'go in a straight line'). This is perhaps more common usage for the older form *kâ-timahâpahtikosilici* 'which go in a continuous straight line', a term used in speaking of caribou.

2 The narrator most likely intended to say *n'kî-mâtahâw* 'I saw the tracks'.

3 Another Cree listener interpreted this as *šâ-â mânisi* 'Oh, my!'

4 i.e., *itikow omisa*.

5 More common form at Moose Factory is *kî-tašîwiw*.

6 According to James Gunner, a more common and better usage is *kêkwân wêhci-anima-tôtahk* or *kêkwân wêhci-anihi-tôtahk*.

7 cf. *ispihtên'tâkosiw nâ kici-kî-tôtahk?* 'Is he strong enough to do it?'

8 Perhaps the verb should have been *kî-pimotaškwâtêw* VTA 'he shot at them', a term more appropriate to a sling-shot or bow and arrow, which the following lines suggest.

9 i.e., *matwê-*; the /w/ glide is typically produced with the lips in relatively straight position.

10 The recording has *'yâkwâmisîyapan n'cakask*, interpreted by a second informant as *'yâkwâmisî êko*. *'yâkwâmisîwipan' n'takask* would mean 'look out where you're

going, my arrow'.

11 i.e., normally *kawahwêw*.

12 i.e., *mîna itohtê ê-kî-ititâpân*.

13 The narrator probably began to say *piko*.

14 *itâcimikosi-* VAI is used for stories about events long ago; *itâcimâkaniwan-* 'be so told about' is used to recount stories of current or recent activities (cf. 6:5).

Notes to Text 6

âtalôhkân. Recorded 1956 or 1957 at CDE's home at Albany Post. Titles by Agnes Hunter (C) and CDE (E). Cf. also Text 17.

1 James Gunner felt this should be *ê-itâtanôhkâtâkaniwit* 'as the story goes'.

2 Suspected loan translation.

3 Note change back to proximate. A folk memory of grizzlies in the Rocky Mountains?

4 Reduplicated from *-mahkišk-* VTI.

5 The narrator began to say *kici-nahînawêhât* 'to satisfy her'.

6 The narrator anticipates *kic'-îtohtêt* in the next clause, then corrects himself.

7 This recalled to James Gunner of Moose Factory the Inuit-type arrow used around Great Whale River and to the north. It was made with small spears at the sides for the more effective shooting of wild fowl.

8 *kâ-pimotaškwâtahk* would be the more usual verb to use for an arrow.

9 cf. *piyêhtahkik*, changed conjunct, from *pêht-*.

10 Chahkabesh seems to be talking to his bow and telling it to 'make the arrow go along the side', i.e., of the line of bears: *ati-lâlipanih-* VTA 'make them go along the side' (cf. *ati-lâlipali-*). This Swampy Cree form seems also to represent a more westerly use with the final *-i* on the imperative.

11 From the rapid speech on the recording it is unclear whether the narrator said *k'-âti-pim'pa...*, *kâ-'ši-pim'panit* 'where it began going along' or *k'-âti-pim'pahtâši...*, *-pim'panit* 'as it began trot..., going along'.

> If the latter reading is correct, the narrator failed to complete the form, *kâ-ati-pim'pahtâšin'ci* 'as they trotted along'. *pim'pahtâši-* VAI, diminutive of *pim'pahtâ-*, is used of a person in a hurry who periodically breaks from a walk into a short trot.

12 i.e., *âta.*

Notes to Text 7

Cyclical *âtalôhkân.* Recorded 1956 or 1957 at CDE's home at Albany Post. Titles by Agnes Hunter (C) and CDE (E); literal translation of the Cree title: 'The legend (told) about Weesakechahk when this land was flooded'. Cf. also Text 28.

1 Identified by James Gunner as a probable metathesis for *môna wîskâc ohci-itên'tam kici-pâhkwânik*; with *kiskên'tam* for *itên'tam*.

2 Identified by James Gunner as an archaism for *nakiskaw*.

3 *ê-* is completely elided in the flow of speech.

4 The narrator palatalizes frequently throughout this section, apparently for stylistic purposes, when recounting actions of a mischievous nature. This is probably an affectation of baby-talk, inviting an indulgent and amused attitude on the part of the listener.

5 Contraction for *n'cîmiš.*

6 The recording is unclear at this point.

7 One informant interpreted the recording as *itwêtokê 'sa* 'he must have said'. The speech is fast and blurred.

8 The subject is *kîhkwahâkêw* 'wolverine'.

9 Or *nêma* (recording is unclear).

10 Alternative usage, *ê-kî-nâspici-niskipotêkopanê*, might have been expected. Clearly a description of Swampy Cree territory.

11 The narrator palatalizes, presumably for stylistic purposes.

12 The new theme of the North brings to mind further tales of Weesakechahk, and the narrator continues right on, in spite of his announced intention of ending the story.

13 i.e., *oški-'škîšiša* 'new little fir trees'.

14 This may have reference to the fact that ptarmigan, at the coast, can be discerned only by two dark eyes and a black spot on the tail.

15 i.e., *mayêw itê ê-itwêt*.

16 i.e., *kâ-natawâpamât wînistam*. The contracted form, *wî'stam*, is used in Moose Cree; *wînistam* to the North in the Albany area.

17 An inverse form might have been expected before now, both here and in the preceding paragraph.

18 This refers to the custom of first chewing pine gum (not spruce, which was too sticky), then rolling it in the palm of the hand into a ball, and then rolling it on the ground. This is what Weesakechahk did with the man who wanted *kâkikê-pimâtisîwin* 'life everlasting'. He rolled him into the ground, which accounts for the rock, *wîlil'wâpisk*, a kind of spotted rock (*ê-pâhpâhtêwašit*) of various colours which sticks out of the ground (*ê-sâsâkiskamikišihk*) here and there (*mâmên*).

19 There is a play on words in Cree between *ininasiniy* 'ordinary stone' and *ininiw* 'an (ordinary) person, an Indian'.

20 Suspected metathesis for *kâ-sâsâkišihk* 'which sticks out here and there'. James Gunner suggested that some speakers would add *mâmên*.

21 *kihtaskamikohk* would sound better according to one informant. James Gunner heard this as *mistâskîhk*, which is seldom used and sounds like a loan translation modelled on English *mainland*. CDE clearly hears *nêsta askîhk*.

Notes to Text 8

âtalôhkân. Recorded 1956 or 1957 at CDE's home at Albany Post. Title (C) based on text, with emendation by James Gunner, (E) by CDE; literal translation of the Cree title: 'Weesakechahk who told about himself, and the birds who flew'. Cf. also Texts 18 and 55.

1 James Gunner suggested that the narrator might have been expected to use *pinêsiwak* with *kâ-papâmihnâcik*.

2 *'wê...*: the narrator probably began to say *'wiyâsîša*.

3 *cahkâpêš*: slip of the tongue. The story is, of course, about Weesakechahk.

4 Narrator uses palatalization stylistically.

5 This narrator uses the form *mâkwa*, rather than the more common *mwâkwa*, until near the end of the story; cf. 8:8.

6 i.e., [ŋkıʃʷá·hıkʊt].

7 i.e., *-pimâponot*.

8 Note VTA instrumental stem-final ...*h*...; the loon is to use his glittering beads as an instrument of deception.

9 i.e., *ta-pimâponow âta*.

10 i.e., *ê-ati-ayihtinici.*
11 i.e., *mâka ê-wâstawêyâpiskitênik.*

Notes to Text 9

Non-cyclical *âtalôhkân*: local legend. Recorded in 1956 or 1957 at CDE's home at Albany Post. Title (C) verbatim from text, (E) by CDE; literal translation of the Cree title: 'An old legend, told about a certain old person, and his son called Ayas'.

1 *ômêniw* might have been expected here.
2 *-nakaci-wêpahwât* 'dumped and left him', and pulled away quickly. Otherwise the form would be simply *-nakatât* 'left him'.
3 i.e., *tâpwêhtawêw âta ê-têpwâtikot.*
4 Roughly synonymous with *môna ohci-kwêskên'tam* 'he didn't change his mind'.
5 i.e., *kî-papâmâšakâmêw*; reduplicated form.
6 *ê-pêtâtakân'ci* 'coming up from the water'. *nipîhk* indicates that the creature was under water.
7 Original transcription read *n'kî-nakatahok nôhtâwiy.*
8 The narrator changes construction to the independent order. Even with this change the omission of *kî-* sounds preferable since, according to James Gunner, "the whistling must still have been going on".
9 Note uncontracted *šawin-*, paralleling *kawin-*.
10 *ê-pâskwahwât* was preferred to *ê-pâskiskwahwât* by James Gunner.
11 For *ka-*; probably influenced by *kê-'ši-šâpoškaman* of preceding sentence.
12 Note transition from obviative to proximate.
13 i.e., *ê-apišîšišit.*
14 i.e., *kê-kî-ati-nipiyân.* On listening to the recording, another Cree speaker claimed to hear the preverbs *kê-kî-ati-*, required by the sense of the passage; CDE could not hear any trace of the missing preverbs.
15 *cîstahikan* is often used for a fork, more properly called *cîstahamâpon.* It is also the term used for a cooking implement made from a half-inch thick willow stick, about eighteen inches in length, whittled to a point and used for turning food over in a stew pot.
16 *mîkiwâminiw* would be expected here. The narrator's first language was Cree; but a relative remarked, "He doesn't finish his words." Yet cf. *mîciminiw* in 9:12, and *mîk'wâminiw kotakîniw* in 9:17.
17 *mistikoniw* would be expected.
18 i.e., *itêw* 'she said to him'.
19 *mîk'wâminiw* would be expected, to show concord with *ê-cimatênik* as in 9:17.
20 Something like *ê-nîpitêkocihkik* would be expected. The narrator seems to have miscalled the gender of *otinîkêkan* NA with the second verb.
21 Probably for *kê-ênikohk* 'as hard as possible'.
22 i.e., *-pimitišahokow.*
23 Note depalatalization of /c/ to /t/.
24 There are a number of caves along the falls on the Abitibi River at Otter Rapids and Fraserdale. They are now obscured by the dam and hydro installations, respectively, at these places. For an older generation of local people, these caves were where *mêmêkwêšiwak* 'mermaids' lived.
25 The narrator stuttered here. The form is probably either *sâkiwêpinêw* VTA 'he throws him up' (to the entrance of the cave), or *sâkiciwêwêpinêw* VTA 'he throws him on a bank'.

26 i.e., almost [tınıpa·t].

27 The recording has *ê-'šiwinât*.

28 The narrator seems to have started to say *mîk'wâminiw*; a plural is intended and the verb is plural in form.

29 Possibly a blend of *nisitawêlimêw* 'he recognizes him' and *nisitâwinawêw* 'he recognizes him by sight'.

30 The recording has *-pîhtokwêsina*.

31 The recording has *-pîhtokwêsinahk*.

32 *kakwê-* occurs on the recording but does not seem to belong.

33 i.e., *ati-wâciyêmêhkâsow*.

34 i.e., *kâ-takošinokopanê*. Palatalization, which is used throughout this section, sometimes seems to signal the speech of the scamp trying to represent himself as lovable, harmless; cf. 3:10 and 4:3, above.

35 cf. *t'-âpatahk kê-wawêšihtâniwahk ôma cîmân?* 'What's the use of fixing this canoe?' *t'-âpatisit kê-cimalâkaniwit awa otâpânâsk?* 'What's the use of standing this sled up?'

36 The verb normally expected when speaking of an arrow would be *pimotahkwê-*.

37 *animêniw* would have been expected.

38 Creeping haplology, corrected in the next two words.

39 lit., 'which make smoke'; probably puff-balls.

40 i.e., *kâ-mânâtašiškîšit;* regressive, non-contiguous assimilation, as *kisêy-iskwêw* for *kišêy-iskwêw*.

41 cf. *otasâmâhtikomi-* VAI 'use it (juniper wood) for snowshoe frames'. It is commonly claimed that tamarack once bent when wet will not straighten again, whereas birch will. Poplar, a lighter wood, is used only for children's or women's snowshoe frames but breaks more easily.

42 Moose Cree equivalent: *ê-mamacitêwêscâk*.

Notes to Text 10

Non-cyclical *âtalôhkân*: local legend. Recorded in 1956 or 1957 at CDE's home at Albany Post. Titles by Agnes Hunter (C) and CDE (E). Cf. also Text 63.

1 *matakwahp-* NI 'an old campsite' (term used mainly by older people).

2 i.e., *nititênihtên*. The /t/ in *-papêtihkwâskopanihoyân* and throughout the following sentence is stylistically affricated. The medial *...âskw...* indicates that the movement was related to a wooden structure, i.e., a coffin.

3 i.e., *kâ-ati-ayitâpoliyân*.

4 i.e., *ati-ayitwêw* 'he kept on repeating'.

5 James Gunner (a Moose Cree speaker) preferred *nîla oš' awa n'kâwiy*, if the mother was thought of as right alongside. If she was eight to ten feet away, *nîla oš' âna n'kâwiy* would seem more appropriate. *ošô* struck the informant as more suited to a context such as *nîla ošô kikâwiy* 'I'm your mother'. *ošô* is, presumably, a contracted variant of *ôš' awa*.

6 James Gunner felt that this sounded like an Ojibwaism for Cree *n'titâw*. There is contact with Ojibwa speakers near Attawapiskat (north), Ogoki (west) and English River (southwest). James Gunner cited a form, *n'titâsi*, as more to be expected. The narrator may have intended, *kîna ošô n'kâwiy* 'you're my mother, you know'. This, however, is only conjecture as the section transcribed is clearly recorded.

7 /š/ in *...šit...*, rather than *...sit...*, is probably due to assimilation. James Gunner supplied the ending which is not on the recording.

It is usual, when a deer has to be carried home on a sled or in a canoe, to cut off the lower legs and antlers for less cumbersome carrying. Care is exercised in cutting the joint to preserve the marrow. The lower leg-bone is then split to provide draw-knife type utensils used to remove the top layer of hide, which is thrown away. The under layer is then tanned. The action used with the bone utensil is that of pushing, as with a spoke-shave, rather than drawing. The process is usually carried out over a peeled, round, smooth log, from 6" to 8" in diameter, running the utensil down the length of the log, which is slanted and pointed with an axe at one end. The skin is draped over the log, with the end over the upper, blunt end. The belly is then pressed against the upper end to hold the skin, and the utensil is run down the log as far as the operator can reach. This is either men's or women's work. It takes between two and three hours to prepare a caribou skin; about four to five hours for a moose hide.

After the hair has been removed from the outer hide with a sharp knife, the hide is then soaked in water for about a week. The longer the hide is soaked, the easier it is to remove the outer hide; cf. 50:6.

8 *kî-*: slip of the tongue; according to James Gunner, *ê'kwân' êši-pôsihak* would be expected, since the deer (caribou) is whole up to the point where the narrator says *ostikwân*. He would still have preferred *ê-otêškaniwêhtinilik ostikwân*.

A live deer with horns is described as *atihk ê-otêškanit* or *otêškana ê-kikiškawât*. If the head of a dead deer retains horns it is described as *atihkwastikwân ê-otêškanêhtihk*.

9 Archaism; modern usage would be *ê'kwâni mâka wêhci-kî-mihcilawêsiyâpân*.

10 Note the stylistic use of palatalization, an invitation to the listener to enter into the atmosphere of the story which appears repeatedly throughout the remainder of the text.

11 Cooked over an *apwâtâkan*, a willow frame of four uprights with two main cross-sticks at the side supporting a floor of slimmer willow sticks about 1" or ½" apart; cf. *apwê-* VAI 'roast' and *apwât-* VTI; also secondary formation in *kêkwân ani kâ-apwâtâcikâtêk* 'What's that which they're roasting (lit., is being roasted)?'

12 James Gunner felt that *tâhtâhkatam* 'he will stab it again and again' would have been the correct form to use here. The term recorded by the narrator really means that he will use the *ê-minwâšihk mîcim* as an instrument with which to stab.

13 i.e., *n'tôtihtên*.

14 The tangled underbrush implies many different kinds of growth with different colours, providing a good hiding place, since the deer cannot spot a person against the background.

15 i.e., *-itihtâkwahk*.

16 i.e., *wâpisakitihp* 'a deer with a white forehead'; i.e., an old deer. This is a near-synonym for *iyâpêwatihkwa* 'real, old buck deer', immediately following.

17 or, 'I didn't allow my arm to rest from moving, ...'

18 i.e., *wêsa êko*.

19 *nimihkonawân* would have been expected, from *mihkonawê-* VAI 'have a red face'.

20 Interpretation of the cry made by a small hawk, *pâpalêkisîw*, after a noise sometimes made at night, "*papapapapapa*", on a high tone.

Various types of noises are made by another bird known as *wâsêhkwanêsiw*, e.g., a fox barking, a dog howling, a baby crying and sounds of other birds. To hear a *wâsêhkwanêsiw* "fooling around" one is an omen of ill luck. Another Cree listener cited several instances of this in two of which he was immediately concerned.

21 The recording is slightly unclear. A second informant insisted that he heard *môna pêhtêyên'tamohkâson* 'I pretended I wasn't in my right senses'. On slower replay, the informant first thought he heard *môna m'pisiskên'tamohkâson* 'I pretended not to pay any attention', but finally decided it was an allegro enunciation of *môna m'pisiskên'tamohkâsohtay* (cf. *pâpisiskênihtamohkâso-*) 'I was pretending not to pay any attention'.

22 A second informant knew no form of the type *mâkošêkwahw-* VTA. As a possibility he suggested *mâkoškaw-* VTA 'jump on and squash s.o. with one's weight'.

23 *nîyak* 'I too' interpreted by Sophia Gunner, a Moose Cree speaker, as Albany usage.

24 May refer either to deer- or caribou-hide.

Notes to Text 11

Non-cyclical *âtalôhkân*: local legend. Recorded in 1956 or 1957 at CDE's home at Albany Post. Titles by Agnes Hunter (C) and CDE (E). This story might be sub-titled, 'The wicked stepfather.'

1 The stylistic use of palatalization here and in 11:4 and 11:5 is an invitation to the listener to enter into the atmosphere of the story.

2 i.e., *ayitâcimikosiw* 'he is the subject of repeated stories'.

3 The narrator seemed to correct himself, first using a word something like *manišôš* or *manicôš* 'insect (i.e., sprite)' and then *mêmišôš*, the name of the conjuror.

4 *-kihcipaniniw* (obviative) might have been expected with *ocîmân*.

5 i.e., *-papâmâšakâminici*.

6 i.e., *itêw*.

7 i.e., *onahâhkišîmiw*.

8 i.e., *ê-pakwanawâspinatât*; cf. *pakwanaw* 'by guess, by memory'. A teacher may say to a child, *êko mâka, pakwanaw itwê* 'now, say it by heart'; or, after following a winding trap line, one might make a guess at a short cut back to camp and say, *pakwanaw n'ka-iši-kihtohtân* 'I'll make a guess at going (to where my camp is)', i.e., by power of the mind, without other guidance or means.

   -âspin- (medial) 'sickness'; cf. *itâspinê-* VAI 'have a certain sickness', e.g., *tân' êtâspinêyin?* 'What sickness do you have?'

9 i.e., *kâ-kî-otonahâhkišîmit*.

10 i.e., *tâwic ... nêtê akohtinôpan ministik*. The verb form sounds more like *akohtinôkwan*.

11 *ninikon* or *ninikwan* 'my son-in-law' (loan from Ojibwa).

12 *kâ-otihtahahkik* would have been more suitable for travel by boat. The term used is more appropriate to walking; cf. *ê-nakatahwât* (11:3). If the son-in-law had been left on land, *ê-nakatât* would have been expected.

13 *manâwinân* 'The Collecting Place', name of a rocky point running out from the mainland about twenty-eight miles south of Albany Post on James Bay. The one mentioned is probably a rocky point off the island in the story.

14 Gulls eggs are eagerly sought, especially around the end of May and beginning of June. The egg is tested to determine whether it is 'birded' or not, by putting it in a pail of water. If it floats, it is replaced in the nest. If it sinks, it is kept. The custom is to hard-boil the eggs.

15 i.e., *kî-itâpicîw*; probably *kîw-itâp... > kîy-otâp...*

16 Probably an alternative form at Albany for *-astahoyâhk*; cf. *astaho-* VAI 'be quilling'.

17 *môna ohci-pisiskên'tam* 'he didn't pay attention (to it)'. James Gunner felt it would be preferable to use *môna ohci-pâpisiskâpahtam* 'he didn't bother looking at it', to

convey the sense of the action, and that the narrator should have used the VTA, i.e., 'didn't bother looking at *him*', rather than the VTI form.

18 i.e., *êhkihk.*
19 i.e., *-wânânik.*
20 i.e., *nâspic.*
21 'a big, little creek', i.e., deep but narrow.
22 i.e., *itikow onahâhkišîma.*
23 i.e., *mihcêt.*
24 Preferred Moose Cree usage seems to be *walastawêw* (or *olastawêw*) *amiskwa.*
25 i.e., *kêkwânên.* This struck James Gunner as an Ojibwaism. The more usual Moose Cree form would be *kêkwânihkân.*
26 *wîyêkitê-* VII 'smell strongly'; possibly for *wînêkitê-.*
27 i.e., *manâ itêw.*
28 i.e., *êhkihk.*
29 i.e., *iskwâskitêskoniw.*

Notes to Text 12

Non-cyclical *âtalôhkân*: local legend. Recorded in 1956 or 1957 at CDE's home at Albany Post. Titles by the narrator (C) and CDE (E). Cf. also Texts 59:2-4, 60.

1 Another name for *wîhtikôwak* or another kind of *wîhtikôwak*, or the name of one of the groups of devils; cf. 12:3 for unpalatalized form, *ociskwatiw.* The term *windigo*, derived from Ojibwa, is more commonly used in English.
2 Baby-talk. Cute little devils are often represented as talking (endearingly?) this way; cf. 4:3; 7:4.
3 *êni*: perhaps for *ênikohk* 'with all his might, as hard as he could', and possibly to be taken with *kînikwânipahtâw.*
4 i.e., *ê-pimiwatêt.*
5 The recording is unclear at this point.
6 The narrator probably started to say *nipâhkâstikwânêšin* 'I've cracked my skull open'.
7 Usually several trees are left standing near a wigwam or camp entrance. When a hunter is disappointed with his catch, he will throw his bag up on a tree rather than bringing it into camp. If proud of his catch, he would take it right to the door of the camp where his wife would reach out and draw the bag in. If a moose, for example, were caught, the heart, liver and kidneys would be brought back in a bag. The moose would be left to cool overnight, making it easier to skin and the meat more tender.
8 *âšay êtokê* 'already apparently'
9 i.e., *mâmîtânaskwan* VII 'the clouds are shitting all around'.
10 i.e., *šâkoc.*
11 i.e., *išpimihk.*
12 Contracted form of *pinalakêskiškamaw-* VTA 'knock the bark down for s.o.'. The man tells the windigo to look out that he doesn't get the bark down his neck.
13 i.e., *itêw.*
14 cf. *pimwêwit-* VTI 'make a noise (in passing)'. When children are told to come in because of stormy weather they may be told, *pêci-pîhtokêk. yâkwâ, kîhkwahâkêw kata- pimwêwitam!* 'Come in. Watch out, the wolverine will be passing and howling!'

   The idea is that the wolverine will be passing through the air. *pimwêwit-* is also used of wolves howling while on the move. *ôlo-* is used when the animal sits howling in one place.

15 Perhaps for *nimošôm* 'my grandfather'; but according to Sophie Gunner, 'the person whom the *ochiskwajiw* planned to kill and eat', perhaps 'my prey'. The word is otherwise unknown.

16 *n'tâšimik* translated by one informant as 'speared'. This seems to be due to uncertainty as to the quantity of the /a/. The meaning might then be, 'My prey has speared me,' an attractive but textually difficult alternative.

17 So on recording. The form seems to be for *kišikamisamaw-* VTA 'heat it up for s.o.'; *kišâpiskisamaw-* might have been expected.

18 Probably for *êko manâ nêkacicâkot* (cf. *nakaciškaw-*) 'so then he was hit head on'.

19 The narrator changes construction from singular to plural.

20 One informant noted that *sâkahikanihk* would be expected here.

21 Baby-talk used stylistically; cf. also 12:1 and 12:13.

22 James Gunner commented that *cîhcîstâkonêhikêw* 'he prods about *in the snow*' would probably have been used if 'snow-bank' had not been explicitly added.

23 The narrator probably had in mind something like *cîstahikêtê* 'in case he would prod'.

24 *t...* presumably some kind of liaison feature in devil speech.

25 Probably for *nawahât-* VTA here and in the next sentence.

26 i.e., *awa ininiw*.

27 i.e., *tâpwê kikitimahtâniwâw mitêwâtisîwin* 'it's a pity the way you're abusing conjuring': more windigo baby-talk. An alternative reading for *mitêwâtisîwin* is *n'kišêwâtisîwin* 'it's a pity you're abusing my kindness'.

Notes to Text 13
Cyclical *âtalôhkân*. Recorded 1960-62 in the recording studio of the Anthropology Department, University of Toronto. Titles by the narrator; literal translation of the Cree title: 'Chahkabesh who reached into the water for the giant beaver'.

1 Chahkabesh is represented as unable to say *nimis*; thus, 'Big Thithter' or 'Big Shishter'.

2 Baby-talk; cf. 12:1 above.

3 On listening to the recording, the narrator inserted *mâka* after *manâ*.

4 The form is mispronounced on the recording as *pêkwâc*.

5 i.e., *tânika*.

6 On listening to the recording, the narrator inserted *anima* after *kêkwâniw*.

7 i.e., [ǯk, ǯk, ǯk].

8 *'ci-* supplied.

9 i.e., *manâ êši-kîwêt*.

10 i.e., [nɪmɪšə].

11 i.e., [žak, žak, žak].

12 i.e., *kakwê-* 'try'.

13 i.e., [wʌnʌwi·pʌnɪnn̥ĵth].

14 The narrator accidentally carries palatalization over into his own narrative.

15 First reading *sîpîhk*. The speech is fairly rapid; but a second informant, on listening to the recording, interpreted this as *sîpîniw*.

16 i.e., *manâ ana awênihkân*.

17 lit., 'he will be said to'.

18 i.e., *ati-ayiskwanêw*, with /a/ raised to /ê/ before /y/.

19 i.e., [óšʌ].

20 i.e., *piko*.

21 i.e., *-pahkišininici*.

22 On listening to the recording, the narrator inserted *manâ itikow omisa* 'that woman said' after *nipiy*.

23 On listening to the recording, the narrator inserted *kî-kîwêw* 'gone home' after *mâka*.

24 On listening to the recording, the narrator inserted *môskamîniw* 'broth' after *ânimêniw*.

25 *âsiniy*: /â/ is long on the recording, with phonetic stress on the penultimate.

26 "Indian style." This is neither squatting nor kneeling. The person sits on the legs which are bent at the knee with the lower leg flat on the floor or ground.

27 i.e., *manâ*.

28 Chahkabesh always kept his bow and arrow buried under the snow.

29 On replay, the narrator preferred *kâ-ati-pimohtênici* 'was starting to walk along'.

30 Baby-talk.

31 Narrator uses vocative form for reasons that remain unclear.

32 On each group of three the pitch is from higher to lower, with a higher pitch on *cit*; i.e., cin^3, cin^2, cin^1; cin^3, cin^2, cin^1, cit^3.

33 On listening to the recording, the narrator gave *êkâ êškwâ ê-ohci-mîcisocik* 'since they had not yet eaten'.

34 i.e., *êkot' âni*.

Notes to Text 14

Cyclical *âtalôhkân*. Recorded 1960-62 in the recording studio of the Anthropology Department, University of Toronto. Titles by the narrator. Cf. also Text 56.

   N.B.: This text was read from a syllabic copy written by the narrator.

1 i.e., [tʌŋŋ, tʌŋŋ, tʌŋŋ].

2 Narrator uses vocative form for reasons that remain unclear.

3 i.e., [tʊŋŋ, tʊŋŋ, tʊŋŋ].

4 cf. *wîhkway-* NI 'bladder'. The modern term is *pîhcipîmân-* NI 'a *pimiy* (fat) container'. The Cree was translated by the narrator as "Gee! I think I ought to take a provision supply."

5 The recording has *iši-kihtohtêw*, with *...hkâsow* following a break; *iši-kihtohtêhkâsow* 'he pretended to go away' makes better sense.

6 i.e., [tʊŋŋ, tʊŋŋ, tʊŋŋ].

7 The narrator began to say what was probably intended to be *otôwîhkwâm* but quickly changed; cf. 14:6, below.

8 i.e., *pimwâhtakonahêw*; cf. 14:5.

9 The narrator probably started to say *ê-âpacihtât* 'using it' and changed his mind.

10 Narrator seems to recall preceding story of Chahkabesh breaking a giant's arm.

Notes to Text 15

Cyclical *âtalôhkân*. Recorded 1960-62 in the recording studio of the Anthropology Department, University of Toronto. Titles by the narrator (C) and CDE (E). Cf. also Text 3.

1 i.e., *itikow omisa*.

2 One Cree listener interpreted the recording as *kiyêkišêpâyânik*, i.e., changed conjunct.

3 *mâši* 'even' seems to fit the sense better.
4 There is an additional but unclear element on the recording here.
5 One Cree listener interpreted the recording as *tiyêpwâtăt*, i.e., changed conjunct.

Notes to Text 16

Cyclical *âtalôhkân*. Recorded 1960-62 in the recording studio of the Anthropology Department, University of Toronto. Titles by the narrator (C) and by CDE or the narrator (E). Cf. also Texts 4, 29.
1 On listening to the recording, the narrator corrected this to *itikow*.
2 On listening to the recording, the narrator added *ka-kî-kohcipanihikohtayak* 'they would have swallowed you right down'.
3 The form recorded seems to be *-kôkamikot*. Several later listeners failed to recognize the form.
4 *n'âpatisiyan*: idiomatic, 'never mind, you're useless'; cf. Glossary.
5 Use of *anima* is probably due to interference from English. On listening to the recording, the narrator replaced *anima* correctly with *anta*.

Notes to Text 17

Cyclical *âtalôhkân*. Recorded 1960-62 in the recording studio of the Anthropology Department, University of Toronto. Titles based on text. Cf. also Text 6.
1 *ê-ânimômâkaniwispan* might have been expected. It looks as though there is interference from ...*wâspan*, VTA conjunct indicative preterit 3–3'.
2 i.e., *manâ*.
3 i.e., *manâ êti-wanawît*.

Notes to Text 18

Cyclical *âtalôhkân*. Recorded 1960-62 in the recording studio of the Anthropology Department, University of Toronto. Titles probably by the narrator (C) and by CDE (E). Cf. also Texts 8 and 55.
1 The six obviative forms in *-a* could equally well be written with final *-h*, e.g., *wêhwêwah, niskawah*, etc.
2 i.e., *tânika itê*.
3 Other Cree speakers who commented seem to lengthen the first vowel of *manipitam*, probably as a contraction of the reduplicated stem, *mamânipit-*; cf. 18:3.
4 Suspected metathesis for *nêtahâšakâmêt*.
5 i.e., [hwæt˺]. Suspected interference from English *what*.
6 On listening to the recording, the narrator inserted *mâka* after *mamânipitam*.
7 The narrator stumbles over several possible sequences here.
8 The narrator stumbles over several possible sequences here.
9 On listening to the recording, the narrator preferred *'ci-ati-tôtamin'ci*.
10 Initial /i/ of *iši-* is devoiced.
11 On listening to the recording, the narrator preferred *itahamâsow* over *itwêw*. Note the similarity of theme with the Comanche story in which Coyote sings to the prairie dogs and clubs them to death as they dance with eyes closed (cf. Elliot Canonge, *Comanche Texts*, Norman, Oklahoma: Summer Institute of Linguistics, 1958; pp. 3-4).
12 cf. *-wanawî-wêpinihcik*, with substitution of /y/ for /w/-glide.
13 *itên'tamwak* is required by the sense, even though the singular *itên'tam* was

recorded. The narrator probably had the loon, whom he was about to mention, in mind.

14 i.e., *mâka*.

15 *-nikwahwât* must be intended.

16 In this whole section Weesakechahk is represented as talking in a little, high, childlike voice.

17 i.e., *âsay*, not *âšay*. Alternative possible reading *'astâw* (cf. *kišâstaw*). If *kišâstaw* is read, then the meaning is, 'Gosh, I want to sleep!'

18 On listening to the recording, the narrator supplied the following explanatory passage after *ê-nipât*:

ininiwak manâ mâka pêci-pimiškâwak. wâpahtamwak manâ iškotêniw; wâpamêwak nêsta wîsakêcâhkwa ê-nipân'ci. wâpamêwak manâ mâka anihi pinêsiwa ê-sâsâkisitêšininici anta iškotêhk. 'kwâni manâ mâka êši-otinâcik, misiwê manâ pôsihêwak ocîmâniwâhk. êkwâni manâ mâka êši-pôsicik.

'some people came paddling along. They saw the fire; they also saw Weesakechahk asleep. And then they saw those birds with their legs sticking up, there on the fire. Straightway they took them, loaded them all into their canoes, then off they went.'

19 On listening to the recording, the narrator inserted *wîsakêcâhk* after *koškopaniw*.

20 On listening to the recording, the narrator inserted *wîsakêcâhkwa* after *ê-ytênimâcik*.

21 On listening to the recording, the narrator inserted *anihi osita* 'those feet' after *piko*.

22 i.e., *-sâsâkihtininiwah*.

23 On listening to the recording, the narrator edited *intiyin* to *ininiwa*.

24 On listening to the recording, the narrator edited *owêhwêma* to *opinêsîma* 'his birds'.

Notes to Text 19

Cyclical *âtalôhkân*. Recorded 1960-62 in the recording studio of the Anthropology Department, University of Toronto. Titles probably by the narrator (C) and by CDE (E). For a shorter version of the same story, cf. text 27:3-4.

1 Bears, as everyone knows, are very cunning and among the most difficult of animals to outwit. This story shows how even the bear is not sufficiently astute to escape being tricked by Weesakechahk.

2 On listening to the recording, the narrator inserted the following after *êši-...*: *ê-'ši-sîhtawipanihot, – omistatâhk êkot' âni mwêhci kâ-i...* 'squeezing himself in between, on his big stomach right there...'.

3 On listening to the recording, the narrator preferred *šâwatêt* 'he was hungry'. The first form is probably due to contamination from the typical, changed form of the preverb, *êši-*, which has occurred in preceding passages.

Notes to Text 20

Cyclical *âtalôhkân*. Recorded 1960-62 in the recording studio of the Anthropology Department, University of Toronto. Titles by the narrator, modified by Agnes Hunter (C), and by CDE (E).

1 Contraction for *wâs' âni*.

2 i.e., *êti-iši-mîcisot*.

3 On listening to the recording, the narrator preferred to substitute *ocêpihkwa* 'roots', rather than the grasses (*maškošîya*) themselves.
4 This touch displays the characteristic greediness of Weesakechahk.
5 This refers to the practice of geese in the fall. After they have fattened themselves, the digestive tract is rid of waste matter before take-off.
6 i.e., *wawênikâpawiwak* 'they stand ready'.
7 *'ti-* for *'ci-*; note the dissimilation from the previous /c/ in *miconi* for *mitoni*.
8 i.e., *êkâ*.
9 The narrator's attention seems to shift from Weesakechahk at *-nipahišihk* to waveys generally at *wêhwêwak*. A singular form would be expected.

Notes to Text 21
Cyclical (thematic) *atalôhkân: pâstâmowin* (cf. Introduction p. xx). Recorded 1960-62 in the recording studio of the Anthropology Department, University of Toronto. Titles by the narrator, modifyed by Agnes Hunter (C), and CDE (E).
1 *nîšo-tipahikan* 'two hours', also used for 'two miles', an instance of cultural updating.
2 lit., 'already'; 'before he was expected', literally, would be *pwâmoši pêhâkaniwit*.
3 *-kîwên'ci* or *-kîwên'c'*. Sometimes the devoiced vowel is audible on the recording as in the present case. Sometimes it is difficult to be sure one has heard the vowel at all and, consequently, whether it should be transcribed or represented as elided. Depending on the decision, both practices are followed in this text.
4 i.e., *mitoni*.
5 Contraction for *kî-sakikâtêpisokopan*.
6 The narrator intended *nihtâ-mitêwiwâkopan* 'they were given to conjuring', but changed instead to *nihtâ-manitôhkêwâkopan* 'they were good at making spirits', i.e., at casting spells.
7 A Cree listener preferred *ê-pâpahitocik*, perhaps 'as they ran again and again', or 'from all sides' towards him; cf. *pimipah-* VTA 'run along with him (e.g., as a dog with a dead rabbit in his mouth)'. The stem used by the narrator, *pimipahito-*, means basically 'run by (each other)'. The reaction of the listener was that this sounded like a non-native speaker, although the narrator was a native speaker; cf. also *pimitâpêpah-* VTA 'run along (e.g., a dog) dragging s.o.'.
8 *wêhci-pêci-kîwêt* seems to be called for grammatically.
9 i.e., *wêhci-takošihk*.
10 On listening to the recording, the narrator interpreted the recording as *kâ-kî-mâkomikot anihi wâpošwa*.

Notes to Text 22
Cyclical (thematic) *atalôhkân: pâstâmowin*. Recorded 1960-62 in the recording studio. Anthropology Department, University of Toronto. Titles by Agnes Hunter (C) and CDE (E).
1 Note the anacoluthon, *pêyakwâ manâ mîna nâpêw ... sakimêwak*.
2 The obviative ending disappears in allegro speech. The narrator later expanded the recording as *kêkwâniw ê-ayât*.
3 Someone replying to a query as to why he had made a poor hunt might say, *môla n'kiskêl'tên âta 'sa n'kî-kocihtân* 'I don't know, I certainly tried'. Someone complaining that he was unable to start a motor might grumble, *âta 'sa misiwê n'kî-ayitôtên* 'I've certainly done everything (and still it won't start)'; cf. *âta isa*

'even though'.

4   The narrator may have intended *ê-kî-pâstâhot* 'because he had said something to bring vengeance on himself', instead of 'because he had brought vengeance on them'.

Notes to Text 23

Cyclical (thematic) *âtalôhkân: pâstâmowin*. Recorded 1960-62 in the recording studio of the Anthropology Department, University of Toronto. Titles by Agnes Hunter (C) and CDE (E).

1   *ana ošîmimâw* would have been preferable. *ana pêyak ošîmimâw* 'one of the younger brothers' suggests that there must have been more than two people involved.

2   The recording has *-pêhtawêna(h)k*; cf. *pêhtawên-* VTI 'hear it (someone coming whom one doesn't see)', i.e., one could hear the crunching on the snow.

3   The recording was variously heard as though the narrator metathesized *ê-'ti-tip...* to *ê-'pitit*, then corrected himself, or as *ê-apit* 'sitting', i.e., in his house.

4   The narrator nearly said *nipîniw* 'water'.

5   i.e., *-âstawêpanik*.

Notes to Text 24

tipâcimôwin: childhood memories. Recorded 1960-62 in the recording studio of the Anthropology Department, University of Toronto. Titles based on text.

1   *iškwâhtêminiw* would be expected.

2   *šîpîšiš* 'creek' would be expected, since a beaver never dams a river.

Notes to Text 25

tipâcimôwin: childhood memories. Recorded 1960-62 in the recording studio of the Anthropology Department, University of Toronto. Titles based on text.

1   i.e., *'ci-*.

2   The narrator probably intended *osôhk* 'on his tail', then changed to *ocihcîhk*.

3   James Gunner felt that *kâ-ohci-pêkopêt* 'where he surfaced from' would have been better.

4   The alternative would have been to use a pole from twelve to fifteen feet long and push it under the ice to its full length. Another hole would then be cut, and so on at intervals. When a line had been extended under the ice to the length of the net, the net would then be attached and pulled into position.

Notes to Text 26

tipâcimôwin: childhood memories. Recorded 1960-62 in the recording studio of the Anthropology Department, University of Toronto. Titles by the narrator (C) and CDE (E).

    Literal translation of the Cree title: 'These ones the sharp-talonned'.

1   i.e., *êkâ wîskâc*.

2   The narrator corrects himself from ...*icik* to ...*iskik*.

Notes to Text 27

Cyclical *âtalôhkân*. Recorded c. September 1957 at CDE's home at Albany Post. Titles by Agnes Hunter (C) and CDE (E). For a fuller version of the same story, cf. text 19:8-9.

1 i.e., *kikiskên'tên*.

2 *kîsiswêw* is probably intended here and in 27:3 as shown by *kâ-kîsiswât* in the sentence which follows it there. The narrator's enunciation was not always distinct.

3 The grammatical sequence is troubled.

4 According to James Gunner, *pâhkân* 'presently' is used like *pâtimâ* at Moose Factory, in the sense of 'until'. The narrator showed many characteristics of Moose Cree.

5 *pîmisi-* VAI 'have a twisted grain (i.e., a tree, and so be hard to chop)'. *pîmâskosi-* VAI may be used to characterize a good, thick trunk or a twisted paddle or sled; *pîmâskwan-* VII may similarly describe an axe-handle.

6 Examples of compounding involving pronouns and particles abound, e.g., *k'-îškw'-ânima-tôtawakiht* 'after we've done that to it' (50:1); *kâ-iškwâ-mistahi-kotawêt* 'after he had kindled a big fire' (19:7); *ê-ispîhc'-êlikohk-mâtot* 'from crying so hard' (46:2); *kâ-k'-antê-misiw'-êhtâlici* 'who were all there' (56:5).

7 The narrator draws out the length of the final vowel.

8 The recording is unclear but sounds like *anihi mêna pimîliw*. The narrator has possibly corrected the ending of *anihi* to *-mêniw* and intended to say *animêliw pimîliw* 'that grease'.

9 The narrator probably began to say *wacask* 'muskrat'.

10 i.e., *-mâkwahpitên*.

11 cf. *wêwêpâliwêpaliho-* VAI or *wêwêpâliwêstâ-* VAI-T 'wag the tail'.

12 Metathesis for *animêliw*.

13 The narrator could have used *môna … âpacihtâw*, referring to *alimêniw* [sic] *pimîniw* above.

14 An obvious break in the construction. *êyâšawakwâškwatiw* for *ayâšiwakwâškwatiw* VAI (redupl.) 'he jumped back and forth across'.

15 cf. *pitihkwahtâ-* VAI 'make a roaring noise (as a child playing)'; *pitihkwêmakan-* VII 'make a roaring noise (as a motor, plane)'.

16 On listening to the recording, the narrator inserted the preverb *pêci-* immediately before the verb: *ê-kî-pêci-šîwatêt*.

17 The passage is hard to interpret from the recording.

18 i.e., *kî-nišiwanâcihitisow*.

19 The speech is rapid and unclear.

Notes to Text 28

Cyclical *âtalôhkân*. Recorded c. September 1957 at CDE's home at Albany Post. Titles by CDE, with the Cree checked by Agnes Hunter; literal translation of the Cree title: 'Weesakechahk makes a person who will live forever'. Cf. also Text 7:9-11.

1 The narrator changes his mind and substitutes *itwêwak manâ* 'they said' for *itikowak manâ* 'he told them'.

2 According to James Gunner, this should perhaps be *anihi*.

Notes to Text 29

Cyclical *âtalôhkân*. Recorded c. 1955 at CDE's home at Albany Post. Titles by CDE, with the Cree checked by Agnes Hunter. Cf. also Texts 4, 16.

1 i.e., *anihi*.

2 i.e., *kâ-wî-kapastawêpanik*, the interpretation of a Cree listener, and the form

required by the grammar. If the reading is *-kapastawêpinahk*, *kêkwâniw* would be expected to follow. The recording is rapid and unclear at this point.

3 cf. *tôhtôskipit-* VTI 'nibble away at s.t. (of a fish or seal)'. The narrator started to use *tôhtôhkipit-* VTI 'widen it (e.g., his mouth)', but finally got the word he wanted. Note the palatalization.

4 i.e., *misiwê wîla, itwêw cahkâpêš.*

5 The recording appears to be *n'ka-kî-mâtâhâw* 'I'll be able to see' ; but *ka-* makes little sense here and probably represents the beginning of a construction abandoned by the narrator.

6 i.e., *awênihkâna.*

7 *kôtawi-pêhtâ-* VAI 'get tired waiting', contracted at Albany Post to *'tôwi-pêhtâ-*.

8 Both the words and actual construction are dubious. The speech on the recording is rapid, poorly enunciated and hard to follow.

9 *pasatah-* VTI 'wear a trail by constant use' (used only of a rabbit who travels back and forth on the same trail). For tracks made by a deer or moose the term is *omayân-* VTI 'make fresh signs'. For a beaver (which seldom travels on the surface in winter) the term is *pimiskanawê-* VAI.

10 Presumably a contraction for *-tâpakwêwat* (relational inflection).

Notes to Text 30

tipâcimôwin: aetiological account. Recorded between 1957 and 1958 at CDE's home at Albany Post. Titles by Agnes Hunter (C) and CDE (E).

Ghost River flows into the Albany River about one hundred miles inland from James Bay.

1 Note *nân'taw'palîstaw-* VTA 'be after s.o.' (cf. *natawipalîstaw-* VTA 'make war on s.o.'), as contrasted with *nân'tawâpam-* VTA 'look for s.o. (without hostile intent)'.

2 *nâtawêw-* NA 'an Iroquois' (*nâtoyêw* heard at Albany). The narrator uses the term *nâtawiyêw-* (cf. *nâtawiyêwastimw-* NA 'a hunting dog'); the usual term is *nâtawêw-*. The Iroquois were reported to tunnel under the river banks and come up suddenly in the settlement, surprising the people and felling them with arrows, spears and tomahawks. Many of the small creeks and gullies running to the bank are attributed to tunnelling operations (cf. *wâtihkê-* VAI 'make a tunnel', *wâti-* NI 'tunnel', pl. *wâta*) of the Iroquois in a bygone day.

3 cf. *tân' êspîš-âpatoyâhk* 'how far are we from each other?'

4 The narrator may have said *tânt'-îhtâcik* 'how far they were on their way', imagining himself in the position of the on-going Iroquois. This bothered James Gunner, who insisted that the Iroquois must have been coming towards the Cree, and thus wanted to substitute *tânt' ê-pêci-ihtâcik.*

5 i.e., *pimâpolo-* VAI 'drift downstream'.

6 i.e., probably *manâ.*

7 i.e., *-awahkâtâcik.*

Notes to Text 31

tipâcimôwin: action tale. Recorded in 1956 or 1957 at CDE's home at Albany Post. Titles by CDE, with the Cree checked by Agnes Hunter.

This story is told of two men who unexpectedly met a polar bear in an area further south than such animals are usually found.

1 An apparent anacoluthon; *wâpask* should probably be in the obviative.

Notes to Text 32

tipâcimôwin. Recorded 1956 or 1957 at CDE's home at Albany Post. Titles by CDE, with the Cree corrected by Agnes Hunter.

Notes to Text 33

tipâcimôwin. Recorded 1956 or 1957 at CDE's home at Albany Post. Titles by Agnes Hunter (C), and by CDE and John Wynne (E). This story might be sub-titled, 'How the Albany Post dog-team beat the Attawapiskat team in a race'.

1 cf. *kotaskaw-* VTA (with elision of initial *ko-*). The recording is not entirely clear; but a Cree listener interpreted it as *-paskilâtôpanîk* rather than *-taskatitôpanîk*, which Agnes Hunter identified as from an archaic form, *kotaskitito-* VAI 'try to beat each other'.

Notes to Text 34

tipâcimôwin: action tale. Recorded 1956 or 1957 at CDE's home at Albany Post. Titles by CDE, with the Cree checked by Agnes Hunter.

1 i.e., *-nanâtawimôswêyâhk*; reduplicated from *natawimôswê-*.
2 i.e., *nikî-*.
3 The narrator here produced a realistic imitation of a moose cough, roughly transcribed as [mhɔ̃ɔ̃ mɔ̃hɔ̃hɔ̃m]. Not to be confused with the bawl of the female which is mimicked by hunters to attract moose, the 'cough' or 'gawunk' is the bull's response to the female call.
4 i.e., *pâskisikanihk* 'in the guns'.
5 i.e., *kâ-kihcihtâyâhk*.

Notes to Text 35

tipâcimôwin: action tale. Recorded 1956 or 1957 at CDE's home at Albany Post. Titles by Agnes Hunter (C) and CDE (E).

1 i.e., *-nanâtawâmôswêt*; reduplicated from *natawimôswê-*.
2 i.e., *animêniw ê-'nâtawâmôswêt*.
3 i.e., *'ci-sîhkacit*.
4 i.e., *ispî*.
5 i.e., *wâwâc*.
6 i.e., *ê-âhkwacišinici*.
7 i.e., *ana ililiw*.
8 Note the use of *anta ohci, môs'-wayânihk*, which is better than *anihi môs'-wayânihk*.

Notes to Text 36

tipâcimôwin: action tale. Recorded 1956 or 1957 at CDE's home at Albany Post. Titles by Agnes Hunter (C) and CDE (E).

1 i.e., *ê-wîcêwak*.
2 i.e., *niwâpamânân*.
3 i.e., alternative Albany area form for *niskâtinâna*.
4 cf. *otatâmišim-* VTA (redupl.) 'bang s.o. on the ground', *otatâmâpiskišim-* VTA 'bang s.o. again and again on the rocks'; to hit once on the rocks would be *otâmâpiskišim-*.

Notes to Text 37

tipâcimôwin: action tale. Recorded in 1956 or 1957 at CDE's home at Albany Post. Titles by CDE, with the Cree checked by Agnes Hunter.

1 i.e., *nitôwanihikaninâniy* 'our traps'.

2 i.e., *ê-natawâpahtahkik*.

3 i.e., *otôwanahikaniwâwa*.

4 i.e., *nînanân* (lit., 'we that other one').

5 i.e., *ê-kî-itohtêyân*. The narrator was following the standard practice of taking a short-cut home after setting out his traps in a wide arc or zig-zag over his trapping grounds. (The zig-zag pattern comes from following the creeks when trapping mink, otter or beaver. Ridges are followed for trapping marten; and in this area these, like the muskeg, run north and south.)

6 *paškosi-* VAI, *paškwâ-* VII 'be clean' (e.g., a mink with hardly any fur). In this case the muskeg was clean as there was no vegetation floating on the surface of the water. Cf. *paškwâliwê-* VAI '(of a mink) have a hairless tail'; *paškwâtihpê-* VAI (of a man) or *paškostikwânê-* VAI 'be bald'. This latter can, however, also be used of a goose or a dog. Cf. also *paškwahamaw-* VTA 'cut s.o.'s hair' and *kâ-paškwahamâkêt* NA 'a barber'. Distinguish between *paškosi-* VAI 'be clean' and *paskisi-* VAI 'have a big mesh (of a net)'.

7 The narrator could have said *tântê kê-ihtakwahkipan*.

8 *cîkahotisôtokwê* would be expected here.

9 Note the change of construction; *môna* is carried over to *kaškihtâwak*.

10 *n'tašêhtêhamân* 'back-track' (cf. *ašêhtêhamâ-* VAI), or, alternatively, *nikîwêhâmân nimêskanaw* might have been expected. The locative, *nimêskanâhk*, would also be acceptable with either of the above verbs. The narrator's usage sounded to another Cree listener "like a White-Man talking Cree", although Cree is the narrator's first language.

11 i.e., *nititênihtên*.

12 *sâkaskêh-* VTI 'come out of the high bush (into the muskeg)'; cf. *sâkâmaciwê-* VAI 'come up over the top of the bank'.

Notes to Text 38

tipâcimôwin: action tale. Recorded 1956 or 1957 at CDE's home at Albany Post. Titles by Agnes Hunter (C) and CDE (E); literal translation of the Cree title: 'Having found again his gun which he had lost'.

1 The contrast is with *n'timišîhk*.

2 *paskêyâ-* VII 'branch off (of a river)'; *paskêyâw-* NI 'a branch stream'; cf. *paski* in *paski n'kî-mîlâw pahkwêsikana* 'I gave him part of my flour'; *paski piko niwâpahtên* 'I see only part of it'.

3 The narrator normally produced *wana...* for *wani...*; note the interchange of /i/ and /a/.

4 i.e., *ê-walastâyân nitôwanahikan*.

5 *apihkanihk* 'on the thwart (of the canoe)' sounds better; this is the regular practice of persons taking a gun in a canoe. The narrator's usage suggests that the canoe was bottom up.

6 i.e., *ê-kakwê-otinamân*.

7 i.e., *manâ nititênihtên*.

8 *kêtâspisopaliho-* VAI 'undress oneself in a hurry'. The common term for 'take off one's clothes, undress' is *kêtâspiso-* VAI.

Notes to Text 39

tipâcimôwin: reminiscence. Recorded 1957 or 1958 at CDE's home at Albany Post. Titles by CDE, with the Cree checked by Agnes Hunter; literal translation of the Cree title: 'Working in the south'.

During the Second World War, about 1941, the tannery in Acton, Ontario sent word north that men were required. Applicants for relief from the settlements of Albany Post, Fort Albany and Attawapiskat were often referred to these job openings. The present account is by one of the (then) younger men from Albany Post who took employment in Acton for a while.

1 i.e., *êkoši mâka iskali-pipon*.
2 i.e., *n'kî-papâ-wanahikân*.
3 i.e., *kici-natawê-nanâtaw'-âpatisiyân* 'that I should go off looking for work'.
4 i.e., *ê-natawê-âpatisiyân*.
5 i.e., *kâ-iši-kîšinihcik*; cf. *kâ-iši-kîšinâkaniwicik* 'where they are tanned', i.e., the hides; cf. *kîšin-*.
6 i.e., *kâ-kî-ihtâyân*.
7 The syntax hangs very loosely together. Another Cree speaker listening to the recording remarked (about the grammar), "Should be better connections than that." The style of narration, however, was ruminative and conducive to anacolutha.
8 *ilikohk* here is almost synonymous with *ispîš*; cf. *ê'kwan' ispîš nipahik* or *ê'kwan' ilikohk nipahik* 'That's enough that you've killed'.
9 i.e., *kêkwânihkân*.

Notes to Text 40

tipâcimôwin: reminiscence. Recorded at Albany Post, date of recording unknown. Titles based on text; literal translation of the Cree title: 'Once long ago'.

1 *wêskac'-ililiwak* 'the old-timers'; a common expression in contexts such as *wêskac'-ililiwak ê-ihtiwâspan* 'the old-timers used to do' or *wêskac'-ililiwak ê-ihtiwâkopanê* 'the old-timers had always done'.
2 Note the use of /r/ in borrowed names and of intrusive /t/ in *hêntriy* 'Henry'. The men named would probably have been travelling with their families. Hence the preceding statement, *ê-mihcêtiyâhk* 'there being a good many of us'.
3 A Cree listener interpreted the recording as *ê-papâmâšihkêyâhk* 'as we were battling our way'.
4 Contraction of *kî-nipahâkaniwanwak* 'there were slain'.
5 A wigwam for four families would have a radius from the fire's edge to the edge of the tent about enough to accommodate a six-foot person from head to foot, i.e., about fifteen feet overall in diameter. Families are generally related and get on well with each other. The wigwam would be made of canvas, each family contributing.
6 i.e., *n'tâpacihânân*.
7 Probably *êy-ocipitak*.
8 The recording is unclear at this point.
9 The recording is unclear at this point.
10 *askonâk* appears to be an alternative for *iskonâk*; note the interchange of /i/ and /a/.
11 i.e., *êkâ ê-ohci-âpacihtâyâhk*.
12 Another Cree listener interpreted the recording as *ê-pimâcihocik* 'in their making a living'.
13 i.e., *alitaw-iškotêw*.

411

14 This may be a reference to the government family allowance.
15 i.e., *niwîcêwâkan*.
16 *kâ-kî-tipâcimoyân* might have been expected.

Notes to Text 41

Conversation. Recorded 19 July 1965 at Gabriel Kiokee's home at Moosonee.

Recording of this conversation (and the two that follow) was agreed to by the participants, who are identified by initials. Gabriel Kiokee, originally from Attawapiskat, is a speaker of Swampy Cree (n-dialect), while Joel Linklater displays the mixed n-l usage characteristic of Kashechewan Cree. The tape recorder, a UHER 4000, was operated by Joel Linklater most of the time since CDE was not present throughout. The recording picks up a conversation already taking place.

1 The stone marker at the Ontario Northland Railway line at Moosonee, on which there is a long inscription in verse.

2 The speaker probably intended *kî-iši-ayaminâniwan* or *kî-iši-nakiškâtonâniwan* 'that's where they had the gathering'.

3 i.e., *namatâwisatamohtâniwan-* VII 'be built out towards a body of water'; the reference is to the Ontario Northland Railway right of way.

4 The construction is continued from *ê-ayamihtâyâhk* 'reading (the names of) those who were killed'.

5 The reference is to the Roman Catholic bishop; the term used for an Anglican bishop is *kihci-ayamihêwikimâw*.

6 With rising intonation, here expressing polite interest.

7 *ê-kî-tipâcimostawât* should perhaps be *ê-kî-tipâcimostâkot* 'he had been told by an old man'.

8 i.e., a person of consequence.

9 *kwâkran* or *kwâkwan* 'Cochrane', 185 miles to the South. *pimitamon-* VII 'cross (of one trail crossing another)'.

10 *kihci-* probably for *kihciwê-otâpâna* 'real trains'; i.e., the transcontinental, not the Cochrane to Moosonee local.

11 *mošê piko anihi* 'nothing but those things'.

12 *papâmipici-* VAI 'travel about with all one's belongings, move camp from place to place lock, stock and barrel'; cf. *pimiwatê-* VAI 'carry'.

13 cf. *pakwantaw* 'trivially, idle, not seriously'; *X 'kwantaw* 'any old kind of X'.

14 *tawikahikê-* VAI 'make a clearing'; cf. *tawâ-* VII 'be room', *tawikahikan-* NI 'township line, frontier line'; cf. also *paškokahikê-* VAI 'clear land'; *paškopit-* VTA 'pluck s.o. (goose, duck, etc.)'.

15 *ohwâsak* NA pl. 'horses'. The word is fairly well established in the Moose area.

16 i.e., *kwayask*.

17 Apparently some children wanted to come into the house at this point to see what was going on.

18 *oš* 'you know', suggests that the adressee had not realized what was alleged; cf. *kišâstaw oša lôtin* 'Oh my! It's blowing (which I hadn't realized)'.

19 *tawâskokahikan-* NI synonym to *tawikahikan-*, above.

20 *pakwataskamik* 'lonely land, solitary land'; cf. *papakwatêliht-* VTI 'be lonesome', e.g., *ê-papakwatêlihtamân ani wêhci-išilawiyân* 'I was lonesome; that's the reason I busied myself about'.

21 Nasalized with rising intonation, signifying that the listener is following the story.

22 Note the change from *'ma takwan* to *'matêw*; another Cree speaker listening to the

recording preferred *'ma takwanôpan ihtâwin.*

23 People probably caught chills which turned to pneumonia.

24 *môšak pêyakwanohk ihtâwak* or *pêyakwahtâwak (tânt')* *ê-ši-tašîhkêcik* 'they always stay in one place'. Cf. *pêpîtoš ihtâwak* or *pêpîtoš iši-tašîhkêwak* 'they live in various places' in the sense of either 'they move from place to place' or 'each one of them lives in a different place'. Cf., however, *âyâhcihtâwak tânt' ê-'ši-tašîhkêcik* 'they move their living quarters from place to place'.

25 i.e., *-iskw-ošihtâ-* VAI-T 'make it to an end'.

26 The statement sounds like sarcasm.

27 i.e., the present settled housing at Moosonee.

28 *mošê*, lit. 'freely', here means 'for next to nothing', as contrasted with present wages. On listening to the recording, Joel Linklater suggested *kêkât mošê* would have been preferable.

29 i.e., *ôta.*

30 *ê-ohtisîwâspan* (3p. conjunct indicative preterit) was probably intended by the speaker, who then selected a different verb: *-tipaham'wâwatipanênak* (VAI-T 3p. conjunct dubitative preterit) 'you must have been paying them'.

31 3p. independent dubitative preterit.

32 i.e., *ê'kô wâsa ani.*

33 i.e., in bringing the railroad up to provide work for many people; many of the section gangs are composed of men from the northern settlements.

34 The word probably would have been *ê-ohcipanit.*

35 The final /ê/ on *misiwê* is sharply reduced phonetically in length.

36 *kîšâc* IPC 'ahead of time'; cf. *nisâwîh-* (VTA) *kîšâc*, *nisâwîhtâ-* (VAI-T) *kîšâc* 'gather up small details ahead of time'.

37 i.e., *kici-ati-ohci-pimâtisinici.*

38 Anacoluthon: 'a person's thinking … they will have it … when I'm an old man'; the grammar matches the desultory thought sequence.

39 Enthusiastic assent, not laughter.

40 *awênihkânak* would be expected, since the reference is to the tourists on the Ontario Northland Railway Sunday excursions to Moosonee and Moose Factory.

41 Private boat owners make a few casual dollars ferrying tourists between Moosonee and Moose Factory.

42 i.e., *kici-kî-ohci-pimâtisit.*

43 At Fraserdale on the Abitibi.

44 The recording has *kâ-yhtakwahk*, which, on replay, was repeated by the other speaker as *kâ-yš'-îhtakwahk*. Joel Linklater was working at Little Long on the Metagami River, about 150 miles southwest of Moosonee.

45 *alîkišak* would be expected. The term is probably a calque. Note the dialect mixture with /l/.

46 *tiskôso-* VAI 'have a crooked back' (in this case from a rock having fallen on it during blasting); cf. *tasôso-* VAI 'catch oneself in a trap (when something accidentally falls on one)', e.g., *mistikwa kî-tasôsow, ê'kwani wêhci-išinâkosit* 'he was pinned by a falling tree, that's why he looks that way'.

47 i.e., *ê-pimišihkik.*

48 i.e., *wêsa.*

49 A stone marker like the one at the end of steel at Moosonee stands on top of the Fraserdale Dam.

50 *âniskôcêhtâ-* VAI-T 'connect them, join them together'. Cf. *âniskôh-, âniskôhtâ-,*

âniskôtâpê-. According to one informant the sense is somewhat like that of *ê-'ti-lahkamohtâniwahk* 'extending it', or *ê-'ti-kihtamohtâniwahk* 'starting out afresh, on a fresh lap'. This latter form was found to be strange by two further native speakers consulted, one of whom preferred *ê-kihcihtâniwahk*.

51 At the end of each lap a stone marker is erected. Four such lengths of line were laid under separate contracts between 1919 and 1931 to bring the railway from Cochrane to Moosonee.

52 The idea is that there must be a main stone some place where all the names are recorded from all over the country. Cf. *mâmaw âlimôtahtâw* 'Let's get together and talk it over'; *mâmaw âlimôtahtâw ôhi* 'Let's talk about (these) several things at the same time'.

53 *môna nêsta* is carried over from above.

54 i.e., *kakîšiwâ-* 'be warm every here and there', reduplicated from *kîšiwâ-* VII 'be warm'; cf. *âskaw-âskaw kakîšiwâyâw* 'it is warm every now and then'.

55 The recording is unclear at this point; it sounds like *kâ-wanastêk* 'which is set up', but on replay a Cree speaking listener interpreted the sequence as *antê* 'there'.

56 *šihkâpêšin-* VAI 'be tapered down' (i.e., the cement rock). *asiniy* probably refers to the concrete of which the dam is built; *asiniy* is commonly used for concrete, from the fuller form, *asiniy kâ-tispahwâkaniwit* 'stone which is mixed'.

57 cf. *nakahw-* VTA, *nakah-* VTI 'reinforce s.o./s.t.'; cf. also *nakâyâskohw-* VTA 'reinforce s.o.' (e.g., a tree which has fallen over and which someone wants to save), *nakâyâskoh-* VTI 'reinforce s.t. (a wooden object)'.

58 The accident in question had happened only a year earlier. Gabriel Kiokee probably thought that this had taken place at Fraserdale some years before.

59 The portion in parentheses was accidentally omitted from the recording and supplied later by Joel Linklater, who had been explaining to Gabriel Kiokee at the time the interest in recording his conversation.

60 Solecism; cf. *išikîšwê-* VAI 'speak a dialect, language'.

61 The recording is unclear at this point.

62 Moose Cree shows certain differences, both grammatical and lexical, from the usage of the Albany area and that of Attawapiskat. The latter two, however, are both Swampy Cree dialects and almost identical.

63 i.e., *tânika itê*.

Notes to Text 42

Conversation. Recorded 19 July 1965 at Gabriel Kiokee's home at Moosonee; cf. Text 41. Joel Linklater later assisted with the transcription and supplied additional contextual information (such as manual gestures).

1 Gabriel Kiokee had been a deck-hand on boats about James Bay. *wînipêk* 'The Bay, James Bay', translated by the informant as 'stinking water'; the name is applied to more than one large, brackish body of water (cf. also Lake Winnipeg, Manitoba); cf. *wînâ-* VII 'be dirty, unclean; stink', and the near-synonyms *wînimâkwan-*, *wihcêkimâkwan-*. Cf. also the expression used when a storm is threatening: *wihcêkinâkwan kîšik* 'the sky looks dirty'. The term is also used of a sore or cut which appears infected: *wihcêkinâkwan, pîhcipômakan mâškôc* 'it looks dirty, maybe poison is setting in'.

2 i.e., *atoskam* 'in spite of everything, willy-nilly'.

3 o- (3rd person singular subject), VII independent dubitative.

4 The recording is too rapid and unclear to allow for a fully certain transcription.

5 i.e., *kâ-ati-ati-kâhcitinamân* [*sic*] 'I kept on getting it'.

6 i.e., *ôma ispîš*.

7 The recording is unclear at this point.

8 What is meant is that only a limited amount of fur can be taken because of the conservation laws.

9 i.e., *kêkwân*.

10 According to another Cree speaker, *ê-mihcêtihk* 'plenty, plentiful' would be better usage.

11 i.e., *tân' înikohk* 'how much'; in contraction, /i/ is here nasalized.

12 *ê-kî-kakêpâtisit* might be a better reading.

13 Another Cree speaker interpreted the recording as *kâ-ayasinihcik šôliyânak* 'when coins are held in the hand'. The speech is rapid and the recording unclear at this point.

14 Another Cree speaker interpreted the recording as *ayâpišîš* 'a little bit at a time'.

15 Loan from English; the usual Cree term for a moving-picture show is *kâ-cahkâstêpalihcikâniwahk* 'that which goes along casting a shadow'; cf. 42:12, below.

16 i.e., *oša*; note the intervocalic /w/ glide.

17 lit., 'who want too much of everything to be used'.

18 Note the variation in Joel Linklater's usage from ...*panihcikâniwan* to ...*palihcikâniwan*, above.

19 cf. *n'kî-kosâpêyâhokon, wêsâ oša ê-kî-pôsihtâsoyân* 'I got swamped by the waves, because I was freighting too much, *you see*'.

20 i.e., *mêšikwani-tipiskâw wîna*.

21 i.e., Moose Factory Island.

22 The Canadian Legion hall, used regularly for film shows.

23 *kanawênimat* translated as though the verb were in the independent indicative in a principal clause by James Gunner, a highly bilingual informant.

24 *kihci-okimâw-* NA 'the government'.

25 i.e., *kêkwânihkâniw*.

26 *âpacihikawi-* 'do a job for, be employed by someone'; *ilâpacihikawi-* refers to a specific job.

27 Another Cree speaker interpreted the recording as something like *êtakipan*, although it is not clear whether the object of the verb is Joel Linklater's son or Gabriel Kiokee's.

28 On listening to the recording, Joel Linklater noted this as a mistake that was corrected a few words further on. The derived passive with ...*âkaniwi-* is generally preferred to the inflected form for indefinite subject.

29 The recording is unclear at this point.

30 Joel Linklater was concerned that CDE, for whom the conversation was recorded, was interested in getting authentic Cree usage.

31 i.e., *apwoy*.

32 On listening to the recording, an older member of the community felt that *ohci* should have been added after *piko* to complete the sense and structure properly. Joel Linklater agreed, with reservations.

33 cf. Gabriel Kiokee's remark (41:20) about his own unmixed speech.

34 Probably *kin'tôpitên*.

35 At Big Lake, up-river from Attawapiskat.

36 Verb used of hauling a toboggan and also for hauling a canoe upstream with a 200

foot tracking line from the bank.

37 i.e., $ 15 (plus supplies) for the whole trip, NOT $ 15 a day.

38 n.b., hypercorrection *hundred-fifty found*. The weight-load suggests toboggan rather than canoe hauling. A twenty-foot canoe would take about 1,000 lbs. of freight.

39 Paradoxically, Joel Linklater is bilingual while Gabriel Kiokee at this point had very little English.

40 At the turn of the century dogs are reported to have been scarce among Indian trappers around Moose Factory and Moosonee. A Hudson's Bay Company servant would have perhaps one or two. An Indian trapper might have one dog to help him rout out beaver.

41 There is contact between Cree speakers on the west coast of James Bay and Ojibwa speakers inland. *šânkwâ*, based on Albany Post, Fort Albany and Attawapiskat *šânk*, is probably from Ojibwa (cf. *šânkwesswi*), as contrasted with Moose Cree *šâkitât* 'nine'.

42 In addition to travelling empty, the existence of the same trail back would help.

43 A second informant interpreted the recording as *ôma wêsa ati-išinâkwan wîna sîpiy* 'for the river gets to look like this'.

44 *wâwâkatamon-* VII 'be a crooked road'; *wâwâkistikwêyâ-* VII 'be a crooked river'.

45 The Hudson's Bay Company probably considered it more economical to use the river, crooked though it was, than to cut a trail through the bush.

46 The recording has either *âtawîn' âpišîš* or *âpihtaw wîn' âpišîš* 'half, a little'.

47 *milotêwêyâ-, milwatêwêyâ-* VII 'be a hard snow crust' (melted by the spring sun during the day and frozen at night), cf. *maškawitêwêyâ-* VII, a near-synonym.

48 The recording is difficult to follow here.

49 *nêmiskâw* 'Namiskau', about one hundred miles up the Rupert's River in Québec.

50 *wêhciy-âlimahk* constructed with *kê'wâ'hkân*.

51 Another Cree speaker, listening to the tape, felt that *ê-wêhtisit* would be better Cree.

52 Probably *êhê* was intended.

53 Mild sarcasm.

54 *kî-masinahamawikopanê* 'if (only) he had written to me' might have been expected here.

55 The reading might perhaps be *n'kî-ihtâhtay* 'I used to be, I used to stay'.

56 On listening to the recording, Joel Linklater supplied the following exchange, missing from the recording:

    JL: *êk' oš' ânima?* 'That one was it?'

    GK: *êk' oš' ânima nîki.* 'That one was my house.'

57 i.e., *kâ-wî-išicišahwâkaniwispan* 'who was going to be sent'.

58 The speaker probably started to say *wîwa* 'his wife'.

59 i.e., *nitihtâhtay*.

60 Rather than pay relief and supply tenting canvas for unemployed Indian trappers, the Indian Agency encouraged people on the reservation at Attawapiskat to build their own houses, remunerating them with rations. The Cree term for Indian Agent is *šôniyânikimâw*.

61 The recording is extremely muffled at this point: phonetically [ŋuŋéne] but clearly intended as *kikiskên'tên*, and interpreted as such by Joel Linklater.

62 The saw at the Roman Catholic mission was run by steam. *pimiy* was probably the oil for the bearings, since the mill was powered by slabs of wood left from the sides

of the logs at the time of squaring.

63 cf. *tipahamôtilâkaniwan* 'he is charged (with costs)'. According to Joel Linklater, Gabriel Kiokee stammered here and intended to say *môna ohci-otinâkaniwanwak* 'they were not taken'.

64 The customary practice of the Roman Catholic mission at Fort Albany, south of Attawapiskat, was for the mill to cut logs brought by the Indians on the understanding that one of every two logs was for the person bringing it, the other for the mission. By supplying oil, the Indian Agent in this case was presumably able to retain all the logs.

65 *kâ-tahkwâpêt* 'short trace', as contrasted with *kâ-kinwâpêt* 'long trace'. The carrying trace, *mîskwâpin-* NI, known as a 'tump-line' or 'portage-strap', was made from soft horse-hide. It was also called the 'hauling-trace', *otâpâniyâpiy-* NI, when used for a toboggan.

66 Joel Linklater drew a distinction between *išikîšwê-* VAI 'speak such and such a language', *kîšawê-* VAI 'have fully grown hair', and *kišawê-* VAI 'speak loudly, make a loud noise' (probably for *kišiwê-*).

67 The form recorded is [kwa·žen]; beginning with a high level, the pitch descends rapidly in the middle of the first syllable to rise again in the second.

68 The recorded line is *kêka môna 'wênihkân tâpwê mâka*. Note the changed word order in the repetition by the second speaker.

69 *aspin* here carries the meaning 'contrary to expectation'. In giving examples of the use of *aspin*, James Gunner, whose perceptive assistance was repeatedly invaluable, cited *kišâspin* as including *aspin*.

70 Immediately in front of the main settlement at Attawapiskat the river is dotted with shoals and banks. The deep water is on the far side.

71 In the gutway between Attawapiskat Island and a smaller island, the landing can be done, but only at high tide.

72 i.e., *oti*.

73 The recording sounds like *pâtâ*.

74 i.e., *ê-mišâk*.

75 i.e., *ê-mêkwâhkahk*.

76 Speech hesitation on the recording: *êy-at'... n'...'takwahk*.

77 The Roman Catholic mission put a dam at the outlet to bring the water-level up.

78 The local English name for the tree while green is *juniper*. After a fire, when the bark is burnt off and the wood dries out, the dead, standing juniper is then known locally as a *tamarack*. Elsewhere, *tamarack* is the normal English name corresponding to Cree *wâkinâkan*. As a verb, *wâkinâkaniskâ-* VII carries the meaning 'be a juniper bluff, be a juniper ridge'. As a noun (NI) in the locative, *wâkinâkaniskâhk* may be translated 'among the junipers'.

    Most ridges of juniper (and others, except poplars) run north and south, like the swamps. Poplars are found along the shoreline. Rock ridges in the Moose area, on the other hand, run mostly east and west. This gives rise to numerous portages on the rivers.

79 This was the Cree name given to the Roman Catholic mission settlement known in French as Lac Ste-Anne.

80 i.e., where the Roman Catholic mission is established. Most of the mission personnel is French Canadian.

81 Analysis of the latter part of this word is doubtful, *...ihtin-* or *...atin-*.

82 i.e., for moose to feed on.

83 *mâmihk* 'down-river'; i.e., at the air base then located at Moosonee.

84 The recording is unclear at this point.

85 Joel Linklater had worked in the hospital power-plant at Moose Factory for three years and had had experience with chemical water purification.

86 i.e., *tahkwâpihkêyâtokê*.

87 i.e., *ê-nîpihk piko*.

88 i.e., *ôma mâka*.

89 The tape recorder had, in fact, already been running and had picked up the remarks on the rocket ship.

90 The recording is unclear at this point.

91 i.e., *kînistam êko*.

92 A bad limp produces the impression of half-hanging as one walks.

93 The final syllable of *išinihkâsow* is devoiced.

94 *pikinwat* is probably a nick-name for the child also called *Dorothy*.

95 The recording is unclear at this point.

96 The final syllable of *n'k'-êtohtân* is devoiced.

97 i.e., *nâkociy*.

98 The recording is unclear at this point.

99 The reference is probably to comic-papers lying nearby.

Notes to Text 43

Conversation. Recorded 19 July 1965 at Gabriel Kiokee's home at Moosonee; cf. text 41.

Joel Linklater and CDE left the house while Gabriel Kiokee recorded himself and two guests of the family. W1 is used to indicate a woman's voice, and W2 marks a second woman's voice intervening.

1 i.e., *ê'kwâni wêhci-itwêyân*.

2 *sapêt* is a common name for a woman at Attawapiskat, perhaps a contraction of *Elizabeth*.

3 *âniy otih, wîci-kišê-'niniwa* 'Annie's old man, that is' suggests that the writer (or reader) omitted something from the preceding sentence, since *sapêt* is not a man's name.

4 *wîci-kišê-'niniwa*, above, is the subject; an obviative verb form would have been expected.

5 The recording is unclear at this point.

6 Final syllable devoiced.

7 The verb used to describe the early stages of child language is *ayamîšihtâ-* VAI 'make speech sounds without pronouncing words properly, stammer, try to talk back (but get only an occasional word right)'.

8 *kâ-wâpamatipan* refers back to *êšinâkosit*.

9 i.e., *'kwâni*.

10 i.e., *môna wâci*.

11 *-mâmîmicimêcik* probably should be *-mani-mîcimêcik; cf. mani-mâcîswê-* VAI 'buy matches', *mani-wîlâhcikê-* VAI 'buy clothes'. On replay, both Joel Linklater and James Gunner felt the term should be *ê-nâci-mîcimêcik* 'going for food'. Alfred Wynne, who assisted with the transcription, preferred *ê-kwâpahi-mîcimêcik* 'scooping for food', almost certainly a flash-back to the days when flour and tea were imported in bulk.

12 The /h/ onset which appears throughout this section is due to the reading style of the speaker.

13 i.e., *manâ otâni*. Joel Linklater interpreted the recording as *manâ oš'âni*.
14 Relational inflection.
15 Relational inflection.
16 Note that the form is not *côsip*, as more commonly heard.
17 The recording is unclear at this point.
18 *'kwêšic* is a contraction (and probably an imitation of child language) *iskwêšiš*.
19 Relational inflection.
20 *ana kâ-a...* refers to CDE. A third Cree speaker listening to the recording interpreted *n'kî-pêhtâk* in the following line as *kê-pêhtâsk* 'who will hear you'. The reading retained seems to fit the context.
21 The recording is unclear at this point.
22 The recording is very noisy and unclear at this point.
23 *ana* probably refers to the child.
24 *siyâkên*, Moose Cree *siyâkêl*. A hunter who had not much meat left might say to another who asked for some, *môla mistahi n'tayân, siyâkêl isa ka-mîlitin* 'I haven't much left, but I'll give you a little at least'.
25 Doll's name, *titima*, palatalized in child language.
26 i.e., child language for *nipâw*; cf. *pâw*, below.
27 i.e., child language for *âhkosiw* 'she is sick'.
28 *awa* refers to CDE, who had returned to the house.
29 i.e., *ayâw*, with raising of initial /a/ to /ê/ before /y/.
30 The speaker probably points towards the microphone plug insert on the recorder. The recording is quite indistinct at this point.
31 i.e., *piko ê-itiht*.
32 *mêmê* 'rock-a-bye'; cf. *mêmêpiso-* VAI 'swing a hammock or suspended cradle'. A mother lulling a baby to sleep will often croon, *mêmê, mêmê, mêmê, mêmê*, etc.
33 The reference is to a group of people outside.
34 *awa* refers to CDE.
35 i.e., the tape recorder, which Gabriel Kiokee, in fact, operated with great effectiveness the first time.
36 The recording continues, much of it quite unclear.

Notes to Text 44
tipâcimôwin: reminiscence and historical narrative. Recorded in 1958 at Moose Factory. Titles based on text (with addition of place name) (C), and by the narrator (E).

This narrative was first written in Cree syllabics, then read into the recorder. The narrator uses a slow, careful reading style, with a literary rather than conversational production of many forms. An interesting account of the same event was published in *The Beaver*, vol. 1, no. 4, January 1922, p.15, under the title, 'A Seaplane Visits Moose Factory'. It is interesting to have a complementary record of the same event in both oral and written history, and sincere appreciation is expressed to D.H. Pentland for bringing this account to the editor's attention.
1 i.e., *-pimihlâmakahk*.
2 i.e., *ninîkihikwak*.
3 So called because the tendon in his ankle was short and he walked only on the fore-part of his foot.
4 i.e., *kêkwânihkân*. *kêkwânihkâniliw* might have been expected with *ômêliw*. Note the agreement of the next two verbs with the proximate form, but agreement for

obviative after *ê-kanawâpahtahkik* in the next sentence.

5 i.e., *-ihkihk*. Final /k/ is dropped colloquially in Moose Cree; cf. *tân' êhki'*.

6 The verbal form would be *mêkwâ-nîpinôpan mêkwâc ôma kâ-ihkih'* 'it was midsummer when this happened'.

Notes to Text 45

Non-cyclical *âtalôhkân*: animal tale. Recorded summer 1958, probably at the narrator's home at Moose Factory. Titles based on text (C), and by the narrator (E); literal translation of the Cree title: 'Why the muskrat's tail looks the way it does'.

1 i.e., *-miloskaminilik*.

2 Archaic vocative form.

Notes to Text 46

Non-cyclical *âtalôhkân*: animal tale. Recorded summer 1958, probably at the narrator's home at Moose Factory. Titles based on text (C), and by the narrator (E).

1 i.e., *nâspic*.

2 i.e., *êlikohk*.

3 A loose compound or, possibly, anacoluthon; cf. 9:7, 22; 19:7; 50:1.

Notes to Text 47

Non-cyclical *âtalôhkân*: animal tale. Recorded summer 1958, probably at the narrator's home at Moose Factory. Titles based on text (C), and by the narrator (E); literal translation of the Cree title: 'Why the loon's feet look the way they do'. Cf. also Text 8:4-5.

1 *omisita*: incorrect form, corrected by Gilbert Faries to *osita*. The translation is deliberately awkward, in imitation of the slip of the tongue in the Cree original.

2 i.e., *ôho mwâkwa*, obviative.

Notes to Text 48

Non-cyclical *âtalôhkân*: animal tale. Recorded summer 1958, probably at the narrator's home at Moose Factory. Titles based on text (C), and by the narrator (E); literal translation of the Cree title: 'Why the bear is short-tailed'.

1 i.e., *nâhtâpwê*.

2 *nisôliw* would be expected.

3 *wî-mâkonatê* 'if you want to grab him' might have been expected in view of the following *wî-kâhcitinatê*.

4 *namêsak* might have been expected; probably attracted into the obviative by preceding *itêlihtam*.

5 *kâ-kîškipalihtwât* might have been expected, indicating use of the force of the whole body. *-kîškipitahk* is suggestive of pulling with the hands.

6 Not to be confused with *akwâkoši-* VAI, *akwâkohtin-* VII 'be rusty, mouldy'.

Notes to Text 49

tipâcimôwin: reminiscence. Recorded summer 1958, probably at the narrator's home at Moose Factory. Titles based on text (C), and by the narrator (E).

1 Another Cree speaker suggested that *ê-'škwâ-kiskisiyân* 'since I first remember' might be more suited to the context of reminiscence.

2 *kinwêš* might have been expected instead of *wêskac ohci*.

3 The narrator came by boat; the form required for travel by canoe would have been

n'kî-pêtaholikawin; cf. *pêtahol-* VTA, *pêtahotâ-* VAI-T 'bring by paddle'; *pêšiw-* VTA, *pêtâ-* VAI-T 'bring'. Note also *-pêšiwikawiyân* for expected *-pêšiwikawiyân*.

4   *walawîmakan-* VII 'go out' (the Old Year).

5   i.e., *nâhtâpwê mâna*.

6   ie., *-nân'tawimôswêcik*.

7   i.e., at the Hudson's Bay Company.

8   The first part of the form is unclear on the recording; *-apihâkaniwicik* would be expected.

9   *wîlistamiwâw* 'they first'. The full set of forms in Moose Cree is:

    1 *nîstam*   1p *nîstaminân*

         21 *kîstaminânaw*

    2 *kîstam*   2p *kîstamiwâw*

    3 *wîstam*   3p *wîstamiwâw*

  The longer 3p form, *wîlistamiwâw*, is heard from some speakers of Moose Cree; cf. *wîstam kata-mîcisow* 'he'll eat first'; *wî(li)stamiwâw kata-mîcisowak* 'they'll eat first'.

10 Obviative. The old-fashioned powder-horn for muzzle-loader guns was known as *pîhcipihkwân-* NA. today the word is applied to cartridges; cf. the currect expression, *niwî-otinikân pîhcipihkwânak* 'I want to buy some shells'.

11 i.e., *êlikohk*.

12 The narrator was probably about to begin a verb in the independent order, i.e., *mâka ati-...*, but changed to the conjunct, *ê-'ti-*.

13 i.e., *makošâniwanôpan*.

14 Probably by the Chief.

15 *pâpihlâ-* VAI 'fly thither'; at the time of the story, planes were not in use in the area and the railroad line had not yet been put through to Moosonee – hence the change to *ê-pâpilispan*.

16 cf. *akwâpicikan-* NI 'seine net'. This is the name for a flat tongue of land which used to be an island, in front of St. Thomas' Church at Moose Factory. It is known in English as 'The Flats'.

17 Slip of the tongue: *kotakiyak* would have been expected.

18 i.e., *êlikohk*.

19 i.e., *kêkwânihkân*.

20 i.e., *n'kî-wâpahtên*.

Notes to Text 50

Description: local technology. Recorded 28 July 1964 at the Moose Fort Indian Residential School. Titles based on text.

1   i.e., *êko*; there is a marked /h/ onset.

2   i.e., *kâ-iskwâ-anima-tôtawakiht*. Note loose composition incorporating the pronoun.

3   i.e., *kici-ihtakwahk*. Note the switch from obviative to proximate.

4   The ends of the hide are overlapped and tied with a string to form a continuous loop, then slung over a pole (inside or outside the house). A shorter stick is then inserted and twisted around, first in one direction, then in the other, until the moose-hide is wrung dry.

5   The brain is added as it boils so that lumps will not form. Where the brain is unavailable, strong yellow soap and coal-oil (kerosene) are used. The soap is then boiled and a little coal-oil is added. The mixture is then dumped into a tub of water.

6 i.e., *nititêhênân*.

7 Snow water is softer.

8 i.e., [stɔ·bɪx] 'on the stove'; loan from English. The Cree word is *iškotêhkân-* NI; locative, *iškotêkânihk*.

9 i.e., *niwakît-astânân*.

10 After the first wringing, the moose-hide is replaced in a tub of clean water, while the brain is simmering on the stove, to make sure the last vestige of blood has left the hide. Otherwise it will not soften. The brain mixture is then poured into the tub of water and the hide allowed to soak another three or four days in the brain mixture. When the mixture can be forced freely through the hide, it is ready to be taken out and wrung again, prior to softening.

11 i.e., *nâsic êlikohk* 'very hard'.

12 According to James Gunner, a contraction of *wâšêyâskohkot-* VTI 'whittle the stick clean'.

13 According to James Gunner, a contraction for *otawicipit-* VTA 'pull away at s.o./s.t.'; cf. *êko mâka wêcipitât*.

14 i.e., *sihtâhkwanak* 'brushwood': a solecism for *cistâhkwan-* NA 'fir tree'; pl. 'fir brushwood'.

15 *êko mâka picêlak kê-kîšinakiht* 'so only then do we begin the finishing stages' might be better stylistically.

16 The process takes about three to five hours of pulling periods of four to five minutes each, alternating with hanging and drying periods of about fifteen minutes each.

17 *nîkânâhtik* 'on the front edge of the stick' might have been expected.

18 Two persons can pull the hide instead of beating it.

19 i.e., *ninânatawâpahtênân*.

20 i.e., from the rotten wood.

21 The hide is laid on a sloping log (about 45°), pointed to dig into the ground, and scraped with a bone tool (*mihkikwat*) to chisel the meat off the hide. The bone tool is often furnished with a wrist strap for ease of operation. The split bone instrument used with a motion like a spoke-shave for getting the top layer of skin off the hide is known as *paškwahcikanâhtik* or *paškwahikan*; cf. 10:5.

22 The speaker corrects *anihi* to *animêliw*. Only the latter part of the form is corrected.

23 i.e., *nîlanân*.

24 James Gunner would have preferred *animêliw* here, followed by *kâ-icikâtêlik*.

25 The women cut the hair off first.

26 i.e., *opîwâliw*.

27 i.e., *anima*.

Notes to Text 51

Description: local technology. Recorded 28 July 1964 at the Moose Fort Indian Residential School. Titles by Agnes Hunter (C) and CDE (E).

1 After being washed, the moss is hung on trees, stumps or branches to dry. Moss is also hung on tetrapods made of branches and, in the old days of potato gardens at Moose Factory, used to be hung on the barbed wire fences.

2 The type of moss used is known as *kihciwêskamikw-* NI 'real moss' – the original disposable diaper. *wâpaskamikw-* NI 'white moss' is not very good as it does not hold dampness very well. *mihkwaskamikw-* NI 'red moss' is no good at all: it causes

the baby to become chafed after urination. When laced into a moss-bag (*wâspisoyân-* NI) properly lined with cleaned, dried moss, a baby can quite easily go a whole day, sometimes longer, without a change and without getting diaper rash.

3   Note the causative, *âpacihtamoh-* VTA 'make s.o. use it'.

4   In this case apparently just 'crawling' worms and not various 'insects', although there are also sometimes small spiders.

5   Note the omission of *ê-* in rapid speech; *ê-kanawêl'cikâtêki* would have been expected here. Note also the /h/ onset on the following *ê-*.

6   i.e., *ê-ayâwâspanak*.

7   Low hanging branches protect the stacked moss from becoming wet or snow-covered.

8   i.e., *sihtâhkwanak* NA pl. 'brushes, brushwood'; cf. 50:3.

9   i.e., *nîlanân*.

10 The narrator's husband often used to spend winters in the bush while trading for Reveillon Frères in the early 1930s. This is what is referred to.

Notes to Text 52

Description: local technology. Recorded c. 13 August 1964 at the Moose Fort Indian Residential School. Titles based on text.

1   The rabbit-skin was cut into strips or strands (*wâšw-* VTA, *wâš-* VTI) or into one long strand if possible.

2   The rabbit-skin is twisted about a stick to produce a strand of skin, evenly furred.

3   i.e., 'has kinks in it'.

4   The recorded segment is *êko šêhkâtâpêt antê kotak ati awâsiš*; *ati* was replaced by a repetition of *antê* after discussion with James Gunner; cf. *šêhkâtâpê-* VAI 'he keeps on drawing it away as fast as it's twisted'.

5   i.e., *êko êkolâkaniwicik*.

6   On listening to the recording, the narrator's husband suggested the addition of *kâ-kî-wašwâkaniwicik wâpoš'-wayânak* 'when the rabbit-skins had been cut into strips' after *ohci* by way of clarification.

7   A frame is usually made about six feet square. The blanket is then netted, working from the outside to the centre or from the top corner back and forth. The frame is usually paralleled by no. 9 twine, which then remains as the outside edge of the blanket.

8   *wâpošo-wayân* is understood.

9   The point is that in a wigwam, where space is restricted, one must start with a four-foot frame, raise the blanket as it progresses, and add on.

10 The singular, *ê-'šihômakahk*, is heard on the recording; the final /i/ is here treated as devoiced.

11 i.e., *ê-ošihtât*.

12 i.e., *wîlâta*.

13 Allegro form for *nêsta nîla*.

14 i.e., *wâspiso-wayân*.

Notes to Text 53

Description: local technology. Recorded August 1964 at the Moose Fort Indian Residential School. Titles based on text, confirmed by Agnes Hunter.

1   i.e., hide subjected to a faster drying process: "fast-drying hide". Cf. *kâhkiso-* VAI, *kâhkitê-* VII 'be dried'.

2   According to James Gunner, *otinikâtêliwa* might have been expected.

3   i.e., *mihcêtwâ*.

4   i.e., *ê-ati-paškišikâtêk*.

5   For netting on the forepart and rear section of a snowshoe the hide of a young moose is used as being thinner and lighter. The central section is laced with babiche from heavier moose-hide, *aškimaniyâpiy-*.

6   The original transcription was *ati*, possibly, though not certainly, an allegro variant for *oti*. This speaker seems to append *ati* as an afterthought to verbs (cf. n. 52:4).

7   Allegro metathesis for *êko*.

8   James Gunner interpreted the recording as *ê-kî-ôškimêyân*, most probably a mispronunciation for *ê-kîšaškimêyân*.

Notes to Text 54

Description: recipe. Recorded August 1964 at the Moose Fort Indian Residential School. Titles probably by Agnes Hunter (C), and by CDE (E); literal translation of the Cree title: 'Cooking whitefish roe'.

1   i.e., *oskwanipiy-* NI 'liver-water'; this actually consists more of the stomach, etc., rather than just the liver. The stomach is probably the largest single organ in the whitefish.

2   *sîn-* VTI 'squeeze it (along)', like a cloth through a wringer. Water is wrung or squeezed out of the gut as out of a tooth-paste tube.

3   i.e., *kici-prâwniwahki* 'so they become all brown'; loan from English. When the water has boiled away, the innards fry in their natural oils.

4   i.e., *anihi*.

5   i.e., *awasitê*.

6   Alternative form of *wîhkašin*.

Notes to Text 55

Cyclical *âtalôhkân*. Recorded August 1964 at the Moose Fort Indian Residential School. Titles probably by Agnes Hunter (C), and by CDE (E). Cf. also Texts 8 and 18.

On the recording of this narrative, the speech is often very rapid with extreme contraction of forms. Final /hk/ varies from [h] to [x] – it is not always easy to decide which. Both *h'* and *hk* have been used in transcription.

The rapid speech also produces contractions throughout: *manâ wt'* for *manâ oti*, *ê-ytat* for *ê-itat*. It is often difficult to determine whether the vowel in question still retains syllabic value or has been reduced to the corresponding glide.

1   Note the Moose Cree form *wîsahkwêcâhk*. James Gunner interpreted the name as something like 'Shrill Spirit'; cf. *wîsahkwê-* VAI 'have a shrill voice'.

2   A feature of Sophie Gunner's speech is the periodic replacement of /i/ with /a/; note /nak.../ in the initial syllable where /nik.../ might have been expected. The narrator has also been heard to say *mahkwacakâš-* NA for *mihkwacakâš-* 'red sucker'. Note also the /h/ in *ninikamôhiniwat*, where the customary form shows /w/. It was suggested that this probably meant 'songs to make people sing'; cf. *nikamohin* 'sing to me', cf. also *nikamôwiniwat*.

3   *ôma* refers to his current activity of carrying moss.

4   i.e., *wî-pêci-itohtêyêkwê*.

5   *askîk'wâm-* NI 'a lodge of logs split to a thickness of about six inches, stood on end and covered with moss'. Seams were usually chinked with blue mud, *wâpitowinaskw-* NI 'clay'. Some times the log faces were alternated, flat-round-flat-

round, etc., to allow water to run off onto the centre-groove of the flat-faced log. The wigwam-like structure was then covered with moss and was very comfortable and warm. Brush was usually put on the floor, with a central fire on the bare ground, perhaps surrounded by rocks, with a vent-hole in the top-centre. A door was made with canvas or hide.

6 i.e., *nâšic*.
7 i.e., *walapihêw*.
8 i.e., *misiwê*.
9 i.e., *ê-wâšakâmênahkik tâpiskôc ê-ati-nîminâniwahk ê-tôtahkik*.
10 *ê-šêšêkošimât* might have been expected.
11 i.e., *kici-kî-itihkasolici*.
12 *kêka* might have been expected; the recording appears to have *êko*.
13 i.e., *awênihkâna*.
14 i.e., *awênihkân*.
15 *âšay wâsêyâliw* seems to be what is on the recording although James Gunner interpreted this as *ê-wâsêyâlik* 'it being clear'.
16 i.e., *âšay*.
17 i.e., *nâspitêpi*.
18 The narrator probably intended *ê-kî-nênîsohtatât* 'having put the two legs of the one bird close together', or perhaps *ê-nênîsohtinilik* 'lying in pairs'. The birds had been shoved under the hot sand with the legs sticking out. Cf. also *šêšêkošimât* (55:4).
19 i.e., *kêkwânihkân*.
20 James Gunner felt that *kotakîliw* would be better.
21 Contraction of *nama wawâc*. The usual Moose Cree form is *môla wâwâc pêyak* 'not even one'.
22 *kêkwâliw* might have been expected.
23 i.e., *wîlâta*.
24 i.e., *nâhitê* for *nâspic tâpwê*.
25 i.e., *miconi*.
26 Extremely allegro speech: *ê'kwâni manâ mâka*.
27 i.e., *kâ-kî-ati-tôtaman*.
28 i.e., *manâ oti*.
29 The recording is unclear at this point.
30 The recording sounds more like *-êhtit*.
31 cf. *kalêkisi-* VAI 'be itchy'.
32 i.e., *ê'kwâni manâ oti ani*.
33 *anihi* refers back to *kâ-wâ'htamahk*; i.e., 'those things which you see which adhere to willows'.
34 i.e., *kâ-ayakwahkêki*.
35 i.e., *kê'wâ'hkâna*.
36 i.e., *ašâtîšišak*.

Notes to Text 56
âtalôhkân. Recorded 28 July 1964 at the Moose Fort Indian Residential School. Titles by CDE, with the Cree checked by Agnes Hunter. Cf. also Text 14.

1 i.e., *apistâpêskwêšiš* 'midget girl'. This form, never fully completed by the narrator, was produced while she searched for the term *mistâpêskwêšiš*. A speaker of Swampy Cree proposed *apisciskwêšiš-* 'midget girl' since ...*âpê*..., to her, implied a

male. A further speaker rejected this term as sounding incorrect and preferred as the correct term for 'midget girl', *apiscininîskwêšiš*.

2   The usual verb is *sakihtatâ* VAI-T 'stick (s.t.) out (and leave it there)'.
3   *ocayâniš* 'his little thing': euphemism for *wîtakay* 'his penis'.
4   *kâ-pâhpihtâyêk* might have been expected.
5   i.e., *-itašilici*.
6   i.e., *awênihkân*.
7   i.e., *âpihcililîš* 'a half person, a small person'.

Notes to Text 57

Conversation. Recorded 1964 at the Moose Fort Indian Residential School. Titles by Agnes Hunter (C) and CDE (E).

The speakers are Sophie Gunner, originally from an area south and east of Moose Factory, and her husband James Gunner of Moose Factory.

1   *ililiwaskiy* is the name of the Indian Reservation about seven miles up the Moose River from Moose (Factory) Island, at the point where the French River enters the Moose River.
2   Particle indicating recognition of a fact, whatever one's judgment on it.
3   i.e., *môla wayêš*.

Notes to Text 58

tipâcimôwin: reminiscence. Recorded 30 July 1964 at the Moose Fort Indian Residential School. Titles by Agnes Hunter (C) and CDE (E); literal translation of the Cree title: 'Doing things when one was a youth'.

The events described here took place around the turn of the century, when the narrator was a young man of eighteen or nineteen years. Cf. also Text 61.

1   n.b., *eighteen poot*. The narrator had been talking in English and periodically introduces English terms into the narrative. The pronunciation of some is clearly influenced by the Cree.

In spite of the intrusion of English words, note the conservative numeral formation with ...*šâpw-* in 58:2: *nêmitana niyâlošâp* 'forty-five'; and in 58:3: *nîšitana n'kotwâs'šâpokonakisiw* 'it is the 26th day'. Once past the '-teen' numbers, younger speakers tend to drop the ...*šâpw-* formation, e.g., *nêmitana niyâlan* 'forty-five'.

2   'Old River', i.e., Fort George. This sometimes used to be known as Big River. Since the building of the Hydro Quebec Project it is commonly known as La Grande.
3   *ôta ohci* would be expected; *ôma ohci* means 'for this reason'.
4   Charlton Island is fifty-two miles from the mouth of the Moose River by ship's log. Canoe travel is ordinarily impossible, according to James Gunner. The water would have to be very smooth.
5   Most likely Strutton Island.
6   cf. *ispîhtakâmêyâ-* VII 'be such a distance (in open, unprotected water) between islands'.
7   The Cree name is *wîpicînak* 'Walrus Island'; cf. *wîpicîw-* NA (Moose Cree *wîpiciw-*) 'walrus'.
8   The distance between Strutton Island and Cape Hope is actually only about twenty-four, not forty-five miles.
9   The meaning is that they were following the course formerly taken by ships from Britain or Montreal, out in the Bay away from the shoals.

10 *ê-otihtahamâhk* 'by paddling' would be expected. The verb used by the narrator usually implies walking rather than paddling. If a vehicle were involved the verb *ê-otihcipaliyâhk* would be expected; cf. also *ôtihtâši-* VAI 'reach one's destination by sail'.

11 i.e., *niwâpahtênân.*

12 *itohtê-* VAI is normally used of walking.

13 *wîhkwêyâw-* NI 'a sack' (as at Albany Post). *wîhkwêyâši-* VAI 'sail into the very end of the bay', NI 'cul de sac'.

14 It is important when travelling by canoe in the late fall to keep between the ice and the shore. Otherwise the tide may carry the canoe out to sea and attempts to get back through the ice can result in cutting a hole in the canoe.

15 i.e., *môla wâwâc* 'not even'.

16 The narrator must have seen *akohciw'lâkana* 'net-floats'.

17 Now called Wemindji; the Cree name is *wîliman'ciy*, cf. *wîliman-* NI 'paint', *waciy-* NI 'hill'.

18 As the year draws to an end, the terms used are *walawîmakan* 'it is going out', and *pîhtokwêmakan* 'it is coming in'. *makošêwi-kîsikâw* 'Feast Day' is used of Christmas at Albany Post (now Kashechewan) and for New Year's Day at Moose Factory.

19 n.b., *pifteenth of January.*

20 i.e., *ê-ohci-kîsiswâkaniwit.*

21 'husky dogs'; possibly a back formation, but related to *askîmêwatimw-* NA 'Eskimo dog'.

22 cf. *wâpišîšin-* NI 'the opposition'; i.e., Reveillon Frères.

Notes to Text 59

tipâcimôwin: reminiscence. Recorded c. 30 July 1964 at the Moose Fort Indian Residential School. Titles by CDE, with the Cree checked by Agnes Hunter.

1 A lengthy preceding pause may account for the anacoluthon; *atihkwa* would be expected.

2 The narrator probably had in mind *môla wîlâta wayêš kî-ohci-ihtiwak* 'there was nothing happened to them'.

3 Note the anacoluthon.

4 i.e., of a family or group.

5 i.e., *ispîš.*

6 For *tahtâpiskipi-* VTI 'trigger s.t.'.

7 James Gunner felt that *nêpahât*, the changed conjunct form, would be preferable here.

8 *wîhtikôwa* would be expected; an /h/ final, barely audible, is perhaps a devoiced /a/.

9 *wêhcîwâkopanê* might have been expected.

10 *kâ-kawahkatêcik* might have been expected.

Notes to Text 60

tipâcimôwin: reminiscence. Recorded 30 July 1964 at the Moose Fort Indian Residential School. Titles by CDE, with the Cree checked by Agnes Hunter.

Usage throughout this text shows considerable grammatical erosion (e.g., absence of obviative forms), even though Cree was the narrator's first language.

1 i.e., *anima ispiš* 'in those days'.

2 *ê-miloskamik* might be better stylistically, since this refers to the period after break-up.

3 *ôho* was preferred here by another Cree speaker, Bertha Metat.

4 The narrator probably made a slip here and meant to say *ninahâhkaniskwêm*, as in the next sentence; a daughter-in-law would not normally be referred to as *iskwêšiš*.

5 Final /ê/ could be /i/, a false start for the next word, *itêw*. This is the first mention of a daughter-in-law. The narrative gives the initial impression that there is only the old man and his son.

6 The narrator does not complete the word; it would be *kê-itêl'tahkik* 'what to think'.

7 i.e., *kata-n'tawihow* 'he will hunt again'. The form in the text may represent a stylistic effect.

8 Contraction for *awa oškinîkiw*.

9 Presumably the two men moved away since the daughter-in-law refused to practise cannibalism.

10 The recording is unclear at this point. Another Cree listener interpreted the recording as *ta-tâhcipôwak* 'they will get fat', although it sounded more like *ta-âhcikwêwak* 'they will move away' to CDE.

11 *ê-itikitilici* would be expected here, and *kikiskêlihtamwân* instead of *kikiskêlihtên* in the next sentence.

12 *omistatâlîw* would have been expected here since in Moose Cree *môswa* is the obviative form.

13 The narrator probably had in mind something like *môla kiskêl'ihtamwak tântê wâ-itohtêcik* 'they didn't know where they were going to go'.

14 *išpacistin-* VII 'be a high drift bank'. This is sought for by Indians camping during the spring period around the shores of James Bay. Camp is pitched atop the drift bank to provide security against flooding. The question may be asked of someone coming into a settlement after Spring Camp: *išpacistin nâ kâ-iši-tašîhkêyin?* 'Is it a high drift bank where you're living?'

15 i.e., *êši-kwâškwatotâtocik* VTA (recipr.) 'they jumped on each other'.

16 cf. *mâših-* VTA 'wrestle s.o.' Many older Indian hunters prefer to take a killed moose whole in a canoe rather than cut it up. Under such circumstances one may hear: *êliwêhk nimâšihâw ê-wî-pôsipitak!* 'Did I ever wrestle (him) as I stowed him!'

17 *môla wâwâc môhkomân* 'not even a knife' would have been better stylistically according to James Gunner.

18 Preferred usage would be *kâ-ohcîlici*. According to James Gunner, the narrator often neglected to use the obviative. There are evidently three persons involved in the fight:

   nîštam kâ-ohcît = *ostêsimâw* 'elder brother'
   âpihta kâ-ohcît = 'middle brother',
   mâhcic kâ-ohcît = *ošîmimâw* 'younger brother';

   cf. also *nîštamošân-* NA 'first child'; *mâhcicošân-* NA 'last child'.

19 *êškaniliw* would be better here, according to James Gunner.

20 The recording is unclear at this point.

21 i.e., *sôhkatâna anima kiwî-tôtênâwâw!* 'So that's what you wanted to do!' The old man evidently thought that the young men were going merely to chisel beaver. He is chagrined that they went after their brother-in-law.

   sôhkatâna corresponds to *tâpwê ot' âni*; if the reading should instead be *êkot' âni*, then the preferred construction, according to Agnes Hunter, would be *êkot' âni mâka wâ-tôtamêkopan!* 'So that's what you had wanted to do!'

22 If *-nipahiht* is to show concord with *ôhtâwiya*, then *kâ-kî-nipahimihci* or

428

-nipahâkaniwilici would be expected. This, however, makes little sense of the story. Presumably the father of the brother-in-law, who was thrown into the hole (*kâ-kî-nipahiht ôhtâwiya*) here makes an appearance for the first time. James Gunner, who preferred *kâ-kî-nipahimihci*, also preferred *nîstânân* to *nîstâwinân*.

23 i.e., *kâ-pîhcihtihk*.
24 *nisitokanê-* VII 'have a taste, flavour (bone)'; it is claimed that a taste of the marrow will indicate whether the meat of a moose will be flavourful or otherwise.
25 Perhaps *-ohpimiht* 'he was lifted up'.
26 i.e., *êkot' âni*.

Notes to Text 61

tipâcimôwin: reminiscence. Recorded 30 July 1964 at the Moose Fort Indian Residential School. Titles by Agnes Hunter (C) and CDE (E); literal translation of the Cree title: 'Other things which had been done'. Cf. also Text 58.

1 i.e., *wâšahâk*
2 The use in the singular indicates a class of birds.
3 lit., 'flying south'. The verb usually used for flying south is *pimah-* VTI 'migrate, fly south'.
4 Note hypercorrect form in Moose Cree; cf. Proto-Algonquian **nyaalanwi* and also Moose Cree *ililiw-* (PA **elenyiwa*).
5 i.e., *ispiš*, or perhaps *ispihc*.
6 The narrator started to say *kâ-nipahtâyân*.
7 The narrator interpolated occasional English expressions, although his control of English was very imperfect.
8 Along the coastline where there are no large trees, only willows are available for building stages. Long grass is laid crosswise over the willows for reinforcement and to distribute the weight; cf. *kici-sôhkahk têšipitâkan* 'to strengthen the stage'.
9 i.e., *ê-âšawahâtakâyân*.
10 Formerly *pêyak šikâk'-wayân* 'one skunk skin' was used for a 'quarter of a dollar'. Hence *šikâk* comes to be used for a 'quarter', in this case 'quarter of a thumb'.
11 i.e., *-kispakisiw*.
12 James Gunner preferred *kâ-pimihtihk*. The streams spoken of here are known locally as 'Partridge Creeks', about fifteen miles east of Moose Factory along the shore of James Bay.
13 The verb indicates that he must have been paddling or swimming by this time.
14 The recording is unclear at this point.
15 The narrator moves from one canoe to seven; perhaps a more impressive figure, as he could not reach any of them.
16 i.e., *ê-ispîhci-kîškâyawâk*. The recording shows an extreme contraction of speech forms here.
17 The recording here is very unclear.
18 i.e., *nâtâpwê*.
19 i.e., *wakîc*.
20 cf. *ôma itaskisow* 'it (a tree) stands at such an angle'. The narrator used *ôtê*, which would be accompanied by a manual gesture showing the angle and direction. Although it remained inaudible to CDE, James Gunner claimed to hear *ôhi* after *itaskitêwa* on the recording.
21 i.e., *aniki*; probable contamination, cf. English *one a' dem* 'one of them'.
22 *-wîhkocîn* might have been expected.

23 *niwâpwayânihk ohci* might be better stylistically.

24 *-wîhkocîn* might have been expected.

25 The narrator uses *n'kî-wîhkocison*; the correct form is *n'kî-wîhkwacihon*.

26 i.e., *wâwâc*.

27 Either *šawiškaw-* VTA 'make a dent or pressure mark on s.o.', or *pâhciškaw-* VTA 'depress s.o.' (both by body action) would be expected, or *matwêškaw-* VTA 'crack s.o.', if he had jumped on the ice. It sounds, from *nimatwênâw*, as though he cracked the ice with his hands.

28 *kâ-iši-kišîciwahk* 'where the current was fast' would be expected.

29 Another Cree speaker interpreted the recording as *maskwamîwanôpan*.

30 *môla n'kî-ohci-wayêš-ihtin* 'I had no bad effects'; note the loose compounding.

Notes to Text 62
Description: local technology. Recorded 30 July 1964 at the Moose Fort Indian Residential School. Titles by CDE, with the Cree checked by Agnes Hunter.

1 cf. *waškway-* NI 'birch bark'.

2 cf. *waškway-* NA 'birch tree'.

3 James Gunner preferred the obviative form *kampanîwa* here.

4 i.e., *êši-'ti-šîpâhocik*; cf. *šîpâhw-* VTA 'squeeze s.o. (cedar ribs) down between'; contrast *šîpahw-* VTA 'stretch it' (as an otter skin). James Gunner felt the form should be *ê-ti-iši-šîpâhocik*.

5 The recording is unclear at this point. Instead of *kâ-môhkotacik*, one Cree listener interpreted the recording as *kâ-napakihkotacik* 'which you plane flat'.

6 i.e., *êkotêni mâka* 'now, that is the way'.

7 James Gunner felt the following should be added, by way of clarification: *ê-ošihtâniwahkwâpan ôhi cîmâna* 'in the process of making these canoes'.

Notes to Text 63
Non-cyclical *âtalôhkân*: local legend. Recorded 21 July 1965 at the narrator's home, a senior citizens' apartment at Moosonee. Titles by Agnes Hunter (C) and CDE (E). Cf. also Text 10.

1 The narrator gave the date in answer to an inquiry by CDE.

2 The obviative form *miščâkalâša* would be expected.

3 i.e., *nicîpayi-ospwâkan*.

4 *ê-pêci-'miškât* was preferred by a second informant.

5 Locative of archaic *ôt-* NI 'canoe', regularly used on the East Coast of James Bay but occurring in Moose Cree only in the derived form *mihtôt-* NI 'raft'.

6 *-pakitinak* would have been expected.

Notes to Text 64
tipâcimôwin: reminiscence. Recorded 21 July 1965 at the narrator's home, a senior citizens' apartment at Moosonee. Title (C) based on the text, and (E) by Bertha Metat, then of Timmins.

1 *pimâtisî-* in Moose Cree.

2 n.b., *Moose Pactory*.

3 *kici-kanawêlimiyamiht* might have been expected.

4 i.e., *otayâna*.

5 James Gunner interpreted this as *nêtê ê-twêwahikêt* [sic] although the recording sounds more like *matê-*; cf. *twêwêhikê-* VAI 'beat time' (as in music); *tatwêwêhikê-*

VAI 'beat the drum, be drumming'.

6 The narrator changed construction here; *askihkwa* should be preceded by *anihi*, but *anima* agrees with *-otatâmaham*.

7 It would have been clearer, according to James Gunner, if the storyteller had prefaced the sound effects with some statement such as *ôma mâka itihtâkwaniliw ê-twêwêhikêt* 'now this is how it sounded as he beat the rhythm', or *ôma mâka itwêwêmakihtâw* 'this is the sound he was making'. From *askihkwa* on, the text would read *ê-otatâmahwât askihkwa ê-itihtâkwahk*.

8 It is a commonplace belief among many older Indian people that trees rubbing against each other in the bush often sound as if they are talking. If one tree is loose at the roots and leaning on another in the wind, the 'screaking' noises produced combine with certain other dull sounds to produce this effect. Old timers believe that the friction produced by two branches rubbing together, as above, in hot dry weather, is a cause of bush fires.

9 *ê'kwânima piko ispiš* might have been expected.

Notes to Text 65

tipâcimôwin: reminiscence. Recorded 21 July 1965 at the home of the narrator, a senior citizens' apartment at Moosonee. Titles based on the text, with the Cree checked by Agnes Hunter; literal translation of the Cree title: 'While I was a child'.

1 *maskwamîwâkamin-* VII 'thicken (the skin surface of ice) on the water' (in the fall).

2 Here used independently as a particle.

3 i.e., *ašikêyân*; the storyteller must have had some kind of moccasin to keep the grass around her foot.

4 In view of the verbal concord, *ôki ililiwak* would have been expected; the narrator probably had in mind that the man was maintaining the family.

5 i.e., Dinah Chum; *iskwêw* would have been clearer and *-âhkosiliwa* would have been expected.

6 cf. *nimitâwih-* VTI 'go along the coast'. An Indian hunter often follows the coast of James Bay, then turns up a creek where he may find moose congregating in a deep spot where they can escape the bull-dog flies and find long, underwater grass (*asisîya* NI pl.) which grows in the eddies and still water. Moose are often found at such spots in creeks or rivers.

7 i.e., *ê-wî-kakwê-pimâcihakiht*.

8 *iši-cimê-* VAI 'go there by canoe'.

9 n.b., *Nort, Nort Plap*.

10 One would expect *kâ-piskwâhkâk*, as the conjunct is required grammatically. This feature is known in English as *North Bluff Shoal*.

11 They could not use a tracking line along the coast where the water is very shallow. They would have to wait till they came to a river to do this.

12 *n'kipotâmoškâkwak* would be expected.

13 The full form would be *ê-pôsihakihcik*.

14 *ispiš âta kâ-kî-ihtât ôta* would be expected. According to James Gunner, even better usage would be *ispîy âta kâ-pêšiwakiht ôta*.

15 i.e., *nâpêwa*.

16 i.e., *-wîcêwêwak*; the narrator began with the preverb *wîci-* and then changed the construction.

17 i.e., *nâspic*.

18 the /â/ is nasalized; cf. *tân' êhtikwê* 'What must be the matter with her?'

19 *mat(w)ê-* is used for things discerned at a distance or in dusk or darkness: i.e., when perceptibility is reduced. One could tell either by seeing or hearing the action.

20 *patotê ispahêw*; cf. *patotêpahêw.*

21 i.e., *piko anta ô*. On query, a child might reply, *piko 'ntaw nimêtawân* 'I'm just playing around.'

22 i.e., *kîwêpalihow* 'she turned back in a hurry'; this fits the context and is probably what was intended. The recording is indistinct and sounds like *kîwêpahkow*, a non-existent form.

23 No concord is shown in the text for *maškošîya*, but it is best taken as loosely constructed with *kî-pêci-pasitêw.*

24 i.e., *-kišiwêwêtêlik* (cf. *kišiwêwêtê-* VII 'make a loud noise'); from the gun report one can gather whether the shells are home or factory loaded; the latter are quieter.

25 Presumably the woman who had been exploding the gun-powder.

26 An obvious but understandable exaggeration; cf. *šâpohkaso-* VAI 'be cooked right through'.

27 Contrast *ê-pâhpihitocik* 'laughing at each other'.

28 *pimâtisî-*: so in Moose Cree; cf. Swampy Cree *pimâtisi-.*

29 This expression indicates that those paddling left the north with no clear-cut idea of heading to Moosonee, but paddled around along the coastline, finally arriving there.

30 *n'kî-ati-atimahwânânak* 'we caught up with them' might have been expected. The narrator's party must have overtaken these people on their way back north.

Notes to Text 66

tipâcimôwin. Recorded 21 July 1965 at the home of the narrator, a senior citizens' apartment at Moosonee. Titles by CDE, with the Cree checked by Agnes Hunter; literal translation of the Cree title: 'A whiskey-jack and a mouse fighting each other'.

1 *sâhkamistikw-* NI 'West River' or 'Kisagami River', flowing from *sâhkamiy sâkahikan* (i.e., Kisagami Lake) to Hannah Bay.

2 i.e., probably, *nôhcimihk.*

3 *nîpisîskâhk* is synonymous with *mêkwêhkop* 'in, amongst the willows'. The usual camping place is *lâlihkop* 'along the edge of the willows', so that the men will not have too far to carry geese but, at the same time, so as to retain some protection for the camp in case of a high wind.

4 i.e., *nititâpin.*

5 i.e., probably, *wêhci-sâkipalihot* 'suddenly emerged, poked out', either from the grass or the snow or around a tree or some other object. To emerge suddenly from snow would more likely be expressed by *sâkâkonêpaliho-* VAI.

6 cf. *wâpikošîša.*

7 Note /ô/ in ...*hôl*... here, though not elsewhere; cf. *pimahol-* VTA 'carry s.o. off', *pimahotâ-* VAI-T 'carry s.t. off' (e.g., as a bird with a fish, a man with a moose in a canoe); *ati-'mahôl-* VTA here means 'fly away with s.o.'.

8 The mouse perhaps defeated the whiskey-jack's efforts by being too heavy to be carried in flight.

9 *šêkopaliho-* VAI 'get under (something) quickly'; the fuller form would be *šêkwâkonêpaliho-*. The narrator's use of the simpler form is regarded as stylistically inferior.

10 i.e., *ê-.*

11 i.e., *awa*.
12 *oskâta piko nîpiwâkêw* 'he [the mouse] was standing on his (hind) legs only' would be expected.
13 *kwêskwêskikwâškototâtowak* 'they were jumping at each other back and forth' would be expected.

Notes to Text 67
Conversation. Recorded 21 July 1965 at the home of Hannah Loon, a senior citizens' apartment at Moosonee.
The conversation is between Hannah Loon (originally from Moose Factory) and her sister, Ellen McLeod .
1 *wâšâhk* is a contraction for *wâšahâhk* 'Hannah Bay' (lit., 'the bay', cf. *wâšahâw-* NI).
2 i.e., the four pound axe used in lumber camps.
3 The usual name for this camping spot is *kâ-mihcâpiskâw*. It is about fifteen miles west of Hannah Bay River at the NW corner of Hannah Bay. This and Netitishi comprise the only two decent camping spots between Hannah Bay River and Moose Factory.
4 *n'kî-ati-atimahwânânak* 'we caught up with them' would have been expected if they had come by canoe; *atiminêhw-* indicates that they caught up by wading.
5 From the form of the verb the plural *nistêsak* would be expected.
6 cf. *n'kâsohtâtonân* 'we're playing hide-and-seek'.
7 The recording is difficult to understand here because of simultaneous talking by several persons.
8 The narrator had probably intended to say *n'têhtapihikawinân* 'we were getting a ride', which was changed to *têhtapihâkaniwan* 'she is given a ride'.
9 *pîhtawânakâw-* NI 'Island-up-against (the mainland)', about two and a half miles from Moose Factory. It is a good spot for fall fishing: herring and whitefish.
10 Willie, the younger brother, was told by Archibald Sailors, the elder brother, to take the girl's axe. Probably she was holding it while running.
11 Particle indicating expostulation, e.g., *'kâwila mâtâna anima tôta!* 'Don't do that, then!'
12 The remainder of this conversation was accidentally erased from the recording.

Notes to Text 68
Non-cyclical *âtalôhkân*: animal tale. Recorded 29 July 1965 at the narrator's home at Moose Factory. Titles based on text.
1 *wînipêkw-* NI (in this case) 'James Bay: any large body of salty water'; cf. *wînâ-* VII 'be stale, rotten'. The water in James Bay is muddy or brackish.
2 The narrator began to say *n'ka-âtalôhkân*.
3 i.e., *ê-išinihkâsot*.
4 *'wênihkâna* would be better stylistically.
5 Note the full form of the negative, *kî-ohci-...*
6 i.e., *iskonâk mâka anima* 'ever since that time, ever since then'. The narrator uses the form *ispihc* for *ispiš*.
7 i.e., *kî-išicišahwâkaniwin*.
8 They must have been expecting that the wolverine would come anyway.
9 James Gunner felt that the form *šêkwâkonakî-* represented better usage.
10 Note the reduplication: *wêwêlâpam-* VTA, *wêwêlâpaht-* VTI 'go around (the circle)

making a choice'.

11 The narrator seems to have changed constructions without a pause. Preferred usage would be *kê-n'tawi-nakiškawâl'ci* 'who would meet him'.

12 The recording sounded initially like *nîla, ninihtâ-naskon* 'I'm good at defending myself', which would make sense in the context; cf. *nasko-* VAI 'defend oneself against attack'; cf. also *naskotamâso-, nâtamâso-*. After several replays before different speakers, the reading adopted was *nâhtâ n'kaškihon* 'I'm very competent'. This is still uncertain.

13 The first /â/ is nasalized.

14 i.e., *mâka*.

15 The narrator might better have used *mêkwêskamik* 'back in the muskeg', *mêkwêyâhtik* 'among the trees' or *mêkwêyâpisk* 'among the rocks'.

16 cf. *nakacâskošin-* VAI, *nakacâskohtin-* VII 'bump into a tree'; note the reduplication and assimilation of /s/ to /š/ by the Moose Cree-speaking narrator.

17 /ê/ is nasalized.

18 /ê/ is nasalized.

19 i.e., *nitati-pêšiwâpahtên*.

20 *itêlihtam* was probably intended by the narrator who then remembered that the wolverine was speaking, not just thinking.

21 The recording is unclear at this point.

22 i.e., *âšay; nâhtâ' âšay sikilêsiw* 'now he was very glad' (with *nâhtâ'* for *nâhtâpwê*) would be better stylistically.

23 *kihciwê-nipîhk* 'proper water', as contrasted with little puddles; cf. *wâlipêyâ-*.

24 Solecism for *ê-tatwêkamâškât* VII 'the rollers are sounding over there'.

25 Contraction of *kêtahtawil* 'suddenly'.

26 The first /â/ is nasalized here and in the previous word.

27 The full form would probably have been *âšaw'kwâškwatiw* 'he jumped across' (e.g., a creek).

28 i.e., *kêka*.

29 *šîwâkamin-* VII 'be sweet or salt water'. Use of the term was probably an afterthought following use of *-šîwâk*; both are not necessary.

Glossary

Stem-Class Codes and Abbreviations

NA	animate noun	NDA	animate noun, dependent
NI	inanimate noun	NDI	inanimate noun, dependent
PR	pronoun	IPV	indeclinable preverb particle
IPC	indeclinable particle	IPN	indeclinable prenoun particle
		IPP	indeclinable pre-particle
VAI	animate intransitive verb	VTA	transitive animate verb
VII	inanimate intransitive verb	VTI	transitive inanimate verb
VAI-T	animate intransitive verb in form with implied or expressed inanimate object	Nom.A	nominal animate
		Nom.I	nominal inanimate
M	medial suffix	F	final suffix
MV	medial suffix with verb only and without related noun form	VAIF	animate intransitive verb final
MF	suffix functioning as medial or final	VIIF	inanimate intransitive verb final
s.o.	someone (animate object of transitive verb)	indecl.	indeclinable
		redupl.	reduplicated
s.t.	something (inanimate object of transitive verb)	recipr.	reciprocal
		conj.	conjunct
sg.	singular	indef.	indefinite
pl.	plural	indic.	indicative
anim.	animate	dubit.	dubitative
inan.	inanimate	subj.	subjunctive
prox.	proximate	MC	Moose Cree
obv.	obviative	SC	Swampy Cree
incl.	inclusive		
excl.	exclusive		

Introduction

Entries in the glossary are listed by stems, e.g., *cîmân-* 'canoe', *nipâ-* 'sleep', with the hyphen used throughout to indicate the point at which inflectional material may be added. All entries are further specified by a stem-class code, a complete list of which appears immediately preceding these comments. The stem-class code is followed by the English gloss, plus a cross-sectional listing of occurrences in the text, noted by text number and paragraph, e.g.,

>   *âpatisi-* VAI work; 2:6; 5:3

These latter references are intended to be typical but not exhaustive. Bracket-enclosed references indicate that the form itself does not occur at that point but is related to one which does or is discussed in the Notes.[1]

Glossary entries also show cross-reference to semantically and derivationally related forms (in the latter case primarily where the relationship is not obvious from proximity in the glossary, with full sentential or phrasal usage illustrated where this is of particular interest). Such illustration normally displays the textual form in which the relevant word or expression occurs.

Lexical entries are by uncontracted form except in a limited number of cases where the contracted form is either by far the more common or the only form under which the item occurs, e.g.,

>   *tântê* (rather than **tânitê*).

Alone among Cree dialects, Moose Cree retains the historic *l* from Proto-Algonquian. In Swampy Cree, this has fallen together with the *n* inherited from the parent language so that it is not possible from the evidence of Swampy Cree alone to distinguish historic *n* sounds from those which were once *l*, e.g.,

>   *ka-kiskênimin* (SC) vs. *ka-kiskêlimin* (MC) 'you will know me'.

The choice of Moose Cree citation forms thus provides information which would otherwise be less immediately accessible. Moose Cree speakers commenting on Swampy Cree and Kashechewan texts often cite equivalent

---

[1] Since text revision continued for some time after the preparation of the glossary, there may be some discrepancies between the paragraphing and spelling in the texts and that cited in the glossary.

forms in Moose Cree, automatically replacing *n* with *l* where Moose Cree has preserved the historic sound. The forms in Kashechewan Cree, a mixed dialect, sometimes display the historic *l* and sometimes show an *n* in its place, e.g.,

> *kihcipali-* or *kihcipani-* VAI/VII 'go off, go away'.

Swampy Cree (n-dialect) forms can be deduced from the Moose Cree (l-dialect) forms by replacing *l* with *n* (except, of course, where an entirely different word is used). Thus, where a Swampy Cree form has not been listed as such it should be looked for under the Moose Cree listing; the stem of *nipwâhkâ* 'be quiet!' (42:3), for example, occurs in both Moose and Swampy Cree forms and is listed here as,

> *lipwâhkâ-* VAI act sensibly, be sensible (MC); SC: *nipwâhkâ-*.

In addition to independent stems of the type outlined above, the glossary also includes certain noun stems in Cree that can never stand alone but must always occur with a possessor prefix to form a full word; the stem *...sit-* NDI 'foot', for example, must occur as *nisit* 'my foot', *osit* 'his foot' or, with the indefinite personal possessor, *misit* 'somebody's foot', commonly translated as 'a foot'.[2] Only when attached to a possessor prefix do they constitute a full stem which may then be followed by any appropriate inflectional material. These dependent stems or medial suffixes are listed at the beginning of the glossary, where they are followed by the full forms which incorporate them.

The triple point, ..., is used to mark the boundary where other elements may be linked as required to build a full stem, e.g.,

> *...hkw...* 'face'; cf. *pâhpi**hkw**êli-* 'have a smile on one's face'.

The marking *.../-* after a suffix shows that as a medial it combines with other elements to build a full stem; as a final it may be followed by inflectional material.

Although the stem-class code adopted is basically that used in the publications edited by H.C. Wolfart, a number of departures from that system, all related to medial suffixes, warrant further comment:

---

[2] Dependent noun stems are also listed under third person and indefinite personal possessors for convenient reference. Kinship terms form an exception. Although built from dependent stems, they exhibit no form with indefinite possessor *mi...* in the Cree of Western James Bay, but when unpossessed take a verbally derived (i.e., deverbal) form under which they are listed.

Stem-class M. Medial suffixes which do not combine directly with personal prefixes to form nouns but occur with other elements to form noun and verb stems or particles are classified simply as M (Medial) e.g.,

...*htâwak*... 'ear'; cf. *kînikihtâwakê-* VAI 'have pointed ears'.

Stem-class MV. Medial suffixes which are restricted to occurrence in verbs only and have no related form occurring in nouns are specified as MV, e.g.,

e.g., ...*hkw*... 'face'; cf. *kâsîhkwê-* VAI 'wash one's face'.

In word-building, medials often occur with an extension ...*ê*..., e.g.,

...*sit*...*ê*...; cf. *kotikositêšin-* VAI 'sprain a foot'.

Stem-classes F and MF. Elements which occur as stem-finals are flagged F (Final): e.g.,

...*hkop*... 'willow'; cf. *mêkwêhkop* IPC 'among the willows'.

Forms occurring as both medial and final are marked MF, e.g.,

...*âskw*.../- 'wooden'; cf. *pîmâskwan-* VII 'be twisted (something wooden, as an axe-handle)', *otâpânâskw-* NA 'sled'.

Stem-classes VAIF and VIIF. In addition to dependent stems, the list of medial suffixes also includes certain intransitive verb finals which carry a basic, concrete (dictionary) meaning, e.g.,

...*pali-* 'move'
...*ciwan-* 'flow'.

These are designated VAIF or VIIF. They also cannot occur alone but require preceding material to form a full stem, e.g.,

pimipali- VAI 'move along'
kišîciwan- VII 'flow swiftly'.

The list of medial suffixes which appears at the beginning of the glossary is designed as an aid in recognizing the structure of complex words. It contains many finals occurring in the text but is not exhaustive.

For a fuller description of stem formation, word building and general grammatical outline the following works are helpful:

Ahenakew, Freda. 1987. *Cree Language Structures: A Cree Approach*.
  Winnipeg: Pemmican Publications.
  (A description of grammatical structure by a linguist whose mother
  tongue is Cree.)

Ellis, C. Douglas. 1983. *Spoken Cree, West Coast of James Bay*. Edmonton:
  Pica Pica Press.
  (A pedagogical grammar of Moose and Swampy Cree with specific
  grammatical points discussed in each lesson.)

Wolfart, H. Christoph, & Janet F. Carroll. 1981. *Meet Cree: A Guide to the
  Cree Language*. Revised edition. Edmonton: University of Alberta Press
  (An excellent, lucid introduction to Plains Cree grammatical structures.)

Wolfart, H. Christoph. 1973. *Plains Cree: A Grammatical Study*. American
  Philposophical Society Transactions, New Series, volume 63, part 5;
  Philadelphia.
  (A more advanced and detailed treatment of the structural features of
  Plains Cree.)

Dependent Stems and Medial/Final Suffixes

...**aci**... VAIF freeze; 48:2; cf. *akoskwaci-*

...**ahamê-** VAIF follow (a course); 20:1; (41:15); cf. *itahamê-, kihtahamê-, pimahamê-*

...**ahkêšiw**.../- MF fox; 36:1; 48:1; 66:1; cf. *âmatahkêšîwi-, mahkêšiw-*

...**ahkon-** NDI ankle; (65:8); cf. *mahkon-, wahkon-*

...**ahtay-** F fur; dollar; 42:12; cf. *nîšohtay*

...**akâm**... MF far side (of water); 11:9; 31:2; 42:47; cf. *têpakâmêpali-, kwêskakâm, lâlakâm, naspâtakâm, têtâwakâm*

...**amahciho-** VAIF sense, feel; 10:10; (23:2; 27:1); cf. *itamahciho-, milomahciho-, pakwâsamahciho-*

...**amêkw-** F fish of a particular species; 54; cf. *atihkamêkw-, namêkos-, wâpamêkw-*

...**amês**.../- MF fish; 16; 16:5; cf. *mistamês-, nôtamêsê-*

...**amiskw**.../- MF beaver; 13; 8; 9; cf. *mistamiskw-, natôkaminamiskwê-*

...**amohkâso-** VAIF pretend to; (n. 10:21); cf. *pêhtêyêlihtamohkâso-, pisiskêlihtamohkâso-*

...**anakway-** NDA sleeve; (13:9); cf. *wanakwaya*

...**anaw**... M cheek; 10:8; cf. *mahkatêwanawê-, ...inaw...*

...**api-** VAIF sit; 9:11; cf. *nahapi-*

...**asiniy-** F rock, stone; 13:14; cf. *mistasiniy-*

...**ask**.../- MF moss, earth; (n. 2:1); 51:1; n. 51:2; cf. *nâtaskê-,* 32:1; *wâpatanask-*

...**askamik**... M land; (2:3); cf. *kišipaskamikâ-*

...**askamikw-** F land, moss; 6:4; 40:2; 41:6; n. 51:2; cf. *kihciwêskamikw-, mihkwaskamikw-, pakwataskamikw-, wâpaskamikw-*

...**askw**... M cloud; 12:5; cf. *mitânaskwan-*

...**askw-** F bear; 31:1; cf. *wâpaskw-*

...**astimw**.../- MF dog; 33; cf. *kêšîciwanastimwak,*

nâtawiyêwastimw-, ...têm-, atimw-

...**ašak**... M skin; (10:7); cf. *wâpašakê-, nîhcikašakê-*

...**ašakay-** NDA skin; (10:7; 21:4); cf. *wašakaya*

...**atay**... M stomach; 16:5; cf. *mahkatayêšin-, ...atay-*

...**atay-** NDI stomach; 4:7; 29:2; cf. *watay-, matay-, ...atay...*

...**atihkw**.../- MF caribou; 10:6; cf. *'nâtawatihkwê-, iyâpêwatihkw-, atihkw-*

...**atin-** VIIF freeze; 48:2; cf. *akoskwatin-*

...**ayâ-** VIIF be; 48:1; 60:7; 66:1; cf. *pakwanêyâ-, maškawitêwêyâ-, tahkâyâ-*

...**âcimo-** VAIF narrate, recount; 1:1; 9:1; 21:1; 41:12; cf. *itâcimo-, tipâcimo-*

...**âhtawî-** VAIF tree-climb; 1:5; 1:7; 12:4; 12:5; 16:5; cf. *kospâhtawî-, nîšâhtawî-*

...**âhtikw**.../- MF wood, tree; 24:1; 67:4; cf. *nîpisiyâhtiko-mistikw-, nôtâhtikwê-, cîpayâhtikw-*

...**âkam**... M liquid; 12:11; cf. *kišâkamitê-, ...kam...*

...**âkamin**... M body of water; 13:8; *natôkaminâmiskwê-*

...**âkamin-** VIIF body of water; 65:9; 68:1; cf. *šîwâkamin-*

...**âkon**... M snow; (48:1); cf. *môskâkonêpit-*

...**âkonak**... MF snow; 21:7; 66:1; (68:2); cf. *môskâkonakî-, šêkwâkonakî-, mostâkonak*

...**âlihkoc**... M midriff; (21:4); cf. *sakâlihkocêpiso-*

...**âliw**... MV tail; 48; cf. *kinwâliwê-, tahkwâliwê-*

...**âmaciwê-** VAIF walk on a slope; 5:1

...**âmatin**... MF land, ground; (42:54); 68:6; cf. *awasâmatin, išpâmatinâ-, mêkwêyâmatin, pimâmatinâ-*

...**ânak**... MF island; 2:3; cf. *kišipânakâ-, awasânak, âstamânak, kwêskânak, otiškawânak*

...**ânakw-** F island; 42:48; cf. *šîpânakohk*

...**âp**... MV line, trace; 42:42; cf.
kinwâpê-, tahkwâpê-

...**âpan**- VIIF dawn; 3:4; 10:4; 42:13; cf.
pêtâpan-, pahkahkâpan-, wâpan-

...**âpan** F dawn; cf. *mêsakwanâpan*

...**âpêk**... M line, string; 1:4; 2:10; 3:11;
4:8; (42:42) et passim; cf. *iskwâpêkan-,
nahkâpêkin-*

...**âpêw**.../- MF male; 10:7; 13; 13:4; 66:3;
cf. *cahkâpêš-, mistâpêw-,
iyâpêwatihkw-*

...**âpi**- VAIF look; 1:4; 9:4; 19:2; 19:4;
66:1; 68:2; cf. *ašawâpi-, itâpi-,
milwêtâpi-, nahâpi-, wîsakâpi-*

...**âpihk**... M line, cord; 1:4; 14:7; 15:5;
52:1; cf. *iskwâpihkêsi-, nîhtâpihkên-*

...**âpisk**... M stone, metal; 33; 42:23;
50:63; cf. *kišâpiskis-, tawâpiskâ-*

...**âpiskw**- F stone, metal; 8:8; 41:4;
42:62; cf. *pîwâpiskw-*

...**âpiy**- F twine, line, rope; (42:42); cf.
pîšâkanâpiy-

...**âpolo**- VAIF drift; 8:5; 10:3; 30:2; cf.
itâpolo-, pimâpolo-

...**âpošw**- F rabbit; cf. 3:10; 21:2; (53:1);
58:5; cf. *kâhkâpošw-, wâpošw-*

...**âpotê**- VIIF drift, slide; (10:4; 13:15;
56:5); cf. *mâhâpotê-, pimâpotê-*

...**âpoy**- F liquid (SC); 9:9; cf.
anôminâpoy-

...**âpôw**- F liquid (MC); 65:1; cf. *kônâpôw-*

...**âpw**... M liquid; (58:5); cf. *tîwâpôhkê-*

...**âskw**.../- MF wood, tree; 40:3; 42:32;
52:2; 60:9; 67:4; cf. *kinwâskohtâ-,
otâpânâskw-, pîmâskwan-*

...**âspinê**- VAIF sickness n. 11:8; cf.
itâspinê-

...**âstan**- VIIF blow (as wind); 9:5; (50:5);
cf. *cîwêyâstan-, wêpâstan-, ...âši-*

...**âšakâmê**- VAIF make one's way
(walking); 9:3; 11:12; cf.
papâmâšakâmê-, pimâšakâmê-

...**âši**- VAIF sail, blow; 42:22; 58:1; 58:2;
cf. *nâmowinâši-, pimâši-, ...âstan-*

...**âtahî**- VAIF slide; 12:15; cf.
*papâmâtahî-, pîhtokwêyâtahî-,
šoškonâtahî-*

...**âtakâ**- VAIF wade, swim; 2:7; 16:3;
61:2; cf. *pimâtakâ-, âšawahâtakâ-*

...**âwaso**- VAIF infant; (1:9; 2:9; 11:1); 51;
cf. *tahkopitâwaso-, wâpamâwaso-*

...**âwikan**... M spine, back; (29:1); cf.
sâkâwikanêstâ-

...**âwikan**- NDI spine, back; (29:1); cf.
wâwikan-

...**câp**... MV eye; 46; cf. *mihkwacâpi-*

...**câš**... M snout; (15:5; 46:2)

...**câš**- NDI snout; (15:5; 46:2); cf. *ocâš-,
napakicâšê-*

...**cêsk**... F mire, mud; (61:2); cf.
liskicêskawišk-

...**cêskaw**... M mud; (61:2); cf.
iskwacêskawê-, liskicêskawišk-

...**cêskawak**... M mud; (61:2); cf.
pasakocêskawakâ-

...**cihc**... MF hand, forepaw; (21:4); cf.
sakicihcêpiso-, nîšocihc

...**cihcân**- F finger; (13:16); cf.
lîlîkicihcân-

...**cihciy**- NDI hand, forepaw; (21:4); cf.
ocihciy-

...**cisk**- NDI arse, backside [animate
when addressed or personalized]; 55:4;
55:5; cf. *ocisk-*

...**ciwan**... M flow, current; (12:5);
môhkiciwanipêkw-

...**ciwan**.../- VIIF flow, current; 61:3; cf.
kišîciwan-

...**ciwanw**... F flow, current; 61:3; 34:1;
39:3; 49:1; cf. *kêšîciwanw-*

...**cîsk(awak)**... M cf. ...*cêsk...,
...cêskawak...*

...**côšimiš**- NDA stepson, stepchild; 48:3;
cf. *ocôšimiša-*

...**êk**... M sheet-like material; 52:3; cf.
iskwêkan-, iskwêkih-

...**êkin**- MF sheet-like material; 42:22;
51:1; cf. *pakwayânêkin-,
apahkwâsonêkin-*

...**hkâso**- VAIF pretend to; 9:20; 13:5; cf.
*kihtohtêhkâso-, kišêwâtotawêhkâso-,
...amohkâso-*

...**hkop**... MF willow; (n. 66:3; 66:1); cf.
lâlihkop, mêkwêhkop, pîkwêhkopâ-

...**hkw**... MV face; 22:3; (46:2); cf.
*macihkwêstâ-, pâhpihkwêli-,
sinikohkwênitiso-, pîmihkwêpali-,
wasaswêhkwêhw-*

...**hlâ**... VAIF fly; 8; cf. *pimihlâ-*,
   kâ-pimihlâmakahk

...**htâwak**... M ear; (15:5); cf.
   kânikihtâwakê-, sakihtâwakêpiso-

...**htâwakay**- NDI ear; cf. *ohtâwakaya*

...**htin**- VIIF lie; 58:4; 61:3; cf. *itêhkêhtin-*,
   pimihtin-, piskwahtin, wâwâcihtin

...**icê**... M main body, main bulk; 4:6;
   19:3; 54:2; 61:1; cf. *mâmihkocêyâ-*,
   pakocên-, pâskicên-

...**ihkâkê**- VAIF use to make s.t.; 41:11;
   cf. *šôliyânihkâkê-*; cf. *...kê-, ...iwâkê-*

...**ihkân**- F surrogate for s.t.; 11:8; 27:7;
   39:4; 42:6; cf. *kêkwânihkân-*,
   pîsimohkân-

...**ihkê**- VAIF make; 11:6; 62; cf.
   apašohkê-, cîmânihkê- mitêhkê-, ...kê-

...**ihkwaši**- VAIF fall asleep; 9:7; 9:17; cf.
   nôhtêhkwaši-, šâkotihkwaši-

...**ihkwâmi**- VAIF sleep; 9:17; 55:5; cf.
   liskihkwâmi-, matwêhkwâmi,
   mošêhkwâmi-, šâpohkwâmi-

...**iht**.../- MF wood; 9:19; (11:7); 23:4;
   14:2; 14:5; cf. *manihtê-, miht-*,
   nâtinihtê-

...**ihtakw**.../- MF wood; (42:54); cf.
   ininâšihtakw-, pîkotôhtakw-,
   têtâwihtak, wakîtihtak

...**ihtâkosi**- VAIF sound; (42:37; 50:5); cf.
   nanêhkâšihtâkosi-, natawêlihtâkosi-

...**ihtâkwan**- VIIF sound; 50:5; cf.
   natawêlihtâkwan-

...**ikamikw**- F structure, building; 41:6;
   42:51; 43:5; cf. *astâsonikamikw-*,
   âhkosîwikamikw-

...**ikamikisi**- VAIF be a dwelling group, a
   family; 21:1; cf. *nîšokamikisi-*,
   pêyakokamikisi-

...**ikâkê**- VAIF use as a means of carrying
   out a general action; (42:59); 50:4; cf.
   manihtâkâkê-, otatâmahikâkê-, ...kê-

...**ikimâw**- F leader, master; 42:39; 49:1;
   cf. *šôliyânikimâw-, okimâw-*

...**ikon**... MV day; (58:3); cf. *nîšokoni-*

...**ikonak**... MV day; 58:3; cf. *nîšitana*,
   nîšokonakisi-

...**ikw**... MV neck; 3:6; 12:3; (18:5); 55:2;
   cf. *nîšokwêšimo-, sakikwêpiso-*,
   ...kwayaw-

...**inaw**... M cheek, face; (10:8); cf.
   nihcikinawê-, wâpiskinawê-, ...anaw...

...**ipê**... M water; 11:7; 18:10;
   lâsipêpahtâ-

...**ipê**- VAIF water; (48:1); 61:3; cf.
   âpihtawipê-, iskopê-, pahkopê-

...**ipêk**... M water; 48:1; cf. *môskipêkipit-*

...**ipêkw**- F water; 9:24; 49:5; 65:9; cf.
   lâlipêkw, pîhtâpêkw-

...**iskâ**- VIIF abound; 41:19; cf. *asinîskâ-*

...**iskw**... MV head; 11:2; 22:3; 27:2; 56:5;
   cf. *itiskwêli-, aspiskwêšimon-*,
   ...stikwân-

...**iskwêw**.../- MF woman; 14:2; 56:2; cf.
   mistâpêskwêw-, nôcîskwêwê-

...**itâpê**- VAIF haul; 4:6; 42:18; 52:1; 65:4;
   cf. *akwâsitâpê-, âwacitâpê-, pimitâpê-*,
   šêhkâtâpê-

...**iwat**.../- MF bag; 14:4; 18:2; cf.
   nikamowiniwat-, wîwaši-

...**iwâkê**- VAIF use as a means to carry
   out a general action; 41:7; 41:10; cf.
   pimâtisîwêkê-, tašîhkêwâkê-, ...kê-

...**îcihkawêsiw**- NDA cousin, brother;
   43:3; cf. *nîcihkawêsiw-*

...**îc'-ililiw**- NDA companion, neighbour;
   cf. *wîc'-îniniwa, nîc'-ililiwak*

...**îci-môsw**- NDA fellow moose; 36:2; cf.
   wîci-môswa

...**îci-nâpêw**- NDA fellow man; 21:3; cf.
   wîci-nâpêwa

...**îk**- NDI home; 3:3; 4:5; 11:6; 37:3; cf.
   nîki, wîki

...**îkiwâm**- NDI tipi; 9:11; 13:4; cf.
   mîkiwâm-, wîkiwâm-

...**îlitihp**- NDI brain; 50:2; cf. *wîlitihp-*,
   ...tihp...

...**îpit**- NDI tooth; (58:2; n. 58:7); cf.
   wîpiciw-

...**îsopiy**- NDA gall bladder; (14:3); cf.
   mîsopiy-

...**îstâw**- NDA brother in law; 60:8; cf.
   wîstâwa

...**îtakay**- NDI penis; (56:2); cf. *âtakay-*

...**îw**... NDA wife; 8:6; 47:1; cf. *wîwa*

...**îwat**- NDI bag, hunting bag; 1:4; 14:4;
   cf. *mîwat-*

...**îyaw**- NDI body; 34:2; 59:4; cf. *mîyaw-*

...**îyâs-** NDI flesh, meat; cf. *wîyâs-,*
wîyaw-

...**kam**... M water; 12:11; cf.
mahkikamâ-, mišikamâ-, ...âkam...

...**kamiy-** F water; 9:7; 60:5; 68:8; cf.
kihcikamiy-

...**kaškam**... M nape of the neck; 12:5; cf.
môhkikaškamêyâhtawî-

...**kaškamâw-** NDI nape of the neck;
12:3; 56:4; cf. *mikaškamâw-,*
okaškamâw-

...**kaškw**... M nail, talon; (42:6); cf.
mihkokaškwênitiso-

...**kâpawi-** VAIF stand; 44:4; 49:5; cf.
nîpitêkâpawi-, wâwâskâpawi-

...**kât**... MF leg; 21:4; (61:2); cf.
âpihtawikât, sakikâtêpiso-, ...skât-

...**kâwiy-** NDA mother; 9:19; cf. *okâwiya*

...**kê-** VAIF use s.t. to carry out an action
[secondary suffix commonly following
...*ihkê-*, as in ...*ihkîkê-*; ...*ikê-*, as in
...*ikâkê-*; and ...*iwê-*, as in ...*iwâkê-*]

...**kitikw-** NDI knee; (11:12; 61:2); cf.
mikitikw-

...**konêw**... MV mouth; 8:8; 21:4; cf.
mahkikonêwê-, pohcikonêwên-, ...tôn-

...**kohtâkan-** NDI throat; (8:8); cf.
okohtâkan-, ...kotaskway-

...**kosis-** NDA son; 9:2; cf. *okosisa*

...**kot-** NDI nose; (46:2); cf. *okot-, ...câš.,*
...*skiwan...*

...**kotaskway-** NDI throat; (8:8); cf.
okotasway-, ...kohtâkan-

...**kwayaw-** NDI neck; 12:6; 66:2; cf.
...*ikw...*

...**lihkw-** NDA tonsil; (42:63); cf. *olihkwa*

...**mâkosi-** VAIF have an odour; (11:12);
cf. *wîhcêkimâkosi-*

...**min**.../- MF berry; 19:1; cf. *môminê-,*
kâhkâkîšimin-, mîniš-

...**mis-** NDA older sister; 3:3; 4:3; 13:1;
15:2; cf. *omisa*

...**mošôm-** NDA grandfather; (n. 12:15);
cf. *omošôma*

...**môsw**... M moose; 35:1; 49:1; cf.
'nâtawamôswê-, môsw-

...**nahâhkaniskwêm-** NDA daughter-in-
law; 60:3; cf. *onahâhkaniskwêma*

...**nahâhkišîm-** NDA son-in-law; 11:3; cf.

onahâhkišîma

...**nâkosi-** VAIF appear, look; 9:17; 11:4;
cf. *lâwinâkosi-*

...**nâkwan-** VIIF appear, look; 37:6;
42:58; cf. *paškonâkwan-*

...**nikon-** NDA son-in-law (Ojibwa); 11:3;
cf. ...*nikwan-*

...**nikwan-** NDA son-in-law (Ojibwa);
11:3; cf. ...*nikon-*

...**nisk**... MV arm; 65:8; cf. *sakiniskêpah-,*
...*spiton-, ...piton*

...**nîkihikw-** NDA parent; 5:3; 6:2; 11:2

...**ohtê-** VAIF go by foot, walk; 1:3; 2:3;
10:6; 11:2; 36:2; 42:1 et passim; cf.
itohtê-, kihtohtê-, pimohtê-

...**ôhkom-** NDA grandmother; 9:8; 27:7;
cf. *ôhkoma*

...**ôhkomis-** NDA stepfather, uncle; 10:4;
10:8; 43:5; 63:1; cf. *ôhkomisa-*

...**ôhtâwiy-** NDA father; 9:9; 9:20; 54:3;
cf. *ôhtâwiya*

...**ôsisim-** NDA grandchild; 9:8; cf.
ôsisima

...**ôtêw**.../- MF family; 1:9; cf.
kistôtêwêskâ-, nîšôtêwisi-, kistôtêw,
nistôtêw

...**ôtênaw-** F dwelling group, family;
60:10; cf. *tân' tahtôtênaw,*
mihcêtôtênaw

...**pahtâ-** VAIF run; 19:8; 19:9; 18:6; 31:2;
34:2; 36:2; 47:2; 56:8; cf. *ispahtâ-,*
kihcipahtâ-

...**pali-** VAI move; 1:2; 2:5; 11:11; 56:8 et
passim; cf. *ispali-, kihcipali-, pimipali-*

...**pali-** VIIF move; 1:2; 2:5; 11:11; 56:8 et
passim; cf. *ispali-, kihcipali-, pimipali-*

...**paliho-** VAIF make oneself go; move
suddenly, move quickly; (65:8); cf.
âkopaliho-, šêkopaliho-

...**pici-** VAIF travel with one's gear; 40:1;
40:4; 41:3; (60:4); cf. *âhcipici-,*
kihcipici-, papâmipici-, pimipici-

...**piskwan**... M back; (9:14); cf.
wâwâhcipiskwanêpaliho-,
mispiskwan-, ospiskwan-

...**piton**... M arm; (42:63); cf.
milîyopitonê-, ...spiton-

...**pîway-** NDI whiskers, bristles; 50:1;
53:1; cf. *opîwaya*

...**po-** VAIF eat; (10:8); cf. *tômiskipo-,*
wîhkipo-

...**pwâm-** NDI thigh; 9:17; cf. *mipwâm-,*
opwâm-

...**sis-** NDA father-in-law; 11:6; cf. *osisa*

...**sisim-** NDA grandchild; 9:8; cf. *osisima*

...**sit**... M foot; (65:8); cf. *kotikositêšin-*

...**sit-** NDI foot; 36:1; 47:1; cf. *osita, misit-*

...**sitân-** NDI toe; (13:16); cf. *lîlîkisitân-,*
misisitân-

...**skan-** NDI bone; 9:15; 11:9; 12:15; 21:9;
50:1; 50:6; cf. *miskan-, oskan-*

...**skanawê-** VAIF leave evidence; 5:2;
29:4; cf. *pimiskanawê-*

...**skât-** NDI leg; 9:17; 21:7; 36:2; cf.
miskât-, oskât-, ...*kât*...

...**skiwan-** NDI bill (of a bird); (46:2); cf.
oskiwan-, ...*câš-,* ...*kot-*

...**skon-** NDI liver; (19:9; 27:4); cf.
miskon-, oskon-, ...*skwan-*

...**skwan-** NDI liver; (19:9; 27:4); cf.
miskwan-, oskwan-, ...*skon-*

...**sôw-** NDI tail (MC); 45; 45:1; cf. *osôw-,*
...*âliw*...

...**sôy-** NDI tail (SC); 13:9; 25:2; n. 25:2; cf.
osôy-, ôsôw-, ...*âliw*...

...**spiskwan-** NDI back; 18:6; cf.
mispiskwan-, ospiskwan-, ...*piskwan*...

...**spiton-** NDI arm; 13:9; cf. *mispiton-,*
ospiton-, ...*piton*...

...**staw-** M snout; 15:5; cf. *kînikistawê-*

...**stês-** NDA older brother; 23:1; 60:9; cf.
ostêsa

...**stikw**.../- MF river; 42:50; 62:3; cf.
pâwistikw-, kinostikwêyâ-,
pâhkostikwêyâ-

...**stikwân**... M head; (37:3); cf.
paškostikwânê-

...**stikwân-** NDI head; 10:5; cf.
mistikwân-, ostikwân-, ...*iskw*...

...**ston**... MV nose; 12:3; cf.
paskostonêhotiso-

...**šân-** F offspring; (1:1); 11:2; cf.
kîwašišân, mâhcišošân

...**šikon**... M tailfin; (29:1); cf.
sâkišikonêšin-, ...*šikwan*...

...**šikwan**... M tailfin; (29:1); cf.
sâsâkišikwanêstâ-, ...*šikon*...

...**šikwanay-** NDI tailfin; (29:1); cf.

mišikwanay-, ošikwanay-

...**šimo-** VAIF lie outstretched; 8:3; cf.
pasakwâpišimo-, pahkopêšimo-

...**šin-** VAIF lie, recline; 19:5; 24:2; 41:14;
43:4; cf. *mâskošin, ohpimêšin,*
otihtapišin, pahkišin, pimišin-,
pimâskošin-, wâwâhcišin

...**šip-** F duck; cf. *kâhkâkišip-*

...**šîm-** NDA younger sibling; 4:6; 16:2;
19:1; 20:2; 27:4; 42:22; cf. *ošîma*

...**šîmiš-** NDA little younger sibling; 65:7;
cf. *ošîmiša*

...**škašiy-** NDA talon, (finger)nail, hoof;
1:7; 2:7; (14:5); cf. *oškašiya;* ...*kaškw*...

...**škîšikw-** NDI eye; 18:6; 19:3; 27:1;
55:2; cf. *miškîšikw-, oškîšikw-*

...**šôkan**... M lower back, backside; 41:13

...**šôkan-** NDI lower back, backside; 8:5;
55:3; cf. *ošôkan-, mišôkan-*

...**tahtahkwan**... M wing; (20:6); cf.
kaškatahtahkwanêh-

...**tahtahkwan-** NDI wing; (20:6); cf.
mitahtahkwan-, otahtahkwan-

...**takiš**... M intestine, gut; 20:4; cf.
sînitakišê-

...**takišiy-** NDI entrails, gut; 19:9; cf.
otakišiy-, otôtakišîm-

...**tamaskay-** NDI gobs of raw meat
adhering to skin; 50:6; cf. *otamaskay-*

...**tâmihkan**... M jaw; (15:5); cf.
kînikitâmihkanê-

...**tâs-** NDI legging(s), trousers [NDA in
some dialects]; 11:11; cf. *mitâs-, otâsa*

...**têlaliy-** NDI tongue; 42:57; cf.
mitêlaliy-, otêlaliy-

...**têm-** NDA dog; 33; cf. *otêma,*
...*astimw-, atimw-*

...**têpo-** VAIF cook; 18:7; 18:9; 55:3

...**têw**... M surface crust; (42:29); cf.
maškawitêwêyâ-

...**tihp**.../- MF skull, cranium; (37:3); cf.
paškwâtihpê-, ...*îlitihp-, wâpisakitihp-*

...**tihtiman-** NDI shoulder; 9:14; 12:3; cf.
mitihtiman-, otihtiman-

...**tilîkêkan-** NDA shoulder blade; 9:15;
cf. *otikîkêkana, mitilîkêkan-*

...**tiy**... MV rump, backside; 68:5; cf.
kwêskitiyêpaliho-, kalakitiyê-

...**ton**... M mouth; (42:63); cf. *milîyotonê-*

...tôhtan- NDI heel; 44:3; cf. *mitôhtan-*, *mâskitôhtan-*

...tôn- NDI mouth; 8:8; 29:3; (ô on analogy of *o*-initial stems with personal prefixes in *t*); cf. *mitôn-*, *otôn-*, *milîyotonê-*

...tôsis- NDA aunt; (63:1); cf. *otôsisa*

...tôskwan- NDI elbow, funny-bone; 9:13; (9:14); 27:4; cf. *mitôskwan-*, *otôskwan-*

...tôtêm- NDA friend; 44:4; cf. *otôtêma*

Stems

acakâš- NA mink (East Coast, James Bay); used at Moose Factory as diminutive of *âtakay-*, cf. *šâkwêšiw-*

acicamoš- NA squirrel; 46:1

acicipahtâ- VAI run down head first (4:6)

acilaw IPC for no good reason; 27:3; *acilaw piko n'kî-âšaw'hênân* we crossed the river for no good reason, no particular reason; cf. Watkins-Faries *aciyaw* a little while, for a short time

acimošiš- NA puppy; 9:15; cf. *apiscacimoš-*

aciwipali- VAI/VII go down, subside; 9:10

ahcâhkw- NA spirit; cf. *wîsahkwêcâhkw-*

ahcâpiy- NA bow (for shooting); 4:1; 13:15

ahlapihkêsiw- NA spider, 'net-maker' (MC); 1:4; *êhêpikw-*; 1:3; SC: *otahnapihkêsiw-*; 2:4

ahlapiy- NA (fish-)net; 25:2; 58:4

akaskw- NA arrow; 4:1; 11:6; 29:1

akâmaskiy- NI [place name] Akimiski, lit., 'land across the water'; (an island offshore from Albany River mouth in James Bay)

akâmihk IPC across the water; 42:18; 58:4; *akâmihk itêhkê ôma sîpiy* on the far side of this river; cf. *...akâm...*, *ênakâm*, *têpakâmêpali-*

akâmiškotêhk IPC to the other side of the fire; 10:4

akâwâc IPC scarcely; 65:3

akâwât IPC scarcely; 65:3

akihcikâtê- VII it is reckoned, calculated; 42:10

akiht- VTI count s.t.; (42:9)

akihtê- VII be counted, pay; 42:4

akim- VTA count s.o.; 42:9

akoci-wêpin- VTA throw s.o. up so it hangs; 11:6

akocin- VAI hang; 12:5

akociw'lâkan- NI net-float; (58:4)

akohcim- VTA put s.o. in water, soak s.o.; 50:1; 50:4

akohcin- VAI float; soak, steep; 50:1

akohkasi- VAI be stuck (because of heat, burning); (48:3)

akohkasikê- VAI weld; (48:3)

akohkatê- VII be stuck (because of heat, burning); (48:3)

akohkê- VAI/VII adhere to, be stuck to, be fastened to; 11:7; 55:9; also as *akwahkê-*

akohtê- VII float; 11:3

akohtitâ- VAI-T put s.t. in water, soak s.t.; 50:1; 50:4

akol- VTA hang s.o.; 14:5; 50:2; 50:3; also as *akwal-*

akomo- VAI sit, float on water (as a duck); 18:1; also as *akwamo-*

akosî- VAI perch, sit on a branch; 12:5; 14:5; 16:1; 66:1

akoškwaci- VAI freeze to the ice; 48:3; cf. *akwâhkwaci-*

akoškwatin- VII freeze to the ice; 48:3; cf. *akwâhkwatin-*

akotâ- VAI-T hang s.t. up; 11:11

akotê- VII hang; 10:3

akwahkê- VAI/VII adhere to, be stuck to, be fastened to; also as *akohkê-*

akwahpiso- VAI be tied up against (something); 65:7

akwal- VTA hang s.o.; 50:6; cf. *akol-*

akwamo- VAI sit, float on water (as a duck); 18:1; cf. *akomo-*

akwanah- VTI cover s.t.; (52:2; 61:4)

akwanahikan- NI cover [sometimes used for 'tarpaulin', which is more accurately called *akwanahotâson*-]; (52:2); cf. *akwanah-, akwanahw-*

akwanahotâson- NI tarpaulin; (52:2); cf. *akwanahikan-*

akwanahotiso- VAI cover oneself; (52:2); 61:4

akwanahw- VTA cover s.o.; (52:2); 61:4

akwani- VAI be covered; 36:2

akwatamon- VII be stuck on (by its own viscosity); (55:9); cf. *ohci-akwatamon-*

akwatamwan- VII be stuck on (by its own viscosity) [alternative form of *akwatamon*-]; (55:9)

akwayâskwah- VTI lever s.t. off the fire (using a stick); (55:7)

akwayâskwahw- VTA lever s.o. off the fire (using a stick); 55:7

akwâhkwaci- VAI be frozen stuck; (48:3); *akwâhkwaciw n'tastis* my mitt is frozen stuck to the ice; cf. *akoskwaci-*

akwâhkwatin- VII be frozen stuck; (48:3); cf. *akoskwatin-, âhkwatin-*

akwâkohtin- VII be rusty, mouldy; (n. 48:6)

akwâkoši- VAI be rusty, mouldy; (n. 48:6)

akwâpasikê- VAI make smoke; (61:6); cf. *pîpotênikê-*

akwâpasw- VTA he smoke-dries s.o.; 50:5

akwâpicikan- NI seining place; 49:5: a tongue of land jutting out from Moose Factory Island, known in English as The Flats

akwâsitâpê- VAI drag (something) ashore; 4:6; cf. ...*itâpê-*

akwâškwaci- VAI be frozen to the ice; (48:3)

akwâškwatin- VII be frozen to the ice; 48:3

akwâtâpât- VTA pull s.o. to shore; 16:5

akwâwân-apašohkê- VAI set up the frame of roasting poles; 19:7; cf. *akwâwânâhtikw-*

akwâwânâhtikw- NI spit (for roasting); 19:9

akwâwê- VAI make a meat stage, roast on a frame over a fire; 19:7

al- VTA set s.o., put s.o.; (23:4); cf. *astâ-*

alisâc IPC hardly, with difficulty; 3:10; cf. *akâwâc*

alitaw-iškotêw- NI an open fire; 40:5

aliwâk IPC over, in excess of; 38:3; 44:2

alîki-pîsimw- NA May, lit., 'frog moon'; cf. *pîsimw-*

alîkiš- NA frog; 41:12

alôminâpoy- NI oatmeal porridge (MC); 9:9; SC: *anôminâpoy-*

alwêpi- VAI take a rest; 42:5

amahkw- NA needle used in snowshoe making; (52:1); cf. *aškimê-, šâponikan-, wâš-*

amiskošiši-wayân- NI pelt of a small beaver; 9:21; cf. *amisk'-wayânišiš*

amisko-wanahikê- VAI trap beaver; 38:1

amisko-wayân- NA beaver skin; 2:10

amisk'-wayânišiš- NA small beaver skin; 9:21; cf. *amiskošiši-wayân-*

amisko-wâpikošîš- NA beaver mouse (little, fat field-mouse); (n. 3:7); cf. *kînikisci-âpikošîš-*

amiskw- NA beaver; 1:7; 13:4; 19:9; 27:4; 40:5

ana PR that one [anim.prox.sing.]; 2:6; cf. *ana kâ-itâpit* that one who looks

anawâniskêpali- VAI rest one's arm between strokes, leave pauses between strokes (of the arm); 10:7

anawâniskêpaliho- VAI rest one's arm from motion; 10:7

anawâniskêšimo- VAI give one's arm(s) a rest; (10:7)

anawêniskêpi- VAI sit and rest one's arm(s); (10:7)

anawêšimo- VAI lie down and take a rest; (10:7)

anâwis IPC scarcely, hardly; 34:2; cf. *akâwâc* (65:3)

ani PR that one [inan.prox.sg.]; 9:5; 15:2

ani IPC [used to emphasize preceding word]; cf. *ê'kwâni, oš' âni*

anihi PR that one [anim.obv./inan.pl.]; 1:4

aniki PR those ones [anim.pl.]; 6:7; 8:5

anima PR that one [inan.prox.sg.]; 3:24 et passim

animêliw PR that one [inan.obv.sg.]; 9:10; 44:4

anišâ IPC given that, seeing that, since fortunately; 3:10; *anišâ mâka piko* given that (it was the only thing to do); *anišâ mâka piko n'kaškihon* but, seeing that I'm smart, (it worked); *anišâ mâka piko ê-kiskên'tamân* but, given that I knew how; *anišâ mâka piko nipatahok* but, since fortunately he missed me, (I was not fatally hurt)

anohc IPC now; 1:3; 30:2; 42:49; *anohc kâ-kîšikâk* today; *anohc oš' âni kâ-wâpahtamân* (it is) only now that I see it, only lately that I see it

anôminâpoy- NI oatmeal porridge (SC); 9:9; MC: *alôminâpoy-*

anta IPC there; 1:4 et passim; *anta itê* along that side; 60:6

antê IPC there, thither; 2:3; 9:8; 41:1 et passim

apahkwân- NI canvas tarpaulin; 51:2; 65:4

apahkwâsonêkin- NI tenting, canvas; 42:22

apašohkê- VAI make a tent-pole; 19:7

apašwoy- NI tent pole; (19:7)

api- VAI sit; 1:4; 2:4; 13:14; 41:1; 42:62 et passim

apih- VTA seat s.o.; 49:1

apihâkaniwi- VAI be seated; cf. *apih-*

apihkan- NA thwart (of a canoe); 11:2; 38:1; n. 38:5; cf. *aspihtitâkan-*

apikanâsamâ- VAI crack the bone open and eat the marrow; 12:7

apiscacimoš- NA small dog (i.e., a pet or house-dog as opposed to a puppy); cf. *acimošiš-* (9:15)

apiscawâšiš- NA small child; 42:63

apiscililîskwêšiš- NA midget girl; (56:2); cf. *apistâpêskwêšiš-*

apiskwêšimon- NI pillow

apiskwêšimonah- VTA make (s.o.) a pillow; 27:2

apiskwêšimo- VAI use for a pillow; 11:12; cf. *aspiskwêšimo-*

apistâpêskwêšiš- NA midget girl; (56:2)

apišâšin- VII be small; 15:5

apišimaniyâpiy- NI small netting line for snowshoes; 53:2; (n. 53:5)

apiši-pakwanêyâ- VII be a small hole; (60:9); cf. *pakwanêyâ-, mahki-pakwanêyâ-*

apišîš IPC a little, a bit; 6:1; 40:4; *apišîš niwî-âtalôhkân* I want to tell a little story; *nâspıc apišîš piko* only a very little

apišîšiši- VAI be small; 3:8; 9:9; 21:1; 24:1; 46:1; 65:4

apwânâskw- NI sharp stick for holding roasting or boiling food (replaced today by a metal *cîstahikan-*) (13:13); cf. *cîstahikan-, kapatêskwê-*

apwâtâkan- NI willow frame for roasting over an open fire; (10:6; n. 10:11)

apwêsi- VAI perspire; 41:7

apwê- VAI roast over an open fire on an *apwâtâkan*; 10:6

asawatâ- VAI-T hold s.t., contain s.t.; 23:3

asâm- NA snowshoe; 53:2

asâmâhtikw- NA snowshoe tree, snowshoe wood; 9:24; snowshoe frame; 42:59; cf. *...âhtikw.../-*

asâtiy- NA poplar; 55:9; n. 55:36

asic IPC along with, together with; 54:2

asicikas- VTI cook s.t. along with; (54:2) *patêtisa n'tasicikasên môso-wîyâsihk* I'm cooking potatoes along with the moose meat

asicikasw- VTA cook s.o. along with; 54:2

asikâpawi- VAI stand together; (18:5; 55:2); cf. *piskokâpawi-, ayasikwêšimo-*

asin- VTA/VTI have a handful of s.o./s.t.; (42:9; n. 42:14)

asinâpiy- NI sinker for a net; (65:9); *mawitônam asinâpiya ê-wî-pakitahwât* she's gathering sinkers to put a net out

asiniy- NA rock, stone; 9:24; 13:14; 41:1

asinîskâ- VII be many rocks, abound in rocks; 41:19

asinîskâw- NI the rocky place, cement

GLOSSARY

asisîya NI [pl.] long, underwater grass which grows in eddies and still water; 65:2

askihkoš- NA little kettle; 9:9

askihkw- NA pail, kettle; 5:10; 23:3

askipôta- NI [pl.] 'husky-boots'; 61:3; cf. *askîmêwaskisin-, âskipôta*

askiy- NI land, earth; 1:1; moss; 18:1; 51:1; soil; 42:55; ground; 62:2

askîkwâm- NI lodge; 55:2; n. 55:5

askîmêwaskisin- NI sealskin boot; (61:3); cf. *âskipôta*

askîmêwatimw- NA 'Eskimo' dog; 58:5; n. 58:21

askîwat- NI moss bag; 18:4

askîwâpiskisi- VAI have white moss on it; 9:24

askîwêtimw- NA 'Husky' dog; 58:5; n. 58:21

askîwi-pimiy- NI coal oil, kerosene; 42:55

askîwi-tipahikan- NI land measure; 37:6; *nîšo-tipahikan, askîwi-tipahikan ê-'špîšinâkwahk* two-measure unit (i.e., land-measure as-it-appeared up-to-such-an-amount; up to two miles)

askonâk IPC since [apparent alternative for *iskonâhk*]; 40:4

aspihtitâkan- NA flooring stay (for a canoe); 62:1; cf. *apihkan-*

aspin IPC away, off; since; contrary to expectation; 1:7; 9:20; 11:4; 13:9; 38:1; 42:13; 42:47; 42:64; 43:14; *aspin mâna* again and again; 66:2

aspiskwêšimon- NI pillow, 'head buffer'; (11:12; 27:2); cf. *aspišimon-*

aspiskwêšimonah- VTA make s.o. into a pillow; 27:2; *asiniya aspiskwêšimonahêw* he made stones into a pillow for him; cf. *aspišimon-, aspiskwêšimon-*

aspiskwêšimo- VAI use s.t. as a pillow; 11:12; 19:5

aspišimon- NI mattress, cushioning medium; (27:2); cf. *aspiskwêšimon-*

astahciko- VAI cache; 64:1

astaho- VAI quill; 11:7

astahw- VTA feather s.o. (an arrow), put

quills on s.o. (an arrow); 11:6; *astahwêw n'takaskwa* he's putting quills on my arrow(s)

astahwât- VTA put quills on s.o. (arrow); (11:6)

astawê- VAI quill [probable alternative form of *astaho-*]; 11:7; cf. *astahw-*

astâ- VAI-T set s.t., put s.t.; 23:4; cf. *al-*

astâsonikamikw- NI warehouse; 42:51; cf. ...*ikamikw-*

astis- NA glove; 41:16

ašah- VTI lie in wait for s.t.; (30:2)

ašahw- VTA lie in wait for s.o., watch for s.o.; 9:17; 30:2; *ašahwêw niska* he's watching for geese; *n'tašahwâw 'ci-pêci-walawît* I'm waiting for him to come out (of a child watching a mouse in a hole); *kî-kiskên'tam ê-ašahokot anihi* he knew that he was being watched by that one; [dialect variants: Peawanuck: *âšwahw-*; Fort Albany: âšwah-]

ašam- VTA feed s.o.; 10:5; 26:2; 27:3; 42:15; 59:2; *pêci-ašamik* bring them food; 43:3; *ašamâkaniwan* he is on rations; 43:6

ašawâpaht- VTI watch for s.t., be on the lookout for s.t.; (66:2; 68:2)

ašawâpam- VTA watch for s.o., be on the lookout for s.o.; 66:2; 68:2

ašawâpi- VAI keep a lookout; (66:2); 68:2; cf. ...*âpi-*

ašêhw- VTA put s.o. (clock) back; (56:1); cf. *âhtahw-, nîkânahw-*

ašê-kâhtin- VTA/VTI push s.o./s.t. away, out of the way; (13:14) *âšê-kâhtinam* he pushes it out of the way; *kitašê-kâhtinâw* you push him away (as from a door); contrast ...*âši-*

âšêstâ- VAI-T back s.t. up, set s.t. back; 13:9

ašic IPC together with, along with; 2:4; 8:1; 18:6; 42:34

ašikanihkê- VAI make (a) sock(s); (65:1); cf. ...*ihkê-*

ašikê- VAI wear socks; 65:1

ašiškiy- NI mud; (32:1); cf. *lêkaw-, wâpatanask-*

ašiwihikê- VAI cf. *ašôhikê-*; 61:1

448

aškimaniyâpiy- NI snowshoe netting line; 53:1; cf. ...*âpiy-*

aškimât- VTA net s.o. (snowshoes); 53:3

aškimê- VAI net a snowshoe frame; (53:1); 53:2; cf. *amahkw-, wâš-, kîšaskimê-*

aškiškâhtikw- NI green wood; 42:60; cf. *nipîwan-*

asôhikê- VAI watch, lie in wait; 61:1

ašwahikê- VAI sit in a blind; 43:5

atâm- VTA sell to s.o.; 62:2

atâmâtim IPC beneath the bank; 42:56

atâmihk IPC at the bottom; 2:3; down inside; 4:7; 9:16; 12:11; 29:2; 42:55; 60:6

atâwâkê- VAI sell, use for selling; 42:37

atâwê- VAI trade; 40:5; 42:23

ati IPV begin to (gradual onset); 1:8; 9:6; 9:18; 19:2; cf. *mâci*

atihkw- NA caribou, deer; 1:7; 10:5; 40:2

atihkamêkw- NA whitefish, 'caribou fish'; 54:1; cf. ...*amêkw-*

atihk'-wayân- NI deer skin, caribou hide; 10:10

ati-lâlipali- VAI/VII go along the side of; (6:11); cf. ...*pali-*

ati-lâlipalih- VTA make s.o. go along the side of; 6:11

atimahw- VTA overtake s.o. by water; n. 65:30; *ka-atimahotin* I'll catch up with you (by canoe)

atimapi- VAI have one's back turned; 56:8; cf. ...*api-*

atiminêhw- VTA overtake s.o. (walking); 67:2; (n. 65:30) *kâ-atiminêhotin* I'll catch up with you (walking); cf. *atimahw-*

atimohtê- VAI go down the road; (41:15); cf. *kihtahamê-, kihtamohtê-, kihtimohtê-, ...ohtê-*

atimokan- NI bone of a dog; (19:9)

ati-oški-pimâtisi- VAI be new-born; 40:6; be young in life; 41:9

atimw- NA dog; 9:15; 42:18

atipis- NI (either) end of a snowshoe; 'small netting', small end; 53:3; *niwâpahtên atipis ê-pahpaskipalik* I see the small end broken in several places; cf. *paskipali-*

atis- VTI dye s.t.; *atisam ostikwân'pîwaya* she dyes her hair; cf. *opîwâwi-*

atisw- VTA dye s.o.

atoskam IPC right away, definitely; 11:5; 42:17; gradually, more so; 42:2; immediately; 68:5

atôskê- VAI labour, work; 40:7

atôspiy- NA black alder; 68:8

atôspiyâhtikw- NA alder tree; (68:8); cf. *mihkopêmakâhtikw-*

awa PR this one [anim.prox.sg.]; 1:8

awahkân- NA captive, slave; pet; 12:9; 24

awahkât- VTA enslave s.o., have (an animal) as a pet; abuse, impose on, detest, abhor s.o.; 9:18; 30:2

awas IPC away with you! be off! 11:7; also as *âwas*; 46:1

awasâmatin IPC on the other side of the mountain; cf. *âstamâmatin, kwêskâmatin-, pâšitâmatin, ...âmatin...*

awasânak IPC on the other side of the island (i.e., *awasitê itêhkê ministikohk*); [synonym: *kaskêw*]; cf. *kaskêwê-, âstamânak, kišipânak, kwêskânak, otiškawânak, šîpânakw-; ...ânak...*

awasitê IPC more; 10:3; 34:3; 41:3 et passim

awas itêhkê IPC back of; 42:51; *awas itêhkê... kâ-'htakwahk* back of where it was

awâšiš- NA child; 1:9; 9:3; 11:6; 40:6

awâšišasâm- NA child's snowshoe; 53:4

awâšišîwi- VAI be a child; 39:1; 50:6; 65:1

awêhtâkwan- VII make sense [usually with negative]; 43:5; *môna kêkwân awêhtâkwan tân' êtwêkwê ê-ayamîšihtât* not a thing that he says makes sense when he prattles on

awênihkân- PR [indef.] some one, some person; 1:3; 2:3

awênihkân- PR [interrog.] who? which person? whoever; 49:4; 16:3; 35:2

awênihkân- NA a person; 9:13; 13:7; 40:6

awênihkâniwi- VAI be someone; 55:7;
ka-kiskêlimin 'lâta 'ê'hkâniwiyân you'll
know who I am now

awêspiso- VAI get dressed; 13:2; cf.
kêtâspiso-, wêspititiso-

awêyâšîš- NA animal, beast, creature; cf.
awiyâšîš; 47:1

awiyân- NA hide, animal skin; 39:2; cf.
wayân-

awiyâšîš- NA animal, beast, creature;
1:7; 3:7; 6:6; 8:1; 8:4; 16:1; 27:3; 46:1;
68:1

awiyâšîši-wayân- NA animal skin, hide;
2:10

ayahâw- NI thing; 40:5; *n'tispahwânân
ayahâhk* we mix it in a thing, 54:1;
kâ-'ši-pim'paniki ayahâwa the
'thingumabobs' that go along, 41:3; as
a pause word: *ay'hâw mâka* well,
then..., well, uh..., 41:12

ayakopâtin- VTA bathe s.o. with water;
64:3

ayakotâ- VAI-T [redupl.] hang s.t. about;
19:7

ayakwahkê- VAI/VII adhere to something
all over; 55:9; cf. *akohkê-*

ayamihcikê- VAI pray, hold a service;
read; 49:6

ayamih- VTA address s.o., speak to s.o.;
1:3; 8:6; 27:7; 53:1; cf. *ayamihtâ-*

ayamihê'-kîšikâ- VII be Sunday; 41:11

ayamihêwikimâw- NA clergyman,
(Anglican) priest; 49:1; cf.
mêhkatêwihkonayêw-, ...ikimâw-

ayamihêwi-masinahikan- NI prayer
book, devotional book; 42:67

ayamihêwiskwêw- NA nun, sister
(religious); 43:1; cf. *...iskwêw.../-*

ayamihitiso- VAI speak to oneself; 19:7

ayamihitowin- NI conversation; 41; 42;
43

ayamihtâ- VAI-T read s.t.; 41:1; 42:66; cf.
ayamih-

ayami- VAI speak; 2:3; 41:4; 41:20; 42:44;
64:2; *kâ-kî-ayamispan* who had been
saying, who had said

ayamiwin- NI word; 11:3; way of
talking; 41:21

ayamîšihtâ- VAI talk on and on, prattle
on (used of a child beginning to speak
or of a drunk); 43:5

ayapi- VAI sit around; 5:9; 42:9; *âskaw
awa ta-ayapîpan* sometimes this fellow
used to sit around

ayasikwên- VTA [redupl.] hold s.o. by
the neck(s) (a clutch of birds); (18:5);
cf. *atasikwêšimôwin-, nîšokwên-,
...ikw...*

ayasikwêšimo- VAI [redupl.] dance with
necks together; (18:5); 55:2.; cf.
*nîšokwên-, nîšokwêšimo-, ayasikwên-,
asikâpawi-, piskokâpawi-, ...ikw...,
...šimo-*

ayasikwêšimôwin- NI dance with necks
together; 18:5; cf. *ayasikwêšimo-*

ayâ- VAI-T have s.t.; 1:8; 6:3; 9:3; cf.
ayâw-

ayâhciw-akocin- VAI limp; (a bad limp
produces the impression of half
hanging as one walks); 42:63;
[synonym: *ayâhciwipali-, mâskipali-*]

ayâhciwipali- VAI/VII limp; (42:63); cf.
mâskipali-, ayâhciwakocin-, ...pali-

ayâhkwacipali- VAI [redupl.] freeze
severally right there; 22:2; cf. *...pali-*

ayâkomo- VAI drift around (on a lake);
8:5

ayâkosikwêkâpawi- VAI stand jostling
each other (to see), stand craning their
necks; 56:6; [*ayâkosikwêyâpam-*
preferred by one Fort Albany speaker];
cf. *...ikw..., ...kâpawi-*

ayâkosikwêyâpam- VTA crane one's
neck to peer at s.o.; (56:6); cf. *...ikw...*

ayâkwâmisî- VAI be careful; 5:7

ayân- NI thing, possession; 11:12; 42:35;
k'-âhtakwakatât oški-'yâniw- that he's
put a new thing on (i.e., a new reel);
43:14; n. 43:31

ayâniskê IPC [redupl.] adjoining,
successive; 1:9; *pîniš ayâniskê*
generation after generation; cf. *âniskê*

ayâniš- NI [dim.] little thing (euphemism
for penis); 56:2; [synonym: *âtakay*]

ayâw- VTA have s.o.; 9:8; 42:42; *êkwâni
misiwê kâ-yš'-êyâwakihcik* so in this
way we had them all

ayêskosi- VAI be tired; 18:8; 21:7; 40:2; 67:5

ayihtâ- VAI [redupl.] be here and there; 10:3

ayihti- VAI [redupl.] act so; 8:7; cf. *ihti-*

ayiskon- VTA [redupl.] roll s.o. up as one walks about; 13:9; *ayiskonêw wanakwaya* he rolls up his sleeves; cf. *iskon-, wanakway-*

ayišilawî- VAI [redupl.] do many things, be 'up to' many things; 10:1.; cf. *išilawî-*

ayitâcimikosi- VAI [redupl.] be widely talked about, be talk about s.o.; 3:1; cf. *itâcimâkaniwan-, itâcimikosi-, itâcimitiso-*

ayitâpi- VAI [redupl.] look around; 8:3; cf. *...âpi-*

ayitâskwan- VTI [redupl.] hold s.t. wooden firmly each time (i.e., prod with s.t. wooden); 9:13; cf. *itâskon-, itâskwan-*

ayitâtalôhkâso- VAI [redupl.] have a legend or myth repeatedly so told about one; 55:3

ayitôt- VTI [redupl.] do s.t. (repeatedly); 3:3; 12:3; cf. *itôt-, ayîtôt-*

ayitwê- VAI [redupl.] keep on saying; 18:4

ayîtahamâso- VAI [redupl.] sing over and over, sing away, hum along; 18:4; *'kwantaw manâ piko ayîtahamâsow* he just sang any old way; cf. *itahamâso-, ayîtahcikê-*

ayîtahcikê- VAI [redupl.] eat any old thing; (18:4); cf. *ayîtahamâso-, ayîtôt-*

ayîtohtah- VTA [redupl.] take s.o. about; 19:2; cf. *itohtah-*; [/i/ raised after preceding /y/, producing effect of lengthening; cf. *ayîtahamâso-, ayîtôt-*]

ayîtôt- VTI [redupl.] do (s.t.) any old way; (18:4); cf. *ayîtahamâso-, ayîtahcikê-*

ayôwin- NI fur; 42:4; 49:2 [variant of *âyowin-*]

âcilaw IPC in spite of everything, willy-nilly; (27:3)

âcistawi IPC weak, ill; 12:3

âcistawi-kiskêlim- VTA more or less know s.o.; 12:12

âcistawi-paskilâko- VAI be overcome in weakness; 12:3

âhay IPC [by] now, already; 55:6 [variant of *âšay*]

âhci IPV change; (11:5); *pošîkipitam ê-wî-âhci-wîskwênahk cîmâniliw* he strips the canvas off the canoe as he's about to change the wrapping

âhcih- VTA alter, change s.o.; make s.o. move; 41:14

âhciho- VAI change one's clothing; (41:20); cf. *kîšawê-*

âhcihtâ- VAI-T alter, change s.t.; make s.t. move; (41:14)

âhcikow IPC worse n. 3:2; *âhcikow nâ ati-ihtiw?* does he fare worse? cf. *âhcîhkên*

âhcikwê- VAI move away; 60:4; [preferred form at Fort Albany: *âhtokwê-*]; cf. *âhcipici-*

âhcipaliho- VAI move with sudden, violent motion; 66:2; cf. *...paliho-*

âhcipêl- NA [proper name] Archibald; 67:4

âhcipici- VAI move away to another place or residence; (60:4); cf. *âhtokwê-, ...pici-*

âhcîhkên IPC still more; 13:3; 14:5; *âhcîhkên ati-âhkosiw* he's taking a turn for the worse; *âhcîhkên ati-kišiwêmakan* it (music) is getting louder and louder; *âhcîhkên môna m'pêhtên* I hear less and less well; [near-synonym: *âhcikow*]: *âhcîhkên piko niwî-minihkwân*; or, *âhcikow piko niwî-minihkwân* I still want to drink some more; *âhcîhkên piko kimiwan* it still keeps raining

âhki IPC 'let's make believe, let's pretend', as it were; 2:9; 55:9; *âhki môswa kâhcišotâw* let's play (make-believe) moose; *âhki mâka tôtam* he's pretending to do it; *âhki wêsa awa šôliyân* pretend this is money; cf. *...hkâso..., nôcîskwêwêhkâso-*

âhkiko-pimiy- NA seal oil; 58:5

âhkikw- NA seal; 58:5

âhkosi- VAI be ill; 40:7

âhkosîwikamikw- NI hospital; 42:56; cf. *...wikamikw-*

âhkwaci- VAI freeze, become frozen; 35:1

âhkwatin- VII freeze; 44:4; 60:5; 61:5

âhtahpit- VTA/VTI tie s.o./s.t. to a different place, different part (of the frame); (52:3); cf. *itahpit-, mâkwahpit-, walahpit-*

âhtahw- VTA change s.o. (clock); (56:1) *n'ka-âhtahwâw pîsimohkân* I'll change the clock; cf. *ašêhw-, nîkânahw-*

âhtawê- VAI change one's coat (as an animal); (56:1); cf. *âhtahw-*

âhtêkipit- VTA/VTI move s.o./s.t. back (e.g., a tent); 50:2

âhtokwê- VAI move to another location; 60:4; standard form for *âhcikwê-*; cf. *âhcipici-*

âkaskiw- NA pheasant, prairie chicken; 58:5

âkôhikâkê- VAI use s.t. to screen oneself, cover oneself with s.t.; (56:2); cf. *âkôšimo-, âkôwiyâskošimo-, âkôwâstêhotiso-*

âkôhtin- VII be out of sight, be concealed; (56:2)

âkôpaliho- VAI take cover quickly, suddenly, in a hurry; (65:8); cf. *...paliho-*

âkôšimôlo- VAI look for cover, take cover; (65:8)

âkôšin- VAI be under cover (behind s.t.) as when being shot at; (65:8)

âkôwâstêhotiso- VAI shade oneself from the sun; (56:2); cf. *âkôšimo-, âkôhikâkê-, âkôwiyâskošimo-*

âkôwiyâskošimo- VAI duck, take cover behind a tree; (56:2); cf. *âyâkôwiyâskošimo-, âkôšimo-, âkôhikâkê-, âkôwâstêhotiso-, âkôwiyâw-, ...âskw.../-, ...šimo-*

âkôwiyâw- NI place of concealment; (56:2) *âkôwiyâhk* in a place where one can't see

âkwânî- VAI be covered with; 10:10

âlikw- NA [proper name] Alec; 40:1; 43:7

âlahkonâw- NA flour; 58:5

âlimakiht- VTI count s.t. as precious, costly; 62:2; seems to be used in 62:2; for *âlimakihtê-*

âlimakihtê- VII be costly, precious; (62:2)

âlimakiso- VAI be costly, precious; (62:2)

âliman- VII be difficult, be expensive; 9:8; 39:1; cf. *âlimisi-*

âlimêliht- VTI be troubled about s.t., in the mind, think of s.t., with disquiet; 39:4

âlimipali- VAI find it hard going; (39:4)

âlimipali- VII be a time of hardship, be 'hard times'; cf. *...pali-*

âlimi-pimipali- VAI have a hard time going about (i.e., have difficulty making ends meet while hunting for a living); 39:4

âlimisi- VAI be difficult; have difficulty, hardship; be expensive; 41:8; 65:1

âlimisîwin- NI difficulty, hardship; 41:8

âlimôcikâso- VAI be reported of s.o.; 41:6; 41:15; cf. *âlimôm-*

âlimôcikâtê- VII be talked about; 42:34; cf. *âlimôt-*

âlimôm- VTA talk about s.o., speak of s.o.; (41:6); 41:2; 49:6; 68:1

âlimôt- VTI talk about s.t., speak of s.t.; cf. *âlimôm-*

âlimôtamaw- VTA talk to s.o. about someone/something; 1:3

âmacastimo- VAI (of a bitch) be in heat; (36:1); cf. *...astimw.../-, itâspinêwin-*

âmacimôso- VAI (of moose) be in heat, rutting; 36:1; cf. *...môsw...*

âmacitihko- VAI (of caribou) be in heat; (36:1); cf. *atihkw-*

âmaciyayahâwi- VAI (of bear) be in heat; (36:1) *nôšêyâpask âmaciyayahâwiw* the female bear is in heat

âmatahkêšîwi- VAI (of a vixen) be in heat; (36:1); cf. *...ahkêšiw.../-*

âmo- VAI (of fish) spawn; (1:9; 2:9; 11:1; 42:55; 51:2); cf. *nihtâwikih-, pâškahâwê-*

âniman- VII be difficult, be expensive; cf. *âliman-*

âniskê IPC adjoining, contiguous, successively; (1:9)

âniskê IPV adjoining, contiguous, successively; (41:15) *misiwê kê-âniskê-pimâtisicik* all future generations; cf. *ayâniskê, âniskotâpân-*

âniskê-âcimostaw- VTA pass the story on to s.o.; 41:17

âniskê-wâhkomâkan- NA ancestor; (41:15)

âniskêyâskwah- VTI join s.t. on by nailing; (52:2); cf. *kîhkêyâskwah(w)-, kîhkêyâskwapit-, wâwiyêyâskwah(w)-, wîhkwêyâskwah(w)-, ...âskw.../-*

âniskêyâskwahw- VTA join s.o. on by nailing; (52:2); cf. *...âskw.../-*

âniskocêhtâ- VAI-T connect them, link them together; 41:15; cf. *...icê...*

âniskoh- VTA join s.o., fasten s.o.; (41:15)

âniskohtâ- VAI-T join s.t. (e.g. two buildings joined by a passageway), fasten s.t.

âniskotâpân- NA great-grandchild; (41:15) *nitâniskotâpânak* my great grandchildren; cf. *...sisim-*, (9:8)

âniskotâpê- VAI make a join (in two lengths of rope); (41:15); cf. *...itâpê-*

âniyw- NA [proper name] Annie; 40:1; [obv.: *anîwa*]

ânkas- NA [proper name] Angus; 65:1

âpacihâkan- NA employee; (41:9; 42:17)

âpacih- VTA use s.o., work for s.o.; 13:10; 25:2; 40:3; 42:10; 42:17; 50:3; 62:1; *âpacihêw* he works for s.o.; *âpacihâkaniwîpan* he was employed by s.o.; 62:1; cf. *n'-âpacihat*

âpacihâkaniwi- VAI be used (i.e., work); 41:9; cf. *âpacih-*

âpacihtamoh- VTA cause s.o. to use it; 51:1

âpacihtâ- VAI-T use s.t.; 13:10; 25:2; 34:2; 38:1; 40:1

âpacihtâwin- NI piece of equipment; something useful; 41:3

âpah- VTI untie s.t.; 3:7

âpahw- VTA untie s.o.; 52:3

âpasâpi- VAI look back; 10:7; cf. *...âpi-*

âpatan- VII be useful, be used; 19:2; 41:1; *môl' âpatan* it's no use; *misiwê piko kêkwân ... kâ-pêci-âpatahki* every single thing ... which was used since,

41:5; *êkâ pakwayânêkin êy-âpatahk* without any cloth being used, 51:1

âpatisi- VAI work; 24:1; cf. n'-âpatisiyan

âpatisîmakan- VII work; 41:11; *kêkwân'hkân êy-âpatisîmakahk* the kind of thing that works (i.e., machinery), 41:16

âpatisîwin- NI work; 41:10

âpawis- VTI thaw s.t. out (e.g., *wîyâs*); (35:2)

âpawisw- VTA thaw s.o. out (e.g., *namês*); 35:2

âpihcacimoš- NA small pet dog; (56:8)

âpihcililîš- NA a small person, midget; 56:8

âpihkopit- VTA/VTI unravel s.o./s.t.; 53:3

âpihta IPC half; 60:9; *âpihta kâ-ohcît* middle brother; *âpihta n'kî-nipân* I slept halfway

âpihtaw IPC half; 1:4; 25:1; *âpihtaw niskâtihk* halfway up my legs, 61:2

âpihtawahtay IPC half a dollar, 'half a pelt', 'half a fur'; 40:5; cf. *...ahtay-*

âpihtawâpisk IPC half way up the blade; 10:9; cf. *...âpiskw-*

âpihtawikâm IPC halfway across the water; 27:5

âpihtawikât IPC halfway up the leg; (61:2); cf. *...kât...*

âpihtawinâkaniwan- VAI/VII be divided in half, be halved; 42:42

âpihtawipê- VII be half in the water; 34:2; cf. *...ipê.../-*

âpihtâ IPV half; *ê-'ti-âpihtâ-tipiskâk* as it was getting to be about midnight, 20:5; *ê-kî-iškwâ-âpihtâ-kîsikâk* in the afternoon, 25:1

âpihtâ-kîsikâ- VII be midday; 25:1

âpihtâ-tipiskâ- VII be midnight; 20:5

âpikošîš- NA mouse; 3:8; 29:4; 66:1; cf. *wâpikošîš-*

âpiscililîš- NA small person, half person; 56:8; cf. *âpihcililîš-*

âsiyân- NA breech-clout; (11:11)

âskaw IPC sometimes; 1:3; 1:4; 39:1

âskipôta NI [pl.] 'husky-boots', (i.e., watertight boots made of sealskin); 65:1; [initial vowel lengthened by narrator]; cf. askipôta-

453

âstam IPC come here! 'facing this way';
11:2; 13:8; 18:3; 27:4; [functions as a
verbal imperative to which ...*ik* may
be added to form the plural: *âstamik*]

âstamâmatin IPC on the facing side of
the mountain; cf. *awasâmatin,
kwêskâmatin, pâsitâmatin, ...âmatin...*

âstamânak IPC on the facing side of the
island; cf. *awasânak, kišipânak,
kwêskânak, otiškawânak, šîpânakw-;
...ânak..., ...ânakw-*

âstamitê IPC on this side; (58:3); cf.
kwêskitê

âstawêh- VTI extinguish, quench (a fire);
12:15

âstawêpali- VII be extinguished, go out;
23:4; cf. *...pali-*

âsawah- VTI cross s.t. (river, stream,
body of water); 9:3; 11:2; 44:4; 58:1;
61:3

âsaw'hâtakâ- VAI wade; 61:2; cf.
pimâtakâ-; ...âtakâ-

âsaw'hol- VTA take s.o. across (a river);
9:4

âsawakan- NA bridge; dock, wharf; cf.
âsôkan; (37:3)

âsawakâkipalih- VTA take s.o. across
the water; 41:12

âsawakâmayâ- VII be a distance across
the water; 58:1; cf. *ispîhtakâmêyâ-,
...akâm..., ...ayâ-*

âsawakâmêyâši- VAI sail across; 58:1;
cf. *pimišakâmêyâši-, ...akâm..., ...âši-*

âsawakâsi- VAI ford (a stream); 37:3

âsawakwâškwati- VAI jump across;
27:5; 68:8; (n. 68:27); cf. *kwâškwati-*

âsay IPC (by) now, already; 1:5; 9:10

âsêtokê IPC already apparently; 12:4;
[contraction of *âsay êtokê*]

âsihkêmo- VAI stab; 12:6; *kâ-âsihkêmot*
cited with some uncertainty by
informant as equivalent of
kâ-tahkamwêt

âsiho- VAI have a sign; (12:16); *âsihow:
wayêš kata-ihtiw* he has a sign:
something is going to happen to him

âsikicišin- VAI sleep on one's back;
(63:2); cf. *kwêtipî-, ohpimêšin-, ...šin-*

âsikitapi- VAI sit with the head back;

(13:14); cf. *...api-*

âsikitastâ- VAI-T push s.t. back; (13:14)
ašikitastâw otastotin he pushes his hat
back (i.e., to the back of his head)

âsikitikâskošin- VAI lie flat on one's
back, lie on the keel of one's back, lie
at full length; 42:67; [synonym:
âšikitišin-]; cf. *ohpimêšin-,
ohpimêyâskošin-, otihtapišin-*

âsikitin- VTA turns s.o. over on his/her
back; 13:14; *kitâšikitinâw* you push
s.o. backwards (with whom you want
to pick a quarrel); e.g., hanging on to
his lapels; cf. *ašêkâhtin-*

âsikitišin- VAI lie on one's back; (42:67);
cf. *âsikitâskošin, ...šin-*

âsim- VTA foretell evil for s.o.; 12:6;
[possibly *asim-* spear s.o.]; cf. n. 12:16,
âsiho-

âsiwah- VTI cross s.t. (river, stream,
body of water); cf. *âsawah-*

âsîš- NA [proper name] Asheesh; 43:7;
44:4

âsôkan- NA bridge; commonly used for
dock, wharf; (37:3); 41:4

âta IPC although [with *ê-* and conjunct];
4:1; 19:3; 41:8; *âta isa, âta oš' âni* even
though [with independent order]; 6:13;
n. 22:3; cf. *ât' ôša*

âtakay- NI penis; (56:2); cf. *wîtakay-,
ayâniš-, acakâš-*

âtakâmišin- VAI have no means of
crossing because of water; 7:8

âtalôhkaw- VTA tell s.o. a legend, an
'old-time' story; 47:1; tell a story about
s.o.; 11:1

âtalôhkân- NI legend; 1:1; 8:8; 12:9

âtalôhkâso- VAI have a legend told
about oneself

âtalôhkê- VAI recount a legend, myth;
1:1; 12:9; 68:1; (n. 68:2); cf.
itâtalôhkâso-

âtalôhkêwin- NI recounting of a legend,
myth; 22:1

âtawâpiskâtw- NI [place name]
Attawapiskat (village located some 128
kms north of Kashechewan on the
west coast of James Bay); the name is
supposed to be an anglicisation of

ê-tawâpiskâk 'it is open and rocky', describing the river valley; 33; 42:23; cf. *tawâpiskâ-*

âtawâpiskâtowastimw- NA dog from Attawapiskat; 33; cf. *...astimw...*/-

âtawêliht- VTI reject or have nothing to do with s.t.; 60:2

âtawêlim- VTA reject or have nothing to do with s.o.; 60:2

âtawîla IPC although, though, nonetheless, anyway; 11:6; 15:2; 37:3; 39:3; 42:11; 42:40; 43:6

âtiht IPC some, several; 7:1; 18:6; 59:1

ât' ôša IPC even though [with independent order] *ât' ôša n'kî-ohcihâw, kiyâpac mâka kî-tôtam* even though I stopped him, he did it just the same; (4:5); cf. *ohcih-*

âwacipalihtwâ- VAI-T haul s.t. (wood, supplies, etc.) by motor, car, truck, boat; (42:18); cf. *âwacitâpê-*

âwacitâpê- VAI haul (wood, supplies) over a period of time; 42:18; *nêw mâka atimwak n'kî-âpacihâhtay êy-âwacitâpêyân* I used to use four dogs when I was hauling; cf. *âwacipalihtwâ-, ...itâpê-*

âwas IPC be off! away with you! 46:1; also as *awas*

âwasâmatin IPC on the other side of the mountain; cf. *awasâmatin, ...âmatin-*

âyâkôwiyâskošimo- VAI [redupl.] take cover, 'duck' behind tree after tree; 56:2; cf. *âkôwiyâskošimo-, ...âskw...*/-, *...šimo-*

âyâpah- VTI [redupl.] keep untying s.t.; (52:3); cf. *âpah-*

âyâpahw- VTA [redupl.] keep untying s.o.; 52:3; cf. *âpahw-*

âyâs- NA [proper name] Ayas (legendary figure); 9:2

âyowin- NI fur; 40:5; [variant of *ayôwin-*]

cacahkaw- VTA [redupl.] poke away at s.o. (as at a fox in his den); cf. *cahkahw-*

cacêmaso- VAI [redupl.] stand together; 19:8; for *cacimaso-* cf. *cimaso-*

cahkah- VTI poke at s.t.; (60:7)

cahkahw- VTA poke at s.o.; 60:7

cahkâpêš- NA [proper name] Chahkabesh (legendary figure); 3:1; 8:2; 56:1; cf. *...âpêw...*/-

cahkâpin- VTA poke s.o. in the eye; (12:3; 21:4); cf. *pohcâpin-, ...âpi-*

cahkâsikê- VAI shine (as the sun), give light; 29:4

cahkâskohtatâ- VAI-T drive s.t. in (e.g., a stick); 12:3

cahkâstêpalihcikâniwan VAI [indef.] one makes it go along casting a shadow, one puts on a picture-show; 42:12; *kâ-cahkâstêpanihcikâniwahk* a moving-picture show

cahkokâpawiši- VAI be short in stature; 13:7; (stylistic palatalization); cf. *tahkokâpawisi-*

cam- NA [proper name] Chum; 65:1

camohkamihtin- VII drop in water with a plop, drop in water with a 'kerplunk'; cf. *...htin-*

camohkamišin- VAI drop in water with a plop, drop in water with a 'kerplunk'; cf. *...šin-*

capašîš IPC (down) below; 1:3; 11:8; 20:6; cf. *tapašîš*

catîtwâskopali- VAI be (physically) stunned; [metathesis for *tacîtwâskopali-*]; 14:7; cf. *...pali-*

câkah- VTA annihilate s.o., kill all of s.o.; 8:2; cf. *câkihtâ-, câkih-*

câkâhkas- VTI burn up s.t.; (60:10); 65:8; cf. *câkâskis-*

câkâhkaso- VAI be burned up; (65:8)

câkâhkasw- VTA burn up s.o.; 60:10; 65:8; *misiwê n'kî-câkâhkaswâwak m'pîhcipihkwânak* I used (burnt) up all my shells; *miconi n'kî-câkipihkwêson* I used up all my powder; cf. *câkâskisw-*

câkâhkatê- VII be burned up; (65:8)

câkâskis- VTI burn s.t. up completely (Kashechewan usage); (11:13); 12:15; elsewhere: *câkâhkas-*

câkâskiso- VAI burn up; (11:13)

câkâskisw- VTA burn s.o. up completely (Kashechewan usage); (11:13); 12:15; elsewhere: *câkâhkasw- câkâhkisw-*

câkâskitê- VII burn up; 9:24; (11:13)

câkih- VTA kill s.o. off, finish s.o. off (as in trapping beaver); 8:2; 12:15; 14:8; cf. *câkah-*

câkihtâ- VAI-T trap it out (i.e., his section of land), deplete s.t.; 8:2

câkin- VTA/VTI use up, exhaust s.o./s.t.; 1:4

câki-nipah- VTA finish killing s.o. off; 21:7

câkipali- VAI/VII be spent, be used up, be consumed; 42:57; 60:11; cf. *...pali-*

câkipihkwêso- VAI burn up or expend one's gunpowder; (65:8)

cân- NA [proper name] John; 42:43; cf. also *cwân-*

cêhkatamon- VII (for the trail) to meet the bush; 42:52

cêkap- NA [proper name] Jacob; 42:35

cêyakoc IPC instead; 43:9

'ci IPV so that, in order to [preverb with conjunct indicative; contraction of *kici-*]; 1:4

cicima NA [proper name] Titima (child's doll); palatalized by child speaker; 43:13

cikêmânima IPC naturally, of course; 3:10; 19:1

cimaso- VAI stick up, be erected; grow up; (9:8); 28:1; 37:3; 41:1; 41:14; *êkot' oš' âni mâka nêšta wakic oskôtim cêmasot an' âsiniy?* and it's right there, of course, too, on top of the dam that that stone stands up?

cimatâ- VAI-T set s.t. up, erect s.t.; 32:1

cimatê- VII stick up, be erected; grow up; 9:8; (28:1); 42:35

cimê- VAI canoe; 11:6; 65:3; 65:6; *êko nêtê kâ-iši-cimêyâhk* so we canoed over there; *ililiwaskîhk n'ka-iši-cimân* I'll canoe to the Indian reserve

cimiyw- NA [proper name] Jimmy; 43:3; [obv.: *cimîwa*]

cipêkisin- VAI be pointed; 9:23

cîhcîstahikê- VAI [redupl.] prod about; 12:12

cîkah- VTI chop s.t.; (37:5)

cîkahikan- NI axe; 67:2; *kâ-mišâk cîkahikan* the big axe; the 4 lb. axe

used in lumber camps

cîkahotiso- VAI chop oneself, cut oneself with an axe; 37:5

cîkahw- VTA chop s.o.; (37:5)

cîkic IPC near; 49:6

cîmân- NI canoe; 18:8; 49:1

cîmânišiš- NI small canoe, small boat; 58:2

cîm- VTA canoe with s.o.; *ôhtâwiya cîmêw* he canoes with his father; cf. *cimê-*

cîmis- NA [proper name] James; 42:42

cîpay- NA ghost, spirit of the dead; 30:2; cf. *ahcâhkw-*

cîpayâhtikw- NA cross (religious symbol); 41:14; cf. *...âhtikw.../-*

cîpayikamikw- NI graveyard; 41:13

cîpayi-mistikwat- NI coffin; 41:15

cîpayi-ospwâkan- NA ghost pipe; 63:2

cîpayi-pastêw- NI ghost smoke; 9:24

cîpayi-sîpiy- NI [place name] Ghost River (flows into the Albany River about 100 miles up from the mouth); 30:2; 36:1

cîposi- VAI be sharp-pointed, be tapered; (61:4) *ati-cîposiw* it (a tree) comes to a point

cîpwâ- VII be sharp-pointed, be tapered; (61:4)

cîstah- VTI jab s.t., stick s.t.; 9:17

cîstahâpwât- VTA/VTI barbecue s.o./s.t.; (55:3); cf. *cîstahâpwê-*

cîstahâpwê- VAI roast on a spit, barbecue; (55:3); cf. *maskatêpwê-*, *sakapwê-*

cîstahikan- NI pointed cooking stick; 9:10: metal pronged instrument used for holding cooked food or for puncturing; 9:17; cf. *apwânâsk-*, *cîstah-*, *cîstahikê-*, *kapatêskwê-*

cîstahikê- VAI prod, jab; (13:13)

cîšim- VTA cheat s.o.; 55:7

cîtawâskopali- VAI stiffen out (as in convulsions); 12:8; cf. *...pali-*

cîtawišôkaninâkosi- VAI appear stiff in the hips or lower back; 41:13; cf. *...cihc...*, *...htâwak...*, *...kât...*, *...nisk...*, *...sit...*, *...šôkan...*; *...nâkosi-*

cîwêhtâwakê- VAI have a singing in one's ears; (9:5); cf. ...*htâwak*...

cîwêyâstan- VII make a whistling or blowing noise (e.g., as wind through a window); 9:5; *paspâpiwin kâ-cîwêyâstahk* a window which whistles; cf. *cîwêhtâwakê-*; ...*âstan-*

cîwêyâsi- VAI make a whistling or blowing noise; 9:5; cf. ...*âši-*

coc- NA [proper name] George; 41:1

côhcôhkipit- VTI widen s.t.; cf. *tôhtôhkipit-*, 29:2

côhcôskipit- VTI nibble away at s.t.; cf. *tôhtôskipit-*, 29:2

côsif- NA [proper name] Joseph; 43:8

côsip- NA [proper name] Joseph; 42:8

côwil- NA [proper name] Joel; 38:2

cwân- NA [proper name] John; 42:43; cf. also *cân-*

ê IPV [aorist preverb particle used with conjunct]

êcika IPC it would appear, so then; 9:21; 12:8; 43:14; 63:2; *âyâs êcika n'kosis kâ-cakošinokopanê* it is Ayas, my son, then, who must have arrived

êcik' âni IPC it would appear, so then [more emphatic than *êcika*]; 9:10; 63:2; *êkw êcik' an' tâpwê [kê-kî-ati-]nipiyân, k'-îtên'tam* it really seems that I'm going to die, he thought; cf. *wêcik' âni*

ê'êci- VAI be sick [child language for *âhkosi-*]; 43:14

êhê IPC yes; 1:3; 9:13; 41:3

êhêpikw- NA spider [archaic form]; 1:3; 1:4; 2:4; SC: *otahnapihkêsiw-*; MC: *ahlapihkêsiw-*

êkâ IPC not [used with conjunct and imperative]; 1:4; 18:9; 19:3; *êkâ wîskât kâ-câkinahk pîšâkanâpîniw* who never exhausts (his) twine (of the spider); *êkâ mâka ... ci-kî-wanawînîsâhtawîcik* and they would not be able to climb out and down, 1:6; *'kâ tôtaw!* don't do (anything) to him! leave him alone! 13:11; [*êkâwina* is normally used with the imperative at Fort Albany and Albany Post except for certain common expressions, e.g., *'kâ kito!* shut up!]

êkâwila IPC not [emphatic form of *êkâ*]

êkâwina IPC not [emphatic form of *êkâ*: used at Fort Albany with imperative only; *êkâ* used with both imperative and conjunct at Moose Factory]; 4:2

êko IPC then, at that point; 9:5; 37:2 et passim

êkocê 'ni IPC in this very direction, in this very way; [palatalized form of *êkotê 'ni*]; 13:5

êko mâka IPC and then, so then; 10:2; cf. *êkw' âni mâka*, 4:2; 9:4

êk' oš' âni IPC so that('s) it, so that's the reason; 3:10; *êk' oš' âni êkâ mâši wêhci-wâpahk* so that's why it didn't even dawn; *êk' oš' ânima* that's the one, y'know, 42:35; *êk' oš' ânima nîki* that's my place, y'know

êkoši IPC so then; 2:4; 39:2; 43:3; 57; *êkoš' isa mâka* let it go at that

êkota IPC there, that very place; 2:4; 11:11

êkot' âni IPC at that point, that very place, that very one; 1:6; 18:2; 26:2

êkot' ânta IPC right there, that's where, it is at that point; 1:6; 8:7; 49:6

êkotê IPC (right) there, thither; 1:3; this very way; 15:2; it is there; 42:49

êkotê 'ni IPC in this very direction, in this very way; 15:3; that's where; 41:2; it was right there; 60:6; cf. *êkocê 'ni*

êkot' ôta IPC right here, this (is) the place; 61:3

êkwa IPC then, so then, at that point; cf. *êko*

êkwâni IPC then, it was then; 37:2; *êkwâni mâka* and now; 4:2; 9:4; [emphatic form of *êko*]

ê'kwâni PR that (very) one [inan.prox.sg.]; 1:5; that's it, that's the one; 9:9

ê'kwânihi PR that very one [anim.obv., inan.prox. & obv.pl.]; 15:5

ê'kwâwa PR this very one [anim.prox.sing.]; 9:13; cf. *êwako*

êkw' êcik' âni IPC so it seems, so it would appear; 9:10

êkwêlâk IPC for the first time; 5:1; 11:9; 37:3

êlikohk IPC hard, strenuously,

vigorously (MC); 9:15; 28:1; 49:4; 50:2;
k'-êlikohk as hard as one can, as hard
as possible

êlikoš- NA little ant; 49:4

êlikw- NA ant; (49:4)

êlikw' IPC hard, strenuously, vigorously
[contraction of *êlikohk*]; 49:4

êlin- NA [proper name] Ellen; 67:1

êliwêhk IPC especially, very much so;
42:6

êmistikôšiw- NA White-Man, European
[alternative form of *wêmistikôšiw-*];
42:62

êmistikôšîwi-mîcim- NI 'White-Man's'
food (as opposed to country food,
pakwataskamik'-mîcim-); 40:2

êmîl- NA [proper name] Emile; 42:65

ênakâm IPC on this side of the river,
near the bank; cf. *akâmihk, ...akâm...*

êncin- NI engine; 42:20

êškan- NA horn, antler; 9:5; (10:5)

êskan- NI chisel; 8:8

êškê- VAI chisel; 13:4; 60:8

êškwâ IPC yet, still; 22:1; 42:16; *êškw'
anima* up to that (point in time); 41:4;
41:6; *êškwâ pitamâ* Wait a minute!
41:21

êtokwê IPC likely, probably, 'I guess',
must be; 14:5; *cahkâpêš oš' ân' êtokwê
mîna kâ-tôtahk* it's likely Chahkabesh
who's doing it again

êwako PR the very one [indeclinable,
intensive]; 6:3

êwakôma PR this very one
[inan.prox.sing.]; 1:3; cf. *êwako*

êwakômêniw PR this very one
[inan.obv.sing.]; 1:8; cf. *êwako*

êwakwâna PR that very one
[anim.prox.sing.]; 1:4; 42:35

êwakwâniki PR those very ones
[anim.pl.], they are the very ones; 5:3;
6:7; 9:10;

êwakwânima PR that very one
[inan.prox.sing.]; 1:9; *ê'k' oš' ânima
nîki* that was my place, y'know; 42:35

gohpâtawîsi- VAI climb up (affected
Ojibwa form for speech of Lynx); 2:7;
cf. *kohpâtawîsi-*

hê IPC yes; [contraction of *êhê*]; 5:4

hêntriyw- NA [proper name] Henry;
40:1; 64:3; [obv.: *hêntrîwa*]

icikâtê- VII be called; 30:2; 34:1

ihkin- VII happen; 2:3; 11:7; *môla
k'-îhkin* it cannot happen, it is
impossible, 40:6; *môna mâka wîn'
anim' ihkin âpatisîwin* but
employment is not like that, 42:5;
môna mâka wîna k'-îhkin anima but it
can't amount to anything, 42:34; *tân'
êhki', tân' êhkihk* what's happening?
43:11; *tâpask môna ta-k'-îhkinôpan* it
probably wouldn't happen (i.e.,
wouldn't work), 43:14; cf. *ihti-*

ihtakwan- VII be (at a place); 1:8 et
passim; *kotak askiy kî-ihtakwan* there
was another land; cf. *ihtâ-*

ihtâ- VAI be (at a place); 1:2; 6:2; 35:1 et
passim; *ôta kâ-yš'-îhtâyahk* here where
we're living, 41:7; cf. *ihtakwan-*

ihtâwin- NI village, settlement; 39:3;
41:6; 42:45; 51:3; 60:8

ihti- VAI fare; n. 3:2; *tân' êhtiyan?*
What's the matter with you? What ails
you? 9:4; *mâtika mâka êy-ihtiyan!*
Look what's happened to you! 16:5;
wêskac oš' êwakwâni wêhc-îhtiyân
because I've been this way for a long
time; 19:2; *wayêš ihtiw* he is in
trouble; 40:6; *ê'kwâni mwêhci ê-'hcicik
kâ-itwêyân* that's exactly what I was
saying happened to them; *misiwê ôma
kâ-k'-îhtiyâhk* all this happened to us;
59:1

iko IPC only; [contraction of *piko*]

ilalâstikw- NA balsam (MC); 68:7; SC:
ininâsihtakw-; cf. *...âhtikw.../-*

ilâpacih- VTA do a specific job for s.o.;
use s.o. for a particular purpose; 42:17;
'kw âni ê'-ilâpacihât that's what he
uses him for; that's how he works for
him; *tân 'êlâpacihât?* how does he
work for him? cf. *âpacih-,
âpacihâkan-, itâpacih-*

ilâpacihikawi- VAI do a kind of work,
work in the capacity of; 42:17;
n'tilâpacihikawihtay kâ-itwêstamâkêt
I used to work as an interpreter

ilâpatisi- VAI work at something; 41:9;
42:31; *êkâ mâka 'wâc apišîš wayêš
ê-'lâpatisiyahk êy-ohtisiyahk mâka
kî'nânaw* even though we work only a
little at it, we're getting paid

ilikohk IPC as much as, until, up to;
1:10; 6:4; 39:4; *pêyakwâ ê-kîsikâk
inikohk* for the space of a day, 6:4;
pîliš nisto-kîsikâw ilikohk up to (as
long as) three days, 39:4; *tân' înikohk
kêškihtâsoyin pêyako-kîsikâw* (up to)
how much can you (earn) in a day? n.
42:11; synonymous with *tân' înikohk
wêhtisiyan?* [near-synonym: *ispîš*]

ililasiniy- NA Indian stone, ordinary
stone (MC); 9:24; SC: *ininasiniy-*

ililâstikw- NA balsam; cf. *ilalâstikw-*

ililiw- NA person (MC); 1:1; 36:1; SC:
ininiw-

ililiwaskiy- NI Indian land, Indian
reservation; 57; cf. *askiy-*

ililîmo- VAI speak Cree (MC); 41:21; SC:
ininîmo-

ililîmowin- NI Cree language, Indian
language (MC); 41:21; SC: *ininîmowin-*

ililî-wêpin- VTI use a Cree word, 'throw
(in)' a Cree word; 42:20

ililîwi- VAI be alive (MC); 1:1; n. 1:2;
kînanânaw ê-ininîwiyahk we [incl.]
who are alive; SC: *ininîwi-*

inikohk IPC as much as, until, up to
(SC); MC: *ilikohk*

ininasiniy- NA Indian stone, ordinary
stone; 7:11; 9:24; cf. *asiniy-*

ininâsihtakw- NA balsam wood (SC);
(42:54); MC: *ilalâstik, ililâstikw-*; cf.
...ihtakw.../-

ininiw- NA person, Indian (SC); 6:2; 10:6
et passim; MC: *ililiw-*

ininîwi-'wâšiš- NA Indian child; 42:7

ininîmo- VAI speak Cree (SC); MC:
ililîmo-

ininîmowin- NI Cree language, Indian
language (SC); MC: *ininîmowin*

ininîwi- VAI be alive (SC); MC: *ililîwi-*

isa IPC in fact, to be sure, indeed, then;
1:2; 2:3; 18:2; 41:1; *êko isa* so then,
well then

iskali IPN the whole, entire; 5:5;
iskali-kîšik all day long; 6:6;
iskali-tipisk all night long;
iskan'-tipiskâw all night; 61:5;
iskali-pipon all winter; 39:2

iskon- VTA roll s.o. up; (13:9)
n'tiskonâwak niwanakwayak I roll up
my sleeves; cf. *ayiskon-, wanakway-*

iskonâk IPC since; 47:2

iskopali- VAI/VII come to an end; 59:4; cf.
iskwâpali-, ...pali-

iskopê- VAI wade up to (such a depth);
(61:2) *âpihtawikât iskopêw* he wades
in water halfway up his leg; cf.
*iskwacîskaw-, iskwâkonê-,
pašakohcîskawakâhk, sâkihkâpi-,
sâkipê-, ...ipê.../-*

iskopêyâ- VII go so far (i.e., water);
ê-iskopêyâk along the water's edge (the
few inches where water and land
meet); cf. *lâlakâm, lâlipêkw, ...ipê...,
...ayâ-*

iskosi- VAI be so long, measure so long;
27:7; 39:4; 52:1; 52:3; *ê-'skosit* to its
full length

iskôliwi- VAI attend school (MC); 42:6;
SC: *iskôniwi-*

iskôniwi- VAI attend school (SC); MC:
iskôliwi-

isk'-ôšihtâ- VAI-T complete s.t., make s.t.
to an end; 41:7; [contracted form of
iskw-ošihtâ-]

iskwacêskawê- VAI be up to such a
depth in mud; (61:2) *kêkât okitikohk
iskwacêskawêw* he's nearly up to his
knees in mud; cf. *iskopê-, iskwâkonê-,
pasakocêskawakâ-, sâkihkâpi-, sâkipê-,
...cêskaw...*

iskwahcikâtê- VII be left over (as after
eating); 19:9

iskwâ- VII be so long, measure so long;
(27:7); 39:4; (52:1; 52:3); 56:8

iskwâkonê- VAI stand up to such a point
in snow; 61:2; *âpihtawikât
iskwâkonêw* he stands in snow
halfway up his leg; cf. *iskopê-,
iskwacîskawê-, ...âkon...,
pašakohcîskawakâhk, sâkihkâpi-,
sâkipê-*

459

iskwâpali- VAI/VII come to an end, be left over; 19:10; 42:46; 44:3

iskw-âpatisi- VAI finish working; 39:3

iskwâpêkan- VII come to an end (as a line or length of rope) 1:4; 2:10; cf. ...*ipêk*...

iskwâpihkêsi- VAI be so long (a line or strand); 52:1; cf. ...*âpihk*...

iskwâpihkêyâ- VII be the end of the line (i.e., of the story); 14:7; 15:5; cf. ...*âpihk*..., ...*ayâ*

iskwâs- VTI burn s.t., scorch s.t.; 11:12

iskwâskitê- VII stand only so high; 52:3; cf. *ispaskitê-, tapahtaskitê-*

iskwâskitêskw- NI charcoal; 11:13

iskwâskoh- VTA make s.o. (of wood) such a length (e.g., snowshoe, toboggan); (52:2); cf. *kinwâskoh-, tahkwâskoh-, ...âskw.../-*

iskwâskohtâ- VAI-T make s.t. (of wood) such a length (e.g., a wooden tool, a stick); 52:2; cf. *kinwâskohtâ-, tahkwâskohtâ-, ...âskw... / -*

iskwâskopit- VTA/VTI raise, pull up s.o./s.t. repeatedly; 52:3

iskwâskosi- VAI be so long (of wood); (52:1)

iskwâskwan- VII be so long (of wood); (52:1); *nêw'-micihcin ê-iskwâskwahk* four inches long (of wood)

iskwâso- VAI be set on fire, be burnt, get scorched; 3:7; 11:12; 27:6; 60:10; 65:8

iskwâsotiso- VAI burn oneself; 55:8; 65:7

iskwâsw- VTA burn s.o., scorch s.o.; (11:12)

iskwâtawînâhtikw- NI ladder; cf. *nîhtin-, ...âhtikw.../-*

iskwâtê- VII be on fire, be burnt, be scorched, be scalded; 11:15; 15:2

iskwêkan- VII be of such a length (cloth); 52:3; cf. ...*êk*...

iskwêkih- VTA make s.o. (cloth or similar material) long; 52:3; cf. ...*êk*...

iskwêkihtâ- VAI-T make s.t. (cloth or similar material) long; (52:3); cf. ...*êk*...

iskwêkisi- VAI be of such a length (cloth); 52:3; cf. ...*êk*...

iskwêšiš- NA girl; 4:5; 6:3; 10:10

[alternative form of *iškwêšiš-*]

iskwêw- NA woman; 1:3; 8:5

iskwêwi- VAI be a woman; 65:6

ispah- VTA run with s.o. in such a way; 65:8; *patotê k'-îspahêw* she ran with her to the side; cf. *patotêpah-*

ispahito- VAI run each other, make each other run; 65:9

ispahtâ- VAI run; 19:8; 19:9; cf. ...*pahtâ-*

ispali- VAI/VII so go; be so; last; be time to... transpire, happen; 1:2; 11:11; transpire, happen; 12:4; 39:1; *môla ispaliw* it does not so happen (i.e., it is not possible); *otâpâna šâposkamik kâ-ispaniki* trains which go through the country; *nâspic mistah' îspaniw antê šôniyân* there is a good deal of money involved there, 41:12; *êliwêhk mistah' ispaliw anima* that sure costs a lot, 42:10; *môna wâwâc pêyak ominikošiš t'-êspanîpan* it wouldn't even take one minute, 42:32; *ê'kwâni mâk' âskani-pipon micon' îspaliwa n'cawâšimišinân anima askiy* and that moss lasted our child the whole winter, 51:3; *kici-ispaliyahk ililiwaskîhk* for us to go to the Indian reservation, 56:8; cf. ...*pali-*

ispaliho- VAI thrust oneself, put oneself there, spring; 9:13; 13:8; 13:11; take over; 13:14; dash (over); 19:9; *tântê kâ-ispalihot?* where did he disappear to? (50:1); cf. ...*paliho-*

ispalihtwâ- VAI-T make s.t. go, have a go at s.t.; 10:7

ispihc IPC up to, till; 62:2; 68:1; *anim' êspihc* at that time, then; cf. *ispiš*

ispihcâ- VII be so big; 52:3; (59:4)

ispihcikiti- VAI be so big; (52:3); 59:4

ispihcisî- VAI be of such an age; 28:1; *nahi n'tispihcisîn* I'm of about average age; cf. *ispîhcisî-*

ispihcî- VAI be so strong; do it meanwhile; (28:1) *ispihcîyâhkê isa* if we have time; cf. *tawipali-*

ispihtâtimâ- VII be such a depth; 38:3

ispihtêkah- VTA make s.o. such a size; 52:2

ispihtêlihtâkosi- VAI be so strong; 5:6;
cf. *...ihtâkosi-. ispihtêlihtâkosiw nâ
kici-kî-tôtahk?* is he strong enough to
do it? *tân' êspihtên'tâkosin'ci* how
strong it was, 5:6

ispihtêlihtâkwan- VII be so strong;
(5:6); cf. *...ihtâkwan-*

ispisêkâ- VII be piled up (as stones);
6:10; *ispisêkâwa* there are mounds of
stones; *kâ-iš'-îspisêkâniki* where there
are mounds of stones

ispiš IPC up to, till; 41:17; *anim' ispiš
wêskac oš' âni* right up till then a long
time ago; cf. *ispîš*

ispit- VTA pull s.o. so; 10:10

ispî IPC when; 1:4; 29:3; 29:4; 37:2

ispîhci IPP so, so much; *ispîhci-mistahi*
so great(ly), 41:7

ispîhci IPV so, so much; to such an
extent; 5:1; 9:7; 32:1; *ê-ispîhci-lôtininik*
because it was so windy;
ê-ispîhci-macênimikawiyân I am
thought so little of, 43:6

ispîhci-išpâ- VII be so high; 41:18

ispîhcipali- VAI/VII travel so much,
travel up to such a point; 34:3; cf.
...pali-

ispîhcisî- VAI be of such an age; 49:4;
tâpiskôc ispîhcisîwak they are both
the same age; cf. *ispihcisî-, ispîhtisî-*

ispîhc'-îšpâ- VII be so high; 41:18; cf.
ispîhci-ispâ-

ispîhtakâmêyâ- VII be such a distance
(over water) n. 58:6; 58:2; 61:2;
[synonym: *ispîhci-âšaw'kâmêyâ-*]; cf.
âšawakâmêyâ-, ...akâm..., ...ayâ-

ispîhtisî- VAI be of such an age (MC);
40:2; 42:17; *âšay n'tispîhtisîn
kišê-il'liw-šôliyân 'ci- mîlikawiyâpân*
I'm old enough now to receive the
old-age pension; cf. *ispîhcisî-*

ispîš IPC so much, up to that amount;
than; instead of; 34:3; 49:6; *pêkwân'
ispîš* that's all, 25:2; *awasitê
kî-kaškihoniwa ispîš wîna-* he was
more powerful than him, 11:3; *ôma
ispîš* right up to now, 42:3; *piko âta
ispîš ê-w'-îspaliyahk* even though we
only wanted to go so far, 57

ispîsinâkosi- VAI appear up to such a
point; (37:6); cf. *...nâkosi-*

ispîsinâkwan- VII appear up to such a
point; 37:6; cf. *...nâkwan-*

iši IPC towards [with locative]; 34:3;
nôhcimihk iši towards the bush

iši IPV/IPN so, thus; there; 1:2 et passim

iši-cimê- VAI paddle to it; 11:3

išicišah- VTI send s.t.; cf. *išitišah-*

išicišahw- VTA send s.o., dispatch s.o.;
42:35; 49:1; *išicišahwâkaniwinôpanak*
they used to be dispatched; 42:35;
êwakwâna kâ-wî-išicišahohtipan that's
the one they were going to send; 68:2;
cf. *išitišahw-*

išihlâ- VAI fly so (MC); 14:5; 20:5

išihnâ- VAI fly so (SC); 20:5; MC: *išihlâ-;
...hlâ-*

išiho- VAI dress oneself so, array oneself
so; (8:6); 9:25; cf. *kihci-ayišiho-*

išihômakan- VII look the same
throughout (as to design, colour, etc.);
52:4; *ê-išihômakahki* a 'suit' of clothes;
niwî-otinikân olâkana ê-išihômakahki
I want to buy a set of dishes; *misiwê
pêyakwan išihowak* they're all dressed
the same (e.g., in a school uniform);
[synonym: *pêyakwan išinâkwanwa*]

išihôwin- NI clothes, apparel; (8:6)

išihw- VTA dress s.o., clothe s.o.; 8:6; cf.
kihci-ayišiho-

išikîšwê- VAI speak a language or
dialect; (41:20); 42:42; *pêyakwan
kit-išikîšwânânaw* we talk the same
language *pêyakwan išikîšwêwak
tâpiskôc kîlanânaw* they talk the same
language as we do; cf. *kišiwê-, kîšawê-*

išilawî- VAI so to fare; be doing things,
be about things; be up to something,
be up to mischief; 3:1; 10:1; (41:5);
56:8; 67:1; *tân' êšilawîcik?* how are
they (sick persons) faring? More non-
committal than *âhcikonâ ati-ihtiw,
nêstapiko ati-milo-ihtiw?* does he fare
still worse, or is he (doing) better? *tân'
êšilawît?* what's he doing? what's he
up to? cf. *pahpakwac, pahpakwatêliht-*

išin- VTI see s.t. as, think s.t. appears so;
19:2; (42:47)

išinaw- VTA see s.o. as, think s.o. appears so, 42:47; *mwêhci wîwa išinawêw* he thinks she looks like his wife *mwêhci niska išinawêw* he thinks it looks like a goose (e.g., of someone who mistakenly begins to call a crow on the blind)

išinâkoh- VTA make s.o. of such an appearance; (9:25)

išinâkoho- VAI make oneself of such an appearance; 9:25

išinâkohtâ- VAI-T dress s.t., prepare s.t., make s.t. of such an appearance; 12:14; 38:2; 54:2; *awasitê mâka wîhkašin anima ê-'šinâkohtâniwahk* it's more delicious when it's dressed that way

išinâkosi- VAI appear so; 19:10; 23:2; 29:3; cf. *...nâkosi-*

išinâkwan- VII appear so; 1:5; 5:1; 7:2; 19:10; 29:3; cf. *...nâkwan-*

išinihkâcikâso- VAI be called, be named; cf. *išinihkât-*

išinihkâcikâtê- VII be called, named; 50:7; *kâ-mahkatêwâk watôw kâ-išinihkâcikâtêk* that black, clotted blood as they call it; cf. *išinihkât-*

išinihkâso- VAI be named, be so called; 2:4; 9:1; 42:63; 54:2

išinihkât- VTA/VTI call s.o./s.t., name s.o./s.t.; 6:7; 9:24; 41:21; 54:1; 58:1

iši-pîhci-wêpin- VTA quickly toss s.o. into; 56:5

išitêpo- VAI cook so; (18:9); 55:3; *tântê kê-išitêpoyân?* What way shall I cook (it)? cf. *milotêpo-, osâmawahahkâtêpo-, ...têpo-*

išitišah- VTI send s.t. (MC); (11:4); cf. *išicišah-*

išitišahw- VTA send s.o. (MC); 11:4; cf. *išicišahw-*

išitiyêli- VAI rub her backside against the male (of a bitch in heat); (68:5); *wîla wêsa k'-îšitiyêliw* (it serves her right) because she rubbed her backside against the male (of a bitch in heat, yelping after the male has mounted her); cf. *kalakitiyê-, kwêskitiyêpaliho-, tahkiskâtitiyêhwê-; ...tiy...*

iši-wêpahw- VTA knock s.o. in a certain way; 49:4

iši-wêpisk- VTI knock s.t.; 47:2

išiwil- VTA take s.o. (somewhere); 29:4

išiwitâ- VAI-T take s.t. (somewhere); 9:17; cf. *pêtiwat-, wîwaši-*

iši-wîl- VTA name s.o. so; 42:62; *ê'kwâni mâk' ê-'ši-wînihcik ôko* that's what they're named

išîhkaw- VTA do something to s.o.; (10:10); cf. *ohcîhkaw-*

išîhkâto- VAI [recipr.] do something to each other; (10:10); cf. *ohcîhkâto-*

išîwî- VAI do things; 43:4; *môna wîskâc wayêš išîwîniwa* he never does anything; cf. *tašîwî-*

iškopali- VAI/VII be left over; 19:10; *mêkwâc mistahi ê-'htakwahk kêkwân kê-mîcinâniwahk êkâ wîskâc 'ci-wêpinikâtêk kêkwân kâ-iškopanik* while there is plenty to eat, something which is left over should never be thrown away; cf. *iškwâpali-, ...pali-*

iškotêhkân- NI stove; (50:2); cf. *stwâp-, ...ihkân-*

iškotêw- NI fire; 3:7; 9:12; 14:5; 23:4; 42:60; *wêsâ kišitêw anta iškotêhk* it is too hot there at the fire

iškotêwan- VII be a fire (there); 11:12

iškwahcikâtê- VII be left over; 19:9; *môna manâ mitoni kêkwân iškwahcikâtêw* not a single thing is left over; cf. *iškwaht-*

iškwaht- VTI leave s.t. (food) after eating the rest; 19:9; 27:4; *môna kanakê kêkwâniw ohc'-iškwahtamwak* they didn't leave anything at all; *âsay osam anihi otôskanima kâ-k'-îškwahtamin'ci awiyâšîša* he (Weesakechahk) boiled the bones of the creatures which they had left after eating

iškwapw- VTA leave s.o. (e.g., *môs, wâpoš*) after eating the rest

iškwâ IPV finish, complete

iškwâhtêm- NI door; 9:13; 12:7; 24:1; 59:3

iškwâpali- VAI/VII come to an end; (19:10); cf. *iškopali-, ...pali-*

iškwâtahw- VTA leave s.o. unscraped; 29:3

iškwêšîš- NA girl; [alternative form of *iskwêšiš*-]

išpacistin- VII be a high drift-bank; 12:11; 60:6; cf. *išpatâwahkâ*-, *išpâmatinâ*-, *išpâpiskâ*-

išpaskitê- VII be high; (52:3) *išpaskitêw wâskâhikan* it is a high house; cf. *iskwâskitê*-, *tapahtaskitê*-

išpatâwahkâ- VII be a high sandy or gravel bank, ridge; (60:6)

išpâ- VII be high; 3:2; 42:32

išpâmatinâ- VII be a high earthen bank; (60:6); cf. ...*âmatin*..., *išpâpiskâ*-, *išpatâwahkâ*-; *ispacistin*-

išpâpiskâ- VII be a high, rocky hill or cliff; 6:4; (60:6); cf. ...*âpisk*...

išpimihk IPC up above, aloft; upstairs; 1:2; 9:23

it- VTA say (something) to s.o., address s.o.; 1:3; 9:4; 43:8

it- VTI say so of s.t., mean s.t.; 43:3

itahamâso- VAI follow for oneself, sing (usually requires name of song or tune to follow verb); 45:11; *itahamâsow nikamôwiniliw* he follows (the words) of a song; *tân' êtahamâsot?* what type of songs does he sing? cf. *ayîtahamâso*-, *otinamâso*-, ...*ahamê*-

itahamê- VAI follow; (18:7); *itahamêw mêskanaw* he follows a path, road; cf. *itahamâso*-, ...*ahamê*-

itahpit- VTA/VTI tie s.o./s.t. this way; (52:2); cf. *âhtahpit*-, *mâkwahpit*-, *walahpit*-

itakiht- VTI value, count, reckon s.t. so, consider s.t. so

itakim- VTA value, count, reckon s.o. so, consider s.o. so; 42:53; 59:2; *môla mistahi n'titakimâw* I don't think much of him

itakiso- VAI cost; 40:5

itakocin- VAI hang so; (47:2)

itakotê- VII hang so; 47:2

itamahciho- VAI feel oneself so; 10:10; cf. ...*amahciho*-

itapi- VAI sit around, sit so; 43:4; cf. ...*api*-

itaskânêsi- VAI belong to a tribe or a nation; 44:4

itaskiso- VAI stand at such an angle (e.g., a tree); 61:4

itaskitê- VII stand at such an angle, be so placed; be stuck so (perpendicularly); 42:45

itastâ- VAI-T place s.t. so; 49:5

itastê- VII be so placed; 41:16

itaši- VAI be so many [used in plural]; 40:1

itašiwât- VTA so order s.o.; 55:7; cf. *olašiwât*-

itâcim- VTA recount (about) s.o. (stories about current or recent activities); 6:2

itâcimâkaniwan- VAI/VII be widely talked about, have stories told about one; [synonym: *itâcimâkaniwi*-, *itâcimitiso*-]

itâcimikosi- VAI be so told about (as in stories about activities long ago); 5:10; 6:1; 8:1; [synonym: *itâcimâkaniwi*-]

itâcimitiso- VAI have stories told about oneself; tell stories about oneself; 10:2; cf. *itâcimâkaniwan*-

itâcimo- VAI recount it so, tell it so; 41:12; cf. ...*âcimo*-

itâcimostaw- VTA tell s.o. about; 44:1; 42:19

itâkaniwi- VAI be called, named; 49:1

itâpatan- VII be so used, be used for something; 42:8; *êkâ mâka wayêš ê-'tâpatahk* when it's not used for anything in particular, 42:11

itâpatisi- VAI work at s.t., s.t. is one's work; 53:4; *cîmânikimâw itâpatisiw* he works as captain, 'a captain' is his job

itâpicî- VAI be absent, be away (for long or short time); 6:6; 11:7; *itâpicîw ê-nâtinihtêt* he is away getting wood; *wayêš nîso-tipahikan kâ-itâpicît* he was away for about two hours

itâpihkêmohtâniwan- VAI the line goes thus; 43:14; cf. ...*âpihk*...

itâpihkêpit- VTI pull the cord thus; 43:11; cf. ...*âpihk*...

itâpipaliho- VAI look suddenly; 14:6; *itâ'palihow* he turns to look; 31:2;

êkoh, ê-itâp'palihoyân then, I would suddenly look around (inattentively), 53:1; *itâpipalihow manâ wt'h* he quickly glanced around, 55:5; cf. *...paliho-*

itâpi- VAI look, see so, look around; 1:4; 9:4; 19:2; 66:1; cf. *...âpi-*

itâpolo- VAI drift so; 10:3; cf. *pimâpolo-, pimâpotê-, pimâstan-, pimâhoko-*

itâskiso- VAI be burnt so; 8:8

itâskwahw- VTA hold s.o. so on a stick; 9:14

itâspinêwin- NI complaint, disease, sickness; (36:1) *tânispî mâhcic kâ-nâtikwêyin iskwêwak otitâspinêwiniwâw?* When did women's sickness last come to you? (standard Cree usage for "When did you have your last menstrual period?"; euphemism in Moose Factory area, not understood by younger girls, is *tânispî mâhcic kâ-nâtisk kôhkom?* When did your grannie last visit you?); cf. *...âspinê-*

itâspit- VTA dress s.o. so; 52:4

itâši- VAI sail thither; 58:1; cf. *...âši-*

itâtalôhkaw- VTA (so) tell s.o. a legend; 46:1

itâtalôhkâsi- VAI be told about in a legend [alternative form of *itâtalôhkâso-*]; 55:9; *ê-'tâtalôhkâsicik aniki mistikwak* as those trees are told about in stories; cf. *âtalôhkâso-*

itâtalôhkâso- VAI be told about in a legend; 1:1; 3:1; 12:16; cf. *itâtalôhkâsi-*

itâtalôhkâtê- VII a legend or myth is (so) told; 2:1; 55:9

itâtalôhkâtiso- VAI tell a legend or myth about oneself; 2:1

itê IPC location, way; in such-and-such a way [in combination with root elements]; 18:1; e.g., *tântê* (cf. *tân...itê*) where; *antê* (cf. *an...itê*) there; *mayê' 'tê* that's not the (right) way; 42:66

itêh- VTI stir s.t.; 50:2

itêhkê IPC -wards, on the side of [with preceding particle and locative]; 49:1; *nîkân itêhkê* ahead of, in front of

itêhkêhtin- VII lie, run so (e.g., of a river); 61:3; *ôtê itêhkêhtin* it runs towards one; *nêtê itêhkêhtin* it runs away from one; *âstamitê itêhkêhtin* it runs in this direction; *awasitê itêhkêhtin* it runs furthest away, towards the far side; cf. *...htin-*

itêliht- VTI think; 3:6

itêlihtâkosi- VAI seem, be so considered; 13:14; 41:15; cf. *...ihtâkosi-*

itêlihtâkwan- VII seem, be so considered; 1:2; 1:3; 40:6; cf. *...ihtâkwan-*; *pîtoš itêl'htâkwan ispîš ôma kâ-tašîhkâtotamahk* it seems different than this one where we make our home

itêlim- VTA think s.o., regard s.o., class s.o.; 2:9; 8:2; 41:1; 41:5

itêlimo- VAI think so of oneself; 10:2

itihkaso- VAI cook in a certain way; 55:3

itihkasw- VTA cook s.o. so; 18:7; *tân'k' êtê mâka kê-itihkaswâwakwênak?* I wonder, though, which way I should cook them?

itiht- VTI imagine s.t. so; 56:1; 64:2; *pôtâcikâniwan n'titihtên* I think I hear a whistle blowing; *pakwantaw ani kititihtênâwâw* you imagine you're hearing things

itihtaw- VTA understand s.o. so, take s.o. in such a way

itihtâkosi- VAI sound so; 9:5; cf. *...ihtâkosi-*

itihtâkwan- VII sound so; 9:5; 13:3; 64:2; cf. *...ihtâkwan-*

itikiti- VAI be so big, be of such a size; 27:2

itin- VTA/VTI hold s.o./s.t. so; 55:2; (Watkins-Faries gives stem form *issen-*, i.e., *išin-*)

itiskwêli- VAI hold one's head so; 56:5; cf. *nâmiskwêstâ-, nânâmiskwêpaliho-, wêwêpiskwêpaliho-, ...iskw...*

itiskwêstâ- VAI-T put one's head in such a way; (56:5) *itiskwêstâ* hold your head so! cf. *itiskwêli-, ...iskw...*

itiškaw- VTA shape s.o. (with bodily action); 8:5

itito- VAI [recipr.] tell each other, say to each other; 10:10; 18:2

itohtê- VAI go there (by walking); 1:3; 11:2; 42:1; cf. *ayîtohtah-*, *...ohtê-*

itôt- VTI do it so to s.t.; 9:2; 11:6; 19:1; 24:2; 27:1; 50:7; *pâpîtoš 'sa itôtamwak* they do it in various ways

itôtaw- VTA do it so to s.o.

itôtêsi- VAI be with one's family; 44:3; [probable contraction of *itôtêwisi-*]; cf. *...ôtêw.../-*

itwâso- VAI profess, think to oneself; imagine; 5:5; 18:3; 55:9; 60:4; a person, jealous of someone else, might say: *"n'kaškihon," itwâsow* he thinks he's smart (lit., "I'm able," he thinks of himself)

itwâtalôhkâtê- VII a legend or myth is (so) told; cf. *itâtalôhkâtê-*, 55:9

itwê- VAI say; 1:3; 9:11 et passim; *itwâniwan* one says, it is said; 1:2

itwêhkâso- VAI cry out, make a noise; 19:6; 20:6; 34:1; *n'kî-pêhtawâw môs ê-itwêhkâsot* I heard a moose making the noise

itwêwêso- VAI make a noise so; 65:8; cf. *kišiwêwêso-*

itwêwêtê- VII make a noise so; cf. *kišiwêwêtê-*

iyâpêwatihkw- NA buck deer; 10:7; 63:3; cf. *...âpêw.../-*; *atihkw-*

îkastê- VII be out (of the tide), be low water; 7:2; [synonym: *pâhkwakastê-*]

îhkât IPC ever; 1:7; [affected Ojibwa form for speech of Lynx]; cf. *wîhkât*

îkatên- VTA/VTI put s.o./s.t. aside, remove s.o./s.t.; 53:3

îkatêpali- VAI/VII go away, go aside; cf. *...pali-*

îkatêsi- VAI get out of the way, remove oneself; 53:2; 60:3

îkatê-wêpinamaw- VTA throw something aside for s.o.; 9:21

îtaw itêhkê IPC on each side; 45:2

ka IPV shall, will [grammatical preverb marking future]; 1:3 et passim; see also *kata-, ta-*

kahikê- VAI fell (timber); [contraction of *kawahikê-*]; 14:2; 14:4

kakêhtâwêliht- VTI be wise, be sensible, think sensibly; 2:9; 12:8

kakêmotamaw- VTA steal from s.o.; 18:9

kakêpah- VTI block up s.t., obstruct s.t.; 24:2; cf. *kipah-*

kakêpahâtâniwan- VII be all closed off; 13:12

kakêpâskwah- VTI close s.t. in on each side, block s.t. off (e.g., a beaver tunnel or a window with wooden panels); 13:8

kakêpâskwahw- VTA close s.o. in on each side, block s.o. off; cf. *...âskw.../-*

kakêpâtisi- VAI be stupid; 42:8

kakêpon- VTI close s.t. (e.g., a door); (14:7); cf. *kakêpwâtâmo-, kakêpwâtâmwâskisw-*

kakêpwâtâmo- VAI gasp for air; (14:7); cf. *kakêpon-, kakêpwâtâmwâskisw-*

kakêpwâtâmwâskisw- VTA cause s.o. to gasp for air; 14:7; cf. *kakêpwâtâmo-, kakêpon-*

kakêskim- VTA advise s.o, counsel s.o. instruct s.o.; 20:5

kakêšiwin- VTA/VTI crash s.o./s.t. down; 28:2

kakihtohtê- VAI move about aimlessly (e.g., a person strolling); 68:8; cf. *...ohtê-*

kakîšowâ- VII be warm every here and there; 41:17; cf. *kîšowâyâ-*

kakwâtakamahciho- VAI feel miserable; (23:2), 58:5; [near-synonym: *pakwâsamahciho-*]; cf. *kakwâtakihtâ-, kitimâkisi-, ...amahciho-*

kakwâtakêlimo- VAI be in misery; (23:2)

kakwâtakihtâ- VAI be pretty poorly off, be miserable; (58:5); [synonym: *êliwêhk kitimâkisi-*]; cf. *kakwâtakimahciho-, kitimâkisi-*

kakwâtakimahciho- VAI feel miserable; cf. *kakwâtakamahciho-*

kakwâtakinâkosi- VAI look miserable; 23:2; cf. *...nâkosi-*

kakwê IPV try; 7:1; 19:1; 20:3; 38:2

kakwêcih- VTA make trial of s.o.; 5:6; 49:3

kakwêcim- VTA ask s.o.; 1:4; 9:4; 20:1; 21:3; 53:4

kalakihtâ- VAI make a soft noise (e.g., as a mouse scratching in a cupboard or someone hammering in the distance so as to hinder sleep); 64:2; cf. *otatâmah-*

kalakitiyê- VAI have an itchy anus; (68:5); *n'kalakitiyân: môla kistinâc kwayêsk n'kî-ohci-kimisâhonâtokwê* my anus is itchy: I can't have wiped myself properly; cf. *kalêkisi-, išitiyêli-, kwêskitiyêpaliho-, tahkiskâtitiyêhw-, kimisah-, kimisaho-, ...tiy...*

kalêkisi- VAI be itchy; 55:9

kampaniy- NA Hudson's Bay Company; 42:24; 64:1

kanakê IPC at all; 13:6; 19:3; 41:5; 41:6; 41:8; at least; 42:12; 42:39

kanawâpaht- VTI look at s.t.; 37:1; 42:66; *ê-papâ-kanawâpahtamâhk n'tônikanâniy* as we looked over our traps

kanawâpam- VTA look at s.o.; 5:10; 13:7

kanawêlihcikâtê- VII be kept; 51:1; cf. *kanawêliht-*

kanawêliht- VTI keep s.t., take care of s.t.

kanawêlim- VTA keep s.o., take care of s.o.; 7:1; 11:2; keep a check on; 58:4

kapahtahan- VII be windy, blow, be the weather side; 12:11; *kâ-iši-kapahtahahk* where the snow is blown by the wind; *nâsic n'kî-âlimisin nahîtâk kapahtahan* I had a hard time, as it happened, windwards; cf. *tipinawâhk*

kapahtahanw- NI windward side; *kapahtahanohk* on the windward side

kapastawêh- VTI put s.t. into the water; 10:3; 13:17

kapastawêhw- VTA put s.o. into the water; 14:5; 29:2; 50:1

kapastawê-kwâškwâti- VAI jump into the water; (4:5); cf. *pahkopê-*

kapastawêpahtâ- VAI run into the water; 18:6; cf. *...pahtâ-*

kapastawêpaliho- VAI throw oneself into the water, jump into the water;

16:3; (38:2); cf. *...paliho-*

kapastawêpali- VAI/VII fall into the water (e.g., an arrow, gun); 4:4; 38:1; cf. *...pali-*

kapastawêpin- VTA/VTI throw s.o./s.t. into the water; 16:4; 29:1; haplology for *kapastawê-wêpin-*

kapastawêšimo- VAI immerse oneself in water, submerge; (38:2); cf. *...šimo-*

kapatêsipahtâ- VAI run ashore; 18:4; cf. *...pahtâ-*

kapatêsipaliho- VAI quickly get out (e.g., of a canoe); 31:2; cf. *...paliho-*

kapatêskwê- VAI take out (e.g., beaver from pot into pan); 13:13; scoop the food out of the pot using a sharp stick; cf. *apwânâskw-, cîstahikan-*

kapatêtâpipahtwâ- VAI-T run s.t. ashore; 31:2

kapatêyâhoko- VAI be washed ashore; (61:3)

kapatêyâhotê- VII be washed ashore; 61:3

kapatêyâhtawî- VAI step on shore or on land; 16:5; cf. *...âhtawî-*

kapâ- VAI step ashore, alight from a vehicle; 9:3; 11:3; 36:1; 65:3

kapâšimo- VAI go swimming, go bathing; 16:4; 22:3; cf. *...šimo-*

kapâšimototaw- VTA swim out to s.o.; 4:4

kapêši- VAI camp, encamp for a night; 40:3; 42:5; 58:5

kapêšiwin- NI a temporary camping place; a day's journey (Watkins-Faries)

kapêšiwinihkâso- VAI make as though to camp, make a sort of camping place; 37:4; cf. *...hkâso-*

kaskêw IPC across the island; [synonym: *awasânakw*]; (n. 2:1)

kaskêwê- VAI go across the island, take a short-cut on a paddling route

kaskêwêhonân- NI short route across, portage

kaskitipiskâ- VII be very dark, be pitch dark; 37:3

kaškatahtahkwanêhw- VTA break s.o.'s wing bone; 20:6; cf. *mitahtahkwan-, wîsakêtahtahkwanêšim-,*

...tahtahkwan...

kaškatahwanêhw- VTA break s.o.'s
wing; (20:6)

kaškatahwanêšimo- VAI break one's
own wing; (20:6)

kaškatahw- VTA break a wing; 20:6;
contrast *kâškâtahw-*

kaškatinisiw- NA November, lit.,
'freeze-up'; cf. *pîsimw-*

kaškêliht- VTI be sad, be depressed, be
lonesome; 19:3; 64:3

kaškêwêhonân- NI [place name] Hay
Creek; lit., 'portage'

kaškiho- VAI be competent at, be clever,
be skilful; 2:7; 42:6

kaškihôwin- NI power, strength, might;
6:10

kaškihtâ- VAI-T be able (to do s.t.),
manage s.t.; 3:9; 9:9; 11:3; 21:6; 32:1;
35:2; 40:3; 64:2

kaškikwêšin- VAI break one's neck;
(12:3); cf. *...ikw...*, *...šin-*

kaškipit- VTA/VTI can pull s.o./s.t., can
budge s.o./s.t.; 60:4

'kat, 'kat IPC slowly, slowly; carefully,
carefully [probable contraction for
pêhkâc, pêhkât]

kata IPV shall, will [grammatical preverb
marking future]; 1:4; cf. *ka-, ta-*

kawacî- VAI be cold, be frozen; 11:11;
23:1

kawah- VTI knock s.t. down; (5:7)

kawahikê- VAI fell (timber); 14:2; cf.
kahikê-

kawahkatê- VAI starve; 27:6; 59:1

kawahw- VTA knock s.o. down; 5:7

kawêšimo- VAI go to bed, retire; 3:4;
11:12; 18:8; cf. *kawišimo-*, *...šimo-*

kawatâpâwê- VAI lose one's life (by
means of water); also heard as
kawatâpwâwê-; cf. *nistâpâwê-*

kawêšimohkâso- VAI pretend to go to
bed, make as if to go to bed; 9:17; cf.
...hkâso-

kawišimo- VAI go to bed, retire; 13:1;
14:3; 55:5; cf. *kawêšimo-*

kawišin- VAI lie; 19:10; cf. *...šin-*

kayâm IPC quietly, tranquilly; all right;
1:4; 11:8; 55:1

kayâš IPC long ago, in days gone by;
42:23

kâ IPV past time, completed action
marker [with conjunct: changed form
of grammatical preverb *kî-*]; with
restrictive usage, who, which, when;
with *iši-*, where; 1:1 et passim

kâ-ayamihêwi-kanawâpit Nom.A = [VAI
changed conjunct] bishop (Roman
Catholic); 41:2; cf.
kihci-ayamihêwikimâw-

kâ(â) IPC [exclamation] oh, so that's it;
43:8

kâhcicišk- VTI catch s.t. with the foot;
9:15

kâhciciškaw- VTI catch s.o. with the
foot; 9:15

kâhcitâpaht- VTI catch sight of s.t.; 55:2

kâhcitin- VTA/VTI lay hold of s.o./s.t.,
grab s.o./s.t.; 7:2; 12:2; 42:1; 48:1; 65:9;
ê-wî-kakwê-kâhcitinamân âpatisîwin
because I wanted to try to get work

kâhkapin- NA moose-hide used for
making snowshoe netting line,
fast-drying hide; 53:1; cf. *kâhkamês-*

kâhkamês- NA dried fish; (53:1); cf.
*kâhkapin, kâhkiso-, kâhkitê-,
kâhkitê-wîyâs-, kâhkâpoš-, ...amês...*/-

kâhkâkîšiminak NA [pl.; place name]
Cockispenny Point, lit., 'crow duck
berries' (located on west coast of
James Bay); cf. *...min...* /-

kâhkâkîšip- NA crow-duck, cormorant;
cf. *...šip...*/-

kâhkâpisi- VAI become discoloured (e.g.,
of something which has been in a
fish's stomach and is not yet quite
digested); 29:3

kâhkâpošw- NA dried rabbit; (53:1); cf.
...âpošw-

kâhkis- VTI sear s.t. (stage prior to
cooking when meat surface dries and
begins to cook over fire); 19:7;
*ê-'ti-kâhkisahk,
kâ-mohci-tômihkâsonici manâ piko
anih' omaskoma* as he started to sear
it, that bear of his just dripped fat

kâhkiso- VAI be dried; (53:1)

kâhkitê- VII be dried; (53:1) *ê-kâhkitêk piko n'tayân* I have only dried meat

kâhkitê-wîyâs- NI dried meat; (53:1)

kâhtin- VTA/VTI push s.o./s.t.; (51:2); cf. *šêšêkon-*

kâhtinikâtê- VII be pushed; 51:2

kâ-iši IPV where (relative) [with conjunct]; 15:3; cf. *kâ-*

kâ-iškwâ IPC after; *kâ-iškwâ anima* after that

kâkê IPC I imagine, probably; 19:7; cf. *kâki*

kâkê oš' â(ni) IPC I thought, as I thought; 9:16; 42:47

kâki IPC I imagine, probably; 18:7; *n'ka-sakapwân kâki* I wonder if I should roast it, I should roast it, I guess; [virtually synonymous with *tâpask n'ka-sakapwân*]; *môla kâki ohci-wâpahtamwak-* I imagine they didn't see it; cf. *tâpask*

kâkikê IPC forever, always, evermore; 28:2

kâ-kinwâwahkâw- NI [place name] Long Ridge, lit., 'long sand ridge' (located on west coast of James Bay)

kâ-mihcâpiskâw NI [place name] Big Stone, traditional name for *kâ-mišikitit asiniy* (located about 27 kilometres west of Hannah Bay River); n. 67:3; cf. *...âpisk...*, *asiniy-*, *mišikiti-*

kâ-mihkopalinâniwahk Nom.I = [VAI indef.conj.indic.] measles; (46:2)

kâ-'mihlâmakahk Nom.I = [VII conj.indic.] aeroplane; 42:28; cf. *kâ-pimihlâmakahk*, *pimihlâ-*

kâ-mišikitit asiniy NA [place name] Big Stone; 67:2; n. 67:3; cf. *kâ-mihcâpiskâw*

kâ-ohci-ayaminâniwahk Nom.I = [VAI indef.conj.indic.] radio, lit., 'that from which one speaks'

kânata- NI [place name] Canada; 1:1

kâ-pimihlâmakahk Nom.I = [VII conj. indic.] aeroplane, 'that which flies'; 42:28; 44:1; cf. *pimihlâ-*

kâ-piskwâhkâšihk Nom.A North Bluff Shoal, lit., '(that) which lies heaped up' (located 27 kilometres north of

Moose Factory on the west coast of James Bay)

kâs- NI [English loanword] 'gas', gasoline; 42:21; cf. *pimiy-*

kâsohtaw- VTA hide from s.o.; 67:2. *n'kâsohtâtonân-* we're playing hide and seek; cf. *kâsostaw-*

kâsostaw- VTA hide oneself from s.o.; 5:7

kâso- VAI hide oneself, conceal oneself; 5:7; 14:4

kâšâ- VII be sharp (edged); (61:4); cf. *cîpwâ-*

kâšikaskiwâkan- NA creature with sharp talons; (26)

kâšikaskiwêsi- VAI [dim.] have sharp little claws; (61:4)

kâšikaskiwê- VAI have sharp talons; 61:4

kâšisi- VAI be sharp (edged); (61:4); cf. *cîposi-*

kâškah- VTI scrape s.t.; (29:3)

kâškahw- VTA scrape s.o.; 29:3

kâškâtahw- VTA scrape s.o.; (20:6)

kâškikwâcikâkê- VAI use it to lace, lace with it; 62:2

kâškikwât- VTI sew s.t.; (62:2)

kâ-tahkwâpêt NA [proper name] Short Trace; 42:42; cf. *tahkwâpê-*, *...âp...*, *...âpêk...*

kâtaw- VTA hide it from s.o.; 5:5

'kâwil' IPC not [with conjunct and imperative]; 4:2; 10:9

'kâwila IPC not; [contraction of *êkâwila*]

'kâwin' IPC not; [contraction of *êkâwina*]

kâwîn IPC not; [affected Ojibwa form for speech of Lynx]; 1:7

kê IPV shall, will [changed form of *ka*, grammatical preverb marking future, with conjunct]; [*kâ-* restrictive with future marker, e.g., *kêy-ohci-pimâtisit* from which he will live]; 40:6

kêcikonah- VTA take off or doff s.o.; 12:7

kêcikonamaw- VTA take it off for s.o.; 12:7

kêcikopali- VII come off; 3:8; cf. *...pali-*

kêciko-wêpin- VTA/VTI throw s.o./s.t. off (i.e., a piece of clothing); 19:8

kêhcin IPC for sure; 9:8; 42:33; *kêhcin ta-nohta-maci-kîšikâw* it's going to be a bad day for sure; *môna kêhcin ka-kî-šâpoškên* for certain you won't be able to pass through it; *kêhcin isa* for sure

kêhcinâho- VAI be sure; 42:6

kê-ilikohk IPC as hard or as much as possible, for all one's worth; 19:6; cf. *k'-êlikohk*

kêka IPC at last, finally; 1:6; 8:2; 9:5; 9:20; 23:5; 34:3

kêkât IPC almost, nearly; 4:7; 13:8; 40:2; 58:2

kêkišêp IPC in the morning; 6:9

kêkišêpânihkwê- VAI have breakfast; 13:2; 14:3

kêkišêpâyâ- VII be morning; 3:2; 13:1; cf. ...*ayâ-*

kêko PR which (one) [indecl.]; 5:2; 41:1

kêkonên- NI sort of thing [possibly an Ojibwa form for *kêkwânihkân*]; 11:12; n. 11:25

kêkwân- NI thing, something; *pêyak kêkwân* one thing

kêkwân- PR what? something [interrog. and indef.]; 1:4; 5:5

kêkwânihkân- NI sort of thing; 27:7; 39:4; 44:2; 49:6; 55:1; cf. *kêkwân*, ...*ihkân-*

kêkwân 'tokwê PR whatever [contraction of *kêkwân êtokwê*]; 68:1

k'-êlikohk IPC as hard as possible, as hard as one can (MC); 20:3; SC: *k'-ênikohk*

k'-ênikohk IPC as hard as possible, for all one is worth (SC); 36:2; *maškošîya manâ k'-ênikohk mîciw* he ate grasses for all he was worth, 36:2; MC: *k'-êlikohk*

kêskaw IPC quickly, hastily; 12:7; *kêskaw pôsipali* jump in quickly; *kêskaw pataskawêpaw* give him an injection quickly

kêskiskawipali- VAI/VII go through the body quickly; 12:7; *kêskiskawipaninitê* if it goes through the body quickly; cf. *sêsikôc*, ...*pali-*

kêšišaw IPC hardly; 41:16

kêšîciwanw- NI [place name] Kashechewan (pronounced in English

as [kəsæ̌čəwʌn]; a village located 160 kilometres north of Moosonee on the Albany River; known in English as Albany Post prior to moving to the north channel of the river around 1959); 34:1; 39:3; 42:53; 49:1; cf. ...*ciwan*.../-

kêšîciwanowastimw- NA dog from Kasechewan or Albany Post; 33; cf. ...*astimw*.../-

kêšîciwanow-ililiw- NA person from Kasechewan; 1:1

kêtahtawêl IPC suddenly; cf. *kêtahtawil*

kêtahtawil IPC suddenly; 9:6; 9:17; 13:3; 20:6; 31:1; 42:35; 42:67; 56:6; 68:8; cf. *sêsikôc*

kêtawatê- VAI remove one's bag; 14:4; cf. ...*wat*.../-

kêtâspiso- VAI undress; (38:2; 65:1); cf. *awêspiso-*, *wêspititiso-*

kêtâspisopaliho- VAI undress quickly; 38:2; cf. ...*paliho-*

kê'wâ'hkân- NI sort of thing [contraction of *kêkwânihkân*]; 41:14

kici IPV so that, in order to [grammatical preverb with conj.indic.]; 1:4; 6:1 et passim; cf. '*ci*

kiciskahol- VTA drop s.o. unintentionally; (66:2); cf. *kiciskipalih-*

kiciskahotâ- VAI-T drop s.t. unintentionally; cf. *kiciskipalihtwâ-*

kiciskin- VTA/VTI drop s.o./s.t.; 66:2; cf. *kiciskahol-*, *kiciskahotâ-*

kicistâpâwahtâ- VAI-T wash s.t.; 19:3

kicistâpâwal- VTA wash s.o.; (20:5)

kicistâpâwalitiso- VAI wash oneself; 20:5; [more usual usage is *kicistâpâwalo-*]

kicistâpâwalo- VAI wash oneself, get washed; 50:2; (68:8); cf. *kistâpâwalo-*

kihci-awênihkâniwi- VAI be a person of importance; 41:14; cf. *awênihkân-*

kihci-ayamihêwikimâw- NA bishop (Anglican); (41:2); cf. *kâ-ayamihêwi-kanawâpit*

kihci-ayišiho- VAI be dressed in fancy things or flashy clothes; (8:6); cf. *išiho-*, *awêspiso-*

kihci-âliman- VII be really difficult; 40:1

kihcicišahw- VTA send s.o. away; 49:5

kihcih- VTA start making s.o., begin to make s.o.; 52:2

kihcihtâ- VAI-T start making s.t., begin to make s.t.; 1:2; 6:2; 34:3; 62:1

kihcikamiy- NI sea; 9:7; 60:5; 68:8; *kwayêsk lâlih kihcikamîhk itohtêwak* they went straight alongside the sea; cf. *...kamiy-*

kihci-kišišawipaliho- VAI be lively, be frisky (of a person, first thing in the morning); (9:16); cf. *kišišaw, ...paliho-*

kihcihlâ- VAI fly away; 14:4; 20:3; 26:1; 61:1; cf. *išihlâ-, pimihlâ-, ...hlâ...*

kihci-okimâw- NA chief manager; 49:5; government; 42:15

kihcipah- VTA run off with s.o.; 65:8; cf. *ispah-, patotêpah-, pêcipah-*

kihcipahtâ- VAI run away; 18:6; 31:2; 34:2; 36:2; 47:2; 56:8; cf. *...pahtâ-*

kihcipalih- VTA make off with s.o.; 16:2

kihcipaliho- VAI take oneself off; 9:6; *êko ... k'-âti-kihcipalihot* so ... he proceeded on his trip, resumed his trip; cf. *...paliho-*

kihcipali- VAI/VII go off, go away; 11:2; 20:5; 41:14; *êkâ mâka 'wâc ê-kî-kihcipalikopanê 'wênihkân* and then (it must have been that) nobody could even go out, 41:14; start off, 42:58; cf. *...pali-*

kihcipici- VAI go away with one's gear; (40:1); cf. *papâmipici-, pêcipici-, ...pici-*

kihci-sîpiy- NI main river; 42:47

kihciskanawê- VAI start to make tracks; 12:13; cf. *pimiskanawê-, ...skanawê-*

kihcišimo- VAI start to dance; 8:3; cf. *...šimo-*

kihciwê IPN real, proper; 49:4; *kihciwê-otâpâna* real trains (i.e., transcontinental express); 41:3; 42:3; 49:4; *kihciwê-nipiy* proper water; 68:8; cf. *wâlipêyâ-*

kihci-wêpin- VTA/VTI heave or throw s.o./s.t.; 13:15; 42:66; *kêy-ohc'-ati-kihci-wêpinahk* where he is to start off from

kihci-wêpinikê- VAI fling with abandon, throw greatly; 8:3; *kihci-wêpinikêw*

ê-nîmiwit he shakes his feet as he dances

kihciwêskamikw- NI 'real moss' n. 51:2; cf. *wâpaskamikw-, mihkwaskamikw-, ...askamikw-; wâspisoyân-*

kihciwil- VTA carry s.o. off, carry s.o. away; 13:14; 40:3; 66:2

kihciwitâ- VAI-T carry s.t. off, carry s.t. away; 31:1

kihtahamêpahtâ- VAI run quickly after; 13:15

kihtahamê- VAI follow a road or trail; go for a walk; (41:15); cf. *pimahamê-, ...ahamê-, atimohtê-, kihtamohtê-, kihtimohtê-*

kihtahol- VTA take s.o. away (in a canoe or plane); used when a bird takes a fish from a net; 9:2; cf. *kihtakihtahol-, pêtahol-, pimahol-*

kihtakihtahol- VTA keep carrying s.o. off; 56:3; cf. *kihtahol-*

kihtamohtê- VAI start out afresh, start on a fresh lap; (41:15); *ê-'ti-kihtamohtâniwahk* starting out afresh, starting on a fresh lap (of a road); cf. *atimohtê-, kihcihtâ-, kihtahamê-, kihtimohtê-, ...ohtê-*

kihtatawêmo- VAI go away crying; 12:8

kihtâcimo- VAI start off telling; 42:62; cf. *tipâcimo-*

kihtân- VTA/VTI dip s.o./s.t., plunge s.o./s.t.; 13:9

kihtâpali- VAI/VII sink; (42:34); cf. *kihtâpêyâ-, ...pali-*

kihtâpêkin- VTA/VTI dip s.o./s.t. into the water (e.g., as in washing a blanket); 48:1; contrast *kapastawêpin-*; cf. *...ipê.../-, ...êkin.../-, kihtâpêkwêpin-*

kihtâpêkwêpin- VTA/VTI toss s.o./s.t. into and keep under the water; (48:1)

kihtâpêyâ- VII be swampy; 42:34; cf. *...ipê.../-, ...ayâ-*

kihtâpihkêpali- VAI/VII set off, start off (of a line or cord); 42:62; cf. *...âpihk..., ...pali-*

kihtâpolo- VAI drift with the current; 10:3; cf. *...âpolo-*

kihtimi- VAI be lazy; 42:8

kihtohtah- VTA take s.o. away; 13:14

kihtimohtê- VAI walk lazily; (41:15); cf. *atimohtê-, kihtahamê-, kihtamohtê-, ...ohtê-*

kihtohtahtâ- VAI-T take s.t. away with one; 15:3; 16:4

kihtohtê- VAI go away; 2:3; 10:6; 36:2; cf. *...ohtê-*

kihtohtêhkâso- VAI pretend to go away; 13:5; cf. *...hkâso-*

kikipaliho- VAI go swiftly or quickly after; 13:10; cf. *...paliho-*

kikisitêšin- VAI lie with the feet attached (i.e., not cut off); 10:5; cf. *...sit...*

kikišk- VTI wear s.t.; 10:5

kikiškaw- VTA wear s.o.

kikitêškanêhtin- VII have horns, have antlers; (10:5) *ostikwân kikitêškanêhtin* the head has horns, antlers; cf. *otêškani-, otêškaniwêhtin-, êškan-*

kilakiškâko- VAI feel 'high', feel slightly intoxicated; 42:65

kilâskim- VTA lie to s.o.; 18:4

kilâski- VAI lie, tell a falsehood; 2:7

kilika-wêpin- VTA/VTI mix s.o./s.t. up; 41:20; 41:21

kilipali- VAI/VII slide smoothly, slide easily (e.g., of a sled with steel shoeing in mild weather); (12:14); cf. *...pali-*

kimisah- VTA wipe s.o. (e.g., a child); (68:5); *kimisay, lipâcihitisôtokê* wipe him, he must have messed his pants

kimisaho- VAI wipe oneself; cf. *kalakitiyê-*

kimiwan- VII rain; 12:5

kimiwaniyân- NI raincoat; 36:2

kimociškw- NA raccoon, 'the robber' (because of his mask; a descriptive rather than traditional term in Moose and Swampy Cree country, since the raccoon does not range so far north)

kimotamaw- VTA rob s.o., steal from s.o.; 18:10; 19:9; 55:4

kimoti- VAI steal, thieve; 13:10

kinikaw IPC mixed (SC); 11:4; MC: *kilika-wêpin-*

kinopali- VAI/VII go long, (fig.) stretch out; 42:15; cf. *...pali-*

kinosi- VAI be long

kinostikwêyâ- VII be a long river; (42:28); cf. *kîškâyawistikwêyâ-, kwayaskostikwêyâ-. pâhkostikwêyâ-, tahkostikwêyâ-, wâwâkistikwêyâ-, ...stikw.../-*

kinošêw- NA pike, jackfish; 4:2

kinošêwi-sîpiy- NI [place name] Canoes River, lit., 'pike river' (located on west coast of James Bay)

kinwâ- VII be long; 6:1; 61:3; *êkâ nâspic kici-kinwâk âtanôhkân* so the story won't be too long

kinwâliwê- VAI have a long tail; (27:4); cf. *tahkwâliwê-, ...âliw...*

kinwâpêkan- VII be long (as a string, cord); 2:4; cf. *...âpêk...*

kinwâpê- VAI be a long trace; (42:42); cf. *tahkwâpê-, mâskwâpin-, otâpâniyâpiy-, ...âp...*

kinwâpihkêmo- VAI move in a long line; 6:9; cf. *...âpihk..., ...ayâ-*

kinwâpihkêyâ- VII be a long line, for the line to be long; cf. *iskwâpihkêyâ-*

kinwâskohtâ- VAI-T make s.t. (of wood) long; (52:2); cf. *iskwâskohtâ-, ...tahkwâskohtâ-, ...âskw.../-*

kinwâskwan- VII be long (e.g., a branch, something wooden); 21:7; 61:3

kinwêš IPC a long time; 1:8; 10:5; 16:4; 20:3; 50:7

kipah- VTI close s.t., shut s.t., cork s.t.; 24:2; 41:21; *kipaha!* shut it off (i.e., the tape recorder)

kipâskwahw- VTA block s.o. off with sticks; (13:4); cf. *pâskihw-, ...âskw... /-*

kipihcipali- VAI stop (suddenly); 13:3; 18:2; cf. *...pali-*

kipihcî- VAI stop, halt; 19:2; 34:1

kipihkwêpit- VTA strangle s.o. by pulling; 18:5; 18:6

kipihtawê- VAI leave off, discontinue (doing s.t.); 55:7

kipihtâciwosopali- VAI/VII stop bouncing around while boiling, stop boiling; 14:6; *kipihtâciywosopaliw askihk* the kettle stops boiling; cf. *mâtâciyosopali-, kipihtin-, oso-, ...pali-*

kipihtâšikowan- VII stop running (of

water), stop dripping; (14:6); cf.
mâtâšikowan-

kipihtin- VTA/VTI stop s.o./s.t. by hand;
(14:6)

kipišk- VTI stop s.t.'s progress with
bodily action, be in the way

kipiškaw- VTA stop s.o.'s progress with
bodily action, be in the way;
kikipiškawin you're in my way; cf.
kipoškaw-

kipiškiš- VTI cut s.t. up

kipiškišw- VTA cut s.o. up; 50:4

kipon- VTA/VTI block s.o./s.t.; 68:5

kipopali- VAI/VII be closed in; 41:19; cf.
...pali-

kipoškaw- VTA block s.o.; *kikipoškawin*
you're in my road; cf. *kipiškaw-*

kipotâmaso- VAI be smothered with
smoke or steam; 56:6

kipotâmâpaso- VAI be smothered with
smoke; 9:20

kipotâmoškaw- VTA suffocate s.o.,
choke s.o.; 65:5

kipwahkâso- VAI be caught in a tide
pool; (54:1) *wâpamêk kipwahkâsow* the
whale is caught in a tide-pool

kipwahkâtê- VII be caught in a tide
pool; (54:1)

kisis- VTI heat s.t. up; cf. *kîsis-*

kisisawisî- VAI be clever at s.t., be
active, be quick; 33; (42:7)

kisisawisîwin- NI cleverness; 42:16;
kisisawisîwinihk itêhkê along smart
lines, in a clever way

kisisâwê- VAI put on heat, heat up; 23:5

kisiso- VAI be warm

kisisw- VTA heat s.o. up; 42:60; cf.
kîsisw-

kisiwâh- VTA anger s.o. (MC); 8:5; 22:1;
27:3; 49:4; *kisiwâhitowak* they anger
each other; SC: *kišiwâh-*; 27:3

kisiwâsi- VAI be angry (MC); 9:2; 18:6;
19:9; 21:5; 23:1; 34:2; 49:4; 63:1; SC:
kišiwâsi-

kiskêlihcikâtê- VII be known; 1:3

kiskêliht- VTI know s.t., know; 2:4; 34:1

kiskêlihtâkwan- VII be known (from
hearsay); 49:4; cf. *...ihtâkwan-*

kiskêlim- VTA know s.o.; 9:8

kiskêlimitotaw- VTA make known to
s.o., advise s.o.; 30:1

kiskinohamaw- VTA teach s.o., instruct
s.o.; 1:4; 1:8; 21:1; *ê-kiskinohamâhcik*
being taught, 42:7;
kâ-k'-îši-kiskinohamâtahkok the way
they taught us, 42:16;
ê-kî-kiskinohamawit that she taught
me, 53:4

kiskinohamâkê- VAI teach; 49:1

kiskinohamâkêmakan- VII teach; 19:10

kiskinohamâtôwikamikw- NI school;
49:1; cf. *...ikamikw-*

kiskinohtah- VTA guide s.o.; 2:8

kiskinowâcicikan- NI mark, sign,
token; 9:24

kiskinowâpi- VAI note, keep track of;
53:2; cf. *...âpi-*

kiskisi- VAI remember; 3:6; 9:8; 9:24;
ê-'ti-mâmawi-kiskisinâniwahki
when the memories are gathered
together

kiskisipali- VAI suddenly recall, have
flash across one's mind, occur to one;
3:5; 15:4; 18:1; 19:10; cf. *...pali-*

kiskisitotaw- VTA recall s.o., bring s.o.
to mind; 43:3

kiskisom- VTA remind s.o.; 42:66

kispakatamwan- VII be getting thick
(i.e., a scab, coat of paint); 55:8

kispakâ- VII be thick

kispakici- VAI be thick; cf. *kispakisi-*

kispakisi- VAI be thick; 61:3

kispakisikwâ- VII be thick (ice on river);
(55:8)

kistakiso- VAI be of considerable
account, be of high position; 49:6

kistamwan- VII be beaten down by
walking (e.g., a trail); (5:6); cf.
kistatah-

kistatah- VTI pack (a trail) down by
walking; 5:6

kistâkan- NI stake, staff (used for an
enclosure); 13:9

kistâpatisi- VAI be useful; 25:1

kistâpâwalo- VAI get washed; 68:8; cf.
kicistâpâwalo-

kistêlihcikâtê- VII be esteemed, be
respected; 49:1

kistêliht- VTI esteem s.t., respect s.t.;
49:6

kistêlim- VTA esteem s.o., respect s.o.;
(49:6)

kistêlimâkaniwan- VAI (passive) be
respected; 2:9

kistinâc IPC surely, certainly; 8:6; 42:12;
55:4

kistinât IPC surely, certainly; cf. *kistinâc*

kistisî- VAI be great, be important, be
eminent; 49:6

kistôtêw IPC (as) a couple (i.e., one man
and one woman, not just any two
people); 1:9; *niwâpamâwak
ê-kistôtêwêskâcik* I see them walking
there as a couple; cf. *nîšôtêw, nistôtêw,
...ôtêw...* / -

kistôtêwêskâ- VAI walk as a couple; cf.
kistôtêw

kišâkamitê- VII be hot liquid; 65:3; cf.
...âkam...

kišâkamitê- NI hot water;
n'tayakopâtinânân kišâkamitêliw we
bathed him with hot water

kišâkolê- VII be a hot flame; 9:19

kišâpiskis- VTI heat s.t. (metal) up; 8:8;
cf. *kišâpiskisikê-, pîwâpiskwahikan-,
...âpisk...*

kišâpiskisikê- VAI warm up the motor
(of car, skidoo, etc.); (8:8)

kišâpiskisamaw- VTA heat metal object
up for s.o.; 12:7; (12:8)
ê-kišâpiskisamâhk in our heating it up

kišâsikê- VAI shine hot (the sun); 15:5

kišâspin IPC if [with conjunct]; 1:5; 2:4;
8:6; 13:4

kišâstaw IPC my goodness! 9:20; 19:9;
42:18; 42:34; *'šâstaw kisiwâsiw* my,
but he was angry! 42:18; *kišâstaw oš'
âni mân' âskaw niwîyatišîhkâhtay*
gosh, y'know, sometimes I used to find
it funny! 42:34

kišê IPV/IPN old; 9:8; 11:2; 41:11

kišê-'ahâwi- VAI be an old person;
[contraction of *kišê-ayahâwi-*]

kišê-ayahâw- NA old person; 44:3; 52:4

kišê-cîmân- NI ship; 58:2

kišê-cîmân ministikw- NI [place name]
Ship-sands Island, lit., 'ship island'

kišê-ililîwi- VAI be an old person; 42:30;
44:4

kišê-iskwêw- NA old woman; 9:11; 56:3;
cf. *nôtokwêw-*

kišê-'liliw- NA old person, old man;
[contraction of *kišê-ililiw-*]; 2:1; 9:1;
11:7; 41:1; 41:2; 58:1

kišê-'liw- NA old person, old man;
[contraction of *kišê-ililiw-*]; cf.
kišê-'niniw, kišê-'niw-

kišê-'niniw- NA old person, old man (SC);
[contraction of *kišê-ininiw-*]; MC:
kišê-ililiw-

kišê-'niw- NA old person, old man (SC);
cf. [contraction of *kišê-ininiw-*]

kišê-pâpîwâtakinam NA January, lit.,
'great- or old-scattered-about moon';
[variant form of
kišê-pâpîwâtakini-pîsimw-]; (58:5); cf.
pîsimw-

kišê-pâpîwâtakini-pîsimw- NA
January, lit., 'great- or old-
scattered-about moon'; [variant form of
kišê-pâpîwâtakinam]; (58:5); cf.
pîsimw-

kišêpâyâ- VII be morning; [contraction of
kêkišêpâyâ-]; 3:2; 10:5; 31:1

kišê-pîsimw- NA February, lit., 'old
moon, great moon'; cf. *pîsimw-*

kišê-sîpiy- NI [place name] Fort George,
Quebec, 'Old River' (otherwise known
as Big River and since construction of
the Hydro-Quebec project as La
Grande); 58:1; n. 58:2

kišê-'skwêw- NA old woman; cf.
kišê-iskwêw-

kišêwâtotaw- VTA have pity on s.o., be
kind to s.o.; 9:20

kišêwâtotawêhkâso- VAI pretend to
have pity on him, pretend to behave
kindly to him; 9:20; cf. *...hkâso-*

kišê-'yahâw- NA old person; 41:2; 41:17;
cf. *kišê-ayahâw*

kišikanisamaw- VTA heat it up for s.o.;
12:8; cf. *kišâpiskisamaw-*

kišipanaskiso- VAI be the (uppermost)
tip; 1:6; (the recording sounds more
like *kišipanaskisi-*); *kišipanaskisow
mistik* it is the tip (top) of the tree

kišipanaskwan- VII be the tip; (1:6)

kišipaskamikâ- VII be an end of the land; (2:3); cf. *pakwataskamikw-*, *...askamik...*

kišipastê- VII stand at an end; 37:3; *pâtimâ kâ-'t'-otihtamân ê-'škwâ-kišipastêki nitôw'nahikana* until I reached the end of my traps; *ê-iškwâ-kišipastêki mihta* at the end of the pile of cord-wood; *ê-iškwâ-kišipastêki cîmâna kapâ* land at the end of (the line of) canoes

kišipâ- VII end, terminate; 1:3; 55:6; *kâ-kišipâk anim' osit* just at the end of his foot

kišipânak IPC at the end of the island; cf. *awasânak, âstamânak, kwêskânak, otiškawânak, šîpânakw-, šîpânakohk*; *...ânak..., ...ânakw-*

kîšipânakâ- VII there is an end to the island n. 2:1; cf. *...ânak...*

kišipânakâhk IPC at the end of the island; *kišipânakâhk tašîhkêw* he dwells at the end of the island; cf. *...ânak...*

kišipâpihkêpali- VAI/VII come to an end (e.g., a line or string); 42:57; 42:60; cf. *...âpihk..., ...pali-*

kišipâskwayâw- NI [place name] 'end-of-big-trees point'; cf. *...âskw.../-*, *...ayâ-*

kišipipali- VAI/VII end (e.g., a story), terminate, conclude; 5:10; 6:15; 9:24; 11:13; 43:14; 59:4; cf. *...pali-*

kišipisk- VTI come to the end of s.t. (e.g., land, trail, track); 2:3; n. 2:1

kišišaw IPC effective(ly), specific(ally), with particular focus; 9:16; 42:8; *'ci-kî-pimâcihitisot kišišaw* to support himself effectively; *môna kišišaw ayitôtam* he's not doing anything of interest or importance; [near-synonym: *kwêkohta*]; cf. *kišišawêliht-, kišišawêlim-, kišišawêpali-, kihci-kišišawêpaliho-*

kišišawêliht- VTI consider s.t. of interest, consider s.t. important; (9:16)

kišišawêlimo- VAI think oneself smart, be conceited; (9:16); cf. *kišišaw*

kišišawinâkwan- VII appear interesting; (42:8) *môna kišišawinâkwan* it doesn't look very interesting; cf. *...nâkwan-*

kišišawipaliho- VAI go along at a brisk walk; (9:16); cf. *...paliho-*

kišitê- VII be hot; 1:3; 22:1; 39:2

kišiwâh- VTA anger s.o.; 27:5; 53:1; 55:5; 55:7

kišiwâsi- VAI be angry; 9:2; 18:6; 19:9; 21:5; 23:1; 34:2; 49:4; 63:1; MC: *kisiwâsi-*

kišiwêmakan- VII make a loud noise; 44:4

kišiwêwêso- VAI make a loud noise; 65:8; cf. *itwêwêso-*

kišiwêwêtê- VII make a loud noise; (65:8); cf. *itwêwêtê-*

kišiwê- VAI speak loudly, make a loud noise; (42:42); n. 42:68

kišiwêwêsikê- VAI shoot with a loud noise; (65:8)

kišîciwan- VII flow swiftly; 61:3; cf. *...ciwan.../-*

kišîhkolê- VII burn fast (e.g, a fast travelling bush or grass fire); (42:60); cf. *ocêhkamahkolê-*

kišîm- VTA affront, vex or anger s.o. by speech; 21:5; 55:6; cf. *nišim-*

kišîpali- VAI/VII go fast; 33; 42:26; 42:31; 68:2; *kišîpaniw 'ci-nipispan* he would be dead in a flash; cf. *...pali-*

kišîpaliho- VAI jump up quickly; 60:3; *pasiko, 'šîpaliho!* stand up, jump up quickly! cf. *...paliho-*

kišîyâpolo- VAI slip by swiftly, slide by (e.g., people shooting rapids or youngsters with sleds on a bank); (12:14); cf. *pîhtokwêyâpolo-, kilipali-, pilêkopali-, ...âpolo-*

kitamaw- VTA eat s.o. up; [possibly for *kitamw-*]; 22:3; 27:3

kitamoh- VTA eat s.o. all up; 21:7

kitamw- VTA eat s.o. up, devour s.o.; (9:9); cf. *kitamaw-, kitâ-*

kitawê-wêpišk- VTI make s.t. clatter, rattle s.t. through bodily contact; 9:15; e.g., someone walking into a heap of tin cans in the dark might remark: *n'kî-kitawê-wêpiškên* I

made them rattle by stumbling into
them

kitawê-wêpiškaw- VTA make s.o.
clatter, rattle s.o. through bodily
contact; (9:15)

kitaw-itâcimo- VAI be tired of telling
about things; [alternative form of
kîtaw-itâcimo-]; 42:65

kitânawêpaliho- VAI gobble everything
up; 19:9; cf. *...paliho-*

kitâ- VAI-T eat s.t. up; 9:9; cf. *kitamw-*

kitimah- VTA injure s.o., ill-treat s.o.,
cause s.o. sorrow or misery; 5:3; 6:7

kitimâkan- VII be in a poor state, be
destitute; 65:1

kitimâkêlim- VTA feel sorry for s.o.,
have compassion for s.o., have pity on
s.o.; 9:3; 42:35

kitimâkisi- VAI be poor, destitute,
pitiable, wretched; (58:5; 65:1) *êliwêhk
kitimâkisiw-* he is pretty poorly off, he
is miserable

kitin- VTA/VTI turn s.o./s.t. over; 13:14

kito- VAI call out, make a noise (of
animals); 27:7; *êkâ kito!* keep quiet!
shut up!

kitoh- VTA call s.o. (wildfowl); 20:4; 20:6

kitohcikêwihamâso- VAI play a tune
for oneself; 55:2

kiyâpac IPC more, still; 2:3; 11:7; 20:3;
40:3

kiyâpac mâka IPC nonetheless, just the
same

kiyâskošiš- NA tern; 11:3

kiyâskw- NA gull; 11:3

kiyâsk'-wayân- NA gull skin; 11:5

kî IPV completed event marker, past time
marker [grammatical preverb]; 1:1; 2:3
et passim; "*êhê*," *kî-itwêwak* "yes," they
said

kî IPV can, able to [grammatical
preverb]; 1:5; 18:2; 35:2 et passim; *êkâ
mâka ... 'ci-kî-walawînîšâhtawîcik* and
that they would not be able to climb
out and down

kîhkânâkwan- VII be clear (i.e., as a
scene); (14:3; 37:6; 42:56); cf.
payahtênâkwan-, *...nâkwan-*

kîhkêyâskwah- VTI nail s.t. in a square;
(52:2); cf. *...âskw...*/-

kîhkêyâskwahw- VTA nail s.o. in a
square; (52:2); cf. *kîhkêyâskwapit-*,
âniskêyâskwah(w)-,
wâwiyêyâskwah(w)-,
wîhkwêyâskwah(w)-, *...âskw...*/-

kîhkêyâskwapit- VTA/VTI tie s.o./s.t. in
a square; 52:2; cf. *kîhkêyâskwapit-*,
âniskêyâskwah(w)-,
wâwiyêyâskwah(w)-,
wîhkwêyâskwah(w)-, *...âskw...*/-

kîhkwahâkêw- NA wolverine; 1:7; 68:1

kîla PR you [sg.]; 9:13

kîlanânaw PR we [incl.] (i.e., including
addressee(s)) (MC); SC: *kînanânaw*

kîmôc IPC stealthily, secretly; 8:4; 9:11;
18:6; 56:2

kînanânaw PR we [incl.] (i.e., including
addressee(s)) (SC); 1:1; 1:9; MC:
kîlanânaw

kî'nânaw PR we [incl.] (i.e., including
addressee(s)) (SC); [contraction of
kînanânaw]; 6:1

kînikâ- VII be pointed n. 3:7; 29:4; 50:6;
ê-kînikâk mistik a pointed stick; cf.
cîpwâ-

kînikicâšê- VAI have a sharp snout;
(15:5); cf. *kînikihtâwakê-*, *kînikistawê-*,
kînikitâmihkanê-, *napakicâšê-*, *...câš...*

kînikihtâwakê- VAI have sharp (i.e.,
pointed) ears; (15:5); cf.
kînikihtâwakê-, *kînikistawê-*,
kînikitâmihkanê-, *napakicâšê-*,
...câš..., *...htâwak...*

kînikikoh- VTI put a point on s.t.; (12:2);
cf. *kînikiko-wêpah-*

kînikiko-wêpah- VTI hurriedly put a
point on s.t.; 12:2

kînikisci-âpikošîš- NA mouse with
pointed nose; 3:8; cf.
amisko-wâpikošîš-

kînikisi- VAI be pointed n. 3:7; 29:4; cf.
cîposi-

kînikistawê- VAI have a sharp snout;
15:5; cf. *kînikicâšê-*, *napakicâšê-*,
kînikihtâwakê-, *kînikitâmihkanê-*,
...staw...

kînikitâmihkanê- VAI have a sharp

chin; (15:5); cf. *kînikistawê-*,
...*tâmihkan*...

kînikwânâciwosw- VTA swirl s.o.
around boiling; 14:5;
*kînikwânâciwoswâkaniwan
mistaskihkohk* he is swirled around
boiling in the big cauldron

kînikwânâciwoso- VAI swirl around
boiling; 14:5; cf. *oso-*

kînikwânâciwohtê- VII spin around
while boiling (e.g., meat or potato);
56:5; cf. *ohtê-*

kînikwân-âpacihtâ- VAI-T work s.t.
around; 1:4

kînikwânâpihkêhtatâ- VAI-T loop s.t.
around and around something; (1:4);
cf. ...*âpihk*...

kînikwânâpihkêšim- VTA loop s.o.
around and around something; (1:4);
cf. ...*âpihk*...

kînikwâninâkosi- VAI seem to spin
around; 13:14; cf. ...*nâkosi-*

kînikwâninâkwan- VII seem to spin
around; cf. ...*nâkwan-*

kînikwânipahtâ- VAI run around; 12:2;
cf. ...*pahtâ-*

kînikwânipali- VAI/VII go around, go in
a circle; 42:47; cf. ...*pali-*

kînikwânišimo- VAI dance around; 55:2;
cf. ...*šimo-*

kînikwânišk- VTI walk around outside
of an s.t. (e.g., house, boat); (55:2); cf.
kînikwânohtê-, têtipâhtê-

kînikwânohtê- VAI walk around
outside; (55:2); cf. *têtipâhtê-,* ...*ohtê-*

kînistam PR you [sg.] first; 42:62; cf.
nînistam, wînistam

kîn'nânaw PR we [incl.] (i.e., including
addressee(s)) (SC); [contraction of
kînanânaw]; 11:11; 41:8

kîpaci-wêpin- VTA/VTI raise s.o./s.t. on
its side, dislodge s.o./s.t.; 13:14

kîsis- VTI cook s.t.; 54:1; cf. *kisis-*

kîsiso- VAI be cooked; 18:8; 65:9

kîsisw- VTA cook s.o.; 13:12; 18:7; 19:9;
58:5; *âhkiko-pimiy
ê-wsi-kîsiswâkaniwit, ê-sâsot namês*
fried fish cooked with seal oil (for *wsi,*
cf. *ohci);* cf. *kisisw-*

kîskwê- VAI be foolish, be mad, be
insane, be out of one's mind; 68:6

kîsaškimê- VAI finish netting
(snowshoes); 53:4; cf. *aškimê-*

kîsawê- VAI have his/her full coat (e.g., a
dog or fox); used for *iši-kîšwê-* in
41:20; n. 42:68; *âšay kîšawêw
ê-kî-âhtawêt* now he has his full coat
(having shed the old one); cf. *âhciho-*

kîšâc IPC ahead of time, in preparation,
with a view to the future; 41:10; *kîšâc
tamahkîw* he is packing ahead of time;
kîšâc n'ka-ayamihâw I'll speak to her
ahead of time

kîši IPV finish, complete; 6:6

kîsih- VTA finish s.o., complete s.o., end
s.o.; 50:1; 50:6; 53:2

kîsihtâ- VAI-T finish s.t., complete s.t.,
end s.t.; 1:4; 18:3; 34:2; 42:61; 58:6;
êko kâ-kîšihtât ê-kihcipahtât so he
finished by running away

kîšikâ- VII be day; 1:9; 20:4

kîšikâstê- VII be brilliant (e.g.,
moonlight); 5:9; cf. *wâstê-*

kîšikâw- NI day

kîšikw- NI sky; 44:2; 57

kîšin- VTA/VTI tan s.o./s.t.; 39:2

kîšinawaso- VAI cook for oneself; (27:2);
56:5

kîšinawân- NI cooking; (54:1)

kîšinawât- VTA cook for s.o. (MC); 19:8;
61:2; 67:2; *kikî-kîšinawatitin* I have
cooked for you; SC: *piminawât-* (Fort
Albany usage)

kîšinawê- VAI cook; 13:12; (54:1; 56:5);
60:5; 67:2

kîšin- VTA/VTI finish s.o./s.t. (by hand),
dress s.o./s.t. (e.g., a hide); 50:4

kîši-nihtâwiki- VAI finish growing, be
full grown; 6:6

kîškahcikâtê- VII be bitten through, be
bitten off; 55:6; cf. *kîškaht-*

kîškaht- VTI gnaw through s.t.; 3:7; 15:5;
bite s.t. off; 55:6

kîškam- VTA gnaw through s.o., bite s.o.
off

kîškâyawâ- VII be deep; 7:1; 31:1; 42:48;
61:3

kîškâyawistikwêyâ- VII be a deep river;

(42:28); cf. *kinostikwêyâ-,
kwayaskostikwêyâ-, pâhkostikwêyâ-,
tahkostikwêyâ-, wâwâkistikwêyâ-,
...stikw.../-, ...ayâ-*

kîskikašêšotisiwin- NI nail clipper;
(14:5); cf. *ninihkikaškwêpali-,
ninihkikaškwê-wêpahw-*

kîskipit- VTA/VTI tear s.o./s.t. by pulling;
48:2; cf. *kîskipalih-, kîskipalihtwâ-*

kîskipali- VAI/VII be cut off; 18:9; cf.
...pali-

kîskipalih- VTA tear s.o. by pulling with
bodily force; (48:2)

kîskipalihtwâ- VAI-T tear s.t. by pulling
with bodily force; cf. *kîskipit-*

kîskipocikan- NI cross-cut saw; (12:14;
42:59); cf. *pilêkopali-*

kîskipol- VTA saw s.o.; (42:59)

kîskipotâ- VAI-T saw s.t.; (42:59); cf.
kîskîskipol-, kîskîskipotâ-

kîskiš- VTI cut s.t. off; (45:2); cf. *mâciš-,
têtipâš-, wîmoš-*

kîskišw- VTA cut s.o. off; (45:2); cf.
mâcišw-, têtipâšw-, wîmošw-

kîskiwêpaht- VTI hurriedly gnaw
through s.t.; 3:8

kîskîskaht- VTI [redupl.] cut s.t. with
one's teeth repeatedly; 24:1

kîskîskipol- VTA saw s.o. again and
again (MC); 42:59; SC: *kîskipol-*

kîskîskipon- VTA saw s.o. again and
again (SC); MC: *kîskîskipol-*

kîskîskipotâ- VAI-T saw s.t. again and
again; (42:59); cf. *kîskipotâ-*

kîskîskis- VTI cut s.t. off (distributively);
18:9

kîskîskisw- VTA cut s.o. off
(distributively); (18:9)

kîskwêh- VTA send s.o. crazy, send s.o.
out of his/her mind (used of going
crazy or wild with enjoyment; e.g., at
meeting a person after a long time, or
of fans with a celebrity, or a man after
a girl); 68:5; *kî-kîskwêhikow* she sent
him crazy; *kîskwêyêlimow* he's crazy
about her

kîskwêhw- VTA knock s.o. senseless,
knock s.o. out; 68:5

kîskwêyêliht- VTI be distraught; 65:9

kîskwêyêlim- VTA be distraught over
s.o., be crazy about s.o.; (68:5)

kîsowâ- VII be warm (referring to an
object); (1:2); cf. *kišowâyâ-*

kîsowâyâ- VII be mild (weather); 1:2;
1:5; 11:11; 41:17; 61:6; *âskaw-âskaw
kakîsowâyâw* it is warm every now
and then; cf. *kîsowâ-, ...ayâ-*

kîsôh- VTA make s.o. warm; 52:4

kîsôsi- VAI be warm (as when wrapped
in a blanket); (1:2)

kîspo- VAI be full

kîsponah- VTA fill s.o.; 60:5

kîsponahtâ- VAI-T fill s.t.; (60:5)

kîspon- VTA fill s.o.; [possibly allegro for
kîsponah-]; cf. *kîspo-, kîsponê-*

kîsponê- VII be full

kîtaw-ihti- VAI be at a loss as to what to
do; cf. *kwîtaw-ihti-*; (42:33)

kîtaw-itâcimo- VAI be at a loss for
story-telling; 42:33; cf. *kwîtaw-itâcimo-*

kîtawi-pêh- VTA get tired waiting for
s.o.; 37:5; *ê-'ti-kîtawi-pêhicik* as they
begin to get tired waiting for me

kîtawi-pêho- VAI get tired waiting; 4:5

kîtawi-pêhtâ- VAI-T get tired waiting for
s.t.; 3:4; 16:4

kîton- VTI search for s.t. (without
finding); 60:8; cf. *kîtowâpaht-, nân'ton-*

kîtonaw- VTA search for s.o. (without
finding); 60:8; cf. *kîtowâpam-,
nân'tonaw-*

kîtowâpaht- VTI search for s.t. by
looking; (60:8)

kîtowâpam- VTA search for s.o. by
looking; (60:8)

kîwasisi- VAI be orphaned; 3:3; 6:5

kîwašišân- NA orphan, 'grief-child'; 11:2;
cf. *mâhcicošân-, nîstamošân-, ...šân-*

kîwê- VAI return, go back, go home; 3:3;
12:13; 16:1; 35:1; 42:26; 58:3

kîwêho- VAI betake oneself back or
home; 65:10

kîwêhol- VTA take s.o. back by water;
65:2

kîwêhtah- VTA take s.o. back; 58:5

kîwêkâpawi- VAI turn back; 9:16; cf.
...kâpawi-

kîwêpah'o- VAI turn back in a hurry; cf.
  kîwêpaliho-; also n. 65:22

kîwêpahtâ- VAI run home, run back;
  56:8; 68:3; cf. *...pahtâ-*

kîwêpaliho- VAI turn back in a hurry;
  65:8; cf. *...paliho-*

kîwêpali- VAI/VII turn back, recede; 49:6;
  come back; 59:3; cf. *...pali-*

kîwêskwêli- VAI turn one's head; 10:8;
  cf. *...iskw...*

kîwêtin- VII blow from the north, be a
  north wind; 12:11

kîwêtin- NI the North; 42:39;
  kâ-tôcikâtêk anta kîwêtinohk what was
  done there in the North, 42:60

kîyôtê- VAI visit; 65:10; [synonym of
  mawâpi-]

koci IPV try; 10:9; 65:5

kocih- VTA try or test s.o.; 3:10; draw,
  extricate s.o.; 4:7

kocihtâ- VAI-T try or test s.t.; 42:2

kocist- VTI taste s.t.; 43:3

kohcipalih- VTA swallow s.o.; 4:2; 4:4;
  4:5; 16:3; 29:1

kohcipalihtwâ- VAI-T swallow s.t.; 29:2

kohpâtawîsi- VAI climb up (affected
  Ojibwa form for speech of Lynx); 1:7;
  cf. *gohpâtawîsi-*

kopâsinâkosi- VAI look miserable; 9:7;
  cf. *...nâkosi-*

kosâpaht- VTI conjure s.t. regarding the
  future; 30:1

kosâpam- VTA conjure s.o. regarding the
  future; (30:1)

kosikomahciho- VAI feel heavy,
  depressed; (9:17)

kosikomahcihtâ- VAI-T feel s.t. as
  heavy; 9:17

kosikwamahcihtâ- VAI-T feel s.t. as
  heavy [alternative form of
  kosikomahcihtâ-]; 48:2; cf. *pwâwatê-*

kosikwati- VAI be heavy; 20:4

kosikwan- VII be heavy; 49:3

koskêwêpišk- VTI bump into s.t. so as to
  cause it to move [alternative form of
  koskowêpišk-]

koskosi- VAI waken, wake up; 10:2; 18:8;
  55:6; 63:2; cf. *koškon-*

koskowêpišk- VTI bump into s.t. so as

to cause it to move; 34:1;
  n'koskowêpiškên cîmân- I rock the
  canoe

kospa-wîcêw- VTA go up (an incline)
  with s.o.; 19:2

kospâhtawî- VAI climb up; 1:7; 12:4

kospâhtawîwâkê- VAI make use of
  it/them for climbing up; 2:7

kospâmaciwê- VAI climb (a hill); 5:1

kospi- VAI go up the bank; 11:7; 49:6

kospihtah- VTA take s.o. up the bank;
  55:7

kospihtatâ- VAI-T take s.t. up the bank;
  (55:7)

kospipahtâ- VAI run up the bank; 18:1;
  (56:8); cf. *...pahtâ-*

kost- VTA/VTI fear s.o./s.t.; 43:15; 68:4

kostâci- VAI be frightened; 11:8; 13:6;
  16:1; 38:2; 55:2; 58:2

kostâtêlimo- VAI be daring, be fearless;
  13:11

kostâtikwan- VII be fearful, be frightful,
  be dreadful, be dangerous; 21:9; cf.
  tâpwêyêlihtâkwan-

kostâtikosi- VAI be fearful, be frightful,
  be dreadful, be dangerous; (21:9)

koško- VAI stir, move; 35:2

koškon- VTA waken s.o. (by touch); 10:4;
  13:5; 15:2; 36:2; cf. *ospâwih-, koskosi-*

koškopali- VAI waken with a start, be
  startled into movement; 18:9; 34:3; cf.
  ...pali-

koškopaliho- VAI start up suddenly,
  move suddenly; 14:7; cf. *...paliho-*

koškwâpišin- VAI be surprised; 9:20

kotak PR other, another
  [anim./inan.prox.sing.]; 1:1; 21:2; 49:1;
  kotakiya [anim.obv./inan.pl.]; 47:1;
  kotakiyak [anim.pl.]; 47:1; 8:5; *kotakiy*
  [inan.sg.] *the* other one; 1:4; 25:2;
  (unlike other pronouns, this form
  occurs in the locative *kotakîhk*); cf.
  25:2

kotaskaw- VTA race s.o., s.o.; 33

kotaskâtito- VAI [recipr.] try to beat
  each other (in a race); 33

kotawaso- VAI build a fire for oneself;
  11:11

kotawê- VAI kindle a fire; 9:19; 19:7; 35:2; 36:1; 39:1; 40:5; 42:5; 61:4

kotawêpaliho- VAI quickly kindle a fire; 18:7; cf. *...paliho-*

kotâwicêškiwakipali- VAI/VII go down in the mud; (32:1); cf. *liskicêškiwakipali-, moškicêškiwakipali-, ...cîskawak...*

kotikon- VTA/VTI disjoint s.o./s.t., dislocate s.o./s.t.; bend s.o./s.t. open; (65:8) *kâ-kotikonikâtêk pâskisikan* a breach-loader (gun)

kotikositêšin- VAI sprain or dislocate a foot or ankle; (65:8); cf. *wahkon-, ...sit...*

kotikošim- VTA dislocate s.o.; (65:8)

kotikotatâ- VAI-T dislocate s.t.; (65:8); *nikotikotatân nahkon* I dislocate my ankle

kôkî- VAI dive; (13:7); 22:3; 25:2; 27:4

kôkîhon- VTA make s.o. dive; 13:7

kôn- NA snow; 5:10; 50:2; 60:6; 66:1

kônâpôw- NI snow-liquid, slush; 65:1; cf. *...âpow-*

kôsîs- NA [proper name] Koosees; 40:1

kôskôskêpali- VAI limp; 43:6; cf. *...pali-*

kôtawi-pêhtâ- VAI-T get tired waiting for s.t.; 29:4; [contracted at Kashechewan to *'tôw'-pêhtâ-*]

'kwancaw IPC trivial(ly), of little account, aimlessly; cf. *'kwantaw, pakwantaw.*; 8:1

'kwantaw IPC casually, aimlessly, idly, not seriously; 4:3; 9:18; 41:2; 41:4; *'kwantaw piko itwêw anima* he says it only lightly, offhandedly (i.e., he doesn't mean it); *'mayêw wîna 'kwantaw 'iniw* he wasn't a person of no account, of no consequence, 41:2; *'kwantaw'-kêkwân* any old thing, 41:4; [contraction of *pakwantaw*]

kwayask IPC straight(ly), proper(ly), correct(ly); 9:19; 23:3; 40:4; 42:27; cf. *kwayêsk*

kwayaskostikwêyâ- VII be a straight river; (42:28); cf. *kîškâyawistikwêyâ-, pâhkostikwêyâ-, kinostikwêyâ-, tahkostikwêyâ-, wâwâkistikwêyâ-, ...stikw..., ...ayâ...*

kwayaskotamon- VII be a straight road; (42:28); cf. *wâwâkatamon-*

kwayêsk IPC straight(ly), proper(ly), correct(ly); 44:4; cf. *kwayask*

kwâcistak IPC oh, my! 9:20; 10:7; what on earth! 18:6; 55:6; *kwâcistak! êliwêhk nimaskâtên kâ-itâcimoyin.* my! I'm surprised at the news you're telling me

kwâhkwâpah- VTI [redupl.] dip s.t. (as with a pail); (5:10)

kwâhkwâpahw- VTA [redupl.] dip s.o. (as with a pail); 5:10

kwâkran- NI Cochrane, Ontario; 41:3

kwân'totaw- VTA set upon s.o., attack s.o.; (12:9); [near-synonym: *kwâškototaw-*]

kwân'tâto- VAI set upon each other, attack each other; 12:9; cf. *kwâškototaw-*

kwân'totaw- VTA attack s.o.

kwâpikê- VAI go for water; 65:3

kwâsipit- VTA/VTI drag s.o./s.t. ashore; 29:2

kwâškocipaliho- VAI give a jump; 48:1; cf. *...paliho-*

kwâškototaw- VTA attack s.o., set upon s.o.; (12:9); 60:9; 66; cf. *kwâškwatotaw-, kwân'tâto-*

kwâškwatahonân- NI jumping place; 11:8

kwâškwati- VAI jump; 9:15

kwâškwatotaw- VTA jump on s.o.; 60:9; cf. *kwâškototaw-*

kwâškwatotâto- VAI jump on each other; 60:9

kwâškwâškwati- VAI [redupl.] hop; 14:5; cf. *kwâškwati-*

kwâškwâškwêyâciwaso- VAI [redupl.] bounce up and down while boiling; 56:5; cf. *oso-*

kwâškwâškwênâkosi- VAI [redupl.] appear to jump, appear to leap; 13:16; cf. *...nâkosi-*

kwâškwâškwênâkwan- VII appear to jump, appear to leap; (13:16); cf. *...nâkwan-*

kwâškwêpicikan- NI fish-hook; 4:6; 16:4; 38:2

kwâškwêpicikê- VAI fish with a hook, angle; 4:6

kwâškwêpit- VTA fish s.o. out with a hook, jerk s.o. out with a hook; 4:6

kwêcih- VTA try s.o., test s.o.; 49:1

kwêcihito- VAI test each other, compete; 49:1

kwêskakâm IPC around the water; 31:2; 42:49; *kwêskakâm itêhkê* around to the water-side, across the water, on the other side of the river; cf. *naspâtakâm, ...akâm..., kwêskânakw*

kwêskâmatin IPC around the mountain; cf. *...âmatin..., awasâmatin, âstamâmatin, pâšitâmatin*

kwêskânak IPC around the island; cf. *awasânak, âstamânak, kišipânak, otiškawânak, šîpânakw-, ...ânak..., ...ânakw-, kwêskakâm*

kwêskinâkosi- VAI turn in appearance (into something); 20:2; cf. *...nâkosi-*

kwêskipaliho- VAI turn around, twist around; 19:9; cf. *...paliho-*

kwêskitê IPC on the other side; 50:7; 58:3; *kwêskitê itêhkê* on the other side, around on the other side; 19:9; cf. *âstamitê*

kwêskitiyêpaliho- VAI suddenly turn one's backside around; 68:5; cf. *išitiyêli-, kalakitiyê-, tahkiskâcitiyêhw-, ...tiy..., ...paliho-*

kwêskwêskikwâškwâškoti- VAI [redupl.] jump back and forth in turn; 66:3; cf. *kwâškwâškwati-, kwêskwêskikwâškototâto-*

kwêskwêskohtê- VAI go back and forth; 52:2; cf. *...ohtê-*

kwêtipah- VTI turn s.t. over with an instrument; (56:7)

kwêtipahw- VTA turn s.o. over with an instrument; 56:7

kwêtipawêpah- VTI fling s.t. over by hitting; (56:7)

kwêtipawêpahw- VTA fling s.o. over by hitting; (56:7)

kwêtipawahikani-sîpiy- NI [place name] Kwetabohigan River, lit., 'stooping river'; 34:1

kwêtipin- VTA/VTI turn s.o./s.t. on the side, tip over; (56:6); (e.g., as a canoe to let water drain out: *'ci-šîkwašikawihk*); cf. *ohpimêl-, otihtapin-, otihtapipalih-, pâhkwâšikawin-, šîkwašikawin-*

kwêtipî- VAI capsize, turn over; 63:2; cf. *âšikicišin-, ohpimêšin*

kwîtaw-ihti- VAI be at a loss as to what to do; (11:13; 42:33); cf. *kîtaw-ihti-, kwîtawi-tôt-*

kwîtawi-iši-ihtâ- VAI be at a loss as to where to stay; 42:44; *âšay ê-kwîtaw'-îš'-îhtât* since now he's at a loss for a place to stay

kwîtaw-itâcimo- VAI be at a loss for story-telling; 42:33; cf. *kîtaw-itâcimo-*

kwîtawi-tôt- VTI be at a loss as to what to do; 11:13; cf. *kwîtaw-ihti-*

lahkamohtâ- VAI-T extend s.t.; *ê-'ti-lahkamohtâniwahk-* extending it (probably referring to a road)

lahkihtâ- VAI-T extend s.t., enlarge s.t.; (41:15)

lalimâ- VII be a head-wind (SC); (42:22); MC: *nâmowinâ-*

lâhkaciši- VAI be light in weight; (61:4)

lâhkašin- VII be light in weight; 61:4

lâlakâm IPC along the shore; cf. *lâlipêkw, iskopêyâ-, ...akâm...*

lâlâšakâmê- VAI walk along the waterline; 9:7; cf. *papâmâšakâmê-, ...âšakâmê...*

lâlâšicihcênitiso- VAI stroke one's hand; (46:2); cf. *...cihc..., sinikocihcênitiso-*

lâlâšihkwênitiso- VAI stroke one's face; (46:2); cf. *sinikohkwênitiso-, ...hkw...*

lâlâšistikwânênitiso- VAI stroke one's head; (46:2); cf. *sinikostikwânênitiso-, ...stikwân...*

lâlâšin- VTA/VTI stroke s.o./s.t.; (46:2); cf. *sinikon-*

lâlêwê- VAI skirt or walk along the edge of the green bush; 9:7; cf. *lâlâšakâmê-*

lâlih IPC alongside of [usually with locative] (MC); 4:2; 9:24; 20:1; 36:1; SC: *nânih*

lâlihkop IPC alongside the willows; (n. 66:3; 66:1); cf. *mêkwêhkop, nîpisîskâhk, ...hkop...*

lâlimâ- VII be a tailwind; 42:22; cf.
nâmowinâ-
lâlipêk IPC along the water's edge; 49:5;
65:9; cf. *lâlakâm, iskopêyâ-,
pîhtâpêkw-, wînipêkw-, ...ipêkw-*
lâsaras- NA [proper name] Lazarus; 40:1
lâsipêpahtâ- VAI run down the bank;
11:7; 18:10; cf. *...ipê.../-, ...pahtâ-*
lâsipêtimihk IPC down the bank; 42:35
lâsipê- VAI go down the bank; 19:5; cf.
...ipê.../-
lâšâpihkên- VTA lower s.o. on a rope
n. 1:9; cf. *nîhtâpihkên-, ...âpihk...*
lâwâpiskâw- NI [place name] 'deep rock'
(a valley located in among the rocks
on the west coast of James Bay); cf.
...âpisk...
lâwinâkosi- VAI appear at a distance;
9:17; 11:4; 64:2; cf. *...nâkosi-*
lâwinâkwan- VII appear at a distance;
37:6; cf. *...nâkwan-*
lêkaw- NA sand; 18:7; 55:4; cf. *askiy-,
ašiškiy-, wâpatanaskw-*
likwah- VTI bury s.t., cover s.t.; (55:3)
likwahw- VTA bury s.o., cover s.o.; 18:7;
55:3
likwahahkatêpo- VAI bake one's food
under sand (MC); 55:3; SC:
nikwâwahahkatêpo-; 18:7; cf. *...têpo-*
lipâcihitiso- VAI mess oneself, dirty
oneself; (68:5); cf. *kalakitiyê-,
kimisaho-*
lipâtan- VII be dirty weather; 57
lipwâhkâ- VAI act sensibly, be sensible;
(to a child) be good; 11:10; *êko mâka!
lipwâhkâ!* see here! be sensible!
nipwâhkâ kîna, torotiy! be quiet, you,
Dorothy! 43:2
liskacistin- VII be buried with drifting
snow, disappear in the drift; 32:1
liskicêskawišk- VTI make s.t. sink into
the mud (as a stick when someone
steps on it); (32:2); cf. *liskipali-,
koyâwicêskiwakipali-,
môskicêskiwakipali-, ...cîskaw...*
liskicêskiwakipali- VAI sink in the
mud; (32:2) *mitoni liskicêskiwakipaliw*
he sinks in the mud (of a heavy man
walking ashore across the mud flats);

cf. *...cêskawak..., ...pali-*
liskicêskawakišk- VTI sink into the
mud (as a stick when someone steps
on it); (32:2); cf. *...cêskawak...*
liskihkwâmi- VAI fall asleep; 9:17; 55:5;
cf. *...ihkwâmi..., šâkotihkwaši-,
nôhtêhkwaši-, ...ihkwaši-*
liskipali- VAI/VII go under, disappear;
(32:1); 34:3; cf. *...pali-*
liskipê- VII be covered by water; (13:15);
cf. *liskiwên-, ...ipê.../-*
liskipotê- VII be flooded, be overflowed
(and so disappear); 7:1; (13:15); cf.
liskiwên-, mâhâpotê-
liskiwên- VTI one's footsteps grow faint;
(13:15); *ê-'ti-liskiwênamin'ci* as
his/their footsteps grow faint; cf.
*liskipê-, liskipotê-, mâhâpotê-,
mâhâpoko-*
lîcin- NI legion; Canadian Legion Hall;
42:13
lîhkitawisi- VAI be forked; 27:3; *miconi
ê-iškwâ-lîhkitawisiyân n'tiskopân* I
waded in up to the crotch
lîlîkicihcân- NI finger; (13:16); cf.
*lîlîkisitân-, micihcân-, misisitân-,
...cihcân-*
lîlîkisitân- NI toe (other than big toe);
(13:16); cf. *lîlîkicihcân-, micihcân-,
lîlîkisitân-, ...sitân-*
lîpisîy- NI leaf; 34:3
lîwakotê- VII hang suspended; (27:3)
lîwâskocin- VAI hang suspended (as
from a tree); (27:3) *nohta-lîwâskocin
pwâmoših askîhk pahkišihk* he got
caught on a branch before he fell to
the ground; cf. *...âskw.../-*
lîwâskocimo- VAI suspend oneself; 27:3;
cf. *...âskw.../-*
lîwâskohtin- VAI for one tree to lean
against another; (27:3); cf. *...âskw.../-*
lôskâ- VII be soft and fluffy; (50:3)
lôskisi- VAI be soft and fluffy; 50:3; cf.
*malôkisi-, malôkâ-, malôkêwikisi-,
lôspisi-, lôspâ-*
lôspâ- VII be friendly; (50:5)
lôspisi- VAI be friendly (e.g., a dog,
horse); (50:5)
lôtin- VII be windy, blow; 12:11; 32:1

macêliht- VTI despise s.t., detest s.t.; run s.t. down (verbally); 42:11

macêlihtâkosi- VAI be mean, be despicable; 42:42

macêlim- VTA condemn s.o., disdain s.o.; run s.o. down (verbally), censure s.o.; 42:11; think little of s.o.; 43:6

maci IPV/IPN bad, evil, wicked; 9:8

macihkwêstâ- VAI make ugly faces; (22:3); *êliwêhk macihkwêstâw!* oh my, he's making ugly faces! cf. *mamacihkwêpaliho-, pâhpihkwêstâ-*

maci-kîšikâ- VII be a bad day, be bad weather; 32:1; cf. *mamacihkwêpaliho-, pâhpihkwêstâ-*

macipali- VAI/VII have a hard time of it; 42:11; cf. *nêsitâmipali-*

macipalih- VTA make the going hard for s.o.; (43:9); [inverse] have a hard time, be given a hard time; 43:9; *kimacipalihikon* you have a hard time

macitêwêyâpiskâ- VII be a point that carries rocks on it; 58:3; cf. *macitêwêyâ-, nêscâ-*

macitêwêyâ- VII be land running out to a point (with trees on it right to the point); 58:3:

macitêwêyâw- NI [place name] North Bluff, lit., 'point of land' (located about 30 kilometres north of Moose Factory on the west coast of James Bay); 65:3

macitêwêyâwi-sîpiy- NI [place name] North Bluff Creek, lit., 'point of land river'

maci-tôtaw- VTA do s.o. ill, wrong s.o., do s.o. harm; 11:11

macostêh- VTI throw s.t. into the fire; 23:4

macostêhw- VTA throw s.o. into the fire; 42:60

macostê-wêpin- VTA/VTI throw s.o./s.t. into the fire; 9:19

mah IPC hush! listen! 41:5; cf. *mâhti*

mahîhkan- NA wolf; 68:3

mahkatayêšin- VAI lie with a huge stomach; 16:5; cf. *...atay...*

mahkatayê- VII have a big stomach, be big in the stomach; (16:5); cf. *...atay...*

mahkatêwanawê- VAI have a black

face; (10:8); cf. *nihcikinawê-, tômiskinawê-, wâpiskinawê-, ...anaw...*

mahkatêwatamwan- VII stick blackly to; 55:9; cf. *akwatamon-, akwatamwan-*

mahkatêwâ- VII be black; 50:7

mahkatêwisi- VAI be black; (50:7)

mahkatêwâkamipali- VAI/VII go black, stay a dark colour (of a liquid); 42:54; *mahkatêwâkam'paniw wâs' ê-wâpâkaminikâtêk* it (the tea) stays black, y'know, when milk is put into it; cf. *...âkam..., ...pali-*

mahkêšiw- NA fox; 48:1; 66:1; cf. *...ahkêsiw-, âmatahkêsîwi-*

mahki IPV large; 11:8

mahkikamâ- VII be large (a body of water); 12:11; [synonym: *mišikamâ-*]; *...kam...*

mahkikonêwê- VAI have a big throat (of a fish); (8:8); cf. *pohcikonêwên-, ...konêw...*

mahki-pakwanêyâ- VII be a big hole; 60:9; cf. *apiši-pakwanêyâ-, pakwanêyâ-*

mahkišk- VTI make a big footprint; (5:2); *ê-mâmahkiškamin'ci* with large footprints

mahki-wâlâ- VII be a very deep depression, be concave; 11:8

mahkon- NDA ankle; (65:8); cf. *...ahkon-, wahkon-, ohkwan-*

makošê- VAI feast; 49:1

makošêh- VTA cause s.o. to feast, make a feast for s.o.; 68:1

makošêwâkê- VAI use for a feast; 49:1

makošêwi-kîšikâ- VII be a feast day; cf. *pîhtokwêmakan-, walawîmakan-*

makošêwi-kîšikâw- NI Feast Day: Christmas at Kashechewan; New Year's Day at Moose Factory; n. 58:18

makošin- VAI be covered over [alternative form of *makwašin-*]; 61:4

makwahtin- VII be covered over; 61:3

makwašin- VAI be covered over; (61:3)

makwâkonêhtin- VII be covered over with snow; (61:3); cf. *...âkon...*

makwâkonêšin- VAI be covered over with snow; (61:3); cf. *...âkon...*

malakwah- VTA bring s.o. bad luck; 27:6

malôkêwikâ- VII be tender, be soft (of food); (50:5); cf. *lôskâ-, lôspâ-*

malôkêwikisi- VAI be tender, be soft (of food); (50:5); cf. *lôskisi-, lôspisi-*

malôkâ- VII be soft (i.e., mattress, bread, rotting canoe); (50:5); cf. *lôskâ-, lôskâ-, malôkêwikâ-*

malôkisi- VAI be soft (i.e., mattress, bread, rotting canoe); (50:5); cf. *lôskisi-, lôspisi-, malôkêwikisi-*

mamacihkwêpaliho- VAI make faces; (22:3); cf. *macihkwêstâ-, ...hkw..., ...paliho-*

mamahkišk- VTI [redupl.] make large footprints (everywhere); 5:2; 5:3; 6:5; *n'kî-mâtâhâw môs ê-mahkiškahk* I saw the tracks of a moose with large footprints; cf. *mahkišk-, mâmahkišk-*

mamaskam- VTA [redupl.] keep taking it from s.o.; 56:3; *mamaskamitowak* they keep taking it from each other; cf. *maskam-*

mamatwêkahikê- VAI [redupl.] make all kinds of noise in the distance, kick up a racket; 13:6; cf. *matwê*

mamâhtawêlihtâkosi- VAI [redupl.] do wondrous(-sounding) things; 5:5; cf. *...ihtâkosi-*

mamâhtâkosi- VAI [redupl.] do wonders; 6:7; cf. *...ihtâkosi-*

mamânipit- VTA/VTI [redupl.] go around pulling up s.o./s.t., gather up s.o./s.t.; 18:3

mamâmawi-tašîhkê- VAI [redupl.] live together in groups; 12:1; cf. *mâmawi-tašîhkê-*

mamihkowâskwan- VII [redupl.] be bloody all over, be bloodstained; 19:9

mamihkwâtakâpi- VAI [redupl.] have red eye-lids; 46:2; cf. *mihkwâtakâpi-, mamihkocâpi-, mihkokotê-, mihkotonê-, mihkotonênitiso-, mihkonawênitiso-, mihkokaškwênitiso-, mihkwanawê-; ...âpi-*

mamišim- VTA [redupl.] tell on s.o., inform on s.o., 'squeal' on s.o.; 60:8; cf. *mišim-*

manah- VTI skim s.t., knock s.t. off; 50:6

manahw- VTA skim s.o., knock s.o. off; (50:6)

manakway- NDA sleeve; (13:9); cf. *...anakway-, wanakwaya*

manawêpaht- VTI take hold of s.t. (as a fish the line), snatch s.t., grab s.t., seize s.t. with the mouth; *âšay manâ piko wêhci-manawêpatahk ana namês kwâškwêpicikaniniw* and immediately that fish took hold of the hook; cf. *manâht-, manipah-, manipahtwâ-*

manâ IPC isn't it so? isn't it the case? (contraction of *nama nâ*); 3:6; 41:8

manâhkatê- VII fall off due to its support being burnt (e.g., clothes hanging on a branch which burns); (11:12); cf. *milâhkatê-*

manâ oti IPC probably, possibly; I suppose then ...

manâht- VTI take hold of s.t.; (16:4); cf. *manawêpaht-*

manâwê- VAI collect eggs

manâwina IPC perhaps, it could be that, isn't it that? I'll wager that; 4:5

manâwinân- NI [place name] No-Man's Land, lit., 'collecting place (for eggs)' (a rocky point located south of Albany Post on James Bay); 11:4; n. 11:13; cf. *manâwê-*

manêsi- VAI be scarce, be poor, be in want of something; 39:4

manêwan- VII be scarce, be lacking, be wanting; 65:1

manicôš- NA insect; worm (diminutive of *manitôw-*); 51:1

manihtâkâkê- VAI use it to gather wood; (42:59); cf. *manihtê-, manihtât-*

manihtât- VTA chop s.o. up for firewood; 42:59; cf. *manihtê-, manihtâkâkê-*

manihtêpaliho- VAI quickly gather firewood; 19:7; cf. *...paliho-*

manihtê- VAI cut wood up, gather wood; 14:2; 14:5; (42:59); cf. *manihtât-*

manikah- VTI chop s.t. off (holding with one hand and chopping with the other); 38:2

manimâcîsê- VAI get (lighting) matches; (14:2)

manimîcimê- VAI get food; (14:2)

manin- VTA/VTI remove s.o./s.t. (by hand); (50:6); (this verb is used even when removal is done with the usual bone instrument); also as *manan-*; *otatâmahwêwak pîliš ê-kîšihâcik pîliš misiwê ê-mananahkik anim' otamaskay kâ-icikâtêk* they beat away at it until they finish, until they remove by hand all that 'meat residue' as it's called

manipah- VTA grab s.o. by hand, seize s.o. by hand; (16:4)

manipahtwâ- VAI-T grab s.t. by hand, seize s.t. by hand; 42:22

manipit- VTA/VTI pull s.o./s.t. off, collect s.o./s.t.; 18:1; 55:9; 65:1

maniš- VTI cut s.t. off; 50:7

manišw- VTA cut s.o. off; (50:7)

manitôhkât- VTA cast a spell on s.o.; 21:5

manitôhkê- VAI commune with the spirits, cast spells; 11:1; 21:5

manitôwi-mâših- VTA fight s.o. with one's spirit; 10:9

maniwîlâhcikê- VAI get clothes; (14:2)

masinahamaw- VTA write to s.o., write it for s.o.; 42:34

masinahikan- NI letter, epistle; 43:7

masinahikâtê- VII be written; 42:66; *kî-masinahikâtêkopanê otih* it could have been written down, that is

masinâso- VAI be marked; 41:15

maskahtwê- VAI rob, take by force; 47:1

maskam- VTA rob s.o., take (something) from s.o.; 8:6; 65:7; cf. *mamaskam-*

maskatêpwê- VAI cook by laying something over a fire; (55:3); describes what may be done with a goose wing while a hunter is on the blind; the meat is usually half cooked but succulent; cf. *cîstahâpwê-, sakapwê-*

maskêkw- NI swamp; 37:3; 42:55

maskisin- NI moccasin, shoe; 29:2

maskisinihkâkê- VAI make moccasins out of it, use to make moccasins; 50:5

masko-cîpay- NA bear spirit; 19:6

maskošiy- NI grass [usually in plural]; 61:2; 65:1; cf. *maskwašiy-*

maskwa- NA bear; 1:7; 19:1; 68:3; cf. *cišêyâkw-*

maskwamîwan- VII be icy; 58:3; 61:6

maskwamîwâkamin- VII thicken on the water (of the ice surface in the fall); 65:1; cf. *...âkamin-*

maskwamîy- NA ice; 12:15; 25:2; 48:1

mašîn- NI [English loanword] machinery; 41:3; *kêkwân mašîn wîna môna kêkwân takwanokopan* anything (by way of) machinery, there wasn't even any

maškawatin- VII freeze hard, be hard packed; (41:16)

maškawatisi- VAI freeze hard, be hard packed; (41:16)

maškawâ- VII be hard; be strong (may also be applied to coffee in sense of strong); 62:3

maškawimahcih- VTA feel s.o.'s strength; 10:9

maškawisi- VAI be hard; 41:16

maškawisî- VAI be strong, be in good health; cf. *maškawî-*

maškawisîmakan- VII be powerful

maškawipaliho- VAI brace oneself; 19:9; cf. *...paliho-*

maškawisîwikamikw- NI power-house (Kashechewan usage); 42:56; MC: *onimiskiwikamikw-*; cf. *...ikamikw-*

maškawitêwêyâ- VII be a strong surface on top of the snow; (42:29); cf. *...ayâ-*

maškawî- VAI be physically strong, powerful; 66:3. cf *sâpisi-, sâpimahciho-, sâpî-*

maškwašiy- NI grass [normally plural], vegetables; 1:6; 20:3; 42:55

matakwahp- NI old campsite (used mainly by old-timers); 10:2

'matakwan- VII not be [contraction of *nama takwan-*]; 41:6; 67:2; cf. *'matê-*

matay- NDI belly; 4:7; 16:5; 29:2; cf. *...atay-, watay-*

matâpêtipwatê- VAI carry out into the open; 51:2

matâpê- VAI come out into an open space (e.g., from the bush or inland); (12:11); 13:3; 34:2; (51:2); 58:4

matâwisipahtâ- VAI come running out

on (an open area); 13:15;
*ati-matâwisipahtâw animêniw
sâkahikaniniw* he came running out
on that lake; cf. *matâpê-*, *...pahtâ-*

matê IPV at or from a distance
[alternative form of *matwê-*]; 4:7

'matê- VAI not be there, 11:2; not exist;
41:1; [contraction of *namatê-*]; cf.
namatakwan-

matwê IPV discernible or perceptible at a
distance; 11:7; *matwê-'mišakâw* he
was heard paddling in the distance

matwê-âskotin- VII crack from the cold
(as trees), crack audibly; 11:13

matwê-âtahikê- VAI make a noise
scraping moose-hide; 56:1; *pêhtawêw
'wê'hkâna ê-matêy-âtahikêl'ci* he hears
someone making a noise scraping
moose-hide; cf. *mâtahikê-*

matwê-âtahw- VTA be heard (but not
seen) scraping s.o. in the distance;
(56:1); cf. *matwê-mâtahw-*

matwêhkwâmi- VAI snore; (11:7); cf.
...ihkwâmi-

matwê-mâtahw- VTA make a noise
(visibly) scraping skins in the
distance; 56:1; *ê-matê-mâtahwâl'ci
amisk'-wayân'* making a noise (in the
distance) scraping beaver-skins (where
someone cannot be seen but can be
heard); cf. *matwê-âtahw-*

matwên- VTA crack s.o.; 61:5; n. 61:27

matwê-nihcikihtin- VII be a dark blotch
in the distance; 19:2

matwê-nohtâkosi- VAI be audible in the
distance making a noise; 66:1

matwê-pihtihkwâsin- VAI fall with an
audible noise; 12:5

matwêškaw- VTA crack s.o. (by gross
body action, e.g., jumping); (61:5)

matwêtê- VII be a sound of a shot fired
(a long way off); 59:4

matwê-wâstê- VII shine at a distance,
show light at a distance; 3:5

mawâpi- VAI visit; (65:10); [synonym:
kîyôtê-]; cf. *...api-*

mawâpîstaw- VTA visit s.o.; 23:2

mawinêhikê- VAI take up pursuit; 13:13

mawiso- VAI gather berries; 65:9

mawitôn- VTA/VTI gather s.o./s.t.
together; 8:2; *mawitônam asiniyâpiya
ê-wî-pakitahwât* she's gathering
sinkers to put a net out

mayâšk- VTI pass s.t. by on foot; 1:7

mayâškaw- VTA pass s.o. by on foot; 2:7

mayâwahw- VTA pass s.o. (on water);
11:6

mayê- VAI/VII not be; [contraction of
namayê-]; 41:2; 41:3; 41:21; *mayêw
wîna, 'kwantaw 'iniw* he wasn't a
person of no account, wasn't a useless
person; *mayêw anima wîna
ininîmowin* that's not Indian
language; *mayêw nîla kâ-tôtamân* it
wasn't I who did it

mâ' IPC but, however; and [contraction of
mâka]; 53:3; 56:5

mâcâ VAI [2 sg.] [Ojibwa loanword] off
with you, away with you, be off; 9:19;
13:12; 13:17; 15:4; 41:5; also as *mâhcâ*;
43:5

mâci IPV begin to; 15:4; 39:3; 49:1; 56:7

mâci VAI on your way! [perhaps
connected with *mâcâ-*]

mâcika IPC lo! behold! 13:13; cf. *mâtika*

mâcikon- VTA/VTI hold s.o./s.t., grip
s.o./s.t.; 27:3

mâcistan- VII break-up (of ice in the
spring); 49:6

mâciš- VTI cut s.t.; (4:7; 16:5; 29:3; 45:2);
cf. *kîškiš-*, *têtipâs-*

mâcišikan- NI scissors; (53:1); cf. *mâciš-*,
môšotowin-

mâcišikâtê- VII be cut; 45:2

mâcišw- VTA cut s.o.; 4:7; 16:5; 29:3; cf.
kîškiš-, *têtipâs-*

mâciwêpiš- VTI slit s.t. down, slash s.t.;
(16:5; 63:1)

mâciwêpišw- VTA slit s.t. down, slash
s.o.; 16:5; 63:1

mâcîs- NA [English loanword] match (for
lighting); 61:3; *nimâcîsimak* my
matches

mâh- VTI go downstream; 62:3; 64:3; cf.
natah-

mâhâpoko- VAI float downstream, drift
downriver; (13:15); cf. *liskipotê-*,
liskiwên-

mâhâpolo- VAI drift down the river; (56:5); cf. ...*âpolo-*

mâhâpotê- VII go downstream on the water; (13:15); cf. *liskipotê-, liskiwên-,* ...*âpotê-*

mâhcic IPC last, lastly, last time; 5:10; 42:63; 43:3; *mâhcic kâ-ôhcît = ošîmimâw;* cf. *ohcî-*

mâhcicošân- NA last child; cf. *kîwašišân-, nîštamošân-,* ...*šân-, ohcî-*

mâhipahtâ- VAI run downriver; 42:29; cf. ...*pahtâ-*

mâhišk- VTI go or walk down the river; 13:3

mâhkiy- NI canvas tent; 37:3

mâhkwapiso- VAI be laced up; (65:7); cf. *akwahpiso-*

mâhkwapit- VTA/VTI tie s.o./s.t.; 59:3; 61:3; cf. *mâkwahpit-*

mâhtâwi IPC strange(ly); 42:38; *mâhtâwi-tôcikâtêw ôta nâspic* things are very strangely done here

mâhti IPC let me see, let's see! 15:3; 18:2; *mâhti mâ!* get away from me! *mâhti pitamâ n'ka-wâpahtên kimasinahikan* let me see your book a minute; *mâhti tânt' êhtâwânê* let's see where I may be, 37:6; *mâhti pêtâ* let's see, bring it here, 43:3; 58:3

mâka IPC but, however; and; 1:2 et passim

mâkohcikê- VAI bite; 21:3; 21:4

mâkoht- VTI bite s.t.; 48:1; cf. *mâkom-*

mâkohw- VTA compress s.o., squeeze s.o., pinch s.o.; 27:3

mâkom- VTA bite s.o.; 16:2; 21:3

mâkon- VTA/VTI grab, grasp, squeeze, take hold of s.o./s.t.; 48:1; 63:1; cf. *mâkwan-*

mâkoškaw- VTA jump on s.o. and squash him with one's weight; 10:10

mâkošêkwahw- VTA compress s.o. (as with a cloth wrapped more and more tightly); 10:10

mâko-wêpam- VTA take a quick bite at s.o.; 21:4; *"niwî-at'-otinâw mâka," manâ itwêw. "êkwâni mâk' ê-pêci-mâko-wêpamit."* "I was just about to take him," he said. "Then he

took a quick bite at me."; cf. *wêpahtêht-*

mâkw- NA large loon; 8:4; [sg.: *mâkwa*]; cf. *mwâkw-*

mâkwahpit- VTA/VTI tie s.o./s.t. up; 27:4; (52:2); cf. *âhtahpit, itahpit-, walahpit-*

mâkwan- VTA/VTI seize s.o./s.t.; 56:4; cf. *mâkon-*

mâlâtan- VII be bad, be ugly; 42:34

mâlâtašiškîši- VAI be ugly with mud (MC); 9:24; SC: mânâtašiškîši

mâlêlihcikê- VAI abuse, torment; 9:24

mâlêlim- VTA abuse, despise, scorn s.o.; tease s.o.; 7:4; 9:24; 21:1; 22:4; 46:1; 67:4

mâmahkicêyâ- VII [redupl.] be really big; 19:3; cf. ...*icê...,* ...*ayâ-*

mâmahkišk- VTI [redupl.] make tracks with large footprints; 5:2; 5:3; 6:5; cf. *mahkišk-*

mâmaskâc IPC wonderful(ly), strange(ly), marvellous(ly); really, very much; 11:1

mâmaskâsinâkosi- VAI be unusual, be out of the ordinary; 41:11; cf. ...*nâkosi-*

mâmaskâsinâkwan- VII be unusual, be out of the ordinary; (41:11); cf. ...*nâkwan-*

mâmaskâtêliht- VTI think it strange, wonder in surprise, marvel at it, look at it with amazement; 12:6; 14:6

mâmaskâtêlihtâkosi- VAI be wonderful; (41:11); cf. ...*ihtâkosi-*

mâmaskâtêlihtâkwan- VII be wonderful; 41:11; cf. ...*ihtâkwan-*

mâmaw IPC all together, together; at one and the same time; 41:15; *mâmaw âlimôtahtâw* let's get together and talk it over; *mâmaw âlimôtahtâw ôhi* let's talk about these things at the same time

mâmawi IPV altogether; 42:34

mâmawi-kiskisi- VAI remember all together, gather memories together; 42:34

mâmawi-kiskisinâniwan- VII the memories are gathered together; 42:34

mâmawipali- VAI/VII run together; 42:34; cf. ...*pali-*

mâmawi-tašîhkê- VAI live (all) together; (12:1)

mâmâhtâwi-tôt- VTI [redupl.] do weird things; cf. *mâhtâwi-*

mâmâkom- VTA [redupl.] bite s.o. again and again, bite s.o. repeatedly; 21:7; 22:1; cf. *mâkom-*

mâmâko-wêpim- VTA bite away at s.o.; 66:3

mâmân IPC I would think, it seems (as if), apparently; 10:7; 14:6; *mâmân ô kata-kimiwan* it seems as if it's going to rain; *mâmân ô âšay n'ka-minawâhtay* it seems as though I should start cooking; *mâmân ta-paskilâkêwak* (of a ball-team) it looks as if they're pretty likely to win

mâmâš IPC carelessly, roughly, haphazardly; 42:8; 42:65; more or less; 43:4; in a hasty way; 67:2; at random; 68:7; *mâmâš piko n'kî-wêpahikân* I swept just any old way

mâmihcêti- VAI [redupl.] be a great many; 42:12; *mâcik' âniki kâ-mâmihcêticik* look at the large families!

mâmihk IPC downriver, downstream; 37:2; often with *itêhkê*, e.g., *mâmihk itêhkê;* cf. *natimihk*

mâmihkocêyâ- VII [redupl.] be red all over (e.g., berries); 19:5; *mîniša kâ-mâmihkocêyâniki* berries which are red all over; cf. *...icê..., ...ayâ-*

mâmihkwâ- VII [redupl.] be really red; 19:3

mâmilotâwê- VAI [redupl.] look resplendent; 2:10

mâmišikiti- VAI [redupl.] be big all over, be enormous; 4:2; 6:6; 65:9; cf. *mišikiti-*

mâmišîhk IPC below a point on a river, downcurrent; 38:1

mâmitonêliht- VTI consider, contemplate; 3:2; have in mind; 11:11; think, reflect; 39:1; think things over; 42:9; give thought to; 42:15; 65:1

mâmitonêlim- VTA think about s.o.; 3:5

mâmîmicimê- VAI [probably for *mani-mîcimê-* buy food]; cf. n. 43:11,

nâci-mîcimê-

mâmîskawi-tôtaw- VTA [redupl.] happen to do it right to s.o.; 12:3; cf. *mîskawi-tôtaw-*

mâmîtânaskwan- VII [redupl.] clouds shit all around; 12:5; cf. *mîtânaskwan-, ...askw...*

mâna IPC frequently, repeatedly, again and again [changed form of *mîna*]; 49:1

mânêniht- VTI mistreat s.t. (SC); 3:11; MC: *mâlêliht-*

mânênim- VTA tease s.o., mistreat s.o. (SC); (3:11); MC: *mâlêlim-*

mân'ênitohk IPC just as though, as if it were the case that; 10:10

mân'sa, mân'si IPC oh my!; cf. *šâ mân'si*

mânišîš IPC a little; 19:3; 49:1; 65:5; cf. *apišîš*

mârtin NA [proper name] Martin; 49:3

mâsihtâkosi- VAI scream; 12:12; cf. *têkwê-, ...ihtâkosi-*

mâsakîskw- NA cedar tree; 62:5; 68:7

mâsikîskw- NA cedar tree; cf. *mâsakîskw-*

mâskâ- VII be defective, be maimed; 9:17

mâskipali- VAI be lame, limp; (42:63); cf. *ayâhciw-akocin-, ayâhciwipali-, ...pali-*

mâskisi- VAI be crippled, be maimed; 9:17

mâskiskaw- VTA cripple s.o.; 47:2

mâskitôhtan- NA [proper name] Lame Heel (nickname: so called because the tendon in the ankle was short, causing the man to walk only on the fore-part of his foot); 44:3; cf. *...tôhtan-*

mâskôc IPC perhaps, maybe; 5:1; 11:6; 35:2 et passim; also as *mâškôc*

mâskostê- VII lie (on something); 38:1; *ê-mâskostêk wakît cîmânihk m'pâskisikan* with my gun lying on top of the canoe; cf. *apîmakan-, astê-*

mâskošin- VAI lie (on something); (38:1); cf. *api-*

mâši IPC even; 3:10; 9:3; one way or another; 27:7; in a sort of a way; 34:2; *êk' oša' ni êkâ mâši wêhci-wâpahk* so that's why it didn't even dawn; *mâši 'sa n'ka-tôtên* I'll do it as nearly as I

487

can to the desired performance (but no guarantee); [synonym: *sêsik*]

mâših- VTA fight s.o.; 63:1

mâšihito- VAI [recipr.] wrestle with each other; 10:9; 60:9; 66:2

mâšihkê- VAI wrestle, struggle; 49:4; 63:1

mâšihkêpalihtwâ- VAI-T cause fighting; 9:2

mâšihtâ- VAI-T fight s.t.; (63:1)

mâtahâmê- VAI follow a path; 14:4; *'kwâni ... êt'-îši-mâtahâmêt* at that ... he started to follow it; cf. *...ahamê-*

mâtahcikê- VAI begin to eat; 56:6; *'kwân' êši-mâtahcikêyân, itwêw manâ* so then I started eating, he said

mâtahikê- VAI scrape moose-hide (to thin it); (56:1); this may be done by both men and women; cf. *mat(w)ê-âtahikê-*

mâtâciyosopali- VAI/VII begin to boil; (14:6); *mâtâciyosopaliw askihk* the kettle begins to boil; cf. *kipihtâciyosopali-, oso-, ...pali-*

mâtâh- VTA/VTI come upon (i.e., just see without looking for) s.o./s.t. (e.g., evident tracks or signs of animals, footprints); 3:2; 5:2; 5:3; 5:5; 5:7; 6:5; 12:2; 29:4; n. 5:1; *mâtâhêw awiyâšîša* he comes upon tracks of animals

mâtâm- VAI come up to the track or trail of it; 3:5

mâtânah IPC [contraction of *manâ ot'âni*]; 57; (65:5); *kîla mâtânah môšak kiwî-okimâwin* you always seem to want to be the boss

mâtânâ IPC [expostulation] then! 65:9; 67:5; *'kâwila mâtânâ anima tôta!* don't do that, then!

mâtâšikowan- VII begin running (i.e., water), begin dripping; (14:6); cf. *kipihtâšikowan-*

mâti(h) IPC look here! see here! 13:7

mâtika IPC look now! see here! 9:7; 11:7; 43:9

mâto- VAI cry, weep; 9:3; 11:2; 60:3; 65:7

mâwac IPC most; 3:10

mâwacih- VTA [recipr.] gather s.o. together; 22:2; 47:1

mâwacihito- VAI [recipr.] assemble themselves, get together; 47:1

mâwacihtâ- VAI-T gather s.t. together, get s.t. together; 19:7; 51:3

mâwatôpah- VTA gather s.o. on the run; 44:2

mêhkatêwihkonayêw- NA priest (Roman Catholic), 'black robe'; (49:1); cf. *ayamihêwikimâw-*

mêkwayêš IPC in the middle, in the centre; 37:3; 68:6; *mêkwayêš mâka 'kwantaw maskêkohk* but some place in the middle of the muskeg; cf. *mêkwêskamik, mêkwêyâhtik, mêkwêyâpisk*

mêkwâc IPC while [as conjunction, with *ê-* with conj.indic.]; 1:3; 8:3; during that time [as adverb]; 42:17

mêkwâhkan- VII be low tide (along the coast); (42:48), 49; cf. *mêkwâhkastê-, mêkwâpêkan-*

mêkwâhkastê- VII be low tide (in the river); (42:48); cf. *mêkwâhkan-, mêkwâpêkan-*

mêkwâ-kîšik IPC at midday; 44:2

mêkwâ-nîpin- VII be midsummer; 22:3

mêkwâ-nîpin IPC in midsummer; 49:1

mêkwâpêkan- VII be high tide; 42:48; cf. *mêkwâhkan-, mêkwâhkastê-, ...ipêk...*

mêkwâšk- VTI run into s.t., fall in with s.t., intercept s.t.; 32:1

mêkwâškamâkê- VAI come right in the midst; 13:12

mêkwâškaw- VTA fall in with s.o., run into s.o.; intercept s.o. (while en route); 6:4

mêkwêhkop IPC among the willows; (66:1; n. 66:3); [synonym: *nîpisîskâhk*]; cf. *lâlihkop, ...hkop...*

mêkwêskamik IPC back in the muskeg; (68:6); cf. *mêkwayêš, mêkwêyâhtikw, mêkwêyâpiskw, ...askamikw-*

mêkwêskamikw- NI muskeg country; 41:6

mêkwêyâhtik IPC among the trees; (68:6); cf. *mêkwayêš, mêkwêskamik, mêkwêyâpisk, ...âhtikw.../-*

mêkwêyâmatin IPC among the knolls; 68:6; cf. *mêkwayêš, mêkwêskamikw,*

*mêkwêyâhtikw, mêkwêyâpiskw,
...âpiskw-*

mêkwêyâpisk IPC among the rocks;
(68:6); cf. *mêkwayêš, mêkwêskamik,
mêkwêyâhtik*

mêmêkwêšiw- NA mermaid; 9:16; (n.
9:24)

mêmêpison- NI swing, hammock; 65:8

mêmišôš- NA [proper name] Memishoosh
(legendary conjuror); 11:1

mêmîskoc IPC [redupl.] in turn, turn
and turn about; 21:2; 39:1; 42:40; cf.
mîskoc

mêriyw- NA [proper name] Mary; 67:4;
[obv.: *mêrîwa*]

mêskanaw- NI trail, path; (rail)road; 5:7;
41:7; 41:14

mêstin- VTA/VTI use s.o./s.t. up, expend
s.o./s.t.; 42:9

mêšakwanâpan IPC every dawn (i.e.,
every day); 42:13; *mêšakwanâpan
nin'taw'-âšawahikân âta êkâ
ê-pâskisikêyân* I go to the blind at
dawn every day, even though I don't
shoot; cf. *...âpan-*

mêšikwani IPN every
mêšikwani-tipiskâw every night; 42:12;
mêšikwan'-pipon every winter; 60:1

mêtawê- VAI play 10:7; 42:9; 49:4

micihcân- NI thumb; (13:16); cf.
*lîlîkicihcân, ...cihcân-, lîlîkisitân,
misisitân*

micihcin- NI an inch; 52:1; 61:3; cf.
ocihciy-, ...cihc...

micihciy- NDI hand; (21:3; 25:2; 36:2;
60:9); cf. *...cihc..., ...cihciy-, ocihciy-*

miconi IPC entirely, very much, utterly
[alternative form of *mitoni*]; 3:4

mihcêt IPC many; 3:1; 23:3

mihcêti- VAI be many; 1:9; 9:8; 21:6;
42:25; 42:40

mihcêtin- VII be many; 19:2; 42:33

mihcêtokamikisi- VAI be many families;
12:7; *nîšitana-nîšo tahtokamikisiwak*
there are twenty-two families; *tâni
tahtokamikisicik?* how many families
are there? cf. *nistokamikisi-,
pêyakokamikisi-, ...ikamikisi-*

mihcêtoyêk IPC many ways, more ways
than one; 3:1; 11:1; 43:5

mihcêtôtênaw IPC many families;
(60:10); cf. *tân' tahtôtênaw, ...otênaw-*

mihcêtwâ IPC many times; 4:3; 9:1; 39:2;
42:1; 42:17

mihcilawêsi- VAI be sorry; 9:7; 11:10

mihcikiw- NA spear; 12:5; cf. *miscikêw-*

mihkikwat- NI bone instrument for
chiselling meat off hide; 50:6

mihkokaškwênitiso- VAI redden one's
nails; (46:2); cf. *mihkonawênitiso-,
mihkotonênitiso-, ...kaškw...*

mihkokotê- VAI have a red nose; (46:2);
cf. *mihkwâtakâpi-, mihkwanawê-,
mihkotonê-, kâ-mihkopalinâniwahk,
okot-, ocâs-, oskiwan-, ...câš..., ...kot...*

mihkonawê- VAI have a red face; 10:8;
cf. *mihkwanawê-, mahkatêwanawê-,
nihcîkinawê-, tômiskinawê-,
wâpinêwipali-, wâpiskinawê-;
...anaw...*

mihkonawênitiso- VAI put rouge on
one's cheeks; (46:2); cf. *mihkwanawê-*

mihkopêmakâhtikw- NA red willow;
(68:8); cf. *atôspiyâhtikw-, ...âhtikw.../-*

mihkosi- VAI be red; 59:3

mihkotonênitiso- VAI put on lipstick;
(46:2); cf. *mihkotonê-, ...ton...*

mihkotonê- VAI have red lips, have a
red mouth; (46:2); cf. *mihkokotê-,
mihkwanawê-, mihkwâtakâpi-, ...ton...*

mihkowan- VII be bloodstained; (21:3)

mihkowi- VAI be bloodstained; 21:3

mihkw- NI blood; 27:7; [sg.: *mihko*]

mihkwacakâš- NA red sucker; 54:2

mihkwacâpi- VAI have red eyes; 46:1; cf.
...câp...

mihkwanawê- VAI have red cheeks;
(46:2); cf. *mihkokotê-, mihkotonê-,
mihkwâtakâpi-, ...anaw...*

mihkwaskamikw- NI red moss n. 51:2;
cf. *kihciwêskamikw-, wâpaskamikw-,
wâpisoyân-, ...askamikw-*

mihkwâ- VII be red; (59:3)

mihkwâpiskiso- VAI be red-hot (of
metal, stone); cf. *...âpisk...*

mihkwâpiskitê- VII be red-hot (of metal,
stone); cf. *wâstawêyâpiskitê-*

mihkwâtakâpi- VAI have red eyes;
(46:2); cf. *mihkokotê-, mihkotonê-,
mihkwanawê-, ...âpi-*

miht- NI log of wood; 9:19; 23:4; [sg.:
mihti, pl.: *mihta*]

mihtawê- VAI be disappointed; (12:4);
complain; (48:2)

mihtâlôw- NA snowdrift; 12:11;
[synonym (and more customary
usage): *ê-piskwacistihk* lump of snow];
cf. *piskwacistin-, piskwasêkâ-*

mihtât- VTA/VTI be sorry for s.o./s.t.,
regret s.o./s.t.; 63:3; *êliwêhk
nimitâhtên ê-kî-atâwakêyin anima
cîmân* I sure am sorry that you sold
that canoe

mihtôt- NI raft; 7:1

mihtôtihkê- VAI make a raft; 7:1; cf.
...ihkê-

mikaškamâw- NDI nape of the neck;
12:3; 56:4; cf. *...kaškamâw...,
okaškamâw-*

mikisimo- VAI bark; 9:15

mikisiw- NA eagle; 4:1

mikisiwi-pîsimw- NA March, lit., 'eagle
moon'; cf. *pîsimw-*

mikitikw- NDI knee; (14:12; 61:2); cf.
...kitikw..., otâšikitikwâna

mikiy- NI scab; 27:7; 55:8

mikohtâkan- NDI throat; (8:8);
[synonym: *mikotaskway-*]; cf.
...kohtâkan-

mikot- NDI nose; (46:2); cf. *...kot..., okot-*

mikotaskway- NDI throat; (8:8);
[synonym: *mikohtâkan-*]; cf.
...kohtâkan-

mikwaškâcih- VTA bother s.o., annoy
s.o., trouble s.o.; 20:4; 23:5; 26:3

mikwaškâcihtâ- VAI-T trouble s.t.,
disturb s.t., bother s.t., worry s.t.; 15:2

mikwaškâtêliht- VTI worry about s.t.;
9:22; 13:17; 23:4

mikwayâw- NDI neck; 12:6; 66:2; cf.
...kwayâw..., okwayâw-

milâhkatê- VII give off a burning smell;
11:12

milâskitê- VII give off a burning smell
(e.g., a stick lying on a stove)

milâkosi- VAI have a strong smell; 50:5

milâkwan- VII have a strong smell;
(50:5)

miliy- NI pus, matter produced by
suppuration; (42:63)

milîwan- VII discharge pus or matter;
(42:63) *milîwaniliw oskât* his leg is
discharging matter; cf. *...kât...,
milîyokâtê-*

milîwi- VAI discharge pus or matter;
(42:63) *milîwiliwa olihkwa* his tonsils
are discharging

milîyocâpi- VAI discharge matter from
the eye; (42:63); 46; cf. *...câp...,
milîwi...*

milîyocihcê- VAI discharge matter from
the hand; (42:63); cf. *...cihc...*

milîyokaškwê- VAI be full of pus (toe-
nails), discharge matter from the
toe-nails; 42:63; cf. *...kaškw...,
milîwi...*

milîyokâtê- VAI be full of pus (leg),
discharge matter from the leg; (42:63);
cf. *...kât..., milîwi...*

milîyopitonê- VAI discharge matter
from the arm; (42:63); cf. *...piton...*

milîyohtâwakê- VAI discharge matter
from the ear; (42:63); cf. *...htâwak...*

milîyotonê- VAI discharge matter from
the mouth; (42:63); cf. *...ton...*

milo IPV/IPN well, good (MC); SC: *mino*

milohtâkosi- VAI sound good; (11:3); cf.
...ihtâkosi-

milohtâkwan- VII sound good; 11:3; cf.
...ihtâkwan-

milo-ihti- VAI be in a good state of mind
or well-being; 65:9; *êkâ ê-wî-milo-ihtit*
since she was not in a good state
(mentally)

milo-itâpi- VAI see well; 19:4; cf. *...âpi-*

milomahciho- VAI feel well; (27:1); cf.
...amahciho-

milomahcihtâ- VAI-T feel (something)
well; 27:1

milonamaw- VTA admire s.o. for
something; fancy something on s.o.;
2:10

milopali- VAI/VII fare well, get along,
make out; 1:4; 9:22; 39:3; cf. *...pali-*

milo-pimâtisî- VAI be in good health, be

in good shape (MC); (27:1); cf.
mino-pimâtisi-

miloskamin- VII be open water; 38:1;
42:2; 45:1; 49:1; cf. *sîkwan-*

milo-tašîhkê- VAI have a good dwelling,
be well fixed as to dwelling; 41:7;
42:43

milotêpo- VAI be a good cook; (18:9;
55:6); cf. *išitêpo-, osâmawahahkâtêpo-,
...têpo-*

milotêwêyâ- VII be a hard crust on top
of the snow; 42:29; [near-synonym:
maškawitêwêyâ-]; cf. *...têw..., ...ayâ-*

milototaw- VTA treat s.o. well, do well
by s.o.; 9:18; 41:8; *ispîhci-mistahi
ê-kî-mino-totâtahkok kî'nânaw* in that
they treated us so well

mil'-ôtâkošin- VII be a fine evening; 5:9

milwahcik ê- VAI eat (and enjoy) good
food, have a good feed; (10:8); 55:6

milwâkamin- VII have good water, be
good water; 42:50; cf. *...âkamin-*

milwâpôw- NI good water; 65:3; cf.
...âpôw-

milwâsin- VII be good, be attractive;
41:7; 42:37

milwâšiši- VAI be good, be attractive;
8:6; 9:24

milwêlihcikâtê- VII be liked, be a good
atmosphere; (figurative: be a good
mood); 42:65; *ta-kî-minwên'cikâtêpan
ê-'yaminâniwahk* we would be in a
mood to talk

milwêliht- VTI like s.t., be happy; 2:10;
19:4

milwêlim- VTA like s.o.; (2:10; 19:4)

milwêlihtâkosi- VAI be good-natured;
25:3; cf. *...ihtâkosi-*

milwêlihtâkwan- VII be enjoyable; 49:4;
cf. *...ihtâkwan-*

minahikoskâ- VII black spruce are
abundant; [sometimes loosely used for
waskiskiy- 'pine']; (42:54); cf. *...iskâ-*

minahikowan- VII be white spruce;
minahikowan ôma šîpîšiš this creek
has only white spruce (along it)

minahikowâmatinâ- VII be a spruce
knoll, be a pine knoll; (42:54); cf.
...âmatin...

minahikw- NA black spruce; 19:8;
(42:54); 50:5; 68:6; cf. *sêsêkâhtak-*

minaho- VAI have a good hunt, make a
good hunt; 61:1

minahwê- VAI have a good hunt, make a
good hunt; cf. *minaho-*

minawaso- VAI cook for oneself
(Kashechewan usage); (27:2);
[synonym: *piminawaso-*]; MC:
kîšinawaso-; cf. *kîšinawê-, minawê-*

minawê- VAI cook; 9:12; 12:8; (27:2)

minâwinân- NI [place name] No-Man's
Land, lit., 'collecting place (for eggs)';
cf. *manâwinân-*

minihkwê- VAI drink; 65:9

ministikw- NI island; 9:2; 11:3; 49:6;
referring to Moose Island, 42:12;
42:56; 58:1; 65:2; cf. *...stikw.../-*

mino IPV/IPN well, good (SC); MC: *milo*

mino-itâpi- VAI see well (SC); 19:4; MC:
milo-itâpi-; cf. *...âpi-*

minokâmo- VAI be nice and fat, be
plump (SC); 19:7; (describes bear as
Weesakecahk prepares to cook him)

mino-pimâtisi VAI be in good health, be
in good shape (SC); 27:1; MC:
milo-pimâtisî-

minotêwêyâ- VII be a hard crust on top
of the snow (SC); MC: *milotêwêyâ-*

minwâšiši- VAI be good, be fine (SC);
9:24; MC: *milwâšiši-*

minwêtâpi- VAI see well; 19:4

mipîway- NDI whisker, bristle; 50:1; 53:1;
cf. *...pîw..., opîwaya, mînistowâkan-,
...pîway-*

misaskêlâ- VII have a bottom (as a lake
or river) which can be easily reached;
34:2

misaskênâ- VII have a bottom (as a lake
or river) which can be easily reached
(SC); MC: *misaskêlâ-*

misawâc IPC anyway, anyhow, in any
case; 41:8; 49:3; 65:7

miscêti- VAI be many; cf. *mihcêti-*; 65:5

miscikêw- NA spear; cf. *mihcikiw-*, 12:5;
cîstahikan-

misisitân- NDI big toe; (13:16); cf.
*lîlîkisitân-, lîlîkicihcân-, micihcân,
...sitân-*

misit- NDI foot; 47:1; cf. *osita, ...sit...*

misitêpit- VTI spread s.t. over; 50:2

misiwê IPC all; 1:4; 9:9; 21:6; 41:21; 59:1; *misiwê piko kêkwân* everything; *misiwê kêkwân piko* only whatever

misiwêsi- VII be whole, entire; 40:3; 60:4

misiwêskamikâk IPC all over the country; 41:15; cf. *...askamik...*

misk- VTI find s.t.; 1:3; 5:7; 37:3; 55:7

miskah- VTI find s.t., discover s.t. with an instrument; (12:12)

miskahw- VTA find s.o., discover s.o. with an instrument; 12:12

miskan- NDI bone; cf. *...skan-, oskan-*

'miskanawê- VAI leave tracks, leave evidence (as one goes along); [contraction of *pimiskanawê-*]; 5:2; cf. *...skanawê-*

miskaw- VTA find s.o.; (1:3; 5:7; 37:3; 55:7)

miskât- NDI leg; cf. *oskât-, ...skât-, ...kât...*

miskon- NDI liver; cf. *...skon-, oskon-, ...skwan-*

miskošk- VTI hit exactly upon s.t. (while walking); (68:8)

miskoškaw- VTA hit exactly upon s.o. (while walking); 68:8; *mwêhci piko kî-miskoškawêw* he hit exactly upon him (e.g., of a person kicking away loose snow to find something he is unable to locate); *môla kî-miskoškawêw* he can't find it

miskwan- NDI liver; cf. *...skon-, oskwan-*

miskwâpin- NI tump-line, portage strap; (42:42); cf. *...âp...*

mispiskwan- NDI back; cf. *ospiskwan-, ...spiskwan-, ...piskwan...*

mispiton- NDI arm; 13:9; cf. *ospiton-, ...spiton..., ...piton..., ...nisk...*

mispon- VII snow; 22:2; 58:3

misponiskâ- VAI run into a snow storm, get caught in a snow storm while travelling; 42:27

mistahi IPC great, greatly; much considerably; 2:3; 19:3; 40:4; *nâspic mistahi* to a considerable extent, 42:11

mistamês- NA giant fish; 16:5; cf. *...amês.../-*

mistamiskw- NA giant beaver; 13:9; cf. *...amiskw.../-*

mistasiniy- NA great rock; 13:14; cf. *...asiniy-*

mistaskihkw- NA big kettle, big cauldron, big pot; 13:12; 56:5

mistatay- NI big stomach, big belly; 19:8; cf. *...atay-*

mistatimw- NA horse; 41:3; cf. *atimw-*

mistâkalâš- NA [proper name] Mistaganash (legendary figure) (MC); (10:1); SC: *mistâkanâš-;* cf. *mišcakalâš*

mistâkanâš- NA [proper name] Mistaganash (legendary figure) (SC); 10:1; MC: *mistâkalâš-*

mistâpêskwêšiš- NA giant girl; 56:2

mistâpêskwêw- NA giant woman; 14:2; 56:2; cf. *...âpêw.../-, ...îskwêw-*

mistâpêw- NA giant; 13:4

mistiko-nâpêwikamikw- NI carpenter shop; 49:1; cf. *...ikamikw-*

mistiko-nâpêwi-môhkotâkan- NI carpenter's plane; cf. *môhkocikê-, môhkotâkan-*

mistikw- NA tree; 1:6; 18:1; 41:4

mistikw- NI stick; 38:2; 52:2

mistikwân- NDI head; 9:4; 9:5; 10:5; cf. *nistikwân-, ostikwân-*

mistosokamikw- NI barn; 42:50; cf. *...ikamikw-*

mišakâ- VAI land, come to shore, arrive by water, paddle in; 10:5; 11:7; 49:1

mišamihtâkosi- VAI have difficulty talking; cf. *...ihtâkosi-*

mišamî- VAI have difficulty doing something; (43); refers to physical difficulty more than *âlimisi-*

mišâ- VII be big; 9:17; 19:2; 37:3; 40:1; 67:2

mišâhtâ- VAI-T make s.t. big; 18:2

mišcâkalâš- NA [proper name] Mishchakalash (legendary figure) (MC); 63:1; SC: *mistâkanâš-*

mišêkan- VII be large (sheet-like, e.g., a tarpaulin); (52:2; 52:3); cf. *...êk...*

mišêkisi- VAI be large (sheet-like, e.g., a skin, hide); 52:2; 52:3; cf. *akwanahikan-, akwanahotâson-, akwanah(w)-*

mišêtwâ IPC many times [variant of *mihcêtwâ*]; 53:1

miši IPV/IPN great, big; 6:4

mišikamâ- VII be large (a body of water); (12:11); [synonym: *mahkikamâ-*]; cf. *...kam...*

miši-kinošêw- NA giant fish, giant pike; 4:4

mišikiti- VAI be big; 4:2; 11:2; 16:5; 41:15

mišikwanay- NDI tailfin; (29:1); cf. *ošikwanay-, ...šikwanay-*

mišim- VTA tell on s.o., inform on s.o.; 60:8; cf. *mamišim-*

miši-maskw- NA giant bear; 6:4

miši-mikisiwi-waciston- NI great eagle's nest; 1:5

miši-pâskisikan- NI cannon; 5:8

miši-šîpîšišihkân- NI deep, narrow creek, 'big creeklet'; 11:8; cf. *...ihkân-*

mišiy-otahnapihkêsiw- NA big spider; 2:4; cf. *êhêpikw-*

miškašîy- NDA hoof; 1:7; 2:7; *kî-wâpahtinêw mâka oškašîya ê-'šinâkosinici* and he showed them what his hooves looked like; *môna n'kî-kospâhtawîwâkân ôko niškašîyak* I can't climb with these hooves of mine, I can't use these hooves of mine for climbing; cf. *...škašîy-, oškašîya*

miškawâšihitiso- VAI run into trouble; 11:10

'miškâ- VAI paddle along, row; swim (of a fish) [contraction of *pimiškâ-*]; 11:6

mišot- VTA/VTI hit s.o./s.t. straight on, score a bull's eye on s.o./s.t.; 37:3

mišôkan- NDI lower back; 8:5; 55:3; cf. *...šôkan-, ošôkan-*

mištâpêskwêšiš- NA giant girl; 56:1; cf. *mistâpêskwêw-*

mištikw- NI stick [variant of *mistikw-*]

mišw- VTA wound s.o., hit s.o. (as in shooting); 34:1

mišwâkanihkât- VTA wound s.o.; 13:13; 14:7

mitâht IPC ten; 37:5

mitahtahkwan- NDI wing; cf. *...tahtahkwan-, otahtahkwan-*

mitâhtomitana IPC hundred; 41:18; 42:24; 42:36; 52:2

mitâhto-piponêsi- VAI be ten years old; 65:4

mitâhtwahtay- NA an amount of ten dollars; 42:14; cf. *nîsohtay, ...ahtay...*

mitâs- NDI legging, trousers (NDA in some areas); 11:11; cf. *...tâs-, otâsa; palacîs-*

mitâsikitikwâna NDI [pl.] leggings; 11:12; [synonym: *mitâs-*]; cf. *mikitikw-*

mitâwisi- VAI come out on something (e.g., a lake in the bush); 12:11; [synonym: *matâpê-*]

mitêhkaw- VTA conjure s.o., cast a spell on s.o.; 11:2

mitêhkât- VTA conjure s.o.; 21:5; 21:8

mitêhkê- VAI do conjuring; 11:6

mitêlaliy- NDI tongue (MC); 42:57; cf. *...têlaliy-*

mitêwi- VAI conjure, be a conjuror; 12:14; 21:5; 59:3

mitêwin- NI conjuring; 12:14; 30:1

mitihtiman- NDI shoulder; 9:14; 12:3; cf. *otihtiman-, ...tihtiman-*

mitilîkêkan- NDA shoulder blade; 9:15; cf. *otilîkêkana-, ...tilîkêkan-*

mitonêlihcikan- NI mind; 5:9; *pîtoš kî-ispaniniw omitonên'cikan* his mind changed

mitoni IPC entirely, very much, utterly; 3:4; 7:1; 41:9; 56:1; cf. *miconi*

mitôhtan- NDI heel; 44:3; cf. *mâskitôhtan-, otôhtan-, ...tôhtan-*

mitôn- NDI mouth; 29:3; cf. *otôn-, ...tôn-, ...ton...*

mîci- VAI-T eat s.t.; 9:8; 19:1; 21:2; 27:2; 40:2; 55:8; 68:1; cf. *mow-*

mîcim- NI food; 9:12; 39:4; 42:10; 43:7

mîciso- VAI eat; 8:2; 9:10; 13:5; 49:1

mîcisonâhtikw- NI table; 49:1; cf. *...âhtikw.../-*

mîcit- VTA defecate on s.o., "mess" on s.o., spray s.o. (of a skunk); 12:5

mîkis- NA bead; 8:6

mîkiwâm- NDI tent (bell style); 9:11; 9:16; 13:4; 14:5; 18:2; 24:1; 27:1; 40:1; 56:3

mîkiwâmišiš- NDI small wigwam; 9:8

mîkwan- NA quill, feather; 11:6; 20:5

mîl- VTA give (to) s.o. (MC); 9:9; 13:12; 42:35; 43:3; SC: *mîn-*

mîlitihp- NDI brain; (50:2); cf. *wîlitihp-, wîlil-, ...îlitihp-, ...tihp.../-*

mîn- VTA give (to) s.o. (SC); MC: *mîl-*

mîna IPC again; 1:7 et passim; cf. *mâna*

mînistowâkan- NI whiskers, beard, feelers; 15:5; cf. *mipîway-, mînistowê-*

mînistowê- VAI have a beard, have feelers (15:5)

mîniš- NI berry; 19:1; 27:1; 65:6; cf. *môminê-, ...min.../-*

mînwâcih- VTA make s.o. feel better; 7:4

mîsâhkwayân- NA sleeping skin (like a small mat); 9:10; 9:14

mîskaw IPC seldom, rarely, once in a while; on the chance that, by chance; 4:6; *kišâspin mîskaw antê êhtâkwê nišîm* on the off-chance that my young brother may be there

mîskawi-tôt- VTI happen to do it right, do it right by chance, hit on the right way to do it (e.g., of someone trying to repair a piece of machinery); 12:3

mîskawi-tôtaw- VTA happen to do it right to s.o.; (12:3)

mîskoc IPC instead, in exchange

mîskoškaw- VTA happen upon s.o., chance upon s.o.; (12:8) *mwêhci piko n'kî-mîskoškawâw* I just happened upon him, I just chanced upon him

mîskoškâto- VAI [recipr.] run into each other; 12:8; cf. *mâmîskoškâto-*

mîskoti-wêpin- VTI switch them around, change their position; 11:12

mîskwah- VTI hit s.t. on the target, hit s.t. squarely; 12:12

mîskwahw- VTA hit s.o. on the target, hit s.o. squarely (e.g., a rock in a river, a ball in baseball); 62:3; cf. *pîstahw-*

mîskwâpin- NI tump line, portage strap, hauling trace; (42:42); cf. *...âp..., otâpâniyâpiy; kinwâpê-, tahkwâpê-*

mîskwâskošimo- VAI stand behind a tree; 56:2; *môla n'kî-pâskiswâw ê-mîskwâskošimot* I couldn't shoot him because he was behind a tree; cf. *...âskw.../-, ...šimo-*

mîsopiy- NDI gall bladder; (14:3); cf. *wîsopiy-, ...îsopiy-*

mîšakipali- VAI have plenty; 39:3

mîtânaskwan- VII clouds shit; 12:5

mîwat- NDI bag; 1:4; 14:4; cf. *wîhkwêyâw-, ...îwat-*

mîwatihkâso- VAI pretend it is a bag, pretend it is a bundle; 18:1; cf. *...hkâso-*

mîwatihkê- VAI make a bag, make a bundle; (18:1); cf. *...îwat-, ...ihkê...*

mohci IPV just; 11:2; 14:5; 19:6; *ê-mohci-otatâmahwât* in just tapping repeatedly; *kâ-mohci-kînikwâninâkosit* he just seemed to spin around, 13:14; *ê-mohc'-otâpâniwahkipan* when they just used to haul, 42:43

mohcihk IPC on the ground; 66:2

mostaskamik IPC on the bare ground; 21:7; 56:6; cf. *...askamikw...*

mostâkonak IPC on top of the bare snow; 21:7; cf. *...âkonak...*

mošê IPC free(ly); *mošê n'kî-mîlik* he gave it to me for nothing; *mošê piko ê-kî-ošihtâniwahk* as it was being done for next to nothing

mošê IPV bare, exposed, in the open; clearly, just as they were, 18:10; 21:9; 41:4; 41:8; 41:9; 65:1; free(ly), for nothing; 42:1; *n'kî-mošê-mîlik* he gave it to me bare or uncovered (cf. also *mošênam kâ-mîlit* he uncovered what he gave me)

mošêhkwâmi- VAI sleep without cover, sleep in the open; 37:4; 39:1; cf. *...ihkwâmi-*

mošên- VTA/VTI uncover s.o./s.t. (by hand), lay s.o./s.t. bare (by hand)

mošêškatê- VAI be naked; 61:5

mošišêyâpiskakocin- VAI hang like a clear stone; 6:14; cf. *akocin-, ...âpisk...*

moškicêškiwakipali- VAI come up in the mud; (32:1); cf. *kotawi..., liski..., ...cîskawak..., ...pali-*

mow- VTA eat s.o.; 12:10; 13:12; 27:2; 53:3; 58:5; 65:6; cf. *mîci-*

mô' 'cê IPC not even [contraction of *môna wâci*]; 43:6

môhkaškamâ- VAI [probable false start for *môhkikaškamêyâhtawî-*]

môhkiciwanipêkw- NI spring which has a fountain-like action and never freezes; (12:5); cf. *...ciwan.../-,* *...ipêkw-*

môhkikaškamêyâhtawî- VAI climb down with back of the neck showing or with neck arched; 12:5; cf. *...kaškam...,* *...âhtawî-*

môhkocikâtê- VII be planed; 52:1; cf. *môhkot-*

môhkocikê- VAI whittle, plane; 6:9; 9:22

môhkomân- NI knife; 10:3; 10:9; 16:4; 60:9

môhkot- VTA/VTI plane s.o./s.t.; (52:1); cf. *napakihkot-*

môhkotâkan- NI (carpenter's) plane; also as *mistiko-nâpêwi-môhkotâkan*

môla IPC no; not [with independent order]; 1:4 et passim; [contraction of *namawila*]

môlâkonêhiwê- VAI dig in the snow; 32:1; cf. *...âkon...*

môl' êškwâ IPC not yet

môlôw- NA grandfather (apparently an archaic form, according to a Fort Albany informant); [synonym: *omošômimâw-*]; 12:6; n. 12:15

mômine- VAI eat berries; 19:1; cf. *kâhkâkîšiminak, ...min.../-, mîniš-*

môsasiniya NI [pl.] moose-shot; 34:2

môsasinî'-pâskisikan- NI [contraction of *môsasinîwi-pâskisikan-*]; 31:1

môsasinîwi-pâskisikan- NI moose-shot gun; 44:3

môskamiwâkamipali- VAI become broth; cf. *môškami-*

môskamiy- NI broth, gravy; cf. *môškamiy-*

môskâkonakî- VAI emerge slowly from the snow; 66:1; cf. *môskî-, ...âkonak...*

môskâkonêpit- VTA/VTI pull s.o./s.t. out of the snow; (48:1); cf. *môskipit-, ...âkon...*

môskinêpê- VII be full of water; 61:3; cf. *...ipê.../-*

môskipali- VAI/VII break out (as a rash or sore); (66:1); cf. *...pali-*

môskipaliho- VAI jump out quickly; (66:1); cf. *...paliho-*

môskipêkipit- VTA/VTI pull s.o./s.t. out of the water; (48:1); cf. *môskipit-, ...ipêk...*

môskipit- VTA/VTI pull s.o./s.t. to the surface; 48:1; dig s.o./s.t. up; 13:15; cf. *môskâkonêpit-, ...âkon...*

môskî- VAI emerge slowly; 66:1

môskôpinê- VAI moan; 11:9; 12:5

môsoniy- NI [place name] Moosonee, Ontario; town upstream from Moose River estuary; 42:34; 44:4

môsonîwi-ministikw- NI [place name] Moose Factory Island; 58:1

môso-wayân- NA moose hide; 35:1; 50:3; often as *môs'-wayân-*

môso-wîyâs- NI moose meat; 49:1; often as *môs'-wîyâs-*

môsokâhcišo- VAI play moose (a children's game: hunter and moose); n. 2:6

môsw- NA moose; 49:1; [sg.: môswa]

môšak IPC always; 3:3; 19:1

môših- VTA feel s.o.; (48:1)

môšihtâ- VAI-T feel s.t.; 41:8; 42:16; 48:1; *nimôšihtân kici-maci-kîšikâk* I feel it is going to be a bad day (said by someone whose rheumatism or arthritis gives forewarning of bad weather)

môškamiwâkamipali- VAI/VII become broth; 13:17; cf. *môškamiwâkamipali-, ...âkam..., ...pali...*

môškamiy- NI broth, gravy; 13:13; 13:17; 14:7; 60:5; cf. *môškamiy-*

môšotôwin- NI scissors; (53:1); cf. *mâciš-, mâcišikan-*

mwâkw- NA loon; 18:1; 47:1; [sg.: mwâkwa]

mwêhci IPC exactly; 1:6; 9:13; 13:8; 42:9; 58:2; *ê'kwâni pêyakwan mwêhci êspanik* that goes exactly the same way 42:9; *mwêhci kišê-cîmân kâ-'ši-pimipalik* right where the ship went 58:2

na IPC see here! 42:62; contrast with *nâ*, the question marker

nahal- VTA put s.o. away, save s.o.; (42:15) *nahalêw ošôliyânima* he saves his money, puts his money away; cf. *nahastâ-*

nahapi- VAI seat oneself; 9:11; cf. *...api-*

nahastamaw- VTA put it away for s.o.; 51:1

nahastamâso- VAI put it away for oneself; 42:15

nahastâ- VAI-T put s.t. away; (42:15); 51:1; *nahastâw ocîmân* he puts his canoe away; *nahastâniwa* they are put away; cf. *nahal-*

nahâpi- VAI see well, see clearly; 19:3; cf. *...âpi-*

nahêliht- VTI be pleased with s.t., be contented with s.t.; 47:1; *môla nahêl'htamwak* they were not pleased, they were offended; *kîla 'sa ê-'ši-nahêl'htaman* just as you please

nahênawêh- VTA satisfy s.o., make s.o. content (SC); 5:4; MC: *nahîlawêh-*

nahi IPC just right, average; 28:1; *nahi n'tispihcisîn* I'm of about average age; *nahi 'ci-ispihcîyân* that I am of about average strength

nahišin- VAI lie comfortably; 10:4; 55:4; 55:5

nahîhk- VTI bury s.t., put s.t. away or aside for safekeeping

nahîhkaw- VTA bury s.o., put s.o. away for safekeeping; 10:2; 41:14

nahîlawêh- VTA satisfy s.o., make s.o. content; 4:3; 5:4; cf. *nahênawêh-*

nahkâpêkin- VTA/VTI extend s.o./s.t.; (42:42); cf. *tahkwâpêkin, ...âpêk...*

nahkon- NDA my ankle (65:8); cf. *wahkon-*

nakacâskohtin- VII bump into a tree; (68:6); cf. *...âskw.../-*

nakacâskošin- VAI bump into a tree; 68:6; cf. *...âskw.../-, nânakacâskošin-, nakacihw-, nakacipah-, tâwatâwiškaw-*

nakacicê-wêpahamaw- VTA drive it through for s.o.; [synonym: *šâpohta-wêpahamaw-*]

nakacih- VTI bump into s.t.; (68:6)

nakacihtâ- VAI-T be familiar with s.t.; 37:3

nakacihw- VTA bump into s.o.; (68:6) *nakacihotômakanwa ocâpân'šiša* the snowmobiles bump into each other

nakacipah- VTA run away from s.o., outruns s.o.; 42:18; 65:8

nakacipahtwâ- VAI-T run away from s.t., leave s.t. behind in running; (42:18; 65:8)

nakacišin- VAI bump into; 12:3; 68:8

nakaciškaw- VTA hit s.o. head on; 12:8; *nakaciškâkow* he is hit head on; for alternate reading, cf. *êko manâ nêkacicâkot* n. 12:18

nakaci-wêpahw- VTA leave s.o. off, dump s.o. and leave him; 9:3

nakamôwiniwat- NI song bag [variant of *nikamôwiniwat*]; 55:1; cf. *...wat-*

nakat- VTA/VTI leave s.o./s.t.; 6:4; 8:6; 21:9; 31:1; 50:5; 58:5

nakatah- VTI leave s.t. (by water); (9:4; 11:4)

nakatahw- VTA leave s.o. (by water); 9:4; 11:4

nakâh- VTI reinforce s.t.; 41:19; parry s.t., ward s.t. off; (63:1)

nakâhikâtê- VII be reinforced; 41:19

nakâhw- VTA reinforce s.o.; (41:19) parry s.o., ward s.o. off; (63:1); cf. *nakâyâskohw-*

nakân- VTI hold s.t. back, stop s.t.; 22:3

nakân- VTA stop s.o. (from doing s.t.); 22:3; e.g., of two people fighting: *nânakânâkaniwanwak* they are being stopped or prevented from fighting; *kata-nakânâkaniwan* he will be stopped

nakâwêpišk- VTI block s.t.; (63:1)

nakâwêpiškaw- VTA block s.o. (as in football, hockey, or when trying to force a passage through a door); (63:1); cf. *nakâhw-, ohcih-*

nakâyâskoh- VTI reinforce s.t., brace s.t. (e.g., a wooden object which has fallen over and which one wants to save); (41:19); cf. *...âskw.../-*

nakâyâskohw- VTA reinforce s.o., brace s.o. (e.g., a tree which had fallen over and which one wants to save); (41:19); cf. *...âskw.../-*

nakicâhk IPC at the far end (e.g., of a hallway)

nakiska IPC a little while; 42:1; [variant of *nakiskaw*]

nakiskaw IPC a little while; 1:6; cf. *nômakê*

nakiškaw- VTA meet s.o. (on land); 21:6; 68:3

nakwâkan- NI snare; 3:5; 21:4

nakwâkaniyâpiy- NI snare wire, snare line; 15:3; 18:3; cf. *...âpiy-*

nakwâkaniyâpîhkê- VAI make snare lines; 18:3; cf. *...âpiy-, ...ihkê-*

nakwâso- VAI be snared, be caught in a snare; 3:6

nakwâtahon- VTA snare s.o.; 8:4

nakwâtaho-wêpin- VTA/VTI loop s.o./s.t. over; 18:5

nakwât- VTA snare s.o.; 3:6

namatakwan- VII not exist, not be; 40:4; 42:54; cf. *'matakwan misiwê kêkwân kî-namatakwan wêmistikôšiwi-mîcim* all kinds of White-Man's food did not exist

namatâwêpali- VAI/VII be going out (as with an outboard motor or canoe); (41:1); cf. *...pali-*

namatâwêpâstan- VII move away from the shore (as a canoe); (41:1); cf. *wêpâstan-*

namatâwisatamohtâ- VAI-T build s.t. towards a body of water; 41:1

namatâwisi- VAI walk towards a body of water; (41:1)

nama tê- VAI not be, be absent; not show up; 4:5; 21:9; cf. *'matê-*

namayê- VAI/VII not be (heard only in contracted form); 41:2; 41:3; cf. *mayê-*

namêh- VTA see signs of s.o.; 6:7; 8:8; 10:7; 12:10; cf. *namêhtâ-*

namêhtâ- VAI-T leave signs of having been there; 10:7; 42:38; cf. *namêh-*

namês- NA fish; 26:2; 48:1; 58:5

namêsi-pimiy- NI fish fat; 14:3

namêsi-wîhkway- NI fish bladder; 14:4

namêsiskâ- VII be plentiful (of fish); 42:29; cf. *nêmiskâw-*

namipalihototaw- VTA lunge at s.o.; 31:2

nanahihtaw- VTA obey s.o.; 6:8

nanâhkaw IPC differently, variously; 3:1; of different colours; 14:6; 42:56

nanâhkawinâkosi- VAI appear differently, have different appearances; (42:55); cf. *pîtošinâkosi-*

nanâskostaw- VTA [redupl.] continually resist s.o., repeatedly fight back against s.o.; 9:2; cf. *naskostaw-*

nanâtawâpaht- VTI [redupl.] go looking for s.t.; 6:6; cf. *nâtawâpaht-*

nanâtawâpam- VTA [redupl.] go looking for s.o.; 3:7; 16:1; cf. *nâtawâpam-*

nanâtawi-pimâciho- VAI look for a living (SC); 3:2; cf. *nânatawi-pimâciho-*

nanêhkâcih- VTA be cruel to s.o., torment s.o., harass s.o., punish s.o.; 22:1; *êškwâ ka-nanêhkâcihitinâwâw* I'll be cruel to you, I'll torment you

nanêhkâci-pimâtisi- VAI live a wretched life, fall on hard times; (42:37)

nanêhkâsihtâkosi- VAI sound poorly, sound sickly, sound pathetic; (42:37); cf. *...ihtâkosi-*

nanêhkâsinâkosi- VAI look poorly, look sickly, look pathetic; 42:37; *êliwêhk nanêhkâsinâkosiw!* he looks really poorly! cf. *nanêhkâci-pimâtisi-, ...nâkosi-*

nanêskamikâ- VII [place name] 'be a point here and there (the land); run out in little points (the ground)'; 9:25; cf. *...askamik...*; the name at Fort Albany for the point in question is *nêscâw-*; at Moose Factory, the name is *macitêwêyâw-*

nanihcî- VAI be nervous; (9:21); 12:12; cf. *šâkwêlimo-*

nanihcîstaw- VTA fear s.o., dread s.o.; (9:21)

nanikwah- VTI [redupl.] bury s.t. here and there; (18:7); cf. *nikwah-, likwah-*

nanikwahw- VTA bury s.o. here and there; 18:7; cf. *nikwahw-, likwahw-*

nanipah- VTA [redupl.] kill s.o. off one after another; 44:1

nanôhtêpali- VAI/VII [redupl.] run short (recurrently); 42:14

napakâ- VII be flat; (18:6); 45:1

napakicâšê- VAI have a flat nose; (15:5); cf. *kînikicâšê-, kînikistawê-, kînikihtâwakê-, kînikitâmihkanê-, ...câš...*

napakicêh- VTA flatten s.o. out (by hand); 19:8

napakicê-wêpah- VTI throw and flatten s.t. out; 19:6

napakih- VTA flatten s.o.; (19:8)

napakihkot- VTA/VTI plane s.o./s.t. flat; 62:5; cf. *môhkot-*

napakisi- VAI be flat; 18:6; (45:1)

napaki-wêpiškaw- VTA flatten s.o. out; 18:6

napatê IPC sideways, with one eye; 55:2

napošêkâ- VII look flat; 8:5

nasko- VAI resist, put up resistance; (68:3)

naskostamâso- VAI defend oneself; (68:3); cf. *nâtamâso-*

naskostaw- VTA resist s.o., fight back against s.o.; (9:2)

naskowâkê- VAI resist by means of, use to resist; 9:10

naspâtakâm IPC wrong side; 42:47; cf. *naspâtaniskêsiw-, kwêskakâm*

naspâtaniskêsiw- NA mole (so called from having the front paws turned backwards); (42:47); cf. *kwêskakâm, naspâtakâm, ...nisk...*

naškwêwaših- VTA answer s.o.; 23:2

natah- VTI go upstream (by water); 62:3; 64:1; cf. *mâh-*

natahâšakâmê- VAI head upstream (walking); 18:1; cf. *...âšakâmê-*

natahi-otâpê- VAI haul upriver; 42:24

natahipahtwâ- VAI-T run s.t. upriver; 42:29

nataho- VAI hunt; 49:1

nataminaho- VAI hunt (usually waterfowl); 10:6; 17:1; 31:1; 59:1

natawah- VTA look for s.o.; 55:5

natawaho- VAI hunt; 21:2; 42:4

natawakotaskê- VAI go to hang moss (to dry); (51:1)

natawatihkwê- VAI go looking for caribou; (63:2)

natawâkošimôlo- VAI go looking for cover; 65:8

natawâmôswê- VAI moose-hunt; cf. *natawimôswê-*

natawâpaht- VTI go to see s.t., fetch s.t., investigate s.t.; 1:4; 13:3

natawâpam- VTA go to see s.o., fetch s.o., investigate s.o.; 1:3; 43:4; 56:2; *kîmôc antê n'tawâp'mêw* he stealthily sneaked up on them there

natawê IPV go to, go after; 44:4; [alternative form of *natawi*]

natawêlihcikê- VAI hunt, look for game; 37:1; 38:1

natawêliht- VTI want s.t.

natawêlim- VTA want s.o.; 9:12; 18:4

natawêlihtâkosi- VAI be necessary; (50:5); cf. *...ihtâkosi-*

natawêlihtâkwan- VII be necessary; 50:5; cf. *...ihtâkwan-*

nataw-êškê- VAI go chiselling (under the ice) for beaver; 60:8; 60:10; cf. *êškê-*

natawi-âšawahikê- VAI go to the (hunting) blind; (42:13)

natawiho- VAI hunt, go hunting; 41:12; 59:1; 65:2; cf. *nataminaho-*

natawi-mawiso- VAI go gathering berries; 65:9; cf. *natawiso-, mawiso-*

natawiminaho- VAI go hunting; 12:1

natawimôswê- VAI moose-hunt; 34:1

natawi-nôtâhtikwê- VAI go logging; 67:4; cf. *...âhtikw.../-*

natawi-pakitin- VTA/VTI go to put s.o./s.t., take s.o./s.t.; 9:2; 59:3

natawipalîstaw- VTA make war on s.o.; 30:1

natawi-papâmohtê- VAI walk about; 59:2; *pakwantaw n'taw'-papâmohtêw* he goes walking about at random; cf. *...ohtê-*

natawi-paškohamâ- VAI go for a haircut; (42:58)

natawi-pîhtokwê- VAI go to enter; 42:5; *kin'taw-pîhtokwân kîkihk* you go into your own home

natawiso- VAI look for berries; 65:9; cf. *natawi-mawiso-, mawiso-*

natawiš- VTI search for s.t. with a knife; (29:3); cf. *natôš-*

natawišipê- VAI hunt duck(s); 49:5; cf.
...*šip...*/-

natawišw- VTA search for s.o. with a
knife; 29:3; cf. *natôšw-*

natâmihk IPC underneath, beneath; at
the bottom [alternative form of
atâmihk]; 55:3; 60:10; 62:2

natimihk IPC upriver, upstream, inland;
37:2; 42:23; often with *itêhkê*, e.g.,
n'timihk itêhkê, or with *sîpiy*, e.g.,
natimihk sîpîhk; 44:3; cf. *mâmihk*

natimišîhk IPC above a point on a river,
up-current; (38:1); cf. *mâmišîhk*

natohkoh- VTA cure s.o., give s.o.
therapy; (41:5)

natohkoliy- NI medicine; (41:5)

natohkoliya kâ-iši-pîhtahikâtêki NI
[pl.] medicine cabinet, 'where
medicines are put in'

natohkoliya kâ-iši-têhtastâniwahki NI
[pl.] medicine shelf, 'where medicines
are placed on'

natohkolîwat- NI medicine chest,
medicine bag; (41:5); cf. ...*wat-*

natohkolon- NA doctor, physician (MC);
41:5; SC: *natohkonon-*

natohkonon- NA doctor, physician (SC);
(41:6)

natohkonon- NI medicine (SC); [the
distinction between *natohkolon-* and
natohkoliy-, as in MC, does not seem to
be made among SC speakers]

natoht- VTI listen to s.t.; 1:8; 13:3

natohtaw- VTA listen to s.o.; 18:3; 43:9

natom- VTA beckon to s.o., call s.o.,
invite s.o.; 55:1; 68:1

natonamaw- VTA 'feel s.o. up' (as in
sexual play); (55:9)

natonaw- VTA go searching for s.o.; cf.
nânatawâpam-

natonikê- VAI feel around; [contraction
of *nânatonikê-*]; 55:9; *kî-pîhtokwêw
nîkihk; misiwê kî-nân'tonikêw* he
entered (broke into) my house; he
ransacked it all over

natopit- VTA/VTI feel about for s.o./s.t.;
9:17; 42:22

natotamâ- VAI-T ask for s.t.; 60:5;
n'totamâw êlikohk k'ci-kimiwahk he

asks hard for it to rain

natôkaminamiskwê- VAI reach for
beaver in the water; 13:8; cf.
...*âkamin...*/-, ...*amiskw...*/-

natôkamin- VTA/VTI reach into the
water for s.o./s.t.; 13:4; 13:7; 13:8;
60:9; cf. ...*âkam...*

natôkaminikê- VAI grope in the water;
(13:9)

natômiskipo- VAI eat fat beaver;
êliwêhk natômiskipow he is eating fat
beaver; cf. *tômiskinawê-*, ...*po-*

natôš- VTI search for s.t. with a knife;
(5:7; 6:12); cf. *natawiš-*

natôšw- VTA search for s.o. with a knife;
5:7; 6:12; cf. *natawišw-*

nawac IPC pretty much, quite; 20:3; 49:1

nawacî- VAI eat en route, have a snack;
14:3

nawah- VTI go after s.t. by water; (34:3)

nawahaht- VTA track s.o. down;
[probable alternative form of
nawahât-]; 12:4; 22:9

nawahâc- VTA track s.o.; 12:2;
palatalized form of *nawahât-*

nawahât- VTA track s.o.; 12:1; 12:4;
12:13; *êkw isa n'tawac nawahâtâtâ* I
guess we'd better track him down 21:9

nawahw- VTA go after s.o. by water; 34:3

nawatin- VTA/VTI grab s.o./s.t., catch
s.o./s.t. in his hand; 10:9; 13:11; 29:2

nawinêhw- VTA get after s.o.; 13:11

nayêwac IPC near the end; 6:1; *nayêwac
piko anta n'ka-ohci-kihtâhtanôhkân*
I'm going to start the story from near
the end

nâ IPC question marker in yes-no
questions; 1:4 et passim;
kiwî-wâpahtênâwâw nâ nêma askiy?
do you want to see yon land?

nâ'c IPC very much [contraction of
nâsic]; 46:2; 49:1

nâcikâpawîstaw- VTA stand close to
s.o.; (19:8); *pêci-nâcikâpawîstawin*
come stand close to me; cf. ...*kâpawi-*

nâci-mîcimê- VAI go for food; 43:6; n.
43:11

nâcipah- VTA run to s.o., run for s.o.;
12:7; 13:17

nâcipahtwâ- VAI-T run to s.t., run for s.t.; 12:4; 50:1; 51:1

nâcistâ- VAI draw close; 19:8; 27:3

nâhic IPC very much [allegro for *nâšic*]; 55:2

nâhitê IPC very, really [allegro for *nâsitê*; contraction of *nâspic tâpwê*]; 55:7

nâhitêpi IPC very much, altogether [allegro for *nâspitêpi*]; 55:6

nâhîtâk IPC as it happened; *nahîtâk êtokwê kâ-wâpamitân* as it happened, I saw you (ran into you)

nâhtâ' IPC very much indeed [contraction of *nâhtâpwê*]; 48:1; 55:7

nâhtâpwê IPC very much indeed; [contraction of *nâspic tâpwê*]; 49:1

nâkacih- VTA watch s.o., look after s.o.; 65:2

nâkê IPC later, later on; 2:7

nâkociy- NA [proper name] Nagochee, 42:65; 44:3

nâmiskwêstâ- VAI bow the head; (56:5) *nâmiskwêstâ* bow your head; cf. *itiskwêstâ-, nânâmiskwêpaliho-, wêwêpiskwêpaliho-, ...iskw...*

nâmowin IPC to leeward; 42:38; cf. *nânim*

nâmowinâ- VII be a tail wind; 42:22; cf. *lâlimâ-*

nâmowinâši- VAI sail with the wind or with a fair wind (on water or in the air); 42:22; cf. *...âši-*

nânakacâskwahtin- VII [redupl.] bump into; (13:9)

nânakacâskwašin- VAI [redupl.] bump headlong into; 13:9; (*amiskwak*) *pêci-nânakacâskwašinwak anta kistâkanihk* (the beaver) are bumping headlong into the enclosure

nânakacih- VTA [redupl.] keep an eye on s.o.; 8:7

nânakânomâso- VAI [redupl.] defend oneself; 12:10

nânapakah- VTI flatten s.t.; (56:7)

nânapakahw- VTA flatten s.o.; 56:7

nânatawâpaht- VTI [redupl.] search for s.t.; 13:2; 55:8; 65:6

nânatawâpam- VTA look for s.o.; (30:1; n. 30:1); cf. *nânatawipalîstaw-*

nânatawiho- VAI [redupl.] hunt around; 60:2

nânatawi-kiskêlimito- VAI [recipr.] search to know each other; 30:1

nânatawi-mîciso- VAI [redupl.] go in search of something to eat; 65:2

nânatawipalîstaw- VTA [redupl.] be 'after' s.o. (as opposed to *nânatawâpam-* look for s.o. quietly and peacefully); 30:1; n. 30:1

nânatawi-pimâciho- VAI [redupl.] look for a living (MC); n. 3:3; [usually contracted to *nân'taw'pimâciho-*]; cf. *nanâtawi-pimâciho-*

nânatawiš- VTI [redupl.] search for s.t. by cutting; (29:3); cf. *nân'tawiš-*

nânatawišw- VTA [redupl.] search for s.o. by cutting; 29:3; cf. *nânatawišw-*

nânaton- VTI search for s.t. by feeling; (60:8); cf. *kîton-, kîtowâpaht-*

nânatonaw- VTI search for s.o. by feeling; (60:8); cf. *kîtonaw-, kîtowâpam-*

nânatonikê- VAI [redupl.] search around; (55:9)

nânâkêh IPC a short while after (MC); 55:5; 56:3; cf. *nâkê(h)*

nânâmiskwêpaliho- VAI [redupl.] nod assent (several nods); (56:5); cf. *itiskwêli-, itiskwêstâ-, nâmiskwêstâ-, wêwêpiskwêpaliho-, ...iskw......paliho-*

nânânatôtamaw- VTA [redupl.] keep on asking s.o. (for it); 2:10

nânâtwâkahihtê- VAI [redupl.] be cutting wood in small lengths; 14:5; [probable contraction of *nânâtwâkahînihtê-*]

nânâtwâkahênihtê- VAI [redupl.] be cutting wood in small lengths; (14:5; 43:4); cf. *...iht.../-*

nânêwê- VAI skirt or walk along the edge of the green bush (SC); MC: *lâlêwê-*

nânih IPC alongside of [usually with locative] (SC); MC: *lâlih*

nânihcî- VAI be nervous; 12:12

nânim IPC to windward; cf. *nâmowin*

nânipah- VTA [redupl.] kill s.o.

repeatedly; 12:8

nânipi- VAI [redupl.] die here and there or all around; 41:14

nânîpawi- VAI [redupl.] stand around; 13:6; 41:1; 43:2

nânîsânisî- VAI risk repeatedly, endanger; 42:33; cf. *nîsânisî-*

nânîwêkotê- VII hang limp; 13:11

nân'tawi-kiskêlimito- VAI [recipr.] search to know each other; 30:1

nân'tawiš- VTI [redupl.] search for s.t. by cutting; (29:3); [contraction of *nânatawiš-*]

nân'tawišw- VTA [redupl.] search for s.o. by cutting; 29:3; [contraction of *nânatawišw-*]

n'-âpacihat [VTA] the heck with him! (43:5); cf. *t'-âpacihat*

n'-âpatisiyan [VAI] you're useless! 16:5; e.g., *n'-âpatisiyan wâ-mîcisoyan* you're useless, but are always wanting to eat

nâpêsis- NA boy; 6:3; 40:7

nâpêw- NA man, husband; 1:3; 21:3; cf. *...âpêw-*

nâsic IPC very much; 38:2; also as *nâsic*; cf. *nâspic*

nâsipê- VAI go down the bank (SC); 55:7; 63:3; 68:6; MC: *lâsipê-*

nâsipêpahtâ- VAI run down the bank (SC); 11:7; 56:8; MC: *lâsipêpahtâ-*; cf. *...pahtâ-*

nâsipêpalih- VTA let s.o. go down (Kashechewan usage); (43:32); MC: *lâsipêpalih-*; SC: *nâsipêpanih-*

nâsipêpalihtwâ- VAI-T let s.t. go down (Kashechewan usage); (43:32); MC: *lâsipêpalihtwâ-*; SC: *nâsipêpanihtwâ-*

nâsipêtâpê- VAI haul down the bank (SC); 65:4; MC: *lâsipêtâpê-*; *...tâpê-*

nâsipê-wêpin- VTA/VTI throw s.o./s.t. down the slope; 42:32; cf. *nâsipêpalih-*, *nâsipêpalihtwâ-*

nâspic IPC very, very much; 1:3; 8:6; 36:2

nâspic mistahi IPC to a considerable extent; 42:11

nâspic têpi IPC very much, altogether; 19:3; *nâspitêpi ninahâpin* I have very good eyesight; cf. *nâspitêpi*

nâspici IPV for good, permanently; 43:2; *kinâspici-kihtohtân* you are going away for good

nâspici-ihtâ- VAI stay for good; 58:6

nâspitahw- VTA kill s.o. outright, kill s.o. stone dead; 9:23; 12:7; *nâspitahokow* he is killed outright

nâspitâskiso- VAI be utterly burned up; 8:8

nâspitêpi IPC very much, altogether; 13:12; 19:3; 42:60; 44:2; 66:2

nâšic IPC very much; 3:4; 38:2; cf. *nâsic*, *nâspic*

nâtahâkonê- VAI go to get snow; 5:9; 6:14; 13:17; cf. *...âkon...*

nâtah- VTI fetch s.t. by water, go after s.t. by water; (4:2; 29:1; 61:6; 64:1)

nâtahamê- VAI head along the track (as when after s.t.); 14:4; *'kwâni manâ mâk' ê-'t'-îši-nâtahamêt pîniš manâ mâka nêtêpêšiwâpahtam* then as he started to head for it, at last he came close to it

nâtahw- VTA fetch s.o. by water, go after s.o. by water; 4:2; 29:1; 61:6; 64:1

nâtakah- VTI paddle towards shore; (9:3); cf. *nimitâwah-*

nâtamâso- VAI defend oneself (without help), take care of oneself; (68:3); cf. *naskostamâso-*

nâtaskê- VAI go to gather moss (for diapers); (51:1; n. 51:2); cf. *nâtawakotaskê-*, *...ask.../-*

nâtaw' IPC [possibly stands for *nâhtâpwê*, very much indeed, 58:3]

'nâtawâkahênihcêši- VAI [redupl.; dim.] chop a little bit of wood (like a small child playing around); 43:4: for *nâtwâkahênihcêši-*; cf. *nâtawâkahênihtê-*

'nâtawâkahênihtê- VAI [redupl.] cut wood in short blocks (i.e., at home after longer pieces have been brought in); (14:5; 43:4): for *nâtwâkahênihtê*; cf. *nânâtwâkahênihtê-*, *...iht.../-*; [contraction of *nanâtwâkahênihtê-*]

'nâtawamôswê- VAI [redupl.] go looking for moose; 35:1; 49:1; [contraction of *nanâtawamôswê-*]; cf. *...môsw.../-*

'nâtawatihkwê- VAI [redupl.] go after
caribou, go caribou-hunting; 10:6;
[contraction of *nanâtawatihkwê-*]; cf.
...atihkw.../-

'nâtawâpam- VTA [redupl.] go looking
for s.o.; 3:7; 12:10; 35:1; [contraction of
nanâtawâpam-]

'nâtawi IPV [redupl.] go to (do
something); 9:13; [contraction of
nanâtawi]

'nâtawim- VTA [redupl.] search for s.o.;
35:2; [contraction of *nanâtawim-*]

'nâtawimôswê- VAI [redupl.] go
moose-hunting; 34:1; [contraction of
nanâtawimôswê-]; cf. 'nâtawamôswê-

nâtawiyêw- NA Iroquois; 30:1; [more
properly: *nâtawêw*]; cf.
nâtawiyêwastimw-

nâtawiyêwastimw- NA hunting dog;
(30:1; n. 30:2); cf. *...astimw-*

nâtâhtawitotaw- VTA go up the tree to
s.o.; 2:7; *pêci-nâtâhtawitotawinân*
come up the tree to us!

nâtinihtê- VAI get wood; (11:7); cf.
manihtê-, miht-

nâtwâ-wêpin- VTA/VTI snap s.o./s.t. off
by hand; 19:9

nâtwâkanêšin- VAI slide and break
one's bones; (12:15)

nâtwâkanê-wêpahw- VTA break s.o.'s
bones; 12:15

nâtwân- VTA/VTI break s.o./s.t. in two,
snap s.o./s.t. in two; 13:11; *aspin manâ
niyâtwânahk* breaking it in two

nâtwânikâtê- VII be broken (in two);
13:11

nâtwâtihtâ- VAI-T break s.t., snap s.t.;
13:14

nâwinâkosi- VAI appear at a distance;
9:17; MC: *lâwinâkosi-*

nâwinâkwan- VII appear at a distance;
(9:17); MC: *lâwinâkwan-*

nêkaw- NI sand (SC); 18:7; MC: *lêkaw-*

nêma PR yonder one [demonstrative
inan.prox.sing]; 1:3; 19:2

nêmiskâw- NI [place name] Namiskau,
Quebec, lit., 'plentiful fish', (settlement
located about 160 kilometres up the
Rupert's River from James Bay);

42:29; cf. *namêsiskâ-*

nênîši- VAI [redupl.] be (continuously)
two; 6:3

nênîšo IPC [redupl.] twice each; 10:7

nênîšohtatâ- VAI-T [redupl.] put two of
s.t. together; 55:6; n. 55:18

nênîšohtin- VII lie in pairs; (55:6)

nêscâ- VII be a point that carries a ridge
of gravel or sand on it; (58:3); cf.
macitêwêyâ-, macitêwêyâpiskâ-

nêšitâmipali- VAI/VII be going wrong,
not go the right way; (42:11); cf.
macipali-, ...pali-

nêsta IPC and, also; 1:1 et passim

nêstapiko IPC or; n. 3:2 et passim

nêtê IPC yonder (further away than
anta; 1:3; 2:2; 36:1

nêtitišiy- NI [place name] Netitishi (one
of two good camping spots between
Hannah Bay and Moose Factory);
(67:2); n. 67:3

nêw IPC four; (41:18); also as *nêyaw*

nêwac IPC right off; 42:22; *nêwac piko
nêwatahtam* he grabs it right off (of a
fish grabbing a hook on the fly)

nêwataht- VTI grab s.t. off; (42:22)

nêwâ IPC four times; 42:12; 42:26

nêwi- VAI be four, be four of them; 21:6;
37:1

nêwin- VII be four, be four of them; 36:2

nêwišâp IPC fourteen; cf. *nêyošâpw*

nêyošâp IPC fourteen; 41:18; 58:1; cf.
nêwišâpw

nihcikašakê- VAI have dark skin, have
dark complexion; (10:7); cf. *wašakaya,
wâpašakê-, ...ašak...*

nihci-kâskis- VTI blacken s.t. by
burning; (11:13); cf. *câkâskis-*

nihci-kâskisêwikin- VTA/VTI blacken
s.o./s.t. by burning, probably with
charcoal; 11:13; cf. *câkâskis-,
câkâskiso-, câkâskitê-*

nihci-kâskiso- VAI be burned black,
burn black; (11:13)

nihci-kâskisw- VTA blacken s.o. by
burning; (11:13); cf. *câkâskisw-*

nihci-kâskitê- VII be burned black, burn
black; (11:13)

nihcikâ- VII be dark coloured; (11:13); cf.

pêci-nihcikâ-

nihcikihtin- VII be a dark blotch; 19:2; cf. *matê-nihcikihtin-*

nihcikinawê- VAI have a dark face; (10:8); considered better usage than *mahkatêwanawê-*; cf. *...anaw...*

nihcikisi- VAI be dark coloured; (11:13)

nihcikišin- VAI be a dark blotch; (19:2); cf. *papâ-nihcikišin-*

nihkwan- NDA my ankle [variant of *nahkon-*]; (65:8); cf. *ohkwan-*; *ohkwana*; *wahkon-*

nihtâ IPV good at (doing s.t.); 11:3; 14:4; 63:1; given to (doing s.t.); *nihtâ-wâwiw* she's a good egg-layer; *kâ-nihtâ-tôtahk* which he was good at doing; *kî-n'tâ-n'tawihow* he was good at hunting

nihtâwiki- VAI be born, grow; (42:55)

nihtâwikih- VTA give birth to s.o., bear s.o.; 1:9; (2:9); 11:1; bring s.o. up; 51:2; cf. *âmo-, okosisi-, pâškahâwê-, wâpamâwaso-*

nihtâwikihcikê- VAI plant a garden; 41:10

nihtâwikihito- VAI [recipr.] bring each other up; 2:9; *kî-nihtâwikihitowak* they brought each other up; [preferred variant: *kî-ohpikihitowak*]

nihtâwikin- VII grow; 42:55

nikamo- VAI sing; 18:2; 60:5

nikamôwiniwat- NI song bag; 18:2; cf. *...wat-*

nikikostikwân(iš)- NI [place name] Otter Head Creek, lit., 'little otter head'

nikâwiy- NDA my mother; 10:5; 63:3; cf. *okâwiya; okâwîmâw-*

nikikw- NA otter; 1:7; 8:6; 40:5

nikiko-wayân- NA otter skin; 2:10

nikosis- NDA my son; n. 12:21; cf. *okosisimâw-; ...kosis-...*

nikotwâs IPC six; 38:3; 39:2

nikotwâsomitana IPC sixty; 41:17; 43:6; *n'kotwâsomitana niyâlošâp* sixty-five; 41:17

nikwah- VTI cover s.t., bury s.t. (as an animal buries food) (SC); (13:15; 18:7); MC: *likwah-*

nikwahw- VTA cover s.o., bury s.o. (as an animal buries food) (SC); 1; 3:15; 18:7; MC: *likwahw-*

nikwâwahahkatêpo- VAI bury under the hot sand and cook (SC); 18:7; MC: *likwahahkatêpo-*; cf. *...têpo-*

nimis- NDA my older sister; 3:3; cf. *omisimâw-, omisa, ...mis-*

nimiš- NDA my older sister; 4:3; affected palatalization to show baby talk, as used by Chahkabesh, who is a small person; [archaic vocative: *nimišê-*, used as normal mention case, 13:16]; cf. *nimis-*

nimitâwah- VTI paddle out from the land; 9:3; cf. *nâtakah-*

nimitâwêhol- VTA take s.o. out in a canoe away from land; 11:3

nimitâwêhtin- VII run out (like a buttress); (41:19)

nimitâwêpali- VAI swim quickly away from shore; 9:6; cf. *...pali-*

nimitâwêšin- VAI run out like a buttress; 41:19

nimitâwê-wêpah- VTI push s.t. (i.e., the canoe) away from shore; 11:4

nimitâwih- VTI go along the coast; 65:2

nimošôm- NDA my grandfather

ninahâhkaniskwêm- NDA my daughter-in-law; (60:3); cf. *onahâhkaniskwêmimâw-, onahâhkaniskwêma, ...nahâhkaniskwêm-*

ninahâhkišîm- NDA my son-in-law; 11:3; cf. *onahâhkišîma, onahâhkišîmimâw-*

ninihkêlimo- VAI be tense, be uptight; (13:9; 14:5)

ninihkikaškwêpali- VAI tremble (as when knocked out); (14:5); cf. *kîškikašêšotisiwin-, ninihkikaškwê-wêpahw-, ...kaškw..., ...pali-*

ninihkikaškwê-wêpahw- VTA sweep s.o. away with talons shaking; hit s.o. so that his claws tremble or shake; 14:5; *kâ-mohci-ninihkikaškwê-wêpahwât* she just swept him away so that his talons were shaking; cf. *ninihkipali-, oškašiya, tâškikaškwêpali-*

503

ninihkinâkosi- VAI appear to shake,
appear to tremble; 13:9; cf.
taši-ninihkinâkosi-, *ninihkipali-*,
ninihki-wêpâstan-, *...nâkosi-*

ninihkinikê- VAI have shaking hands or
arms; (13:9); cf. *ninihki-wêpâstan-*

ninihkipali- VAI/VII be shaking, be
trembling; (13:9; 14:5); cf. *...pali-*

ninihki-wêpâstan- VII blow trembling;
(13:9) *ninihki-wêpâstanwanîpîša* the
leaves are trembling in the breeze; cf.
ninihkinâkosi-, *ninihkipali-*

ninikon- NDA my son-in-law; cf.
ninikwan, *...nikon-*

ninikwan- NDA my son-in-law; 11:3;
11:9; cf. *onikwana*, *...nikwan-*

ninîkihikwak NDA [pl.] my parents; 5:3;
6:2; 11:2; cf. *onîkihikwa*, *...nîkihikw-*

nipah- VTA kill s.o.; 5:3; 10:10; 13:10;
21:7; 27:2

nipahikêwâkê- VAI kill using s.t., use
s.t. to kill; 9:17

nipahišin- VAI kill oneself falling, die
from a fall; 20:6; 41:14

nipahito- VAI [recipr.] kill each other;
9:14

nipahiwê- VAI kill; 60:9

nipahtamaw- VTA kill it for s.o.; 60:3;
êko mâka, ka-nipahtamâkowâw mîcim
and then, he'll kill some meat for you

nipahtâ- VAI-T kill s.t.; 40:2

nipâ- VAI sleep; 3:4; 8:7; 18:8; 35:1;
nipâtê when he's asleep; cf.
...ihkwâmi-, *...ihkwaši-*

nipâhkâso- VAI pretend to sleep; 9:17;
cf. *nipâ-*, *...hkâso-*

nipâkan- NI bed roll; 37:4

nipâwiyi- VAI yawn; 55:4

nipêwin- NI bed; cf. *nîhtin-*

nipi- VAI die; 9:9; 11:2; 44:4; 59:2

nipiy- NI water; 4:2; 38:3; cf. *...âkam...*,
...kam..., *...kamiy-*

nipîwan- VII be wet, be 'green' (of wood);
42:59; cf. *aškiškâhtikw-*

nipîwi- VAI be wet; 61:3

nipîwihtâ- VAI-T wet s.t., get s.t. wet;
11:11

nisâwîh- VTA gather up small details of
s.o. all at once; (41:10); often with

kîšâc ahead of time, in preparation

nisâwîhtâ- VAI-T gather up small details
of s.t. all at once; (41:10); cf. *nisâwîh-*

niscikikonêwênâkosi- VAI appear dark
throated; 8:8; cf. *nihci...*, *...konêw...*,
...nâkosi-

nisitawêniw- VTA recognize s.o.; 9:18;
[possibly a blend of *nisitawênim-* and
nisitawinaw-]

nisitawin- VTI recognize s.t. by sight;
37:3

nisis- NDA my father-in-law; (11:16); cf.
osisimâw-; *osisa*

nisitawinamêh- VTA recognize s.o. from
the signs (e.g., one might recognize
another's work in cutting down a tree
from the axe cut); 4:5;

nisitawinaw- VTA recognize s.o. by
sight; (37:3)

nisitohtâto- VAI understand each other;
2:10

nisitokanê- VII have a (rich) taste or
flavour (as a bone); 60:10

nisitosi- VAI have feeling, have
sensation; 43:5; *môna nisîtosiw
ocihcîhk* he has no feeling in his
hand(s); *môna nisitosiw ositihk* he has
no feeling in his foot/feet

nisitospakwan- VII have a taste, have
flavour; (60:10); cf. *...ispakwan-*

nisitwâ- VII have a nice taste, have a
good flavour; 60:10

nisk- NA goose; 18:1; 55:3; 61:1

niski-pîsimw- NA April, lit., 'goose
moon'; cf. *pîsimw-*

niskihkwâmi- VAI fall asleep; sleep
soundly (SC); 9:17; MC: *liskihkwâmi-*

nistâpâwê- VAI drown; 27:5; (61:6); cf.
kawatâpâwê-

nisti- VAI be three; 21:6

nistikwân- NDI my head; 9:4; cf.
ostikwân-, *...stikwân-*, *...iskw...*

nisto-kîšikâw IPC period of three days,
for three days; 35:2; 39:4

nist'-ominikošiš IPC [calque] three
minute period, for three minutes; 19:4;
cf. *ominikw-*, *ominikošiš-*

nistomitana IPC thirty; 44:2; 61:1

nistopahtâ- VAI run as three together; 21:6; cf. ...*pahtâ-*

nisto-pipon IPC three year period, for three years; 39:3

nistošimo- VAI dance three together; cf. ...*šimo-*

nistôtêw IPC (as) three couples, (as) three families; (1:9); *niwâpamâwak nistôtêw nêtê ê-pimohtêcik* I see three families walking over there; cf. *kistôtêw, nîšôtêw,* ...*ôtêw...*

nistôtêwisi- VAI be (travelling as) three families; (1:9)

nistwâ IPC three times; 42:26

nišiwanâcih- VTA destroy s.o.; 6:7; 6:10; 59:3; 60:10

nišiwanâcihitiso- VAI completely destroy oneself, cripple oneself; 27

nišiwanâciho- VAI destroy oneself; 65:9

nišiwanâcihtâ- VAI-T spoil s.t., destroy s.t.; 68:4

nišîm- NDA my younger sibling; 4:6; 19:1; 20:2; cf. *ošîma,* ...*šîm-*

ništam IPC first (ordinal); 37:2; at first; 39:1; cf. *nîštam*

ništi- VAI be three [variant of *nisti-*]; 60:8

nitêm- NDA my dog; (33); cf. ...*têm-, atimw-, âtawâpiskâtowastimw-, kêšîciwanowastimw-,* ...*astimw-*

nitôtêm- NDA my friend; 44:4; cf. *otôtêmimâw-, otôtêma,* ...*tôtêm-*

niyâlan IPC five; 40:5; 42:25

niyâli- VAI be five; 58:4

niyâlomitana IPC fifty; 42:24; 42:36; 52:2

niyâlošâp IPC fifteen; 41:17; *n'kotwâsomitana niyâlošâp* sixty-five (not seventy-five, as in French)

niyâlošâp'-ahtay- NA (amount of) fifteeen dollars; 42:24; n. 42:38

niyânânêwi- VAI be eight; 13:6

niyânânêwimitana IPC eighty; 41:18

niyânânêw'-pipon IPC eight year period, eight years; 42:3

nîcihkawêsiw- NA my cousin or brother; 43:3; cf. ...*îcihkawêsiw-*

nîci-iskwêšiš- NA my girl companion; 65:7; cf. *wîci-*

nîhci-twêho- VAI alight on the ground, land; 14:5; cf. *twêho-*

nîhtahw- VTA knock s.o. down; 6:12

nîhtan- VTA/VTI take s.o./s.t. down; [variant of *nîhtin-*]; *êko mîn' nîhtanâkaniwicik aniki wâpoš-'iyânak* then those rabbit skins are taken down, 52:1

nîhtâpihkên- VTA/VTI lower s.o./s.t. on a line or rope; 1:4; [synonym: *lâsâpihkên-*]; cf. *pakitâpihkên-,* ...*âpihk...*

nîhtin- VTA/VTI take s.o./s.t. down, lower s.o./s.t.; 52:1; (n. 2:1) *nîhtin nipêwinihk ohci* lower him from the bed; *nîhtin mêmêpisonihk ohci* lower him from the swing; *nîhtin iskwâtawînâhtikohk ohci* lower him off the ladder

nîkân IPC ahead, out front, in advance; in the future; 30:2; 41:10; 42:6; 42:16; 49:1; *ki'y-at'-ohci-pimâtisin'ci nîkân ocawâšimiša 'ntê itêhkê* so their children will make a living from it in the future ahead 41:10; *ta-kîy-ati-pimâcihitisowak nîkân itêhkê* they will be able to begin supporting themselves in the future 42:6

nîkânahw- VTA put (clock) ahead; (56:1); cf. *ašêhw-, âhtahw-*

nîkânipali- VAI/VII be out ahead, be in the lead; 49:3; cf. ...*pali-*

nîkânisî- VAI be leader; 46:1

nîkânî- VAI be foremost, be ahead, be in the lead; 20:4; *kâ-nîkânît wêhwêw* the chief wavey

nîki NDI [sg.] my home; 4:5; cf. *wîki,* ...*îk-*

nîla PR I (MC); 9:4; SC: *nîna*

nîlanân PR we [excl.] (i.e., excluding addressee(s)) (MC); 34:3; 40:2; 49:1; SC: *nînanân*

nîmâ- VAI take provisions for travelling; 14:3

nîmâskwahw- VTA hang s.o. on a pole; 52:1; cf. ...*âskw...*/-

nîmi- VAI dance; 8:2; 18:4; 49:5; 55:2; *nîminâniwan* one gives a dance, a

dance is given; cf. *ayasikwêšimo-*,
...*šimo-*

nîmihiwê- VAI throw a dance; 8:2

nîmihkâso- VAI pretend to dance; 55:2;
cf. ...*hkâso-*

nîna PR I (SC); 10:7; MC: *nîla*

nînanân PR we [excl.] (i.e., excluding
addressee(s)) (SC); MC: *nîlanân*

nînistam PR I first, I in my turn; 10:7

nîpawi- VAI stand; 2:3; 13:11; 43:10;
56:2; 65:9; 66:3; *ê-matwê-nîpawit*
(discerned) standing (at a distance);
kî-nîpawiw wêhwêw he turned into
(lit., 'stood as') a goose; cf. ...*kâpawi-*

nîpin- NI summer; 41:14

nîpin- VII be summer; 22:1; 39:2; 44:2

nîpinohk IPC last summer; 41:12; 42:64

nîpisiy- NI willow; 55:9; 66:1

nîpisiyâhtiko-mistikw- NI willow-wood
stick; 24:1; cf. ...*âhtik...*/-, *mistikw-*

nîpisîskâhk IPC in among the willows;
66:1; [synonym: *mêkwêhkop*]; cf.
lâlihkop, ...*hkop*...

nîpitêhpiso- VAI hang from a line in a
row, be strung from a line in a row;
9:15

nîpitêhpitê- VII hang from a line in a
row, be strung from a line in a row;
9:15

nîpitêkâpawi- VAI stand in line; 49:5;
cf. *pîhtinikêkâpawi-*, ...*kâpawi-*

nîpîš- NI leaf

nîpîšišiwan- VII have little leaves, be
small leaves; 42:58

nîsânisî- VAI risk; 42:33; *ta-nîsânisîw
'ci-cîkahotisot* he will risk cutting
himself; cf. *nânîsânisî-*

nîstâw- NDA my brother-in-law; (60:8);
cf. *wîstâwimâw-*, *wîstâwa*, *nîstâw-*,
...*îstaw-*

nîswâs IPC seven; 39:2

nîswâsi- VAI be seven; 13:13

nîswâskwan- VII be seven (of something
wooden); 61:3; cf. ...*âskw...*/-

nîswâsomitana niyâlan IPC seventy-
five; 61:1; note hyper-corrected form,
niyâlal; cf. n. 61:4

nîswâso-pipon IPC seven year period,
for seven years; 42:3

nîswâsošâp IPC seventeen; 41:18

nîšâhtawî- VAI go down; 1:5; cf.
walawî-nîšâhtawî-

nîšâhtawîpali- VAI go down; 41:19; cf.
nîšâhtawîyâpihkêpali-, ...*pali-*

nîšâhtawîtah- VTA bring or take s.o.
down; 1:8; 2:8

nîšâhtawîtatâ- VAI-T bring or take s.t.
down; (1:8; 2:8)

nîšâhtawîyâpihkêpali- VAI/VII go down
on a line or cord (used for an elevator);
(41:19); cf. ...*âhtawî-*, ...*âpihk*...,
...*pali-*

nîšâpihkên- VTA/VTI lower s.o./s.t. on a
line; 2:5; cf. ...*âpihk*...

nîši- VAI be two; 2:2; 6:3; 9:17; 11:3; 29:1;
42:42; 64:2; *n'kî-ati-nîšinân* we began
to team up

nîšin- VII be two; (2:2; 6:3; 9:17; 11:3;
29:1; 42:42; 64:2)

nîšitana IPC twenty; 42:25; 58:5;
nîšitanawêkonakisiw January it is the
twentieth of January; (58:5)
*nîšitana-n'kotwâs' šîpokonakisiw
October* it is the twenty-sixth of
October

nîšo IPC two; 1:3; 8:6; 25:1; *nîšo mîna
âpihtaw* half past two

nîšocihc IPC with both hands; 13:10; cf.
...*cihc*...

nîšohkaw- VTA they work at s.o. two
together; 50:5; cf. *pêyakohkaw-*

nîšohtay IPC amount of two dollars;
42:12; cf. ...*ahtay-*

nîšokamikisi- VAI be two families; 21:1;
cf. *pêyakotênaw, pêyakokamikisi-*,
...*ikamikisi-*

nîšokonakisi- VAI be the second day;
(58:3); cf. ...*ikonak*...

nîšokoni- VAI be away two days (and
nights), as when hunting; (58:3); cf.
...*ikon*...

nîšokwên- VTA hold two of s.o. by the
neck; (18:5); cf. *ayasikwên-*, ...*ikw*...

nîšokwêšimo- VAI two dance with necks
together; (18:5; 55:2); (for any number
higher than 'two', usage reverts to
ayasi...)

nîšo-piponêsi- VAI be two years old; 65:2

nîšošâp IPC twelve; 58:5

nîšo-tašîhkê- VAI dwell two together; 56:1

nîšôtêw IPC (as) two families, two couples (i.e., of a man and woman each); cf. *kistôtêw, nistôtêw, ...ôtêw...*

nîšôtêwisi- VAI be (travelling) as two families

nîšo-tipahikan IPC period of two hours (i.e., two measures); 18:8; 21:3; distance of two miles; 37:6

nîštam IPC first (in order); 1:2; 6:2; 19:5; 37:1; 41:14; 62:1. [*nîštam kâ-ohcît:* synonym for *ostêsimâw*]; cf. *ništam, ohcî-*

nîštamišk- VTI come upon s.t. first; 9:18

nîštamošân- NA first child; cf. *mâhcicošân-, ...šân-, ohcî-*

nîšwâ IPC twice; 2:4; 11:11; 41:18; 42:36

nîšwâskon- VTA/VTI hold two stick-like entities; *nîšwâskona* hold two sticks! cf. *pêyakwâskwamo-, ...âskw.../-*

nîšwâskosi- VAI (trees) stand two together; 19:8; cf. *...âskw.../-*

nîšwâskwamo- VAI (two sticks) stand side by side, be two sticks; 19:8; cf. *pêyakwâskwamo-*

nîwatiyâskocimo- VAI squeeze one's belly with trees

nîyak PR I too; 10:10; cf. n. 10:23

n'kotwâs IPC six; 38:3; cf. *nikotwâs*

nohtâkosi- VAI call, sound; [allegro for *nôhtâkosi-*]; 9:5; 43:10

nohtâkwan- VII sound; [allegro for *nôhtâkwan-*]; 9:15; 55:4

nôcih- VTA hunt s.o., work at s.o., busy oneself with s.o., follow her (as a dog a female); 13:4; 21:2; 43:7; 47:1; *namêsa nôcihêwak* they go after fish

nôcihtâ- VAI-T work with s.t.; 40:6; *wanahikan' âta ê-nôcihtât* even though he tends his traps

nôcihtâhkâso- VAI pretend to work on it; 11:12; cf. *...hkâso-*

nôcîskwêwê- VAI court, flirt; cf. n. 2:6

nôcîskwêwêhkâso- VAI pretend to flirt, pretend to court; cf. n. 2:6,

...iskwêw.../-, ...hkâso-

nôhcimihk IPC in the forest, in the bush; 19:2; 34:1; 40:1; 51:3

nôhcimîw'-ililiw- NA man of the forest (description of *pakwacililiw-*); 64

nôhkom- NDA my grandmother; (9:8; 27:7); cf. *ôhkomimâw-, ohkoma*

nôhkomis- NDA my step-father, my uncle; 10:8; cf. *ôhkomisa, ...ôhkomis-*

nôhtaw IPC short of; 7:3; 42:33; *nôhtaw kî-nistâpâwêw* he drowned short of his destination

nôhtawi IPV short of; *n'kî-nôhtawi-kapêšin* we camped short of our destination

nôhtâkosi- VAI make a sound; 9:15 et passim; cf. *nohtâkosi-, ...ihtâkosi-*

nôhtâkwan- VII make a sound; (9:15) et passim; cf. *nohtâkwan-, ...ihtâkwan-*

nôhtâwiy- NDA my father (9:9; 9:20; 54:3); cf. *ôhtâwimâw-, ôhtâwiya, ...ôhtâwiy-*

nôhtê-âhkosi- VAI fall sick (e.g., before one can do something)

nôhtêhkwaši- VAI fall asleep because one cannot stay awake any longer (as a child when adults are talking), fall asleep in spite of oneself; (9:7); cf. *liskihkwâmi-, šâkotihkwaši-, ...ihkwaši-*

nôhtêkâmêhâ- VAI not make it, fall short (e.g., when jumping across something, a ditch or space); 11:8; cf. *...akâm...*

nôhtêkâmêpali- VAI not make it when jumping (e.g., a creek) (MC); (11:8); cf. *...pali-*

nôhtê-kipihcihtâ- VAI-T put a stop to s.t.; 42:46; *payihtaw mâka kî-nôhtê-kipihcihtâwak* the trouble is, though, they finally put a stop to it; cf. *nôhtê(y)-âhkosi-, nôhtê-kipihcî-* or *nôhtaw kipihcî-, nôhtê-pîkopali-*

nôhtê-kipihcî- VAI stop short (of a destination); *kî-nôhtê-kipihcîw* or *nôhtaw kî-kipihcîw* he stopped short (of a place)

nôhtêpali- VAI/VII run short (of some commodity); 39:4; 42:34; *êko wâs' âni* *ê-nôhtêpaliyahk* so we're running short; *kêhcin n'ka-nôhtêpalin cîstâskwâna* I'll run short of nails for sure; cf. *...pali-*

nôhtê-pâšici-kwâškwati- VAI fail to jump over it; (11:8)

nôhtê-pîkopali- VAI/VII break up short of

nôkosi- VAI appear, come into sight; 5:7; 34:1

nôkwan- VII appear, come into sight; 41:2; 41:9; 60:5

nômakê IPC [archaic form] a little while; (9:7); [synonym: *nakiskaw*]

nômakê IPV a little while; 9:7; *ê-'ti-nômakê-kihtohtêt* as he began to walk away for a short while

nômakê-kihtohtê- VAI go away for a short while (but not yet have reached one's destination); 9:7; cf. *kihtohtê-, ...ohtê-*

nômakêpi- VAI sit for a while; (9:7); cf. *...api-*

nôsonêh- VTI follow s.t.; (2:8; 67:2)

nôsonêhw- VTA follow s.o.; 2:8; 67:2

nôsoškaw- VTA follow s.o.; (8:4)

nôso'-tahkiškât- VTA kick s.o. while pursuing him; 47:1; 55:3; [contraction of *nôsowi-tahkiškât-*]

nôso'-wêpiškât- VTA kick s.o. away while pursuing him; 8:4; [contraction of *nôsowi-wêpiškât-*]

nôsowi-tahkiškât- VTA kick s.o. while pursuing him; 47:2

nôsowi-wêpiškât- VTA kick s.o. away while following him; 8:4

nôspinêhw- VTA follow s.o.; 59:3

nôtamêsê- VAI fish, be fishing; (67:4); cf. *...amês.../-*

nôtâhtikwê- VAI log, be logging, fell timber; 42:40; 67:4; cf. *...âhtikw.../-*

nôtêh- VTI fall short of s.t. (as a target); (11:8)

nôtêhw- VTA fall short of s.o. (as a target); (11:8)

nôtimâ- VII be round (as a solid); (55:7); cf. *wâwiyêyâ-*

nôtimêsi- VAI be round (as a solid); (55:7); cf. *wâwiyêsi-*

nôtimi-wêpahw- VTA knock s.o. down in a lump; (55:7)

nôtin- VTA fight s.o.; 43:5; 63:1; cf. *otâmi-nôtin-*

nôtokwêw- NA old woman; (56:3); cf. *kišê-iskwêw-*

n'tawâc IPC just a well; 1:4; 16:2; 19:2; 39:2; *n'tawâc âpatisîwin 'ci-kakwê-kâhcitinamân* just as well that I try to get work

n'timihk IPC upriver, upstream; 37:2; [contraction of *natimihk*]

ocâš- NDI his/her snout (of an animal); (46:2); cf. *okot-, oskiwan, ...câš-*

ocêhkamahkolê- VII catch fire quickly, burn up fast (with a flash); 42:60; [more common usage: *kišîhkolê-*]

ocêk- NA fisher; 1:7; *kî-wâpamêwak misiwê awiyâšîša: nikikwa, ocêka ...* they saw all the creatures: the otter, the fisher ...

ocêm- VTA kiss s.o.; 43:1

ocicipit- VTA pull away at s.o./s.t. [contraction of *otawicipit-*]; 50:3; n. 50:13

ocihcipali- VAI/VII come to pass, happen; 42:50; palatalization of *otihcipali-*

ocihciy- NDI his/her hand, paw; 21:3; 25:2; 36:2; 60:9; cf. *micihciy-, ...cihciy-, ...cihc...*

ocipah- VTA get s.o., grab s.o.; 18:3; 19:6; 65:8

ocipahtwâ- VAI-T get s.t., grab s.t.; 13:11

ocipaliho- VAI back up, draw back; 9:16; cf. *ohcipaliho-, ...paliho-*

ocipicikê- VAI pull (and pull); withdraw (e.g., money from the bank); [regarded by some speakers as preferred over *ocipitakê-*]; (50:3); *mâhcâ, n'taw'-ocipicikê!* Go on, go get some money (from the bank)!

ocipit- VTA/VTI draw s.o./s.t., pull s.o./s.t.; 5:9; 13:9; 16:5; 28:2; 40:3; 55:6

ocipitakê- VAI pull (and pull); withdraw (e.g., money from the bank) [less preferred variant of *ocipicikê-*]; 50:3

ocisk- NDI his/her arse, rear end [animate when addressed or personalized]; 55:4; 55:5; cf. *micisk-,*

...cisk-

ociškawaskitê- VII stand facing one; 12:2

ociškawikâpawi- VAI stand facing one; (12:8) *nitôciškawikâpawîstawik* he stands facing me; cf. ...kâpawi-

ociškwaciw- NA ochiskwajiw; another name for *wîhtikôw*, supposedly the one left over when every one else was frozen; (since such a person was assumed to survive through cannibalism, he was supposed to turn into a devil, a *wîhtikôw*; the term is also used as 'bogeyman' to frighten children)

ociškwacîwi- VAI be a devil, be an *ociškwaciw*; 12:15

ocîhcîhkwanapipaliho- VAI go and kneel; 13:14; cf. ...paliho-

ocîkahikani- VAI own an axe; 67:4

ocôšimiša NDA [dim.] his/her step-son; 43:8; cf. *otôsisa*, ...côšimiš-, ...tôsis-

ohci IPC from, for; 1:5; about; 3:1 et passim

ohci IPV (1) from that point, as a result of; 1:8; *êkota kâ-ati-ohci-mihcêticik ililiwak* it is from that point that people began to multiply; (2) completed action marker in negative clauses (colloquial usage for *kî-ohci-*); *môna kinwêš ohci-natohtam* he didn't listen for long

ohci-akwatamon- VII be connected; (55:9); *nispitôn nitihtimanihk ohci-akwatamon* my arm is connected to my shoulder; [near-synonym: *ohci-akohkê-*]; cf. *akwatamon-*

ohcih- VTA forbid s.o., prevent s.o.; 4:5; 42:67; 63:1; cf. *nakâhw-, nakâwêpiškaw-*

ohcihiwê- VAI prevent (things happening), get in the way; 42:44

ohci-itâpi- VAI peek out, look about (from what one is doing); 18:6; 20:5; *'kâwina mâka wîskâc ohc'-îtâpi* but don't ever look about; *mwâkwa manâ mâka ohc'-îtâpiw kîmôc* and then the loon suddenly peeked out stealthily; cf. ...âpi-

ohci-nâcipahtwâ- VAI-T go fetch from (a place); 51:2

ohci-osâwêyâkamipaliho- VAI churn the water up frightfully making it brown; 56:6; cf. *osâwâ-*, ...âkam..., ...paliho-

ohcipahtwâ- VAI-T (suddenly) grab s.t.; 55:2

ohcipali- VAI/VII proceed from, come from; 41:10; cf. ...pali-

ohcipaliho- VAI suddenly appear; (9:16); cf. *ocipâliho-*

ohci-pâpahtâ- VAI suddenly come running; 65:7

ohci-pêci-walawîpaliho- VAI come tumbling out; 13:9; cf. *walawî-*, ...paliho-

ohci-pimâtisi- VAI live off, make one's living from [with locative]; 42:43

ohcitaw IPC purposely, deliberately; 9:23

ohci-tôt- VTI do s.t. from (somewhere); 9:16

ohci-walawî-kwâškwati- VAI jump out from; 56:7

ohci-wâpaht- VTI suddenly descry s.t., suddenly catch sight of s.t.; 16:1

ohci-wâpam- VTA suddenly descry s.o., suddenly catch sight of s.o.; (16:1)

ohcî- VAI come from, originate from; 1:1; among siblings: *nîštam kâ-ohcît* = *ostêsimâw* 'elder brother'; *âpihta kâ-ohcît* 'middle brother'; *mâhcic kâ-ohcît* = *ošimimâw* 'younger brother'; cf. *nîštamošân-, mâhcicošân-*

ohcîhkaw- VTA prevent s.o. (from getting at s.t. or s.o.); 10:10; cf. *išîhkaw-*

ohcîhkâto- VAI [recipr.] bother or fight each other; 10:10; cf. *išîhkâto-*

ohcîmakan- VII come from, originate; 3:1; 42:13

ohkohtin- VII be heaped up; (42:35)

ohkwan- NDA ankle (variant of *wahkon-*); *nihkwan*; *ohkwana*; (65:8)

ohkwana NDA his/her ankle (65:8)

ohpaho- VAI fly up; 11:5; 49:5; take off (in flight); 20:4; 27:5

ohpahôwi-pîsimw- NA August, lit., 'flying-up moon'; cf. *pîsimw-*

ohpiki- VAI grow up; 1:3; 40:4

ohpikih- VTA bring s.o. up, raise s.o. from childhood; 42:16

ohpikihâwiso- VAI bring up one's family, raise children; 51:2; [variant of *ohpikihâwaso-*] cf. *...âwaso-*

ohpimêl- VTA lay s.o. (e.g., a kettle) on its side; 56:6; cf. *al-*

ohpimêšin- VAI lie on one's side; (42:67); cf. *âšikitâskošin-, âšikitišin-, kwêtipî-, ohpimêyâskošin-, otihtapišin-*

ohpimêyâskošin- VAI lie stretched out on one's side; (42:67); cf. *ohpimêšin-, ...âskw.../-*

ohpipali- VAI/VII go up, ascend, rise; 59:3; cf. *...pali-*

ohpwêkahikê- VAI hoist sail; 42:22

ohtê- VII boil; 9:12; (13:12)

ohtin- VTA/VTI take s.o./s.t. from; 41:9; *ê-ohtinahk šôniyân* and we took money from it

ohtisi- VAI earn wages; 41:9

ohtohtê- VAI be coming from, on the way from; 13:3; 37:5; cf. *...ohtê-*

ohwâs- NA horse (term fairly well established in Moose area); 41:1

okakêhtâwêlihtamow- NA (the) wise one; 12:7

okaškamâw- NDI nape of the neck; 12:3; 56:4; *okaškamâhk piko iši-nôkosiw* the only part of him which shows is the back of his neck; *n'kaškamâhk n'tatinik* he grabs me by the scruff of my neck; *nisakaškamâwênik* he's hanging on to the back of my neck; cf. *mikaškamâw-, kaškikwêšin-, sakikâtêpiso-, sakikwêpiso-, ...kaškamâw-, tatin-*

okâsakaskiwêsiw- NA hawk, 'the sharp-talonned one'; 26:1

okâsakimi- VAI be greedy; 48:2; *êliwêhk kitokâsakimitayân* my! you're awfully greedy! *n'kâsakimiyâpiy nôhtâkosiw* or *mihtawêw* my greedy-gut is sounding or complaining (when empty stomach growls)

okâwiya NDA his/her mother; 9:19; cf. *okâwimâw-*

okâwî- VAI have a mother; 65:1; cf. *...kâwiy-*

okâwîmâw- NA a mother; (9:19); cf. *nikâwiy-, okâwiya*

okimâhkat- VTI be boss (over s.t.); 13:14; VTA does not seem to occur; cf. *onîkâni-*

okimâw- NA manager, boss; 49:1

okimâwi- VAI be leader; 13:8

okitikw- NDI his/her knee; (61:2); cf. *mikitikw-, ...kitikw-, iskwacîskaw-*

okîcišim- VTA lay s.o. on top of; cf. *wakîcišim-*; 50:6

okîtapi- VAI sit on top of; cf. *wakîtapi-*; 55:7

okîtohtak IPC on deck, on the deck; cf. *wakîtohtak*; (55:2)

okohtâkan- NDI his/her throat; (8:8); cf. *...kohtâkan-, mikohtâkan, okotaskway-*

okosisa NDA his/her son; 9:2; 12:15; cf. *okosisimâw-....kosis-*

okosisimâw- NA a son; 9:2; cf. *okosisa, ...kosis-*

okot- NDI his/her nose (of a human); (46:2); cf. *...kot-, ...câš-, ocâš-, ...skiwan-, oskiwan-*

okotaskway- NDI his/her throat; (8:8); cf. *...kotaskway-, mikotaskway-, okohtâkan-*

okwayâw- NDI his/her neck; 12:6; 66:2; cf. *mikwayâw-, ...kwayâw-*

olahlapê- VAI get a/one's net ready; cf. *walahlapê-*; (55:2)

olapih- VTA seat s.o., make s.o. sit down; cf. *walapih-*; 55:2

olašiwât- VTA give s.o. instructions, order s.o., enjoin s.o.; cf. *walašiwât-, itašiwât-*

olašowâtikowin- NI instruction; 1:6; cf. *walašawê-*

olâkan- NI dish; 36:2; 50:2

olâkanišiš- NI small dish; 54:1

olâpihkên- VTI set up a line; cf. *walâpihkên-*

olâskwah- VTI make or lay down a canoe frame; 62:1; *olâskwaham cîmânâhtikoliw* he is making a canoe frame

olihkwa NDA his/her tonsil(s); (42:63); cf. *...lihkw-*

omayân- VTI make fresh tracks (e.g., a
moose or caribou); (29:4; n. 29:9)
n'kî-mâtâhâw atihk ê-omayânahk I
saw fresh tracks of a caribou; cf.
pasatah-, pimiskanawê-

omâhkîmi- VAI own a tent, have a tent;
66:1

omikiy- NI his/her scab; 55:8; cf. *mikiy-*

omikîwi- VAI have a scab

ominikošiš- NI [calque] minute; cf.
nist'-ominikošiš

ominikw- NA pintail duck

ominiskiw- NA thunder [pl.:
ominiskiwak thunder(-birds)]; 9:4;
[metathesis for *onimiskiw-*]; cf.
onimiskiwikamikw-

ominiskîskâ- VII be an abundance of
thunder, be a storm; 9:5; cf.
ominiskiw-, ...iskâ-

omisa NDA his/her older sister; 13:1;
15:1; cf. *omisimâw-, ...mis-*

omisimâw- NA an older sister; (60:5)

omišwâkan- NA wounded man; 14:7

omošôma NDA his/her grandfather; cf.
...mošôm-, n. 12:15

omošômimâw- NA a grandfather; cf.
...mošôm-

onahâhkaniskwêma NDA his/her
daughter-in-law; 60:3; cf.
*onahâhkaniskwêmimâw-,
...nahâhkaniskwêm-*

onahâhkaniskwêmimâw- NA a
daughter-in-law; (60:3)

onahâhkišîma NDA his/her son-in-law;
11:3; cf. *onahâhkišîmimâw-,
...nahâhkišîm-*

onahâhkišîmi- VAI have him/them as
son(s)-in-law; 11:1

onahâhkišîmimâw- NA a son-in-law;
(11:1; 11:3)

onahkitiy- NI tail end of a bird where
oil glands are situated; 47:2

onâpêma NA her husband; (12:8; 21:3)

onâpêmi- VAI have a husband, be
married (of a woman); 12:8

onikwana NDA his/her son-in-law (11:3;
11:9); cf. *ninikwan*

onimiskiw- NA thunder; 9:4; [occurs in
text as *ominiskiw-*]

onimiskiwikamikw- NI power house; cf.
maškawisîwikamikw-, ...ikamikw-

onîkânî- NA leader, head; boss; (13:14);
cf. *okimâhkat-*

onîkihikomâw- NA a parent; (11:12)

onîkihikowi- VAI have parents; 6:9

onîkihikwa NDA his/her parents; 11:12;
cf. *ninîkihikwak, onîkihikomâw-,
...nîkihikw-*

opaskowi-pîsimw- NA July, lit.,
'moulting moon'; 63:1; cf. *pîsimw-*

opihkwâciwâkamipali- VAI bubble (of
water); (16:1); cf. *...âkam..., ...pali-*

opimahâmowi-pîsimw- NA October, lit.,
'migrating moon'; (58:3); cf. *pîsimw-*

opistikwayâw- NA French Canadian;
(42:45); 42:50; cf. *wapistikwayâw-*

opîskâkani- VAI own a coat, possess a
coat; 2:10

opîwaya NDI [pl.] his/her whiskers or
bristles; 50:1; 53:1; cf. *mipîway-,
...pîway-*

opîwâwi- VAI have feathers, be feathery;
have hair, be hairy; 26:1; cf. *atis-*

opîwâwitonâniwan- VII for hair to be
around the mouth; 29:3; cf. *...ton...*

opwâm- NDI his/her thigh; 9:17; cf.
mipwâm, ...pwâm-

os- VTI boil s.t.; (13:12)

osa IPC then, you know, as you can see;
(suggests that what is stated had not
been fully realized); 10:4; 14:3; 41:5;
42:12; *ki-pêhtâkosin oš' anta* you can
be heard there, you know; *wêsâ 'sa
pwâ'tâpêw* he's dragging too heavy a
load, you see

osâm IPC especially; 22:1

osâm'ahkâtêpo- VAI overcook
[contraction of *osâmawahahkâtêpo-*]

osâmawahahkâtêpo- VAI overcook;
18:9; (55:6); cf. *likwahahkatêpo-,
nikwâwahahkatêpo-, milotêpo-,
išitêpo-, ...têpo...*

osâmâskiso- VAI be overcooked; 18:9

osâmâskitê- VII be overcooked; (18:9)

osâminâkosi- VAI look spectacular, look
outstanding; look quite a sight, look
frightful; (42:50); cf. *...nâkosi-*

osâminâkwan- VII look spectacular, look outstanding; look quite a sight, look frightful; 42:50; cf. *...nâkwan-*

os' âna IPC 43:1; that one, mind you; cf. *oš' âna*

os' âni IPC 9:20; indeed, to be sure; cf. *oš' âni*

os' âtawîna IPC of course; 42:60

osâwa-pasw- VTA smoke s.o. yellow; 50:3; 50:5

osâwaškâ- VII be yellow grass (as in autumn); 63:2

osâwâ- VII be yellow/brown (area of spectrum including both colours); (9:24); 10:9

osâwisi- VAI be yellow/brown (area of spectrum including both colours); 9:24; (10:9)

osisa NDA his/her father-in-law; 11:6; cf. *osisimâw-, ...sis-*

osisimâw- NA a father-in-law; (11:6); cf. *osisa, nisis*

osita NDI [pl.] his/her feet; 36:1; 47:1; cf. *misit-, ...sit-*

oskac IPC at first, in the beginning [unchanged form of *wêskac*]

oskan- NDI his/her bone; 9:15; 12:15; 21:9; 50:1; 50:6; *otôskanim-*; (27:4) his bone (i.e., an animal bone which belongs to someone); for *miskan-*; 11:9; cf. *miskan-, ...skan-*

oskât- NDI his/her leg; 9:17; 21:7; 36:2; cf. *miskât-, ...skât-, ...kât...*

oskâtihkâkê- VAI make legs or supports out of it, use to make legs or supports; 41:4

oskâtihkê- VAI make legs or supports; 41:1

oskisk- NA jack-pine; fir tree; 28:1; cf. *oškiškîsiš-*

oskiwan- NDI his/her bill (of a bird); (46:2); cf. *miskiwan-, ocâs-, okot-*

oskon- NDI his/her liver; (19:9; 27:4); cf. *miskon-, oskwan-, otôskonim-*

oskôtim- NI dam; 41:12

oskwan- NDI his/her liver; (27:4); cf. *miskwan-, oskan-, otôskanim-, otôskwan-*

oskwanipiy- NI liver water (often cooked up with wild berries); 54:1; n. 54:1

oso- VAI boil; (13:12)

osôw- NDI his/her tail (MC); 45:1; SC: *osôy-;* cf. *...sôw-*

osôy- NDI his/her tail (SC); 13:9; 25:2; *nisôyê* my tail (archaic vocative); MC: *...osôw-;* cf. *...sôy-*

ospâwih- VTA waken s.o. (accidentally by making a noise); (13:5); cf. *koškon-*

ospiskwan- NDI his/her back; (9:14); 18:6; cf. *mispiskwan-, ...spiskwan-, ...piskwan...*

ospiton- NDI his/her arm; 13:9; cf. *mispiton-, ...spiton-, ...piton..., ...nisk...*

ostêsa- NDA his/her older brother; cf. *...stês-*

ostêsimâwi- VAI be an older brother; 23:1; 60:9

ostikwân- NDI his/her head; 9:5; 10:5; cf. *mistikwân-, ...stikwân-, ...iskw...*

osw- VTA boil s.o.; 13:12; 50:4; cf. *os-*

oša IPC then, you know, as you can see [variant of *osa*]

ošašâšipit- VTI stutter; (13:9; 14:5)

oš' âna IPC that one it must be, that one you realize; 18:2; *hêy, wîsakêcâhk oš' âna* that's Weesakechahk to be sure; cf. *oš' âwa*

oš' ân' êtokwê IPC it must be (then); 13:7

oš' âni IPC to be sure you realize; 5:3; that one, after all; 8:2

ošâšihtâkwan- VII sound snippy, sound cheeky or not too polite; 43:7

oš' âwa IPC this one it must be, this one to be sure; 56:8; 64:2; cf. *oš' âna*

ošâwasko-pilêšiš- NA [proper name] Blue Bird; 10:9; alternate reading for *ošâwaško-'pwoy* Green Paddle or Blue Paddle

ošâwasko-'pwoy- NA [proper name] Green Paddle; 10:9

ošâwaskosi- VAI be green/blue (area of spectrum including both colours); (10:9); contrast *osâwisi-*

ošâwaskwâ- VII be green/blue (area of spectrum including both colours); (10:9); contrast *osâwâ-*; cf. *osâwaškâ-*

oših- VTA make s.o.; 5:5; 41:4; 50:5; *âšokanak êy-ošihihcik* bridges being built; 41:4; *'kwân' êh-tôtawakiht môso-wayân êy-oš'akiht* that's what we do to moose hide when we make it

ošihtamaw- VTA do or make it for s.o.; 52:4; 62:1

ošihtâ- VAI-T make s.t.; 1:4; 9:18; 13:17; 18:2; 41:4; 42:36; *êkw'ani mâka wêhci-kîy-ošihtâyâpân* that's why I had made it; *ošihtâniwan* be made

ošikwanay- NDI his/her tailfin; (29:1); cf. *...šikwanay-, mišikwanay-, sâsâkišikwanêstâ-*

ošimo- VAI escape; 12:2; 31:2

ošîma NDA his/her younger sibling; 16:2; 27:4; 42:44; cf. *...šîm-, ošîmimâw-, nišîm-*

ošîmimâw- NA a younger sibling; 23:1; 60:9; cf. *ošîma*

ošîmiša NDA his/her little younger sibling; 65:7; cf. *...šîmiš-, ošîma*

oškašiya NDA his/her talons or nails, fingernails; form *miškašiy-* supplied by informant as unpossessed form; (14:5); cf. *...škašiy-, ...kaškw...*, *ninihkikaškwêwêpahw-*

oški IPV/IPN new; 40:6; *k'-ât'-oški-p'mâtisicik awâš'šak* when children are new-born

oški-kîšikâ- VII be Monday

oški-kîšikâw- NI Monday

oškiškîšiš- NA new little fir tree; 7:8 cf. *oskisk-*

oškinîkiw- NA young man; 9:3; 23:1; 38; (41:17); 49:4; 60:2

oškinîkiwi- VAI be a young man; 41:17

oškîšikw- NDI his/her eye; 18:6; 19:3; 27:1; 55:2; cf. *miškîšikw-, ...škîšikw-, ...câp...*

oškway- NI birch bark; cf. *waškway-*

oš' ô IPC here then; 27:7; 43:2; cf. *oš' awa, oš' âna, ô*

ošôkan- NDI his/her lower back, backside; 8:5; 55:3; cf. *mišôkan-, ...šôkan-*

otahtahkwan- NDI his/her wing; 14:7; (20:6); cf. *otakahkwan-, mitahtahkwan-, ...tahtahkwan-*

otahtapišin- VAI lie upside down; 13:14

otakahkwan- NDI his/her wing; 55:2; 66:3; [solecism for *otahtahkwan*]

otakišiy- NDI his/her 'innards', entrails, guts; firehose; 19:9; 54:1; cf. *mitakišiy-, ...takišiy-*, cf. *pîmâstêyâ-*

otam- VTA suck, draw on s.o. (e.g., a pipe), seize s.o., grab s.o.; 16:2; *ka-kîy-otamikohtayak* they would have grabbed hold of you

otamaskay- NDI his (i.e., moose's) bits of meat left sticking to the hide, his meat residue; 50:6; often refers to meat plus (clear) membrane; cf. *...tamaskay-*

otami IPV be busy at; 65:4

otami-nôtin- VTA be busy fighting s.o.; 43:5

otahnapihkêsiw- NA spider, 'net-maker' (SC); 2:4; MC: *ahlapihkêsiw-*; cf. *êhêpikw-*

otaskî- VAI have (one's) trapping ground; 64:1; *kâ-k'-îši-otaskîspan môsak* where he always used to have his trapping grounds; cf. *askiy-*

otatâmah- VTI [redupl.] bang s.t., hit s.t. repeatedly; 13:9; 64:2; cf. *otâmah-, kalakihtâ-*

otatâmahikâkê- VAI [redupl.] use s.t. to hit away with; 50:4; cf. *...kê-*

otatâmahw- VTA [redupl.] tap or hit s.o. repeatedly, beat s.o.; 11:12; 13:10; 21:7; 50:4; 50:6; 56:7; 64:2; cf. *otâmahw-*

otatâmâpiskahikê- VAI [redupl.] bang away or drum away on metal; 64:3; cf. *...âpisk...*

otatâmâpiskišim- VTA [redupl.] bang s.o. repeatedly on the rocks; 36:2; cf. *otâmâpiskišim-, ...âpisk...*

otatâmâskwah- VTI [redupl.] bang sticks, knock sticks, rattle sticks; 13:6; cf. *...âskw.../-*

otawahkâni- VAI have as a pet; have as a slave or captive; 24:1

otawâšimiši- VAI have a child or children; 11:2

otawicipit- VTA/VTI pull away at s.o./s.t.; 50:3; cf. *ocicipit-*

otayâni- VAI-T own s.t., have as a possession; 43:10

otâkošin- VII be evening, be late afternoon; 5:2; 22:1; 61:2; *mîna kotakiy otâkošihk* the next evening

otâkošîhk IPC yesterday; 41:1; 41:7

otâmahikan- NI hammer; (68:6)

otâmahw- VTA hit s.o., strike s.o.; (11:20); 43:2

otâmâpiskišim- VTA bang s.o. on the rocks; (36:2); cf. *...âpisk...*

otâmâskwah- VTI strike it on the handle; 60:9; cf. *tâpâskwah-, ...âskw.../-*

otâmikâtêhw- VTA club s.o. on the leg; 60:10; cf. *...kât..., ...skât-*

otâmišin- VAI strike very hard; 20:6

otânâhk IPC back, behind; formerly; 11:7; 42:10; 47:2

ot' âni IPC that is to say, namely, then [emphatic form of *oti*]

otâpân- NI train; 41:1; 41:3; 41:11; *kihciwê-otâpân* real train (i.e., transcontinental express)

otâpânâskw- NA sled; 40:3; 42:32; 52:2; 67:4; cf. *...âskw-/-*

otâpâniyâpiy- NI hauling trace; (42:42); cf. *miskwâpin-, kinwâpê-, tahkwâpê-, ...âp..., ...âpiy-*

otâpât- VTA haul s.o.; 67:5

otâpê- VAI haul (e.g., a toboggan or canoe upstream with a tracking line); 40:3; 42:3; 42:23; cf. *...itâpê-*

otâsa NDI [pl.] his/her leggings, trousers [NDA in some dialects]; 11:11; cf. *mitâs-:...tâs-*

otâsikitikwâna NI [pl.] leggings; 11:12; [synonym: *otâsa*]; cf. *mikitikw-, ...kitikw-*

otêlaliy- NDI his/her tongue; 42:57; cf. *mitêlaliy-, ...têlaliy-*

otêma NDA his/her dog; cf. *...têm-, ...astimw-, atimw-*

otêškani- VAI have antlers or horns; 9:4; (10:5); cf. *otêškaniwêhtin-, kikitêškanêhtin-, êškan-*

otêškaniwêhtin- VII have horns or antlers attached to the head; 10:5; cf. *otêškani-, kikitêškanêhtin-*

oti IPC namely, that is to say; 3:6; 27:7; 29:3; 41:8; *manâ oti* I suppose, then

otihcipali- VAI/VII come, arrive; 1:5; come about; 40:7; cf. palatalized variant, *ocihcipali-*, 42:50; cf. *...pali-*

otiht- VTA/VTI reach s.o./s.t., arrive at s.o./s.t.; 1:4 et passim

otihtah- VTI reach s.t. with an instrument; (20:4)

otihtahw- VTA reach s.o. with an instrument; 20:4

otihtapa-wêpin- VTA/VTI overturn s.o./s.t.; 13:13

otihtapihtin- VII lie upside down; (13:14)

otihtapin- VTA/VTI turn s.o./s.t. bottom up; (56:6); cf. *kwêtipin-, ohpimêl-, otihtapipalih-*

otihtapipalih- VTA turn s.o. bottom up in a hurry; 56:6; cf. *kwêtipin-, ohpimêl-, otihtapin-*

otihtapišin- VAI lie upside down; 13:14; (42:67); cf. *âšikitâskošin-, âšikitišin-, ohpimêšin-, ohpimêyâskošin-*

otihtiman- NDI his/her shoulder; 9:14; 12:3; cf. *mitihtiman-, ...tihtiman-*

otihtin- VTA/VTI reach out to s.o./s.t.; 11:5

otilîkêkana NDA his/her shoulder blade; 9:15; cf. *mitilîkêkan-, ...tilîkêkan-*

otin- VTA/VTI take s.o./s.t.; 4:1; 10:3; 13:11; 29:3; 38:2; 50:3

otinikâtê- VII be taken; 52:1; cf. *otin-*

otinikê- VAI buy; 42:14

otinimâso- VAI take for oneself; 11:1

otiškawaskitâ- VAI-T place s.t. facing towards; 12:2

otiškawânak IPC on the facing side of the island; cf. *awasânak, âstamânak, kwêskânak, kišipânak, šipânakw-; ...ânak...; ...ânakw-*

otôhtan- NDI his/her heel; 44:3; cf. *mitôhtan-, mâskitôhtan-, ...tôhtan-*

otôn- NDI his/her mouth; 29:3; cf. *mitôn-, ...tôn-, ...ton...*

otôsisa NDA his/her aunt; (63:1); cf. *otôsisimâw-, ...tôsis-, ôhkomisa*

otôskanima NDA his/her bones (of another creature) 27:4; cf. *oskan-*, *...skan-*

otôskonim- NDI his/her liver (i.e., an animal's liver which belongs to someone) [variant of *otôskwanim*]; 19:9; contrast *otôskwan-*; cf. *miskon-*, *oskon-*, *...skon-*, *atimokan-*

otôskwan- NDI his/her elbow, funny-bone; 9:13; (9:14); 27:4; cf. *mitôskwan-*, *...tôskwan-*

otôskwanahoto- VAI elbow each other; 9:14

otôskwanahw- VTA elbow s.o.; 9:13

otôskwanêsiwak NA [pl.] 'The Elbowed Ones'; 9:13; cf. *otôskwan-*

otôskwanim- NDI his/her liver [variant of *otôskonim-*]; 19:9; 19:10; *nêtê manâ mâka k'-îši-wêpinamôpan otôtakišîm, otôskwanim* they (the animals, after eating Weesakechahk's bear) threw away the intestines and the liver which belonged to him (Weesakechahk); cf. *otôskan-*

otôtakišîm- NDI his/her 'innards', entrails, guts; 19:9; cf. *otakišiy-*, *...takišiy-*

otôtapîma NA his/her roots (i.e., roots of a plant which belong to someone); 18:5; note parallel with *otôwîyâs* his flesh vs. *wîyâs* NDI and *otôskanim*; cf. *watapiy-*

otôtêma NDA his/her friend; 44:4; cf. *otôtêmimâw-*, *...tôtêm-*

otôtêmimâw- NA a friend

otôwîhkwâm- NDI his/her bladder (i.e., an animal bladder which belongs to someone); 14:6; cf. *wîhkway*

otôwîyâs- NDI his/her meat (i.e., animal meat which belongs to someone vs. *wîyâs* his/her flesh)

ô IPC see here! 9:20; 18:2; 67:4; normally used with exclamatory particle or with a pronoun: *kwâcistak ô!* surely indeed! *nîla ô!* it's me! *'kwantaw ô kêkwân* nothing serious, just some stuff; 18:2; *pakwantaw ô nimîcin mîniša* I'm just eating berries; [contraction of *awa*]; 60:9

ôhkoma NDA his/her grandmother; 9:8; 27:7; cf. *ôhkomimâw-*, *nôhkom-*, *...ôhkom-*

ôhkomimâw- NA a grandmother; (9:8; 27:7)

ôhkomisa NDA his stepfather, uncle; 10:4; 43:5; 63:1; cf. *ôhkomisimâw-*, *...ôhkomis-*, *nôhkomis-*, *otôsisa*

ôhkomisi- VAI have him as a stepfather; 10:9

ôhkomisimâw- NA a stepfather; (10:8); cf. *nôhkomis-*, *...ôhkomis-*

ôho PR this one [anim.obv.]; 6:4; these ones [inan.prox./obv.pl.]

ôhtâwiya NDA his/her father; 9:9; 9:20; 54:3; cf. *ôhtâwîmâw-*, *...ôhtâwiy-*

ôhtâwîmâw- NA a father; (9:9; 9:20; 54:3); cf. *ôhtâwiya*, *nôhtâwiy-*, *...ôhtâwiy-*

ôki PR these ones [anim. prox. pl.]; cf. *ôko*

ôko PR these ones [anim.prox.pl.]; 6:3; cf. *awa*

ôma IPC at this time, at this point; 68:5

ôma PR this one [inan.prox.sg.]

ômêliw PR this one [inan.obv.sg.] (MC); 44:4

ôsisima NDA his/her grandchild; 9:8; cf. *...ôsisim-*

ôta IPC here; 2:2

ôtê IPC this way, hither; 10:7; 39:3; 49:1; 60:7

ôtôtâpânâskwâhtikohkê- VAI make sled runners; 11:13; cf. *otâpânâskw-*, *...âskw.../-*, *...âhtikw.../-*, *...ihkê-*

pahkahkâpan- VII be broad daylight; 55:6; cf. *...âpan-*, *wâpan-*

pahkân IPC apart, separately; 60:4; cf. *pahkânisi-*, *pahkânihito-*

pahkânihito- VAI separate from each other; (60:4); cf. *pahkân*

pahkânisi- VAI separate (e.g., two married people), part; (60:4); cf. *pahkân*

pahkicipit- VTA/VTI pull s.o./s.t. out so he/it falls; 42:62

pahkis- VTI blow s.t. up; (41:13; 65:7)

pahkisâwê- VAI blow things up (with dynamite or powder); (41:13)

pahkisikê- VAI be dynamiting; 41:13

pahkiso- VAI explode, blow up; 65:8; *êko mâk' awa kâ-pahkisot pihkoliw iskwêw* then this woman exploded some gunpowder

pahkisotiso- VAI blow oneself up, explode oneself; 65:7

pahkisw- VTA blow s.o. up; (41:13); 65:7; *pahkiswêw maskomîya* he blows the ice up

pahkihtin- VII fall; (4:2; 20:6; 34:2; 41:13); cf. ...*htin-*

pahkišimo- VAI be sunset, (for) the sun (to) set; 61:3; cf. ...*šîmô-*

pahkišin- VAI fall; 4:2; 20:6; 43:2; 41:13; cf. ...*šin-*

pahkon- VTA skin s.o.; 11:5; 14:4; 35:1; cf. *pakocên-, pošîkipit-*

pahkopê- VAI wade (out in the water); 4:5; 16:2; 29:1; 34:2; 65:1; 68:8; cf. ...*ipê-*

pahkopêšimo- VAI go into the water (to swim); cf. *pahkopê-,* ...*ipê-,* ...*šimo-*

pahkwatah- VTI remove s.t. with a tool

pahkwatahw- VTA remove s.o. with a tool

pahkwêhtahw- VTA tear chunks off s.o.; 11:5

pahkwêpicikâtê- VII be pulled off in chunks; 51:1; cf. *pahkwêpit-*

pahkwêpin- VTA pull the skin off s.o. by hand; 14:4; 19:7

pahkwêpit- VTA/VTI tear s.o./s.t. off; (51:1)

pahkwêšikan- NI flour; 54:1

pahkwêšikanâpoy- NI flour soup; 9:9; cf. ...*âpoy-*

pahpakwac IPC keeping occupied, by way of keeping busy; 43:4; cf. *pahpakwatêliht-*

pahpakwatêliht- VTI keep oneself occupied; (41:5) *ê-pahpakwatêlihtamân, ani wêhci-išilawîyân* keeping myself occupied, that's the reason I was doing things; cf. *pahpakwac, išilawî-*

pahpaškiš- VTI [redupl.] keep on cutting s.t. here and there; 53:1

pahpawipalih- VTA beat s.o.; 20:5;

pahpawipanihêwak omîkwaniwâwa they beat their quills

pahpîtôš- VTI slice s.t. (e.g., a roast) back and forth in layers without cutting through, so as to produce a long piece of meat; *âšay man' âti-pahpîtôšam omîcim* now then he began to slice his food (back and forth)

pakasôwin- NI marrow; (60:10); cf. *wîlil-, wînin-*

pakici-wêpin- VTA/VTI drop s.o./s.t. off; 9:6

pakitahwâ- VAI set nets; 25:2; 65:6

pakitâpihkên- VTA lower s.o. by rope; 2:5; cf. *lâšâpihkên-, nîhtâpihkên-,* ...*âpihk...*

pakitin- VTA/VTI put s.o./s.t., allow s.o.; 9:11; 12:11; 27:1; 27:3; 49:1; 54:1; 68:4

pakitinikâtê- VII be put; 42:56; 49:1; 52:1

pakocên- VTA eviscerate s.o., disembowel s.o.; 4:6; 54:2; 61:1; cf. ...*icê...*

pakosêlim- VTA expect s.o., hope s.o., desire s.o., request s.o.; 44:1

pakosêlimo- VAI wish; 28:1; 43:2

pakwacililiw- NA [proper name] Bushman, person from the bush (imaginary being inhabiting the forest); 64:2; [near-synonym: *nôhcimililiw*]

pakwanawâspinat- VTA make s.o. ill by casting an evil spell; 11:2; cf. ...*âspin-*

pakwanêcâpi- VAI have a hole for the eye; 52:1; cf. ...*câp...*

pakwanêh- VTI make a hole in s.t.; 60:7; 60:9

pakwanêhw- VTA make a hole in s.o.; (60:7; 60:9)

pakwanêyâ- VII be a hole, have a hole in it (referring to a hole in the ice above a spring which never freezes); 48:1; 60:7; 66:1; contrast *twâhikan-* a hole bored in the ice; cf. ...*ayâ-*

pakwantaw IPC casually, idly, aimlessly, at random; 13:2; 19:1; 41:14; cf. *'kwantaw*

pakwataskamikw- NI wilderness, open country, hinterland; 6:4; 40:2; 41:6;

42:20; *kî-papâmohtêwak
pakwataskamikohk* they went about in
the hinterland; cf. *papakwatêliht-,
kišipaskamikâ-, ...askamikw-*

pakwataskamik'-mîcim- NI country
food (e.g., game as opposed to
êmistikôšîwi-mîcim- White-Man's
food); 40:2

pakwatošân- NA illegitimate child; cf.
pakwacililiw, (64); *...šân-*

pakwayânêkin- NI cloth; 51:1; cf.
...êkin.../-

pakwânêkin- NI shirt; 42:22; cf.
...êkin.../-

pakwâsamahciho- VAI feel
uncomfortable; (23:2); [near-synonym:
kakwâtakamahciho-]; cf. *...amahciho-*

pakwât- VTA/VTI dislike s.o./s.t., hate
s.o./s.t.; 8:5; 19:3; 23:1; 42:44; 44:2;
45:1

palacîs- NA trousers; 52:4; cf. *mitâs-,
...tâs-*

panaškatin- VTA/VTI stick s.o./s.t. to
something; 55:9; *m'panaškatinâw
m'pikîm mistikohk* I stick my gum on
a tree

papanaškatin- VTA/VTI [redupl.] stick
s.o./s.t. around here and there; 55:9;
cf. *panaškatin-*

papaskiw- NA birch grouse, ruffed
grouse; 27:5; *ošahwêw papaskiwa* he
flushes a birch grouse

papâ IPV walking around about; 18:10;
19:2; 37:1; 39:1

papâ-itohtê- VAI walk around about;
37:1

papâmahamê- VAI walk around
following the road, trail; 42:51; cf.
...ahamê-

papâmâšakâmê- VAI [redupl.] walk
along the shore line; 9:3; 11:2; cf.
pimâšakâmê-, ...âšakâmê-

papâ-mâšihkê- VAI fight one's way
along; battle on one's way; 40:1 (the
recording, which is unclear at this
point, should perhaps be read as
ê-papâ-'mâtisiyâhk)

papâmâtahî- VAI slide all over, skate;
(12:15); cf. *pîhtokwêyâtahî-,*

šôškonâtahî-, ...âtahî-

papâmâtakâ- VAI swim around, move
around; 29:2; 45:1; 60:10; 65:1;
ê-'pâmâtakâyân kônâpôhk walking
around in the slush; cf. *...âtakâ-*

papâmâtêmo- VAI go around crying;
45:1

papâ-'mâtisi- VAI live on the move; 40:1;
cf. *papâ-mâšihkê-*

papâmêliht- VTI concern oneself about
s.t., worry about s.t.; 29:4

papâmihlâ- VAI fly about; 42:20; cf.
...hlâ-

papâmipahtâ- VAI run around; 25:3;
68:2; cf. *...pahtâ-*

papâmipali- VAI/VII travel about, move
about; 42:1; 20; 44:4; *kîšikohk
kâ-papâm'palik* which moved about in
the sky; cf. *...pali-*

papâmipici- VAI travel about (with one's
gear) camping; 40:1; 41:3; cf.
kihcipici-, pêcipici-, ...pici-

papâ-miskanawê- VAI make footprints
(walking about); 18:10

papâmiškâ- VAI paddle about; 64:1; cf.
pimiškâ-

papâmohtê- VAI walk about; 2:7; 6:4;
13:2; 36:2; 40:3; 55:1; 56:1;
kâ-kî-pêci-papâmohtêyâhk when we
were coming along; cf. *papâmôtê-,
...ohtê-*

papâmohtêmakan- VII rove about; 40:2

papâmôtê- VAI travel about; (44:20); cf.
papâmohtê-

papâ-nanâtawâpaht- VTI walk around
searching for s.t.; 65:6

papâ-natawiho- VAI hunt here and
there; 56:1

papâ-nânîpawi- VAI stand (shuffling)
around; 61:5

papâ-nihcikišin- VAI move about like a
dot against the background; 19:1; cf.
...šin-

papâ-nîši- VAI walk about two together;
60:1

papâ-nôkosi- VAI appear going about;
(19:4)

papâ-nôkwan- VII appear going about;
19:4

papâpilâškâ- VAI wander about; 56:1

papâ-wîcêwito- VAI go around together, keep each other company; 19:2

papêmâwatamwan- VII [redupl.] criss-cross into blocks; 42:47; cf. *pêmâwatamwan-, pimitatamwan-*

papêtihkwâskopaliho- VAI (of a partridge) make a thundering noise beating his wings as he takes off; 10:3; cf. *pitihkohtâ-; ...paliho-*

papêwêyâ- VII atmospheric conditions prevail in which one can hear clearly (e.g., a train) in the distance (a sign of impending bad weather); cf. *paswêwêpali-*

papimi-wêpin- VTA/VTI throw s.o./s.t. around; 13:10

papîwahâhkê- VAI spill or scatter feathers in all directions (used of shooting several geese at once); 10:9; cf. *tašiwâhkwê-*

pasakocêskawakâ- VII be miry mud, be sticky mud; (61:2) *pasakocêskawakâhk pimohtêw* he walks in sticky, soft mud; cf. *iskwacêskawê-; ...cêskawak...*

pasakohikan- NI glue; (42:34); cf. *pasakopêyâ-*

pasakopêyâ- VII be swampy or marshy or 'sticky' water; 42:34; [more usual usage is *kihtâpêyâ-*]; cf. *wâlipêyâ-, ...ipê-, ...ayâ-*

pasakwâpišimo- VAI dance with eyes closed; 8:3; cf. *pasakwâpi-, tôhkâpi-, tôhkâpišimo-, nistošimo-, ...âpi-, ...šimo-*

pasakwâpi- VAI have one's eyes closed; 18:5; 19:5; *pasakwâpîhkan* close (your) eyes! cf. *...âpi-*

pasakwâpišimôwin- NI Shut-eye Dance; 18:5; cf. *pasakwâpišimo-*

pasatah- VTI wear a trail by constant use (used only of a rabbit); 29:4; n. 29:9; cf. *omayân-, pasatamwatâ-, pimiskanawê-*

pasatamwatâ- VAI-T wear a trail by constant use; 6:4

pasâhtakwâtâ- VAI-T use wood chips; 50:3; *ê-wî-osâwâ-pasokiht wîla, nipasâhtakwâtânân* as we want to smoke it yellow, we use wood chips

pasiko- VAI arise, stand up; 20:6; 23:5; 60:3

pasikohtah- VTA raise s.o. up, open s.o.; (41:10)

pasikowitâ- VAI-T raise s.t. up, 'open up' s.t. (e.g., a work project); 41:10; cf. *nisâwîhtâ-*

pasiso- VAI burn; 9:24

pasitê- VII be on fire, burn (as a prairie fire); 9:23; 42:60; 65:8

pasitêpali- VAI/VII flare up; 23:4; cf. *...pali-*

paskam- VTA gnaw s.o. through (e.g., a net or cord); 29:4; cf. *pêkotaht-, pêkotam-*

paskê- VAI branch off (from the main trail); n. 3:5

paskêlâ- VII fork (as a river); [possible hyper-correction]; cf. *paskêyâ-*

paskêwê- VAI be very thin, be skinny, be lean; (n. 3:5)

paskêwil- VTA part company with s.o., take s.o. aside; 37:2

paskêyâ- VII fork, branch off (as a river); 38:1; *ministik akohtin anta cîpayi-sîpiy kâ-iši-paskêyâk* there was an island there where Ghost River branches off; cf. n. 38:2, *paski, ...ayâ-*

paski IPC in part, partly; cf. n. 38:2

paskilaw- VTA beat s.o., get the better of s.o. (in a contest or game), surpass s.o., overcome s.o.; 11:3; 11:9; 12:11; 23:5; cf. *šâkoh-*

paskilâkê- VAI overcome; 33

paskilâto- VAI [recipr.] beat each other (in competition), overcome each other; 33; *kî-kakwê-paskilâtôpanîk atimwak* the dogs were trying to beat each other

paskipali- VAI/VII be broken (e.g., rope, line, string); (53:3); cf. *...pali-*

paskisi- VAI have a big mesh (net); (37:3)

paskitâmaciwê- VAI go over the ridge; 3:2; cf. *...âmaciwê-*

paskocêh- VTI burst s.t. open (e.g., as when a charge of shot bursts open the stomach of a goose); 60:7; cf. *...icê-*

paskocêhw- VTA burst s.o. open; (60:7); cf. ...*cê*...

paskocê-wêpah- VTI burst s.t. open; (60:10)

paskocê-wêpahw- VTA burst s.o. open; (60:10)

paskocê-wêpahikâtê- VII be burst open; 60:10; *paskocê-wêpahikâtêliw oskan* his bone was burst open; cf. *pîši-wêpah-*

paskostonêhotiso- VAI make one's (own) nose bleed; 12:3; cf. *pohcicâšênitiso-*

paskostonêhw- VTA make s.o.'s nose bleed; (12:3); cf. ...*ston*...

paskwahciy- NI stump; (51:1), 61:4; 63:3

paskwahcîwi-sîpiy- NI [place name] White Top Creek, lit., 'stump river'

paskwahcîwi-sîpisis- NI [place name] Little White Top Creek, lit., 'stump creek'

paso- VAI be singed; 3:9

paspâpi- VAI peek in, peep in; 12:7; cf. ...*âpi-*

paspâpikâpawi- VAI stand peeping or peeking in; 10:8; cf. ...*âpi-*..., ...*kâpawi-*

paswêwêpali- VII echo (as in mountains); cf. *papêwêyâ-*, ...*pali-*

paškiš- VTI cut s.t.; 53:1; cf. *pahpaškiš-*; contrast *pâškiš-*

paškišikâtê- VII be cut; 53:1

paškišw- VTA cut s.o.; 53:1

paškocâpipitiso- VAI pluck one's (own) eyebrows; (46:2); cf. *sinikocâpinitiso-*, ...*câp*...

paškohtâ- VAI-T clear s.t.; 42:58

paškokahikê- VAI clear land (with an axe or by pulling up material); 42:38

paškonâkwan- VII look bare, look cleared; 42:58; cf. ...*nâkwan-*

paškopicikê- VAI pluck; (42:58); 55:4

paškopit- VTA pluck s.o. (e.g., goose, duck); 55:4

paškosi- VAI be clean (e.g., a mink with hardly any fur); 37:3; contrast *paskisi-*; cf. *paškwâliwê-*, *paškostawê-*, *paškostikwânê-*, *paškwâtihpê-*

paškostawê- VAI have one's whiskers

sheared off; 15:5

paškostikwânê- VAI be bald (also used for a goose or dog); (37:3); cf. *paškwâliwê-*, *paškwâtihpê-*, ...*stikwân*...

paškwahamâ- VAI have a haircut; (42:59); 50:6; cf. *natawi-paškwahamâ-*, *paškwahtâniwan-*, *paškwahikê-*

paškwahikan- NI split bone instrument for removing top layer of skin from hide; (50:6); cf. *paškwam-*, *paškwaht-*, *paškwahw-*, *paškwahamâ-*, *paškwapit-*, *mihkikwat-*

paškwahcikanâhtikw- NI wood on which hide is scraped; (50:6); cf. ...*âhtikw*.../-

paškwahikê- VAI make a clearing; (42:58)

paškwaht- VTI remove s.t. by chewing (of a wolf or fox removing hair from a moose head to get at the meat); (50:6); cf. *paškwam-*

paškwahtâniwan- VII be cleared to the ground; 42:58; cf. *paškwahamâ-*

paškwahw- VTA scrape away from s.o. the layer of skin which holds the hair; scrape hair off s.o. (moose) 50:1; (50:6)

paškwam- VTA chew s.o. (of a mouse chewing hair off a mink to get at the flesh); (50:6); (refers only to chewing the hair off; for other body parts, which are normally dependent stems and so possessed; cf. *paškwahtamwê-*; e.g., *paškwahtamwêw ospitôninîw* he chews off his arm

paškwatawêšw- VTA cut the hair off s.o.; 50:1

paškwâ- VII be clean, be cleared land; 37:3; 42:38; cf. *paškosi-*

paškwâliwê- VAI (of a mink) be without hair on the tail; (37:3); cf. *paškostikwânê-*, *paškwâtihpê-*, ...*âliw*...

paškwâtihpê- VAI (of a man) be bald; (37:3); cf. *paškostikwânê-*, *paškwâliwê-*, ...*tihp*..., ...*îlitihp-*

paškwâ- VII be clean, be cleared land; 37:3; 42:38; cf. *paškosi-*

patah- VTI miss s.t.; 42:9

patahw- VTA miss s.o.; 60:9

pataskišin- VAI run into, drive oneself into; 12:2; *n'kî-pataskišin cîstâskwân* I ran into (stepped on) a nail; cf. *...šin-*

patêtisa NI [pl.] potatoes

patotê IPC a little way off; 13:5; aside, on one side; 65:8

patotêpah- VTA run with s.o. to the side; 65:8

pawapit- VTA/VTI shake s.o./s.t. out; 51:1; *pawapitâkaniwanwak nêsta* they are also shaken out

pawayâskopali- VAI/VII make a shadow while travelling; 12:12; cf. *pawêhtin-*

pawâmowin- NI dream; 44:4

pawêhtin- VII make a shadow (in one place); (12:12); cf. *pawayâskopali-*, *...htin-*

pawipicikâtê- VII be shaken, be pulled; 51:1; contrast *pwâwipicikê-;* cf. *pâhpawipicikâtê-*

payahtênâkwan- VII become light, brighten, look clear; 14:3; 37:6; 42:56; *'kwâni manâ mâka tâpw' êši-kihtohtêt, ê-'ti- payahtênâkwaninik* at that he set off in real earnest, as soon as it began to look clear; *ê-'ti-payahtênâkwaninik* as soon as dawn breaks; cf. *kîhkânâkwan-*, *...nâkwan-*

payêhkisi- VAI be clean; 51:2

payihtaw IPC the trouble is that... (alleges an excuse); 42:36; *payihtaw kî-pîkopaliw nipâskisikan* it is because my gun broke (that I didn't do such and such); *payihtaw n'kî-pîkoškawâw n'tasâm, wêhci-êkâ-kî-ohci-nipahak môs* it was that I broke my snowshoe, which is why I didn't kill a moose; *payihtaw isa mâhtâwi-tôcikâtêw ôta nâspic;* the trouble is, things are very strangely done here, 42:38

pâhciškaw- VTA press down on s.o., depress s.o. (by body action); (61:5); cf. *matwên-*, *matwêškaw-*, *šawiškaw-*

pâhkah- VTI crack s.t. open (e.g., an egg or abscess); (12:3) *pâhkaham wâwiliw* he cracks open an egg; cf. *pâškahw-*

pâhkân IPC presently, after a short time; 27:3; 32:1; used in 27:3 like

pâtimâ 'until' at Moose Factory

pâhkâstikwânêšin- VAI crack one's skull (open); (12:3); cf. *...stikwân...*

pâhkisw- VTA shoot s.o. [variant of *pâskisw-*]; 34:3

pâhkopali- VAI/VII go dry; 50:2; cf. *...pali-*

pâhkosi- VAI be dry; 61:3

pâhkostikwêyâ- VII be a shallow river; (42:28); cf. *kinostikwêyâ-*, *kîškâyawistikwêyâ-*, *kwayaskostikwêyâ-*, *tahkostikwêyâ-*, *wâwâkistikwêyâ-*, *...stikw...*, *...ayâ-*

pâhkwahkastê- VII (for) the tide (to) be out, be low water; (7:2); [synonym: *îkastê-*]

pâhkwahkâso- VAI boil dry; (54:1) *niwâpamâw âhkik ê-pâhkwahkâsot* I see a seal marooned 'high and dry'; cf. *kipwahkâso-*

pâhkwahkâtê- VII boil dry, evaporate till dry; also used of a river bottom in a dry summer; 54:1; *kî-pâhkwahkâtêw n'kîsinawân* my cooking has boiled dry; cf. *kipwahkâtê-*, *pâhkwâ-*

pâhkwâ- VII it is dry; 7:2; 42:29; 42:61

pâhkwâw- NI the dry (land); 4:5; 9:6; [loc.: *pâhkwâhk* on the dry part]

pâhkwâpiskâ- VII be dry rocks; 42:49; cf. *...âpisk...*

pâhkwâšikawin- VII drain out (e.g., a canoe on its side); (56:6); cf. *kwêtipin-*; for draining from a hole, cf. *šîkwašikawin-*

pâhkwâšin- VII [dim.] be shallow; 29:2

pâhkwâšin- NI the shallows

pâhpahkišin- VAI [redupl.] fall in all directions, keep falling; 9:7; 13:16

pâhpahtâ- VAI-T laugh at s.t.; cf. *pâhpih-*, *pâhpihtâ-*; 63:1

pâhpawêyâskohtê- VAI be visible now and then walking in the bushes or going between the trees; (56:2); cf. *pawêhtin-*, *...âskw.../-*, *...ohtê-*

pâhpawêyâskošimo- VAI be visible now and then going between the trees; (56:2); cf. *...âskw.../-*, *...šimo-*

pâhpawipicikâtê- VII [redupl.] be shaken and pulled; (51:1); cf.

pawipicikâtê-

pâhpâskâtikohtâ- VAI-T make bubbles or ripples by breaking the surface; 16:1

pâhpâškicê-wêpin- VTI crush and throw s.t.; 19:6

pâhpêyak IPC one apiece, one by one; one at a time, by themselves; 12:9; by himself; 42:40; cf. *pâpêyak, pêhpêyak*

pâhpi- VAI laugh; 13:7; 21:4; 56:3

pâhpih- VTA laugh at s.o., make fun of s.o.; 13:7; 21:1; 46:1; 56:8

pâhpihkwêli- VAI have a smile on one's face; (22:3); cf. *...hkw...*

pâhpihkwêstâ- VAI pretend to smile; (22:3); cf. *macihkwêstâ-, ...hkw...*

pâhpihtâ- VAI-T laugh at s.t.; 56:3

pâhpipali- VAI burst into laughter; 21:3; cf. *...pali-*

pâhtakoškaw- VTA press down on s.o., crush s.o. with body action; 9:17

pâhtakwahw- VTA crush s.o.; 9:17

pâkašiy- NI [place name] Pagashi River (a tributary flowing into the Albany River about 20 kms east of Ghost River); 38:1

'pâmâtakâ- VAI move around; swim around [contraction of *papâmâtakâ-*]; 65:1

pâmihlâ- VAI fly about; 4:4; cf. *...hlâ-*

'pâmiškâ- VAI paddle about [contraction of *papâmiškâ-*]; 64:1; 65:7; 65:10

'pâmohtê- VAI walk about [contraction of *papâmohtê-*]

pânaskihkw- NA frying pan, skillet; 54:1

pâpah- VTA run s.o., cause s.o. to run hither; (65:8); cf. *ispah-, kihcipah-*

pâpahito- VAI run toward each other; 65:9

pâpahtâ- VAI run hither; 65:8; cf. *...pahtâ-*

pâpahtwâ- VAI-T run s.t., cause s.t. to run hither; 65:8

pâpalêkisîw- NA type of small hawk; (10:8); n. 10:20

pâpali- VAI/VII come, approach; 41:11; 44:1; cf. *...pali-*

pâpâskis- VTI [redupl.] shoot at s.t. repeatedly; 44:3

pâpâskisikê- VAI [redupl.] begin to fire (a gun); 49:6

pâpêyak IPC one apiece, one by one; one at a time [redupl.; variant of *pâhpêyak-*]; cf. *pêhpêyakw*

pâpihlâ- VAI fly hither; 49:5; cf. *...hlâ-*

pâpisiskêlihtamohkâso- VAI [redupl.] pretend to pay attention; (10:8); cf. *pisiskêlihtamohkâso-, ...hkâso-*

pâpîhtokwê- VAI [redupl.] enter here and there; 22:3; cf. *pîhtokwê-*

pâpîmin- VTA/VTI [redupl.] twist s.o./s.t.; 27:3; cf. *pîmih(w)-*

pâpîwâtakinam NA December, lit., 'little scattering moon'; [variant form of *pâpîwâcakinišîš*]; also as *pîwâtakinam-*; cf. *pîsimw-*

pâpîwâcakinišîš- NA December, lit., 'little scattering moon'; [variant form of *pâpîwâtakinam*]; also as *pîwâcakinišîš-*; cf. *pîsimw-*

pâs- VTI dry s.t.; 11:11; 27:7; 61:5

pâsicipotê- VII be flooded or overflowed, be covered by water; 49:6

pâsikâtê- VII be dried; 51:1

pâsinâso- VAI dry one's clothes; 11:12; [synonym: *pâsam otayâna*]; cf. *pâsinât-*

pâsinât- VTA dry s.o. else's clothes; 11:12; *nipâsinâtâw cîmis* I'm drying James' clothes; [synonymous phrase: *nipâsamwân cîmis otayân*]

pâsitêniko- VAI have heartburn; 14:3

pâskac IPC ostensibly, affirmatively; 9:22

pâskâhkotê- VII be clear ground (i.e., not covered by snow); 51:3

pâskicên- VTA/VTI open s.o./s.t. up; 14:6; cf. *pâškicên-, ...cê...*

pâskih- VTI block s.t. off with sticks; (13:4); cf. *kipâskwah-*

pâskihtên- VTA/VTI open s.o./s.t., throw s.o./s.t. open; (19:3); [synonym: *âpah(w)-*]

pâskihw- VTA block s.o. off with sticks (as a beaver lodge); 13:4; cf. *kipâskwahw-*

pâskis- VTI shoot s.t.

pâskisikan- NI gun; 10:3; 31:1; 34:2;

49:5; *môs'asinî-pâskisikan-* moose-shot rifle

pâskisikê- VAI shoot; 59:4

pâskiskwah- VTI strike (as a thunderbolt 'with fiery explosion'); (9:6)

pâskiskwahikê- VAI strike (as a thunderbolt 'with fiery explosion'); 9:6

pâskiskwahw- VTA strike s.o. (with a fiery burst, as lightning); 9:6

pâskiso- VAI be shot; 20:7

pâskisw- VTA shoot s.o.; 10:7; 20:4; 21:6; 34:2

pâskwah- VTI burst s.t., break s.t. open

pâskwahw- VTA burst s.o., break s.o. open; 9:6

pâso- VAI dry; 50:3

pâstâh- VTA bring evil on s.o., cast an evil spell on s.o.; (21:1); 22:4

pâstâho- VAI utter s.t. which brings evil or bad luck on oneself; (21:1); *'yâkwâ 'sa, ka-pâstâhon!* look out, you're doing something that will do you harm!

pâstâm- VTA speak so as to bring evil on s.o.; (21:1)

pâstâmo- VAI say s.t. which brings one bad luck, blaspheme; 21:9; 22:3

pâstâmowin- NI speaking evil of sacred things, blasphemy which brings retribution; 21; 21:9

pâstân- VTA/VTI put pressure on s.o./s.t. to the point of cracking; (21:1); *pâstânam paspâwiwinâpiskoliw* he puts pressure on a piece of glass to the point where it cracks

pâstin- VTA/VTI crack s.o./s.t. (e.g., an egg) while holding it; (21:1); contrast *pâstân-*

pâšic IPC over (and across); *pâšic mêskanâhk* over across the road; cf. *pâšitâmatin, awasâmatin, kwêskâmatin*

pâšici-iškohtêhkân IPC over beyond the stove; (9:15)

pâšici-kwâškwati- VAI jump over; 9:15; *êko mâka piyâšici-kwâškwatit* so then he leaped over

pâšitah- VTI step over s.t.; (11:8)

pâšitahw- VTA step over s.o.; (11:8)

pâšitâmatin IPC over the mountain; cf. *awasâmatin, âstamâmatin, kwêskâmatin, ...âmatin...*

pâškahâwê- VAI break the egg (as a mother bird for the chick to hatch); (1:9; 2:9); also used of animals stealing and breaking eggs

pâškahw- VTA burst s.o. (e.g., a boil, pimple); cf. *pâhkah-*

pâškicên- VTA/VTI crush s.o./s.t. with the fingers; 19:3; *ê'kwânihi kâ-iši-pâhpâškicênimâpân* those are the ones which I crushed successively (into my eyes); cf. *...icê...*

pâškin- VTA/VTI crush s.o./s.t.; (19:3)

pâškipali- VAI/VII explode, burst; 27:4; cf. *...pali-*

pâškiš- VTI burst s.t. open by cutting (as a balloon); (53:1); contrast *paškiš-*

pâškišw- VTA burst s.o. open by cutting (as a balloon); (53:1); contrast *paškišw-*

pâtimâ IPC until, later on, bye and bye; 1:4; 1:10; 11:10; 19:3; 35:2; 41:10; 58:4

'pâtin- VTA/VTI wring s.o./s.t. out by hand [contraction of *sînipâtin-*]; 50:4

pâtrik- NA [proper name] Patrick; 40:1

pâw VAI [3 sg.] he/she is sleeping, he/she is asleep [child language for *nipâw*]; 43:13; also as *pâ;* cf. *nipâ-*

pâwanaci- VAI dry in the frost; 50:7

pâwanahtin- VII dry in the frost; (50:7); cf. *...htin-*

pâwistikw- NI rapids; 62:3; cf. *...stikw.../-*

pêci IPV hither, towards speaker; 1:1; 1:7; 39:3 et passim

pêci-api- VAI come to sit, come and sit; 42:62; *pêc'-api ôta* come sit here

pêci-âpatisi- VAI come to work; 41:8

pêci-âpišîšiši- VAI be small approaching, come being small; 13:7; cf. *apišîšiši-*

pêci-itohtê- VAI come; 42:1

pêci-kaškihtâ- VAI arrive at the point where one is able; 65:4

pêci-kâhcinâkosi- VAI approach with alacrity; 13:8; cf. *...nâkosi-*

pêci-kîwêho- VAI paddle back home; (63:3); cf. *pêtâstamiškâ-*

pêci-kîwê- VAI come back, come home, return; 5:10

pêci-nâcistâ- VAI approach, come close; 19:8; *"êko mistikwak, pêci-nâcistâk,"* manâ itêw anihi mistikwa then to the trees he said, "Trees, come close together"

pêci-nâtahw- VTA come to fetch s.o., come to get s.o. (64:1); cf. *pêti-nâtahw-*

pêci-nihcikâ- VII come as a black cloud; cf. *nihcikâ-, nihcikisi-*; (11:13)

pêci-nôkosi- VAI appear, come into sight; 2:7

pêci-nôkwan- VII appear, come into sight; (2:7)

pêci-ošihtâ- VAI-T come to make s.t., come to build s.t.; 41:8; *kâ-kî-pêci-ošihtâcik* who had come to build it; *mêkwâc kâ-pêci-ošihtâniwahk* while the building was coming along; cf. *oših-, ošihtâ-*

pêcipah- VTA come running with s.o.; 19:6; cf. *ispah-, patotêpah-*

pêci-pahkišin- VAI came and fall; 59:3; cf. *...šin-*

pêcipahtâ- VAI-T come running with s.t.; (19:6); cf. *ispahtâ-, kihcipahtâ-, ...pahtâ-*

pêcipici- VAI come in (to camp) with his gear; (40:1); this is hardly ever used for arrival at a post, where *takošin-* is the term normally employed; in the bush, however, if one family joins another already in camp, *pêcipici-* is used, or more frequently, *nipêcipicîstâk* he is coming to camp beside me; or, *kipêcipicîstâkonaw* he's moving in alongside of us; cf. *papâmipici-, kihcipici-, ...pici-*

pêci-takwan- VII come; (to be); 41:14; cf. *takwan-*

pêci-wâwâkipah- VTA make s.o. come zig-zagging; (43:6); cf. *wâwâkiškâ-, ispah-, pecipah-*

pêci-wâwâkipahtâ- VAI-T come running from side to side; (43:6); cf. *wâwâkiškâ-, ispahtâ-, pêcipahtâ-, ...pahtâ-*

pêh- VTA wait for s.o., await s.o.; 21:7

pêhkâc IPC slowly, carefully; 4:7; 16:5; 29:3

pêhkâcî- VAI be slow; 68:3

pêhkât IPC slowly, carefully [variant of *pêhkâc*]

pêhpêyak IPC one by one; 5:7; 12:8; each one way; 10:10; one each; 40:3; *pêhpêyak n'tôtâpânân atihkwak ê-misiwêsicik* one by one we hauled whole caribou; cf. *pâhpêyak, pêhpêyakwâskotâpê-*

pêhpêyakwâ IPC once each; 1:8; 10:7

pêhpêyakwâskotâpê- VAI haul one by one (on a sled) *nipêhpêyakwâskotâpânân atihkwak* one by one we hauled whole caribou; cf. *...âskw.../-, ...itâpê-*

pêhtawêšin- VAI be audible walking; 56:7

pêht- VTI hear s.t.; 2:3

pêhtaw- VTA hear s.o.; 9:4; 18:2; 34:1; 43:10; 64:3

pêhtâkosi- VAI be audible, make a sound; 41:5; cf. *...ihtâkosi-*

pêhtâkosîwin- NI sound (as of the voice); 2:3

pêhtâkwan- VII be audible, make a sound; 64:2; cf. *...ihtâkwan-*

pêhtêyêlihtamohkâso- VAI [usually with negative] pretend not to be in one's right mind or right senses; (10:8), n. 10:21; *môla pêhtêyêlihtamohkâsow* he pretended that he was not in his right mind; cf. *...amohkâso- ...hkâso-*

pêkotah- VTI drill a hole through s.t.; (25:2)

pêkotahw- VTA drill a hole through s.o.; 25:2; also as *pêkwatah(w-)*

pêkotaht- VTI chew through s.t.; (29:4)

pêkotam- VTA chew through s.o.; (29:4); cf. *paskam-*

pêkwacâ- VII be a hole; (51:2); cf. *pakwanêyâ-, wîhkwêyâ-*

pêmâwatamwan- VII cross; (42:47); cf. *papêmâwatamwan-, pimitatamwan-*

pêpêyak IPC one each; 40:3; [variant of *pêhpêyak*]

pêpîtoš IPC [redupl.] different in many

ways; 1:3; in many different ways; 41:21; *pêpîtoš ihtâwak* or *pêpîtoš iši-tasîhkêwak* they live in various places; cf. *pîtoš*

pêsin- NA/NI [English loanword] basin; 50:2; gender varies with speaker: either *pêšiw pêsin* or *pêtâ pêsin* bring me a basin; for variable gender, cf. *pikîw-, šôkâw-*

pêšinâkosi- VAI approach, draw near; 6:12; 12:10

pêšinâkwan- VII draw near, get near; 3:5; 60:9; cf. *pêšonâkwan-*

pêšiw- VTA bring s.o.; 9:20; 13:11; 49:1; 65:2

pêšiwâpaht- VTI near s.t., draw near to s.t.; 3:6; 16:3; 68:7

pêšiwâpam- VTA near s.o.; draw near to s.o.; (3:6; 16:3; 68:7)

pêšiwêlim- VTA sense that s.o. is coming near; 12:14

pêškiš IPC on account of; 8:2; 9:7; *pêškiš ê-otakikomiyân, nitâhkosin mîna* on account of getting a cold, I'm sick again; *pêškiš ê-kî-kišiwâhikot, wêhci-anima-tôtawât* because he had been annoyed (by him), that's why he did it to him

pêškiš mâka IPC but even so; 18:3; 42:8

pêškiš nêsta IPC on that account; 42:60

pêšoc IPC close by, near; 19:3; 42:50; 65:8

pêšohtâkosi- VAI make a sound nearby; 12:6; cf. *...ihtâkosi-*

pêšohtâkwan- VII sound close at hand; 13:3; cf. *...ihtâkwan-*

pêšonâkwan- VII draw near; 9:6; 12:4; 36:1; 37:6; cf. *pêšinâkwan-*

pêtahol- VTA bring s.o. back (as a moose which one has shot); (56:3); cf. *kihtahol-, pimahol-*

pêtahotâ- VAI-T bring s.t. back; 63:3

pêtâ- VAI-T bring s.t.; 40:2; 43:7; 63:3

pêtâpan- VII be dawn; cf. *...âpan-, wâpan-*

pêtâstamiškâ- VAI paddle towards someone; 63:3; cf. *âstam, pêci-kîwêho-*

pêtâtakâ- VAI swim towards someone; 9:4; cf. *...âtakâ-*

pêti-nâtahw- VTA come to fetch s.o., come to get s.o. [variant of *pêci-nâtahw-*]; 64:1

pêtiwatâm- VTA carry s.o. (a person, e.g., a baby in a cradle); (60:4)

pêtiwatê- VAI bring back; 12:4; 60:2

pêtiwêhtin- VII be audible coming (e.g., a train); (13:13); (VII refers to the beat in the 'choo-choo' sound; VAI *pêtiwêsin-* refers to the 'thud-thud' of walking); cf. *pêtiwêpali-, pêtiwêšin-, pimiwêpali-*

pêtiwêpali- VAI/VII come towards one (e.g., a car or boat) with a smooth sound; (13:13); cf. *pimiwêpali-, ...pali-*

pêtiwêšin- VAI be audible walking (of a person whose footsteps can be heard); 13:13; 56:7

pêtwêwin- VTI hear s.t. coming; 12:15

pêtwêwit- VTI be audible approaching; 9:7; *pêtwêwitamwak ominiskiwak* the thunder can be heard approaching; *pêtwêwitamwak niskak* the geese can be heard approaching

pêyak IPC one; 1:3; 9:15

pêyako- VAI be alone [variant of *pêyakwê-*]; 9:18

pêyakohk- VTI work s.t. alone; (50:4)

pêyakohkaw- VTA work s.o. alone; 50:4; cf. *nîšohkawê-, (n. 50:18), niyâlohkawê-, nîswâsohkawê-, pêyakošâpohkawê-*

pêyakohtâ- VAI stay in one place; (41:6); *pêyakohtâwak ê-'ši-tašîhkêcik* they stay in one place

pêyakokamikisi- VAI make up one dwelling group; (21:1); in singular: make up one's own dwelling unit; [synonym: *pêyakokwê-*]; cf. *nîšokamikisi-, ...ikamikisi-*

pêyakokwê- VAI live by oneself, live alone in one's dwelling; (21:1); [synonym: *pêyakokamikisi-*]

pêyako-piponêsi- VAI be one year old; 65:2

pêyako-tawâstêw- NI one-week period; 39:1; 40:6; 42:34

pêyako-tipahikan IPC period of one hour; 18:8

pêyako-twâhikan- NI single hole (bored through the ice); 25:2; contrast *pakwanêyâ-*; cf. *twâhikê-*

pêyakoyêk IPC at one place; 42:50

pêyakôtê- VAI be one family, be alone with one's family

pêyakôtênaw IPC as one family; (1:9; 21:1); 60:2; *êko, pêyakotênaw kî-miskawêw ililiwa* so, he found people (Indians) living as one family or one dwelling group; also as *pêyakwatênaw*; cf. *kistôtêw, ...ôtênaw*

pêyakôtêw IPC one family; cf. *nistôtêw*

pêyakôtêwisi- VAI be (travelling) as one family

pêyakwan- VII be one, be the same; 4:1; n. 4:1; 11:10; *'kwâni pêyakwan* it's the same (thing)

pêyakwanohk IPC in the same place, in one place; 41:7; *môšak pêyakwanohk ihtâwak* they always stay in one place; synonymous with *môšak pêyakwahtâwak ê-'ši-tašîhkêcik*; cf. *pêyakohtâ-*

pêyakwayak itêhkê IPC in one direction; 19:9

pêyakwâ IPC once; 1:3; 1:8; 7:1; 31:1; 42:64

pêyakwâhtik IPC one stick; 59:4; *pêyakwâhtik ê-matwêtêk pâskisikan* a single-shot gun; *pêyakwâhtik pâskiswêw* he fired a single shot at him

pêyakwâskokâpawi- VAI stand by oneself (e.g., a lone tree); 13:16; cf. *nîšwâskosi-, ...âskw.../-, ...kâpawi-*

pêyakwâskwamo- VAI be a lone stick; (19:7); cf. *nîšwâskwamo-, nîšwâskon-*

pêyakwê- VAI be alone; 9:18

picêlak IPC as yet only; 11:6; just then 50:4

picênak IPC some time later; 42:64

pihkw- NI gunpowder; 65:8; [sg.: *pihko*]

pihkwâhkocihcân- NI fist; (13:10); cf. *...cihcân-*

pihkwâhkocihcêni- VAI make a fist; 13:10; cf. *...cihc...*

pikinwât- NA [proper name] Pikinwat (nickname); 42:63; n. 42:97

pikîw- NA/NI pitch, tar, gum, resin; 42:60; 55:9; for variable gender cf. *pêsin-, šôkâw-*

pikîwi- VAI be pitchy, be full of pitch or resin; 42:60

piko IPC only; 1:2 et passim; *piko mâka pîtoš ê-itêlihtakwahk* except that it seems different

pilêkopali- VAI/VII slide roughly or heavily; (12:14); used of a steel-shod sled in very cold weather, or a buck-saw sticking due to improper setting: *pilêkopaliw kîškipocikan* the cross-cut saw is sticking; cf. *kîškipotâ-, ...pali-*

pilêsiw- NA bird; 8:2; 47:1; 55:1

pilêšiš- NA [dim.] small partridge; 27:5

pilêšîš- NA [dim.] bird; 10:9; 16:1; 61:4

pilêw- NA partridge (MC); 14:3; 27:5; 58:5; SC: *pinêw-*

pimahamê- VAI follow the track; (14:4); cf. *...ahamê-*

pimahol- VTA carry s.o. along, carry s.o. off; 49:6; (56:3); 66:2; cf. *kihtahol-, pêtahol-*

pimahotâ- VAI-T carry s.t. along, carry s.t. off; (49:6; 56:3; 66:2)

pimatah- VTI [archaism] go over the ridge, trudge; 5:3

pimatamwatâ- VAI-T wear a trail; 6:6

pimatâhkê- VAI pursue; doubtful form; 3:2; cf. *pimicišahikê-*

pimâcih- VTA save s.o., rescue s.o.; 65:8

pimâcihitiso- VAI maintain oneself; 6:3; 42:19

pimâciho- VAI keep alive, get a livelihood, make a living; 1:8; 2:4; 7:1; 21:1; 40:7

pimâh- VTI migrate, fly south; 20:1; 20:2

pimâhoko- VAI be adrift (as on a lake after losing a paddle); (10:4)

pimâmatinâ- VII be a high ridge, be high land all along; (42:54); cf. *...âmatin...*

pimâpihkêšin- VAI lie along (as a line); 62:2

pimâpolo- VAI drift with the current, drift downstream; 8:5; 30:2; cf. *itâpolo-, ...âpolo-*

pimâpotê- VII drift with the waves (e.g., a log); (10:4); cf. ...*âpotê-*

pimâskohtin- VII lie along (associated with wood); (43:4); cf. ...*âskw.../-,* ...*htin-*

pimâskošin- VAI lie along (associated with wood); 43:4; cf. ...*âskw.../-,* ...*šin-*

pimâstan- VII drift with the wind; (10:4); cf. ...*âstan-*

pimâšakâmêpicikê- VAI track a canoe, tow a canoe with a line from the bank; 65:5

pimâšakâmê- VAI walk along the shore, skirt the river bank; 11:2; 18:1; 18:2; 19:1; 20:1; cf. ...*âšakâmê.../-*

pimâši- VAI sail about, sail along; 58:2; *kêkât n'kî-kostâcin ê-pimâšiyân antê tâwic* I was almost scared as I sailed away out there; cf. ...*âši-*

pimâtakâ- VAI wade (of a man); swim (of a fish or four-footed animal); 2:7; 16:3; 61:5; cf. *âšawahâtakâ-,* ...*âtakâ-*

pimâtisi- VAI live (SC); 1:3; 21:4; 28:2; 43:4; MC: *pimâtisî-*

pimâtisiwin- NI life (SC); (1:3); MC: *pimâtisîwin-*

pimâtisî- VAI live (MC); 64:1; SC: *pimâtisi-*

pimâtisîwâkê- VAI make a living by using it, use it to make a living; 41:10; cf. ...*kê-*

pimâtisîwin- NI life (MC); 1:2; 6:4; 10:1; (64:1); SC: *pimâtisiwin-*

pimi-akocin- VAI hang along, coast along; 42:31; *išpimihk ê-pimiy-akocihk* coasting along away up

pimicipali- VAI/VII go sideways; 1:6; cf. ...*pali-*

pimicicišahikê- VAI pursue (MC); cf. *pimicišahw-*

pimicišahw- VTA chase after s.o., pursue s.o.; (21:6); 31:2; 47:2

pimihlâ- VAI fly; 8:2; 20:5; 42:28; 44:1

pimihtin- VII lie; 58:4; cf. *pimišin-,* ...*htin-*

pimikalakâpiskipalih- VTA make s.o. (of metal) rattle going along; 49:1; cf. *kalakihtâ-,* ...*âpisk...,* ...*pali-*

piminawaso- VAI cook for oneself (SC);

27:2; [synonym: *minawaso-*]; MC: *kîšinawaso-;* cf. *kîšinawê-, minawê-*

piminawât- VTA cook for s.o. (SC); [near synonym: *kîšinawât-* (MC); (27:2)

pimipah- VTA run with s.o. (i.e., carrying s.o.); 58:5; 67:4; cf. *ispah-, kihcipah-, pâpah-*

pimipahtâ- VAI run along; 6:12; 21:6; cf. ...*pahtâ-*

pimipahtâši- VAI [dim.] periodically break from a walk into a trot; 6:12; cf. *pimipahtâ-,* ...*pahtâ-*

pimipali- VAI/VII go along, travel along; 1:4; 2:5; 20:5; 41:3; 42:20; 57; cf. ...*pali-*

pimipici- VAI go about with one's gear; 40:4; cf. *kihcipici-, papâmipici-,* ...*pici-*

pimiskanawê- VAI leave footprints, leave tracks (e.g., on the snow); 5:2; n. 5:1; 29:4; n. 29:9; used of a beaver which seldom travels on the surface in winter; *ê-'miskanawên'ci* making tracks; cf. *miskanawê-, papâmiskanawê-, pasatah-,* ...*skanawê-*

pimišakâ- VAI come in by paddle; 65:4; cf. *'mišakâ-*

pimišakâmêyâši- VAI sail along; 58:2; cf. *âsawakâmêyâši-, mišakâmêyâši-,* ...*akâm...,* ...*âši-*

pimišim- VTA lay s.o. down, place s.o. down; 10:3

pimišin- VAI lie, recline; 19:5; 24:2; 41:14; 41:19; cf. ...*šin-*

pimiškâ- VAI paddle along, row; swim (of a fish); 11:2; 11:6; 18:8; 34:1; 34:3; 58:1

pimitah- VTI walk over the ridge; 6:7

pimitamon- VII be upon s.t.; 41:3

pimitatamwan- VII meet; (42:7); cf. *pêmâwatamwan-, papêmâwatamwan-*

pimitâpê- VAI drag along; 65:4; cf. ...*itâpê-*

pimitišahw- VTA chase s.o., run after s.o.; 9:16

pimiwatê- VAI carry over one's back; 12:3; 18:1; cf. *pimiwitâ-, pohciwatê-*

pimiwêpahw- VTA knock s.o. down and kill him; 14:4; clear s.o. right out of the way

pimiwêpali- VAI/VII go by (as an ordinary motor vehicle); (13:13); cf. *pêtiwêpali-, ...pali-*

pimiwêyâkonêhikê- VAI make a noise coming and going on the snow; 60:7; cf. *wêpahâkonê-, ...âkon...*

pimiwil- VTA carry s.o.; 9:4

pimiwitamaw- VTA carry it for s.o.; 40:3; cf. *pimiwitâ-*

pimiwitâ- VAI-T carry s.t., convey s.t.; 40:3; 42:31; cf. *pimiwitamaw-*

pimiwitâso- VAI transport (something by canoe); 42:29

pimiwitâsowâkê- VAI use it for transporting, use it for carrying; 42:62; cf. *...kê-*

pimiy- NI grease, fat, oil; 23:3; 27:4; 42:41; fuel; 42:21

pimocikê- VAI shoot (by arrow); 9:23; 13:16; cf. *pimotahkwê-*

pimohtah- VTA carry s.o. off; 13:11

pimohtahtâ- VAI-T carry s.t., portage s.t.; 42:30; 61:4

pimohtê- VAI walk along; 1:7; 2:7; 13:7; cf. *...ohtê-*

pimohtêmakan- VII walk along; 15:1

pimohtêwâkê- VAI walk (using something); 36:2; *ê-'mohtêwâkêyâhk nisitinâna nêsta nicihcînânîy* as we walked using our feet and hands; cf. *...ohtê-, ...kê-*

pimot- VTA/VTI throw s.t. at s.o./s.t.; 4:4; 5:6; 14:4; also used of shooting an arrow. *pimotêw asiniya ostikwânilîhk* he threw a stone at him, at his head

pimotahkwê- VAI shoot (by arrow); (9:23); cf. *pimocikê-*

pimotaškwât- VTA shoot at s.o. with bow or sling shot; 6:10; n. 6:8

pimwâhtikonah- VTA throw (something) at s.o.; 14:5; *pimwâtihkonahihk pîwikahikaniniw* throw a chip at him! also as *'mwâtihkonah-*; cf. *...âhtikw.../-*

pimwêwit- VTI make a noise in passing; 12:6; used of wolves howling while on the move

pinakêskiškamaw- VTA knock the bark down for s.o. [contraction of *pinalakêskiškamaw-*]; 12:5

pinalakêskiškamaw- VTA knock the bark down for s.o.; 12:5; cf. *walakêskw-*

pinêw- NA partridge (SC); 14:3; MC: *pilêw-*

pinko- NI [English loanword] bingo; 42:10

pipâhkwatiwêšimâhkâso- VAI pretend to dry water off s.o. (i.e., off his fur); 13:10; cf. *...hkâso-*

pipâhkwatiwêšim- VTA dry water off s.o. (i.e., off his fur); 13:10

pipêskwahpit- VTA/VTI tie s.o./s.t. together; 18:5

pipon- VII be winter; 13:4; 20:2; 35:1; 40:5; 41:7

pipon- NI winter, year; 44:2

piponasiw- NA partridge hawk; 26:1

piponiši- VAI spend the winter (somewhere); 58:4

pisiskâpaht- VTI notice s.t.; (14:5)

pisiskâpam- VTA notice s.o.; 14:5

pisiskêliht- VTI pay attention to s.t.; (11:7)

pisiskêlihtamohkâso- VAI pretend to pay attention; 10:6; cf. *pâpisiskêlihtamohkâso-*

pisiskêlim- VTA pay attention to s.o.; 11:7

pisiskêniht- VTA/VTI notice s.o./s.t.; 20:6; *môna pisiskênihtam* he didn't notice

pisiskihtawêhkâso- VAI pretend to hear; 18:2; cf. *...hkâso-*

piskokâpawi- VAI stand in a hump or bunch; 13:15; (55:2); cf. *asikâpawi-, ayasikwêšimo-, ...kâpawi-*

piskosi- VAI have a lump, have a knob; 50:4; cf. *piskwâ-*

piskošim- VTA throw s.o. in a heap; 55:3

piskwacistin- VII be a pile of snow made by the wind; (12:11); cf. *mihtâlôw-*

piskwahtin- VII lie in a heap; 61:5; *piskwahtinwa mihta* the (drift)wood lies in a heap (as after high tide or break-up of the ice in spring); cf. *...htin-*

piskwasêkâ- VII be humpy; be a hump or mound of stones; 5:6; cf. *ispisêkâ-*

piskwastê- VII be heaped up; 42:35; [synonym: *ohkohtin-*]

piskwâ- VII have a lump, a knob; 50:4; cf. *piskosi-*

piskwâmiskw- NI [place name] Piskwamisk, lit., 'hump' (located on west coast of James Bay)

piskwâmiskošiš- NI [place name] Little Piskwamisk, lit., 'little hump' (located on west coast of James Bay)

piskwâskwayâ- VII be a heavy clump of bushes or trees; 12:2; cf. *...âskw.../-, ...ayâ-*

piskwâšin- VAI lie piled up in a heap; 13:17; cf. *...šin-*

piskwâwahkâ- VII be a sandy shoal; 65:3

piskwâwahkâšin- VII [dim.] be a little sandy shoal; (65:3); *kâ-piskwâ'hkâšihk* North Bluff Shoal (located 27 kilometres north of Moose Factory on the west coast of James Bay)

pistah- VTI hit s.t. by accident; (62:3); cf. *mîskwah-*

pistahw- VTA hit s.o. by accident; (62:3); cf. *mîskwahw-*

pišišik IPC simply, nothing other than, always, invariably, consistently, throughout, constantly, exclusively; 1:2; 8:6; 10:8; 21:7; 39:1; 41:4; 42:9; 42:53; 51:2; 59:1; 62:1; *pišišik mîcim* nothing but (country) food

pišišikohtê- VAI travel empty, travel without a load; 42:26; cf. *...ohtê-*

pišišikwâ- VII be empty; 2:2; 43:6

pišiw- NA lynx; 1:7; 2:7

pitamâ IPC first (of all), for now; 2:4; 13:3; 30:1; 42:20 42:21; *êškwâ pitamâ* wait a minute! *ê'kwâni pitamâ* that's enough for now!

pitihkohtâ- VAI make a beating, flapping or booming noise; 18:5; cf. *pitihkwahtâ-, pitihkwê-, papêtihkwâskopaliho-*

pitihkopaliho- VAI make a roaring noise; 27:5; cf. *...paliho-*

pitihkwahtâ- VAI make a beating, flapping or booming noise; 18:6; cf. *pitihkohtâ-*

pitihkwahtin- VII hit the ground with a noise; 60:2; *pêci-pitihkwahtin mîn' anta mîwat* again the bag resounded loudly

pitihkwašin- VAI hit the ground with a noise (as in falling); 12:5; cf. *...šin-*

pitihkwê- VAI make a loud noise; *pêci-pitihkwêwak ominiskiwak* the thunder is sure making a loud noise; *pêci-pitihkwêw maskwamiy* the ice (breaking up) is making a loud noise

pîhci IPC inside [with locative]; 9:12; 18:2; 29:2; 55:2

pîhcihtin- VII lie inside; 12:4; 59:4

pîhcipali- VAI/VII go into; 1:5; 43:14; cf. *...pali-*

pîhcipaliho- VAI jump in; 9:16; cf. *...paliho-*

pîhcipihkwân- NA cartridge, shell; 49:1

pîhcipihkwât- VTI load s.t. (e.g., a gun); 59:4

pîhcipîmân- NI fat container, bladder or any kind of container for grease or gasoline; (14:3); cf. *pîhcipimê-, wîhkway-*

pîhcipimê- VAI pour fat into a bladder or container; put gas into an engine; (14:3); cf. *pimiy-*

pîhcišin- VAI lie inside; 49:3; 56:7; cf. *...šin-*

pîhciškaw- VTA get inside of s.o.; 11:5

pîhtah- VTI put s.t. into (something); 27:4; 51:1; *pîhtahikâtêwa mâka mîwatihk* they are then put in a bag

pîhtahw- VTA put s.o. into (something); 22:2

pîhtawânakâw- NI [place name] Peehtawanagaw, lit., 'island-in-against (the mainland)'; 67:4; cf. *pîhtwêstah-, ...ânak...*

pîhtawê IPC in between; (14:4)

pîhtawên- VTA/VTI put s.o./s.t. in between; (14:4); *pîhtawênik n'tastisak* put a lining in my mitts; *pîhtawêna nipâkan* put a new lining on the quilt, eiderdown; cf. *pîhtôšakêpit-, pîhtwêstah-*

pîhtâpêkw- NI lagoon, pond; 9:24; 42:54; *pîhtâpêkohk kâ-cimasot âskaw* *wâkinâkan* the tamarack which sometimes sticks up in the lagoon; cf. *...ipêkw-*

pîhtâpêkw- NI [place name] Fort Albany, lit., 'pond, lagoon'; village located on the south branch of the Albany River

pîhtikom IPC inside; (55:2); 56:4; cf. *têtipâhtê-*

pîhtikomihk IPC inside the house; 23:3; cf. *pîhtikwamihk, pîhtokwamihk*

pîhtinikêkâpawi- VAI stand with one's hands in one's pockets; 41:8; cf. *nîpitêkâpawi-, ...kâpawi-*

pîhtikwamihk IPC inside, within; 66:1; cf. *pîhtokwamihk, pîhtikomihk*

pîhtokatâ- VAI-T bring s.t. in; 43:6

pîhtokwah- VTA bring or take s.o. in; 42:59

pîhtokwahtâ- VAI-T bring or take s.t. in; (42:59)

pîhtokwamihk IPC indoors; 18:2; cf. *pîhtikwamihk, pîhtikomihk*

pîhtokwê- VAI enter, go in; 9:8; 18:2; 21:3; 41:5

pîhtokwêcin- VTA/VTI push s.o./s.t. in by hand; (9:19)

pîhtokwê-kwâškwati- VAI jump in; 13:13

pîhtokwêmakan- VII come in (especially referring to the new year); (58:4); n. 58:18; cf. *makošêwi-kîšikâ-, walawîmakan-*

pîhtokwêpah- VTA make s.o. run or scurry; 44:2

pîhtokwêpaliho- VAI jump in, come rushing in; 13:14; 14:6; cf. *...paliho-*

pîhtokwêpit- VTA/VTI pull s.o./s.t. inside; 60:3

pîhtokwê-wêpin- VTA/VTI throw s.o./s.t. inside; 13:12; 14:5

pîhtokwêyâpolo- VAI slip in, slide in; 12:14; cf. *kilipali-, kišîyâpolo-, pilêkopali-, ...âpolo-*

pîhtokwêyâtahî- VAI slide in; 12:15; cf. *papâmâtahî-, šôškonâtahî-, ...âtahî-*

pîhtômo- VAI tuck (something) inside one's clothing, carry (something) under one's coat; 14:4

pîhtôšakêpit- VTA/VTI strip the skin off s.o./s.t.; 14:4; cf. *pîhtawê..., pîhtawên-, wašakaya*

pîhtwâ- VAI smoke; 41:20; 58:5; 63:2

pîhtwêstah- VTI put lining in s.t.; (67:4); cf. *pîhtawânakâw-, pîhtawên-*

pîkišênâkwan- VII be blurry, be blurred; (19:2); cf. *...nâkwan-*

pîkišêpali- VAI/VII steam; 9:24; cf. *...pali-*

pîkišêyâ- VII be foggy, be hazy, be misty; 19:2; cf. *...ayâ-*

pîkohikâtê- VII be broken with an instrument; 12:15

pîkon- VTA/VTI break s.o./s.t. (by hand); 1:6

pîkopali- VAI/VII break

pîkositêšin- VAI blister one's feet; 9:21; cf. *...sit..., ...šin-*

pîkošim- VTA smash s.o.; 42:32

pîkotôhtakw- NI rotten-wood; 50:5

pîkotôwan- VII it is rotten (wood); 50:5

pîkwahtin- VII be broken, get broken; 62:3

pîkwêhkopâ- VII be bushy, be thick; 42:58; cf. *...hkop...*

pîkwêhkopâw- NI willow thicket; 42:58; *pîkwêhkopâhk* where the willows are thick, in the willow thicket; cf. *wîkopiy-, ...hkop...*

pîkwêsi- VAI have thick fur; (42:58); cf. *pîkwêhkopâ-, pîkwêyâliwê-, pîkwêyâskwêyâ-*

pîkwêyâliwê- VAI have a bushy tail; (42:58); cf. *kinwâliwê-, tahkwâliwê-, ...âliw...*

pîkwêyâskwêyâ- VII be thick (of trees); (42:58); cf. *...âskw.../-, ...ayâ-*

pîkwêyâskwêyâw- NI tree thicket; (42:58); *pîkwêyâskwêyâhk* where the trees are thick, in the tree thicket; cf. *pîkwêyâskwêyâ-*

pîliš IPC until, up to, at last (MC); 6:8; 36:2; 39:1; 42:38; 50:5; *ôtê pîniš* right up to here; *pîliš pîliš* at long last; MC: *pîniš*

pîmâpiskahikan- NI screw-driver; (27:3); cf. *...âpisk...*

pîmâskosi- VAI be twisted (something wooden, e.g., tree trunk, paddle or sled); (27:3); n. 27:5

pîmâskwan- VII be twisted (something wooden, e.g., an axe-handle); (27:3); n. 27:5; cf. *...âskw...*/-

pîmastêh- VTI twist s.t.; (52:1); cf. *taŝwâpihkêpit-*

pîmâstêhw- VTA twist s.o.; (52:1); cf. *taŝwâpihkêpit-*

pîmâstêhwâkaniwan- VAI be twisted, have kinks put in it; 52:1

pîmâstêpali- VAI/VII go into kinks while being handled; (52:1); cf. *...pali-*

pîmâstêsi- VAI have kinks; (52:1); *pimâstêsiw pîŝâkanâpiy* the rope has kinks in it

pîmâstêyâ- VII have kinks; (52:1); *pimâstêyâw otakišiy* the fire hose has kinks in it; cf. *...ayâ-*

pîmih- VTI spin s.t., twist s.t.; (52:1)

pîmihkwêpali- VAI face be twisted; 43:5; cf. *...hkw...*, *...pali-*

pîmihw- VTA spin s.o., twist s.o. (as yarn); 52:1

pîmisi- VAI have twisted grain (as a tree); 27:3; cf. *pîmâpiskahikan-*, *pîmâskosi-*, *pîmâskwan-*

pîm'pâtâskwah- VTI wring s.t. using a stick; (50:2); cf. *...âskw...*/-

pîm'pâtâskwahw- VTA wring s.o. using a stick; 50:2; cf. *pîm'pâtin-*

pîm'pâtin- VTA/VTI wring s.o./s.t.; (50:2)

pînîš IPC until, up to, at last (SC); 1:4; 5:1; 27:3; MC: *pîliš*

pîpotênikê- VAI make a smoke or smudgefire; 6:16

pîpotêpali- VAI/VII make smoke; 9:24; cf. *...pali-*

pîsawêpah- VTI knock s.t. in pieces; 6:10

pîsawêpahw- VTA knock s.o. in pieces; (6:10)

pîsimw- NA sun, luminary; month; 3:6; 15:10; 39:2; 50:7; 63:1; *pêyako-pîsim* period of one month; cf. *tipiski-pîsimw-, kisê-pâpîwâtakinam, kišê-pîsimw-, mikisiwi-pîsimw-, niski-pîsimw-, alîki-pîsimw-, sâkipakâwi-pîsimw-,*

opaskowi-pîsimw-, ohpahôwi-pîsimw-, wêhwêsi-pîsimw-, opimahâmowi-pîwimw-, kaškatinisiw, pâpîwâcakinišîš

pîsimohkân- NA clock; 42:6; cf. *...ihkân-*

pîsiwêpah- VTI shatter s.t. in pieces; 5:6; (60:10)

pîsiwêpahw- VTA shatter s.o. in pieces; (5:6; 60:10)

pîskâkan- NI coat, jacket, shirt; 2:10; 19:8; 52:4; [contraction of *pîsiskâkan-*]

pîstêw- NI foam, froth, scum; 9:6

pîŝâkanâpiy- NI twine, line, rope, cord; 1:4; 52:2; cf. as NA with *pîmâstêsi-*, *...âpiy-*

pîtoš IPC different(ly); 1:2; 9:11; 13:4; 37:5; 39:4; 42:5

pîtošinâkosi- VAI look different; (42:55); cf. *nanâhkawinâkosi-*, *...nâkosi-*

pîtošinâkwan- VII look different; 42:55; cf. *nanâhkawinâkwan-*, *...nâkwan-*

pîwâpiskw- NI metal; 41:4; cf. *...âpiskw-*

pîwâpiskohikan- NI flat-iron; (8:8); 42:62; cf. *...âpiskw-*

pîwâpiskwahikan- NI flat-iron [variant of *pîwâpiskohikan-*]; (8:8)

pîwikahikan- NI wood chip; 14:5

pîwit- VTI run or shoot (a rapid); 62:3; *pîwitam (pâwistikoliw)* he shoots (the rapid)

pohcâpin- VTA put a hand or finger in s.o.'s eye, poke s.o.'s eye; (12:3; 21:4); cf. *cahkâpin-*, *...câp...*

pohcicâšên- VTA put a finger in s.o.'s nose; (12:3; 21:4); cf. *...câš...*

pohcicâšênitiso- VAI put one's finger up one's nose, pick one's nose; (12:3; 21:4)

pohcikonêwên- VTA put a hand in s.o.'s mouth, poke (something down) s.o.'s throat; 21:4; cf. *mahkikonêwê-, okotaskway-, okohtâkan-, ...konêw...*

pohcikonêwêyâskohw- VTA poke (something long and wooden) down s.o.'s throat

pohcikonêwêyâsko-wêpahw- VTA shove (something wooden) down s.o.'s throat; 8:8; cf. *...konêw...*, *...âskw...*/-

pohtêlikomên- VTA shove something up s.o.'s nose

pohcišk- VTI put s.t. on; 52:4; 61:3; 65:1; cf. *tâpiskon-*

pohciškaw- VTA put s.o. on; 11:6; cf. *tâpiskon-*

pohciwatê- VAI sling one's packsack over one's back; 12:3

pohci-wêpin- VTA/VTI throw s.o./s.t. in a box or hole (where fit is required); 60:9

pohci-wêpiškaw- VTA put s.o. on quickly, throw s.o. on quickly; 14:4; *'kwâni manâ mâka êši-pohci-wêpiškawât anihi wîskacâniši-wayâna* then he quickly put on the whiskey-jack skin

pohpohtât- VTI [redupl.] blow at s.t.; 28:1

pohpohtâtaw- VTA [redupl.] blow at s.o.; (28:1)

pošîkipit- VTA/VTI strip the bark off s.o./s.t.; (11:5) *pošîkipitam nîpisîliw* he strips the bark off a willow; *pošîkipitam ê-wî-âhci-wîskwênahk cîmâniliw* he strips the canvas off the canoe with the intention of 'changing the wrapping'; cf. *âhci-, wîskwên-*

pôn- VTI make a fire, fuel a fire; 9:19

pônêliht- VTI stop thinking about s.t.; 57; *n'tawâc êkoši m'pônêl'htên nîla* I may as well stop thinking about it (i.e., personally, I don't care)

pôni IPV discontinue; 8:5; 44:4

pônih- VTA stop s.o., hold s.o. up; 27:3; 50:3

pônihtâ- VAI-T stop s.t., desist (from) s.t., leave s.t. alone; 11:1; 42:1; 42:7; 50:2; *êkâ oti kâ-pônihtâcik* the ones, that is, who don't give up

pôni-'mâtisi- VAI pass away, die; [contraction of *pôni-pimâtisi-*, lit., 'cease living', a frequent euphemism for *nipi-*]; 44:4

pôni-pimâtisi- VAI 'pass away', die; 8:5; *kâ-ati-pôni-pimâtisit* he gradually died

pôsi- VAI embark, set out; 1:4; 10:4; 11:4; 18:8; 58:1; 60:7; 65:3

pôsih- VTA load s.o., aboard, cause s.o. to embark or depart by boat; 18:8; 64:1; 64:2; n. 65:13

pôsihtâ- VAI-T load s.t. aboard; 10:5

pôsikâciš- NA [English loanword] cat (from pussy-cat); 26:3

pôsipali- VAI embark by jumping aboard; 42:47; cf. *...pali-*

pôsipaliho- VAI embark quickly, jump aboard and shove off; 11:4; cf. *...paliho-*

pôsitahkoskê- VAI step into a canoe; 65:4

pôsiwêpin- VTA/VTI throw s.o./s.t. in a canoe; (60:9); cf. *pohci-wêpin-*

prâwniwan- VII [English loanword] become brown in frying; 54:1

pwâkit- NI [English loanword] pocket; 43:6; 49:1; *nipwâkitim* 'my pocket'

pwâmošê IPC before [with conjunct, variant of *pwâmoši*]; 58:4

pwâmoši IPC before [with conjunct]; 1:4; 9:9; 19:1; 40:1

pwâwanî- VAI be weak from hunger; (48:2)

pwâwatê- VAI be heavily loaded, burdened; (48:2); *êliwêhk m'p'âwatân kâ-wîwašiyân* I'm loaded down with my burden; cf. *kosikwamahcihtâ-*

pwâwihotâ- VAI-T drag s.t. around; 45:1

pwâwipicikê- VAI pull or drag with difficulty (because of weight); (51:1); cf. *pwâwatê-, pwâwitâpê-*

pwâwitâpê- VAI drag a (too) heavy load; (42:12) *wêsâ 'sa pwâ'tâpêw* for he's dragging too heavy a load; cf. *...itâpê-*

rêmiy- NA [proper name] Rémi; 43:8

sakapwê- VAI roast (meat), barbecue; 18:7; 55:3; cf. *cîstahâpwê-, maskatêpwê-*

sakâlihkocêpiso- VAI be snared by the middle; (21:4); cf. *...âlihkoc...*

sakâskosi- VAI be thick (i.e., branches); 51:2; cf. *...âskw.../-*

sakicihcêpiso- VAI be snared by the hand or forepaw; (21:4); cf. *...cihc...*

sakihtâwikêpiso- VAI be snared by the ears; (21:4); cf. *...htâwak...*

sakihtin- VII be caught or hooked on something; (21:4); cf. *...htin-, sakipâson-*

sakikâtêpiso- VAI be snared by the leg; 21:4; cf. *...kât...*

sakikwêpiso- VAI be snared by the neck; 3:6; (21:4); cf. ...*ikw*...

sakimêskâ- VII mosquitoes abound; 42:58; cf. ...*iskâ-*

sakimêw- NA mosquito; 22:1; 65:51

sakiniskêhtah- VTA walk s.o. along holding his/her hand; (65:8); cf. ...*nisk*...

sakiniskêpah- VTA run s.o. along holding his/her hand; 65:8; *nisakiniskêpahâhtay kâ-kotikositêšihk* I was running with him by the hand (arm) when he dislocated his ankle; cf. ...*nisk*..., *kotikositêšin-*

sakipâson- NA button, clasp; (21:4)

sakisitêpiso- VAI be snared by the foot; (21:4); cf. ...*sit*...

sakistikwânêpiso- VAI be snared by the head; (21:4); cf. ...*stikwân*.../-

sakišin- VAI be caught or hooked on something; (21:4) cf. ...*šin-*, *sakipâson-*

sapêt- NA [proper name] woman's name at Attawapiskat; 43:4; [contraction of Elizabeth]

saskah- VTI set fire to s.t.; (12:15)

saskahw- VTA set fire to s.o.; 12:15

saskamoci-wêpil- VTA put something into s.o.'s mouth quickly (MC); [probable hypercorrection for *saskamoci-wêpin-*]; 60:10

saskamoci-wêpin- VTA put something into s.o.'s mouth quickly; 12:15; cf. *saskamôtil-*

saskamôtil- VTA put something into s.o.'s mouth; (12:15; 60:10)

sayman- NA [proper name] Simon; 43:5

sâhkamistikw- NI [place name] West River, Kisagami River; 66:1; n. 66:1; cf. ...*stikw*.../-

sâkahikan- NI lake; 1:6; 8:5; 9:24; 16:1; 42:50

sâkasâkin- VTA/VTI [redupl.] stick s.o./s.t. out every now and then; 56:2; [more usual usage: *sâkihtatâ-*]

sâkaskêh- VTI come out of high bush into the muskeg; 37:6

sâkaškamikišin- VAI lie partially covered by earth (i.e., moose or other animal); (29:1); cf. ...*askamik*..., ...*šin-*

sâkâkonêpaliho- VAI quickly poke out or emerge from the snow; (66:1; n. 66:5); cf. ...*âkon*..., ...*paliho-*

sâkâmaciwê- VAI climb up a bank, come up over the top of the bank; 9:16; (37:6); cf. ...*âmaciwê-*

sâkâstawê- VAI rise (i.e., the sun); 15:2

sâkâstawêpali- VAI suddenly rise (i.e., the sun); 3:8; cf. *sâkâstê-*, ...*pali-*

sâkâstê- VII be sunrise; cf. *wâstê-*

sâkâwikanêstâ- VAI-T show the dorsal fin; (29:1); cf. *wâwikan-*; ...*âwikan*...

sâkêwêskawê- VAI come around the bend; 13:6

sâkiciwêwêpin- VTA throw s.o. on a bank; 9:16

sâkih- VTA love s.o.; 26:2

sâkihkâpi- VAI stand out, protrude; (61:2); *âpihtawikât sâkihkâpiw lêkâhk* he stands in sand half way up his leg; cf. *iskopê-*, *iskwâkonê-*, *pašakohcîskawakâhk*, *sâkipê-*

sâkihtatâ- VAI-T stick s.t. in so that it protrudes; 55:6; cf. *sâkasâkin-*

sâkihtâ- VAI-T love s.t.; (26:2)

sâkihtin- VII stick up (above a surface), protrude; 9:16; 12:6; cf. *sâkišin-*, ...*htin-*

sâkin- VTA/VTI stick s.o./s.t. out; 56:3

sâkipakâ- VII bud, bloom (i.e., flower or plant); 9:16; (29:1)

sâkipakâwi-pîsimw- NA June, lit., 'budding moon'; 9:16; cf. *pîsimw-*

sâkipakî- VII break through the surface (as flowers, grasses, etc.); (29:1)

sâkipali- VAI/VII come out, stick out; 13:9; cf. ...*pali-*

sâkipaliho- VAI quickly poke out, emerge; 66:1; cf. *sâkâkonêpaliho-*, ...*paliho-*

sâkipalihtwâ- VAI-T quickly poke s.t. out; 56:3

sâkipê- VAI stand out of the water; (61:2); *âpihtawikât sâkipêw* he stands out of the water half way up his leg; contrast *âpihtaw niskâtihk n'tiskwâkonân kôn* the snow was half way up my leg; 61:2; cf. *iskopê-*, *iskwâkonê-*, *iskocêškaw-*, *sâkihkâpi-*,

pasakocêškawakîhk, ...ipê.../-
sâkipit- VTA/VTI pull s.o./s.t. out; 13:9
sâkiskwêli- VAI face (to) protrude, face come to the surface; 22:3; cf. *...iskw...*
sâkiskwêpaliho- VAI pop one's head up (as a child playing among blankets); (22:3); cf. *...iskw...*, *...paliho-*
sâkistikwânêpali- VAI head (to) pop out; 60:3; *kawahkatêw mâka âpihta, wêhci-pêci-sâkistikwânêpalit* half starved, all of a sudden a girl's head popped out; cf. *...stikwân...*, *...pali-*
sâkišikonêšin- VAI show the tail fin (at one point) above the surface of the water; (29:1); cf. *...šikon...*, *...šin-*
sâkišin- VAI protrude, stick up above a surface; (9:16); 12:6; 58:4; cf. *sâkihtin-*, *...šin-*
sâkiwêpin- VTA/VTI throw s.o./s.t. up; 9:16; cf. *pohci-wêpin-*
sâmin- VTA/VTI touch s.o./s.t.; 10:9
sâmišk- VTI make body contact with s.t.; 1:5; cf. *sâmin-*
sâmiškaw- VTA make body contact with s.o.; (1:5)
sâpêliht- VTI be content with s.t. [usually with negative]; 9:2; 42:44; *môla ohci-sâpêlihtam* she wasn't keen about it; cf. *šaškatêliht-*
sâpimahciho- VAI feel weak, feel unwell; 58:5; not used independently; must occur in context supplying reason: *êkâ ê-sâpimahcihoyâhk anima ê-'ši-mîcisoyâhk* because we didn't feel well in ourselves from eating that; cf. *sâpî-, sâpisî-, maškawî-, ...amahciho-*
sâpisî- VAI be in a state of strength (of body), be in good physical shape [used only with negative]; 58:5; *môna sâpisîw* he is weak (from ill health)
sâpî- VAI be strong of body, be able-bodied [used only with negative]; 58:5; *môna sâpîw* he is not strong (opposite of *maškawî-*); cf. *sâpimahciho-, sâpisi-*
sâs- VTI fry s.t.; (54:1; 58:5)
sâsâkâskon- VTA/VTI [redupl.] stick s.o./s.t. out in the open repeatedly or every now and then; 56:4

sâsâkihtatâ- VAI-T [redupl.] stick s.t. in here and there; 18:9; 55:6
sâsâkihtin- VII [redupl.] lie sticking up (distributively); 18:9; cf. *sâkihtin-*, *...htin-*
sâsâkikâpawi- VAI stand with the body sticking out and showing repeatedly; 56:3; cf. *...kâpawi-*
sâsâkilicihcê- VAI be bare-handed; (11:13); cf. *...cihc...*
sâsâkilikâtê- VAI be bare-legged; 11:13; cf. *...kât...*
sâsâkilisitê- VAI be bare-footed; (11:13); 61:5; cf. *...sit...*
sâsâkilistikwânê- VAI be bare-headed; (11:13); cf. *...stikwân...*
sâsâkisitêšim- VTA lay s.o. here and there with s.o.'s feet sticking up; 18:7; cf. *...sit...*
sâsâkisitêšin- VAI lie all around with feet sticking up; 18:8; cf. *...sit...*, *...šin-*
sâsâkišikonê- VAI show the tail fin periodically above the water surface; (29:1); cf. *sâkâwikanêstâ-, sâkišikonêsin-, ošikwanay-, wâwikan-, ...šikon...*
sâsâkišikonêni- VAI show the tail fin (as a mermaid); (29:1); cf. *...šikon...*
sâsâkišikwanê- VAI show the tail fin intermittently above the water surface [variant of *sâsâkišikonê-*]; 29:1
sâsâkišikwanêstâ- VAI-T break surface with the tail fin repeatedly; (29:1); cf. *ošikwanay-, ...šikwan...*
sâsikâtê- VII be fried; 54:1; cf. *sâs-, sâsw-*
sâsîkahahtaw- VTA [redupl.] pour liquid all over s.o., drench s.o.; 14:7; cf. *sîkahahtaw-, sîkahahtâso-*
sâso- VAI fry; 58:5; *ê-sâsot namês* frying fish
sâsw- VTA fry s.o.; (54:1; 58:5)
sêkah- VTA frighten s.o.; 8:7; 12:5; *ê'kotânta kê-sêkahak* that's where I'll frighten him
sêkim- VTA frighten s.o. (by word); 14:2; 17:1; 23:2
sêkisi- VAI be afraid, be scared; 3:10; 37:5; 60:3; 65:9

sêlors- NA [proper name] Sailors; 64:3

sêsêkâhtakw- NA white spruce; (42:54); cf. *minahikw-, ...htakw.../-*

sêsik IPC (1) near; (12:9); *'kâwila sêsik anta itohtê; kostâtikwan* don't go near that place; it's dangerous; (2) in a sort of way; (27:7); [synonym: *mâši(h)*]

sêsikêh- VTA get near s.o.; (12:9) *môla n'kî-sêsikêhâw* I can't get near him; cf. *sêsik*

sêsikêhito- VAI [recipr.] go near each other; (12:9)

sêsikôc IPC suddenly, without warning, unexpectedly; (12:7); cf. *kêtahtawil*

sêskah- VTI put ashore; 8:7; *pêci-sêskaham* he comes ashore, he comes and beaches it

sêskipahtâ- VAI run ashore; 34:3; cf. *...pahtâ-*

sihkosiw- NA weasel; 19:9; 68:2

sihkwâht- VTI spit s.t. out; (21:4); [less preferred synonym for *wêpatêht-*]

sihtâhkwanak NA [pl.] brushwood; 50:3; 51:2 [solecism for *cistâhkwan-*]

sikilêsi- VAI be glad; 10:5; 53:4

sikilêyâpamo- VAI feel happy; 12:5

sinikocâpinitiso- VAI rub one's eyes; 46:2; cf. *paškocâpipitiso-, ...câp...*

sinikocihcênitiso- VAI rub one's hand(s); 46:2; cf. *...cihc...*

sinikohkwênitiso- VAI rub one's face; (46:2); cf. *...hkw...*

sinikon- VTA/VTI rub s.o./s.t.; (46:2); cf. *lâlâšin-*

sinikostikwânênitiso- VAI rub one's head; (46:2); cf. *...stikwân...*

siyâkêl IPC at least, anyhow, at any rate (MC); 43:12; SC: *siyâkên*

siyâkên IPC at least, anyhow, at any rate (SC); MC: *siyâkêl*

sîhcâ- VII be tight-packed, be close-fitting; (63:2); cf. *sîhtâskinê-*

sîhcišk- VTI fit s.t. closely, be tight-packed or crowded in s.t.; (63:2); *wêsâ sîhciškam opîskâkan* his coat is too small

sîhciškaw- VTA fit s.o. closely, be tight-packed or crowded in s.o.; 63:2; *wêsâ sîhciškawêw opalacîsa* his pants are too tight

sîhkaci- VAI be cold, be chilled; 23:1; 35:1

sîhkatim- VTA chill s.o.; 23:2; cf. *tahkahcihtâ-*

sîhtawi-ošim- VTA push s.o. in between two things; (62:5)

sîhtawipaliho- VAI squeeze oneself in between; 19:8; cf. *...paliho-*

sîhtâškinê- VAI be too crowded (in a house); (63:2); cf. *sîhcâ-*

sîkahahtaw- VTA baptize s.o., pour water on s.o.; (14:7); cf. *sâsîkahahtaw-, sîkahahtâso-*

sîkahahtâso- VAI get baptized; (14:7)

sîkin- VTI pour s.t.; 50:2

sîkwan- VII be early spring (before open water); 22:3; 42:49; 43:5; 60:1; cf. *miloskamin-*

sîkwanw- NI early spring; (43:5)

sîkwanohk IPC last spring; 43:5

sîkwêpahâht- VTI pour s.t.; 23:4

sîkwêpin- VTA/VTI pour s.o./s.t. out; 13:13

sîn- VTA/VTI squeeze s.o./s.t. along (like a cloth through a wringer, or fish or bird intestines when cleaning them); 54:1

sînipâtah- VTI wring s.t. out by an instrument; (50:4); cf. *sînipâtin-*

sînipâtahw- VTA wring s.o. out by an instrument; (50:4); cf. *sînipâtin-*

sînipâtin- VTA/VTI wring s.o./s.t. out by hand by torsion; 50:5; 61:5

sînitakišê- VAI purge oneself, purge one's gut; 20:4; cf. *...takiš...*

sîpiy- NI river; 1:5; 13:3; 34:2; cf. *...stikw.../-*

sôhka IPC strongly, mightily; 40:6; 43:5

sôhkatâna IPC so that's it! 60:10 [synonym: *tâpwê ot' âni*]

sôhkatâni IPC so that's it! [alternative form of *sôhkatâna*]

sômis- NA [proper name] Soomis; 44:4

sôp- NA [English loanword] soap; 50:4

sôpâpôw- NI soap liquid: made by cutting up and dissolving soap in water for use in tanning moose hide; cf. *...âpôw-*

sôsâskohtâ- VAI-T make glare ice (by

smoothing off bumps with a shovel);
12:14

sôsâskwan- VII be glare ice; (12:14)

stîpin- NA [proper name] Stephen; 40:1;
42:44

stwâp- NI [English loanword] stove 50:2;
cf. *iškotêhkân-*

šamacikâpawi- VAI stand erect; 1:8;
šâmacikâpawiw ê-môminêt he's
standing erect eating berries (e.g., a
bear); cf. *...kâpawi-*

šamatâskohotiso- VAI prop oneself up
with a wooden frame (as a sick person
in bed); (1:8)

šamatâsko- VAI climb (of a bear); be
upright against the wood of a tree (of
four-legged animals only); 1:8; for a
person *wî-ati-kospâhtawî-* is used; cf.
...âsw.../-

šašiwin- VTA/VTI rub s.o./s.t. on; 50:2; cf.
šišôpêhikê-

šaškatêliht- VTI be fed up with s.t., be
tired of s.t.; 42:8; cf. *sâpêliht-*

šaškatêlim- VTA be fed up with s.o., be
tired of s.o.; (42:8)

šawahw- VTA harm s.o., 59:4

šawin- VTA/VTI move, dislodge or budge
s.o./s.t.; 9:6; *môla n'šawinên* I'm not
budging it, I can't budge it

šawipit- VTA/VTI move or budge s.o./s.t.
by pulling; *môla n'šawipitên* I can't
budge it (e.g., a canoe); *môla
n'šawipitâw* I can't move it (e.g., a
tree)

šawiškaw- VTA make a dent or pressure
mark on s.o. (by body action); (61:5);
cf. *matwên-, matwêškaw-, pâhciškaw-*

šâ IPC tsk! tsk! darn it! 5:3; 12:8

šâ mân'sa IPC oh my! 5:3; 29:2

šâ mân'si IPC oh my! [variant of *šâ
mân'sa*]

šâk- NI [English loanword] shack; 41:6

'šâkanâpiy- NI twine, line, rope, cord
[contraction of *pišâkanâpiy-*]; 53:1;
55:2; 65:5

šâkitâto-kîšikâw IPC a nine-day period;
58:5; cf. *pêyako-tipahikan*

šâkoc IPC to be sure, for sure, certainly,
however; 1:3; 9:1; 9:2; 40:6; 41:18

šâkoc mâka IPC but

šâkocih- VTA overcome s.o., beat s.o.,
conquer s.o., defeat s.o.; 23:5

šâkocihtâ- VAI-T overcome s.t., beat s.t.,
get the best of s.t.; 10:3

šâkoh- VTA overcome s.o., overpower s.o.,
master s.o. (as in a fight); 42:18; 60:9;
66:2; for a game cf. *paskilaw-*

šâkohtâ- VAI-T overcome s.t., overpower
s.t., master s.t.; (42:18; 60:9; 66:2)

šâkotihkwaši- VAI fall asleep, drowse;
9:17; cf. *liskihkwâmi-, nôhtêhkwaši-,
šâpohkwâmi-, ...ihkwaši-*

šâkotwâ- VAI win; 49:4

šâkwêh- VTA get the better of s.o.; 60:9

šâkwêlimo- VAI be nervous, be hesitant,
be diffident; 11:9; cf. *nanihcî-*

šâkwêšiw- NA mink; 1:7; 9:16; 19:9;
40:5; cf. *acakâš-*

šâkwêši-wayân- NI mink skin; 9:10

šâmišk- VTI make body contact with s.t.;
1:5; [variant of *sâmišk-*, with
idiosyncratic palatalization by
speaker]

šânkwâ IPC nine times; 42:26; n. 42:42

šâpatîs- NA [proper name] Jean-
Baptiste; 43:8

šâpohkwâmi- VAI sleep soundly; 8:8; cf.
*liskihkwâmi-, ...ihkwâmi-, šâpopali-,
šâpohtawêsk-, nôhtêhkwaši-,
šâkotihkwaši-; ...ihkwaši-*

šâpohtawêpahamaw- VTA drive it
through for s.o.; (12:7)

šâponikan- NI (sewing-)needle; (52:1); cf.
amahkw-, aškimê-, wâš-

šâposkamik IPC through the world;
41:3; cf. *misiwêskamikâk, ...askamikw-*

šâposkamikipali- VAI/VII go through the
country; 41:3; cf. *...askamik..., ...pali-*

šâpošk- VTI pass through s.t.; 9:8

šâpoškaw- VTA pass through s.o.; (9:8)

šâpotawêyâtihkê- VAI dig (something)
right through; (60:6); cf. *wâtihkê-*

šâpwâpâwê- VAI be soaked right
through; 61:5; cf. *tihkâpâwê-*

'šâstaw IPC my goodness! goodness
gracious! [contraction of *kišâstaw*];
9:20

sâwanohk IPC in the south, to the south; 61:1

sêhkâtâpê- VAI draw (something) away; 52:1; cf. ...*itâpê-*

sêhkêl IPC by itself, automatically (MC); *sêhkêl ta-âpahipaliw* it will open automatically; MC: *sêhkên*

sêhkên IPC by itself, automatically (SC); MC: *sêhkêl*

sêko- VAI squeeze under (a little place); (52:2)

sêkoh- VTI squeeze in behind by canoe; cf. *sêkošimo-, sêkotâcimo-, sêkwâhkâw-*

sêkopali- VAI/VII get in a crack; (52:2); cf. ...*pali-*

sêkopaliho- VAI get under (something) quickly; 66:2; cf. *sêkwâkonêpaliho-, ...paliho-*

sêkošim- VTA shove s.o. under; (55:4); cf. *sêsêkošim-*

sêkošimo- VAI squeeze under a little place (for shelter); (52:2); cf. *sêkotâcimo-, têpa-sêko-*

sêkotâcimo- VAI crawl under a shelter, crawl into a tight place; (52:2); cf. *têpa-sêko-*

sêkwâhkâw- NI [place name] Jarvis Bluff (topographical feature on west coast of James Bay); [possible contraction of *sêkwâwahkâw-* 'sand or gravel shoal']; cf. *sêkoh-, sêkotâcimo-*

sêkwâkonakî- VAI tunnel under the snow; (68:2); [variant of *sêkwâkonêwi-*]

sêkwâkonêpaliho- VAI get under the snow quickly; (66:2); cf. *sêkopaliho-, ...âkon..., ...paliho-*

sêkwâkonêwi- VAI tunnel under the snow; 68:2; cf. *sêkwâkonakî-, ...âkonak...*

sêmâcišin- VAI move over and straighten out (as a person in bed); 10:3; cf. ...*šin-*

sêsêkon- VTA/VTI [redupl.] shove s.o./s.t., ram s.o./s.t., jam s.o./s.t., push s.o./s.t.; (51:2); [near-synonym: *kâtin-*]

sêsêkonikâtê- VII [redupl.] be shoved, be squeezed in; 51:2; cf. *sêsêkon-*

sêsêkošim- VTA [redupl.] shove s.o. under, one after another; 55:4; cf.

šêkošim-

'šêyâkw- NA bear (East Coast, James Bay); (n. 2:5); [contraction of *cišêyâkw-*]; cf. *maskw-*

šihkâpêšin- VAI be tapered down (e.g., *asiniy*, concrete); 41:19

šihkošiw- NA weasel; 68:2; cf. *sihkosiw-*

šikâkw- NA skunk, quarter; 61:3; 68:4; *pêyak šikâko-wayân* one skunk skin; (this was at one time worth a quarter of a dollar and so came to be used for 25¢; *šikâkw-* then came to be the general term for quarter)

šiki- VAI urinate; (12:5)

šikit- VTA/VTI urinate on s.o./s.t.; 12:5

šimatâsko- VAI get up on the hind legs; 1:8; cf. *šamatâsko-*

'šin'kâcikâtê- VII be called, be named [contraction of *išinihkâcikâtê-*]; 54:1; *oskwanipiy 'sin'kâcikâtêw* it is called 'liver water'; cf. *oskwan-*

šinkipiš- NA [proper name] Shingibish (legendary figure); probably the small or hooded merganser; 8:6; 8:7; 8:8; 47:1; cf. *šihkipiš*, form used at Attawapiskat. The species is more common in Ojibwa speaking country, which may account for the Ojibwa form of the name in the legend.

šišôpêhikê- VAI paint; cf. *šašiwin-, ...ipê-*

šîhkicišahw- VTA encourage or urge s.o., order, direct or get after s.o. (to do s.t.); 42:17

šîhkih- VTA urge s.o. on, encourage s.o.; 49:4

šîhkim- VTA persuade s.o.; 8:2

šîkwašikawin- VII drain out (as of a pail with holes); (56:6); cf. *kwêtipin-, pâhkwašikawin-*

šîpahw- VTA stretch s.o. (e.g., an otter skin); (62:1); contrast *šîpâhw-*

šîpâ IPC beneath [with locative]; 25:2

šîpâhw- VTA squeeze s.o.; 62:1; contrast *šîpahw-*

šîpânakohk IPC behind the island, in the channel; 42:48

šîpânakw- NI channel, strait, branch river; cf. *awasânak, âstamânak,* *kišipânak, kwêskânak, otiškawânak, šîpânakohk*; *...ânak..., ...ânakw-*

šîpâso- VAI go underneath; 9:15

šîpîšiš- NI creek; 8:5; 45:1; cf. *sîpiy-*

šîpwâstêpali- VAI/VII be discernible coming through, come translucently; 60:7; *kâ-pêci-šîpwâstêpalik mistik* where the stick could be discerned coming through; cf. *šîpwâstê-, ...pali-*

šîpwâstê- VII be translucent, be almost transparent; 60:7

šîšîp- NA duck; 18:1; 49:5; 61:1

šîšîpišimo- VAI do the duck dance; contrast *wâpošo-nîmiwin nîmiwak* they do the rabbit dance; cf. *...šimo-*

šîwatê- VAI be hungry; 18:10; 19:7; 27:6; cf. *kawahkatê-*

šîwâ- VII be sweet, be salty; be candy; be fresh (of fruits); 43:3; 68:8; *kâ-šîwâki mînîša* fresh fruits

šîwâkamin- VII be salt (water), be sweet (tea); 65:9; 68:1; 61:8; cf. *...âkamin.../-, šîwâpôwan-, šîwihtâkan-, šôkâw-*

šîwâpôw- NI salt water (MC); 65:9; SC: *šîwâpôy-*; cf. *...âpôw-*

šîwâpôwan- VII be salt water; (68:1); cf. *šîwâkamin-, šîwihtâkan-, šôkâw-*

šîwâpôy- NI salt water (SC); 65:9; MC: *šîwâpôw-*; cf. *...âpôw-*

šîwihtâkan- NI salt; (68:1); cf. *šîwâkamin-, šôkâw-*

šîwîyatihkân- NI stomach of a caribou used as a bag; 12:3; cf. *...atay..., ...ihkân-*

šôkâw- NI [English loanword] sugar [sometimes NA]; 58:5; for variable gender cf. *pêsin-, pikîw-*

šôliyân- NA money; 39:3; 41:9; 42:9

šôliyânihkâkê- VAI make money (out of it), use it to make money; 41:11; cf. *...ihkâkê-*

šôliyânikimâw- NA Indian Agent 'paymaster'; 42:39

šôšawakohtin- VII spread floating; 14:6; *šôšawakohtin pimiy* the fat spread over the top (of the water)

šôšawâpawâcikê- VAI spill and have (something) spread; (14:6); cf. *šôšawakohtin-*

šôškonâtahî- VAI slide down (the hill); (12:15); cf. *papâmâtahî-, pîhtokwêyâtahî-, ...âtahî-*

šôw- NI [English loanword] (moving picture) show; 42:9; n. 42:16

ta IPV shall, will; 1:4; [contraction of *kata*]; used with 3rd person subjects only

tacipali- VAI/VII come to a short stop, be checked, stick; (42:36); cf. *...pali-*

tacipalihiko- VAI be stopped short (in time, funds, etc.), held in check; 42:36; cf. *tacipali-, tatâpêpali-*

tacîtwâskopali- VAI be (physically) stunned, 14:7; *kâ-mohci-catîtwâskopanin'ci manâ piko, ê'kwâni misiw' ê-kî-câkihât* then as he was simply stunned with shock, at that point he finished them all off; (note metathesis in the text)

tahkahcihtâ- VAI-T cool s.t. off (as food); (23:2); cf. *sîhkatim-*

tahkam- VTA stab s.o., spear s.o.; 10:9; 12:5; 60:9; cf. *tâtahkam-*

tahkamwê- VAI stab; (12:6)

tahkâši- VAI be in a cold draft; (41:7); cf. *...âši-*

tahkâyâ- VII be cold; 1:2; 22:2; 35:1; 40:5; 41:7; cf. *...ayâ-*

tahkâyânipali- VAI suddenly become cold; 11:11; cf. *tahkâyâ-, ...pali-*

tahkêliht- VTI feel chilly; (41:7)

tahkikamihtin- VII become cool (liquid); (27:4); cf. *...kam..., ...htin-*

tahkikamihtitâ- VAI-T cool it (liquid) off; (27:4); cf. *...kam...; tatahkikamihtitâ-*

tahkipali- VAI get a chill; 41:7; cf. *tahkâši-, tahkêliht-, ...pali-*

tahkiškâcitiyêhw- VTA kick s.o. in the behind; (68:5); cf. *išitiyêli-, kalakitiyê-, kwêskitiyêpaliho-, ...tiy...*

tahkiškât- VTA/VTI kick s.o./s.t.; 18:6; cf. *wêpiškât-*

tahkoh- VTI steer s.t.; 65:5

tahkokâpiwisi- VAI be short in stature; 13:7; cf. *...kâpawi-*

tahkon- VTA/VTI hold s.o./s.t.; 5:10; 9:20; 19:8; 53:1; 65:7

tahkon-apwoy- NA rudder handle, steering wheel; 42:31; cf. *apwoy-*

tahkopit- VTA/VTI tie s.o./s.t.; 25:2; cf. *tahkwapiso-*

tahkopitâwaso- VAI have a (new) baby (tied up); 51; cf. *...âwaso-*

tahkostikwêyâ- VII be a short river; (42:28); cf. *kinostikwêyâ-, kîškâyawistikwêyâ-, kwayaskostikwêyâ-, pâhkostikwêyâ-, wâwâkistikwêyâ-, ...stikw...*

tahkotâmaciwê- VAI get to the top of the hill; 5:1; cf. *...âmaciwê-*

tahkwapiso- VAI be laced in; 51:1; also as *tahkopiso-*; cf. *tahkopit-*

tahkwâliwê- VAI have a short tail (e.g., a moose); (27:4); cf. *kinwâliwê-, pîkwêyâliwê-, ...âliw...*

tahkwâpêkin- VTA/VTI shorten s.o./s.t.; (42:42); cf. *nahkâpêkin-, ...êkin.../-*

tahkwâpê- VAI be a short trace, be a short leash; 42:42; cf. *kâ-tahkwâpêt, kinwâpê-, nahkâpêkin-, tahkwâpêkin-, mîskwâpin-, otâpâniyâpiy-, ...âp...*

tahkwâpihkêyâ- VII be short (of a cord, line, rope); 42:57; cf. *...âpihk..., ...ayâ-*

tahkwâskohtâ- VAI-T make s.t. short (of wood); (52:2); cf. *iskwâskohtâ-, kinwâskohtâ-, ...âskw.../-*

tahkwâ- VII be short; 8:1

tahtakwah- VTI [redupl.] make s.t. fall (with an instrument); (13:16)

tahtakwahw- VTA [redupl.] make s.o. fall with an instrument (as ice chunks in one's way on the river or shrubs in the way of putting up a tent); knock s.o. down (as in fighting or goose hunting); 13:16; *n'kî-tahtakwahwâwak* I knocked them all down; cf. *wani-tahtakwahw-*

tahtâpiskipit- VTI trigger s.t.; (59:4); cf. *...âpisk...*

tahtin- VTA/VTI unbutton s.o./s.t., loosen s.o./s.t.; (10:9)

tahto IPV/IPN each, every; much, as many as; 6:12; 13:2; 41:14; *tahto-nîpin* every summer; *tân' tahto-piponêsit* how old is she?

tahto-nipâ- VAI sleep so many times

(i.e., on a trip), camp so many times; 42:26

tahto-pimiy- NI so much fat, every kind of fat; 23:3

tahto-piponêsi- VAI be of such an age, be of so many winters; 41:18

tahto-tipahikanêyâ- VII be so many miles; 42:25; cf. *...ayâ-*

tahtowêkinâkosi- VAI be of every kind; 8:3; cf. *tahtoyêk, ...nâkosi-*

tahtoyêk IPC of every kind; 18:1

tahtwâ IPC every time; 25:3; 41:10; 42:5; *tahtwâ ê-kîšikâk* every day; *tahtwâ êyamihê-kîšikâki* whenever it is Sunday, every Sunday

takohikana NI [pl.] pliers, pincers; (42:32)

takopali- VAI/VII arrive; 42:47; 44:4; cf. *...pali-*

takositêhotiso- VAI jam one's (own) foot; (42:32); cf. *...sit..., takwahw-*

takositêhw- VTA jam s.o.'s foot, crush s.o.'s foot; (42:32); 42:62; *ta-takositêhokow* it will (fall and) crush her foot

takošin- VAI arrive; 1:8; 9:8; 16:4; 35:2

takwah- VTI jam s.t., catch s.t. (accidentally, e.g., a finger or toe in a door), crush s.t. by dropping something on it, pound s.t.; (13:16) *n'kî-takwahên nimisisitân* I dropped something on my big toe; cf. *lîlîkicihcân-, lîlîkisitân-, micihcan-, misisitân-*

takwahw- VTA jam s.o., catch s.o. (accidentally), pound s.o., bray s.o.; 42:32; (13:16); cf. *takositêhw-, takositêhotiso-, takohikana*

takwan- VII be, exist; 40:1; 40:6; 41:12; 60:8; *môna kîy-ohci-takwan anima tôwi-kêkwân kanakê* that kind of thing didn't exist at all

takwâkin- VII be autumn; 20:1; 36:1; 49:1; 58:3; 61:2

tapahtaskitê- VII be low; (52:3) *tapahtaskitêw wâskâhikan* it is a low house; cf. *iskwâskitê-, ispaskitê-*

tapasih- VTA dodge s.o., evade s.o. (as in playing tag or avoiding a blow); (43:6)

taskatito- VAI beat each other; n. 33:1;
cf. *paskilâto-*

tasôso- VAI be caught by something
which has fallen on one (e.g., trap,
tree, rock); 41:13; *mistikwa kî-tasôsow,
ê'kwâni wêhci-išinâkosit* a tree fell on
him, that's why he looks that way;
ê-kî-pahkišin'ci ê-kî-tasôsot asiniya he
was pinned when a rock fell on him

tastawic IPC in the middle, between;
42:45

tašihtâkwan- VII sound there; 13:3; cf.
...ihtâkwan-

taši-nanêhkâsinâkwan- VII look so
poorly, remain looking poorly; 42:37;
cf. *...nâkwan-*

tašinawî- VAI busy oneself (SC); 5:5; MC:
tašîwî-

tašinê IPC all the time, continually,
incessantly, repeatedly; 7:8; 8:7; 22:1;
23:4; 40:6; 41:7; *nikamow mâka tašinê*
and he is forever singing

taši-ninihkinâkosi- VAI appear to
shake there violently (from the
thrashing of the beaver); 13:9; cf.
ninihkinâkosi-, ...nâkosi-

tašiwâhkwê- VAI spread one's wings
(i.e., geese); (10:9); cf. *papîwahâhkê-*

tašîhkaw- VTA take such a time to make
s.o., spend such a time on s.o.; 52:3;
*nisto-kîšikâw n'kî-tašîhkawâw ê-ošihak
wâpoš'-'êyân* it took me three days to
make the rabbit blanket; cf.
wâpošo-wayân-

tašîhkâtot- VTI use (s.t.) for a dwelling
(referring to a place); 1:1; [reference to
a house requires *tašîhkê-*]

tašîhkê- VAI dwell; 1:3; 41:7; cf.
milo-tašîhkê-

tašîhkêm- VTA live with s.o.; 9:18

tašîhkêwâkê- VAI use for a dwelling;
41:7; cf. *...kê-*

taš'-îšinâkwan- VII it looks such a way;
42:36; *wa, ê'kwâni kê-taš '-îšinâkwahk!*
oh, let it go the way it looks there! cf.
...nâkwan-

tašîwî- VAI busy oneself around, potter
around, fritter around (MC); 5:5; 53:2;
58:2; *pêyakwanohk tašîwîw* he's

busying himself in one place *anta piko
tašîwîw* he's just working around
there (pointing); SC: *tašinawî-*; cf.
išîwî-

tašwâpihkêpit- VTA/VTI stretch s.o./s.t.
out, uncoil s.o./s.t., unravel s.o./s.t.;
(52:1); cf. *pîmastêhwâkaniwan-,
pîmastêpali-, pîmastêsi-, ...âpihk...*

tašwâpihkêšim- VTA spread s.o. out to
one side; 18:3; cf. *...âpihk...*

tatahkikamihtitâ- VAI-T [redupl.] cool
s.t. (liquid) off, make s.t. (liquid) cold;
27:4; cf. *tahkikamihtitâ-,
tahkikamihtin-, ...kam...*

tatašiwêkišim- VTA [redupl.] spread s.o.
about; 9:21; cf. *...êk...*

tatawêh- VTI make a noise there; 14:5;
cf. *tatawêkahikê-*

tatawêht- VTI be heard (one's voice)
from such a place; 20:5; *'kâwina
wîskâc ohc'-îtâpi kâ-tatawêhtahkik*
don't ever look about when they call

tatawêkahikê- VAI make a noise; 14:5;
cf. *tatawêh-*

tatâpêpali- VAI/VII be stopped short, be
checked (as a canoe held by a rope
from drifting, or a dog restrained by a
chain from attacking); 42:36; cf.
...tâpê-, ...pali-

tatêliht- VTI make a guess at its being
there; 68:6; *ninân'tawa'htên
otâmahikan; ôta mâka n'tatêl'htên* I'm
looking around for the hammer; my
guess is, it's around here

tatêlim- VTA think s.o. there; 12:13;
60:7

tatêpipali- VAI/VII [redupl.] have
enough, get along adequately; 42:65;
cf. *têpipali-*

tatin- VTA/VTI grab s.o./s.t. to try to
separate them; 10:9; 13:9; contrast
tahtin-

tatwêkamahâšikê- VII (rollers, waves)
sound over there [solecism for
tatwêkamâškâ-]; 68:8

tatwêkamâškâ- VII (rollers, waves)
sound over there; 68:8; cf.
tatwêkamahâšikê-, ...kam...

tatwêwêhikê- VAI [redupl.] beat the
drum, be drumming; (64:2); cf.
twêwêhikê-

tawâpiskâ- VII be open and rocky; cf.
âtawâpiskâtw-, ...âpisk...

tawâskitê- VII an open path be burnt, a
trail be blazed; 15:1

tawâskokahikan- NI railway-cut
through the bush; 41:6

tawâstê- VII be a week; 39:1; 42:12;
pêyakwâ ê-tawâstêk once a week

tawâstêw- NI week

tawikahikan- NI clearing; township
line, frontier line; railway cut; 41:4

tawikahikê- VAI cut a clearing, cut a
trail; 41:4

tawipali- VAI/VII be an opening; (28:1)
tawipaliyâhkê isa if there is time, if
we have time; [near-synonym:
ispihcîyâhkê isa]; cf. *ispihcî-, ...pali-*

'tawi-pêh- VTA get tired waiting for s.o.;
16:4; cf. *kîtawi-pêhtâ-*

tayna- NA [proper name] Dinah; 65:1

tâcikwê- VAI scream; 60:3

tâhcipo- VAI be fat, be stout (applied to
human beings and round islands, as
along the north shore of Lake
Superior); (19:1); contrast
'ci-wî-kakwê-tâhcipohitisoyan; 20:3

tâhcipoh- VTA make s.o. fat, fatten s.o.;
(19:1)

tâhcipohitiso- VAI make oneself fat;
19:1

tâhkihtin- VII touch, tip; (5:7); cf.
...htin-

tâhkišin- VAI touch, tip; 5:7; cf.
tâhtâhkišin-, ...šin-

tâhtakošin- VAI [redupl.] arrive
one-by-one; 10:7; cf. *takošin-, ...šin-*

tâhtâhkihtin- VII [redupl.] skip along
touching; (5:7); cf. *tâhkihtin-, ...htin-*

tâhtâhkišin- VAI [redupl.] skip along
touching; 5:7; cf. *tâhkišin-, ...šin-*

tâhtâpišah- VTI [redupl.] thread s.t.,
string s.t.; (52:2)

tâhtâpišahw- VTA [redupl.] thread s.o.,
string s.o.; 52:2

tâni IPC how; 2:8; cf. *tahto*

tânika IPC (1) [with conj.indic.]: would

that; I hope; 3:5; 7:2; *tân'ka wîcêwakik*
how I'd like to go with them! 20:1; (2)
[with conj.dubit.]: what in the
world...? 3:5; 9:22; what can it be, I
wonder whether...; 13:3; 14:1; 14:3;
tân'k' êtokwê what must it be... 65:7;
tân'ka kipakwâtên how you must hate
it! [indep.indic.] 19:3

tânika itê IPC I wonder [with
conj.dubit.]; 18:1; 18:7; *tâ'ka ytê
kê-kî-tôtamowâpânê* I wonder what I
should do; *tân'ka 'tê kê-tôtamwânê* I
wonder what I should do; 38:2; *tân'ka
itê mâka mîna k'êtâcimoyin* I wonder
what story you'll tell now; 41:21;
tân'ka 'tê kê-išitêpoyân ôkih? I wonder
how I'll cook these? 55:3

tânispî IPC when? 20:3; 42:63

tân' tahtôtênaw IPC how many
families? 60:10; cf. *mihcêtôtênaw,
...ôtênaw-*

tântê IPC where? [allegro for *tân' itê*];
1:1; 9:3 et passim

tântê piko IPC wherever; 22:3

t'-âpacihat [VTA] have nothing to do
with him! what's the use of him?
(regarded as MC by SC speakers of
Albany Post and Fort Albany); 43:5;
e.g., t'-âpacihat! môla wayêš itâpatisiw
have nothing to do with him! he's good
for nothing; cf. *n'-âpacihat*

tâpakwê- VAI set snares; 3:2; 21:2; 29:4

tâpask IPC probably not, doubt that;
18:7; 42:63; *tâpask n'ka-sakapwân* I
wonder whether I shouldn't roast;
[virtually synonymous with
n'ka-sakapwân kâki]; *tâpask ana tâpw'
ê'kwân' êšinihkâsot* I wonder if that's
really her name 42:63

tâpâskwah- VTI put a handle on an axe;
(60:9); cf. *otâmâskwah-*

tâpêkâ IPC now then (mild
expostulation), isn't it the case that ...;
5:8; 13:9; 42:66; *tâpêkâ 'kâwina mîna
itohtê* seriously I told you or didn't I
tell you, don't go there again;
sometimes wistful: *tâpêkâ
ê-sâkihtâyâpân* I sure liked it! (of a
lost canoe); *tâpêkâ ê-sâkihakipan!* I

was really fond of him (of a dog lost or dead)

tâpêk' âni IPC [emph.] isn't it so that ...; *tâpêkâ;* 5:8; 42:58; *tâpêk' âni ê-sâkihakwâpan!* I was really fond of them!

tâpikâ IPC even though; even so; [possible variant of *tâpêkâ*]; 11:13; 63:2; *tâpikâ kici-pôsiyân 'kišêpâyâkê* nonetheless I have to go tomorrow (i.e., even though it's stormy); *tâpikâ kici-pâpalik otâpân* the train has got to come in (i.e., even though there's been a washout); *tâpikâ nâspic ê-sâkihak n'kosis* indeed I love my son very much, 63:2; *tâpikâ mîna 'ci-nipâyan wâpahkê* I'll bet you're going to sleep in tomorrow

tâpinâ IPC since not, inasmuch as not; 65:3; *tâpinâ ('nsi) n'kî-ohci-naskomâhtay kici-wîkimak* after all, I didn't promise to marry her; *tântê kê-kî-ohci-masinahikêhâkaniwit mîna, tâpinâ 'nsi kî-ohci-tipahikêpan?* how can he expect to get more credit, since he didn't square up what he got last year?

tâpisikohtatâ- VAI-T insert s.t. into something (used of an electric plug in a socket or outlet); 52:1

tâpisiko-wêpahw- VTA lasso s.o.; 55:2

tâpiskâkan- NA kerchief; 59:3

tâpiskon- VTA/VTI slip s.o./s.t. on; 50:6; *âšay kî-tâpiskonêw otastisa* he's already put his mitt on; cf. *pohcišk(aw)-*

tâpiskôc IPC like, as, as if; 1:1; 1:4; 9:2; alike, together; 11:3; 21:2; 36:2; 41:6; 45:1; 55:4; *kî-pôsiwak anima tâpiskôc* they embarked at that point together; *tâpiskôc kit-îtihkasol'ci* so they would all be roasted alike (i.e., evenly)

tâpwê IPC truly, indeed; really, seriously; 3:6; 9:20; 15:3; 41:8

tâpwê- VAI tell the truth; 1:7

tâpwêht- VTI believe s.t.; 11:7; 16:5

tâpwêhtaw- VTA believe s.o., give in to s.o., listen to s.o., 6:8; 9:3; 19:8; 29:4

tâpwêyêlihtâkwan- VII be safe, be sure; (21:9) *tâpwêyêlihtâkwan nâ kici-âšaw'kâskonâniwahk?* Do you think it's safe to walk across the ice? cf. *kostâtikwan-, ...ihtâkwan-*

tâstakât- VTI consider s.t. distasteful, dislike s.t., detest s.t.; 42:22; *tâstakâcikâtêw ê-êškâniwahk* people hate chiselling (through the ice)

tâšipwâ IPC no wonder! 63:3; cf. *tâšipwâm*

tâšipwâm IPC [archaism] that's why; 10:5; *tâšipwâm ê-mihcilawêsiyâpân nkosis ê-nipit* that's why I was sorry that my son died

tâškikaškwêpali- VAI/VII break, split (of a nail); (14:5); cf. *ninihkikaškwêwêpahw-*

tâškipali- VAI/VII be cracked; 60:10; cf. *...pali-*

tâškipocikan- NI rip-saw, pit-saw; 42:41

tâškipocikê- VAI (rip-)saw; 42:41

tâtahkam- VTA [redupl.] jab at s.o. repeatedly, poke at s.o.; 60:10; cf. *tahkam-*

tâtahkiškât- VTA [redupl.] kick away at s.o.; 27:5

tâtahkoskât- VTA [redupl.] tread here and there on s.o.; 9:24

tâtâhkoskê- VAI [redupl.] step here and there; 9:21

tâtwah- VTI rip s.t., tear s.t.; (59:4)

tâtwahw- VTA rip s.o., tear s.o.; 59:4

tâwahw- VTA hit s.o. dead on (as with an arrow or moving object); 9:23; cf. *pistahw-*

tâwatâwišk- VTI [redupl.] stagger around (bumping) into s.t.; (68:7)

tâwatâwiškaw- VTA [redupl.] stagger around (bumping) into s.o.; (68:7)

tâwatonêwêhkwâmi- VAI sleep with one's mouth open (SC); 8:8; MC: *tâwatihkonêwêhkwâmi-*; cf. *...ihkwâmi-*

tâwic IPC away from shore, in midstream; 4:4; 9:8; 58:2; 65:2; 66:1

têho- VAI land, alight; 42:48; (44:4); 66:2

têhômakan- VII land, alight; 42:47; 44:4

têhtapi- VAI sit or ride upon; 9:4; 18:4; cf. *têhtapiwin-, ...api-*

têhtapih- VTA cause s.o. to sit or ride upon; 67:3

têhtapiwin- NI chair, seat; (9:4; 18:4; 67:3

têhtâ- VII be a raised platform or support surface; *walawîtim astâ kâ-itêhtâk* put it outside on the gallery; cf. *têšipitâkan-*

têhtinikan- NI stretcher-like hand-barrow for hay-loading; (67:3); n. 67:8

têkwê- VAI scream; cf. *mâsihtâkosi-*

têpakâmêpali- VAI reach far enough over, reach far enough in a jump (MC); 11:9; cf. *akâmihk, ...akâm..., ...pali-*

têpakâmêpani- VAI reach far enough over, reach far enough in a jump (SC); MC: *têpakâmêpali-*

têpa-šêko- VAI be able to wiggle under with enough to cover oneself; 52:2; cf. *šêko-, šêkopali-, šêkošimo-, šêkotâcimo-*

têpâpaht- VTI catch sight of s.t.; 1:5

têpâpam- VTA catch sight of s.o.; (1:5)

têpihtâkosi- VAI be heard sufficiently; 28:1; cf. *...ihtâkosi-*

têpihtâkwan- VII be heard sufficiently; (28:1); cf. *...ihtâkwan-*

têpilâhk IPC provided that, as long as (MC); (4:3; 42:15); SC: *têpinâhk*

têpinâhk IPC provided that, as long as (SC); 4:3; 42:15; MC: *têpilâhk*

têpinâkosi- VAI be within (range of) sight; 65:3; cf. *...nâkosi-*

têpinâkwan- VII be in sight; 1:5; cf. *...nâkwan-*

têpipali- VAI/VII have enough, be enough (MC); (42:63); 50:2; cf. *...pali-*

têpipani- VAI/VII have enough, be enough (SC); MC: *têpipali-*

têpihtin- VII fit in; (60:9); cf. *...htin-*

têpišin- VAI fit in; 60:9; cf. *...šin-*

têpi-tôtamâso- VAI do it adequately for oneself; 43:15

têpwât- VTA call s.o.; 11:4; 13:8; 15:5; 18:1; 31:2

têpwê- VAI shout, call out, cry out; 5:7; 14:6; 19:8; 27:3; 63:1

têšipitâkan- NI stage on trapping grounds for securing food from dogs or for building a tent secure from flood-water; 60:9; 61:2; cf. *têhtâ-*

têtapânakih- VTI paddle all around the island; (55:2); cf. *têtipahânakih-*

têtâw IPC in the centre of; 55:7; *têtâw'-iškotêw* in the centre of the fire; *têtâwi-sîpiy* half way across the river; cf. *têtâwic, têtâwihtak, têtâwi-sâkahikan, têtâwiskanaw*

têtâwakâm IPC at midstream; 11:6; 34:2; 60:9; cf. *...akâm.../-*

têtâwic IPC in the middle, in the centre; amidst, in the midst of; (11:6); 18:4; 55:4; (55:7)

têtâwihtak IPC in the centre of the floor; (55:7)

têtâwi-sâkahikan IPC half way across the lake; (55:7)

têtâwiskanaw IPC half way across the road; (55:7)

têtipa IPV all around; 55:2; 55:7; cf. *têtipahânakih-, têtipahânakišk-, têtipâhtê-, kînikwânitê-, kînikwânišk-*

têtipa-apih- VTA seat s.o. all around; 55:2

têtipahânakih- VTI paddle all around the island; (55:2); [preferred variant of *têtipânakih-*; sometimes heard as *têtipayânakih-*]

têtipahânakišk- VTI walk around the island; (55:2); [sometimes *têtipayânakišk-*]; cf. *têtipânakohtê-, kînikwânišk-, ...ânak.../-*

têtêtipa-šêšêkwahw- VTA shove s.o. around under; 55:4

têtipâhtê- VAI walk around inside [with *pîhtikom*]; (55:2) *têtipâhtêw pîhtikom* he walks around inside; cf. *têtipa, kînikwânohtê-, kînikwânišk-*

têtipânah- VTI paddle around s.t.; (55:2) *têtipâna'* paddle around it (i.e., an island)!

têtipânahw- VTA paddle around s.o.; (55:2)

têtipânakohtê- VAI walk around the island; (55:2); cf. *...ânak..., ...ohtê-*

têtipâš- VTI cut around s.t.; (45:2)

têtipâšikâtê- VII be cut around; (45:2);
*têtipâšikâtêliw osôw
ê-'ši-oskaniwanilik* his tail is cut
around the bone (i.e., flesh is cut off);
cf. *kîškiš-, mâciš-, wîmoš-*

têtipâšw- VTA cut around s.o.; (45:2)

tihkâpâwê- VAI dissolve; (61:5); cf.
šâpwâpâwê-

tihkinâkan- NI Indian cradle (carried on
the back); 65:7

tihkis- VTI melt s.t.; (13:12)

tihkisomâkaniwi- VAI be melted; 12:15

tihkiso- VAI melt; 23:2

tihkisw- VTA melt s.o.; 13:12

tihtipanipali- VAI/VII wind up; 52:1; cf.
...pali-

tihtipipaliho- VAI roll over; 19:6; cf.
...paliho-

tipah- VTI pay s.t.; (40:5)

tipahamaw- VTA pay (it to) s.o.; 41:8;
41:9; 42:36; *âta... ê-tipahamâhcik*
although they were being paid;
kišâspin... tipahamawiyanê if you pay
me

tipahamâso- VAI pay back, get one's
revenge; 22:2

tipahamôtil- VTA charge s.o. (an amount
of money); (42:41)

tipahikan- NI a measure; 61:2; a mile;
58:1; *pêyak tipahikan ispîtakâmêyâw*
it (the river) is one mile wide

tipahikâtê- VII be paid; 40:4; cf. *tipah-*

tipahikê- VAI pay, measure; 41:9; 42:28

tipâcim- VTA tell about s.o., recount a
story about s.o.; 41:1; 45:1

tipâcimikosi- VAI be told about in story,
be spoken of; 10:1

tipâcimikowisîwin- NI account of
events, story; 5:10; 6:15

tipâcimo- VAI recount, tell, narrate; 1:1;
9:1; 21:1; 41:1; 41:7

tipâcimostaw- VTA tell s.o. a story,
recount for s.o.; 3:3; 6:5; 13:3; 16:1;
21:3; 41:2; 41:17

tipâcimôwin- NI story, news, narrative;
5:10; 9:19; 21:1; 42:33; 43:3

tipâpêskocikan- NA pound; 42:24

tipâtocikâtê- VII be talked about; 1:3;
anima išpimihk k-tipâtocikâtêk askiy

that land above which is talked about

tipâtot- VTI tell about s.t., testify about
s.t.; 10:1; 41:16

tipêliht- VTI control s.t., be in charge of
s.t.; 10:6; 20:4; 68:4

tipi IPV enough; 6:10; 2:5; 6:10; *tipi-ayâw*
he has enough; *tipi-ispihcâw* it is large
enough; [alternative form of *têpi-*, e.g.,
têpi-ayâ-]

tipilawê IPC own, self; individually; 2:1;
42:6; *nîla tipilawê nitipêlihtên* that is
my personal belonging

tipinawâhk IPC in the lee, sheltered
from the wind; (12:12); cf. *kapahtahan*

tipiskâ- VTI be night, be dark; 3:4; 10:4;
20:4; 22:1; 55:4; *kê-tipiskâlik* this
(coming) evening

tipiski-pîsimw- NA moon; 5:9; cf.
pîsimw-

tipiskôc IPC over against, directly across
from; above; 1:7; 12:4

tiskôso- VAI have a back injury, have a
crooked back from an injury; 41:13

tispah- VTI mix s.t., stir s.t.; (54:1)

tispahw- VTA mix s.o., stir s.o.; 54:1

titima- NA [proper name] Titima (child's
doll); 43:13; cf. *cicima-*

tîwâpohkê- VAI make tea; cf. *tîy-,
...âpw..., ...ihkê-*

tîy- NI [English loanword] tea; 58:5

torotiyw- NA [proper name] Dorothy;
[sometimes *toltiyw-*]; 42:63; 43:12

tôcikâtê- VII be done; 2:4; 12:8; 41:1;
42:4; 51:1

tôhkâpi- VAI have one's eyes open; 8:4;
19:4; cf. *...âpi-*

tôhkâpišimo- VAI dance with one's eyes
open; (8:3; 8:4); cf. *...âpi-...šimo-*

tôhtôhkipit- VTI [redupl.] widen s.t.
(e.g., one's mouth); 29:2

tôhtôskipit- VTI [redupl.] nibble away at
s.t. (as a fish or seal); 29:2

tômâ- VII be oily, be greasy, be fat; (14:3)

tômihkâso- VAI drip fat; 19:7

tômisi- VAI be oily, be greasy, be fat;
14:3; *wêsâ êkâ ê-tômisit* because he is
not fat enough

tômiskinawê- VAI have a greasy face;
(10:8)

tômiskipo- VAI eat fat beaver; (10:8); cf. *milwahcikê-, wîhkipo-, ...amisk..., ...po-*

tôt- VTI do s.t.; 2:3; 15:2; 42:64; cf. *tôtaw-*

tôtamaw- VTA do (something) for s.o.; 67:2

tôtamâso- VAI do (something) for oneself; 22:4; 41:11

tôtaw- VTA do (something) to s.o., do (something) for s.o.; 2:3; 8:4; 19:4; 42:67; *'kwantaw niwî-tôtâkonân* he wants to do something to us; *k'-îškwâ-tôtâtânê* after I've done it for you; *ê'k'oš'âni mâna nîna ê-tôtawak an' awâšiš* that's what I do repeatedly to that child

tôtâso- VAI do (something) to oneself; 37:5

tôwa- NA kind; 41:15; 42:8

tôwhân- NA ball; 28:2

tôwi IPN kind of...; 19:9; 41:12

tôwihkân- NI kind, sort; 55:1

'tôwi-pêhtâ- VAI-T get tired waiting for s.t.; 29:4; [contraction of *kôtawi-pêhtâ-*]

twâhikan- NI ice-hole, hole bored in ice; 13:9; cf. *pakwanêyâ-*

twâhikê- VAI bore holes (through the ice for setting hooks); (25:2)

twâhtwâhikê- VAI bore a number of holes; 25:2; cf. *twâhikê-*

twâmas- NA [proper name] Thomas; 43:5

twêho- VAI land, alight (a bird or pilot); 14:4; cf. *têho-, nîhci-twêho-*

twêwêhikê- VAI beat time (as to a tune); 64:2; cf. *tatwêwêhikê-*

twoyêhk IPC right away, immediately, directly; 2:4; 21:6; 42:36; 65:9

wacaskw- NA muskrat; 27:4; 45:1

waciston- NI nest; 4:1

wacistoni- VAI be nesting; 4:1

waciy- NI hill, mountain; 3:2; cf. *wîliman-, wîliman'ciy-*

wahkêwâskitê- VII burn easily (of wood); 23:3

wahkon- NDI his/her ankle; (65:8); cf. *nikotikotatân nahkon* I dislocate my ankle; cf. *mahkon-, ...ahkon-, ohkwan-*

wakic IPC on top of (with locative)

[variant of *wakîc*]; 42:55

wakîc IPC on top of (with locative); 9:6; 50:1

wakîcišim- VTA lay s.o. on top of; (50:6); *'kwân ê-'ši-okîcišimâcik ant' akolêwak* then laying it on [something], they hang it up there; cf. *okîcišim-*

wakît IPC on top of (with locative) [variant of *wakîc*]

wakîtapi- VAI sit on top of, sit thereupon; 55:7; cf. *...api-*

wakît-astâ- VAI-T set s.t. on top; 50:2; *stwâpihk n'tôkît-astânân* we lay it on top of the stove (as though from *okît-*, with o lengthened after *nit...*)

wakîtâmatin IPC on top of a hill; 19:2; cf. *...âmatin...*

wakîtihtak IPC on deck, on the deck; (55:2); cf. *...ihtakw.../-*

walahpit- VTA/VTI wrap s.o./s.t. up; (52:2); cf. *âhtahpit-, itahpit-, mâkwahpit-*

walahlapê- VAI get one's net ready; (55:2); cf. *olahlapê-, ...ahlapiy-*

walakêskw- NA bark (of a tree); 42:60

walapi- VAI get settled (in sitting posture); 13:8; cf. *...api-*

walapih- VTA seat s.o., make s.o. sit down; 55:2

walastaw- VTA set up (traps) for s.o. (MC); (11:11) *walastawêw amiskwa* he sets traps for beaver; SC: *wanahâmaw-*

walastâ- VAI-T set s.t. up, arrange s.t.; 38:1; 49:5

walašawê- VAI give orders; 12:7

walašiwât- VTA give s.o. instructions, order s.o., enjoin on s.o.; 1:4

walawî- VAI go or come out; 1:5; 4:2; 4:8; 32:1

walawîcišahikê- VAI drive out; 13:9

walawîcišahw- VTA send s.o. out, chase s.o. out; 13:8

walawîhtah- VTA take s.o. outside; 43:5; [imp.: *walawîhtay* take him out]

walawîmakan- VII go out (referring especially to the old year) n. 58:18; (58:4); cf. *makošêwi-kîšikâ-, pîhtokwêmakan-*

walawî-nîšâhtawî- VAI climb out and

down; 1:5; cf. ...*âhtawî-*

walawîpahtâ- VAI run out; 18:6; 56:7; cf. ...*pahtâ-*

walawîpali- VAI burst out, come or go abruptly out; 9:20; 56:4; cf. ...*pali-*

walawîpaliho- VAI dash out; 8:4; 13:9; cf. ...*paliho-*

walawîtah- VTA take s.o. out, make s.o. go out; 22:2

walawîtim IPC outside (MC); 60:2; [contraction of *walawîtimihk*]

walawîtimihk IPC outside; 14:5; 41:5; 42:35

walawî-wêpin- VTA/VTI scatter s.o./s.t. out around; 22:2; 42:35

walawîyâhtawî- VAI come out (on one's feet or crawling); 5:7

walâpaht- VTI choose s.t.; (68:3)

walâpam- VTA choose s.o.; (68:3)

walâpihkên- VTI set up a line; 55:2; cf. ...*âpihk...*

wanahâmaw- VTA set traps for s.o. (SC); 11:11; *wanahâmawêw amiskwa* he sets traps for beaver; MC: *walawastaw-*

wanahikê- VAI set traps; 11:11; 32:1; 39:1; 39:2; cf. *wanihikê-*

wanahikan- NI trap; 37:1; 40:6

wanakohkê- VAI hang on (in some set way); 48:2; *kata-wanakohkêwak* they will be hanging on here and there; *miconi kâ-ati-wanakohkêcik* there's a whole string hanging on (e.g., sturgeon on a night-line)

wanakwaya NDA his/her sleeve(s); (13:9); cf. *manakway-*, ...*anakway-*, *ayiskon-*, *iskon-*

wanal- VTA set s.o. up, arrange s.o., establish s.o.; (42:15)

wanastâ- VAI-T set s.t. up, arange s.t., establish s.t.; 42:15

wanâh- VTA disturb s.o., trouble s.o.; 42:8; *ê'kw'âni kâ-wanâhikot 'wênihkân* that's what spoils a person

wanâhtâkosi- VAI drown other sound out; (41:5); cf. ...*ihtâkosi-*

wanâhtâkwan- VII drown other sound out; (41:5); cf. ...*ihtâkwan-*

wanêliht- VTI think wrongly, have the wrong idea; (55:3); cf. *wawânêliht-*

wanih- VTA lose s.o.; 9:12; 35:2

wanihikê- VAI set traps, trap; 11:11; 38:1; 42:4; cf. *wanahikê-*

wanihtâ- VAI-T lose s.t., miss s.t.; 6:3; 27:4; 39:4

wani-kiskisi- VAI forget, 'misremember'; 9:21

wanišin- VAI go astray, get lost; 37:5; cf. ...*šin-*

waniškâ- VAI get up from sleep, arise; 6:9; 10:2; 13:1; 35:2; 42:17; 55:5; *waniškâhkan* get up!

waniškâpahtâ- VAI leap out of bed and start running; 55:5; cf. ...*pahtâ-*

waniškâpaliho- VAI get up suddenly, get right up; 13:15; cf. ...*paliho-*

wani-tahtakwahw- VTA [redupl.] cause s.o. to collapse one after the other; 13:16; cf. *tahtakwahw-*

wapistikwayâw- NA French Canadian; 42:45; also as *opistikwayâw-*; cf. *wêmistikôšiw-*

wasaswê IPC dispersedly, diffusely; 14:7

wasaswêhkwêhw- VTA knock s.o.'s face to pieces; (9:7); cf. ...*hkw...*

wasaswê-wêpin- VTA/VTI scatter s.o./s.t. about; 14:7

waskiskiy- NA pine; (42:54); cf. *minahikw-*, *minahikoskâ-*

waswêhkwakwahw- VTA knock s.o.'s face to pieces; cf. *wasaswêhkwêhw-*; 9:7

waswêhw- VTA knock s.o. to pieces; 9:7

wašakaya NDA his/her skin; (10:7); cf. *mašakay-*, ...*ašakay-*, *nihcikašakê-*, *wâpašakê-*, *pîhtôšakapit-*

waškway- NA birch tree; (68:6)

waškway- NI birch bark; 62:1

waškwayâhtikw- NA birchwood tree; 68:6; cf. ...*âhtikw.../-*

waskwayi-cîmân- NI birch bark canoe; 62:1; 62:2

watapiy- NA root; 18:3; 62:2; cf. *otôtapîma*

watay- NDI his/her stomach; 4:7; 29:2; cf. *watânîhk, matay-*, ...*atay-*

watêm- VTA have s.o. in one's belly; 29:2; cf. ...*atay...*

watên- VTI be held up or supported on top of ice, snow, etc.; 61:5

watoy- NA blood clot (SC); 9:7; MC: *watôw-*

watôw- NI blood clot (MC); 50:7; 53:1

watôw- NA blood clot (MC); 56:3

wawâc IPC even; 1:4; 11:1; [variant of *wâwâc*]

wawâlawî-wêpin- VTA/VTI [redupl.] keep on throwing s.o./s.t. out; 18:5

wawânêliht- VTI wonder; 55:3; cf. *wanêliht-*

wawânihtakoskâ- VII [redupl.] be tangled bushes, be tangled underbrush; 10:7; cf. *wânihtakoskâ-*, *...htakw.../-*, *...iskâ-*

wawêlapi- VAI settle oneself, sit down comfortably; 13:9

wawêlêliht- VTI make up one's mind; 57

wawêlikâpawi- VAI stand in readiness; 20:5; cf. *...kâpawi-*

wawêlî- VAI get ready, prepare; 14:4; 23:3

wawêšiho- VAI dress (up); 10:8

wawêšihtâ- VAI-T prepare s.t., fix s.t. up; 42:37

wawocipah- VTA [redupl.] quickly snatch s.o.; 18:5; cf. *ocipah-*

wayahtâkan- NI barrel; 51:3; cf. *wâhtâkan-*

wayân- NA animal hide, animal skin; 2:10; 9:21; 50

wayêš IPC about, approximately; thereabouts; 5:9; 11:2; 13:5; 22:1; 35:2; *môla wayêš* nothing in particular; *môla wayêš n'kî-âšaw'hên* I've no way to get across; *môna wayêš n'k'-îtohtân* I can't go anywhere; *môna mâka wayêš kî-tôtam* he couldn't do anything about it; *wayêš nîswâso-mitâhtomitana tipahikan* (a distance of) about seven hundred miles

wayêših- VTA deceive s.o., trick s.o. (by some device); 8:6; 19:6

wayêšim- VTA deceive s.o., trick s.o. (by speech); 1:7

wâ IPV want to, going to [changed form of *wî-* in conjunct clause]; 1:4; 9:8; 43:9

'wâc IPC even [contraction of *wawâc*]; 41:3; 41:9; 42:19

wâcêm- VTA shake hands with s.o. [contraction of *wâciyêm-*]; 9:21

wâci IPC even; 42:19; 50:1; *êkâ wâci pêyak* not even one; *êkâ wâci mân'šîš kit'-ihtakwahk* not even a little is there

wâciyê IPC hello, good-bye; 43:7

wâciyêm- VTA shake hands with s.o.; 9:21

wâciyêmêhkâso- VAI pretend to shake hands; 9:21; cf. *wâciyêm-*, *wâcêm-*, *...hkâso-*

wâciyi IPC hello, good-bye [variant of *wâciyê*]; (43:7)

wâhkomâkan- NA relative; 42:35; 49:6

wâhkonak NA [pl.] roe (of fish and frogs); 54:2

wâhnaw IPC far, distant (SC); 5:1; 19:2; MC: *wâlaw*

wâkâ- VII be bent, be crooked; (41:13)

wâkihkotâkan- NI crooked knife; (65:9)

wâkin- VTA/VTI bend s.o./s.t.; 11:13; 62:5

wâkinâkan- NA tamarack, juniper; 9:24; 11:13; (42:51)

wâkinâkaniskâ- VII abound with juniper, be a juniper bluff or ridge; 42:51; 42:59; n. 42:81; cf. *...iskâ-*

wâkinâkaniskâhk IPC among the junipers; 42:51; n. 42:81

wâkipit- VTA/VTI bend s.o./s.t. by pulling; 13:16

wâkisi- VAI be bent, be crooked; 41:13

wâlaw IPC far, at a distance (MC); 5:1; 9:2; 11:4; 35:1; SC: *wâhnaw*

wâlâ- VII be concave, be hollowed (in shape of basin); 11:8

wâlâtimâ- VII be a deep hole in the river bed; (2:10) *milwâšinôtokwê anta; wâlâtimâw wêsa.* It ought to be good there (for fishing); for there's a deep hole

wâlipêyâ- VII be a little puddle; (42:34); n. 68:23; cf. *kihtâpêyâ-*, *pasakopêyâ-*, *...ipê.../-*, *...ayâ-*

wânêliht- VTI be at a loss, be stuck; 42:65; e.g., of a person in a bad storm:

môla kata-wanêlihtam kê-tôtahk (or *kê-ihtit*) he won't be stuck for what to do

wânihtak IPC any way one wishes, as one will; 11:3; *wânihtak piko n'kî-ayitôtawâw* I can handle him whichever way I want; also in stem composition: *kici-wânihtak-ayitôtawât* to do whatever he wanted to him

wânihtakoskâ- VII be tangled bushes, be tangled underbrush; 10:7; *tânta ani wiyân'takoskâk* (or *wayântakoskâk*)? where is that place where the bush is tangled?

wâpahcikâtê- VII be seen; 51:1; cf. *wâpaht-*

wâpahkê VII tomorrow [conj.subj.]; 15:2; cf. *wâpan-*

wâpahkê- VAI see; cf. 52:4

wâpaht- VTI see s.t.; 2:6 et passim

wâpahtamol- VTA show s.o., give s.o. evidence; 49:6

wâpahtil- VTA show s.o.; 1:7

wâpahtilamoh- VTA let s.o. see it, cause s.o. to see it; 21:9

wâpam- VTA see s.o.; 8:6; 26:3 et passim

wâpamâwaso- VAI be in childbirth, give birth; (1:9; 2:9; 11:1; 42:55; 51:2); cf. *...âwaso-, nihtâwikih-*

wâpamêkw- NA whale; (54:1); cf. *...amêkw-*

wâpan- VII be dawn, be morning; 3:4; 10:4; 20:6; 37:6; 42:17

wâpaskamikw- NI white moss; n. 51:2; cf. *kihciwêskamikw-, mihkwaskamikw-, ...askamikw-, wâspisoyân-*

wâpask'âw- NI [place name] Halfway Point (located on west coast of James Bay); [contraction of *wâpaskoskâw*, 'white bears abound']

wâpaskw- NA polar bear; 31:1; cf. *...askw-, wâpask'âw*

wâpašakê- VAI have light skin; (10:7); cf. *nihcikašakê-, ...ašak..., wašakaya*

wâpatanask- NA clay; (32:1); cf. *ašiskiy-, lêkaw-, ...ask...*

wâpâ- VII be white; 19:2; cf. *wâpisi-*

wâpâkamin- VTI put milk ('white liquid') in s.t. (e.g., tea); (42:54); cf. *...âkamin.../-*

wâpâkaminikâtê- VII have milk ('white liquid') put in it; 42:54; cf. *...âkamin.../-*

wâpâspicikâtê- VII be dressed in white; (50:5) *wâpâspicikâtêw miyaw* the body is dressed in white; cf. *wâpâspit-*

wâpâspit- VTA dress s.o. in white; (50:5); cf. *wâpih-, wâpihtâ-*

wâpâspitâkaniwan- VAI be dressed in white; *wâpâspitâkaniwan apiscawâšiš* the baby is dressed in white

wâpâspitâkaniwi- VAI be dressed in white; (50:5)

wâpi- VAI see; 9:11; 19:2

wâpih- VTA whiten s.o.; (50:5)

wâpihtâ- VAI-T whiten s.t.; 50:5; *wâpihtâw cîpayi-mistikwatiliw* he's making the coffin white; cf. *wâpâspit-*

wâpikalow- NA white owl

wâpikalowi-sîpiy- NI [place name] White Owl Creek, lit., 'white owl river'; (located on the west coast of James Bay)

wâpikošîš- NA mouse; 15:5; cf. *âpikošîš-*

wâpikwan- NI flower; (1:6; 20:3)

wâpinêwipali- VAI turn pale; (10:8); *mitoni wâpinêwipaliw ê-ispîhci -kisiwâsit* he turns pale because he's so angry; cf. *mihkonawê-; ...pali-*

wâpipêh- VTI paint s.t. white; (41:14)

wâpipêhikâso- VAI be painted white; 41:14; cf. *wâpišašôhikâso-, wâpišašôh-, ...ipê.../-*

wâpipêhikâtê- VII be painted white; (41:14); cf. *wâpišašôhikâtê-, wâpišašôh-*

wâpipêhw- VTA paint s.o. white; (41:14)

wâpipêhwâkaniwan- VAI be painted white; 41:14; cf. *wâpipêh(w)-*

wâpisakitihp- NA deer with a white forehead (i.e., an old deer); 10:7; [near synonym: *iyâpêwatihkw-*]; cf. *...tihp.../-*

wâpisi- VAI be white; 1:10; 50:7

wâpisîwi-sîpiy- NI [place name] 'swan river' (on west coast of James Bay)

wâpiskâ- VII be white; (20:5)

wâpiskinawê- VAI have a light complexion; (10:8); cf. *wâpašakê-, nihcikašakê-, nihcikinawê-*

wâpiskisi- VAI be white; 20:5

wâpistân- NA marten

wâpišakê- VAI have white skin, have light-coloured skin; (10:7); cf. *nihcikašakê-, ošakaya, wašakaya; ...ašak...*

wâpišakitihp- NA deer with a white forehead; 10:7; [alternative form of *wâpisakitihp-*]

wâpišašôh- VTI paint s.t. white; 41:14

wâpišašôhikâso- VAI be painted white; 41:14

wâpišašôhikâtê- VII be painted white; (41:14)

wâpišîšin- NI the 'Opposition' (to the Hudson's Bay Company; i.e., Reveillon Frères); 58:6

wâpitanask- NA clay; cf. *wâpatanask-, ...ask.../-*

wâpitowinaskw- NI clay; (55:2)

wâpošw- NA rabbit; 3:10; 21:2; 58:5

wâpošo-wayân- NA rabbit skin; 35:1; 52:1

wâpwayân- NI blanket; 42:22

wâsa IPC as you know, you realize (northern West James Bay usage); 5:8; 7:1; 10:2; 20:3; 41:5; 41:17; 42:16; 42:49; 42:58; *ê-pêhtâkosiyin wâsa ka-ytwân* you'll speak and you'll be heard, you realize; cf. *wêsa*

wâs' âni IPC for, as you know, you realize [emphatic form of *wâsa*]; 42:49

wâsêhkwanêsiw- NA bird which mimics various types of noises and animal cries; 10:8; n. 10:20

wâsêskwan- VII be clear sky; 6:14; 17:1; 60:5; cf. *...askw...*

wâsêyâ- VII be clear; 55:6; cf. *...ayâ-*

wâsitê- VII shine, be bright; 19:2

wâskaminahikoskâ- VII be abundance of black spruce around the edge; (42:54); cf. *minahikw-, ...iskâ-, wîhpi-minahikoskâwihtin-*

wâskâhikan- NI house; 49:6; 60:8

wâskâhikanihkâso- VAI make a house for oneself; 42:40; cf. *...ihkê-*

wâskâhikanihkê- VAI make a house; (42:40); cf. *...ihkê-*

wâskâkâpawîstaw- VTA stand around s.o.; 14:6

wâskâškowâkaniwan- VAI be surrounded (by other people); (42:54)

wâskâškowâkaniwi- VAI be surrounded (by other people); cf. *wâskâškowâkaniwan-*

wâspiso-wayân- NI moss bag (for baby); 51:1; n. 51:2; 52:4; cf. *kihciwêskamikw-, mihkwaskamikw-, wâpaskamikw-*

wâspisoyân- NI moss bag (for baby) [contraction of *wâspiso-wayân-*]; 51:1; n. 51:2

wâspit- VTA/VTI lace s.o./s.t.; 52:2

wâstawêyâpiskitê- VII be white hot; 8:8; cf. *mihkwâpiskiso-, mihkwâpiskitê-, ...âpisk...*

wâstê- VII be light, show light, glow; 3:5; *ê'kot' ânta piko mêtê-wâstênik mwêhci onakwâkanihk* at that very point light was showing in the distance right in his snare

wâstêpali- VII grow light, lighten, brighten; 3:8; 29:4; cf. *...pali-*

wâstêyâpiskihkâso- VAI be white (i.e., glowing) hot (stone, metal, glass); 55:7; cf. *mihkwâpiskihkâso-*

wâstêyâpiskihkâtê- VII be white hot (stone, metal, glass); (55:7); cf. *mihkwâpiskihkâtê-*

wâš- VTI cut s.t. into strips or strands; (52:1); cf. *wâšw-*

wâša IPC as you know, you realize [variant of *wâsa*]; 12:6

wâšahâ- VII be a bay; 58:3

wâšahâw- NI [place name] Hannah Bay, lit., 'bay'; 61:1; 67:1

wâšakâm IPC around in a circle, around the bend; 18:4; 52:2

wâšakâmên- VTI join hands; 55:2

wâšakâmêpi- VAI sit around; 18:4; *wâsakâmêpiwak manâ* they sit around in a circle; cf. *...api-*

wâšêyâkamin- VII be clear liquid, (for) liquid; (to) be clear; 42:55; cf. *...âkamin-...*/-

wâšêyâskohkot- VTI whittle a stick clean; 50:3; cf. *...âskw...*/-, *môhkot-*, *napakihkot-*

wâšêyâskot- VTI whittle the stick clean [contraction of *wâšêyâskohkot-*]; 50:3

wâšw- VTA cut s.o. into strips or strands (e.g., rabbit skin or moose hide for snow shoe netting); 52:1; *wâšwêw môso-wayâna ê-aškimaniyâpîhkêt* he cuts strands of moose hide as he makes babiche; cf. *amahkw-*, *šâponikan-*, *wâš-*

wât- NI den, lair [sg. *wâti*]; 6:11; 13:8

wâtihkê- VAI dig a tunnel, dig a den; 60:6; cf. *šâpotawêyâtihkê-*, *...ihkê-*

wâwâc IPC even; 2:4; *môn' êškwâ wâwâc âpihtaw* not yet even half; cf. *wawâc*

wâwâhcihtin- VII lie facing away from each other; (9:14); cf. *...htin-*

wâwâhcikâpawi- VAI stand facing away from each other; (9:14)

wâwâhciniskêpaliho- VAI jostle with one's arms; (9:14); cf. *wâwâhcipiskwanêpaliho-*, *...nisk...*

wâwâhcipiskwanêpaliho- VAI jostle with one's back; 9:14; cf. *mispiskwan*, *wâwâhcihtin-*, *wâwâhcišin-*, *wâwâhcikâpawi-*, *wâwâhtapi-*, *wâwâhtal-*, *wâwâhtastâ*, *...piskwan...*, *...paliho-*

wâwâhcišin- VAI lie facing away from each other; (9:14); cf. *...šin-*

wâwâhtal- VTA set s.o. facing away from each other; (9:14)

wâwâhtapi- VAI sit facing away from each other; (9:14); cf. *...api-*

wâwâhtastâ- VAI-T set s.t. facing away from each other; (9:14)

wâwâkatamon- VII be a crooked road; 42:28; cf. *wâwâkistikwêyâ-*, *kwayaskotamon-*, *kwayaskostikwêyâ-*

wâwâkistikwêyâ- VII be a crooked river; (42:28); n. 42:45; cf. *kinostikwêyâ-*, *kâškâyawistikwêyâ-*, *kwayaskostikwêyâ-*, *pâhkostikwêyâ-*, *tahkostikwêyâ-*, *...stikw...*/-, *...ayâ-*

wâwâkiškâ- VAI [redupl.] walk zig-zag; (43:6); cf. *pêci-wâwâkipah-*, *pêci-wâwâkipahtâ-*, *tapasih-*

wâwâskâpawi- VAI [redupl.] stand around; 44:4; cf. *...kâpawi-*

wâwâskêsiw- NA deer; (1:7; 10:5; 40:2)

wâwi- VAI lay eggs; 11:3; 27:5

wâw- NI egg [pl.: *wâwa*]; 11:3

wâwikan- NI dorsal fin; (29:1); spine, back; cf. *...âwikan-*

wâwiyêsi- VAI be round (disk-like); 5:9; cf. *nôtimêsi-*

wâwiyê-wêpin- VTA/VTI spin s.o./s.t. around; 28:1

wâwiyêyâ- VII be round (disk-like); (5:9); cf. *nôtimâ-*, *...ayâ-*

wâwiyêyâskwah- VTI nail s.t. in a circle; (52:2); cf. *âniskêyâskwah-*, *kîhkêyâskwah-*, *kîhkêyâskwapit-*, *wîhkwêyâskwah-*

wâwiyêyâskwahw- VTA nail s.o. in a circle; (52:2); cf. *âniskêyâskwahw-*, *kîhkêyâskwahw-*, *kîhkêyâskwapit-*, *wîhkwêyâskwahw-*

wâwîcihito- VAI [redupl.] help each other all 'round; 42:40

wêcik' âni IPC as you would expect; cf. *êcik' âni*, 29:4; 63:2

wêcik' âwa IPC this one then [mild surprise noting the unexpected]; cf. *êcika, êcik' âni*; 61:4

wêcik' ô IPC so then! [expression of surprise]; 10:3; [variant: *êcik' ô kîna, êcik' o*! oh, it's you!]

wêhci IPC from, why [changed form of *ohci* with conjunct]; 1:1; 1:9; *ê'kwâni wêhci-ihtâyahk ôma askiy* that's why we're in this land

wêhtan- VII be easy, be inexpensive; 25:3; 40:6; 42:19; 62:1

wêhtisi- VAI have an easy time, do (something) easily; 25:3

wêhwêw- NA the 'wavey', snow goose, blue goose; 18:1; 20; 55:1; 61:1

wêhwêwi-pîsimw- NA September, lit., 'wavey moon'; cf. *pîsimw-*

wêhwêwi-sîpiy ministikw- NA [place name] Sandy Island, lit., 'wavey-river island'

wêmistikôšiw- NA White-Man,
European; 2:10; 40:1; 41:12; 42:43;
43:15; cf. *opistikwayâw-*

wêmistikôšiwi-mîcim- NI White-Man's
food; 40:4; 59:1

wêmistikôšîmowin- NI English
(language); 41:21

wênâpêmit Nom.A = [VAI changed conj.
indic.] one who has a husband; 12:8;
cf. *onâpêmi-*

wêpahâkonê- VAI shovel snow; (60:7);
cf. *pimiwêyâkonêhikê-*; *...âkon...*

wêpanâskwân- NI sling shot, catapult;
(n. 4:4); cf. *pimotâskwât-*; *...âskw.../-*

wêpanâskwât- VTA throw or sling a
stone at s.o.; (n. 4:4); cf. *pimotâskwât-*,
...âskw.../-

wêpanâskwê- VAI shoot with a sling
shot; (n. 4:4; n. 9:36); cf. *pimotâskwât-*,
...âskw.../-

wêpatêht- VTI spit s.t. out; [preferred
synonym for *sihkwâht-*]; 21:4

wêpawêpâliwêpaliho- VAI [redupl.]
wiggle the tail; 27:4; cf. *...âliw...*,
...paliho-

wêpâši- VAI blow away; (50:5); cf. *...âši-*

wêpâstan- VII blow away; (50:5); cf.
...âstan...

wêpin- VTA/VTI throw s.o./s.t.; 3:8

wêpinamaw- VTA throw it to s.o.; 42:67

wêpinikâtê- VII be thrown; (away);
19:10

wêpipalih- VTA fling s.o. or s.o. off (as in
wrestling); 9:6

wêpipaliho- VAI fling oneself off; 9:6; cf.
...paliho-

wêpiškât- VTA/VTI kick s.o./s.t.; 13:14;
(23:2); cf. *tahkiškât-*

wêsa IPC for, as you realize (alleges
reason); often translated as 'because';
cf. *wâlâtimâ-*

wêsâ IPC too much, too; 3:7; *wêsâ kišitêw
anta iškotêhk* it is too hot there at the
fire

wês' âni IPC for [emphatic form of *wêsa*];
(with emphasis: idiomatically matches
English use of 'necessarily' in the
example below) 42:15; 60:3; 64:2; *môla
wês' âni môšak anima n'tiši-mîcisonân*

we don't necessarily always eat like
that

wêskac IPC long ago [changed form of
oskac]; 2:2; 9:1; 18:6; 40:1; 41:2; 41:3;
41:12; 59:1; 68:1; cf. *kayâs*

wêskaci IPN of old times; 40:1;
wêskaci-ililiwak old timers, people of
long ago

wêškinîkit Nom.A = [VAI changed
conjunct indicative] one who is a
young man [contraction of *oškinîkiwi-*];
10:8

wêskwâhtêmihk IPC back of the tent
(opposite the door); 9:11; cf. *iskwâhtêm*

wêspititiso- VAI get dressed, dress
oneself; 65:1; cf. *awêspiso-, kêtâspiso-*

wewêlat IPC openly, unimpeded; 42:44;
note *wewêlit* in *wewêlit kî-kakwêcimêw*
he inquired of them diligently (Matt.
2:7)

wewêlâpaht- VTI [redupl.] go around
(the circle) making a choice of s.t.;
(68:3); cf. *walâpaht-*

wewêlâpam- VTA [redupl.] go around
(the circle) making a choice of s.o.;
68:3; cf. *walâpam-*

wewêpâliwêpaliho- VAI [redupl.] wag
the tail; 27:4; cf. *wewêpâliwêstâ-,
kinwâliwê-, tahkwâliwê-, ...âliw...*,
...paliho-

wewêpâliwêstâ- VAI-T [redupl.] wag the
tail; (27:4)...*âliw...*

wewêpâstan- VII [redupl.] blow in the
wind; (50:5; 52:1) *ayamihêwêkin
wewêpâstan* the flag is flying in the
breeze; cf. *wêpâstan-, ...âstan-*

wewêpâši- VAI [redupl.] blow in the
wind; 50:5; 52:1; cf. *wêpâši-, ...âši-*

wewêpiskwêpaliho- VAI [redupl.] shake
one's head; (56:5); cf. *itiskwêli-,
itiskwêstâ-, nâmiskwêstâ-,
nânâmiskwêpaliho-, ...iskw...*,
...paliho-

wewêpiškât- VTA/VTI [redupl.] kick
s.o./s.t. more than once, kick s.o./s.t.
around; 23:2; cf. *wêpiškât-*

wî IPV going to, want to; 1:2; 6:1; 43:7 et
passim

wîcêwâkan- NA mate, partner; 40:7;

58:6; cf. *wîciwîkan-*

wîcêwâkanih- VTA be a companion to s.o.; 64:3

wîcêw- VTA accompany s.o.; 2:3; 10:5; 13:17; 19:1; 34:1; 37:1; 58:1; 58:6

wîcêwito- VAI accompany each other; 19:2; cf. *papâ-wîcêwito-*

wîci IPV together with, co-; 9:20; *wîci-tašîhkêmêw* he dwells together with s.o., he cohabits with s.o.

wîci IPN fellow; *wîci-kišê-'n'niw* his old partner, fellow old person

wîcih- VTA help s.o.; 42:16; 53:1

wîcihito- VAI [recipr.] help each other; 42:40

wîcihiwê- VAI help; 62:2; 65:5

wîcihkawêsiwa NDA his/her cousin(s) or brother(s); 43:3; cf. *...îcihkawêsiw-*

wîc'-ililiwa NDA his/her companion(s), neighbour(s) (MC); 40:3; cf. *wîc'-îliliwa, ...îc '- ililiw-*; SC: *wîc'-ininiwa* 21:4

wîci-môswa NDA his/her fellow moose; 36:2; cf. *nîci-môs, kîci-môs,* etc., *...îci-môsw-*

wîci-nâpêwa NDA his partner, his fellow man; 21:3; contrast *onâpêma* her husband; cf. *...îci-nâpêw-*

wîci-pimâtisîm- VTA live with s.o.; 6:5

wîci-tašîhkêm- VTA dwell with s.o.; 3:3; 6:5; 8:2; 9:18; 29:1; 39:1

wîciwâkan- NA companion, partner; 58:3; [variant of *wîcêwâkan-*]

wîc'-îliliwa NDA his/her companion(s) (MC); cf. *wîc'-ililiwa*; SC: *wîc'îniniwa* 12:14

wîhcêkimâkosi- VAI have foul odour, stink; (11:2); to a child who has messed his pants a mother may say: *awas, kiwîhcêkimâkosin!* away with you, you smell dirty! cf. *...mâkosi-*

wîhcêkisi- VAI have a bad odour, stink; (11:12); to a child who has messed his pants a mother may say: *awas, kiwîhcêkisin!* away with you, you stink!

wîhcikâtê- VII be told, named; 41:21; cf. *wîht-*

wîhkacîši- VAI be delicious; (54:1)

wîhkašin- VII be delicious; 54:1

wîhkât IPC ever; 2:7; [Ojibwa form for speech of Lynx]; cf. *îhkât, wîskâc*

wîhkipo- VAI enjoy one's food; (10:8); cf. *milwahcikê-, tômiskipo-, ...po-*

wîhkociso- VAI escape, extricate oneself; [variant of *wîhkwaciho-*]; 61:5

wîhkocî- VAI wiggle out (of a blanket, snow, etc.); 61:4

wîhkwaciho- VAI escape, extricate oneself; 61:5; cf. *wîhkociso-*

wîhkway- NI bladder (often made from urinary bladder of caribou or moose or from fish skin; ptarmigan and partridge also have a bladder for food before it goes to the stomach, but these are not used to hold grease); 14:3; 14:6; 27:4; n. 14:4; cf. *otôwîhkwâm, otôskwanim, pîhcipimân-, pîhcipimê-, wîsopiy-*

wîhkwayêkiwatê- VAI carry (in a bundle on one's back); 51:2; cf. *...êk..., ...wat.../-*

wîhkwêyâskwah- VTI crate s.t.; (52:2); cf. *âniskêyâskwah-, kîhkêyâskwah-, kîhkêyâskwapit-, wâwiyêyâskwah-, ...âskw.../-*

wîhkwêyâskwahw- VTA crate s.o.; (52:2); cf. *âniskêyâskwahw-, kîhkêyâskwahw-, kîhkêyâskwapit-, wâwiyêyâskwahw-, ...âskw.../-*

wîhkwêyâši- VAI sail into the very end of the bay; 58:3; cf. *wîhkwêyâw-, ...âši...*

wîhkwêyâw- VII be a bay [used at Kashechewan for 'bag, sack' with drawstring closure] (58:3)

wîhpâ- VII be hollow; (9:16)

wîhpâpiskâ- VII be a cave (in a rock face); 9:16; cf. *wîhpâ-, ...âpisk...*

wîhpi IPV enclose; (42:54)

wîhpihtin- VAI be an enclosure; (42:54); cf. *wîhpi..., ...htin-*

wîhpi-mêniskâhtikohikê- VAI build an enclosing fence; (42:54); cf. *...âhtikw.../-*

wîhpi-mêniskâhtikwâ- VII be a(n enclosing) fence; (42:54)

wîhpi-minahikoskâwihtin- VII lie
enclosed by an abundance of black
spruce; 42:54;
*wîhpi-minahikoskâwihtinwa os'âni
sâkahikana* the lakes lie surrounded
by a continuous ridge of black spruce
(i.e., the lakes with good water in
them); cf. *minahikw-, ininâsihtakw-,
sêsêkâhtakw-, waskiskiy-;
wâskaminahikoskâ-*

wîhpisi- VAI be hollow; (9:16)

wîht- VTI tell s.t.; (41:21)

wîhtamaw- VTA tell (it to) s.o.; 1:4; 9:2;
13:3; 28:1; 41:5; *kî-wîhtamâkopan* she
had warned him; *wîhtamawik êkâ
'ci-pêci-pîhtokwêcik* tell them not to
come in

wîhtikôw- NA windigo, cannibal devil;
12; n. 12:1; 44:3; cf. *ociškwaciw-*

wîkatên- VTA/VTI store s.o./s.t. away, put
s.o./s.t. aside; (51:1); [form with initial
w, normal transition glide, seems to
have become lexicalized as such in
speech of the MC narrator of this text];
n'ka-wîkatênên n'tiškohtêhkân I'll be
storing my stove away; cf. *îkatên-*

wîkatêpali- VAI/VII go aside, go away;
50:1; *misiwê âšay kî-wîkatêpaliw
maskwamiy* all the ice has already
gone away; cf. *îkatêpali-, ...pali-,
wîkatên-*

wîkatêpit- VTA/VTI pull s.o./s.t. apart,
pull s.o./s.t. aside; 51:1;
wîkatêpitâkaniwanwa they are pulled
away, pulled aside; cf. *îkatêpit-,
wîkatên-*

wîki NDI his/her home; 3:3; 4:5; 11:6;
37:3; cf. *...îk-*

wîki- VAI dwell, lodge, tent, have one's
home; 9:18; 42:35; 42:52; 65:8; *nêtê
oš'ân' n'kî-wîkihtay* I used to live over
there

wîkim- VTA marry s.o.; 60:8

wîkimâkan- NA spouse, wife; 2:3; 9:1;
9:18

wîkiwâm- NDI his/her tent, wigwam;
55:2; cf. *mîkiwâm-*

wîkopiy- NI grey willow (bark of the
wîkopiy was formerly used for tying

net-sticks); 68:7; cf. *...hkop...,
akociw'lâkan-, asinâpiya*

wîkopiyâpiy- NI willow strand; (68:7)

wîla PR he, she; it (MC); 1:4 et passim;
SC: *wîna*

wîla IPC as for [emph.] (MC); SC: *wîna*

wîlawâw PR they (MC); 2:1; 37:5;
wîlawâw tipilawê ililiwak kâ-itihcik
those who are themselves called
Indians (people); SC: *wînawâw*

wîlâhcikan- NI clothing (MC); 41:16;
42:10; SC: *wînâhcikan-*

wîlâht- VTI wear s.t. (MC); (2:10); SC:
wînâht-

wîlâkaniwi- VAI be dressed, be
apparelled; 44:4

wîlâm- VTA wear s.o. (SC); 2:10; SC:
wînâm-

wîlâta IPC however, although, though
(MC); 52:4; SC: *wînâta*

wîlil- NI fat (animal or human), marrow,
blubber (seal or whale) (MC); 12:15;
60:10; SC: *wînin-*; cf. *pakasôwin-;
...îlitihp-*

wîlili- VAI be fat (of an animal) (MC);
19:7; SC: *wînini-*

wîliman- NI paint; (58:4); cf.
wîliman'ciy-, waciy-

wîliman'ciy- NI Paint Hills; (58:4);
known in y-dialect of East Coast,
James Bay as *wîy'man'ciy*

wîlistamiwâw PR they first (MC); 49:1;
n. 49:9; SC: *wînistamiwâw*

wîlitihp- NDI his/her brain; 50:2; cf.
mîlitihp-, ...îlitihp-, ...tihp.../-, wîlil-

wîlitihpâpôw- NI brain liquid (MC);
50:2; SC: *wînitihpâpoy-*; cf. *...âpôw-*

wîliyw- NA [proper name] Willie; 67:4;
[obv.: *wîlîwa*]

wîmoš- VTI cut s.t. off entirely, amputate
s.t.; (45:2); cf. *kîškiš-, mâciš-, têtipâš-*

wîmošw- VTA cut s.o. off entirely,
amputate s.o.; (45:2); cf. *kîškišw-,
mâcišw-, têtipâšw-*

wîna PR he, she; it (SC); 1:4 et passim;
MC: *wîla*

wîna IPC as for [emph.] *anohc wîna*
right now; 41:7; *misiwê kêkwâniw
wîna* everything

wînawâw PR they (SC); 2:1; 37:5; *môna nêsta wînawâw kiskên'tamwak* they too did not know; MC: *wîlawâw*

wînâ- VII be stale, rotten (applied to water in James Bay which is muddy, brackish); (68:1); cf. *wînisi-*

wînâht- VTI wear s.t. (SC); (2:10); MC: *wîlâht-*

wînâm- VTA wear s.o. (SC); 2:10; MC: *wîlâm-*

wînini- VAI be fat (of an animal) (SC); 19:7; MC: *wîlili-*

wînipêkw- NI body of muddy or brackish water (applied to James Bay); 20:1; 42:1; 68:1; cf. *...ipêkw-*

wînisi- VAI be dirty, be filthy, be foul; (11:12); to a child who has messed his pants a mother may say: *awas, kiwînisin!* away with you, you're dirty! cf. *wînâ-*

wîpac IPC soon, early; 6:6; 21:3

wîpâ- VII be hollow; 9:24

wîpiciw- NA walrus (MC); (58:2; n. 58:7); SC: *wîpicîw-, ...îpit-*

wîpicînakw- NI [place name] Cape Hope Island, lit., 'walrus island'; (n. 58:7)

wîpicîw- NA walrus (SC); (58:2; n. 58:7); MC: *wîpiciw-*

wîsahkwê- VAI have a shrill voice; *kihci-wîsahkwêw* he has a loud, squeaky voice (which stands out among others); cf. *wîsahkwêcâhkw-, wîsahkwêhtâkosi-*

wîsahkwêcâhkw- NA [proper name (MC)] Weesahkwechahk (legendary trickster figure); 55:2; 68:1; SC: *wîsakêcâhkw-*

wîsahkwêhtâkosi- VAI have a loud, shrill voice; *wîsahkwêhtâkosiw ê-ayamit* he has a loud, squeaky voice; cf. *wîsahkwêcâhkw-, ...ihtâkosi-*

wîsakâpi- VAI eye(s) smart; 19:3; cf. *...âpi-*

wîsakêcâhkw- NA [proper name (SC)] Weesakechahk (legendary trickster figure); 7:1; 8:1; 18:8; 55:2; MC: *wîsahkwêcâhkw-*

wîsakêliht- VTI suffer, be in pain, ache; 65:3

wîsakêtahtahkwanêšim- VTA hurt

s.o.'s wing bone; (20:6); cf. *kaskatahtahkwanêh-, mitahtahkwan-, ...tahtahkwan.../-*

wîsakêtahtahkwanêšimo- VAI hurt one's (own) wing bone; (20:6); cf. *...šimo-*

wîskacân- NA whiskey-jack; 14:4

wîskacâniš- NA [dim.] little whiskey-jack; 66:1

wîskâc IPC ever; 1:4; 14:2; 40:2; 42:65

wîskât IPC ever; [variant of *wîskâc*]; *êkâ wîskât* never

wîskâta IPC after a (long) time; 11:10; *wîskâta nawac* later on

wîskwêkonî- VAI wrap up by covering oneself; 35:1; cf. *akwani-*

wîskwên- VTA/VTI wrap s.o./s.t. about; (11:5; 35:1)

wîskwêpaliho- VAI wrap oneself quickly around; 22:3; cf. *...paliho-*

wîskwêyêkî- VAI wrap oneself up; (35:1); cf. *...êk...-*

wîsopiy- NDI his/her gall bladder; (14:3); cf. *mîsopiy-, ...îsopiy-*

wîstâwa NDA his/her brother-in-law; 60:8; cf. *wîstâwimâw-, nîstâw-...îstâw-*

wîstâwimâw- NA a brother-in-law; (60:8)

wîst- NI beaver lodge; [sg.: *wîsti*]; 13:9

wîsâm- VTA invite s.o. (to accompany one, or to a wedding feast); 11:8; [near synonym: *natom-*]

wîtakay- NDI his penis; (56:2); cf. *âtakay-, ayâniš-*

wîwa NDA his wife; 8:6; 47:1; cf. *...îw-*

wîwaši- VAI carry (on the back); 60:4

wîwat- NDI his/her bag; 14:4; *êkâ ê-'yâspanak wîla mîwatiliw wêskac awê'hkânak* when people long ago didn't have a bag; 14:4; cf. *mîwat-, ...îwat-*

wîwi- VAI marry; 12:9

wîyašinaw- VTA think s.o. funny, think s.o. amusing; 56:3

wîyašinâkosi- VAI look funny; (42:18); cf. *...nâkosi-*

wîyašim- VTA fool with s.o., kid s.o. along; 55:5

wîyatisîhkê- VAI be funny by doing s.t.;
42; cf. ...*ihkê-*

wîyaw- NDI his/her body; 34:2; 59:4; cf.
mîyaw-, ...*îyaw-*

wîyâs- NDI his/her flesh, meat; cf. ...*îyâs-*

wîyêkitê- VII have a strong odour; 11:12;

[possibly for *wînêkitê-*]

yâkwâ IPC watch out! look out!

'yâkwâmisî- VAI be careful; 5:7;
[contraction of *ayâkwâmisî-*]